östberg™

Library of Design Management

Praise for the
ALMANAC *of* ARCHITECTURE & DESIGN

"The reader who uses this book well will come away with a richer sense
of the texture of the profession and of the architecture it produces."
—Paul Goldberger
Pulitzer Prize-winning architecture critic, *The New Yorker*

"The essential and definitive tool for architecture and design facts.
Very well done and valuable."
—William Stout Architectural Books

"Indispensable for any public library, any design firm, and any school of
architecture, landscape architecture, or interior design...
solid, reliable, and remarkably complete."
—Robert Campbell
Pulitzer Prize-winning architecture critic, *The Boston Globe*

"The only source book of its kind,
this almanac is the design professional's definitive resource."
—MSN.com

"A goldmine of facts."
—HOK

"It won't tell you when the high tide will be next June 28 or
who won the 1976 World Series, but the *Almanac of Architecture & Design*
does fill you in on the field's best and little known facts...
Where else can you find one book that lists the world's tallest buildings,
average salaries for your region, and Ralph Adam Cram's birthday?"
—*Architecture* magazine

DesignIntelligence®

ALMANAC of ARCHITECTURE

& DESIGN 2006
SEVENTH EDITION

DesignIntelligence®

ALMANAC of ARCHITECTURE & DESIGN 2006
SEVENTH EDITION

Edited by James P. Cramer and
Jennifer Evans Yankopolus

✚ Greenway Communications

östberg™

| Editors: | James P. Cramer and |
| | Jennifer Evans Yankopolus |

Assistant Editor and Consulting
Architectural Historian:
Jane Paradise Wolford PhD
Editorial and Research Staff:
Corinne Aaker, Susan Boling,
Austin Cramer, Ryan Cramer,
Lee Cuthbert, Ann Perkins Delatte PhD,
Daniel Downey, Mary Pereboom

| Layout: | Karen Berube, K.Designs |
| Index: | Kay Wosewick, Pathways Indexing |

Greenway Communications,
a division of The Greenway Group
30 Technology Parkway South, Suite 200
Atlanta, GA 30092
(800) 726-8603
www.greenway.us

Publisher's Cataloging-in-Publication

Almanac of architecture & design / James P.
  Cramer and Jennifer Evans Yankopolus, editors.
  2006 ed.
  p. cm.
  Almanac of architecture and design
  Includes bibliographical references and index.
  ISBN–13: 978-0-9755654-2-7
  ISBN–10: 0-9755654-2-7

  1. Architecture—Directories. 2. Architectural
design. 3. Architecture—United States. I. Title:
Almanac of architecture and design

NA9.A27 2006   720

Contents

Contents

} LEADERSHIP IN DESIGN

4 RECORDS, RANKINGS & ACHIEVEMENTS

Contents

7 DESIGN EDUCATION

8 ORGANIZATIONS

Contents

Introduction: Inspiring Change through Architecture and Design

Welcome to the world of architecture and design. As we look forward, we believe that 2006 will be an important time for architecture and design as we consider issues of vital importance to our planet, including safety, security, and sustainability. Design takes on new importance and relevancy when taking into account the pressing issues of our time.

The hurricane damage to New Orleans and the Gulf States, for instance, was not an unforeseen event, but rather, one of the inevitable "surprises" we knew were forthcoming. The only questions, then, were *when*, and *how bad?* Now that we have our answers, it is apparent that we were (by any measure) woefully unprepared. How can design leaders address this problem? What can we do differently?

Scientific discovery and responsive governance, combined with foresight, often lead to new action plans. Plans, however, are without value unless they are well-laid *before* tragedy strikes.

In the case study of hurricane Katrina in 2005 we found that the annual planning, budget requests, and political energy never led to meaningful execution that could have protected New Orleans from the worst of this disaster. For the last five consecutive years, budgets and actions plans were put on the shelf and/or turned down. Additionally, the US Army Corp of Engineers' budgets in the affected areas were cut in half. The bottom line is that we have paid—and will continue to pay—a high price for our lack of collective wisdom and failings of leadership in our governmental organizations.

We believe the architectural profession, along with the other design professions, is among the noblest of all professions, combining the essences of human health, safety, and welfare. Architects, engineers, designers, and related creative professionals hold an important public trust and must understand that the protection and safety of the human condition requires more than a rear-view- mirror understanding of the importance of design to the future. Foresight isn't just advisable, it's mandatory.

Ask yourself:

- Are we moving the entrusted value of the architect and designer forward?
- What makes a profession (like a human cell) divide and grow? Is the design profession dividing against itself or growing toward new relevance?
- Are we as designers pioneers in the new scientific revolution?

Introduction: Inspiring Change through Architecture and Design

- It's been approximately three centuries since the beginning of the industrial revolution. How does this timeframe relate to the age of today's design profession? Are we teenagers? How do we grow and advance relevancy through architecture and design beyond the information age into what will emerge?
- How might foresight and design leadership models redefine the design professions?

The latest research reveals that between now and the year 2030 the built environment in the United States will double. The baby-boomer generation (a crowd of 75 million born between 1946 and 1964) will have a soon-to-come retirement range of nearly two decades. These and so many other game-changing events will have signal impact on architects and construction. Combining demographics with new technology will create situations that will require leadership with foresight, agility, and wisdom. Massive change is just ahead of us.

We believe that the design professionals will become increasingly essential to solving the vast dilemmas associated with the environment and population growth. But foresight is required or our gene growth could backfire and mutate toward increasingly marginalized relevancy.

It is time to learn anew. As professionals, we must not squander this period of change. Today, architects and designers are taking lead roles in our communities and are inspiring change. And, just as design solutions outlined in this seventh edition of the *Almanac of Architecture & Design* show more efficient and beautiful design applications at the macro level, there are hundreds of other micro initiatives designers are becoming proficient with, leading to a new and, hopefully, safer world.

The pioneering spirit of designers is important today more than ever before. Your next-level leadership and design strategies are needed just as our once single-cell profession grows into new relevancy, new growth, and its next life.

We both want to especially thank the following for their essential contributions to this edition: Mary Pereboom our principal for administration and research who organizes us and manages our schedules and circulation; Jane Paradise Wolford, our consulting architectural historian and associate editor; Austin Cramer, one of our capable graphic designers and chartists; Karen Berube, our lead designer for this edition who brought us color, chapter tabs, and fresh clarity. We would also like to thank

Corinne Aaker and Chelsie Butler, who most ably read and reread every word in their proofing text after text, and Daniel Downey, who lent much needed editorial support despite only recently joining our team.

We especially want to thank all the firms and associations who have contributed their time and talent to make sure our data and research is the latest and most accurate of any in the industry.

This edition will set another circulation record. We are grateful to each reader, whether you are in the new central library in Seattle (Office for Metropolitan Architects and LMN Architects) or the new library at Ohio State University's School of Architecture (Mack Scogin Merrill Elam Architects). Or perhaps you've just picked up this book at one of the hundreds of bookstores around the world who retail the *Almanac of Architecture & Design*.

Our mission is to serve your data needs, fill information gaps, and provide valuable perspective for you consistently, year after year. Already we are working on the eighth edition. Please let us hear from you and put our research team to work on your priorities as well.

We wish you a safe and prosperous 2006!

James P. Cramer   Jennifer Evans Yankopolus
jcramer@di.net   jyank@di.net

1

Speeches
& Essays

Acceptance speeches from many of the past year's notable award recipients (including Santiago Calatrava and Jeremy Harris) as well as award-winning essays from design students can be found in this chapter.

Douglas Steidl. Photo courtesy of the American Institute of Architects.

To be truly accountable, we must
design projects that elevate and
enrich the quality of life.

Douglas L. Steidl

Architects as Stewards: The 2005 AIA President Takes Office

Douglas L. Steidl

Doug Steidl was inaugurated as the 2005 AIA president on December 3, 2004, at a ceremony held in Washington, DC. The following remarks were excerpted from his acceptance speech.

What a thrill this is to stand here, tonight; yet, what an obligation. This organization has come a long way over the course of the last few years. Gene [Hopkins] mentioned some specific actions that have been well addressed. I could expand that list exponentially. But perhaps the most significant thing we've accomplished is to focus our vision.

First, our strategic plan. It's a living document that hones in with purpose on four key areas. Gene mentioned these: knowledge, for the practitioner; advocacy, for the profession; community, for the member and the citizen; and value, the resources to support the first three.

This past March, the [AIA] Board specifically tackled our approach to advocacy. How do we advocate? What do we advocate? And for whom do we advocate?

In wrestling with these questions, we came up with an ambitious and far-reaching statement: We said we are challenged to see the world in its totality, to see it in all 360 degrees of its needs and desires and dreams. In other words, to see the really big picture. Central to this 360-degree context is a statement that defines our responsibilities as a profession: Architects: creating safe, healthy, sustainable communities for future generations.

This past year we have also clarified the vision of our public policies. As rewritten and approved by the board this week, they now state more emphatically what we believe, what we cherish, and what we value. They're divided into three parts: the architect, the practice, and the world.

The first deals with collaboration and how everything we do in life is relational— it affects others. We do not stand alone. The second addresses the built environment and our responsibility to form it in ways that serve all of humanity by creating safe, healthy, sustainable communities that raise the quality of life for our clients and all citizens of the world. The third policy calls us to respect the natural environment. It speaks to the obligation architects have to sustain earth's unique resources so that future generations are served. This focused vision facilitates continuity from president to president. More importantly, it provides a platform from which to see the future.

When I began my remarks, I characterized the challenge ahead as an obligation.

4

Architects as Stewards: The 2005 AIA President Takes Office

Believe me, I have more in mind than the responsibilities of this particular office. If architects can see the preferred future—and I believe we do—there is an obligation to act. If we can see the options available to our society and the consequences associated with these options, we as individuals and collectively, we as the American Institute of Architects, have an obligation to work with clients and the public to make sure the right decisions about our common future are made.

Nearly 150 years ago, 13 men met in New York and set out to change the practice of architecture; to formalize professional education, to share their knowledge through an architectural library and through fellowship, to raise the standards by which we practice, and to standardize expectations of those who would hire us. This was their incredibly ambitious goal. Amazingly, they achieved it. They created a profession, one that today provides value to clients and earns a living for those who practice the art and science of architecture.

Today, the AIA still protects and promotes the business of architecture. We are working to ensure that laws treat the profession fairly, that contracts do not place us at a disadvantage, that the public understands what we do, and that critical knowledge and practices are not only developed but also shared.

Some years ago, when I was considering becoming a candidate for treasurer, I went back to my office and asked my partners if I should run since it would undoubtedly take some time away from the office. Immediately a response rang out from the individual who gave the invocation here this evening, You've got to do it. I asked why? The answer went something like this: Every time you attend an AIA meeting you bring back an idea, a procedure, an insight, or a suggestion that makes Braun & Steidl better able to serve our clients. The firm reaps value from your service. I believe that's the answer all of us would give. The AIA, our professional community, continues to deliver value to us and, consequently, prosperity to their firms and better service to our clients.

We serve one another, our professional community. But our work, the vision we've painted this year, fills a far larger canvas. It stretches beyond our offices, beyond the communities in which we practice, even beyond the nation in which we live as citizens. What we do touches the world. It embraces all mankind. I stand before you tonight to say I will be president of an honored professional society that will serve both the architect and the citizen. We will focus on our obligations to both.

As you have already heard, last September the board voted unanimously, and with fantastic enthusiasm, to partner with the Enterprise Foundation to define, evaluate, and facilitate half a billion dollars worth of green, affordable housing communities. This action has not been typical of AIA in the past. But it certainly is indicative of the big picture I spoke about earlier. It reflects our commitment to go beyond words when we talk about serving our clients and society. This is just a beginning. I pledge to you to extend the grasp of our vision. I pledge to explore with your help ways to take action that reflect our values.

There are several Clemson fans here tonight. I noted an article on the sports page last week that speaks to the importance of values. It said the presidents of Clemson and the University of South Carolina had banned their teams from post-season bowl games. They did so because the brawl that occurred at the end of the game between these two schools did not reflect the values for which the schools stand.

I was impressed. Think about the money they will lose from television rights to the games. Think about the response of many alumni who are big donors. Yet, they turned down the counterfeit currency of dollars for the gold coin of their beliefs and values. We must do the same.

When a conflict arises between our values and a potential benefit to the organization, I will choose values. I ask that each of us take on that commitment within our own firms. Our ability to make a positive difference depends on our serving the public's interest first as trusted advisors and advocates. To earn that credibility means we must act first and foremost to benefit those we serve, not ourselves.

Former Supreme Court Justice Brandeis made a statement that has imprinted itself in my mind. He said, "A profession is an occupation primarily in service to others." I believe that. I trust that you do too. Barry Posner the dean of the business school at Santa Clara University and a former public director on our board put it even more strongly. He challenged us to be guided by what he called our "moral obligation as architects."

Tonight, I suggest we define that moral obligation as stewardship. Let me offer what I believe anchors, and stewardship is an acceptance of accountability. To be a steward is to be accountable for all we have been given as architects and as citizens of this unique planet.

Accepting accountability for how we use our training and our talent and how we relate to others is what nourishes our values. Stewardship is our moral compass. It guides us in many ways:

If we truly love our profession, we are good stewards for those who will come after us. We accept our accountability to future generations of architects by being

Architects as Stewards: The 2005 AIA President Takes Office

mentors and role models.

Since our work literally shapes the face of the land, we are called upon to be faithful stewards of the fragile beauty of this planet. We are accountable for how this planet's resources are allocated and how life will be meaningful in the future.

Since our work results in community, we are accountable for the quality of life where we live and practice. To be truly accountable, we must design projects that elevate and enrich the quality of life. We must be engaged with our neighbors in leading conversations whose outcome will guide how our communities grow and how they facilitate positive social relationships.

Many architects, as well as community leaders and legislators still see the AIA as primarily self-serving. They criticize it for being, as they see it, hardly more than a trade organization dedicated to a narrow agenda of self-service and self-interest. This is not the organization I joined. It's not the organization I serve. And it certainly is not the organization I will lead in the months ahead.

I believe in an AIA that serves its members. But, service to society, the true measure of stewardship, must be foremost in our vision. If we serve society well, we will be valued and we as a profession will flourish. On the other hand, if we seek selfish interests first, we will squander our legacy and lose our capacity to lead significant change. What is in our hearts—our motives—are readable by the public. Our motives are the foundation of our reputation, and our reputation is what gains us access to the public trust.

Architects are blessed by the talents we've been given, the skills we are taught, and the opportunities to serve that come naturally with the territory of the profession. We're trained to envision the non-existent, to pull ideas from a client and flesh them out for all to see. We're trained to see the shapes of visions, which others can only feel as needs. To be of service, we must direct our gifts to help our clients and the public to turn our visions into reality. It is our obligation to build a better future—a future for all citizens.

That is the full measure of our stewardship. That is the obligation that is conveyed with the title "architect." Let us joyfully and unselfishly help build safe, healthy, sustainable communities for future generations. The future is in our hands. I believe we will build a better world, and I invite each one of you to join me in service to both our members and all citizens of this world. It is our legacy—and our call to service— as members of the American Institute of Architects. Thank you.

8

Brian Knight.

Like a comma in a sentence, the space is a pause in the built environment that allows one to step back and more clearly read the character of the city as a whole.

Brian Knight

The Belmont Tunnel and Toluca Yard

Brian Knight

Brian Knight's first-place winning essay in the 2005 Berkeley Prize Essay Competition (see page 504) responded to the question: What makes a place truly public? Go out into a community that you know well and find an exceptional, built example of one such place. In most likelihood, among other attributes, this place will embody the traditions of local culture and be a reflection of the world at large. Describe this place in a way that makes it a compelling demonstration of how other places might remain similarly vital to their own communities. Be both evocative and specific in your tribute to this place.

Brian Knight graduated from the Southern California Institute of Architecture in May 2005 with a BArch degree. He was awarded the Henry Adams Medal for academic achievement and given SCI-Arc's graduation with distinction award. He is also the winner of the 2005 SOM Traveling Fellowship award for undergraduate students. He is currently working as an architectural designer in Los Angeles.

Urban planning has always been about colonization, the marking of boundaries, of order and form. Architecture is the instrument of this organization. It transforms the cluttered into the cultivated, the fallow into the productive, and the void into the built. It is the power of accumulation, of accretion, of addition. But very little consideration is given to the act of subtraction in urban design and planning. Although the modernist's edict of the tabula rasa is one example of subtraction as urban planning, its results are not what I am interested in. I am interested in a type of urban space that falls outside the scope of what we call normal or significant. These subtractive spaces—vacant lots, self-regulating zones, and residual spaces—act as counterpoints to the way order and consumption control the city.

At the intersection of Glendale and Beverly boulevards near downtown Los Angeles there is a tunnel embedded in a hillside at the end of a flat, empty lot. The small utilitarian building alongside the tunnel is covered with graffiti, and homeless people are known to live in and around it. Locals call this lot "The Tunnel." Most people don't remember what it was used for and simply think of it as urban decay. But this tunnel was once a significant entry point into downtown Los Angeles.

Even though Los Angeles has a modern subway line running from downtown to North Hollywood, few are aware that the city once had a subway more than 75 years ago. This portal was part of that system. The Belmont Tunnel and Toluca Yard, as the lot is now known, is situated in an area of Los Angeles called Westlake. The area

The Belmont Tunnel and Toluca Yard

could be described as an urban backwater, a neighborhood left behind when the construction of the Hollywood Freeway bypassed it in the mid-1950s. The Belmont Tunnel site has been vacant for decades, and the remaining vestiges of its original infrastructure are run down and frequented almost exclusively by graffiti artists and the homeless. People from the nearby neighborhood use the former Toluca Yard area just outside the mouth of the tunnel for tarasca games. This game is derived from a Pre-Columbian ball game that the Aztecs and Mayans played in Mexico. The playing field at Belmont is the only known tarasca ball court in the United States. The tunnel location is also well known among graffiti artists and aficionados of their work. It has been a semi-legal meeting place for West Coast graffiti artists to practice their art over the years. On some weekends there can be 40 to 50 people of all ages using this site—playing tarasca, creating art, cooking, drinking, and catching up on the latest neighborhood news.

The initial view of this space is that it is unacceptable due to the socio-economic deterioration and abandonment implied in it. It disrupts the image of order. A second view holds that this space offers room for spontaneous, creative appropriation and informal uses. These are the kind of uses that would normally have a hard time finding room within the urban fabric and its demands of commerce and commodity. Although it is not the revenue-generating site that the city of Los Angeles would like it to be, it is a historically significant and open area that supplies its residents with services that the city is not able to supply. Like a comma in a sentence, the space is a pause in the built environment that allows one to step back and more clearly read the character of the city as a whole. But before I describe more of the site itself, it may be interesting to look at some historical inquiries into this idea of what I call subtractive spaces.

In the 1950s, a group of French urban theorists calling themselves Situationists attempted to reveal the real city, the one that lay hidden under layers of marketing, commerce, and capital. They began to layout a plan for the Situationist City. Roughly basing it on experiments they conducted in Paris and Amsterdam, they felt that once the thin veil of refinement—the spectacle of advertising, images, and products—had been lifted, the real life of the city could be found.

The Situationists felt that the indigenous living patterns of the inner cities were best nurtured through the clustering of the city. They began cutting up maps of Paris and started to identify working-class zones worthy of study. These were clusters of the city that commerce, advertising, and marketing had left behind. One could begin to see a new pattern of the indigenous city take form in these collaged map studies they were producing. Their main grievance was that the Modernist architects were placing more importance on purely functional issues like automobile traffic. To the Situationists, one aspect of city life was no more important than any other. They called for a "unitary urbanism," a planning scheme that weaves the entire urban fabric together. They treated traffic, the home, commercial life, industry, and civic life, with equal importance.

The philosopher Henri Lefebvre heavily influenced the Situationists. Lefebvre saw the essence of the city as a place of play, spontaneity, and festivity and saw these as necessities of daily life. These were the forces that combated the suffocating power of top-down bureaucratic planners. His idea of the "moment" was based on the fleeting epiphanies—sensations of delight, surprise, horror, or outrage—that occur in the urban environment.

The closest the Situationists came to constructing their ideas was in the work of one of its founding members, Constant Nieuwenhuys. Constant's 10-year project, New Babylon, was his attempt to realize some the Situationists' desires for life in the new urban setting. A city of shock, surprise, and fun, it was the architectural development of the idea of a unitary urbanism. He was drawing upon the story of the legendary Babylon with the phenomenon of the modern city. But whereas Babylon was a parable about disarray, fragmentation, and collapse, New Babylon was an ideal of the modern city with its technological prowess and moments of spontaneity, surprise, and play. But the most important aspect of Constant's work is its questioning of the way we consider planning and zoning practices. Under the modernists' functional ideal there was no room for individual, idiosyncratic conditions of city dwelling. He combined the Situationists idea of intense neighborhoods and the architect's ability to initiate situations, moments, and epiphanies through non-rational combinations of constructions.

Another way of looking at the idiosyncratic urban space is through the policies and politics of real estate. In the 1970s the works of the artist Gordon Matta-Clark looked at the dissolution of building components and the breakdown in composition that revealed flaws in the buildings and flaws in the political system that made these buildings possible. In his most famous work "Splitting," Matta-Clark highlighted these flaws by sawing a single-family residence in half and separating the two halves by a few inches. And in his work "Reality Properties: Fake Estates" he bought 15 tiny lots of land in New York that had been left over in property deals. These sites included a foot strip down somebody's driveway, a square foot of sidewalk, and tiny sections of curbs and gutters. Some sites could not even be accessed from the street. Buying these ridiculously unusable lots was part of Matta-Clark's interest in the reactivation

The Belmont Tunnel and Toluca Yard

of severed and disused surfaces. It is an example of his idiosyncratic reinterpretation and manipulation of the economies of real estate. Matta-Clark's art embraced the abandoned and disowned. He worked in old buildings and neighborhoods and would nurture back to life those forgotten spaces that had lost their reason to exist.

In more recent times, the architect Ignasi de Sola-Morales Rubio has coined the term "terrain vague" to describe the residual spaces of the post-industrial city. The terrain vague considers the underlying complexities inherent in the empty, disused, and abandoned spaces of the city. There is a dynamic relationship between the absence of use and activity and the sense of freedom and expectancy. This concept is critical to understanding the evocative potential of the city's terrain vague. These are the spaces of pause, void, and absence and also promise, possibilities, and expectations. The terrain vague act as counterpoints to the efficient, productive city. These spaces are a critique of city planning in that they allow for individual and flexible usage and can be looked at as possible alternatives to city living. These sites have all had previous lives, and by looking at them as such one can see the city as a fluid collection of traces. The city is a palimpsest that can be revised, and these spaces help to define those revisions by revealing the evolving cultural, economic, and political establishments that define our existence in the urban environment.

This continual process of erasure can never reach a final outcome. For the city to continue to be a dynamic, exciting experience there must always be a trace of something no longer there and the anticipation of something that will be. There must always be the residue of something that has occurred and the expectation of something about to occur. Constant and the Situationists showed us that the process of becoming lies in the revelatory moments of urban exploration and re-examination. Matta-Clark showed us the potential of fragmentation and reuse. And finally there is the concept of the terrain vague and its continual flux of presence and absence and their mutual necessity. It is in a sense, the presence of an absence that is the absence of presence. Which brings us to the public space in question.

Before Southern California was known for its freeways, it had the largest trolley system in the world, the Pacific Electric Railway. The system spanned 1,100 miles throughout Southern California, and it was the main means of transportation before the construction of the freeways. Downtown Los Angeles had an active, bustling city center typical of those in New York or Chicago at the time. Downtown Los Angeles was also the hub of the Pacific Electric Railway. In the 1920s, the rising presence of automobiles led to congestion and traffic jams, which in turn slowed down the speed of the Pacific Electric Railway, which ran mostly on tracks in the middle of the streets.

The Pacific Electric decided to build a subway for trolleys going to Hollywood or the San Fernando Valley. The Hollywood Subway was only one mile long, but it allowed trolleys going to and from Hollywood to completely bypass downtown's street traffic. Trains entered the subway at the Belmont Tunnel portal and stopped downtown at the Subway Terminal Building on Hill and 4th streets.

The subway opened on November 30, 1925, and was in operation for about 30 years—until June 19, 1955. Since that time, the Belmont Tunnel site, with its adjoining trolley maintenance area known as the Toluca Yards, has been a vacant lot owned by the city and undeveloped.

Today the site is exactly the type that the Situationists, Gordon Matta-Clark, and Ignasi de Sola-Morales Rubio would have loved. It lies in an urban hinterland, and as such it has been immune from the homogenizing effects of mass marketing, advertising, and speculative real estate development. The men from the nearby neighborhood who use the site for their tarasca games seem to have chosen this site for very specific reasons.

In the Pre-Columbian era tarasca was a part of both the Mayan and Aztec religion. The game symbolized a portal to the underworld and functioned in a ceremonial capacity. The Aztec ball court bears a striking resemblance to the Toluca Yard site. Ten-foot high walls bound the traditional courts on both sides of a 40-foot-wide by 300-foot-long field. The citizenry would sit on top of the walls and watch the unfolding drama and pageantry of the game. At the Belmont Tunnel the game survives on a site that was once a portal to downtown Los Angeles—another, almost foreign world that the residents of the neighborhood visit occasionally. Nine-foot high walls bound the yard on three sides of its plain and on the fourth side by the gradual slope of a hill. This hillside is used as seating for the onlookers of this ancient game in its reincarnated form.

The walls bounding the space have been transformed by the brightly colored, collaged representations that characterize the exuberant style of the graffiti artists and their artworks. Sometimes these works tell a story, and often they offer a critique of the politics, culture, and economics of the neighborhood. This simultaneous mix of artistic and sporting ceremony, coupled with the news and commentary on the walls creates a juxtaposition of startling urban spontaneity that is exciting and fun and, at the same time, relaxing and pleasurable.

The Belmont Tunnel is a space at the crossroads of the post-industrial urbanization that has created many more sites like this, sites that raise questions about the very nature of the city. This particular public space is internal to the city fabric yet external

The Belmont Tunnel and Toluca Yard

to its everyday use. The Tunnel can be seen as a laboratory for a new idea of urbanity that can offer an intense, vital experience of the city. This site acts as a foil against the standardized and hyper-planned public spaces that increasingly inhabit most of our cities. There is a tendency in the creation of new public spaces to over-design a situation that leaves little room for the idiosyncrasies of juxtaposed materials and the richness that can accompany the unexpected. What is important in the development of public spaces is the ability to leverage what exists to help generate new ways of experiencing the city. The Belmont site is an amalgamation of disparate components that, when brought together, help to enrich the experience of the space in particular and our conception of the new post-industrial city in general.

When the generic is seen as unique and when the obvious is seen as enlightening, there comes a forgetfulness that threatens to severely limit the way we are able to experience our day-to-day lives. Our current bureaucratic, top-down urban planning and zoning policies have, for the most part, created public spaces that are monotonous and trivial when one considers the critical roles these spaces should play. Our public spaces and our life in the city should be rich with history; they should be dynamic, exciting, and sublime. When the commoditization and co-option of everything we experience in the city becomes the norm, the absolutely particular and individual spaces we can and should create become our post-industrial cities' most vital assets. These spaces are all around us if we wish to see their potential. The neighborhoods of disregard, the urban backwaters and eddies that are ignored by the marketing guru, advertising executive, and master planner are, in all actuality, home to some of the most dynamic public spaces in the city. The Belmont Tunnel and Toluca Yard, located in the Westlake district of Los Angeles is just the type of public space we need more than ever today.

© Brian Knight

Left to right: Henry Hope Reed, Richard H. Driehaus, Quinlan Terry. Photo courtesy of the University of Notre Dame School of Architecture.

Classical architecture is a tradition that has worked and would go on providing a sustainable environment if we would have the courage to follow that example more closely.

Quinlan Terry

Defining Classical Architecture for Today: The 2005 Driehaus Prize Recipient

Quinlan Terry

Quinlan Terry received the 2005 Richard H. Driehaus Prize for Classical Architecture (see page 166) from the University of Notre Dame School of Architecture and Richard H. Driehaus, chair of Driehaus Capital Management. When accepting the award on March 19, 2005, at the University Club of Chicago, Terry presented the following remarks.

There are many ways to describe classical architecture today; and with over 300 people here this evening, I am sure there would be a variety of definitions. But clearly it should be more than a Corinthian column tacked onto a steel frame or a tempietto on top of a skyscraper. It is much deeper than that.

To me, classical architecture is primarily the right way to build a permanent structure in traditional materials with a preference for using brick, stone, lime mortar, timber, and pitched roofs covered in slate or tile. It is working within the disciplines of solid load-bearing masonry construction with all that that implies: a limit in height, a preoccupation with the size and position of windows to provide comfortable conditions within the building, a natural bias towards simple solid geometry, a willingness to use ornament, and a desire to express the classical orders in all their fullness as they are appropriate to the fabric of the building and its neighbors. In short, we should carry on the great classical tradition of our forefathers.

Alongside this, we should—and will soon have to—consider a more modest consumption of the earth's resources to service our buildings. The classical tradition developed over thousands of years in ages, which had no lifts, no electric light, no air conditioning, no hi-fi, no easy transport, and yet they lived and prospered in all climates, took little out of the earth, produced no toxic chemicals and no waste—everything was recycled. Classical architecture is a tradition that has worked and would go on providing a sustainable environment if we would have the courage to follow that example more closely. Only in this way will we produce buildings which are not only beautiful to behold [but] not harmful to the environment.

To do this will require a life of painstaking labor, commitment, and dedication to achieve even modest satisfaction. And one has to acknowledge that one seldom reaches a level worthy of comparison with the architectural achievements of our forefathers.

This process is doubly difficult in our generation because of the attractions of an alternative way of building with a preference for using steel, glass, reinforced concrete, and plastics, which can provide structures which are higher, cheaper, lighter,

Defining Classical Architecture for Today: The 2005 Driehaus Prize Recipient

and quicker to erect. Such buildings are less permanent (probably only lasting for a few decades), have no beauty or charm, and are wholly dependent on high consumption of energy to survive. However, they have captivated the minds of virtually all the academies, seats of learning, and leaders of the architectural establishment, which means that anyone who wants to pursue contemporary classicism seriously will have to plough a lonely furrow, enduring conflict, obloquy and insults throughout their career. But their days are numbered as a new generation seeks a more beautiful, natural, and sustainable world.

In my case I have had to fight every step of the way for the last 40 years against entrenched opposition with the architectural establishment, not to mention closet Modernists in the conservation bodies. I only survive because I have been fortunate to have been commissioned by those independently minded clients looking for a long-term solution to an age-old problem. I have also had the support of friends and patrons, many of whom are here this evening. This is why an event like this is so enjoyable.

And as we think of patrons we should remember how crucial they have been at critical points in the history of classicism. There would hardly have been a Renaissance without a Medici or the Farnese. Without the vision of Julius II we would not have heard of Michelangelo, Bramante, Sangallo, or Vignola. Without John D. Rockefeller Jr. we would have hardly heard of Colonial Williamsburg.

Richard Driehaus, your encouragement and support is crucial for the revival and survival of classicism today.

Source: The Richard H. Driehaus Prize and the University of Notre Dame. © *Quinlan Terry and the University of Notre Dame*

Hannah Teicher.

Just as design-build is gaining ground as a way for architects to expand their role in the building economy, development-design might offer a promising avenue for extending publicly engaged practice beyond school.

Hannah Teicher

Engaging the Everyday

Hannah Teicher

Hannah Teicher's essay won the first prize in the 2005 ArchVoices Essay Competition (see page 500), where entrants were asked to reflect on the engagement of contemporary architectural practice with the general public. She is currently working toward an MArch degree at the University of British Columbia, focusing her design thesis on the inner suburban strip. She received a Bachelor of Arts in sociology and anthropology from Swarthmore College and became interested in architecture after interning at Metropolis *magazine.*

Considering the oft-quoted statistic that architects are involved in a paltry 5 percent of building in North America, one would almost have to conclude that not only has the field of architecture been marginalized by external forces, but it has actively contributed to its own marginalization. If the latter is in fact the case, many factors contribute to this state of affairs, but the most fundamental is a denial of the dominant built fabric of the contemporary metropolis as "city," and therefore the concern of the architectural profession. Driving through a landscape of strip malls, big boxes, and subdivisions, very little well-crafted building grabs the eye. Thumbing through an architectural journal, very little of the territory of the suburb jumps out, as the central concern of practitioners remains in the city center. Denying the places where most people live and work as a meaningful preoccupation can't help but alienate those people from the practice of architecture. From the perspective of those on the periphery of practice, i.e., most people, architecture is thought of as the rarefied province of cities hungrily seeking the Bilbao effect, if it is thought about at all.

Under the aegis of post-modern urbanism, and even more recently through the emerging construct of landscape urbanism, some theoreticians have begun to think through urban praxis differently, a first step toward communicating that everyday surroundings should comprise the domain of design. Accepting and even embracing the post-industrial landscape as a field pulsing with the latent potential of urban systems that might refashion the built environment, this school of thought devalues the conventional desire to operate on a greenfield blank slate. This is no accident, as urban spread will inevitably render the greenfield a thing of the past. From different positions, this theoretical approach and the concerns of people outside the profession pull architecture toward the vast middle ground stretching from the 19th-century urban core to the rural fringe. Young practitioners can play a pivotal role in staking out this territory, rather than luxury showcases, as a central concern of the design professions. In so doing, contact, and by extension engagement, with the general public would be

Engaging the Everyday

fostered as widespread versions of daily life would become a common point of concern. Just as the hierarchy of center and periphery might be flattened into a more evenly grained field, the hierarchy of professional, client, and public might be tempered through the multiplication of points of contact.

Despite theoretical leanings in this direction, that goal poses a seemingly insurmountable challenge to young practitioners as current development forces persist. Though architects have at times adopted radical avant-garde positions, it can be extremely challenging to carry those out when projects are typically built in response to client initiative. This would seem to suggest that demand must be manipulated to request an alternative, but that situates the architect as social engineer, once again reserving power for the marginal elite. Rather than manipulating the uneducated masses to demand the production of the visionary architect, it would be far more fruitful to engage in dialogue that raises the awareness that for every ingrained typology and production methodology, alternatives exist. That the built environment is highly malleable as it has, embodied shifting social, political, and economic currents and will continue to do so. Neither the downtown core nor the suburbs, neither the office park nor the strip mall are an inevitable outcome of unalterable forces of development. Heightening awareness of this complex reality could offer people a radically new perception of their surroundings in which they become powerful actors rather than passive inhabitants.

Still, that possibility seems farfetched. But academia, where students have the luxury of reflecting on the built environment outside of status quo client demands, can further foster interrogation of the aspirations of architectural practice. Having considered whether architecture should remain elite, potentially rendering itself obsolete, or whether it should reengage with everyday building, students might reposition their role as they enter the professional world. Design studios present the perfect place to frame alternatives to the frequent fascination with the urban gallery space or the rural retreat, positing a role for carefully considered design in the developer-driven middle ground where architects have been edged out or were never invited in to begin with.

Equally important to this reconstruction of program and site priorities is a reconstruction of the methodological response. Rather than measuring dimensions, either at the physical site or the most readily accessible GIS site, students might begin to construct the context for their interventions through a greater understanding of the underlying social, political, economic, and ecological systems. This would require a much deeper interrogation of a given site, demanding contact with many different constituents, whether surrounding residents, local politicians, or the storm sewer. Though a full grasp of these systems might be an overly ambitious goal for a studio semester, establishing an active interest in aspects of them would lay the groundwork for developing a greater understanding of the context in which architecture operates as well as encouraging emerging architects to engage with the public as an implicit part of their practice. Frequent interaction with the public might elicit an enlivened interest in the role of architecture, as it begins to be seen as an active ingredient in development.

With an eye to improving business, a pawnshop owner in a dying strip mall welcomed the idea of architectural intervention as I proposed a merely theoretical thesis project. Recognizing the inadequate lighting and signage and the relative inaction of the management, he embraced the enhanced visibility he inferred as a result of architectural attention. On the other hand, the bartender serving the afternoon regulars at the strip mall's Chinese-American restaurant had no interest in speaking to me after I mentioned the potential project. This response, as well as the less hostile but equally disinterested responses of the part-time workers in most of the other stores, serves to temper any naïve idealism about latent public interest in architecture. However, the few positive responses suggest that merely broaching the topic could initiate far broader public participation in shaping the built environment than is currently manifest.

Just as design-build is gaining ground as a way for architects to expand their role in the building economy, development-design might offer a promising avenue for extending publicly engaged practice beyond school. Rather than accepting defeat in the face of unabated conventional suburban development, architects might obtain parcels of land, whether greenfield or greyfield, to explore new typologies. Rather than accepting that they are beholden to market demand as construed by targeted surveys, architects might engage in their own surveying methods, uncovering a different type of demand. It is telling that in the first round of post-World War II suburban development many new homeowners, driven by the need to obtain affordable, efficient housing, found other desires underserved by their cul-de-sac homes.

Delores Hayden offers a perspective tempering this post-war panacea, "The sitcom suburbs offered the cheapest housing available in the postwar years. However inconvenient, however remote from railroad stations or bus routes, families coped with them because they had few other choices. In the late 1940s and early 1950s, not everyone did own a car. Men sometimes carpooled to work. Women walked to shops if they could or begged a ride from a neighbor. Because of dispersed houses, the demand for cars rose, including the demand for second cars and the market for used cars." (Hayden, p.161) Similarly now, affordability trumps all, potentially leaving many other desires unheeded, in spite of the conventional wisdom concerning the American desire for a private lawn. If architects engage in field work as they enter the field, they might

Engaging the Everyday

find ways to achieve affordability as they develop, design, and build while considering a broad scope of public desires unearthed through multiple dialogues.

Making inroads into the predominantly greenfield territory of large, well-financed developers remains a tall order, so adopting the conventionally less desirable but culturally more challenging sites left in those developers' lengthening wake may be more realistic. As strip malls decline and die and cheaply built ranch houses deteriorate, they may provide a fruitful territory for emerging architects to test a more engaged methodology, bringing their education to bear on the economic and social issues identified by pockets of people afloat amidst this urban aggregate. Though younger architects may be uniquely poised to take this risk intellectually, more established architects may be better positioned to take the risk financially. An ethic may emerge among those leaving school that suggests taking this on, but more mature architects attuned to pressing urban issues might just as readily adopt the challenge.

Any sector of the architectural profession that does challenge entrenched normative development patterns in a process that involves the public will likely find that their expenditure of resources, time, and effort is repaid and exceeded by mounting interest in architecture as a tool in everyday life. This awareness could foster a much higher demand for the thoughtful, rather than merely expedient, articulation of spaces for a continually increasing urban population. Though fraught with stumbling blocks, this could become a win-win situation in which architects find themselves in higher demand and multiple publics find their lifestyles better accommodated by a reshaped built environment. At the same time, both might find the experience of their immediate and distant urban surroundings far more pleasurable.

If carefully crafted design were to infiltrate large and small pieces of the built fabric, popping up in the ageing subdivision, the gas station, and the freeway off-ramp, the architectural profession might find itself operating on a scale unprecedented in North America. Architects have no absolute responsibility to engage the general public, but in so doing they might first and foremost fulfill a responsibility to themselves, addressing an innate desire to expand their opportunity to practice. Architects espousing vastly divergent ideologies might be able to commonly support an architectural version of the Hippocratic Oath, which would charge thoughtful design with supplanting rudimentary building to the greatest extent possible.

Reference: Delores Hayden. Building Suburbia: Green Fields and Urban Growth, 1820-2000. New York: Vintage Books, 2003.

Thom Mayne. Photo by Mark Hanauer, courtesy of the Hyatt Foundation.

Architecture, this thing we call architecture, is a way of seeing, thinking, and questioning our world and our place in it.

Thom Mayne

The Great Power of Architecture: The 2005 Pritzker Prize Laureate

Thom Mayne

Thom Mayne, the 2005 Pritzker Prize Laureate, delivered the following acceptance speech at the Jay Pritzker Pavilion in Chicago's Millennium Park on May 31, 2005.

I have these wonderful memories as a child, coming to this city with my mother and my brother. I wish my mother could be here right now. And I was somewhere between the years of five and nine years old. And as I think back, it's as it was yesterday, I can remember looking at construction sites and the energy a young boy senses with that activity. And I remember the L. I remember the sound of the L. I think at one point I had seen some very terrible accident, and it somewhat frightened me. To this day, when I'm in a subway, I always think about standing back a bit—that I'm convinced I'm going to get sucked up.

And it always seemed to end at Marshall Field's, with something good to eat or something I wanted. I have to say, I can't imagine a more wonderful way to come back to my first city, here on this occasion, in this place, this particular place, which strangely brings me back to California. And Frank, it's been said already a couple times this evening, but I know I speak for all of us when I acknowledge this place that's so filled with optimism, with energy, and this complete and total commitment to your artistic expression and your enterprise, which all of us so admire, which is a guide for all of us architects to follow you.

For me, standing here at this moment, I have to say it's even more personal. It feels as though this pavilion was made for this particular event for me. I would like to thank Mayor Daley. It's a pleasure to be in your city. I would like to thank Lord Palumbo for reminding me and the audience of my bad-boy status and my revolutionary place in the '60s. I would like to thank Tom and Cindy Pritzker, the whole Pritzker family, for your support of architecture. Your contributions elevate the entire field of power and visibility in this country and the world. And Tom, I have to tell you, the words were really lovely. You captured so much of what I'm going to talk about tonight.

And of course, for the members of the jury, for your faith in me. To my clients. What can I say? Through your suspension of disbelief, your ability to translate visions into realities, and now you're here all tonight, so many of you, all at once, trading stories. My god—an architect's potential, a frightening thing for somebody like myself.

My Morphosis colleagues, I see a whole group of you here today. Our work is a result of a collective engagement. Morphosis, a collective. Not my work—our work.

The Great Power of Architecture: The 2005 Pritzker Prize Laureate

My role is the part of a leader and to focus this group. I thank you all, and I receive this honor, this prize, in honor of your commitment and your energy. The 35 of you here this evening represent 200 years of collective work. I actually did the math myself—and that's normal people's 200 years. As all of you know, in architectural terms, that would translate to at least 300 years. So it's kind of amazing—that amount of time that we've worked together, just this group in front of you today.

To my friends, this is an immensely amazing event. I've been running around saying to other people: this is my whole world sitting in this audience today, for 40 years I have gained so much from the people here and these immense friendships over this period of time. And it means a huge amount to me that you're here tonight. It would be meaningless without you here, and you know that our relationships have shaped me. I wouldn't be here tonight without the engagement.

My family: Richard, Sam, Cooper, I'm proud to be your dad. And of course, my wife, life wife, what can I say? I met my match. You're everywhere in my life. This prize we share completely.

Architecture, this thing we call architecture, is a way of seeing, thinking, and questioning our world and our place in it. It requires a natural inquisitiveness, an openness to our observations, and a will to act in affirmation. There's no choice. The growth of an architect takes quite a bit of time. One thinks, constructs, assembles, thinks, and repeats this process again and again until a personal vision, a reality of this thing that's in our brain, emerges, and it becomes the basis of our work.

The great power of architecture is to take this personal vision out of the realm of the private and into something that is immersed in the complexities, the conflicts, and the tensions that define the human character and our community. These connections and intersections are where the generative material, the DNA matter, of my work exists—it's the beginning point. One begins intuitively, through a hunch, a speculation, looking for some essential part of a problem—a human problem that can be grasped and nurtured and slowly tease it into the development of a piece of work.

Very seldom do I have any preconceived idea of what my projects will be, much less what they'll look like. I need only at the beginning an embryonic impression, which, when worked on and put in collaboration with the huge numbers of forces, will develop in a unique way. The outcome of this process will be intensely specific. It'll talk about a project and a circumstance that relate to only this time and place and the people that are involved in this piece of work. This is what I value in architecture, and this is what I strive for.

Of course, there are inevitable similarities among my projects in building—characteristics that make them recognizable as the work of Morphosis. But this is not what interests me. I'm engaged more in the process than the result. I am engaged more in the notion of captivating what emerges and develops from the smallest piece of information and absorbs the huge number of realities—the human realities that come to impact us.

In this process, the end cannot be known in the beginning. One starts with just questions. Like life, it's evolutionary, adapting, transforming—growing out of, but not enslaved by, our profession's overinvestment in history with its A-priority solutions. Which takes me back to the city. To me, the city is a beginning point. It's the most profound creation of human activity. To me, it's continually changing, evolving, mysterious, and, therefore, in important ways, unknowable.

Its lack of fixity in the unthinkable number of its random interaction, exchanges, and encounters, in the sheer magnitude of the variety of intelligences that make up these places we call cities, here rests the potential of a true creativity where serendipity and spontaneous behaviors, spontaneous combustion, can take place. Our cities have a location of continuous regenerative forces, places of infinite possibility, which demand in us an attitude of expansiveness and a continued notion of questioning.

Yet, today, we seem to find ourselves in this first decade of the 21st century infused by fear, immobilized by the complexity of realities that have come with living in the present, the now—insisting instead on seeing our diverse society through a simplistic lens, resisting its reality, demanding uniformity in the face of the obviousness of diversity. And the refuge, especially in architecture, as it's always been in these cycles, is in nostalgia—a desire for the illusion of order, consistency and safety, qualities that we all enjoyed from childhood.

Okay, this is maybe a bit strong, but I'm saying it for rhetorical affect. This is temporary. It has to be. I believe during periods of great cultural expansion and optimism that was mentioned in the '60s, I felt the intoxication that happens when an entire generation decides to stop looking backward and deals with its problems and looks before it for its own direction. I see in this pavilion, in the work of my peers, a harbinger of better things, a fierce optimism of looking forward. Isn't it always that way? One looks to artists to remind us that we're moving forward, empowered. I'm chasing an architecture that engages and demands inquiry, an architecture that's not passive, certainly not decorative. It's essential. It affects us directly and profoundly. It

The Great Power of Architecture:
The 2005 Pritzker Prize Laureate

has potential to impact our human behavior and the qualities of our day-to-day lives.

As architects, our works are embedded with our values. We cannot escape society's layered and complex problems. Early in our careers we start with smaller work. We're criticized a bit. This allows us to tune our artistic skills and to hone our internal esthetic, something more private.

At this early point, these values are implicit. As the work grows in magnitude and becomes engaged with broader issues (for me, this has taken place in the last five years, as you know) architects grow up very late—I'm 61 years old. These embedded values become more explicit, and they offer a larger contribution to our society and something more substantial.

The Pritzker Prize recognizes the power of architecture to shape our lives, and it helps empower, not only its recipient, but all architects as they impact our society. In this way, it brings honor. But more than honor, it brings a responsibility.

I am very deeply humbled to receive this award, this prize, and I accept it with huge happiness, with pride, with a deep sense of responsibility. I'm honored that my work has been deemed deserving of such recognition and that my name will join others who I have such huge admiration for. You have given me the supplies as a young architect. I'm aware of that. And herein lies my challenge: to bring honor to the Pritzker Prize, to my future endeavors, is exactly what I intend to do. I thank you very much. It's an immense pleasure to be here tonight.

Courtesy of the Hyatt Foundation

Jeremy Harris. Photo courtesy of the American Institute of Architects.

Just one architect can transform the face of an American city.

Jeremy Harris

One Architect Can Make a Difference: The 2005 Keystone Award Recipient

Jeremy Harris

The American Architectural Foundation presented Jeremy Harris, the former mayor of Honolulu, with its Keystone Award (see page 128). The following is excerpted from his acceptance speech delivered at the 16th-annual Accent on Architecture Gala at the National Building Museum in Washington, DC, on Feb. 11, 2005.

I want to thank the Board of Regents of the American Architectural Foundation for this prestigious award. The Mayor's Institute on City Design, a program of the NEA, managed by the Foundation in partnership with the NEA and the US Conference of Mayors, is providing real leadership in promoting good urban design in this nation. But rather than recognizing the urban design accomplishments of a mayor, what this award tonight really represents is the impact that one architect can have on the rebuilding of an American city.

Today, other than the Mayor's Institute, there is an enormous void in leadership in this country when it comes to articulating a vision for the future of our cities. No one has picked up the torch to lead our cities as they confront the challenges of urban sprawl, the death of downtowns, and all of the issues of urban sustainability that fundamentally revolve around design.

In Honolulu, we are perhaps uniquely fortunate to have AIA architects play a prominent leadership role in local government. The seeds of that strong relationship began 20 years ago when a young architect joined city government as the deputy director of the Land Utilization Department. Because of this architect's strong personal commitment to good design, the relationship between the city and the design community began to change. In the past, the city simply didn't focus on design—and when it hired architects to design public facilities, the city was largely an uninvolved client. With the client showing no interest in design, the result was predictable— mediocrity in urban improvements.

However, with this new design-oriented architect in a city leadership role, the city's role as client changed dramatically. Now, excellence was the standard, and architects were challenged to make every city project a design award winner. Expectations and understanding began to change throughout the city. Hard-bitten engineers and bureaucrats began to learn and appreciate the importance of good design for the city's future. This architect within city government became a teacher of design to other cabinet officials, the managing director, and ultimately the mayor. The result

One Architect Can Make a Difference:
The 2005 Keystone Award Recipient

was that city design standards and expectations went up across the board.

Government responds to success, and so more architects were hired to lead other city departments such as planning, building, housing, and design and construction, positions traditionally held by civil engineers. This evolution of the city's focus on design also brought AIA architects into focus as talented leaders within the community. As a result, more architects were appointed to boards and commissions, and their role in city government increased. Largely because of the efforts of our local AIA, Honolulu recently received the first-place, Gold Award as the most livable large city in the world.

I think there are lessons to be learned from the Honolulu experience. The first is that it is possible for AIA architects to play a greatly expanded role of leadership at their local level. The second is that educating government officials and community leaders in design and architecture will have long-lasting, positive affects on a city's future. The third is that by contributing more time and talent to the local community, AIA architects can build a stronger relationship with their local government, and in so doing they can assume a leadership role in the future of our cities and establish their identity as true community builders.

The final lesson is that one architect can make a difference. Just one architect can transform the face of an American city. That one architect for Honolulu is with us here tonight. Please help me thank him for making Honolulu number one—Mr. Ben Lee, FAIA.

Courtesy of the American Architectural Foundation.

2

Awards
& Honors

The results of major national and international design awards programs (both project and individual recognition awards) are included in this chapter along with information about their scope, purpose, and winners. Other award programs related to sustainable/green design, historic preservation, and design education can be found in their respective chapters.

Aga Khan Award for Architecture

Granted once every three years by the Aga Khan Trust for Culture, the Aga Khan Award for Architecture recognizes outstanding contributions to the built environment in the Muslim world. The diversity of winning projects includes individual buildings, restoration and reuse schemes, large-scale community developments, and environmental projects. In addition to the physical, economic, and social needs of a region, this award seeks to emphasize the importance of the cultural and spiritual aspects of a project. The steering committee, comprised of internationally distinguished architects and scholars, governs this complex three-year process of nominations and technical review as well as the selection of the master jury, which chooses the final winning entries. Eligible projects must have been completed within the past 25 years and in use for a minimum of two years. An award of $500,000 is apportioned among each cycle's winners.

For more information, as well as photographs, drawings, and descriptions of the winning projects, visit the Aga Khan Award for Architecture's Web site at *www.akdn.org*.

The Ninth Award Cycle (2002–2004) Recipients

Bibliotheca Alexandrina
Alexandria, Egypt
Snøhetta Hamza Consortium
(Egypt and Norway)

Primary School
Gando, Burkina Faso
Diébédo Francis Kéré (Burkina Faso)

Sandbag Shelter
Prototypes worldwide
California Institute of Earth Art and
Architecture (US)

Restoration of Al-Abbas Mosque
Asnaf, Yemen
Marylène Barret (France) with Abdullah
al-Hadrami (Yemen)

Old City of Jerusalem Revitalization Program
Jerusalem, Israel
OCJRP Technical Office (Israel)

B2 House
Ayvacık, Turkey
Han Tümertekin (Turkey)

Petronas Towers
Kuala Lumpur, Malaysia
Cesar Pelli & Associates (US)

Jury
Ghada Amer, artist (US)
Hanif Kara, Adams Kara Taylor Structural and
Civil Engineering Consultancy (UK)
Rahul Mehrotra, Urban Design Research
Institute (India)
Farshid Moussavi, Foreign Office Architects (UK)
Modjtaba Sadria, Chuo University (Japan)
Reinhard Schulze, University of Berne
(Switzerland)
Elías Torres Tur, Martínez Lapeña–Torres
Arquitectos (Spain)
Billie Tsien, Tod Williams Billie Tsien
Architects (US)
Jafar Tukan, Consolidated Consultants for
Engineering and the Environment (Jordon)

Primary School. This school is the result of one man's mission to improve conditions in his village. Not only did architect Diébédo Francis Kéré, the first person from Gando to study abroad, design the school and raise the funds to build it, he secured government support to train people in building with local materials. **Photo courtesy of the Aga Khan Trust for Culture.**

Chairman's Awards

On three occasions the Chairman's Award has been granted. It was established to honor individuals who have made considerable lifetime achievements to Muslim architecture but whose work was not within the scope of the Master Jury's mandate.

1980	Hassan Fathy (Egypt)
1986	Rifat Chadirji (Iraq)
2001	Geoffrey Bawa (Sri Lanka)

Source: Aga Khan Trust for Culture

AIA Gold Medal

The Gold Medal is the American Institute of Architects' highest award. Eligibility is open to architects or non-architects, living or dead, whose contribution to the field of architecture has made a lasting impact. The AIA's board of directors, with rare exception, grants a single gold medal each year, occasionally granting none.

For more information, contact the AIA's Honor and Awards Department at (202) 626-7586 or visit its Web site at *www.aia.org*.

1907	Sir Aston Webb (UK)	1966	Kenzo Tange (Japan)
1909	Charles Follen McKim (US)	1967	Wallace Kirkman Harrison (US)
1911	George Browne Post (US)	1968	Marcel Lajos Breuer (US)
1914	Jean Louis Pascal (France)	1969	William Wilson Wurster (US)
1922	Victor Laloux (France)	1970	Richard Buckminster Fuller (US)
1923	Henry Bacon (US)	1971	Louis I. Kahn (US)
1925	Sir Edwin Landseer Lutyens (UK)	1972	Pietro Belluschi (US)
1925	Bertram Grosvenor Goodhue (US)	1977	Richard Joseph Neutra*
1927	Howard Van Doren Shaw (US)		(Germany/US)
1929	Milton Bennett Medary (US)	1978	Philip Cortelyou Johnson (US)
1933	Ragnar Östberg (Sweden)	1979	Ieoh Ming Pei (US)
1938	Paul Philippe Cret (France/US)	1981	Jose Luis Sert (Spain)
1944	Louis Henry Sullivan (US)	1982	Romaldo Giurgola (US)
1947	Eliel Saarinen (Finland/US)	1983	Nathaniel Alexander Owings (US)
1948	Charles Donagh Maginnis (US)	1985	William Wayne Caudill* (US)
1949	Frank Lloyd Wright (US)	1986	Arthur Charles Erickson (Canada)
1950	Sir Patrick Abercrombie (UK)	1989	Joseph Esherick (US)
1951	Bernard Ralph Maybeck (US)	1990	E. Fay Jones (US)
1952	Auguste Perret (France)	1991	Charles W. Moore (US)
1953	William Adams Delano (US)	1992	Benjamin Thompson (US)
1955	William Marinus Dudok	1993	Thomas Jefferson* (US)
	(Netherlands)	1993	Kevin Roche (US)
1956	Clarence S. Stein (US)	1994	Sir Norman Foster (UK)
1957	Ralph Walker (US)	1995	Cesar Pelli (US)
1957	Louis Skidmore (US)	1997	Richard Meier (US)
1958	John Wellborn Root II (US)	1999	Frank Gehry (US)
1959	Walter Adolph Gropius	2000	Ricardo Legorreta (Mexico)
	(Germany/US)	2001	Michael Graves (US)
1960	Ludwig Mies van der Rohe	2002	Tadao Ando (Japan)
	(Germany/US)	2004	Samuel (Sambo) Mockbee (US)
1961	Le Corbusier (Charles Édouard	2005	Santiago Calatrava (Spain)
	Jeanneret) (Switzerland/France)		
1962	Eero Saarinen* (US)	* Honored posthumously	
1963	Alvar Aalto (Finland)		
1964	Pier Luigi Nervi (Italy)	*Source: American Institute of Architects*	

AIA Honor Awards

The American Institute of Architects' Honor Awards celebrate outstanding design in three areas: architecture, interior architecture, and regional and urban design. Juries of designers and executives present separate awards in each category.

Additional information and entry forms may be obtained by contacting the AIA Honors and Awards Department at (202) 626-7586 or by visiting their Web site at *www.aia.org.*

2005 Honor Award for Oustanding Architecture

Agosta House
San Juan Island, WA
Patkau Architects, Inc.

Conservatory of Flowers
San Francisco, CA
Architectural Resource Group

Contemporaine at 516 North Wells
Chicago, IL
Perkins + Will

Emerson Sauna
Duluth, MN
Salmela Architect

Gannett/USA Today Headquarters
McLean, VA
Kohn Pedersen Fox Associates

University of Michigan Hill Auditorium
Ann Arbor, MN
Quinn Evans | Architects with Albert Kahn
    Associates, Inc.

Holy Rosary Catholic Church Complex
St. Amant, LA
Trahan Architects

Jubilee Church
Rome, Italy
Richard Meier & Partners Architects

Mill City Museum
Minneapolis, MN
Meyer, Scherer & Rockcastle

Mountain Tree House
Dillard, GA
Mack Scogin Merrill Elam Architects

Seattle Central Library
Seattle, WA
OMA/LMN—A Joint Venture

Shaw House
Vancouver, BC, Canada
Patkau Architects, Inc.

Somis Hay Barn
Somis, CA
SPF:architects

Architecture Jury

Thomas W. Ventulett, Thompson, Ventulett,
    Stainback & Associates (chair)
Frank Harmon, Frank Harmon Architect
Amira Joelson, architect
Brenda A. Levin, Levin & Associates
Susan Lipka, Anderson Cancer Center
Vivian Loftness, Carnegie Mellon University
Thomas Phifer, Thomas Phifer and Partners
Joseph M. Valerio, Valerio Dewalt Train
    Associates
Danielle S. Willkins, American Institute
    of Architecture Students

AIA Honor Awards

2005 Honor Awards for Outstanding Interiors

AM International
London, UK
Elliott + Associates Architects

Boys Club of Sioux City
Sioux City, IA
Randy Brown Architects

Chanel
Paris, France
Peter Marino + Assoc. Architects
    with Vigneron Architects

East End Temple
New York, NY
BKSK Architects

Elie Tahari Fashion Design Office
    & Warehouse
Millburn, NJ
Voorsanger Architects

Hyde Park Bank Building Hall
Chicago, IL
Florian Architects

McMaster University James Stewart Centre
    for Mathematics
Hamilton, ON, Canada
Kuwabara Payne McKenna Blumberg
Architects

Jigsaw
Los Angeles, CA
Pugh + Scarpa Architects

l.a. Eyeworks Showroom
Los Angeles, CA
Neil M. Denari Architects

Paul & Lulu Hilliard University Art Museum
Lafayette, LA
Eskew + Dumez + Ripple

Pavilion in the Sky
London, UK
Peter Marino + Assoc. Architects

Interior Architecture Jury
Mark C. McInturff, McInturff Architects (chair)
Judith DiMaio, New York Institute of Technology
Karen I. Fiene, Karen Fiene Architects
Douglas A. Garofalo, Garofalo Architects
Nancy Tessman, Salt Lake City Public Library

Did you know...

In the last 10 years, the following firms have won the most AIA Honor Awards:
Skidmore, Owings & Merrill – 20
Elliot + Associates Architects – 7
Herbert Lewis Kruse Blunck
    Architecture – 7
Hardy Holzman Pfeiffer Associates – 6
Richard Meier & Partners,
    Architects – 7
Morphosis – 6
Murphy/Jahn Architects – 6
Polshek Partnership Architects – 5
Pugh + Scarpa Architecture–5
Shelton, Mindel & Associatesv5
William Rawn Associates,
    Architects, Inc. – 5

Source: **DesignIntelligence**

43

AIA Honor Awards

2005 Honor Awards for Outstanding Regional and Urban Design ——

Anacostia Waterfront Initiative Framework Plan
Washington, DC
Chan Krieger & Associates, Inc. with Beyer
  Blinder Belle; Ehrenkrantz, Eckstut and Kuhn
  Architects; Simon Martin-Vegue Winkelstein &
  Moris; Greenberg Consultants Ltd.; Wallace,
  Roberts & Todd

Battery Park City Streetscapes
New York, NY
Rogers Marvel Architects

Cady's Alley
Washington, DC
Sorg & Associates PC with Frank Schlesinger
  Associates Architects; McInturff Architects;
  Martinez & Johnson Architecture; Shalom
  Baranes Associates Architects; The Fitch
  Studio

City of Santa Cruz Accessory Dwelling Unit
  Program
Santa Cruz, CA
RACESTUDIOS with Mark Primack Architect;
  David Baker Partners Architects; CCS
  Architecture; SixEight Design; Boone/Low
  Architects and Planners; Peterson Architects;
  Eve Reynolds Architects

Chongming Island Master Plan
Shanghai, China
Skidmore, Owings & Merrill with W. Cecil
  Steward, associate architect

Jackson Meadow, Marine on St. Croix
St. Croix, MN
Salmela Architect; Coen + Partners

North Allston Strategic Framework for Planning
Boston, MA
Goody, Clancy & Associates

Northeastern University West Campus
  Master Plan
Boston, MA
William Rawn Associates, Architects, Inc.

Ramsey Town Center
Ramsey, MN
Elness Swenson Graham Architects Inc.
  with Close Landscape Architects

Riparian Meadows, Mounds & Rooms:
  Urban Greenway
Warren, AR
University of Arkansas Community
  Design Center

West Harlem Waterfront Park
New York, NY
W Architecture & Landscape Architecture

Regional and Urban Design Jury
Michael E. Willis, Michael E. Willis Associates
  (chair)
John C. Guenther, Mackey Mitchell Associates
Rosemarie M. Ives, City of Redmond, WA
Stephen L. Quick, Perkins Eastman
Karen Van Lengen, University of Virginia

Source: American Institute of Architects

AIA Honors for Collaborative Achievement

The American Institute of Architects presents their Honors for Collaborative Achievement award to recognize achievements in influencing or advancing the architectural profession. Recipients may be individuals or groups. Nominees must be living at the time of their nomination and may have been active in any number of areas, including administration, art, collaborative achievement, construction, industrial design, information science, professions allied with architecture, public policy, research, education, recording, illustration, writing, and scholarship.

For more information, refer to the AIA's Web site at *www.aia.org* or contact its Honors and Awards Department at (202) 626-7586.

1976
Edmund N. Bacon
Charles A. Blessing
Wendell J. Campbell
Gordon Cullen
James Marston Fitch
Institute for Architecture and Urban Studies
New York City Planning Commission and New
    York City Landmarks Preservation Committee
Saul Steinberg
Vincent J. Scully Jr.
Robert Le Ricolais

1977
Claes Oldenburg
Louise Nevelson
Historic American Buildings Survey
Arthur Drexler
G. Holmes Perkins
Baroness Jackson of Lodsworth DBE
    (Barbara Ward)
Walker Art Center
City of Boston
Pittsburgh History & Landmarks Foundation
Montreal Metro System

1978
Frederick Gutheim
Richard Haas
August Komendant
David A. Macaulay
National Trust for Historic Preservation

Stanislawa Nowicki
John C. Portman Jr.
Robert Royston
Nicholas N. Solovioff
Robert Venturi

1979
Douglas Haskell
Barry Commoner
John D. Entenza
Bernard Rudofsky
Steen Eiler Rasmussen
National Endowment for the Arts
Christo
Bedford-Stuyvesant Restoration
Charles E. Peters
Arthur S. Siegel*

1980
Cyril M. Harris
Sol LeWitt
Robert Campbell
Committee for the Preservation of Architectural
    Records
Progressive Architecture Awards Program
Rouse Company for Faneuil Hall Marketplace
John Benson
M. Paul Friedberg
Jack E. Boucher
Mrs. Lyndon B. Johnson

AIA Honors for Collaborative Achievement

1981

Kenneth Snelson
Paul Goldberger
Sir Nikolaus Pevsner
Herman Miller, Inc.
Edison Price
Colin Rowe
Reynolds Metals Company
Smithsonian Associates

1982

"Oppositions" (Institute for Architecture
  & Urban Studies)
Historic New Harmony, Inc.
MIT Press
Jean Dubuffet
Sir John Summerson
Plan of St. Gall
Washington Metropolitan Area Transit Authority
William H. Whyte

1983

Christopher S. Bond
Donald Canty
Fazlur Khan*
Knoll International
Christian Norberg-Schultz
Paul Stevenson Oles

1984

Reyner Banham
Bolt, Beranek & Newman
Cooper-Hewitt Museum
Inner Harbor Development of the City
  of Baltimore
Aga Khan
Tung-Yen Lin
Steve Rosenthal
San Antonio River Walk
Bruno Zevi

1985

Ward Bennett
Kenneth Frampton
Esther McCoy
Norman McGrath
John F. Seiberling

Weidlinger Associates
Nick Wheeler
Games of the XXIII Olympiad
Cranbrook Academy of Art
Central Park

1986

Cathedral Church of St. John the Divine
Antoinette Forrester Downing
David H. Geiger
Gladding, McBean & Company
William H. Jordy
Master Plan for the United States Capitol
Adolf Kurt Placzek
Cervin Robinson
Rudolf Wittkower*

1987

James S. Ackerman
Jennifer Bartlett
Steven Brooke
Chicago Architecture Foundation
Jules Fisher & Paul Marantz, Inc.
Charles Guggenheim
John B. Jackson
Mesa Verde National Park
Rizzoli International Publications, Inc.
Carter Wiseman

1988

Spiro Kostof
Loeb Fellowship in Advanced Environmental
  Studies, Harvard University
Robert Smithson*
Society for the Preservation of New England
  Antiquities
Sussman/Prejza & Company, Inc.
Robert Wilson

1989

Battery Park City Authority
American Academy in Rome
Eduard Sekler
Leslie E. Robertson
Niels Diffrient
David S. Haviland
V'Soske

AIA Honors for Collaborative Achievement

1990

Association for the Preservation of Virginia
    Antiquities
Corning Incorporated
Jackie Ferrara
Timothy Hursley
Marvin Mass
Mary Miss
Peter G. Rolland
Joseph Santeramo
Taos Pueblo
Emmet L. Wemple

1991

James Fraser Carpenter
Danish Design Centre
Foundation for Architecture, Philadelphia
J.M. Kaplan Fund
Maguire Thomas Partners
Native American Architecture (Robert Easton
    and Peter Nabokov)
Princeton Architectural Press
Seaside, Florida
Allan Temko
Lebbeus Woods

1992

Siah Armajani
Canadian Centre for Architecture
Stephen Coyle
Milton Glaser
Mayors' Institute on City Design
Municipal Art Society of New York
John Julius Norwich
Ove Arup & Partners Consulting Engineers
Peter Vanderwarker
Peter Walker

1993

ADPSR (Architects/Designers/Planners
    for Social Responsibility)
Michael Blackwood
Conservation Trust of Puerto Rico
Benjamin Forgey
Gamble House
Philadelphia Zoological Society
Princeton University Board of Trustees, Officers
    and the Office of Physical Planning

Jane Thompson
Sally B. Woodbridge
World Monuments Fund

1994

Joseph H. Baum
Beth Dunlop
Mildred Friedman
Historic Savannah Foundation
Rhode Island Historical Preservation
    Commission
Salvadori Educational Center on the Built
    Environment
Gordon H. Smith
Stuart Collection
Sunset magazine
Judith Turner

1995

Art Institute of Chicago, Dept. of Architecture
ASAP (American Society of Architectural
    Perspectivists)
Friends of Post Office Square
University of Virginia, Curator and Architect
    for the Academical Village/The Rotunda
Albert Paley
UrbanArts, Inc.
Yoichi Ando

1996

Boston by Foot, Inc.
William S. Donnell
Haley & Aldrich, Inc.
Toshio Nakamura
Joseph Passonneau
Preservation Society of Charleston
Earl Walls Associates
Paul Warchol Photography, Inc.

1997

Architecture Resource Center

1998

Lian Hurst Mann
SOM Foundation
William Morgan

AIA Honors for Collaborative Achievement

1999

Howard Brandston
Jeff Goldberg
Ann E. Gray
Blair Kamin
Ronald McKay
Miami-Dade Art in Public Places
Monacelli Press
New York Landmarks Conservancy

2000

Aga Khan Award for Architecture
Douglas Cooper
Christopher Jaffe
Donald Kaufman and Taffy Dahl
William Lam
San Antonio Conservation Society
F. Michael Wong

2001†

Vernon L. Mays Jr.
John R. Stilgoe

2003

Kathryn H. Anthony
Herve Descottes
Gilbert Gorski
Jane Merkel
J. Irwin Miller
New York, New Visions
Joan Ockman
Martin Puryear
Robin Hood Foundation

2005

ArchVoices
Randall Arendt
John James
Barbara A. Nadel
Schoolyards to Skylines

* Awarded posthumously

† Beginning in 2001, the award schedule became biennial.

Source: American Institute of Architects

AIA Housing Awards

The Housing Professional Interest Area of the American Institute of Architects established the Housing Awards to recognize the importance of good housing as a necessity of life, a sanctuary for the human spirit, and a valuable national resource. AIA-member architects licensed in the United States are eligible to enter US-built projects. Winning projects are published in *Architectural Record* and displayed at the annual AIA National Convention and Expo.

For additional information, contact the AIA Honors and Awards department at (202) 626-7563 or visit them on the Internet at *www.aia.org*.

2005 Recipients

Community Design
LeMoyne Revitalization
Memphis, TN
Torti Gallas and Partners, Inc.

The Garlands of Barrington
Barrington, IL
Torti Gallas and Partners, Inc.

Innovation in Housing Design
F10 House
Chicago, IL
EHDD Architecture

Multi-Family
Soma Studios and 8th + Howard Apartments
San Francisco, CA
David Baker + Partners, Architects
with I.A. Gonzales Architects

Single-family Market
Greenwood Avenue Cottages
Shoreline, WA
Ross Chapin Architects

Urban Infill 01
Milwaukee, WI
Johnsen Schmaling Architects

Single-family Custom
Lake Austin Residence
Austin, TX
Lake/Flato Architects Inc.

Canyon House
Julietta, ID
Paul Hirzel, Architect

Jury
Edward M. Hord, Hord Coplan Macht
   Architects (chair)
Donna Kacmar, Architect Works, Inc.
Jane Kolleeny, *Architectural Record*
Jonathan S. Segal, Jonathan S. Segal, Architect
Gina Van Tine, Vine Tine | Guthrie Studio

Source: American Institute of Architects

Canyon House. This 40-acre, year-round retreat contains two buildings: a bunkhouse nestled into a ravine and, 300 yards away, a studio house (above) perched on a ridge overlooking the Clearwater River. Derivative of the canyon's mining structures, the studio house is a simple rectangular box inserted into a moment-resisting wooden frame that mimics the 30-percent slope of the site. **Photo by Art Price.**

AIA/HUD Secretary's Housing and Community Design Award

Innovative, affordable, and accessible building designs are honored by the HUD Secretary's Housing and Community Design Award, presented jointly by the American Institute of Architects and the US Department of Housing and Urban Development. The AIA's Center for Livable Communities and the AIA Housing Professional Interest Area, in partnership with HUD, created this biennial award program to recognize the best in residential and community design. The three award categories are mixed-use/mixed-income development for projects that revitalize neighborhoods through a combination of residential and non-residential uses; community design to honor projects that rebuild poor neighborhoods; and the Alan J. Rothman Housing Accessibility Award, named in honor of the late HUD senior policy analyst, an expert on disability issues.

Additional information can be found on the AIA's Web site at *www.aia.org*.

2005 Winners

Mixed-Use/Mixed-Income Design
Main Street North
Boulder, CO
Wolff Lyon Architects; Gebau Inc.; Boulder
    Engineering Co.; Deneuve Construction

Community Design
Linden Court and Chestnut Court
West Oakland, CA
David Baker + Partners, Architects; Michael
    Willis Architects; OLMM, Pattillo + Garrett
    Associates; Roberts/Obayashi Corporation;
    Shift Design Studio; Design Mesh

Jury
Edward M. Hord, Hord Coplan Macht (chair)
Donna Kacmar, Architect Works Inc.
Jane Kolleeny, *Architectural Record*
Carlos Martín, HUD
Marina L. Myhre, HUD
Jonathan S. Segal, architect
Gina Van Tine, Van Tine|Guthrie Studio

Source: American Institute of Architects

Alice Davis Hitchcock Book Award

The Alice Davis Hitchcock book award has been granted annually by the Society of Architectural Historians since 1949. It is given to a publication by a North American scholar, published within the preceding two years, that demonstrates a high level of scholarly distinction in the field of architectural history.

For more information contact the SAH at (312) 573-1365 or visit their Web site at *www.sah.org*.

1949
Colonial Architecture and Sculpture in Peru by Harold Wethey (Harvard University Press)

1950
Architecture of the Old Northwest Territory by Rexford Newcomb (University of Chicago Press)

1951
Architecture and Town Planning in Colonial Connecticut by Anthony Garvan (Yale University Press)

1952
The Architectural History of Newport by Antoinette Downing and Vincent Scully (Harvard University Press)

1953
Charles Rennie Mackintosh and the Modern Movement by Thomas Howarth (Routledge and K. Paul)

1954
Early Victorian Architecture in Britain by Henry Russell Hitchcock (Da Capo Press, Inc.)

1955
Benjamin H. Latrobe by Talbot Hamlin (Oxford University Press)

1956
The Railroad Station: An Architectural History by Carroll L.V. Meeks (Yale University Press)

1957
The Early Architecture of Georgia by Frederick D. Nichols (University of N.C. Press)

1958
The Public Buildings of Williamsburg by Marcus Whiffen (Colonial Williamsburg)

1959
Carolingian and Romanesque Architecture, 800 to 1200 by Kenneth J. Conant (Yale University Press)

1960
The Villa d'Este at Tivoli by David Coffin (Princeton University Press)

1961
The Architecture of Michelangelo by James S. Ackerman (University of Chicago Press)

1962
The Art and Architecture of Ancient America by George Kubler (Yale University Press)

1963
La Cathédrale de Bourges et sa Place dans l'Architecture Gothique by Robert Branner (Tardy)

1964
Images of American Living, Four Centuries of Architecture and Furniture as Cultural Expression by Alan Gowans (Lippincott)

Alice Davis Hitchcock Book Award

1965

The Open-Air Churches of Sixteenth Century Mexico by John McAndrew (Harvard University Press)

1966

Early Christian and Byzantine Architecture by Richard Krautheimer (Penguin Books)

1967

Eighteenth-Century Architecture in Piedmont: the open structures of Juvarra, Alfieri & Vittone by Richard Pommer (New York University Press)

1968

Architecture and Politics in Germany, 1918–1945 by Barbara Miller Lane (Harvard University Press)

1969

Samothrace, Volume III: The Hieron by Phyllis Williams Lehmann (Princeton University Press)

1970

The Church of Notre Dame in Montreal by Franklin Toker (McGill-Queen's University Press)

1971

No award granted

1972

The Prairie School: Frank Lloyd Wright and his Midwest Contemporaries by H. Allen Brooks (University of Toronto Press)

The Early Churches of Constantinople: Architecture and Liturgy by Thomas F. Mathews (Pennsylvania State University Press)

1973

The Campanile of Florence Cathedral: "Giotto's Tower" by Marvin Trachtenberg (New York University Press)

1974

FLO, A Biography of Frederick Law Olmstead by Laura Wood Roper (Johns Hopkins University Press)

1975

Gothic vs. Classic, Architectural Projects in Seventeenth-Century Italy by Rudolf Wittkower (G. Braziller)

1976

No award granted

1977

The Esplanade Ridge (Vol.V in The New Orleans Architecture Series) by Mary Louise Christovich, Sally Kitredge Evans, Betsy Swanson, and Roulhac Toledano (Pelican Publishing Company)

1978

Sebastiano Serlio on Domestic Architecture by Myra Nan Rosenfeld (Architectural History Foundation)

1979

The Framed Houses of Massachusetts Bay, 1625–1725 by Abbott Lowell Cummings (Belknap Press)

Paris: A Century of Change, 1878–1978 by Norma Evenson (Yale University Press)

1980

Rome: Profile of a City, 312–1308 by Richard Krautheimer (Princeton University Press)

1981

Gardens of Illusion: The Genius of Andre LeNotre by Franklin Hamilton Hazelhurst (Vanderbilt University Press)

1982

Indian Summer: Luytens, Baker and Imperial Delhi by Robert Grant Irving (Yale Univ. Press)

Alice Davis Hitchcock Book Award

1983

Architecture and the Crisis of Modern Science
by Alberto Pérez-Goméz (MIT Press)

1984

Campus: An American Planning Tradition
by Paul Venable Turner (MIT Press)

1985

*The Law Courts: The Architecture of George
Edmund Street* by David Brownlee (MIT Press)

1986

*The Architecture of the Roman Empire: An Urban
Appraisal* by William L. MacDonald (Yale
University Press)

1987

*Holy Things and Profane: Anglican Parish
Churches in Colonial Virginia* by Dell Upton
(MIT Press)

1988

*Designing Paris: The Architecture of Duban,
Labrouste, Duc and Vaudoyer* by David Van
Zanten (MIT Press)

1989

*Florentine New Towns: Urban Design in the Late
Middle Ages* by David Friedman (MIT Press)

1990

*Claude-Nicolas Ledoux: Architecture and Social
Reform at the End of the Ancient Régime* by
Anthony Vidler (MIT Press)

1991

The Paris of Henri IV: Architecture and Urbanism
by Hilary Ballon (MIT Press)

*Seventeenth-Century Roman Palaces: Use and the
Art of the Plan* by Patricia Waddy (MIT Press)

1992

Modernism in Italian Architecture, 1890–1940
by Richard Etlin (MIT Press)

1994*

Baths and Bathing in Classical Antiquity
by Fikret Yegul (MIT Press)

1995

*The Politics of the German Gothic Revival: August
Reichensperger* by Michael J. Lewis (MIT Press)

1996

Hadrian's Villa and Its Legacy by William J.
MacDonald and John Pinto (Yale University
Press)

1997

*Gottfried Semper: Architect of the Nineteenth
Century* by Harry Francis Mallgrave
(Yale University Press)

1998

The Dancing Column: On Order in Architecture
by Joseph Rykwert (MIT Press)

1999

*Dominion of the Eye: Urbanism, Art & Power in
Early Modern Florence* by Marvin Trachtenberg
(Cambridge University Press)

2000

The Architectural Treatise in the Renaissance by
Alina A. Payne (Cambridge University Press)

2001

The Architecture of Red Vienna, 1919–1934
by Eve Blau (MIT Press)

2002

*Modernism and Nation-Building: Turkish
Architectural Culture in the Early Republic* by
Sibel Bozdogan (University of Washington
Press)

Marcel Breuer: The Career and the Buildings
by Isabelle Hyman (Harry N. Abrams)

2003

*The Chicago Auditorium Building: Adler and
Sullivan's Architecture and the City* by Joseph
Siry (University of Chicago Press)

Alice Davis Hitchcock Book Award

House and Home in Modern Japan. Author Jordan Sand explores the history of the Japanese house as both a site (the bounds and focus of a community) and a material extension of its occupants' lives. Photo courtesy of Harvard University Press.

2004

The Chicago Tribune Tower Competition: Skyscraper Design and Cultural Change in the 1920s by Katherine Solomonson (Cambridge University Press)

2005

House and Home in Modern Japan: Architecture, Domestic Space, and Bourgeois Culture, 1880–1930 by Jordan Sand (Harvard University Press)

* At this time the SAH altered their award schedule to coincide with their annual meeting; therefore, no award for 1993 was granted.

Source: Society of Architectural Historians

American Academy of Arts and Letters Academy Awards for Architecture

The American Academy of Arts and Letters grants its annual Academy Awards for Architecture to an American architect(s) whose work is characterized by a strong personal direction. The prize consists of a $7,500 cash award. Recipients must be citizens of the United States. Members of the academy are not eligible.

For more information, contact the American Academy of Arts and Letters at (212) 368-5900.

1991	Rodolfo Machado and Jorge Silvetti
1992	Thom Mayne and Michael Rotondi, Morphosis
1993	Franklin D. Israel
1994	Craig Hodgetts and Hsin-Ming Fung
1995	Mack Scogin and Merrill Elam
1996	Maya Lin
1997	Daniel Libeskind
1998	Laurie Olin
1999	Eric Owen Moss
2000	Will Bruder
	Jesse Reiser and Nanako Umemoto
2001	Vincent James
	SHoP/Sharples Holden Pasquarelli
2002	Rick Joy
	Office dA/Mónica Ponce de León with Nader Tehrani
2003	Greg Lynn
	Guy Nordensen
	Andrew Zago
2004	Preston Scott Cohen
	Marion Weiss and Michael Manfredi
	James Corner
2005	Gisue Hariri and Mojgan Hariri
	Toshiko Mori
	Massimo and Lella Vignelli

Source: American Academy of Arts and Letters

American Academy of Arts and Letters Gold Medal for Architecture

The American Academy of Arts and Letters annually grants a gold medal in the arts, rotating among painting, music, sculpture, poetry, and architecture. The architect's entire career is weighed when being considered for the award. Only citizens of the United States are eligible.

For more information, contact the American Academy of Arts and Letters at (212) 368-5900.

1912	William Rutherford Mead	1973	Louis I. Kahn
1921	Cass Gilbert	1979	I.M. Pei
1930	Charles Adams Platt	1984	Gordon Bunshaft
1940	William Adams Delano	1990	Kevin Roche
1949	Frederick Law Olmsted	1996	Philip Johnson
1953	Frank Lloyd Wright	2002	Frank Gehry
1958	Henry R. Shepley		
1963	Ludwig Mies van der Rohe		
1968	R. Buckminster Fuller		

Source: American Academy of Arts and Letters

Did you know...

Swanke Hayden Connell Architects is restoring the gilded dome of the West Virginia State Capitol to its original 1932 appearance, which the building's architect, Cass Gilbert, modeled after the 17th-century dome of the Hotel des Invalides in Paris.

Annual Interiors Awards

The Annual Interiors Awards recognizes interior design excellence in multiple commercial categories. A jury of design professionals selects winning projects based on aesthetics, design creativity, function, and achievement of client objectives, which are published in *Contract* magazine. Winners are also honored at the Annual Interiors Awards Breakfast in New York.

For more information, visit *Contract*'s Web site at *www.contractmagazine.com*.

2005 Recipients

Education
Pomerantz Student Union, Drake University
Des Moines, IA
Herbert Lewis Kruse Blunck Architecture

Environmental
Genzyme Center
Cambridge, MA
Behnisch, Behnisch & Partner

Exhibit
Keep Off the Grass!
Los Angeles, CA
Griffin Enright Architects

Hotel
Lodge at Turning Stone
Verona, NY
BBGM Interiors

Large Office
Human Rights Campaign
Washington, DC
Skidmore, Owings & Merrill

Restaurant
IniAni Coffee Shop
New York, NY
Lewis.Tsurumaki.Lewis

Restoration
Boston Opera House
Boston, MA
Martinez & Johnson Architecture

Retail
Fornarina Mandalay Bay
Las Vegas NV
Giorgio Borruso Design

Service Retail
Tsunami Wash
Palm Springs, CA
RoathDesign

Showroom
DuPont Antron Chicago Showroom
Chicago, IL
Perkins+Will/Eva Maddox Branded
    Environments

Small Office
M-E Engineers Offices & Studio
Culver City, CA
HKS Architects

Sports/Entertainment
McClendon Athletic Facility, Heritage
    Hall School
Oklahoma City, OK
Elliott + Associates Architects

Student/Conceptual
Tango Nuevo
California State University at Long Beach
Mandy Chan

Annual Interiors Awards

Pomerantz Student Union. With the inauguration of the Pomerantz Student Union, Drake students now have a unique, fun place to gather, including a coffee/smoothie shop, e-mail terminals, pool tables, dart boards, and a stage. The design fosters a real student union atmosphere, something the campus previously lacked. **Photo courtesy of Drake University.**

Jury

Robert Brown, Childs Bertman Tseckares/CBT
Shashi Caan, The Shashi Caan Collective
Wing Chao, Walt Disney Imagineering
Julie Eizenberg, Koning Eizenberg Architecture
Michael Gabellini, Gabellini Associates

Source: Contract *magazine*

APA Journalism Awards

The American Planning Association honors outstanding newspaper coverage of city and regional planning issues each year with its Journalism Awards. This accolade is presented to daily and weekly newspapers in three classes: circulation below 50,000; circulation of 50,000 to 100,000; and circulation above 100,000. Papers in the United States and Canada are eligible; nominations may be made by an editor, publisher, or the readers. Winning articles must render outstanding public service in their coverage, perspective, interpretation, and impact.

Additional information is available on the Internet at *www.planning.org* or by contacting the APA at (312) 431-9985.

2005 Recipients

Large Newspaper
(circulation 100,000+)
"The Last Drop"
Rocky Mountain News (Denver, CO)
Jerd Smith, Todd Hartman, Ken Papaleo

Medium Newspaper
(circulation 50,000–100,000)
"Downtown: Beyond Perception"
Green Bay Press-Gazette (Green Bay, WI)
Richard Ryman, Karen Rauen

Small Newspaper
(circulation under 50,000)
"Little Pink Houses"
Lebanon Democrat (Lebanon, TN)
Brian Harville

Source: American Planning Association

Architectural Photography Competition

The American Institute of Architects' St. Louis chapter sponsors the Architectural Photography Competition each year. Winners are awarded a cash prize and are eligible for inclusion in the American Architectural Foundation's yearly calendar. All architects, AIA associate members, and members of the American Institute of Architecture Students from the United States are eligible to enter. The subject matter must have an architectural theme or contain some element of the manmade environment.

Winning photos can be seen on the AIA St. Louis chapter's Web site at *www.aia-stlouis.org.*

2005 Winners

First Place
"Yard"
Leadville, CO
Val Glitsch

Second Place
"Civic Reflection"
Chicago, IL
Jonathan Wirth

Third Place
"Desolate Shade"
Atacama Desert, Chile
Steven House

Louise Bethune Award
"Palouse Hills"
Washington state
Richard Cardwell

Judges Special Commendation Awards
"Green Barn 1"
Quebec, Canada
Tom Cullins

"DC Underground"
Washington, DC
Thomas Peterson

"New Stair"
Ettal Monastery, Germany
Gerald Moorehead

"Composition with Roof and Rail"
Milwaukee, WI
Mehernosh Mistry

"Untitled"
Gweta, Botswana
John Shorb Jr.

"Street Theatre"
Barcelona, Spain
Yves Gosselin

"Last Frontier"
Grand Canyon, AZ
Daniel Langer

"Symbiotic Sidesway"
Granville, ND
Gerald Shonkwiler

"Monterey Bay Aquarium"
Monterey, CA
Eleanor Choi

"Stripes"
Houston, TX
Val Glitsch

Source: AIA St. Louis

Architecture Firm Award

The American Institute of Architects grants its Architecture Firm Award, the highest honor the AIA can bestow on a firm, annually to an architecture firm for "consistently producing distinguished architecture." Eligible firms must claim collaboration within the practice as a hallmark of their methodology and must have been producing work as an entity for at least 10 years.

For more information, visit the AIA on the Internet at *www.aia.org* or contact the AIA Honors and Awards Department at (202) 626-7586.

1962	Skidmore, Owings & Merrill
1964	The Architects Collaborative
1965	Wurster, Bernardi & Emmons
1967	Hugh Stubbins & Associates
1968	I.M. Pei & Partners
1969	Jones & Emmons
1970	Ernest J. Kump Associates
1971	Albert Kahn Associates, Inc.
1972	Caudill Rowlett Scott
1973	Shepley Bulfinch Richardson Abbott
1974	Kevin Roche John Dinkeloo & Associates
1975	Davis, Brody & Associates
1976	Mitchell/Giurgola Architects
1977	Sert, Jackson and Associates
1978	Harry Weese & Associates
1979	Geddes Brecher Qualls Cunningham
1980	Edward Larrabee Barnes Associates
1981	Hardy Holzman Pfeiffer Associates
1982	Gwathmey Siegel & Associates, Architects
1983	Holabird & Root, Architects, Engineers & Planners
1984	Kallmann, McKinnell & Wood, Architects
1985	Venturi, Rauch and Scott Brown
1986	Esherick Homsey Dodge & Davis
1987	Benjamin Thompson & Associates
1988	Hartman-Cox Architects
1989	Cesar Pelli & Associates
1990	Kohn Pedersen Fox Associates
1991	Zimmer Gunsul Frasca Partnership
1992	James Stewart Polshek and Partners
1993	Cambridge Seven Associates Inc.
1994	Bohlin Cywinski Jackson
1995	Beyer Blinder Belle
1996	Skidmore, Owings & Merrill
1997	R.M. Kliment & Frances Halsband Architects
1998	Centerbrook Architects and Planners
1999	Perkins & Will
2000	Gensler
2001	Herbert Lewis Kruse Blunck
2002	Thompson, Ventulett, Stainback & Associates
2003	The Miller/Hull Partnership
2004	Lake/Flato Architects Inc.
2005	Murphy/Jahn

Source: American Institute of Architects

ar+d award

The ar+d award for emerging architecture is an international annual competition intended to bring wider recognition to a talented new generation of architects and designers. It is open to architects and designers age 45 and under. Encompassing the full range of design activity, entries can be made for any building, interior, landscape, urban site, or product design as long as it is a completed work. Each year the jury selects the award categories and chooses any number of winners and highly commended entries. A total of £10,000 in prize money is awarded. Sponsored by the British periodical *The Architectural Review*, d line™ international, a Danish architectural firm; and Buro Happold, a European engineering firm, the ar+d award was inaugurated in 1999.

Additional information and an entry form can be found on the ar+d award Web site, *www.arplusd.com.*

2004 Winners

Maritime Youth Centre
Amager, Copenhagen, Denmark
PLOT (Denmark)

Porciuncula de La Milagrosa
La Calera, Colombia
Daniel Bonilla Arquitectos (Columbia)

Peregrine Winery
Gibbston Valley, Otago, New Zealand
Architecture Workshop (New Zealand)

Cell Brick House
Tokyo, Japan
Atelier Tekuto (Japan)

Architectural Documentation Centre
Madrid, Spain
Aparicio + Fernandez-Elorza (Spain)

2004 High Commendations

Urban renewal around Palazzo Arese
Cesano Maderno, Italy
Marco Castelletti Architetto (Italy)

Mausoleum
Murcia, Spain
Manuel Clavel Rojo (Spain)

City Museum of Ljubjlana extension
Ljubjlana, Slovenia
Ofis Arhitekti (Slovenia)

ar+d award

2004 Commendations

64

Ecole Sauvage
Luong Son, Vietnam
Theskyisbeautiful Architecture (France)

House
Antiparos, Greece
Deca Architecture (Greece)

Interfaith Spiritual Center, Northeastern
   University
Boston, MA
Office dA (US)

Garden hut
Sant Miquel de Cruilles, Spain
eightyseven (UK)

Fenestration system, No. 1 Moulmein Rise
Singapore
WoHa Designs (Singapore)

Bathing establishment on Lake Segrino
Como, Italy
Marco Castelletti Architetto (Italy)

Glowgo lamp
Carl Fredrik Svenstedt (France)

Worb Railway Station
Bern, Switzerland
Smarch (Switzerland)

House
Malahide, Dublin, Ireland
David McDowell (Ireland)

Museum of Natural Science
Matsunoyama, Niigata, Japan
Tezuka Architects (Japan)

Fishmouth-inspired landscaping
Dujiangyan City, China
Turenscape (China)

2004 Honorable Mention

First Presbyterian Church of Encino
Encino, CA
Abramson Teiger Architects (US)

Swiss Pavilion for ARCO
Madrid, Spain
2B Architectes (Spain)

Erica Mann Elementary School
Berlin, Germany
Die Baupiloten (Germany)

Jury
Mario Cucinella, MCA (Germany)
Kevin Daly, Daly Genik (US)
Ryue Nishizawa, Kazuyo Sejima + Ryue
   Nishizawa/SANAA (Japan)
Gert Wingårdh, Wingårdh Architects (Sweden)
Peter Davey, *Architectural Review* (UK)

Source: ar+d award

Peregrine Winery. Peregrine's state-of-the-art winery is both the functional center of the label's winemaking and a piece of art in harmony with the landscape. The winery operations are actually housed underground topped by the free-floating, translucent roof, which represents the wing of the native Peregrine bird and the schist rock rising out of the ground throughout the area. Photo by Patrick Reynolds, courtesy of Architecture Workshop.

Arnold W. Brunner Memorial Prize

With the Arnold W. Brunner Memorial Prize the American Academy of Arts and Letters annually recognizes an architect who has contributed to architecture as an art. A prize of $5,000 is granted to each recipient. Eligibility is open to architects of any nationality.

For more information, contact the American Academy of Arts and Letters at (212) 368-5900.

1955	Gordon Bunshaft (US)
	Minoru Yamasaki (US), *Honorable Mention*
1956	John Yeon (US)
1957	John Carl Warnecke (US)
1958	Paul Rudolph (US)
1959	Edward Larrabee Barnes (US)
1960	Louis I. Kahn (US)
1961	I.M. Pei (US)
1962	Ulrich Franzen (US)
1963	Edward Charles Basset (US)
1964	Harry Weese (US)
1965	Kevin Roche (US)
1966	Romaldo Giurgola (US)
1967	*No award granted*
1968	John M. Johansen (US)
1969	Noel Michael McKinnell (US)
1970	Charles Gwathmey and Richard Henderson (US)
1971	John Andrews (Australia)
1972	Richard Meier (US)
1973	Robert Venturi (US)
1974	Hugh Hardy with Norman Pfeiffer and Malcolm Holzman (US)
1975	Lewis Davis and Samuel Brody (US)
1976	James Stirling (UK)
1977	Henry N. Cobb (US)
1978	Cesar Pelli (US)
1979	Charles W. Moore (US)
1980	Michael Graves (US)
1981	Gunnar Birkerts (US)

1982	Helmut Jahn (US)
1983	Frank O. Gehry (US)
1984	Peter K. Eisenman (US)
1985	William Pedersen and Arthur May (US)
1986	John Hejduk (US)
1987	James Ingo Freed (US)
1988	Arata Isozaki (Japan)
1989	Richard Rogers (UK)
1990	Steven Holl (US)
1991	Tadao Ando (Japan)
1992	Sir Norman Foster (UK)
1993	Jose Rafael Moneo (Spain)
1994	Renzo Piano (Italy)
1995	Daniel Urban Kiley (US)
1996	Tod Williams and Billie Tsien (US)
1997	Henri Ciriani (France)
1998	Alvaro Siza (Portugal)
1999	Fumihiko Maki (Japan)
2000	Toyo Ito (Japan)
2001	Henry Smith-Miller and Laurie Hawkinson (US)
2002	Kazuyo Sejima + Ryue Nishizawa (Japan)
2003	Elizabeth Diller and Ricardo Scofidio (US)
2004	Hans Hollein (Austria)
2005	Shigeru Ban (Japan)

Source: American Academy of Arts and Letters

ASLA Design Medal

The ASLA Design Medal recognizes an individual landscape architect who has produced a body of exceptional design work at a sustained level for at least 10 years. Medals are conferred by the board of trustees of the American Society of Landscape Architects and are presented during the organization's annual meeting.

For additional information, visit the ASLA on the Web at *www.alsa.org* or call (202) 898-2444.

2003	Lawrence Halprin
2004	M. Paul Friedberg
2005	Laurie D. Olin

Source: American Society of Landscape Architects

We cannot live in pictures, and therefore a landscape designed as a series of pictures robs us of an opportunity to use that area for animated living.

James Rose

Laurie D. Olin. A founder and principal of the Olin Partnership, Ltd. in Philadelphia, Laurie Olin's notable projects range from Bryant Park and Battery Park City in New York, to the J. Paul Getty Center in Los Angeles, to Independence Historical Park in Philadelphia and the Washington Monument in Washington, DC. Photo by James B. Abbott, courtesy of the Olin Partnership.

ASLA Firm Award

The American Society of Landscape Architects presents its ASLA Firm Award annually to landscape architecture firms that have produced bodies of distinguished work influencing professional practice for a sustained period of at least 10 years. It is the highest award the ASLA may bestow on a landscape architecture firm. The organization's board of trustees selects the recipient on the following criteria: the firm's influence on the profession of landscape architecture; the collaborative environment of the firm; the consistent quality of the firm's work; and its recognition by fellow practitioners, teachers of landscape architecture, members of allied professions, and the general public.

For more information, contact the ASLA online at *www.asla.org* or (202) 898-2444.

2003	Jones & Jones
2004	Wallace Roberts & Todd, LLC
2005	SWA Group

Source: American Society of Landscape Architects

ASLA Medal

The American Society of Landscape Architects anually awards its highest honor, the ASLA Medal, to an individual who has made a significant contribution to the field of landscape architecture. The following individuals were chosen for the unique and lasting impact of their work in landscape design, planning, writing, and/or public service. Eligibility is open to ASLA members and non-members of any nationality.

For more information, contact the ASLA at (202) 898-2444 or visit its Web site at *www.asla.org.*

1971	Hideo Sasaki	1990	Ray Freeman
1972	Conrad L. Wirth	1991	Meade Palmer
1973	John C. Simonds	1992	Robert S. (Doc) Reich
1974	Campbell E. Miller	1993	A.E. (Ed) Bye Jr.
1975	Garrett Eckbo	1994	Edward D. Stone Jr.
1976	Thomas Church	1995	Dr. Ervin Zube
1977	Hubert Owens	1996	John Lyle
1978	Lawrence Halprin	1997	Julius Fabos
1979	Norman T. Newton	1998	Carol R. Johnson
1980	William G. Swain	1999	Stuart C. Dawson
1981	Sir Geoffrey Jellicoe	2000	Carl D. Johnson
1982	Charles W. Eliot II	2001	Robert E. Marvin
1983	Theodore O. Osmundson	2002	Morgan (Bill) Evans
1984	Ian McHarg	2003	Richard Haag
1985	Roberto Burle Marx	2004	Peter E. Walker
1986	William J. Johnson	2005	Jane Silverstein Ries
1987	Phillip H. Lewis Jr.		
1988	Dame Sylvia Crowe		
1989	Robert N. Royston		

Source: American Society of Landscape Architects

Did you know...

In 2005, Peter Walker was named the first recipient of the International Federation of Landscape Architects' Sir Geoffrey Jellico Gold Medal for the lasting impact his work has had on the welfare of society and the environment.

ASLA Medal

Jane Silverstein Ries. In 1929 Jane Silverstein Ries enrolled at the Lowthorpe School of Landscape Architecture and, upon graduating, became the first female landscape architect in the state of Colorado. Shortly thereafter, she started her own firm. Throughout her 56-year career, Ries became an early advocate of sustainable design, was the creative force behind such civic improvement projects as the Denver Botanical Gardens and the Denver Art Museum, and, in her residential work, endeavored to make the garden another room of the house.

ASLA Professional Awards

The American Society of Landscape Architects' annual Professional Awards program is intended to encourage the profession by rewarding works of distinction and to generate increased visibility for the winners and the profession in general. Entries are accepted for placement in one of four areas: design, analysis and planning, residential design (cosponsored by *Garden Design* magazine), and communication. Eligibility is open to any landscape architect or, in the case of communication projects, any individual or group. Juries for each category are comprised of landscape professionals and appointed by ASLA's Professional Awards Committee.

For additional information, visit the ASLA's Web site at *www.asla.org* or contact them at (202) 898-2444.

2005 Design Award Recipients

Award of Excellence
Kreielsheimer Promenade at Marion Oliver
    McCaw Hall
Seattle, WA
Gustafson Guthrie Nichol Ltd

Heart of the Park at Hermann Park
Houston, TX
SWA Group with Olin Partnership, Ltd.

Award of Honor
South Campus, Toyota Motor Sales, USA, Inc.
Torrance, CA
LPA, Inc.

Ben Gurion International Airport
Lod, Israel
Shlomo Aronson Architects

Shenyang Architectural University Campus
Shenyang City, Liaoning Province, China
Peking University Graduate School of Landscape
    Architecture; Turenscape

Stanford University Medical School Campus
    Underground Parking Garage
Palo Alto, CA
Peter Walker and Partners

12,000 Factory Workers Meet Ecology in the
    Parking Lot
Canton, GA
Michael Van Valkenburgh Associates, Inc.

Illinois Institute of Technology Campus
Chicago, IL
Peter Lindsay Schaudt Landscape
    Architecture, Inc.

Ute Cemetery Restoration
Aspen, CO
BHA Design, Inc.

Capitol Plaza
New York, NY
Thomas Balsley Associates

Mount St. Helens National Volcanic Monument,
    Coldwater/Johnston Recreation Complex
Castle Rock, WA
Charles Anderson Landscape Architecture;
    EDAW, Inc.; USDA Forest Service

Parc Diagonal Mar
Barcelona, Spain
EDAW, Inc.; EMBT Arquitectes

ASLA Professional Awards

Capitol Plaza. Located in the emerging Chelsea Heights neighborhood, this new public open space, which connects 26th and 27th streets, just east of Sixth Avenue, features garden seating areas, a promenade, and cafes. In an area of Manhattan with too few public open spaces, the aim of the Capitol Plaza was to offer people a place to pause among lush bamboo groves, ornamental grass plantings, distinctive contemporary seating, and adjacent cafes and shops–all in a synergistic composition that ensures long term enjoyment and use. **Photos by Michael Koontz.**

ASLA Professional Awards

2005 Residential Design Recipients

Award of Excellence
Stone Meadow
Martha's Vineyard, MA
Stephen Stimson Associates

Award of Honor
Cane River Residence
Natchitoches, LA
Jeffrey Carbo Landscape Architects/
    Site Planners

Private Residential Garden
Minneapolis, MN
oslund.and.assoc.

Island Modern
Key West, FL
Raymond Jungles, Inc.

Private Residence/Garden of Planes
Richmond, VA
Gregg Bleam Landscape Architects

Private Residence
Rowena, OR
Koch Landscape Architecture

Ivy Street Roof Garden
San Francisco, CA
Andrea Cochran Landscape Architecture

Livingood Residence
Jackson, WY
VLA, Inc.

Reyrosa Ranch
Waxahachie, TX
MESA Design Group

2005 Analysis & Planning Award Recipients

Award of Excellence
"The New American City: The Noisette
    Community of North Charleston, SC"
North Charleston, SC
BNIM Architects; Burt Hill Inc.

Award of Honor
"Lloyd Crossing Sustainable Urban Design Plan"
Portland, OR
Mithun Architects + Designers + Planners

"Clearings, Clusters, and Cloisters: A Garden
    of Trees for Two Rivers Park"
Little Rock, AR
University of Arkansas Community
    Design Center

"The Growth Pattern of Taizhou City Based on
    Ecological Infrastructure"
Taizhou City, Zhejiang Province, China
Peking University Graduate School of Landscape
    Architecture; Turenscape

"Brightwater Siting Project"
King and Snohomish Counties, WA
King County Department of Natural Resources
    and Parks-Wastewater Treatment Division;
    CH2M Hill; Environmental Science Associates

"Calumet Plans"
Chicago, IL
City of Chicago, Department of Planning;
    Wolff Clements & Associates; Planning
    Resources Inc

"Gateway Valley Development"
Orinda, CA
Hart Howerton

"Burlingame Ranch Affordable Housing"
Aspen, CO
DHM Design

ASLA Professional Awards

"Battery Park City Streetscapes"
New York, NY
Rogers Marvel Architects

"Dasve Village"
Maharashtra, India
HOK Planning Group

2005 Communications Award Recipients

Award of Honor

The Grand Concourse Authority Walkway
   Maintenance Manual
The Grand Concourse Authority

Urban Ecology; Landscape Design Principles and
   Practices for Water Quality Improvement in
   the Lower Boise River
Ecosystem Sciences Foundation

Jury

Gary R. Hilderbrand, Reed Hilderbrand
   Associates, Inc. (chair)
Beth Dunlop, *Miami Herald*
Edward A. Feiner, Skidmore, Owings & Merrill
Terence Harkness, University of Illinois at
   Urbana–Champaign
Suzanne Turner, consultant
Mia Lehrer, Mia Lehrer + Associates
Todd Johnson, Design Workshop, Inc.
Bill Marken, *Garden Design* magazine
Barbara E. Wilks, W Architecture and Landscape
Karen Jessup, National Trust for Historic
   Preservation

Source: American Society of Landscape Architects

Auguste Perret Prize

The International Union of Architects (UIA) grants the triennial Auguste Perret Prize to an internationally renowned architect or architects for work in applied technology in architecture. The prize is named after notable French architect Auguste Perret, a leading pioneer of reinforced concrete design.

For more information, visit the UIA's Web site at *www.uia-architectes.org.*

1961
Felix Candela (Mexico)

Honorary Mention
The architects of the British Ministry for Education office and the architects of the office for the study of industrial and agricultural buildings of Hungary

1963
Kunio Mayekawa (Japan)
Jean Prouvé (France)

1965
Hans Scharoun (GFR)

Honorary Mention
Heikki and Kaija Siren (Finland)

1967
Frei Otto and Rolf Gutbrod (GFR)

1969
Karel Hubacek (Czechoslovakia)

1972
E. Pinez Pinero (Spain)

1975
Arthur C. Erickson and team (Canada)

Honorary Mention
J. Cardoso (Brazil)

1978
Kiyonori Kitutake (Japan)
Piano & Rogers (Italy/UK)

1981
Günter Behnisch (GFR)

Honorary Mention
Jacques Rougerie (France)

1984
Joao Baptista Vilanova Artigas (Brazil)

1987
Santiago Calatrava (Spain)

Honorary Mention
Clorindo Testa (Argentina)

1990
Adien Fainsilber (France)

1993
KHR AS Arkitekten (Denmark)

1996
Thomas Herzog (Germany)

1999
Ken Yeang (Malaysia)

2002
Sir Norman Foster (UK)

2005
Werner Sobek (Germany)

Source: International Union of Architects

Austrian Frederick Kiesler Prize for Architecture and the Arts

The biennial Austrian Frederick Kiesler Prize for Architecture and the Arts is presented for extraordinary achievement in architecture and the arts as relates to the work and philosophy of the award's namesake, Frederick Kiesler. A native of Vienna, Kiesler worked as a theatrical producer, architect, painter, and sculptor (among other things) and was a prolific author. His nontraditional ideas about the correlated arts were both visionary and theoretical. This award honors that spirit. The Austrian Frederick and Lillian Kiesler Private Foundation organizes the award, which is presented alternately by the Republic of Austria and the City of Vienna.

Additional information is available at *www.kiesler.org.*

1998	Frank O. Gehry (US)
2000	Judith Barry (US)
2002	Cedric Price (UK)
2004	Asymptote/Hani Rashid + Lise Anne Courture (US)

Source: Austrian Frederick and Lillian Kiesler Private Foundation

Austrian Frederick Kiesler Prize for Architecture and the Arts

Hani Rashid and Lise Anne Couture. In 1989 Hani Rashid and Lise Anne Couture founded Asymptote, a collaborative design, architecture, and art practice in New York. Interactive digital design is at the forefront of their work, such as the virtual trading floor for the New York Stock Exchange and the Guggenheim Virtual Museum, which are both fully navigable, interactive, multidimensional architectural environments. Photos courtesy of the Kiesler Foundation.

Best in American Living Award

Each year the National Association of Home Builders and *Professional Builder* magazine jointly present the Best in American Living Award for residential housing. Judging criteria include not only appearance but the interior floor plans, how the project relates to its local market, and construction techniques and materials. The competition is open to builders, developers, architects, land planners, and designers nationwide who may enter designs in one of more than 40 categories, including the HUD Secretary's Award for Excellence, which recognizes design excellence produced through cooperative public/private efforts that expand homeownership opportunities for underserved Americans. Awards are presented at platinum, gold, and silver levels in addition to regional winners.

For a complete list of all winners with photos and floor plans, or to obtain an entry form, visit the Best in American Living Award page on the Internet at *www.housingzone.com*.

2004 Home of the Year

Altamura at Nellie Gail Ranch, Residence 3
Laguna Hills, CA
Bassenian/Lagoni Architects

2004 Platinum Winners

Best Single-Family Detached Home
Under 1,500 square feet
Baywood, Residence 1
Hercules, CA
Dahlin Group Architecture Planning

Best Single-Family Detached Home
1,501-1,800 square feet
Baywood, Residence 3
Hercules, CA
Dahlin Group Architecture Planning

Best Single-Family Detached Home
1,801-2,400 square feet
Carneros Inn
Napa, CA
William Rawn Associates, Architects, Inc.

Best Single-Family Detached Home
2,401-3,000 square feet
Ledges at Turtle Ridge, Residence 2Z
Irvine, CA
Robert Hidey Architects

Best Single-Family Detached Home
3,001-4,000 square feet
Nautilus, Residence 3
Newport Coast, CA
Robert Hidey Architects

Best Single-Family Detached Home
4,001 square feet and more
The Cortile Collection at the Bridges, Residence 2
Rancho Santa Fe, CA
Bassenian/Lagoni Architects

Best in American Living Award

Altamura at Nellie Gail Ranch, Residence 3
Laguna Hills, CA
Bassenian/Lagoni Architects

The Cortile Collection at The Bridges, Residence 3
Rancho Santa Fe, CA
Bassenian/Lagoni Architects

Best Attached Home
Up to and including 8 units per acre
The Strand at Crystal Cove
Newport Beach, CA
Scheurer Architects

Best Attached Home
20 units per acre and over
Sutter's Mill, Plan 4
Ladera Ranch, CA
Bassenian/Lagoni Architects

Best One-of-a-Kind Custom Home
Up to and including 4,000 square feet
Rivera Barn
Napa, CA
Dahlin Group Architecture Planning

Alexander Residence
Newport Beach, CA
Scheurer Architect

Best One-of-a-Kind Custom Home
4,001–6,500 square feet
Color Me Kiawah
Kiawah Island, SC
Wayne Windham Architect

Private Residence
Scottsdale, AZ
Urban Design Associates, Ltd.

Best One-of-a-Kind Custom Home
6,501 square feet and over
Childhood Memories, Re-created
Kiawah Island, SC
Christopher Rose Architects

Best Rental Development
5 units and over
The Prado
Valencia, CA
Thomas P. Cox Architects, Inc.

Watermarke
Irvine, CA
Meeks + Partners

Best Neighborhood
151 units and over
Habersham
Beaufort, SC
Duany Plater-Zyberk & Company; Stephen
    Fuller; Moser Design Group Inc.; William T.
    Baker; Brown Design Studio

Best Urban Smart Growth
Neighborhood/Community
Fall Creek Place
Indianapolis, IN
Rottmann Architects

Best Smart Growth Community
151 units and over
Stapleton
Denver, CO
Forest City Stapleton, Inc.

Suburban Smart Growth
Neighborhood/Community
Daniel Island
Charleston, SC
The Daniel Island Company

Fruitvale Transit Village
Oakland, CA
McLarand Vasquez Emsiek & Partners

HUD Secretary's Award for Excellence
No platinum award granted

Best in American Living Award

Jury
Jody Beck, New Jersey Institute of Technology
Patty Carmichael, John Laing Luxury
Armando Cobo, Armando Cobo Designer
Cheryl O'Brien, C. O'Brien Architects
Douglas Gilliland, The Triwest Group, Inc.
Barry Glantz, Glantz & Associates
Sarah Dreo, Lita Dirks & Co.
Kent DeReus, Orren Pickell
Pa Darcy Garneau, EDI Architects
Carol Lavender, Lavender Design Group
Rick Leach, Paragon Construction
Heather McCune, *Professional Builder*
Elton Parsons, Builders Inc
Dennis Rodriguez, SheaHomes Colorado
Stephen D. Shelley, HUD Chicago Office
Ed Tombari, NAHB
Andrea Vrankar, HUD Cleveland Office
Robin Ward, Municipality of Anchorage
Rita Williams, merchandisingplus

Source: Professional Builder *magazine*

None of us has invented the house;
that was done many thousands of
years ago.

Arne Jacobsen

Best of NeoCon

The Best of NeoCon Competition honors new products introduced to the US market during the past year. The program's sponsor's include: *Contract* magazine; Merchandise Mart Properties, Inc.; International Interior Design Association; International Facility Management Association; and McMorrowreport.com. A jury of industry professionals selects gold, silver, editor's choice, and innovation award winners. From these, one product is chosen as the best of competition. Winners are announced at NeoCon, the interior design industry's annual showcase for the newest products and trends.

For more information and a list of all winners, including photos, visit *Contract* on the Web at *www.contractmagazine.com.*

2005 Best of Competition

Art Center College of Design, Seating Collection
Bernhardt Design

Art Center College of Design, Tables Collection
Bernhardt Design

2005 Gold Winners

Alternative Office
44 (For Four)
Hettich

Architectural Products
Bricks, Boards and Sticks Collection
Joel Berman Glass Studios

Carpet: Broadloom
Colouresce
Monterey Carpets

Carpet: Fiber
Enviro6ix nylon
Zeftron

Carpet: Modular
L7
Shaw Contract Group

Case Goods & Desks
Aerial
Nucraft

Education Solutions
More Collection
Howe Furniture

Files & Storage
Reach
Allsteel Inc.

Flooring
Five New Textures for Roundel Rubber
    Flooring Line
Johnsonite

Furniture Systems
Align
Allsteel Inc.

Furniture Systems: Enhancements
Elective Elements
Steelcase Inc.

Healthcare Products
Narrative
Patrician Furniture, Inc.

Best of NeoCon

Lighting
Halley, LED Task Lamp
Lucesco Lighting

Office Accessories
Lapjack
Colebrook Bosson Saunders

Seating: Ergonomic Desk/Task
Silver Office & Conference Seating
Interstuhl Buromoebel GmbH & Co. KG

Seating: Guest
Liberty side chair
Humanscale

Seating: Sofas & Lounge
Art Center College of Design, Seating Collection
Bernhardt Design

Seating: Stacking
Daylight
KI

Surfacing Materials
Infused Imagery Collection
Deepa Textiles

Tables: Conference
a_con conference table
Haworth, Inc.

Tables: Occasional
Art Center College of Design, Tables Collection
Bernhardt Design

Technology Support
"FYI" Flat Panel Monitor Arm
Details

Textiles: Drapery/Cubicle/Shade
Natural Intelligence
Deepa Textiles

Textiles: Upholstery
Art of the Line: Upholstery
Deepa Textiles

Wall Treatments
Mother of Pearl
Maya Romanoff Corporation

Workplace Technologies
Babble, Voice Privacy without Walls
Sonare Technologies | A Herman Miller
    Company

Source: Contract *magazine*

83

Best of Seniors' Housing Awards

The National Council on Seniors' Housing, a council established by the National Association of Home Builders in 1989, annually presents the Best of Seniors' Housing Awards. Winning projects are chosen for their ability to meet the demands and needs of the ever-changing seniors' housing market, including the constraints of seniors' housing in marketability, budget, density, and programs. Platinum, gold, and silver awards are presented in a range of categories based on project type and size.

For a complete list of all winners, including photos and full project credits, visit NCOSH online at *www.nahb.org*.

2005 Platinum Recipients

Active Adult Community, Midsize
The Villages on Mount Hope Bay
Tiverton, RI
Bloodgood Sharp Buster

Active Adult Community, Large
Four Seasons at Palm Springs
Palm Springs, CA
Perlman Architects

Active Adult Community Center, Midsize
Riviera at Freehold
Freehold, NJ
Minno & Wasko Architects and Planners

Active Adult Community Center, Very Large
Club Renaissance at Sun City Center
Sun City Center, FL
JBZ Architecture + Planning

Active Adult Community Center Interior Design, Midsize
Four Seasons at Farmington
Macungie, PA
M. Ford and Associates

Active Adult Community Center Interior Design, Large
Jubilee at Hawks Prairie
Lacey, WA
DesignWorks, Inc.

Active Adult Home Design
1,501–2,100 Square Feet
Canoa Ranch – Valle
Green Valley, AZ
Freeline

Riviera at Freehold
Freehold, NJ
Toll Architecture

Active Adult Home Design
2,101–2,800 Square Feet
Courtyard at Rolling Hills – Conifer
Denver, CO
Kephart

Village of Five Parks – The Gentry
Arvada, CO
Bloodgood Sharp Buster

Active Adult Community On the Boards, Large
Central Parke at Victoria Falls
Laurel, MD
Martin Architectural Group

Continuing Care Retirement Community, Large
Classic Residence by Hyatt at Aventura
Aventura, FL
Mouriz, Salazar & Associates

Best of Seniors' Housing Awards

Maravilla
Santa Barbara, CA
Mithun; Cearnal Architect

Park Springs
Stone Mountain, GA
Foley Design Associates

Continuing Care Retirement Community Common Area Interior Design, Large
Maravilla
Santa Barbara, CA
Mithun; Cearnal Architect

Montereau in Warren Woods
Tulsa, OK
Reese Lower Patrick & Scott, Ltd.

Continuing Care Retirement Community On the Boards, Large
The Hill at Whitemarsh
Lafayette Hill, PA
EGA, P.C.

Assisted Living Facility, Large
Willow Towers Assisted Living Residence
New Rochelle, NY
Perkins Eastman

For-Sale Condominiums
Touchmark at Mount Bachelor Village
Bend, OR
Touchmark Development & Construction Co.

Affordable Rental Apartments
Kenaitze Point
Anchorage, AK
Koonce Pfeffer Bettis

Silver Lake Commons
Pittsburgh, PA
Perkins Eastman

For-Sale Condominiums On the Boards
Sensara, Benalmadena Costa
Malaga, Spain
Guillen y Asociados

Aging in Place, New Production Home
St. Andrews Court – Drummond
Overland Park, KS
Wancour Residential Architects

Aging in Place, Remodeled Home
Old Naples Residence
Naples, FL
Abbie Joan Enterprises

Renovated Service-Enriched Seniors Housing
The Crossings at Woodbury Mews
Woodbury, NJ
J. Randolph Parry Architects

Renovated Multifamily Seniors Housing
Frisco Senior Apartments
Joplin, MO
Stark Wilson Duncan Architects, Inc.

Mixed-Use Project
Village of Five Parks
Arvada, CO
Village Homes

Source: National Council on Seniors' Housing, National Association of Home Builders

Bottom Line Design Awards

Business 2.0 and frog design launched the Bottom Line Design Awards to recognize the positive effects of experience-driven industrial design on businesses and their brands. Jurors analyzed entries for such factors as sales record, brand fit, relevance to the target consumer, marketing program, utilization of technology, impact on the corporate culture, improvement over previous models, ease of use and understanding, noteworthy design, and the generation of world-of-mouth recommendations and customer loyalty. One winner was chosen from each category.

For more information, visit frog design on the Web at *www.frogdesign.com* or *Business 2.0* at *www.business2.com.*

2005 Winners

Grand Prize
LiveStrong Wristband

Environments
Virgin Atlantic Upper-Class Cabin

Personal Computers
Apple Flat-Panel iMac G5

Household Goods
Fiskars Posthole Digger

Media
The Incredibles

Architecture
Millau Viaduct
Millau, France

Mobile Devices
Motorola Razr V3

2005 Honorable Mentions

Fashion
Tumi Flow Collection

Household Goods
OXO Good Grips Mandoline

User Interfaces
Google Gmail

Mobile Devices
Sony PlayStation Portable

Audio Equipment
Belkin PureAV Line

Furniture
Allsteel Sum Chair

Jury
Nanette Bisher, *San Francisco Chronicle*
Hartmut Esslinger, frog design
Rob Forbes, Design Within Reach
Karen Francis, Publicis & Hal Riney
Arnie Freeman, American Association of
    Advertising Agencies
Jeffrey Jones, Gap
Sam Lucente, Hewlett-Packard
Michael Moritz, Sequoia Capital
Patricia Roller, frog design

Source: Business 2.0 *and frog design*

Bridge Awards

The Engineers' Society of Western Pennsylvania annually recognizes outstanding achievements in bridge engineering through their Bridge Awards. The George S. Richardson Medal is awarded to bridges that demonstrate outstanding design, construction, research, or education. The Gustav Lindenthal Medal recognizes bridges for their technical and material innovation, aesthetic merit, harmony with the environment, or successful community participation. The Eugene C. Figg Medal is awarded to bridges that, through vision and innovation, provide an icon to the community for which it was designed. The focus of the Arthur G. Hayden Medal is on innovation in special-use bridges, such as pedestrian, people-movers, or non-traditional structures.

For more information, visit the Engineers' Society of Western Pennsylvania on the Web at *www.eswp.com.*

George S. Richardson Medal

1988	Sunshine Skyway Bridge St. Petersburg–Bradenton, FL
1989	Honshu-Shikoku Bridge Routes (specifically the Kojima-Sakaide Route) Kobe–Sakaide, Japan
1990	Ben Sawyer Bridge Mt. Pleasant–Sullivans Island, SC
1990	Oakland Bay Bridge San Francisco–Oakland, CA
1991	Roosevelt Lake Bridge Roosevelt, AZ
1992	Lake Washington Floating Bridge Seattle, WA
1993	Hanging Lake Viaduct Glenwood Canyon, CO
1994	Natchez Trace Parkway Bridge Franklin, TN
1995	Normandy Bridge Le Havre–Honfleur, France
1996	LRFD Design Specifications
1997	George P. Coleman Bridge Yorktown, VA
1998	Akashi-Kaikyo Bridge Honshu–Awaji, Japan
1999	Confederation Bridge Northumberland Strait, Port Borden, PE–Cape Tormentine, NB, Canada
2000	Storrow Drive Bridge Boston, MA
2001	Tagus River Suspension Bridge Rail Addition Project Lisbon, Portugal
2002	Lions Gate Bridge Vancouver, BC, Canada
2003	Leonard P. Zakim Bunker Hill Bridge Boston, MA
2004	Al Zampa Memorial Bridge (New Carquinez Bridge) Vallejo, CA
2005	Rion–Antirion Bridge (Harilaos Trikoupis Bridge) Rion–Antirrion, Greece

Bridge Awards

Gustav Lindenthal Medal

1999	Interstate H-3 Winward Viaduct Oahu, Hawaii
2000	Golden Gate Bridge San Francisco, CA
2001	Oresund Fixed Link Bridge Project Copenhagen, Denmark–Malmö, Sweden
2002	Broadway Bridge Daytona Beach, FL
2003	President JK Bridge Brasilia, Brazil
2004	Mingo Creek Viaduct (Joe Montana Bridge) Washington County, PA
2005	Viaduct of Millau Millau, France

Eugene C. Figg Jr. Medal for Signature Bridges

2002	Jiangyin Bridge Jiangyin, China
2003	Rama 8 Bridge Chaiyuth Na Nakorn, Bangkok, Thailand
2004	Lu Pu Bridge Shanghai, China
2005	Sundial Bridge at Turtle Bay Redding, CA

Arthur G. Hayden Medal

2003	Duisburg Inner Harbor Footbridge Duisburg, Germany
2004	Esplanade Riel Pedestrian Bridge Winnipeg, MB, Canada
2005	Liberty Bridge Greenville, SC

Source: Engineers' Society of Western Pennsylvania

Did you know...

When it opened on Dec. 14, 2004, Sir Norman Foster's Millau Viaduct (France) became, at 1,125 feet, the world's tallest bridge as well as the longest cable-stayed bridge, stretching 1.6 miles over the Tarn Gorge.

BusinessWeek/Architectural Record Awards

The *BusinessWeek/Architectural Record* Awards are given annually to organizations that prove "good design is good business." Sponsored by the American Institute of Architects, in conjunction with *Architectural Record* and *BusinessWeek* magazines, the award's special focus is on collaboration and the achievement of business goals through architecture. Eligible projects must have been completed within the past three years and be submitted jointly by the architect and the client. Projects may be located anywhere in the world.

For additional information, call (202) 682-3205 or visit the AIA on the Internet at *www.aia.org*.

2004 Winners

Humane Society/SPCA of San Antonio
and Bexar County
San Antonio, TX
Alamo Architects Inc. with Connolly
Architects Inc.

Limerick County Hall
County Limerick, Ireland
Bucholz McEvoy Architects

MoMA QNS
Long Island City, NY
Cooper, Robertson & Partners with
Michael Maltzan Architecture

Israeli Foreign Ministry
Jerusalem, Israel
Diamond and Schmitt Architects Inc.
with Kolker, Kolker Epstein Architects

Iron Studio, Penland School of Crafts
Penland, NC
Frank Harmon Architect

Finn Center, Community School of Music
and Arts
Mountain View, CA
Mark Cavagnero Associates

Ehime Prefectural Budokan
Matsuyama City, Ehime, Japan
Ishimoto Architectural & Engineering Firm Inc.

James M. Wood Community Center
Los Angeles, CA
Lehrer Architects

Fisher Pavilion at Seattle Center
Seattle, WA
Miller/Hull Partnership

Britomart Transport Centre
Auckland, New Zealand
JASMAX Ltd. and Mario Madayag Architecture
Ltd. with Salmond Reed Architects

BusinessWeek/Architectural Record Awards

Jury

Moshe Safdie, Moshe Safdie and Associates
(chair)
Betsy Z. Cohen, Resource Asset Investment Trust
Rand Elliott, Elliott + Associates Architects
Douglas Gardner, Catellus Development
Corporation
Lee Green, IBM Corporation
Paul Herzan, Cooper–Hewitt, National Design
Museum
Frances P. Huppert, Empire State Development
Corporation
Marianne McKenna, Kuwabara Payne McKenna
Blumberg Architects
Paula S. Wallace, Savannah College of Art and
Design
Allison G. Williams, Ai Architecture/San
Francisco

Source: BusinessWeek/Architectural Record

Did you know...

The Ehime Prefectural Budokan, a new martial arts facility in Ehime, Japan, has seen a 700-percent increase in attendance and boosted the community's economy by $13 million.

Charter Awards

Presented annually by the Congress for the New Urbanism, the Charter Awards honor projects that best comply with the Charter of the New Urbanism. The Charter provides principles for development at three levels: the region; the neighborhood, district, and corridor; and the block, street, and building. Dedicated to improving and restoring the quality of life in urban neighborhoods as well as preserving the built environment, the CNU's Charter Awards specifically address how plans and projects respond to and integrate with their environment and, consequently, how they improve the human experience of blocks, neighborhoods, and regions. All architects, urban designers, planners, landscape architects, transportation planners, and civil engineers are eligible to enter, as are developers, institutions, government agencies, and the owners of the submitted projects.

For additional information as well as entry materials, visit the CNU on the Web at *www.cnu.org.*

2005 Winners

The Region: Metropolis, City, and Town

Chongming Island Master Plan
Shanghai, China
Skidmore, Owings & Merrill

Crozet Master Plan
Crozet, VA
Renaissance Planning Group

Dasve Village
Maharashtra, India
HOK Planning Group

Getting it Right: Preventing Sprawl
    in Coyote Valley
San Jose, CA
Wallace Roberts & Todd, LLC/Solomon E.T.C.

Western Sydney Urban Land Release
Sydney, Australia
NSW Department of Infrastructure, Planning
    and Natural Resources

The Neighborhood, the District, and the Corridor

Waukegan Lakefront Downtown Master
    Plan/Urban Design Plan
Waukegan, IL
Skidmore, Owings, & Merrill

Beall's Hill Urban Design and
    Architectural Guidelines
Macon, GA
Ayers Saint Gross Architects + Planners

Belmar
Lakewood, CO
Continuum Partners

Westgate Pasadena
Pasadena, CA
Thomas P. Cox Architects, Inc.

East Bayfront Precinct Plan
Toronto, ON, Canada
Koetter Kim & Associates

Charter Awards

Campus Åkroken, Mid Sweden University
Sundsvall, Sweden
Arken Arkitekter AB

The Block, the Street, and the Building
A Pattern Book for Norfolk Neighborhoods
Norfolk, VA
Urban Design Associates

The Intergenerational Learning Center
Chicago, IL
Office dA

Student/Faculty Submissions
Charrette #1: Envisioning International Avenue
Calgary, AB, Canada
University of Calgary

Honorable Mention
Buckwood Village
Greenville, SC
Clemson University

Jury
John Francis Torti, Torti Gallas and Partners
   (chair)
Stephanie Bothwell, Urban and Landscape
   Design
Maurice Cox, Professor, University of Virginia
Douglas Kelbaugh, University of Michigan
Paul Murrain, The Prince's Foundation
Linda Pollak, Marpillero Pollak Architects
Jeff B. Speck, National Endowment for the Arts

Source: Congress for the New Urbanism

The complexity of functions, the precision of the urban spaces, and particularly the revalorization of public space (as an alternative to the introverted and alienating tyranny of the privacy of suburbia) will be instrumental in the necessary revitalization of social and civic life, the redevelopment of urban freedom and autonomy, the emancipation of real citizenship in the renaissance of the traditional urban neighborhood!

Lucien Steil

da Vinci Awards

The da Vinci Awards, sponsored by the Engineering Society of Detroit and the Detroit chapter of the National Multiple Sclerosis Society, recognizes individuals, organizations, and corporations that improve the quality of life for people with disabilities and encourage universal design of products and environments that enable people and improve accessibility. Product entries must currently be on the market, and facility entries must be completed. Submissions categories include, but are not limited to, assistive technology, information technology, personal mobility, vehicular mobility, materials, applied research as well as commercial, public or residential facilities. Winners are celebrated at the annual Dinner with da Vinci™ gala.

For more information on the da Vinci Awards, visit *www.davinciawards.com.*

2004 Winners

The Application of Selective Laser Sintering Techniques to Improve the Functional Mobility for Those with Lower-Limb Disabilities
Richard R. Neptune, University of Texas at Austin

All Kids Playground
Waterford, MI
National Council of Jewish Women

HomeSaver1 Stove Sensor
Lee Sesinger

A Universally Accessible Treehouse at Crotched Mountain
Greenfield, NH
Forever Young Treehouses, Inc.

BoardSpeaker
Afforda Speech

Bruno Lift-Up Power Mobility Seat
Bruno Independent Living Aids, Inc.

IBM's Web Adaptation Device
IBM Accessibility Center

IKAN Bowler
MGT Corporation

Sanyog: A Multilingual Iconic Communication System for Children with Severe Speech and Multiple Disorders
Indian Institute of Technology

WheelchairBackpack Holder and Retriever
Chandler Macocha

Jury
Charles Wu, Ford Motor Company (chair)
Leonard Bertin, Mobile Music USA
John Fillion, DaimlerChrysler
Ann Gale, National Multiple Sclerosis Society
Beth Gibbons, SMART
Michael Harris, Paralyzed Veterans of America
Sue Littles, DTE Energy
David Miller, Construction Association of Michigan

Source: Engineering Society of Detroit and National Multiple Sclerosis Society, Detroit Chapter

Dedalo Minosse International Prize for Commissioning a Building

The biennial Dedalo Minosse International Prize, sponsored by the Associazione Liberi Architetti (Italian Association of Professional Architects), *l'Arca*, and Caoduro Lucernari, honors outstanding clients of architecture. The International Prize recognizes a client who has commissioned an architect from any country, whereas the ALA-Assoarchitetti Prize is given for commissioning an Italian architect. Both awards are also granted for hiring architects under 40 years old. In addition to these main prizes, 10 special awards and 12 acclamations are granted along with the Quinquennial Honorary Award, which commemorates the program's fifth anniversary. The prize takes its name from the Greek myth of Daedalus whose design for the elaborate labyrinth to imprison the Minotaur pleased his client, King Minos of Crete. But it was the clarity of Minos' vision that made such a design possible. Thus this prize celebrates that ineffable part of the creative process—the client's participation.

For additional information about the award and a complete list of winners, visit *www.assoarchitetti.it.*

2003–2004 Winners

International Prize for Commissioning a Building
KLIA Consultancy Services, client
Kuala Lumpur International Airport
Sepang, Selangor, Malaysia
Kisho Kurokawa Architect & Associates (Japan)

International Prize for Commissioning a Building, Architect Under 40
Aluminum Center Foundation, client
Aluminum Center Foundation Headquarters
Houten, Utrecht, Netherlands
Micha de Haas (Netherlands)

ALA-Assoarchitetti Prize
Italian Ministry of Foreign Affairs, client
Chancellery of the Italian Embassy
Washington, DC
Piero Sartoga Architects (Italy)

ALA-Assoarchitetti Prize, Architect Under 40
City of Syracuse, Italy, client
Internal Piazza Courtyard
Ortigia Island, Italy
Vincenzo Latina, Daniele Catania, Sebastiano Fortuna, Silvia Sgariglia, Nadia Montouri, Rudiano Macalone, Luca Sipala (Italy)

Quinquennial Honorary Award
Rome Vicarage, client
Jubilee Church
Rome, Italy
Richard Meier & Partners, Architects (US)

Dedalo Minosse International Prize for Commissioning a Building

Aluminum Center Foundation Headquarters. Micha de Haas' design for the Aluminum Center Foundation Headquarters is an innovative collaboration between design and industry calculated to demonstrate the metal's versatility. The 3,200-square-foot box is balanced atop a forest of canted aluminum columns. **Photo courtesy of the Associazione Liberi Architetti.**

Jury

Stanislao Nievo, writer and environmentalist (chair)
Dante O. Benini, architect
Paolo Caoduro, Caoduro Lucernari
Cesare Maria Casati, *l'Arca*
Odile Decq, architect
Bruno Gabbiani, ALA Assoarchitetti
Giovanni Gabetti, real estate agent
Guido Gentili, *Il Sole 24 Ore*
Richard Haslam, art historian

Hideto Horike, architect
Boris Podrecca, architect
Adriano Rasi Caldogno, Veneto Region Planning Office
Roberto Tretti, Centro Studio per le Lebere Professioni
Stefano Battaglia, architect
Marcella Gabbiani, ALA architect

Source: Associazione Liberi Architetti

Design for Humanity Award

Every year the American Society of Interior Designer grants the Design for Humanity Award to an individual or institution that has made a significant contribution toward improving the quality of the human environment through design-related activities that have had a universal and far-reaching effect. A committee appointed by the ASID board reviews the nominations. The award is presented at ASID's annual national convention.

For additional information about the Design for Humanity Award, contact the ASID at (202) 546-3480 or on the Internet at *www.asid.org*.

1990	The Scavenger Hotline	1998	William L. Wilkoff
1991	E.I. Du Pont de Nemours & Company	1999	AlliedSignal, Inc., Polymers Division
1992	The Preservation Resource Center	2000	Victoria Schomer
1993	Neighborhood Design Center	2001	ASID Tennessee Chapter, Chattanooga
1994	Elizabeth Paepcke and International Design Conference in Aspen	2002	Cynthia Leibrock
		2003	Habitat for Humanity International
1995	Cranbrook Academy of Art	2004	Architecture for Humanity and
1996	Wayne Ruga and the Center for Health Design		Cameron Sinclair
1997	Barbara J. Campbell, *Accessibility Guidebook For Washington, DC*		*Source: American Society of Interior Designers*

Architecture for Humanity represents the finest of the new breed of architectural leadership, employing architectural skills and directing them for the larger good. Committed, unapologetically architectural in name and mission, Architecture for Humanity stands up for people in need.

Robert Ivy,
Architectural Record

Designer of Distinction Award

The Designer of Distinction Award is granted by the American Society of Interior Designers to an ASID interior designer whose professional achievements have demonstrated design excellence. Eligibility is open to members in good standing who have practiced within the preceding 10 years. Nominations are accepted by ASID's general membership body and reviewed by a jury selected by the national president. This is a merit-based award and, thus, is not always granted annually.

For more information, visit the ASID on the Internet at *www.asid.org* or contact them at (202) 546-3480.

1979	William Pahlman		1997	Phyllis Martin-Vegue
1980	Everett Brown		1998	Janet Schirn
1981	Barbara D'Arcy		1999	Gary E. Wheeler
1982	Edward J. Wormley		2000	Paul Vincent Wiseman
1983	Edward J. Perrault		2001	William Hodgins
1984	Michael Taylor		2002	Hugh Latta
1985	Norman DeHaan			Margaret McCurry
1986	Rita St. Clair		2003	Eleanor Brydone
1987	James Merricksmith		2004	Deborah Lloyd Forrest
1988	Louis Tregre			
1994	Charles D. Gandy			
1995	Andre Staffelbach			*Source: American Society of Interior Designers*
1996	Joseph Minton			

edra/*Places* Awards

Places and the Environmental Design Research Association sponsor the annual edra/*Places* Awards to promote excellence in environmental design research and practice. This program emphasizes the relationships between people and place-based research and design by granting two categories of awards: place design and planning awards for completed projects that demonstrate excellence as human environments and research awards for exemplary projects that investigate the relationship between physical form and human activity or experience. Entries are accepted from designers and researchers from a wide range of backgrounds, including architecture, landscape architecture, planning, urban design, interior design, lighting design, environmental graphic design, public art, environmental psychology, sociology, anthropology, geography, and related fields.

For detailed submission requirements, visit edra on the Internet at *www.edra.org*.

2005 Winners

Place Design
Los Altos School District Master Plan Update
Los Altos, CA
Gelfand Partners Architects

Landscape Park Duisburg Nord
Duisburg, Germany
Latz + Partner

Place Planning
Lloyd Crossing Sustainable Urban Design Plan
Portland, OR
Mithun Architects + Designers + Planners

Iqaluit Core Area & Capital District Plan
Nunavut, Canada
Office for Urbanism; FoTenn Urban Planners
   and Designers; Laird and Associates

Place Research
"People and Places on the Outer Cape:
   A Landscape Character Study"
Jack Ahern, University of Massachusetts

"The Dignity of Resistance: Women Resident's
   Activism in Chicago Public Housing"
Roberta M. Feldman and Susan Stall

Jury
Gail Brager, University of California, Berkeley
Galen Cranz, University of California, Berkeley
Peter Bosselman, University of California,
   Berkeley
Larry Vale, Massachusetts Institute of Technology
Hugh Hardy, Hardy Holzman Pfeiffer Associates

Source: Environmental Design Research Association

First life, then spaces, then buildings—
the other way around never works.

Jan Gehl

Edward C. Kemper Award

Edward C. Kemper served as executive director of the American Institute of Architects for nearly 35 years, 1914–1948. The Edward C. Kemper Award honors an architect member of the AIA who has similarly served as an outstanding member.

For more information, visit the AIA on the Internet at *www.aia.org* or contact the AIA Honors and Awards Department at (202) 626-7586.

1950	William Perkins	1981	Robert L. Durham
1951	Marshall Shaffer	1982	Leslie N. Boney Jr.
1952	William Stanley Parker	1983	Jules Gregory
1953	Gerrit J. De Gelleke	1984	Dean F. Hilfinger
1954	Henry H. Saylor	1985	Charles Redmon
1955	Turpin C. Bannister	1986	Harry Harmon
1956	Theodore Irving Coe	1987	Joseph Monticciolo
1957	David C. Baer	1988	David Lewis
1958	Edmund R. Purves	1989	Jean P. Carlhian
1959	Bradley P. Kidder	1990	Henry W. Schirmer
1960	Philip D. Creer	1991	John F. Hartray Jr.
1961	Earl H. Reed	1992	Betty Lou Custer*
1962	Harry D. Payne	1993	Theodore F. Mariani
1963	Samuel E. Lunden	1994	Harry C. Hallenbeck
1964	Daniel Schwartzman	1995	Paul R. Neel
1965	Joseph Watterson	1996	Sylvester Damianos
1966	William W. Eshbach	1997	Harold L. Adams
1967	Robert H. Levison	1998	Norman L. Koonce
1968	E. James Gambaro	1999	James R. Franklin
1969	Philip J. Meathe	2000	James A. Scheeler
1970	Ulysses Floyd Rible	2001	Charles F. Harper
1971	Gerald McCue	2002	*No award granted*
1972	David N. Yerkes	2003	C. James Lawler Jr.
1973	Bernard B. Rothschild	2004	Robert A. Odermatt
1974	Jack D. Train	2005	Norbert W. Young Jr.
1975	F. Carter Williams		
1976	Leo A Daly		* Honored posthumously
1977	Ronald A. Straka		
1978	Carl L. Bradley		
1979	Herbert E. Duncan Jr.		*Source: American Institute of Architects*
1980	Herbert Epstein		

Engineering Excellence Awards

The American Council of Engineering Companies' annual Engineering Excellence Awards begin at the state level, with finalists moving to the national competition. Each year one project receives the Grand Conceptor Award, and up to 23 other projects receive either grand or honor awards. Projects are judged by a panel of 20–25 engineers and infrastructure experts on the basis of uniqueness and originality, technical value to the engineering profession, social and economic considerations, complexity, and how successfully the project met the needs of the client. Projects must be entered in one of nine categories: studies, research, and consulting engineering services; building support systems; structural systems; surveying and mapping; environmental; water and wastewater; water resources; transportation; and special projects. Any firm engaged in private practice, consulting engineering, or surveying is eligible to participate. Entries must be submitted to an ACEC member organization.

For more information and winning project descriptions, visit *www.acec.org* on the Internet.

2005 Winners

Grand Conceptor Award
Everglades Restoration, Stormwater
  Treatment Area
Palm Beach/Broward County, FL
Burns & McDonnell

Grand Awards
Ode to Poseidon, Rion Antirion Bridge
Rion, Gulf of Corinth, Greece
Langan Engineering and Environmental
  Services; Parsons Transportation Group

Seattle Central Library
Seattle, WA
Magnusson Klemencic Associates

Russia Wharf – Supporting Occupied Historic
  Buildings During Tunneling
Boston, MA
Mueser Rutledge Consulting Engineers

Millennium Park
Chicago, IL
McDonough Associates, Inc.

Brownfield Redevelopment of a Former
  BP Refinery
Casper, WY
The Retec Group, Inc.

MIT Ray and Maria Stata Center for Computer,
  Information, and Intelligence Sciences
Cambridge, MA
Judith Nitsch Engineering, Inc.

Renaissance of a Junction
Kansas City, MO/Kansas City, KS
TranSystems Corporation

Honor Awards
Iraq Reconstruction Program Master Plan
Baghdad, Republic of Iraq/Washington, DC
Michael Baker Jr., Inc.; Stanley Consultants, Inc.

Engineering Excellence Awards

Columbus Biosolids Flow-through Thermophilic
    Treatment Investigation
Columbus, GA
Brown and Caldwell

Seattle Central Library
Seattle, WA
Sparling

Maria Fareri Children's Hospital at Westchester
    Medical Center
Valhalla, NY
Syska Hennessy Group

Earthquake Building Instrumentation
San Francisco, CA
Degenkolb Engineers

Kyrene Monte Vista Pedestrian Bridge
Phoenix, AZ
SVR, Inc.

Bunker Hillsides Revegetation Project
Kellogg, ID
CH2M HILL

Geysers Recharge Project
Santa Rosa, CA
CH2M HILL

Morris Forman WTP Alternative Solids Project
Louisville, KY
Black & Veatch Corporation

Overcoming Site Challenges to Create
    Constructed Wetlands in Clayton County,
    Georgia
Morrow, GA
CH2M HILL

Newark Brackish Water Desalination
Newark, CA
CDM

I–75 Alligator Alley Barrier
Collier County, FL
American Consulting Engineers of Florida, LLC

Pier T Container Terminal Development
Long Beach, CA
KPFF Consulting Engineers

Route 29 South Riverwalk Park
Trenton, NJ
Vollmer Associates LLP

Mustard Agent Decontamination System
Aberdeen Proving Ground, MS
Merrick & Company

Afghanistan Reconstruction Group
    Temporary Compound
Kabul, Afghanistan
PAE/Louis Berger Group

Source: American Council of Engineering Companies

Did you know...

At 6.5 million square feet, the
Pentagon is three times the size
of the Empire State Building.

Excellence on the Waterfront Awards

Lauding projects that convert abandoned or outmoded waterfronts into constructive spaces in the public interest, the Excellence on the Waterfront Awards are presented annually by the nonprofit Waterfront Center. Any built project on any body of water, new or old, is eligible to enter. Judging criteria include the design's sensitivity to the water, quality and harmony, civic contribution, environmental impact, and educational components. The group also presents a Clearwater Citizens Award that recognizes outstanding grassroots initiatives.

Additional information about the awards are available on the Waterfront Center's Web site at *www.waterfrontcenter.org*.

2004 Top Honor: Project

Mill City Museum
Minneapolis, MN
Meyer, Scherer & Rockcastle

Minneapolis Riverfront District
Minneapolis, MN
City of Minneapolis Department of Community
    Planning and Economic Development

2004 Top Honor: Plan

Oakland Waterfront Trail, Bay Trail
    Feasibility and Design Guidelines
Oakland, CA
EDAW Inc.

Eastshore State Park General Plan
San Francisco, CA
Wallace Roberts & Todd

2004 Honor Awards: Projects

Environmental Protection and Enhancement
Northwest Maritime Center Demonstration Dock
Port Townsend, WA
Miller/Hull Partnership

Historic Preservation and Adaptive Reuse
San Francisco Ferry Building
San Francisco, CA
SMWM

Beerline Neighborhood
Milwaukee, WI
Vetter Denk Architects

Parks/Recreation
Millennium Park Recreation Core
Kent County, MI
O'Boyle, Cowell, Blalock & Associates

Corvallis Riverfront Commemorative Park
Corvallis, OR
Walker Macy Landscape Architects

Hudson River Park
New York City, NY
Han-Padrom Associates

Excellence on the Waterfront Awards

Residential

False Creek North/Concord Pacific Place
Vancouver, BC, Canada
Concord Pacific Group Inc.

National Anpin Harbor Historic Park
Tainan City, Taiwan
National Cheng-Kung University

2004 Honor Awards: Planning

Ashbridge Bay Treatment Plant Site Design
Toronto, ON, Canada
architectsAlliance

2004 Clearwater Citizen's Awards

Penn's Landing Forums
Philadelphia, PA

Jury

Alex Lifschutz, Lifschutz Davidson (chair)
Michael Dawson, The River Alliance
Sylvia McLaughlin, Waterfront Action
Robert Searns, project development consultant
George Stockton, Moriyama & Teshima Planners

Source: Waterfront Center

Did you know...

The Clearwater Citizen's Award is named for the Clearwater organization that has worked for years to clean up the Hudson River in New York. Led by Pete Seeger, this grassroots group's programs include environmental education, advocacy, and the annual River Revival Festival.

Exhibition of School Architecture Awards

As part of the juried Exhibition of School Architecture, outstanding school design and educational environments are honored each year with two awards: the Walter Taylor and Shirley Cooper awards, named in honor of the original organizers of the School Architecture Exhibit. Additional citations may be presented at the discretion of the jury. The program is sponsored by the American Association of School Administrators, American Institute of Architects, and Council of Education Facility Planners International and is open to registered architects and landscape architects.

For more information, contact the AASA at (703) 528-0070 or visit them on the Internet at *www.aasa.org.*

2005 Recipients

Walter Taylor Award
Matapeake Elementary School
Stevensville, MD
Grimm & Parker Architects

Shirley Cooper Award
Knapp Forest Elementary School
Forest Hills, MI
Kingscott Associates

Citation Honorees
John M. Langston High School Continuation
    and Langston-Brown Community Center
Arlington, VA
BeeryRio

Medina High School and Community Center
Medina, OH
Fanning/Howey Associates, Inc.

Sprague Elementary School
Wellesley, MA
HMFH Architects, Inc.

Daniel Hand High School
Madison, CT
Jeter, Cook & Jepson Architects, Inc.

Central High School
Hollywood, CA
Perkins+Will

Irvington Middle School/High School
    Community Campus
Irvington, NY
Peter Gisolfi Associates

San Jose City College Student and Career
    Services Center, San Jose/Evergreen
    Community College
San Jose, CA
tBP/Architecture

Source: American Association of School Administrators

Gold Key Awards for Excellence in Hospitality Design

For more than 20 years the Gold Key Awards for Excellence in Hospitality Design have honored excellence in hospitality design in eight design categories: spa, restaurant–casual dining, guest room, lounge/bar, lobby/reception area, restaurant–fine dining, suite, and best hotel design. The awards are presented by the International Hotel/Motel & Restaurant Show and sponsored by *Interior Design* and *HOTELS* magazines. Winners in each category are profiled in both sponsoring publications.

For a description of eligibility requirements and an entry form, visit *www.ihmrs.com.*

2004 Recipients

Best Hotel Design
W Mexico City
Mexico City, Mexico
KMD Mexico

Guest Room
Mandarin Oriental New York
New York, NY
HBA/Hirsch Bedner Associates

Lobby/Reception Area
Le Meridien Minneapolis
Minneapolis, MN
Yabu Pushelberg/Graves Hospitality

Lounge/Bar
Le Meridien Minneapolis
Minneapolis, MN
Yabu Pushelberg/Graves Hospitality

Restaurants–Casual Dining
Spoon Hong Kong, Intercontinental Hotel
Hong Kong
Tony Chi & Associates

Restaurants–Fine Dining
Asiate at the Mandarin Oriental New York
New York, NY
Tony Chi & Associates

Spa
Sasanqua Spa
Kiawah Island, SC
Clodagh Design

Suite
Soho Grand Penthouse Lofts
New York, NY
Soho Grand Hotel

Jury
Clodagh, Clodagh Design
Deborah Lloyd Forrest, ForrestPerkins
Peter Gorman, Brennan Beer Gorman
    Monk/Interiors
D.B. Kim, Starwood Hotels & Resorts
    Worldwide, Inc.
Meg Prendergast, Gettys Group
John Segreti, New York Palace

Source: International Hotel/Motel & Restaurant Show

Gold Key Awards for Excellence in Hospitality Design

Le Meridian. Yabu Pushelberg's extensive use of elegant materials—glass, wood vein-cut marble floors, striking acrylic walls, comfortable leather seating—in the lounge and lobby coalesce to help make this hotel a fashion and design destination for the city. **Photos courtesy of the International Hotel/Motel & Restaurant Show.**

GSA Design Awards

The US General Services Administration presents its biennial Design Awards as part of its Design Excellence Program, which seeks the best in design, construction, and restoration for all Federal building projects. The awards were developed to encourage and recognize innovative design in Federal buildings and to honor noteworthy achievements in the preservation and renovation of historic structures.

For additional information about the GSA Design Awards or to view photographs and descriptions of the winners, visit GSA's Web site at *www.gsa.gov.*

2004 Honor Award Recipients

On the Boards
Federal Building
San Francisco, CA
Morphosis

Preservation/Conservation
Robert F. Kennedy Department of Justice
    Federal Building
Washington, DC
Heery/Tishman, a joint venture; Burt Hill Kosar
    Rittleman; Page Conservation Inc.; Gilbane
    Building Company

Construction Excellence
United States Courthouse
Seattle, WA
J.A. Jones/Absher Construction Company,
    a joint venture

2004 Citation Award Recipients

Architecture
United States Courthouse
Hammond, IN
Pei Cobb Freed & Partners Architects; Browning
    Day Mullins Dierdorf Architects

Architecture/Interior Design
United States Courthouse
Seattle, WA
NBBJ

Architecture/Engineering
ATF National Laboratory Center
Beltsville, MD
Kallmann McKinnell & Wood Architects, Inc.;
    Whiting-Turner Contracting Company

On the Boards
United States Courthouse
Buffalo, NY
Kohn Pedersen Fox Associates

United States Courthouse
El Paso, TX
Antoine Predock Architect

United States Port of Entry
Del Rio, TX
Charles Rose Architects Inc.

GSA Design Awards

Modernization
United States Courthouse and Federal Building
Phoenix, AZ
Thomas Phifer and Partners; Gould Evans
    Associates

Preservation
United States Courthouse
Erie, PA
KSBA/DPK&A, a joint venture

Art
River of Light, United States Courthouse
Wheeling, WV
Mikyoung Kim

First Impressions
Richard Bolling Federal Building
Kansas City, MO
BNIM Architects

Graphic Design
World War II Memorial Book
Washington, DC
Cox & Associates

Construction Excellence
United States and Canada Shared Border Station
Sweet Grass, MT/Coutts, AB, Canada
Abide International, Inc.

World War II Memorial
Washington, DC
Tompkins/Grunley-Walsh Joint Venture

Jury
Mack Scogin, Mack Scogin Merrill Elam (chair)
Cindy Allen, *Interior Design* magazine
Maurice Cox, University of Virginia and the City
    of Charlottesville, VA
Thomas Geismar, Chermayeff & Geismar, Inc.
Steve Hamline, J.E. Dunn Construction Co.
Thomas Gunny Harboe, McClier
Michael Maybaum, Cosentini Associates
Robert Rogers, Rogers Marvel Architect
Mary Donovan Young, National Gallery of Art

Source: US General Services Administration

Healthcare Environment Award

Since 1989 the annual Healthcare Environment Awards have recognized innovative, life-enhancing designs that contribute to the quality of healthcare. The award is sponsored by the Center for Health Design, *Contract* magazine, Medquest Communications, and the American Institute of Architecture Students and is open to architects, interior designers, healthcare executives, and students. The winners are honored at the annual Healthcare Design Conference as well as featured in an issue of *Contract* magazine.

For additional information, contact the Center for Health Design on the Web at *www.healthdesign.org.*

2005 Winners

Acute Care Facilities
Northwestern Hospital Neuroscience/
    Orthopaedic/Spine Patient Care Center
Minneapolis, MN
Ellerbe Becket

Honorable Mention
Lacks Cancer Center at Saint Mary's
Grand Rapids, MI
Trinity Design

Ambulatory Care Facilities
Mary Bridge Children's Health Center
Tacoma, WA
Bainbridge Design, Inc.

Honorable Mention
Emory University's Winship Cancer Institute
Atlanta, GA
Stanley Beaman & Sears

Long-Term Care/Assisted Living Facilities
No awards granted

Health and Fitness Facilities
Price Medical
Washington, DC
Forma Design

Miami Institute for Age Management &
    Intervention
Miami, FL
Perkins+Will

Honorable Mention
Orthodontist Office for
    Alec N. Elchahal, MD, MS, PC
Suwanee, GA
Kohl Gramigna Monardo Architects;
    Luke & Associates

Conceptual
No awards granted

Student Category
"A Green Wellness Clinic as Center of
    Community: The New Joseph F. Sullivan
    Center"
Emily Bland, Allen Buie, Amanda Schmaltz,
    Clemson University

Honorable Mention
"The New Joseph F. Sullivan Center: A Green
    Wellness Clinic"
Paula Froehbrodt, Megan Gerend, Clemson
    University

"The Methodist Specialty and Transplant
    Hospital"
Josh Pierce, University of Texas at San Antonio

Healthcare Environment Award

Miami Institute for Age Management & Intervention.
This surgical center and medical spa was
designed for maximum patient comfort, privacy,
and convenience. Ambient light and textures, as
well as organic touches, such as juniper stools,
Asian teak, and soothing fabrics create a pleasant
and delightfully recuperative space. Photo by Glen
Daidone.

Jury
Linda Bishop, Watkins Hamilton Ross Architects
Barbara Dellinger, HDR
Ana Maregatti, Maregatti Interiors
Norman Rosenfeld, Norman Rosenfeld
    Architects
Trinity Simons, American Institute of
    Architecture Students

Source: Center for Health Design

Henry C. Turner Prize for Innovation in Construction Technology

The Henry C. Turner Prize for Innovation in Construction Technology is presented jointly by the National Building Museum and Turner Construction Company for notable advances and high achievement in the process of construction. The award is named for the founder of Turner Construction Company, which began operation in New York City in 1902. It recognizes invention, innovative methodologies, and/or exceptional leadership by an individual or team in construction technology. At the discretion of the jury, the Turner Prize and its $25,000 cash award are presented annually.

For additional information about this award, contact the National Building Museum at (202) 272-2448 or visit them online at *www.nbm.org*.

2002	Leslie E. Robertson
2003	I.M. Pei
2004	Charles A. DeBenedittis
2005	US Green Building Council

Source: National Building Museum

> Architecture is really the product of a collaboration among a client, an architect, and a builder. Every party brings the best of the talents to the project of constructing a building.
>
> **Tado Ando**

Rick Fedrizzi. The US Green Building Council was selected to receive the Henry C. Turner Prize for its role as a major catalyst in the sustainable design movement spearheaded by its green building rating program, LEED. Rick Fedrizzi, president, CEO, and founding chair of the USGBC, said of this honor, "Five years ago, when USGBC staff and volunteers created LEED, we never could have imagined the market transformation that would follow. USGBC and LEED bring together the entire building industry in an effort to lead a national consensus on green building." Photo by Sam Holden, courtesy of the National Building Museum.

Hugh Ferriss Memorial Prize

The Hugh Ferriss Memorial Prize is awarded annually by the American Society of Architectural Illustrators to recognize excellence in architectural illustration. This international awards program is open to all current members of the Society. A traveling exhibition, *Architecture in Perspective,* co-sponsored by the Otis Elevator Company, highlights the winners and selected entries, raising awareness of the field.

To view the winning drawings, visit the ASAI's Web site at *www.asai.org.*

1986
Lee Dunnette and James Record

1987
One Montvale Avenue
Richard Lovelace

1988
Proposed Arts and Cultural Center
Thomas Wells Schaller

1989
Edgar Allen Poe Memorial (detail)
Daniel Willis

1990
The Interior of the Basilica Ulpia
Gilbert Gorski

1991
Affordable Housing Now!
Luis Blanc

1992
BMC Real Properties Buildings
Douglas E. Jamieson

1993
Additions and Renovations to Tuckerton Marine Research Field Station
David Sylvester

1994
3rd Government Center Competition
Rael D. Slutsky

1995
The Pyramid at Le Grand Louvre
Lee Dunnette

1996
Hines France Office Tower
Paul Stevenson Oles

1997
World War II Memorial
Advanced Media Design

1998
Baker Library Addition, Dartmouth College
Wei Li

1999
Five Star Deluxe Beach Hotel
Serge Zaleski

2000
1000 Wilshire Blvd.
Thomas W. Schaller

2001
The Royal Ascot, Finishing Post
Michael McCann

2002
Chicago 2020
Gilbert Gorski

2003
Edge City
Ronald Love

2004
Project Japan
Michael Reardon

2005
Resort, Evening
Chris Grubbs

Source: American Society of Architectural Illustrators

I.D. Annual Design Review

I.D. magazine's Annual Design Review began in 1954 and today is considered America's largest and most prestigious industrial design competition. Entries are placed in one of seven categories and reviewed by juries of leading practitioners. Within each category, projects are awarded on three levels: best of category, design distinction, and honorable mention. Winning entries are published in a special July/August issue of *I.D.* magazine.

For additional information about the Annual Design Review, including descriptions of all the winners, visit *I.D.* magazine online at *www. idonline.com.*

2005 Best of Category Winners

Concepts
Urban Nomad Shelter
Electroland

Consumer Products
Wisecracker Crab Shell Cracker/Splitter
Chef'n Corporation

Environments
Huyghe + Le Corbusier Puppet Theater
Michael Meredith

Equipment
Search + Rescue CommVest
Nike EXPLORE Advanced Concept Studio

Furniture
Foamz—Furniture for Kids
Disorder Collectiv

Graphics
America (The Book)
Pentagram Design

Interactive
DIM Mobile Retail Unit
Inbar Barak; LOT–EK

Packaging
1-2 Paint
FLEX/the INNOVATIONLAB

Jury
Bruce Ancona, A2
Richard Baker, *Life* magazine
Ted Boerner, Ted Boerner, Inc.
Laurene Leon Boym, Boym Partners
Mark Gobé, Desgrippes Gobé and Associates
Markus Dochantschi, studioMDA
Alex Grossman, Richardson Sadeki
Jessica Helfand, Winterhouse
Debera Johnson, Pratt Institute
Shelia Kennedy, Kennedy & Violich
    Architecture, Ltd.
Ellen Lupton, Maryland College of Art
Lisa Mahar, Kid O
David Revere McFadden, Museum of Arts
    & Design
Debbie Millman, Sterling Group
Gregg Pasquarelli, ShoP/Sharples Holden
    Pasquarelli
David Rockwell, Rockwell Group
Andrea Ruggiero, designer
Allen Sayegh, INVIVIA, Inc.
Bibi Seck, Birsel + Seck
Susan Sellers, 2x4
Bonne Siegler, Number Seventeen
Rosanne Somerson, Rhode Island School
    of Design
Mark Tribe, artist
David Weeks, David Weeks Studio

Source: I.D. *magazine*

IDSA Personal Recognition Award

The Industrial Designers Society of America presents its Personal Recognition Award to an individual whose involvement in and support of design makes him or her a special friend of the profession and a major contributor to its long-term welfare and importance. Nominees are chosen for final consideration by a nominating committee; IDSA officers select the final winners.

For nomination forms and additional information visit the IDSA Web site at *www.idsa.org*, or contact IDSA by phone at (703) 707-6000.

1968	Dave Chapman	1996	Jane Thompson
1969	John Vassos	1997	Eva Zeisel
1978	Raymond Loewy	1998	Donald Dohner
1980	William Goldsmith	1999	Victor Papanek
1981	George Nelson	2000	Robert Schwartz
1982	Jay Doblin	2001	William Stumpf
1985	Deane Richardson	2002	Viktor Schreckengost
1986	Carroll Gantz	2003	Sam Farber
1991	Budd Steinhilber	2004	Henry Dreyfuss
1992	Cooper Woodring		Bruce Nussbaum
	Ellen Manderfield	2005	*No award granted*
1993	Ray Spilman		
	Brooks Stevens		
1994	Belle Kogan		
1995	David B. Smith		

Source: Industrial Designers Society of America

> If you want to be creative, don't try to do something new. Doing something new means not doing what's been done before, and that's a negative impulse. Negative impulses are frustrating. They're the opposite of creativity, and they never yield good ideas—not even in business or technology.
>
> **Eva Zeisel**

IIDA/*Hospitality Design* Product Design Competition

Hospitality Design magazine and the International Interior Design Association jointly grant the IIDA/Hospitality Design Product Design Competition awards, which recognize the manufacturers and designers of innovative product designs for the hospitality industry. The jury evaluates the entries for design innovation, technical advancements, cost and value, environmental responsibility, aesthetics, need, and usage within hospitality applications. Performance, comfort, safety, suitability for intended use, durability, accessibility, and client/user benefits are also considered. The awards are announced at the annual Hospitality and Design Expo and Conference. The winning products, manufacturers, and designers are published in *Hospitality Design* and *Perspective* magazines.

For additional information about this award program, visit IIDA on the Internet at *www.iida.org*.

2005 Best of Competition

Raleo Wood Surfacing Panels
Architectural Systems, Inc.

2005 Award of Excellence

Wall Coverings and Treatments
LeatherLok
C.C. Leathers, Inc.

Textiles/Upholstery
Wind China & Lilly Pond
Arc-Com Fabrics

Textiles/Bedspreads, Drapery, or Casement Fabrics
Solar Satin
Fabricut Contract

Individual Seating, Dining
Dimpled Chair
Janus et Cie

Individual Seating, Outdoor
Equinox Sun Lounge
Barlow Tyrie, Inc.

Group Seating, Lounge
Bent Woven Chairs/Settee
Janus et Cie

Individual Lighting
Solaris
Leucos USA, Inc.

Group Lighting
The Regent by Electric Mirror LLC

Accessories
KWC Murano
KWC America

IIDA/*Hospitality Design* Product Design Competition

2005 Honorable Mentions

Wallcoverings and Treatments
Mother of Pearl Beadazzled Relief
Maya Romanoff Corp.

Textiles/Upholstery
Genoise
Designtex

Group Seating, Lounge
Diesis
Loewenstein

Neo Contour Double Chaise Lounge
CMS Commercial Furniture

Flooring
Damask Abaca Jacquard, Bubbles Abaca
  Jacquard, Vicky, Cynthia, Jumbo, Lisa,
  Hempster, Kami, Woolnona Raffia, and
  Rudy Fawn
The Natural Carpet Company

Jury
Maria Mendoza, Marigold Interior Design
Conrad Bonet, Bonet & Associates International
Michael Dalton, Visions Design, Inc.
Robert Ledingham, Robert Ledingham, Inc.

Source: International Interior Design Association

Industrial Design Excellence Awards

The Industrial Design Excellence Awards, co-sponsored by *BusinessWeek* and the Industrial Designers Society of America, are presented annually to honor industrial design worldwide. Any designer, student, or design worldwide is eligible. A jury of business executives and design professionals issues as many awards as it deems necessary, evaluating more than 1,000 entries on the following criteria: design innovation, benefit to the user, benefit to the client/business, ecological responsibility, and appropriate aesthetics and appeal. Citations at the gold, silver, and bronze level are granted.

For detailed descriptions, photographs, and contact information for all winners, visit the IDSA on the Internet at *www.idsa.org*.

IDEA 2005 Gold Award Winners

Business & Industrial Products
Terabeam 3200i Optical Transceiver
Lakeside Product Development; Terabeam

Nike ACG Search and Rescue CommVEST
Nike, Inc.

TOPTURN X Self-propelled Compost Turner
heufler design

Johnson Controls 9100 Series Environmental
  Room Control Sensors
Design Continuum

Computer Equipment
Mac Mini
Apple Computer, Inc.

NetGear Platinum II
NewDealDesign LLC; NetGear Inc.

Intous3
ZIBA Design

Consumer Products
Stanley FatMax Hacksaw
The Stanley Works

Motorola Razr V3 Mobile Phone
Motorola, Inc.

Gerber SippySnacker
Fitch; Gerber

Nike Considered Boot
Nike, Inc.

Sony QUALIA 016 Digital Camera
Sony Corp.

iPod Shuffle
Apple Computer, Inc.

Spring Roll
Design Edge

CafeSolo
Tools Design

Barrel Grill
Tools Design

byo lunchbag
Built NY Inc.

Industrial Design Excellence Awards

Design Exploration
SHIFT Concept Bike
Scott Shim, Matt Grossman and Ryan Lightbody
    (Purdue University)

Toshiba Red Transformer Laptop
fuseproject

Mitsubishi E Boost Concept Car
Mitsubishi Motors R & D

IBM Audio Video Speech Recognition System
IBM Corp.

Civic Exchange
Antenna Design New York Inc.

The food experience
Alto Design Inc

Design Strategy
MINI_motion Strategy
fuseproject; MINI USA

Digital Media & Interfaces
Eastman Innovation Lab
The Brewery Ltd

Environments
Ambient Experience for Healthcare
Philips Design

Rubbermaid 9s09 Folding Safety Cone
    (a.k.a. Mr. Twister)
Rubbermaid Commercial Products

Clinton Presidential Center
Ralph Appelbaum Associates

Furniture
Kohler Purist Hatbox Toilet
Kohler Co.

Medical & Scientific Products
GMP LifeSync Wireless ECG Monitor
Design Continuum; GMP Companies; Robrady
    Design; Motorola Energy Systems Group;
    Stonestreet One, Inc.; Heatlhcare Technology
    Group; Motorola, Inc.

VIOlight Toothbrush Sanitizer
Philippe Starck Network; VIOlight LLC

Heart Stabilizer
CardioVations ETHICON, Inc.; Herbst LaZar
    Bell Inc.; Avail Medical Products Inc.;
    StrategixVision

Niton family of XRF Analyzers & Accessories
Altitude, Inc; Niton, LLC

Packaging & Graphics
1-2 Paint
FLEX/the INNOVATIONLAB

Research
Moen Revolution Showerhead
Design Continuum

**In the past five years, the following
design firms have won the most
IDEAs:**
IDEO – 48
Design Continuum – 18
Smart Design – 18
fuseproject – 17
ZIBA – 16
Lunar Design – 15
Pentagram – 12
Herbst LaZar Bell – 9
Altitude – 7
RKS Design Inc. – 7

**Source: Industrial Designers
Society of America**

Industrial Design Excellence Awards

Student Designs

'Spotlight the music and touch the light' —
    Audio system interfacing with Lighting
Suk-woo Lee, Hong-ik University

MOTUS: Inegrated Automotive Interior for
    Active Paraplegics
T. Jon Mayer, Eugene Bae, John Caswell, Ryan
    Dickman, and Morgan Wise, Art Center
    College of Design

I/O Brush
Kimiko Ryokai and Stefan Marti, Massachusetts
    Institute of Technology

Transportation

No gold award granted

Jury

Tucker Viemeister, Springtime-USA (chair)
Peter Arnell, Arnell Group
Eric Chan, Ecco Design
Chris Conley, Gravity Tank
Natascha Drabbe, Premsela
Marc Gobé, Desgrippes Gobé and Associates
Nasir Kassamali, Luminaire
Larry Keeley, Doblin Inc
Michael McCoy, McCoy&McCoy,
    Fahnstrom/McCoy
Pierre-Yves (PY) Panis, Legrand
Chee Pearlman, Chee Company
Ivy Ross, Old Navy, Gap, Inc.
Celso Santos, Rio 21 Design
Budd Steinhilber, designer
Peter Stathis, Virtual Studio
Susan Yelavich, Parsons School of Design

Source: Industrial Designers Society of America

In the past five years, the following corporations have won the most IDEAs:

Samsung – 19
Apple Computer – 17
IBM – 15
Nike Inc. – 13
Hewlett-Packard – 12
Philips Design – 10
Art Center College of Design – 9
BMW – 9
Logitech – 9
DaimlerChrysler – 8
Microsoft – 8

**Source: Industrial Designers
Society of America**

Industrial Design Excellence Awards

IDEA 2005 winners, clockwise from top left: VIOlight, Cafe Solo, QUALIA 016. Photos courtesy of the Industrial Designers Society of America.

Interior Design Competition

The Interior Design Competition is presented jointly each year by the International Interior Design Association and *Interior Design* magazine. The competition was established in 1973 to recognize outstanding interior design and to foster new interior design ideas and techniques. Winning projects appear in *Interior Design* magazine, and the best-of-competition winner receives a $5,000 cash prize.

For more information, contact IIDA at (888) 799-4432 or visit its Web site at *www.iida.org.*

2005 Recipients

Haworth Center
Chicago, IL
Perkins+Will/Eva Maddox Branded
    Environments

2005 Best of Competition

The Orange Room
Toronto, ON, Canada
munge//leung: design associates

Anthony Nak
Austin, TX
M.J. Neal Architects

Mason Hall/Juliet Rosch Recital Hall
Fredonia, NY
Pasanella + Klein Stolzman + Berg Architects

Boston Convention and Exhibition Center
Boston, MA
HNTB/Rafael Vinoly Architects (joint venture)

Jury
Lauren Rottet, DMJM/Rottet
Stephen Apking, Skidmore, Owings & Merrill
Todd Degarmo, Studios Architecture
Gordon Leney, HLW International Ltd.

Source: International Interior Design Association

James Beard Foundation Restaurant Design Award

Since 1995 the James Beard Foundation has awarded the James Beard Restaurant Design Award to the project executed in the United States and Canada that most demonstrates excellence in restaurant design or renovation. Architects and interior designers are eligible to enter restaurant projects that have been completed within the proceding three years. The award is presented at the annual Beard Birthday Fortnight celebration.

Entry forms and additional information can be found at *www.jamesbeard.org* or by calling the awards office at (212) 627-2090.

1995
Fifty Seven Fifty Seven
New York, NY
Chhada Siembieda and Partners

1996
Bar 89
New York, NY
Ogawa/Depardon Architects

1997
Paci Restaurant
Westport, CT
Ferris Architects

1998
Monsoon
Toronto, ON, Canada
Yabu Pushelberg

1999
MC Squared
San Francisco, CA
Mark Cavagnero Associates

2000
Brasserie
New York, NY
Diller & Scofidio

2001
Russian Tea Room
New York, NY
Leroy Adventures

2002
Blackbird Restaurant
Chicago, IL
Thomas Schlesser & Demian Repucci

2003
L'Impero Restaurant
New York, NY
Vicente Wolf Associates

2004
PUBLIC
New York, NY
AvroKO

2005
Solea Restaurant, W Mexico City
Mexico City, Mexico
Studio Gaia

Avec
Chicago, IL
Thomas Schlesser Design

Source: James Beard Foundation

Solea Restaurant. Inside W's first Latin American hotel, the Solea Restaurant is anchored by a white-stone tunnel with banquette seating-areas separated by red glass partitions (top). An eye-catching, intimate 12-seat dining room is sunken several feet so that the lower half, which is enclosed by glass walls, is transparent to people in the lobby (left). Photos courtesy of Studio Gaia.

J.C. Nichols Prize for Visionary Urban Development

The Urban Land Institute created the J.C. Nichols Prize for Visionary Urban Development to honor an individual or an institution who has made a commitment to responsible urban community development. As a founding member of the Urban Land Institute and whose work as a visionary developer includes the Country Club Plaza in Kansas City (MO), the award's namesake, J.C. Nichols, embodied the ULI's commitment to fostering responsible land use and reputable development. Nominees can be drawn from a wide range of disciplines, such as architects, researchers, developers, journalists, public officials, and academics, and must be US or Canadian citizens. A jury of urban experts, each representing diverse backgrounds and experiences, reviews the nominations. Recipients receive a $100,000 honorarium.

For additional information, visit the prize on the Web at *www.nicholsprize.org* or contact them at (202) 624-7000.

2000	Joseph P. Riley Jr.
2001	Daniel Patrick Moynihan
2002	Gerald D. Hines
2003	Vincent Scully
2004	Richard D. Baron

Source: Urban Land Institute

Cities have the capability of providing something for everybody, only because, and only when, they are created by everybody.

Jane Jacobs

J.C. Nichols Prize for Visionary Urban Development

Richard D. Baron (right) and 2003 laureate Vincent Scully. Richard D. Baron, co-founder, chair, and CEO of McCormack Baron Salazar, Inc., specializes in the development of economically integrated urban neighborhoods. Jury member Ronald Ratner said of Baron's contributions, "Richard Baron's long-term impact is successfully demonstrating the benefits of inclusivity in neighborhoods and showing that diversity makes for a rich environment. Housing patterns have long been determined by race and income, but he is a shining example of how that can be changed." **Photo courtesy of the Urban Land Institute.**

Jean Tschumi Prize

The Jean Tschumi Prize is awarded by the International Union of Architects (UIA) to individuals for a significant contribution to architectural criticism or architectural education.

For more information, visit the UIA's Web site at *www.uia-architectes.org.*

1967
Jean-Pierre Vouga (Switzerland)

1969
I. Nikolaev (USSR)
Pedro Ramirez Vazquez (Mexico)

1972
João Batista Vilanova Artigas (Brazil)

1975
Reyner Banham (UK)

1978
Rectory and Faculty of Architecture
of the University of Lima (Peru)

1981
Neville Quarry (Australia)

Honorary Mention
Jorge Glusberg (Argentina) and
Tadeusz Barucki (Poland)

1984
Julius Posener (GDR)

1987
Christian Norberg-Schultz (Norway)
Ada Louise Huxtable (US)

1990
Eduard Franz Sekler (Austria)

Honorary Mention
Dennis Sharp (UK) and Claude Parent
(France)

1993
Eric Kumchew Lye (Malaysia)

1996
Peter Cook (UK)
Liangyong Wu (China)

Honorary Mention
Toshio Nakamura and the Mexican editor
COMEX

1999
Juhani Pallasmaa (Finland)

Honorary Mention
Jennifer Taylor (Australia)

2002
Manuel Tainha (Portugal)
Elia Zenghelis (Greece)

Honorary Mention
The authors of the collection of books:
World Architecture: A Critical Mosaic (China)

2005
QUADERNS magazine (Spain)
Peter Davey (UK)

Honorary Mention
Selim Khan-Magomedov (Russia)

Source: International Union of Architects

Keystone Award

Created by the American Architectural Foundation in 1999, the Keystone Award honors individuals who have furthered the Foundation's vision "of a society that participates in shaping its environment through an understanding of the power of architecture to elevate and enrich the human experience." The award's objective is to recognize and encourage leadership that results in citizen participation in the design process and advances communication with key decision-makers about how design issues affect a community's quality of life. Nominees may include, but are not limited to, patrons, advocates, critics, activists, clients, government representatives, and educational leaders. The award selection committee is comprised of experts in the fields of community development, communication, design, preservation, and government. Presentation of the award is made at the annual Accent on Architecture Gala in Washington, DC.

For additional information, contact the AAF at (202) 626-7500 or on the Web at *www.archfoundation.org.*

1999	Richard M. Daley
2000	Rick Lowe
2002	Joseph P. Riley Jr.
2004	US General Services Administration, Public Buildings Service
2005	Jeremy Harris

Source: American Architectural Foundation

> All over the world, you have the same buildings—totally without connection, without quality, with only an emphasis on occupancy and maximum space. I understand business is business, but I pay every day because I'm seeing your ugly building.
>
> **Piero Lissoni**

Lewis Mumford Prize

Every two years the Society for American City and Regional Planning History grants the Lewis Mumford Prize for the best book on American city and regional history. Winners are chosen based on originality, depth of research, quality of writing, and the degree to which the book contributes to a greater understanding of the rich history of American city or regional planning. The presentation of a plaque and $500 cash prize is made at the Society's biennial conference.

129

For additional information, visit the Society on the Internet at *www.urban.uiuc.edu/ sacrph/*.

1991–93
The New York Approach: Robert Moses, Urban Liberals, and Redevelopment of the Inner City by Joel Schwartz (Ohio State University Press)

1993–95
The City of Collective Memory: Its Historical Imagery and Architectural Entertainments by M. Christine Boyer (MIT Press)

1995–97
City Center to Regional Mall: Architecture, the Automobile, and Retailing in Los Angeles, 1920–1950 by Richard Longstreth (MIT Press)

1997–99
Boston's Changeful Times: Origins of Preservation and Planning in America by Michael Holleran (Johns Hopkins University Press)

Honorary Mention
Remaking Chicago: The Political Origins of Urban Industrial Change by Joel Rast (Northern Illinois University Press)

1999–01
Downtown: Its Rise and Fall, 1880–1950 by Robert Fogelson (Yale University Press)

2001–03
The Bulldozer in the Countryside: Suburban Sprawl and the Rise of American Environmentalism by Adam Rome (Cambridge University Press)

2003–05
Downtown America : A History of the Place and the People Who Made It by Alison Isenberg (University of Chicago Press)

Source: Society for American City and Regional Planning History

In my country, we are just learning that sidewalks are relatives of parks— not passing lanes for cars.

Enrique Peñalosa

Library Buildings Awards

The American Institute of Architects and American Library Association present the biennial Library Buildings Awards to encourage excellence in the architectural design and planning of libraries. Architects licensed in the United States are eligible to enter any public or private library project from around the world, whether a renovation, addition, conversion, interior project, or new construction. The jury consists of three architects and three librarians with extensive library building experience.

Additional information is available on the ALA's Web site at *www.ala.org* or by contacting the AIA Awards Office at (202) 626-7586.

2005 Winners

Landman Library at Arcadia University
Glenside, PA
R.M. Kliment & Frances Halsband Architects

Austin E. Knowlton School of Architecture
　Library at the Ohio State University
Columbus, OH
Mack Scogin Merrill Elam Architects with
　Wandel and Schnell Architects

Carnegie Library of Pittsburgh
Brookline, PA
Loysen + Kreuthmeier Architects

The Georgia Archives
Morrow, GA
Hellmuth, Obata & Kassabaum

Harry Elkins Widener Memorial Library
　Renovation at Harvard University
Cambridge, MA
Einhorn Yaffee Prescott

Issaquah Public Library
Issaquah, WA
Bohlin Cywinski Jackson

Salt Lake City Public Library
Salt Lake City, UT
VCBO Architecture with Moshe Safdie
　and Associates

Seattle Central Library
Seattle, WA
Office for Metropolitan Architecture and
　LMN Architects, joint venture

Jury

Michael Mills, Ford, Farewell, Mills & Gatsch
　Architects (chair)
Charles Forrest, Robert W. Woodruff Library
Sheila Kennedy, Kennedy & Violich
　Architecture Ltd.
Anne Larsen, Massachusetts Board of Library
　Commissioners
Jeffrey Scherer, Meyer, Scherer & Rockcastle Ltd.
Jonalyn Woolf-Ivory, Sno-Isle Library System

Source: American Institute of Architects

Lighting Design Awards

Presented for lighting installations that couple aesthetic achievement with technical expertise, the Lighting Design Awards are bestowed annually by the International Association of Lighting Designers and *Architectural Lighting* magazine. The Awards emphasize design with attention to energy usage, economics, and sustainable design. Projects are judged individually, not in competition with each other. The Radiance Award recognizes the finest example of lighting design excellence among all submissions. Awards of excellence and merit are awarded at the jury's discretion.

For additional information, visit the IALD on the Internet at *www.iald.org.*

2005 Radiance Award

Galleria West
Seoul, Korea
Arup Lighting

2005 Award of Excellence

Pulrose Power Station
Isle of Man, UK
Speirs and Major Associates

Berlin Medical Society
Berlin, Germany
L-Plan Lighting Design

Lath and Plaster Showroom
New York, NY
SBLD Studio

Bridge of Aspiration
London, UK
Speirs and Major Associates

Crown Fountain
Chicago, IL
Schuler Shook

St. Franziskus
Regensburg, Germany
Lightplanung

2005 Award of Merit

Adotta
Vicenza, Italy
Archingegno

Stone & Youngberg
San Francisco, CA
Architecture & Light

Hilton Hotel
Athens, Greece
dpa lighting consultants

Semiramis Hotel
Athens, Greece
Focus Lighting, Inc.

Lighting Design Awards

Frost Bank Tower
Austin, TX
Cline Bettridge Bernstein Lighting Design, Inc.

Pier 1 Imports Headquarters
Fort Worth, TX
Cline Bettridge Bernstein Lighting Design, Inc.

Restoration of Paseo del Ovalo
Teruel, Spain
Artecluminotecnia

Bullring WCs
Birmingham, UK
dpa lighting design

Carlos Miele
New York, NY
Focus Lighting, Inc.

Montage, Inc.
Boston, MA
Light This! Architectural Theatrical
   Lighting Design

Morongo Casino Resort & Spa
Palm Springs, CA
Visual Terrain

DeVos Performance Hall Renovation
Grand Rapids, MI
Schuler Shook

Jubilee Church
Rome, Italy
Fisher Marantz Stone; ERCO Leuchten GMBH

Monumen Nasional
Jakarta, Indonesia
Auviz Lumina Plano Pt.

Rion–Antirion Bridge
Corinth Gulf, Greece
Concepto Agency

2005 Special Citation

Kingsdale School
London, UK
Fulcrum Consulting

Source: International Association of Lighting Designers

Architecture is the shaping of space
with objects in light to create practical
and emotive places.

Michael B. Lehrer

Lighting Design Awards

Bridge of Aspiration. The Bridge of Aspiration walkway connects London's Royal Ballet School and Royal Opera House. The primary design challenge was to capture the dynamic form and innovative drama of the heliotropic design that changes levels as it spans the street. Twenty-three square aluminum frames twist in four-degree steps that achieve a 90-degree shift from end to end. Photos by Edmund Sumner, courtesy of the International Association of Lighting Designers.

Lynn S. Beedle Achievement Award

The Lynn S. Beedle Achievement Award recognizes individuals who have made extraordinary contributions to tall buildings and/or the urban environment, which enhance cities and the lives of their inhabitants. The award is named after Lynn S. Beedle, founder and director of the Council on Tall Buildings and Urban Habitats from 1969 to 2000. Candidates may be from any area of specialization, including architecture, structures, building systems, construction, academia, planning, development, or management. Their contribution(s) may take any form, such as completed projects, research, technology, methods, ideas, or industry leadership, that are consistent with the values and mission of the CTBUH and its founder.

For more information, visit the CTBUH Web site at *www.ctbuh.org* or call (312) 909-0253.

2002	Lynn S. Beedle
2003	Charles A. DeBenedittis
2004	Gerald D. Hines
2005	Alan G. Davenport

Source: Council on Tall Buildings and Urban Habitats

Marcus Prize

In 2005 the Marcus Corporation Foundation initiated a $100,000 biennial gift to a budding architect with international aspirations who agrees to apply his or her talents to a Milwaukee urban design challenge. The Marcus Prize recognizes architects "at the beginning of greatness, rather than at the end of it, and focuses the best talent in the world on Milwaukee issues," according to Bob Greenstreet, dean of the School of Architecture and Urban Planning at the University of Wisconsin–Milwaukee, which is a partner in the effort along with the city. Greenstreet states that the idea "is to find people of the caliber of [Santiago] Calatrava" who, before he became an international superstar, came to Milwaukee in the mid-1990s to work on the winged expansion of the Milwaukee Art Museum. Half of the cash prize will be awarded to the winning architect, and the other half will be given to the UWM School of Architecture and Urban Planning to administer the prize and the recipient's work with faculty and students focusing on design challenges in city. The recipient will also serve as a guest lecturer and workshop studio participant at UWM, leading discussions about challenges in urban planning and design both in the school and the community.

For additional information about the Marcus Prize, visit the University of Wisconsin–Milwaukee on the Web at *www.uwm.edu*.

2005   MVRDV (Netherlands)

Source: University of Wisconsin–Milwaukee

The American city is experienced as an incessant series of happenings, as a never-resting process that engages and fascinates.

Christian Norberg-Schultz

Michelangelo Award

The Construction Specifications Institute established the Michelangelo Buonarroti Award to pay tribute to an exceptional individual for a lifetime of distinguished, innovative service to the design and construction industry. Recipients have exhibited excellence in the mastery of creating and sustaining the built environment. About the genesis of the award, CSI had said, "Michelangelo is one of the greatest artists of all time, a man whose name has become synonymous with the word 'masterpiece.' As an artist he was unmatched, the creator of works of sublime beauty that express the full breadth of the human condition. Because of his lifetime devotion to art and architecture, he was venerated after his death as the 'father and master of all the arts.'" Recipients are honored at the annual CSI Show and presented with a bust of Michelangelo.

For more information on this award visit, the Construction Specifications Institute on the Web at *www.csinet.org*.

2005   Lawrence Halprin

Source: Construction Specifications Institute

Mies van der Rohe Award for European Architecture

Established in 1987 by the European Commission, the European Parliament, and the Mies van der Rohe Foundation, the Mies van der Rohe Award for European Architecture seeks to highlight notable projects within the context of contemporary European architecture. Works by European architects that are constructed in the member states of the European Union and associated European states within the two years following the granting of the previous award are eligible for the program. Winning projects are chosen for their innovative character and excellence in design and execution by an international panel of experts in the field of architecture and architectural criticism. The award consists of a cash prize of 50,000 euros and a sculpture by Xavier Corberó, a design inspired by the Mies van der Rohe Pavilion in Barcelona, Spain.

For more information, visit the Mies van der Rohe Foundation's Web site at *www.miesbcn.com.*

1988
Borges e Irmão Bank
Vila do Conde, Portugal
Alvaro Siza (Portugal)

1990
New Terminal Development, Stansted Airport
London, England
Norman Foster & Partners (UK)

1992
Municipal Sports Stadium
Badalona, Barcelona, Spain
Esteve Bonell and Francesc Rius (Spain)

1994
Waterloo International Station
London, England
Nicholas Grimshaw & Partners (UK)

1996
Bibliotèque Nationale de France
Paris, France
Dominique Perrault (France)

1999
Art Museum in Bregenz
Bregenz, Austria
Peter Zumthor (Switzerland)

2001
Kursaal Congress Centre
San Sebastian, Spain
Rafael Moneo (Spain)

Emerging Architect Special Mention
Kaufmann Holz Distribution Centre
Bobingen, Germany
Florian Nagler, Florian Nagler Architekt
    (Germany)

2003
Car Park & Terminal Hoenheim North
Strasbourg, France
Zaha Hadid (UK)

Emerging Architect Special Mention
Scharnhauser Park Town Hall
Ostfildern, Germany
Jürgen Mayer (Germany)

Mies van der Rohe Award for European Architecture

2005

Netherlands Embassy Berlin
Berlin, Germany
Office for Metropolitan Architecture
(Netherlands)

Emerging Architect Special Mention

Basket Bar
Utrecht, Netherlands
NL Architects (Netherlands)

Source: Mies van der Rohe Foundation

You don't do a thing because you like
to do it but because it is right.

Mies van der Rohe

Modern Healthcare/AIA Design Awards

Each year registered architects are invited to enter the *Modern Healthcare*/AIA Design Awards competition, which recognizes excellence in the design and planning of new and remodeled healthcare facilities. Sponsored by *Modern Healthcare* magazine and the American Institute of Architects' Academy of Architecture for Health, all types and sizes of patient care-related facilities are eligible for submission. Winners are recognized in an issue of *Modern Healthcare* magazine and at the annual AAH convention.

Entry details and winning project profiles are available on the Internet at *www.modernhealthcare.com.*

2004 Recipients

Awards of Excellence

MIND Institute, University of California,
   Davis Medical Center
Sacramento, CA
Hammel, Green and Abrahamson

Parker Adventist Hospital
Parker, CO
HKS

Rumsey Community and Wellness Center
Brooks, CA
Chong Partners Architecture

Honorable Mention

Central DuPage Health Integrative
   Medicine Centre
Geneva, IL
Loebl Schlossman & Hackl

D'Amour Center for Cancer Care
Springfield, MA
Steffian Bradley Architects

Weinberg Building, University of Maryland
   Medical System
Baltimore, MD
Kohn Pedersen Fox Associates

Citation

CentraCare Health Plaza
St. Cloud, MN
Hammel, Green and Abrahamson

St. Joseph Outpatient Center
Tacoma, WA
Callison Architecture

Jury

Peter Bardwell, Bardwell & Associates
Carol Bentel, Bentel & Bentel,
   Architects/Planners
David Brems, Gillies Stransky Brems Smith
Sue Brody, Bayfront Medical Center
Ray Grady, Evanston Hospital
Edward Huckaby, FKP Architects
Rebecca Lewis, Damberg Scott Gerzina Wagner
Randy Peterson, Salina Regional Health Center
Louis Pounders, Williamson Pounders Architects

Source: Modern Healthcare *magazine*

MIND Institute. The placement of the institute's four buildings creates a series of courtyards and reception quads connected by garden-trellis walkways. This results in an environment that is conducive to scholarly interaction as well as offers a warm and inviting space for the families of individuals with neurodevelopmental disorders to find hope.   Photo: Richard Barnes, courtesy of HGA.

National Building Museum Honor Award

Since 1986 the National Building Museum has honored individuals and organizations that have made an exceptional contribution to America's built history with its Honor Award. The award is presented each year at an elegant gala held in the Museum's Great Hall, which since 1883 has often been the site of the Presidential Inaugural Ball.

For more information, contact the National Building Museum at (202) 272-2448 or visit their Web site at *www.nbm.org.*

1986	J. Irwin Miller	1998	Riley P. Bechtel and Stephen D. Bechtel Jr. of the Bechtel Group
1987	*No award granted*	1999	Harold and Terry McGraw and the McGraw-Hill Companies
1988	James W. Rouse		
1989	Daniel Patrick Moynihan	2000	Gerald D. Hines
1990	IBM	2001	Michael D. Eisner and the Walt Disney Company
1991	The Rockefeller Family		
1992	The Civic Leadership of Greater Pittsburgh	2002	DuPont
1993	J. Carter Brown	2003	National Football League and Major League Baseball
1994	James A. Johnson and Fannie Mae		
1995	Lady Bird Johnson	2004	US General Services Administration
1996	Cindy and Jay Pritzker	2005	Forest City Enterprises
1997	Morris Cafritz, Charles E. Smith, Charles A. Horsky and Oliver T. Carr Jr.		

Source: National Building Museum

National Design Awards

Each year the Smithsonian Institution's Cooper-Hewitt, National Design Museum honors American designers with its National Design Awards. Presented in seven categories for excellence, innovation, and enhancement of the quality of life, awards are bestowed for a body of work and not a specific project. Journalists, designers, filmmakers, architects, authors, and other professionals are invited by the Smithsonian to make nominations for the awards.

Complete information is available from the award's Web site, *www.ndm.si.edu.*

2004 Recipients

Architectural Design
Polshek Partnership
Rick Joy

Communications Design
@radical.media

Corporate Achievement
Aveda Corporation

Design Patron
Amanda M. Burden

Environment Design
William McDonough + Partners

Fashion Design
Yeohlee Teng

Lifetime Achievement
Milton Glaser

Product Design
Yves Béhar

Jury
Eliza Bolen, Oscar de la Renta, Ltd.
Ralph Caplan, editor, writer and
    design consultant
Deborah Nevins, landscape designer
    and historian
Andy Proehl, Sony Design Center
Christopher Pullman, WGBH Public
    Broadcasting
Álvaro Siza, architect

> Not until there is nothing ugly left to buy, not until it is as cheap to buy what is beautiful as it is to buy what is ugly, not until then can beauty for everyone become a reality.
>
> **Ellen Key**

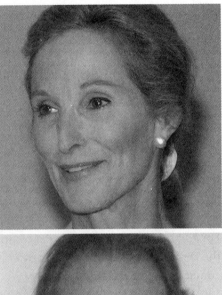

2004 National Design Award recipients, clockwise from top left: Rick Joy (Photo: Bill Timmerman), Amanda M. Burden, William McDonough, Milton Glaser, and Yves Béhar (Photo: Todd Hido). Photos courtesy of the Cooper-Hewitt, National Design Museum.

National Design-Build Awards

Every year the Design-Build Institute of America honors exemplary design-build projects through its National Design-Build Awards with the goal of promoting the design-build process as an effective project delivery method. Submitted entries in each category are evaluated for their overall success in fulfilling the owner's project goals. The projects' achievement within the design-build approach of efficiency, performance, architecture, risk management, and problem solving and the design team's use of innovation to add value are also considerations. Projects completed within the last three years that meet the criteria of a qualified design-build contract are eligible. When merited, the jury may choose to grant the Design-Build Excellence Award to those projects that were outstanding but fell short of the National Design-Build Award.

For additional information and a complete list of all the National Design-Build and the Design-Build Excellence Award winners, visit DBIA's Web site at *www.dbia.org* or contact them at (202) 682-0110.

2004 National Design-Build Award Recipients

Public Sector Building Over $15 Million
Wellington E. Webb Municipal Office Building
Denver, CO
Hensel Phelps Construction Co.

New Embassy Complex
Abu Dhabi, UAE
J.A. Jones International

Transportation Over $15 million
Metro Gold Line
Los Angeles-Pasadena, CA
Kiewit/Washington, joint venture

Water Over $15 million
Morris Forman Wastewater Treatment Plant
   Alternative Solids Project
Louisville, KY
Black & Veatch/Alberici Constructors,
   joint venture

Water Under $15 million
Gilbert and Mosley Project
Wichita, KS
Camp Dresser & McKee Inc.

Under $5 million
Cubs Care Park at New City YMCA
Chicago, IL
Weiss-Wight Cubs Care Joint Venture

Design-Build Rehabilitation/ Renovation/Restoration
Paramount Theater Renovation
Denver, CO
M.A. Mortenson Company

Legacy
ConAgra Foods Corporate Campus
Omaha, NE
Opus Northwest

Source: Design-Build Institute of America

National Medal of Arts

The National Medal of Arts was established by Congress in 1984 to honor individuals and organizations "who in the President's judgment are deserving of special recognition by reason of their outstanding contributions to the excellence, growth, support, and availability of the arts in the United States." All categories of the arts are represented; although awards are not always granted in each category every year. No more than 12 medals may be awarded per year. Individuals and organizations nationwide may make nominations to the National Endowment for the Arts. The National Council on the Arts reviews these nominations and makes recommendations to the president of the United States for final selection of the annual medal. The following individuals received this honor for their work in the design professions.

Visit the NEA's Web site at *www.arts.endow.gov* for additional information and nomination forms.

1987	Isamu Noguchi
1988	I.M. Pei
1989	Leopold Adler
1990	Ian McHarg
1991	Pietro Belluschi
1992	Robert Venturi
	Denise Scott Brown
1995	James Ingo Freed
1997	Daniel Urban Kiley
1998	Frank Gehry
1999	Michael Graves
2002	Florence Knoll Basset
	Lawrence Halprin
2004	Vincent Scully

Source: National Endowment for the Arts

Did you know...

Among the many honors Florence Knoll Bassett has received is the Design Excellence Award from the Philadelphia Museum of Art, which hosted an exhibit on her work in 2005 titled "Florence Knoll Bassett: Defining Modern."

Outstanding Planning Awards

The American Planning Association's annual Outstanding Planning Awards honor group achievement and planning excellence. Winners may be a planning agency, planning team or firm, community group, or local authority and are judged on criteria ranging from project originality to public participation to community acceptance. Four Outstanding Planning Awards may be presented each year: Outstanding Planning Award for a Plan, which may include housing plans, historic conservation plans, economic development plans, and other types; Outstanding Planning Award for a Project/Program/Tool, for a project, program, or tool that is a significant advancement to specific elements of planning; Outstanding Planning Award for a Special Community Initiative; Outstanding Planning Award for a Small Town or Rural Community; and Outstanding Planning Award for Implementation, for an effort that shows significant achievement in accomplishing positive change.

For additional information about the Outstanding Planning Awards, call the American Planning Association at (202) 872-0611, or visit the group's Web site at *www.planning.org*.

2005 Winners

Outstanding Planning Award for a Plan
"Queen City Hub: Regional Action Plan for Downtown Buffalo"
Buffalo, NY
Office of Strategic Planning, the City of Buffalo; Buffalo Place Inc.; School of Architecture and Planning, the University at Buffalo/SUNY

Outstanding Planning Award for a Project/Program/Tool
City of Santa Cruz Accessory Dwelling Unit Development Program
Santa Cruz, CA
City of Santa Cruz Department of Planning and Community Development

Outstanding Planning Award for Implementation
"Extending the Vision for South Broad Street—Building Philadelphia's Avenue of the Arts in the 21st Century"
Philadelphia, PA
Philadelphia City Planning Commission

Outstanding Planning Award for a Special Community Initiative
Atchison Riverfront Park
Atchison, KS
HNTB

Source: American Planning Association

P/A Awards

The P/A Awards were first granted in 1954 by *Progressive Architecture* magazine and are now presented annually by *Architecture* magazine. The awards recognize design excellence in unbuilt projects. A jury of designers and architects selects the winners.

For more information, call (212) 536-6221 or visit the magazine on the Internet at *www.architecturemag.com*.

2005 Recipients

L.A. Now: Volume 3
Los Angeles, CA
Department of Architecture and Urban Design,
   University of California, Los Angeles

2005 Citations

2:1 House
Berkeley, CA
Iwamoto Scott Architecture

Perth Amboy High School
Perth Amboy, NJ
John Ronan Architect

Troia/Temporary Residences for
   Intelligence Agents
Multiple locations, Europe
Neil Denari Architects

Intergenerational Learning Center
Chicago, IL
Office dA

8 Container Farmhouse
Puerto Rico
LOO: LinOldhamOffice

In the Margins
Hollywood, CA
UrbanRock Designs

Jury
Maurice Cox, RBGC Architecture,
   Research & Urbanism
Teddy Cruz, Estudio Teddy Cruz
Roger Duffy, Skidmore, Owings & Merrill
Maxine Griffith, Philadelphia City Planning
   Commission
Brian Healy, Brian Healy Architects

Source: Architecture *magazine*

Philip Johnson Exhibition Catalogue Award

With its Philip Johnson Exhibition Catalogue Award, the Society of Architectural Historians annually recognizes an outstanding architectural exhibition catalogue. In order to be eligible, the catalogue must have been published within the preceding two years.

For more information, contact the SAH at (312) 573-1365 or visit their Web site at *www.sah.org.*

1990

Los Angeles Blueprints for Modern Living: History and Legacy of the Case Study Houses by Elizabeth A.T. Smith (The Museum of Contemporary Art and MIT Press)

1991

Architecture and Its Image: Four Centuries of Architectural Representation, Works from the Collection of the Canadian Centre for Architecture by Eve Blau and Edward Kaufman, eds. (The Canadian Centre for Architecture and MIT Press)

1992

No award granted

1993

The Making of Virginia Architecture by Charles Brownell (Virginia Museum of Fine Arts and the University Press of Virginia)

Louis Kahn: In the Realm of Architecture by David Brownlee (The Museum of Contemporary Art and Rizzoli International)

1994

Chicago Architecture and Design 1923–1993: Reconfiguration of an American Metropolis by John Zukowsky (Prestel and Art Institute of Chicago)

1995

The Palladian Revival: Lord Burlington, His Villa and Garden in Chiswick by John Harris (Yale University Press)

1996

The Perspective of Anglo-American Architecture by James F. O'Gorman (The Athenaeum of Philadelphia)

An Everyday Modernism: The Houses of William Wurster by Marc Treib (San Francisco Museum of Modern Art and the University of California Press)

1997

Sacred Realm: The Emergence of the Synagogue in the Ancient World by Steven Fine (Yeshiva University Museum and Oxford University Press)

1998

Building for Air Travel: Architecture and Design for Commercial Aviation by John Zukowsky (Art Institute of Chicago and Prestel)

1999

The Work of Charles and Ray Eames: a Legacy of Invention by Donald Albrecht (The Library of Congress, Vitra Design Museum, and Abrams Publishing)

2000

E.W. Godwin: Aesthetic Movement Architect and Designer by Susan Weber Soros (Yale University Press)

2001

Mapping Boston by Alex Krieger and David Cobb, editors (MIT Press)

Philip Johnson Exhibition Catalogue Award

Thomas Jeckyll: Architect and Designer. This abundantly illustrated book is the definitive study of Thomas Jeckyll, a major figure in the English Aesthetic movement. The authors examine his most important architectural commissions and diverse examples of his decorative arts. Photo courtesy of Yale University Press.

2002

Mies in Berlin by Terry Riley, Barry Bergdoll, and the Museum of Modern Art (Harry N. Abrams)

2003

Richard Neutra's Windshield House by Dietrich Neumann, ed. (Yale University)

2004

Central European Avant-Gardes: Exchange and Transformation, 1910–930 by Timothy O. Benson, ed. (The MIT Press)

2005

Thomas Jeckyll: Architect and Designer, 1827–1881 by Susan Soros and Catherine Arbuthnott (Yale University Press)

Source: Society of Architectural Historians

Praemium Imperiale

The Praemium Imperiale is awarded by the Japan Art Association, Japan's premier cultural institution, for lifetime achievement in the fields of painting, sculpture, music, architecture, and theater/film. The following individuals received this honor for architecture, which includes a commemorative medal and 15,000,000 yen ($140,000) honorarium.

For more information, visit the Japan Art Association's Web site at *www. praemiumimperiale.org.*

1989	I.M. Pei (US)
1990	James Stirling (UK)
1991	Gae Aulenti (Italy)
1992	Frank Gehry (US)
1993	Kenzo Tange (Japan)
1994	Charles Correa (India)
1995	Renzo Piano (Italy)
1996	Tadao Ando (Japan)
1997	Richard Meier (US)
1998	Alvaro Siza (Portugal)
1999	Fumihiko Maki (Japan)
2000	Richard Rogers (UK)
2001	Jean Nouvel (France)
2002	Sir Norman Foster (UK)
2003	Rem Koolhaas (Netherlands)
2004	Oscar Niemeyer (Brazil)

Source: Japan Art Association

Pritzker Architecture Prize

In 1979, Jay and Cindy Pritzker, through the Hyatt Foundation, established the Pritzker Architecture Prize to inspire greater creativity among the architectural profession and to generate a heightened public awareness about architecture. Today, it is revered as one of the highest honors in the field of architecture. The prize is awarded each year to a living architect whose body of work represents a long-standing, significant contribution to the built environment. Nominations are accepted every January from any interested party. Architects from all nations are eligible. Laureates of the Pritzker Prize receive a $100,000 grant, citation certificate, and bronze medallion.

For additional information, visit their Web site at *www.pritzkerprize.com.*

1979	Philip Johnson (US)	1994	Christian de Portzamparc (France)
1980	Luis Barragán (Mexico)	1995	Tadao Ando (Japan)
1981	James Stirling (UK)	1996	Rafael Moneo (Spain)
1982	Kevin Roche (US)	1997	Sverre Fehn (Norway)
1983	I.M. Pei (US)	1998	Renzo Piano (Italy)
1984	Richard Meier (US)	1999	Sir Norman Foster (UK)
1985	Hans Hollein (Austria)	2000	Rem Koolhaas (Netherlands)
1986	Gottfried Boehm (Germany)	2001	Jacques Herzog and Pierre de Meuron
1987	Kenzo Tange (Japan)		(Switzerland)
1988	Gordon Bunshaft (US)	2002	Glenn Murcutt (Australia)
	Oscar Niemeyer (Brazil)	2003	Jørn Utzon (Denmark)
1989	Frank O. Gehry (US)	2004	Zaha Hadid (UK)
1990	Aldo Rossi (Italy)	2005	Thom Mayne (US)
1991	Robert Venturi (US)		
1992	Alvaro Siza (Portugal)		
1993	Fumihiko Maki (Japan)		*Source: The Pritzker Architecture Prize*

Pulitzer Prize for Architectural Criticism

As one of the many lasting contributions he made to the field of journalism, Joseph Pulitzer established the Pulitzer Prize as an incentive to excellence in journalism, music, and letters. Over the years, the scope of the award has been expanded from its original 1917 configuration. Since 1970, the Pulitzer Prize Board has awarded a prize for distinguished journalistic criticism, and since 1980, they have also acknowledged the finalists. This category includes winners in the arts, culture, and literary fields as well as architecture. The following individuals received this honor for their work in architectural criticism, as well as those that were finalists.

Visit the Pulitzer Prize's Web site at *www.pulitzer.org* for a detailed history, chronology, and archive of past winners.

1970
Ada Louise Huxtable
New York Times

1979
Paul Gapp
Chicago Tribune

1981 finalist
Allan Temko
San Francisco Chronicle

1983 finalist
Beth Dunlop
Miami Herald

1984
Paul Goldberger
New York Times

1988 finalist
Allan Temko
San Francisco Chronicle

1990
Allan Temko
San Francisco Chronicle

1996
Robert Campbell
Boston Globe

1997 finalist
Herbert Muschamp
New York Times

1999
Blair Kamin
Chicago Tribune

2002 finalist
John King
San Francisco Chronicle

2003 finalist
John King
San Francisco Chronicle

Nicolai Ouroussoff
Los Angeles Times

2004 finalist
Nicolai Ouroussoff
Los Angeles Times

Source: The Pulitzer Prize Board

RAIA Gold Medal

The Gold Medal is the highest honor bestowed by the Royal Australian Institute of Architects. It is presented annually to recognize distinguished service by architects who have designed or executed buildings of high merit or have advanced the architecture profession. Gold medallists are nominated by their peers in confidence, and a jury comprised of past medallists and the national president make the final selection. Since 1970, the Gold Medallist traditionally delivers the A.S. Hook Address, named in memory of the early RAIA promoter Alfred Samuel Hook, providing insight into the life, work, and principles of the Gold Medalist and the state of the profession at the time.

For additional information about the Gold Medal or to read past A.S. Hook Addresses, visit the RAIA on the Internet at *www.architecture.com.au.*

1960	Leslie Wilkinson
1961	Louis Layborne-Smith
1962	Joseph Charles Fowell
1963	Sir Arthur Stephenson
1964	Cobden Parkes
1965	Sir Osborn McCutcheon
1966	William Rae Laurie
1967	William Purves Race Godfrey
1968	Sir Roy Grounds
1969	Robin Boyd
1970	Jack Hobbs McConnell
1971	Frederick Bruce Lucas
1972	Edward Herbert Farmer
1973	Jørn Utzon
1974	Raymond Berg
1975	Sydney Edward Ancher
1976	Harry Seidler
1977	Ronald Andrew Gilling
1978	Mervyn Henry Parry
1979	Harold Bryce Mortlock
1980	John Hamilton Andrews
1981	Colin Frederick Madigan
1982	Sir John Wallace Overall
1983	Gilbert Ridgway Nicol and Ross Kingsley Chisholm
1984	Philip Sutton Cox
1985	Richard Norman Johnson
1986	Richard Butterworth
1987	Daryl Sanders Jackson
1988	Romaldo Giurgola
1989	Robin Findlay Gibson
1990	Peter McIntyre
1991	Donald Campbell Rupert Bailey
1992	Glenn Murcutt
1993	Kenneth Frank Woolley
1994	Neville Quarry
1995	*No award granted*
1996	Denton Corker Marshall
1997	Roy Simpson
1998	Gabriel Poole
1999	Richard Leplastrier
2000	John Morphett
2001	Keith Cottier
2002	Brit Andresen
2003	Peter Corrigan
2004	Gregory Burgess
2005	James Birrell

Source: Royal Australian Institute of Architects

RAIC Gold Medal

The Royal Architectural Institute of Canada began its Gold Medal program in 1967 to recognize the achievements of an architect or individual in a related field and their contribution to Canada's built environment. As the RAIC Gold Medal is merit-based, awards are not always granted yearly.

For more information, contact the RAIC at (613) 241-3600 or visit its Web site at *www.raic.org.*

1967	Jean Drapeau (Canada)	1991	Phyllis Lambert (Canada)
1968	Vincent Massey (Canada)	1992	Doug Shadbolt (Canada)
1970	Eric R. Arthur (Canada)	1994	Barton Myers (Canada)
	John A. Russell* (Canada)	1995	Moshe Safdie (Israel)
1973	Serge Chermayeff (Georgia)	1997	Raymond Moriyama (Canada)
1976	Constantinos Doxiadis (Greece)	1998	Frank O. Gehry (US)
1979	John C. Parkin (Canada)	1999	Douglas Cardinal (Canada)
1981	Jane Jacobs (Canada)	2001	A.J. (Jack) Diamond (Canada)
1982	Ralph Erskine (Sweden)		
1984	Arthur Erickson (Canada)		*Honored posthumously
1985	John Bland (Canada)		
1986	Eberhard Zeidler (Canada)		
1989	Raymond T. Affleck (Canada)		*Source: Royal Architectural Institute of Canada*

red dot design awards

The red dot design awards are one of the oldest world-wide product design competitions. The Design Zentrum Nordrhein Westfalen in Essen, Germany, founded the program in 1955 to celebrate outstanding design. Any product launched world-wide within the past two years is eligible to enter in one of 11 categories. An international panel of jurors reviews the entries for degree of innovation, functionality, formal quality, symbolic and emotional content as well as ergonomics and ecological compatibility. The winners are exhibited at the museum and receive the red dot trophy, an international seal of quality for outstanding design.

For more information about the Best of the Best winners, including photos, and a full list of all winning designs, visit red dot online at *www.red-dot.de.*

2005 Best of the Best Recipients

Architecture and Interior Design
LiTraCon - Light-Transmitting Concrete
LiTraCon Bt. (Hungary)

Pinc House Prefabricated Houses
Pinc AB (Sweden)

Bathroom, Heating, Sanitary Installations, and Air Conditioning
Axor Citterio Bathtub-Sink Unit
Antonio Citterio (Germany)

Axor Starck X Faucet
Philippe Starck (France)

Household and Kitchen
Hansacanyon Fittings Series
octopus productdesign (Germany)

touch! Design for the Sense dinnerware
speziell produktgestaltung (Germany)

Varino II, Variable Organization System
Miele & Cie. KG (Germany)

Industry and Crafts
MS12 Air Supply Unit
Festo AG + Co. KG (Germany)

HSW Handling Module
Festo AG + Co. KG (Germany)

Linde T20/T24 SP Electric Pallet Truck
Porsche AG (Germany)

Jewelry, Fashion, Accessories, Textile Design, and New Materials
Akashi Handbag
Studio Vertijet (Germany)

Birkenstock Birki Pro/Birki Clogs
fuseproject (US)

MONACO V4 Concept Watch
Ross Lovegrove (UK)

P'8404 Porsche Design Sunglasses
Peter Kövari (Germany)

Leisure, Sports, Wellness, and Caravanning
Bikamper Tent
Topeak Design Team; Lutz Scheffer (Taiwan)

Initech Geologic Bow
Decathlon Sportartikel GmbH (Germany)

red dot design awards

SILVERFISH Underwater Camcorder Housing
RWE Mechatronics GmbH (Germany)

Life Science and Medicine
c.cam SPECT-Scanner
Siemens Medical Solutions (US)

OES Pro-2 Resectoscope
Held + Team (Germany)

Unilateral Orthotic Joint System
Otto Bock HealthCare GmbH (Germany)

Lighting and Lamps
Mouette Pendant Lamp
Jean-Michel Wilmotte (France)

One Line Table Lamp
Artemide GmbH (Germany)

Living Rooms and Bedrooms
Diamond Tables
Patricia Urquiola

Facett Armchair
Ronan & Erwan Bouroullec Design (France)

platten_bau Shelving System
Florian Petri (Germany)

Media and Home Electronics
Apple Cinema Displays
Apple Computer (US)

HDR-FX1 HDV1080i-Camcorder
Sony Corporation (Japan)

Spheros R 37 Masterpiece LCD-TV
Loewe AG (Germany)

Wave Music System
Bose Corp. (US)

Office and Administration
Sqr Carpet
Peter Maly (Germany)

Transport
K 1200 S Motorrad
BMW Group (Germany)

Porsche 911 Carrera
Porsche AG (Germany)

Z-Tech Tugboat
Robert Allan Ltd. (Canada)

Jury
Werner Aisslinger, Studio Aisslinger (Germany)
Masayo Ave, MasayoAve creation
   (Japan and Italy)
Martin Bergmann, EOOS (Austria)
Mårten Claesson, Claesson Koivisto Rune
   (Sweden)
Björn Dahlström, graphic, industrial, and
   product designer (Sweden)
Joachim H. Faust, HPP Hentrich-Petschnigg
   & Partner KG (Germany)
Luigi Ferrara, George Brown College and
   the Architectural Literacy Forum (Canada)
Andrea Finke-Anlauff, Mango Design and Mango
   Objects (Germany)
Naoto Fukasawa, Naoto Fukasawa Design (Japan)
Kenneth Grange, Kenneth Grange Design (UK)
Flemming Bo Hansen, goldsmith and designer
   (Denmark)
Tapani Hyvönen, ED-design Ltd. (Finland)
Chul-ho Kim, Korea Institute of Design
   Promotion (Korea)
Odo Klose, Odo Klose & Partner (Germany)
Annette Lang, designer (Germany)
Kristiina Lassus, Kristiina Lassus Studio (Finland)
Stefan Lengyel, designer (Germany)
Wolfgang K. Meyer-Hayoz, Meyer-Hayoz Design
   Engineering Group (Germany)
Francesco Milani, designer (Switzerland)
Giuliano Molineri, Frimark Srl (Italy)
Marcello Morandini, designer (Italy)
Ron Nabarro, Israel Institute of Technology
   (Israel)
Danny Venlet, designer (Australia)
Helen Yardley, AZ Studios (UK)

Source: Design Zentrum Nordrhein Westfalen

red dot design awards

2005 red dot design award winners, clockwise from top left: Akashi Handbag, MONACO V4 Concept Watch, Bikamper Tent, and LiTraCon - Light-transmitting Concrete. Photos courtesy of the red dot design awards.

Religious Art & Architecture Design Awards

The annual Religious Art & Architecture Design Awards, co-sponsored by *Faith & Form* magazine and the Interfaith Forum on Religion, Art and Architecture (a professional interest area of the American Institute of Architects), acknowledge the highest standards in architecture, liturgical design, and art for religious spaces. Awards are presented for religious architecture in three categories: new facilities, renovations, and restorations. Additional categories may include visual arts, liturgical furnishings, and ceremonial objects. Licensed US architects, liturgical consultants, interior designers, artists, and craftpersons are eligible to enter. Winning projects are featured in *Faith & Form* magazine.

For additional information and entry forms, visit *www.faithandform.org* on the Internet or contact *Faith & Form* magazine at (919) 489-3359.

2004 Honor Awards

New Facility

Saint Francis de Sales Parish Church
Morgantown, WV
Rafferty Rafferty Tollefson Architects

Temple Bat Yahm Torah Center
Newport Beach, CA
Lehrer Architects

Holy Rosary Catholic Church Complex
St. Amant, LA
Trahan Architects

Jubilee Church, Dio Padre Misericordioso
  Tor Tre Teste
Rome, Italy
Richard Meier & Partners, Architects

Renovation

Rodef Shalom Congregation
Pittsburgh, PA
The Design Alliance

First Unitarian Church
Providence, RI
Centerbrook Architects and Planners

Restoration

Immaculate Conception Cathedral
Kansas City, MO
Shaughnessy Fickel & Scott Architects Inc.

Visual Arts

Doctors of the Church Project, St. Catharine
  of Siena Catholic Church
Columbus, OH
Sarah Hall Studio Inc.

Crucifix, St. Gabriel's Catholic Church
McKinney, TX
John Collier

Holocaust Sculpture, "Kriah," Congregation
  Beth Israel
San Diego, CA
Laurie Gross Studios

Liturgical Furnishings

Peninsula Temple Sholom
Burlingame, CA
Herman & Coliver: Architecture

Religious Art & Architecture Design Awards

2004 Merit Awards

New Facility

Temple De Hirsch Sinai
Bellevue, WA
Weinstein A/U Architects + Urban Designers

Al Hidayah Mosque
Port Coquitlam, BC, Canada
Studio Senbel, architecture + design

Christ Chapel
Madison County, OH
Phillip Markwood Architects

Saints Cyril & Methodios Orthodox Church
and Heritage Center
Mercer, PA
Huelat Parimucha Ltd.

Renovation

Immanuel Lutheran Church
East Dundee, IL
David F. Schultz Assoc.

St. Stephen's Episcopal Church
Belvedere, CA
Goring & Straja Architect

First Presbyterian Church of Encino
Encino, CA
Abramson Teiger Architects

Restoration

Cathedral of Saint Andrew
Grand Rapids, MI
Quinn Evans Architects

Liturgical/Furnishings

Peninsula Temple Sholom
Burlingame, CA
Herman & Coliver: Architecture

Visual Arts

Ambulatory Window, Old Saint Mary's
Catholic Church
Chicago, IL
Kessler Studios, Inc.

Jury

Judith Dupre, author and critic (chair)
Frances Halsband, RM Kliment & Frances
Halsband Architects
Michael Mills, artist
John Buscemi, liturgical designer
James Howell, clergy

Source: Faith & Form *magazine*

159

Did you know...

Pittsburgh architect Louis D. Astorino was the first American architect to design a building at the Vatican, the 1996 Chapel of the Holy Spirit.

residential architect Design Awards

In 2000, *residential architect* magazine established a design award program to honor the best in American housing. Projects may be submitted in one of eight categories, though judges may eliminate, add, or combine categories—bestowing as many awards (or none) as they see fit. The jury, comprised of top residential architects, also selects the best residential project of the year from among the winning entries. Winning projects are published in *residential architect* magazine.

For photographs and descriptions of all the winning projects, visit *www.residential architect.com* on the Internet.

2005 Best Residential Project of the Year

Contemporaine at 516 North Wells
Chicago, IL
Perkins+Will

2005 Grand Prize Winners

Custom Home
3,500 square feet or less
Chicken Point Cabin
Northern Idaho
Olson Sundberg Kundig Allen Architects

Custom Home
More than 3,500 square feet
The Prospect
La Jolla, CA
Jonathan Segal

Rye Residence
Eastern Pennsylvania
Bohlin Cywinski Jackson

Renovation
Dog Team Too
San Antonio, TX
Lake/Flato Architects

Multifamily
Skybridge @ One North Halsted
Chicago, IL
Perkins+Will

Kitchen
Potrero Hill Residence
San Francisco, CA
Serrao Design/Architecture

On the Boards
Schindler Residence
San Francisco, CA
Serrao Design/Architecture

Fahrenheit
San Diego, CA
Studio E Architects

Cabin on a Pond in Maine
Eastbrook, ME
Perfido Weiskopf Architects

residential architect Design Awards

2005 Merit Winners

Custom Home
3,500 square feet or less
Matthew Residence
Brainerd, MN
Salmela Architect

Pacific Palisades Residence
Pacific Palisades, CA
PAASTUDIO

Custom Home
More than 3,500 square feet
Orleans Residence
Orleans, MA
Charles Rose Architects

Veber Residence
Rye, NY
Kaehler Moore Architects

Feinstein Residence
Malibu, CA
Kanner Architects

Renovation
Wilson Residence
Alexandria, VA
Envision

Via de la Paz Residence
Pacific Palisades, CA
Nonzero/Architecture

Folsom Street Residential Laboratory
San Francisco, CA
Petersen + Verwers

Farmhouse
Virginia
Rill & Decker Architects

Multifamily
Harper Court: Seven Fountains
West Hollywood, CA
Moule & Polyzoides

Bentley Massachusetts Apartments
Los Angeles, CA
Kanner Architects

Affordable Housing
Soma Studios and 8th + Howard Apartments
San Francisco, CA
David Baker & Partners, Architects

Eucalyptus View Cooperative
Escondido, CA
Studio E Architects

Chelsea Court
New York, NY
Louise Braverman, Architect

City West: Phase II
Cincinnati, OH
Torti Gallas and Partners

Single-Family Production
Housing, Attached
110 Chattanooga Duplex
San Francisco, CA
Zack/Devito Architecture

Cannery Lofts
Newport Beach, CA
Tanner Hecht Architecture

Campus Housing
Ramapo College 300-bed Dormitory
Mahwah, NJ
Paulus, Sokolowski & Sartor Architecture

residential architect Design Awards

CCAC Clifton Street Housing
Oakland, CA
Mark Horton/Architecture

Residential Suites, California State Polytechnic
    University, Pomona
Pomona, CA
Sasaki Associates

Outbuilding
Broadford Farm Pavilion
Hailey, ID
Lake/Flato Architects

Private Wine Silo
Teton County, WY
Carney Architects

Poolhouse
Amherst, MA
Austin Design

Bath
Winter Residence
Tucson, AZ
Ibarra Rosano Design Architects

Architectural Design Detail
House Ocho
Carmel Valley, CA
Feldman Architecture

Stud Skeleton Library
Winchester, VA
Reader and Swartz Architects

On the Boards
Loblolly House
Taylors Island, MD
KieranTimberlake Associates

Jury
Kirk V. Blunck, Herbert Lewis Kruse Blunck
    Architecture
Stuart Cohen, Stuart Cohen & Julie Hacker
    Architects
Laura Hartman, Fernau & Hartman Architects
William P. Lecky, The Lessard Group
Dan Rockhill, Rockhill and Associates
Edward Weinstein, Weinstein A/U Architects +
    Urban Designers

Source: residential architecture *magazine*

Home is a name, a word, it is a
strong one: stronger than a magician
ever spoke, or spirit ever answered
to, in the strongest conjuration.

Charles Dickens

RIBA Royal Gold Medal

The Royal Institute of British Architects' Royal Gold Medal was inaugurated by Queen Victoria in 1848. It is conferred by the Sovereign annually on a distinguished architect, person, or firm "whose work has promoted, either directly or indirectly, the advancement of architecture."

For additional information, visit the RIBA on the Internet at *www.riba.org.*

1848	Charles Robert Cockerell (UK)
1849	Luigi Canina (Italy)
1850	Sir Charles Barry (UK)
1851	Thomas L. Donaldson (UK)
1852	Leo von Klenze (Germany)
1853	Sir Robert Smirke (UK)
1854	Philip Hardwick (UK)
1855	Jacques Ignace Hittorff (France)
1856	Sir William Tite (UK)
1857	Owen Jones (UK)
1858	Friedrich August Stuler (Germany)
1859	Sir G. Gilbert Scott (UK)
1860	Sydney Smirke (UK)
1861	Jean-Baptiste Cicéron Lesueur (France)
1862	Rev. Robert Willis (UK)
1863	Anthony Salvin (UK)
1864	Eugène Emmanuel Violett-le-Duc (France)
1865	Sir James Pennethorne (UK)
1866	Sir Matthew Digby Wyatt (UK)
1867	Charles Texier (France)
1868	Sir Henry Layard (UK)
1869	C.R. Lepsius (Germany)
1870	Benjamin Ferrey (UK)
1871	James Fergusson (UK)
1872	Baron von Schmidt (Austria)
1873	Thomas Henry Wyatt (UK)
1874	George Edmund Street (UK)
1875	Edmund Sharpe (UK)
1876	Joseph Louis Duc (France)
1877	Charles Barry Jr. (UK)
1878	Alfred Waterhouse (UK)
1879	Marquis de Vogue (France)
1880	John L. Pearson (UK)
1881	George Godwin (UK)
1882	Baron von Ferstel (Austria)
1883	Francis Cranmer Penrose (UK)
1884	William Butterfield (UK)

1885	H. Schliemann (Germany)
1886	Charles Garnier (France)
1887	Ewan Christian (UK)
1888	Baron von Hansen (Austria)
1889	Sir Charles T. Newton (UK)
1890	John Gibson (UK)
1891	Sir Arthur Blomfield (UK)
1892	Cesar Daly (France)
1893	Richard Morris Hunt (US)
1894	Lord Leighton (UK)
1895	James Brooks (UK)
1896	Sir Ernest George (UK)
1897	Petrus Josephus Hubertus Cuypers (Netherlands)
1898	George Aitchison (UK)
1899	George Frederick Bodley (UK)
1900	Rodolfo Amadeo Lanciani (Italy)
1901	*No award granted due to the death of Queen Victoria*
1902	Thomas Edward Collcutt (UK)
1903	Charles F. McKim (US)
1904	Auguste Choisy (France)
1905	Sir Aston Webb (UK)
1906	Sir Lawrence Alma-Tadema (UK)
1907	John Belcher (UK)
1908	Honore Daumet (France)
1909	Sir Arthur John Evans (UK)
1910	Sir Thomas Graham Jackson (UK)
1911	Wilhelm Dorpfeld (Germany)
1912	Basil Champneys (UK)
1913	Sir Reginald Blomfield (UK)
1914	Jean Louis Pascal (France)
1915	Frank Darling (Canada)
1916	Sir Robert Rowand Anderson (UK)
1917	Henri Paul Nenot (France)
1918	Ernest Newton (UK)
1919	Leonard Stokes (UK)
1920	Charles Louis Girault (France)
1921	Sir Edwin Landseer Lutyens (UK)

RIBA Royal Gold Medal

1922	Thomas Hastings (US)
1923	Sir John James Burnet (UK)
1924	*No award granted*
1925	Sir Giles Gilbert Scott (UK)
1926	Ragnar Östberg (Sweden)
1927	Sir Herbert Baker (US)
1928	Sir Guy Dawber (US)
1929	Victor Alexandre Frederic Laloux (France)
1930	Sir Percy Scott Worthington (UK)
1931	Sir Edwin Cooper (US)
1932	Hendrik Petrus Berlage (Netherlands)
1933	Sir Charles Reed Peers (UK)
1934	Henry Vaughan Lanchester (UK)
1935	Willem Marinus Dudok (Netherlands)
1936	Charles Henry Holden (UK)
1937	Sir Raymond Unwin (UK)
1938	Ivar Tengbom (Sweden)
1939	Sir Percy Thomas (UK)
1940	Charles Francis Annesley Voysey (UK)
1941	Frank Lloyd Wright (US)
1942	William Curtis Green (UK)
1943	Sir Charles Herbert Reilly (UK)
1944	Sir Edward Maufe (UK)
1945	Victor Vesnin (USSR)
1946	Sir Patrick Abercrombie (UK)
1947	Sir Albert Edward Richardson (UK)
1948	Auguste Perret (France)
1949	Sir Howard Robertson (UK)
1950	Eleil Saarinen (Finland)
1951	Emanuel Vincent Harris (UK)
1952	George Grey Wornum (UK)
1953	Le Corbusier (C.E. Jeanneret-Gris) (Switzerland)
1954	Sir Arthur George Stephenson (Australia)
1955	John Murray Easton (UK)
1956	Walter Adolf Gropius (Germany)
1957	Hugo Alvar Henrik Aalto (Finland)
1958	Robert Schofield Morris (Italy)
1959	Ludwig Mies van der Rohe (Germany)
1960	Pier Luigi Nervi (Italy)
1961	Lewis Mumford (US)
1962	Sven Gottfrid Markeluis (Sweden)
1963	The Lord Holford (UK)
1964	E. Maxwell Fry (UK)
1965	Kenzo Tange (Japan)
1966	Ove Arup (UK)

1967	Sir Nikolaus Pevsner (UK)
1968	Richard Buckminster Fuller (US)
1969	Jack Antonio Coia (UK)
1970	Sir Robert Matthew (UK)
1971	Hubert de Cronin Hastings (UK)
1972	Louis I. Kahn (US)
1973	Sir Leslie Martin (UK)
1974	Powell & Moya (UK)
1975	Michael Scott (Ireland)
1976	Sir John Summerson (UK)
1977	Sir Denys Lasdun (UK)
1978	Jørn Utzon (Denmark)
1979	The Office of Charles and Ray Eames (US)
1980	James Stirling (UK)
1981	Sir Philip Dowson (UK)
1982	Berthold Lubetkin (Georgia)
1983	Sir Norman Foster (UK)
1984	Charles Correa (India)
1985	Sir Richard Rogers (UK)
1986	Arata Isozaki (Japan)
1987	Ralph Erskine (Sweden)
1988	Richard Meier (UK)
1989	Renzo Piano (Italy)
1990	Aldo van Eyck (Netherlands)
1991	Sir Colin Stansfield Smith (UK)
1992	Peter Rice (UK)
1993	Giancarlo de Carlo (Italy)
1994	Sir Michael and Patty Hopkins (UK)
1995	Colin Rowe (UK)
1996	Harry Seidler (Australia)
1997	Tadao Ando (Japan)
1998	Oscar Niemeyer (Brazil)
1999	Barcelona, Spain
2000	Frank Gehry (US)
2001	Jean Nouvel (France)
2002	Archigram (UK)
2003	Rafael Moneo (Spain)
2004	Rem Koolhaas (Netherlands)
2005	Frei Otto (Germany)

Source: Royal Institute of British Architects

Frei Otto. German architect and engineer Frei Otto is the world's leading authority on lightweight tensile and membrane structures. His most
famous projects include the West German Pavilion at the Montreal
Exposition in 1967 and the roofs over several of the sports structures
at the 1972 Olympic Park in Munich. Photo © Morley von Sternberg, courtesy
of the RIBA.

Richard H. Driehaus Prize for Classical Architecture

The Richard H. Driehaus Prize for Classical Architecture was established, endowed, and named for the founder of Chicago's Driehaus Capital Management Company and presented by the University of Notre Dame's School of Architecture. The annual award honors a major contributor in the field of traditional and classical architecture or historic preservation. Each year a panel of educators and leading architects selects one recipient. Winners receive $100,000 and a bronze and stone model of the Choregic Monument of Lysikrates in Athens, Greece.

For additional information about the Driehaus Prize, visit the Notre Dame School of Architecture on the Web at *www.driehausprize.org*

2003	Léon Krier (UK)
2004	Demetri Porphyrios (Greece)
2005	Quinlan Terry (UK)

Source: University of Notre Dame, School of Architecture

A work is classical not because it is immutable, eternal, and sacred but because it continually searches for and brings out the new. Classicism is not a style. Classicism is not a doctrine; it is philosophy of life. It is the philosophy of free will nurtured by tradition.

Demitri Porphyrios

Richard H. Driehaus Prize for Classical Architecture

Corinthian Villa, Regent's Park, London, UK. Terry Quinlan's Baroque style design for the Corinthian Villa takes its influences from Borromini and late Roman work. The serpentine, triple-curved facade, which was occasionally used in Italy and Central Europe during the 17th century, is here used for the first time in the history of English architecture. Photos courtesy of Quinlan and Francis Terry Architects and University of Notre Dame, School of Architecture.

Rudy Bruner Award for Urban Excellence

The biennial Rudy Bruner Award for Urban Excellence is awarded to projects that approach urban problems with creative inclusion of often competing political, community, environmental, and formal considerations. Established in 1987, the award grants one gold medal, along with a $50,000 cash prize, and four silver medals, which each receive $10,000. Any project that fosters urban excellence is eligible to apply. A multidisciplinary jury performs an on-site evaluation of the five finalists before selection of the gold-medal recipient.

For photographs and project descriptions, visit the Bruner Foundation on the Internet at w*ww.brunerfoundation.org* or contact them at (617) 876-8404.

2005 Winners

Gold Medal
Portland Streetcar Project
Portland, OR

Silver Medal
Paducah Artist Relocation Program
Paducah, KY

Heidelberg Project
Detriot, MI

Fruitvale Village
Oakland, CA

Downtown Silver Spring and Discovery
   Communications World Headquarters
Silver Spring, MD

Jury
Andrew Altman, Anacostia Waterfront Corp.
Lee Cott, Bruner/Cott & Associates
Maurice Cox, University of Virginia
Shirley Franklin, City of Atlanta
Christopher B. Leinberger, Arcadia Land Co.
Louise Manuel, Local Initiatives Support Corp.
Dee Walsh, REACH Community
   Development Corp.

Source: Bruner Foundation

The Rudy Bruner Award is more than an award for excellence. It is an award for those who believe that social equity, economic opportunity, and environmental stewardship can be embraced to sustain all America's communities.

Norman B. Rice

The Heidelberg Project. In 1986 Tyree Guyton **(left)**, a world-renowned painter, sculptor, and mixed media and urban environmental artist, began the Heidelberg Project to revitalize and restore Detroit's East Side neighborhood, where he was born and raised, by using art as a catalyst. For example, the Dotty Wotty House **(top)** is adorned with polka dots, which are meant to symbolize and celebrate the city's, as well as the world's, diversity. **Photos courtesy of the Heidelberg Project Archives.**

Russel Wright Award

Established by Manitoga, The Russel Wright Center in Garrison, NY, the Russel Wright Award honors individuals who are working in the tradition of the mid-20th-century design pioneer Russel Wright (1904–1976) to provide outstanding design to the general public. Russel Wright was a well-known home furnishings designer in the 1930s through the 1950s who throughout his career maintained the importance of making well-designed objects accessible to the public. The 75-acre wooded landscape he sculpted, Manitoga, is listed in the National Register of Historic Places. It includes Dragon Rock, a home he designed that exemplifies his philosophy that architecture should enhance rather than dominate its surroundings.

For additional information about the Russel Wright Award, contact Manitoga at (845) 424-3812 or *www.russelwrightcenter.org*.

2000
Michael Graves

2001
Lella and Massimo Vignelli
William T. Golden
Cooper-Hewitt National Design Museum,
 Smithsonian Institution

2002
Murray Moss
Frances S. Reese
Eva Zeisel

2003
Jack Lenor Larsen
Harvey Keyes Flad
Rob Forbes

2004
Jens Risom
Michael and Stephen Maharam
The Institute of Ecosystems Studies

2005
Knoll, Inc.
Palisades Interstate Park Commission

Source: Manitoga, The Russel Wright Center

Did you know...

When Russel and Mary Wright purchased land in Garrison, NY, in 1942 to build their country retreat, Manitoga, the property was a quarry-pitted, lumber-stripped industrial site. Russel Wright spent the next 30 years reclaiming the property.

SADI Awards

The SADI (Superior Achievement in Design and Imaging) Awards are presented each year by *Retail Traffic* magazine, formerly *Shopping Center World* magazine, for retail design achievement and trendsetting. Award categories range from restaurants to renovated shopping centers, plus a best-in-show Grand SADI Award, and honorable mentions at the judges' discretion. The jury is comprised of leading retail architects and designers from across the United States who score projects based on such criteria as construction problem solving, general aesthetics, image-building, and implementation. The competition is open to any architectural or design firm, retailer, or developer responsible for the design of a new or renovated retail store, shopping center, or restaurant.

For additional information, visit *Retail Traffic* magazine's Web site at *www.retailtrafficmag.com.*

2005 Grand SADI Winner

Namba Parks
Osaka, Japan
The Jerde Partnership with Obayashi
    Corporation Architectural Department

2005 Winners

New Retail Store Interior
Less than 5,000 Square Feet
Fornarina
Las Vegas, NV
Giorgio Borruso Design; Gensler Architects

Miss Sixty
Aventura, FL
Giorgia Borruso Design; Brand & Allen

New Retail Store
5,000 Square Feet or More
Home Economist Market
Charlotte, NC
Little Diversified Architectural Consulting

Safeway-Mission Place
San Francisco, CA
SGPA Architecture & Planning;
    King Retail Solutions

**Renovated or Expanded
Enclosed Center**
Estacion de Tren Principe Pio
Madrid, Spain
RTKL Associates Inc. with Fernandez del Amo

Cincinnati Mills
Cincinnati, OH
FRCH Design Worldwide

**Best Adapted Reuse of
Original Space**
Bloomingdale's SoHo
New York, NY
Mancini Duffy with Tucci, Segrete + Rosen

SADI Awards

Renovated or Expanded Community/Power Center
30,000–600,000 Square Feet
Eton Chagrin Boulevard
Woodmere, OH
Bialosky + Partners; David Benjamin Meleca
    Architecture & Urban Planning

New Open-Air Center
80,000–800,000 Square Feet or More
Namba Parks
Osaka, Japan
The Jerde Partnership with Obayashi
    Corporation Architectural Department

Legacy Town Center
Plano, TX
RTKL Associates Inc. with
    Michael Twitchell Architects

Best New Quick-Serve Restaurant
Cosi
Avon, CT
Little Diversified Architectural Consulting

New Enclosed Center
The Shops at Columbus Circle/
    Time Warner Center
New York, NY
Elkus Manfredi Architects; Skidmore,
    Owings & Merrill

Jury
Vilma Barr, Barr Publicity & Editorial Services
Arthur Benedetti, The Jerde Partnership
Annmarie Brintnall, Callison Architecture
Mark Carter, Thompson, Ventulett, Stainback &
    Associates Inc.
Christian Davies, FRCH Design Worldwide
Kevin Dougherty, Dougherty Schroeder &
    Associates, Inc.
Dennis Gervais, GHA Shoppingscapes
Jeff Gill, MCG Architecture
Jennifer Johanson, Engstrom Design Group
Y.E. Smith, Sienna Architectural Co.

Source: Retail Traffic *magazine*

Did you know...

At $1.8 billion, the mixed-use Time Warner Center (2004) by Skidmore, Owings & Merrill, with two glass-sheathed towers atop a two-block curved base, is the most expensive single building ever erected in the United States.

SCUP/AIA-CAE Excellence in Planning Awards

The Society for College and University Planning and the American Institute of Architects' Committee on Architecture for Education jointly present the annual Excellence in Planning Awards to honor planning and design that recognizes excellence in higher education environments. The jury considers the quality of the physical environment as well as the comprehensiveness of the planning process. The award is open to any professional who has prepared plans for higher education institutions and the institutions themselves and is presented to all members of the project team.

Additional information can be found at the SCUP Web site, *www.scup.org*, or by calling (734) 998-6595.

2005 Honor Award

Nicola Valley Institute of Technology
Merritt, BC, Canada
Busby Perkins + Will Architects, Co.

2005 Merit Award

Campus Architecture
Rothermere American Institute,
   University of Oxford
Oxford, UK
Kohn Pedersen Fox Associates

Campus Heritage
"Brooklyn College Master Plan,"
   Brooklyn College, CUNY
Brooklyn, NY
Gruzen Samton; RM Kliment & Frances
   Halsband Architects

District Planning
"Gateway to the Sciences: Chemistry Research
   and Life Sciences Complex," Pennsylvania
   State University
State College, PA
BLT/Payette Joint Venture Architects

Planning for an Established Campus
"The 2001 Campus Master Plan,"
   University of North Carolina at Chapel Hill
Chapel Hill, NC
Ayers/Saint/Gross, Architects + Planners

"Yale University: A Framework for
   Campus Planning"
New Haven, CT
Cooper, Robertson & Partners

Planning for a New Campus
"The North Allston Strategic Framework for
   Planning: Building a Social, Economic, and
   Intellectual Future for Campus, City, and
   Community," Harvard University
Cambridge, MA
Goody Clancy

SCUP/AIA-CAE Excellence in Planning Awards

"The New West Campus Master Plan,"
    Northeastern University
Boston, MA
William Rawn Associates, Architects, Inc.

"The University of North Texas at
    Dallas Campus Master Plan"
Dallas, TX
Sasaki Associates, Inc.

Jury

Calvert W. Audrain, consultant
Anthony (Tony) G. Catchot, JJR
Daniel Mark Fogel, University of Vermont
Lenell Kittlitz, Connecticut Community-
    Technical College System
David J. Neuman, University of Virginia
Martha Thorne, Art Institute of Chicago

*Source: Society for College and University Planning and the American
    Institute of Architects' Committee on Architecture for Education*

SEGD Design Awards

The Society for Environmental Graphic Design's Design Awards recognize the best in environmental design—the planning, design, and specifying of graphic elements in the built and natural environments. Eligible projects include signage, wayfinding systems, mapping, exhibit design, themed environments, retail spaces, sports facilities, and campus design. A jury of professionals reviews the entries to determine which projects best help identify, direct, inform, interpret, and visually enhance our surroundings. Three levels of awards are granted: honor awards, merit awards, and the juror award. Winners are announced at SEGD's annual conference each spring and are honored in an annual exhibition and biannual publication.

For a list of all winning entries, visit SEGD's Web site at *www.segd.org.*

2005 Honor Awards

Capital Metro Experience Design
Austin, TX
fd2s, inc.

Children's Museum of Pittsburgh
Pittsburgh, PA
Pentagram Design

M.D. Anderson Access System
Houston, TX
fd2s, inc.

Mini Store
Multiple locations, US
Apple Computer

National Constitution Center
Philadelphia, PA
Ralph Appelbaum Associates

NYCHHC Interior Signage Standards
New York, NY
Hillier Environmental Graphic Design

"Picture This: Windows on the American Home,"
National Building Museum
Washington, DC
Matter Practice; MGMT. design

Shake Shack
New York, NY
Pentagram Design

Social Studies/ASU, Lattie F. Coor Hall,
Arizona State University
Tempe, AZ
Krivanek+Breaux/Art+Design

Temporary WTC Path Station, World Trade
Center Site
New York, NY
Pentagram Design

Voices
Barcelona, Spain
Ralph Appelbaum Associates

Wave Hill
Bronx, NY
Pentagram Design

Jury
Kiku Obata, Kiku Obata & Company (chair)
Judy Cunningham, Mesa Design Group
Ellen Lupton, Cooper–Hewitt, National Design
Museum
Tom Mnich, The Mills Corporation
Merritt Price, J. Paul Getty Museum
Tom Quirk, D'Agostino Izzo Quirk Architects

Picture This: Windows on the American Home. Of this exhibit the jury said, "This is a show about windows, a pretty tough subject to make vivid and interesting. When designing exhibitions about the history of applied arts and technology, it's always tempting to simulate the past in a literal, Disneyesque way. I admire the way the designers set the windows into an abstract wall structure that gives visitors a sense of how the windows would have functioned in space without creating a decorative environment around them. The graphics are beautifully integrated with this architectural display system. The typography is simple, distinctive, and dramatic, and the whole effect of the exhibition is to present a modern view on history." **Photos: Harry Zernike.**

Sir Patrick Abercrombie Prize

The triennial Sir Patrick Abercrombie Prize is awarded by the International Union of Architects (UIA) to an internationally renowned architect or architects for significant work in town planning and territorial development. The prize is named after the distinguished British architect and planner Sir Patrick Abercrombie, who is known for the post-World War II replanning of many British towns, most notably London.

For more information, visit the UIA's Web site at *www.uia-architectes.org.*

1961
Town Planning Service of the City of Stockholm (Sven Markelius and G. Onblahd, Sweden)

1963
Constantinos Doxiadis (Greece)

1965
Colin Buchanan and team (UK)
T. Farkas and team (Hungary)

1967
Giancarlo De Carlo (Italy)

1969
H. Bennet and team (UK)

Honorary Mention
Belaunde Terry (Peru)

1972
Centre for Experimentation, Research and Training (Morocco)

1975
Iosif Bronislavovitch Orlov and Nilolai Ivanovitch Simonov (USSR)

1978
The City of Louvain la Neuve (Belgium)

1981
Warsaw architects (Poland) for the reconstruction of their capital

Honorary Mention
M. Balderiotte and team (Argentina)

1984
Hans Blumenfeld (Canada) and Lucio Costa (Brazil)

1987
AIA Regional/Urban Design Assistance Team (US)

Honorary Mention
Eduardo Leira (Spain); L. Bortenreuter, K. Griebel, H.G. Tiedt for the remodeling of the city center of Gera (GDR)

1990
Edmund N. Bacon (US)

1993
Jan Gehl (Denmark)

1996
Juan Gil Elizondo (Mexico)

1999
Karl Ganser (Germany)

Honorary Mention
Master plan of the city of Shenzhen (China)

2002
Group 91 Architects for the Temple Bar district in Dublin (Ireland)

2005
Nuno Portas (Portugal)

Honorary Mention
Hermann Sträb (Germany)

Source: International Union of Architects

Sir Robert Matthew Prize

The International Union of Architects (UIA) grants the triennial Sir Robert Matthew Prize to an internationally renowned architect or architects whose work has improved the quality of human settlements. The prize is named after notable Scottish architect Sir Robert Matthew, who is known for his contributions to social architecture, among other achievements.

For more information, visit the UIA's Web site at *www.uia-architectes.org*.

1978
John F.C. Turner (UK)

1981
Hassan Fathy (Egypt)

Honorary Mention
Rod Hackney (UK) and
Hardt Walther Hamer (GFR)

1984
Charles Correa (India)

1987
Housing Reconstruction Program for the
City of Mexico (Mexico)

1990
Department of Architecture of the
Singapore Housing & Development
Board (Singapore)

1993
Laurie Baker (UK)

1996
Giancarlo De Carlo (Italy)

Jury Citation
Oberste Baubehörde (the German team
under the guidance of architect Benno
Brugger and led by Hans Jörg Nussberger)

1999
Martin Treberspurg (Austria)

Honorary Mention
Development & Construction Branch of the
Hong Kong Housing Department (China)

2002
Justin Kilcullen (Ireland)
Jaime Lerner (Brazil)

Honorary Mention
Kooperation GdW-BDA-DST (Germany)

2005
Stefan Forster (Germany)
Xiaodong Wang (China)

Source: International Union of Architects

Spirit of Nature Wood Architecture Award

The Spirit of Nature Wood Architecture Award was established in Finland in 1999 by the Wood in Culture Association to promote the use of timber in architecture. An international jury of architects meets biennially to select the recipient, a person or group of persons whose work exemplifies a progressive and creative use of timber. Through this award, the organizers hope to increase the respect for timber buildings and improve their quality.

More information about the Spirit of Nature Wood Architecture Award is available online at *www.spiritofnature.net.*

2000	Renzo Piano (Italy)
2002	Kengo Kuma (Japan)
2004	Richard Leplastrier (Australia)

Source: Wood in Culture Association

I try to design places which are not in conflict with the stream of the past...for the present, however inspired by the future, is built upon the past.

Christopher Day

Spiro Kostof Book Award

The Society of Architectural Historians grants the annual Spiro Kostof Award to a publication that has made the greatest contribution to understanding the historical development of the change in urbanism and architecture.

For more information, contact the SAH at (312) 573-1365 or visit their Web site at *www.sah.org.*

1994

Architecture Power and National Identity by Lawrence J. Vale (Yale University Press)

1995

In the Theatre of Criminal Justice: The Palais de Justice in Second Empire Paris by Katherine Fischer Taylor (Princeton University Press)

1996

The Topkapi Scroll: Geometry and Ornament in Islamic Architecture by Gülru Necipoglu (Getty Center for the History of Art and Humanities)

1997

The Projective Cast: Architecture and Its Three Geometries by Robin Evans (MIT Press)

Auschwitz: 1270 to the Present by Debórah Dwork and Robert Jan van Pelt (Norton)

1998

The Architects and the City by Robert Bruegmann (University of Chicago Press)

Magnetic Los Angeles by Gregory Hise (Johns Hopkins Press)

1999

City Center to Regional Mall: Architecture, the Automobile and Retailing in Los Angeles, 1920–1950 by Richard Longstreth (MIT Press)

Housing Design and Society in Amsterdam: Reconfiguring Urban Order and Identity, 1900–1920 by Nancy Stieber (University of Chicago Press)

2000

The Architecture of Red Vienna 1919–1934 by Eve Blau (MIT Press)

2001

The Creative Destruction of Manhattan, 1900–1940 by Max Page (University of Chicago Press)

2002

Buildings on Ruins: The Rediscovery of Rome and English Architecture by Frank Salmon (Ashgate Publishing Company)

2003

Architecture in the Age of Printing: Orality, Writing, Typography and Printed Images in the History of Architectural Theory by Mario Carpo (MIT Press)

Concrete and Clay: Reworking Nature in New York City by Matthew Gandy (MIT Press)

2004

Archaeologies of the Greek Past: Landscape, Monuments, and Memories by Susan E. Alcock (Cambridge University Press)

2005

The Birth of City Planning in the United States, 1840–1917 by Jon A. Peterson (Johns Hopkins University Press)

Source: Society of Architectural Historians

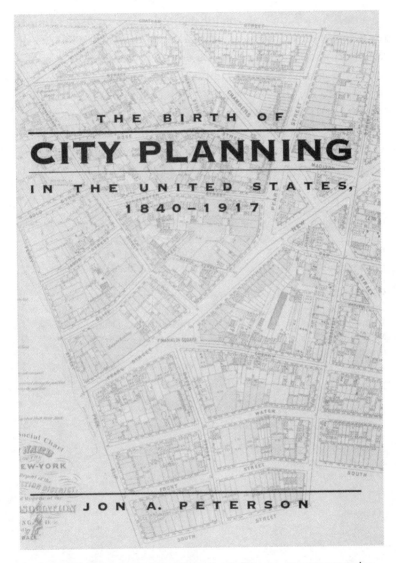

The Birth of City Planning in the United States. Jon A. Peterson presents a sweeping narrative history of the origins of city planning in the United States, from its 19-century antecedents to its flowering in the early 20th century supplemented by historic plans, illustrations, and photographs. Photo courtesy of John Hopkins University Press.

Star Award

Through its Star Award, the International Interior Design Association recognizes individuals who have made an outstanding contribution to the interior design profession. No more than one award is granted each year. However, as this is merit based, awards are not always given annually. Although non-members are eligible for the Star Award, the IIDA board of directors (the selection body) only accepts nominations from IIDA fellows, chapter presidents, and directors.

For more information about the Star Award, visit IIDA's Web site at *www.iida.org* or contact them at (888) 799-4432.

1985	Lester Dundes		1997	Michael Wirtz
1986	William Sullivan		1998	Charles and Ray Eames
1987	Orlando Diaz-Azcuy		1999	Michael Brill
1988	Paul Brayton		2000	Eva L. Maddox
1989	Florence Knoll Bassett		2001	Andrée Putman
1990	Beverly Russell		2002	Karim Rashid
1991	Stanley Abercrombie		2003	Ray Anderson
1992	M. Arthur Gensler Jr.		2004	Kevin Kampschroer
1993	Sivon C. Reznikoff		2005	Target Corporation
1994	Michael Kroelinger			
1995	Douglas R. Parker			

Source: International Interior Designers Association

Tau Sigma Delta Gold Medal

Presented annually by Tau Sigma Delta, the honor society of architecture and the allied arts, the Gold Medal honors an individual who has made outstanding contributions in the fields of architecture, landscape architecture, or an allied profession.

More information about the medal can be found online at *www.tausigmadelta.org.*

1970	Norman Fletcher		1989	Richard Meier
1971	Gunnar Birkerts		1990	Joseph Esherick
1972	O'Neil Ford		1991	Denise Scott Brown
1973	Arthur Erickson		1992	Charles Moore
1974	Ian McHarg		1993	Harold L. Adams
1975	Hugh Stubbins		1994	Harvey B. Gantt
1976	Vincent G. Kling		1995	Peter Eisenman
1977	Harry Weese		1996	Vincent Scully
1978	William Wayne Caudill		1997	Cesar Pelli
1979	Edmond Bacon		1998	William Pedersen
1980	Alexander Girard		1999	William Curtis
1981	Charles Moore		2000	Pierre Koenig
1982	Moshe Safdie		2001	Malcolm Holzman
1983	Ricardo Legorreta		2002	Cynthia Weese
1984	E. Fay Jones		2003	Michael Graves
1985	Pietro Belluschi		2004	Mary Miss
1986	Walter A. Netsch		2005	Martha Schwartz
1987	Lawrence Halprin			
1988	Kenneth Frampton			

Source: Tau Sigma Delta

Did you know...

Architect Ann M. Beha and landscape architect Martha Schwartz received the 2004 Women in Design Awards from the Boston Society of Architects for the "spirit, innovation, transformation, and enhanced level of design women have brought to the profession of architecture."

Tau Sigma Delta Gold Medal

Martha Schwartz. Martha Schwartz is a landscape architect and artist with a focus on urban projects and the execution of site-specific public art installations. Her work explores the relationship among art, culture, and landscape, challenging traditional concepts of landscape design. Recent projects include the HUD Plaza improvements in Washington, DC; Jacob Javitz Federal Building East Plaza in New York; Minneapolis Courthouse plaza; and Gifu Kitagata Apartments in Japan.

Thomas Jefferson Award for Public Architecture

The Thomas Jefferson Award for Public Architecture is presented by the American Institute of Architects to recognize and foster the importance of design excellence in government and infrastructure projects. Awards are presented in three categories: private sector architects who have amassed a portfolio of accomplished and distinguished public facilities, public sector architects who produce quality projects within their agencies, and public officials or others who have been strong advocates for design excellence.

For more information, visit the AIA on the Internet at *www.aia.org* or contact the AIA Honors and Awards Department at (202) 626-7586.

1992
James Ingo Freed
George M. White
Patrick J. Moynihan

1993
Jack Brooks

1994
Richard Dattner
M.J. "Jay" Brodie
Joseph P. Riley Jr.

1995
Herbert S. Newman
Edward A. Feiner
Henry G. Cisneros

1996
Thomas R. Aidala
Douglas P. Woodlock

1997
John Tarantino
Richard A. Kahan
Hunter Morrison

1998
Arthur Rosenblatt

1999
Lewis Davis
Robert Kroin

2000
Charles Emil Peterson
Jay Chatterjee

2001
Terrel M. Emmons
J. Stroud Watson

2003*
Edmund W. Ong
Susan Williams

2005
Carol Ross Barney
Diane Georgopulos
Charles Atherton

* At this time the AIA altered the schedule for this award from annual to biennial.

Source: American Institute of Architects

There exists neither authoritarian nor democratic architecture. There exist only authoritarian and democratic ways of producing and using architecture.

Léon Krier

Thomas Jefferson Medal in Architecture

The Thomas Jefferson Medal in Architecture is granted jointly by the Thomas Jefferson Foundation and the University of Virginia School of Architecture for notable achievements in design or for distinguished contributions to the field of architecture. Recipients need not be architects. This award, along with the Thomas Jefferson Medal in Law, is the highest outside honor offered by the university, which does not grant honorary degrees.

For additional information, visit the school online at *www.virginia.edu/arch/*.

1966	Mies Van der Rohe	1988	Romaldo Giurgola
1967	Alvar Aalto	1989	Paul Mellon
1968	Marcel Breuer	1990	Fumihiko Maki
1969	John Ely Burchard	1991	John Lindsay
1970	Kenzo Tange	1992	Aldo Rossi
1971	Jose Luis Sert	1993	Andrés Duany and
1972	Lewis Mumford		Elizabeth Plater-Zyberk
1973	Jean Labatut	1994	Frank Gehry
1974	Frei Otto	1995	Ian McHarg
1975	Sir Nikolaus Pevsner	1996	Jane Jacobs
1976	I.M. Pei	1997	Jaime Lerner
1977	Ada Louis Huxtable	1998	Jaquelin Robertson
1978	Philip Johnson	1999	Richard Rogers
1979	Lawrence Halprin	2000	Daniel Patrick Moynihan
1980	Hugh A. Stubbins	2001	Glenn Murcutt
1981	Edward Larrabee Barnes	2002	James Turrell
1982	Vincent Scully	2003	Tod Williams and Billie Tsien
1983	Robert Venturi	2004	Peter Walker
1984	Aga Khan	2005	Shigeru Ban
1985	Léon Krier		
1986	James Stirling		
1987	Dan Kiley		

Source: University of Virginia

Paper Temporary Studio, Paris, France. When Shigeru Ban Architects received the commission to design the Pompidou Center Metz in Metz, France, they needed temporary office space. The director of the Pompidou Center in Paris agreed to let the firm retrofit an unused terrace on the sixth floor of this landmark building. This tubular structure (above) is composed of 29 semi-circular arches with ribs made of paper tubes and covered by a waterproof membrane. Photos © Didier Boy de la Tour, courtesy of Shigeru Ban Architects.

Twenty-five Year Award

Awarded annually by the American Institute of Architects, the Twenty-five Year Award is presented to buildings that excel under the test of time. Projects must have been completed 25 to 35 years ago by an architect licensed in the United States, though the buildings may be located anywhere in the world. To be eligible, submissions must still be carrying out their original program and demonstrating continued viability in their function and form.

For more information, visit the AIA on the Internet at *www.aia.org* or contact the AIA Honors and Awards Department at (202) 626-7586.

1969
Rockefeller Center
New York, NY, 1931–40
Reinhard & Hofmeister with Corbett,
Harrison & MacMurray and Hood &
Fouilhoux

1971
Crow Island School
Winnetka, IL, 1939
Perkins, Wheeler & Will and Eliel and Eero
Saarinen

1972
Baldwin Hills Village
Los Angeles, CA, 1941
Reginald D. Johnson with Wilson, Merrill &
Alexander and Clarence S. Stein

1973
Taliesin West
Paradise Valley, AZ, 1938
Frank Lloyd Wright

1974
Johnson and Son Administration Building
Racine, WI, 1936-39
Frank Lloyd Wright

1975
Philip Johnson Residence
(The Glass House)
New Canaan, CT, 1949
Philip Johnson

1976
860-880 North Lakeshore Drive Apartments
Chicago, IL, 1948–51
Ludwig Mies van der Rohe

1977
Christ Lutheran Church
Minneapolis, MN, 1948–51
Saarinen, Saarinen & Associates
with Hills, Gilbertson & Hays

1978
Eames House
Pacific Palisades, CA, 1949
Charles and Ray Eames

1979
Yale University Art Gallery
New Haven, CT, 1954
Louis I. Kahn with Douglas Orr

1980
Lever House
New York, NY, 1952
Skidmore, Owings & Merrill

1981
Farnsworth House
Plano, IL, 1950
Ludwig Mies van der Rohe

1982
Equitable Savings and Loan Building
Portland, OR, 1948
Pietro Belluschi

Twenty-five Year Award

1983
Price Tower
Bartlesville, OK, 1956
Frank Lloyd Wright

1984
Seagram Building
New York, NY, 1957
Ludwig Mies van der Rohe

1985
General Motors Technical Center
Warren, MI, 1951
Eero Saarinen & Associates with Smith,
  Hinchman & Grylls Associates

1986
Solomon R. Guggenheim Museum
New York, NY, 1959
Frank Lloyd Wright

1987
Bavinger House
Norman, OK, 1953
Bruce Goff

1988
Dulles International Airport
  Terminal Building
Chantilly, VA, 1962
Eero Saarinen & Associates

1989
Vanna Venturi House
Chestnut Hill, PA, 1964
Robert Venturi

1990
Gateway Arch
St. Louis, MO, 1965
Eero Saarinen & Associates

1991
Sea Ranch Condominium I
The Sea Ranch, CA, 1965
Moore Lyndon Turnbull Whitaker

1992
Salk Institute for Biological Studies
La Jolla, CA, 1966
Louis I. Kahn

1993
Deere & Company Administrative Center
Moline, IL, 1963
Eero Saarinen & Associates

1994
Haystack Mountain School of Crafts
Deer Isle, ME, 1962
Edward Larrabee Barnes

1995
Ford Foundation Headquarters
New York, NY, 1968
Kevin Roche John Dinkeloo and Associates

1996
Air Force Academy Cadet Chapel
Colorado Springs, CO, 1962
Skidmore, Owings & Merrill

1997
Phillips Exeter Academy Library
Exeter, NH, 1972
Louis I. Kahn

1998
Kimbell Art Museum
Fort Worth, TX, 1972
Louis I. Kahn

1999
John Hancock Center
Chicago, IL, 1969
Skidmore, Owings & Merrill

2000
Smith House
Darien, CT, 1967
Richard Meier & Partners

2001
Weyerhaeuser Headquarters
Tacoma, WA, 1971
Skidmore, Owings & Merrill

189

Twenty-five Year Award

2002
Fundació Joan Miró
Barcelona, Spain, 1975
Sert Jackson and Associates

2003
Design Research Headquarters Building
Cambridge, MA, 1969
BTA Architects Inc.

2004
East Building, National Gallery of Art
Washington, DC, 1978
I.M. Pei & Partners

2005
Yale Center for British Art
New Haven, CT, 1977
Louis I. Kahn

Source: American Institute of Architects

Did you know...

Louis Kahn and Eero Saarinen are both tied for the most buildings to receive the Twenty-five Year Award – 5.

UIA Gold Medal

Every three years at its World Congress, the International Union of Architects (UIA) awards its Gold Medal to a living architect who has made an outstanding achievement to the field of architecture. This honor recognizes the recipient's lifetime of distinguished practice, contribution to the enrichment of mankind, and the promotion of the art of architecture.

For more information, visit the UIA Web site at *www.uia-architectes.org.*

1984	Hassan Fathy (Egypt)
1987	Reima Pietila (Finland)
1990	Charles Correa (India)
1993	Fumihiko Maki (Japan)
1996	Rafael Moneo (Spain)
1999	Ricardo Legorreta (Mexico)
2002	Renzo Piano (Italy)
2005	Tadao Ando (Japan)

Source: International Union of Architects

Did you know...

MIT awarded Spanish-born architect Santiago Calatrava its 2005 McDermott Award and $70,000 prize "for the highest standard of creative achievement."

Urban Land Institute Awards for Excellence

The Urban Land Institute Awards for Excellence follow the organization's mission "to provide responsible leadership in the use of land in order to enhance the environment." Since it was established in 1979, the program has evolved from recognition of one development in North America to separate juried competitions for the Americas, Europe, and Asia Pacific. The awards recognize the full development process, not just a project's architecture or design, and include such building types as office, residential, recreational, urban/mixed-use, industrial/office park, commercial/retail, new community, rehabilitation, and public projects. Winning entries represent superior design, improve the quality of the built environment, exhibit a sensitivity to the community, display financial viability, and demonstrate relevance to contemporary issues.

For additional information about the awards, contact the Urban Land Institute at (800) 321-5011 or visit their Web site at www.uli.org.

2004 Recipients

Americas

Baldwin Park
Orlando, FL

Fall Creek Place
Indianapolis, IN

First Ward Place/The Garden District
Charlotte, NC

Playhouse Square Center
Cleveland, OH

The Plaza at PPL Center
Allentown, PA

Technology Square at Georgia Institute
of Technology
Atlanta, GA

University Park at MIT
Cambridge, MA

Walt Disney Concert Hall
Los Angeles, CA

WaterColor
Seagrove Beach, FL

Americas Jury

Diana Permar, Permar, Inc. (US, chair)
Robert A. Alleborn, Robert Alleborn
  Properties, Inc. (US)
Jan A. de Kreij, Corio, N.V. (Netherlands)
Barbara Faga, EDAW Inc. (US)
Richard F. Galehouse,
  Sasaki Associates, Inc. (US)
J. Brad Griffith, Griffith Properties (US)
John S. Hagestad, Sares-Regis Group (US)
Richard E. Heapes, Street-Works (US)
Pamela J. Herbst, AEW Capital
  Management (US)
Frederick A. Kober, The Christopher
  Companies (US)
Isaac H. Manning, Trinity Works (US)
James D. Motta, Arvida (US)
James F. Porter, Altoon & Porter Architects (US)
Leonard A. Zax, Latham & Watkins (US)

Urban Land Institute Awards for Excellence

Europe

Brindleyplace
Birmingham, UK

Bullring
Birmingham, UK

Casa de les Punxes
Barcelona, Spain

Diagonal Mar
Barcelona, Spain

Promenaden Hauptbahnhof Leipzig
Leipzig, Germany

Regenboogpark
Tilburg, Netherlands

Europe Jury

Jan A. De Kreij, Corio N.V.
(Netherlands, co-chair)
Michael Spies, Tishman Speyer Properties
(UK, co-chair)
Willi Alda, Deka Immobilien Investment,
(Germany)
William P. Kistler, ULI Europe (UK)
Frederick A. Kober, The Christopher
Companies (US)
Carlos Lamela De Vargas,
Estudio Lamela, (Spain)

2005 Recipients

Americas

34th Street Streetscape Program
New York, NY

731 Lexington Avenue/One Beacon Court
New York, NY

Fourth Street Live!
Louisville, KY

The Glen
Glenview, IL

Harbor Town
Memphis, TN

The Market Common, Clarendon
Arlington, VA

Millennium Park
Chicago, IL

Pueblo del Sol
Los Angeles, CA

Time Warner Center
New York, NY

Ville Placido Domingo
Acapulco, Mexico

Chautauqua Institution
Chautauqua, NY

Americas Jury

Diana Permar, president, Permar, Inc.
(US, chair)
Barbara Faga, EDAW Inc. (US)
Richard F. Galehouse,
Sasaki Associates, Inc. (US)
John S. Hagestad, Sares-Regis Group (US)
Lee T. Hanley, Vestar Development Co. (US)
Marty Jones, Corcoran Jennison Cos. (US)
Isaac H. Manning, Trinity Works (US)
James D. Motta, The Motta Group (US)
Frank Ricks, Looney Ricks Kiss Architects (US)
Robert M. Weekley, Lowe Enterprises, Inc. (US)

193

Urban Land Institute Awards for Excellence

194

Europe

Cézanne Saint-Honoré
Paris, France

Danube House
Prague, Czech Republic

Government Offices Great George Street
London, UK

De Hoftoren
The Hague, Netherlands

Meander
Amsterdam, Netherlands

Europe Jury

Michael Spies, Tishman Speyer Properties
(UK, co-chair)
Jan de Kreij, Corio NV (Netherlands, co-chair)
Timothy Cyr, Group France Terre (France)
Francis Duffy, DEGW (UK)
Ayse Hasol Erktin, Has Mimarlik Ltd. (Turkey)
John Gomez Hall, Hines, (Spain)
Gilberto Jordan, Planbelas SA (Portugal)

Asia Pacific

Federation Square
Melbourne, Australia

Hangzhou Waterfront
Hangzhou, China

The Loft
Singapore

Marunouchi Building
Tokyo, Japan

Pier 6/7, Walsh Bay
Sydney, Australia

Asia Pacific Jury

C.Y. Leung, DTZ Debenham Tie Leung Limited
(Hong Kong, chair)
Sean Chuan-Sheng Chiao, EDAW Urban Design
Ltd. (Hong Kong)
James M. DeFrancia, Lowe Enterprises
Community Development, Inc. (US)
Akio Makiyama, Forum for Urban
Development (Japan)
Edmund N.S. Tie, DTZ Debenham
Tie Leung (SEA) Pte. Ltd. (Singapore)
Peter Verwer, Property Council
of Australia (Australia)
Stephany N. Yu, Shanghai Luting
Group Ltd. (China)

Note: During the 2005 award year, the schedule shifted from the
fall to spring/summer and saw the addition of the Asia
Pacific Awards.

Source: Urban Land Institute

Did you know...

In 2005, Mary Jordan Taylor, a
partner in Skidmore, Ownings and
Merrill's New York office, became
chair of the ULI—the first woman,
as well as the first architect, to hold
this position.

Veronica Rudge Green Prize in Urban Design

Established by Harvard University in 1986, the Veronica Rudge Green Prize in Urban Design recognizes excellence in urban design with an emphasis on projects that contribute to the public spaces and improve the quality of urban life. The prize is awarded biennially by a jury of experts in the field of architecture and urban design. Nominations are made to Harvard's Graduate School of Design by a panel of critics, academics, and practitioners in the field of architecture, landscape architecture, and urban design. Eligible projects must be larger in scope than a single building and must have been constructed within the past 10 years. Winners receive a monetary award and certificate.

Additional information about the award can be found on the Internet at *www.gsd.harvard.edu.*

1988
Byker Redevelopment
Newcastle upon Tyne, UK
Ralph Erskine (Sweden)

Malagueira Quarter Housing Project
Evora, Portugal
Alvaro Siza (Portugal)

1990
Urban Public Spaces of Barcelona
Barcelona, Spain
City of Barcelona (Spain)

1993
Hillside Terrace Complex
Tokyo, Japan
Fumihiko Maki (Japan)

Master Plan and Public Buildings
Monte Carasso, Switzerland
Luigi Snozzi (Switzerland)

1996
Restoration of the Historic Center of Mexico
City and Ecological Restoration of the
District of Xochimilco
Mexico City, Mexico

1998
Subway System
Bilbao, Spain
Sir Norman Foster and
Foster and Partners (UK)

Development of Carré d'Art Plaza
Nîmes, France
Sir Norman Foster and
Foster and Partners (UK)

2000
Favela-Bairro Project
Rio de Janeiro, Brazil
Jorge Mario Jáuregui and Jorge Mario
Jáuregui Architects (Brazil)

2002
Borneo-Sporenburg Housing Project
Amsterdam, The Netherlands
West 8 Urban Design & Landscape
Architecture (Netherlands)

2004
City of Aleppo
Aleppo, Syria
German Technical Corporation (Germany)

Source: Harvard Graduate School of Design/School of Architecture

Vincent J. Scully Prize

The National Building Museum founded the Vincent J. Scully Prize to recognize practice, scholarship, and criticism in the design professions—architecture, landscape architecture, historic preservation, city planning, and urban design. By naming the prize after Vincent J. Scully, America's renowned architectural scholar, mentor, and critic whose lifetime of work made a tremendous impact on the profession, the museum hopes to celebrate others who have yielded a significant contribution to the betterment of our world. The award carries a $25,000 honorarium, and the recipient is invited to present a lecture at the museum.

For more information about the Vincent J. Scully Prize, contact the National Building Museum at (202) 272-2448 or visit them on the Internet at *www.nbm.org*.

1999	Vincent J. Scully
2000	Jane Jacobs
2001	Elizabeth Plater-Zyberk
	Andrés Duany
2002	Robert Venturi
	Denise Scott Brown
2005	Aga Khan

Source: National Building Museum

Good art cannot be universally liked in its time...the issue is do the right people hate it.

Robert Venturi

Vincent J. Scully Prize

His Highness the Aga Khan. The National Building Museum honored the Aga Khan with the Vincent Scully Prize in recognition of his contributions to promoting design excellence and improving the built environment in the Muslim world. In 1977 he established the Aga Khan Award for Architecture, the world's largest prize for architecture; and through the Aga Khan Trust for Culture, which was established in 1988, the Aga Khan has supported numerous conservation and urban revitalization projects in culturally significant sites of the Islamic world. Photo © Vivian Ronay/www.vivianronay.com, courtesy of the National Building Museum.

Whitney M. Young Jr. Award

The American Institute of Architects bestows the Whitney M. Young Jr. Award annually upon an architect or architecturally oriented organization that makes a significant contribution toward meeting the challenge set forth by Young to architects: to assume a professional responsibility toward current social issues. These issues are ever present and flexible and include such things as housing the homeless, affordable housing, minority and women participation in the profession, disability issues, and literacy.

For more information, visit the AIA on the Internet at *www.aia.org* or contact the AIA Honors and Awards Department at (202) 626-7586.

1972	Robert J. Nash
1973	Architects Workshop of Philadelphia
1974	Stephen Cram*
1975	Van B. Bruner Jr.
1976	Wendell J. Campbell
1980	Leroy M. Campbell*
1981	Robert T. Coles
1982	John S. Chase
1983	Howard Hamilton Mackey Sr.
1984	John Louis Wilson
1985	Milton V. Bergstedt
1986	Richard McClure Prosse*
1987	J. Max Bond Jr.
1988	Habitat for Humanity
1989	John H. Spencer
1990	Harry G. Robinson III
1991	Robert Kennard
1992	Curtis J. Moody
1993	David Castro-Blanco
1994	Ki Suh Park
1995	William J. Stanley III
1996	John L. Wilson
1997	Alan Y. Taniguchi
1998	Leon Bridges
1999	Charles F. McAfee
2000	Louis L. Weller
2001	Cecil A. Alexander Jr.
2002	Robert P. Madison
2003	Hispanic American Construction Industry Association
2004	Terrance J. Brown
2005	Stanford R. Britt

* Honored posthumously

Source: American Institute of Architects

Wolf Prize for Architecture

Ricardo Wolf established the Wolf Foundation in 1976 to "promote science and arts for the benefit of mankind." In this vein, the Wolf prize is awarded annually to outstanding living scientists and artists in the fields of agriculture, chemistry, mathematics, medicine, physics, and the arts. The awards, an honorarium of $100,000 and a diploma, are presented each year in Jerusalem's Chagall Hall. In the arts category, the Wolf Prize rotates annually among architecture, music, painting, and sculpture. The following individuals received this honor for their contribution to the field of architecture.

For more information about the Wolf Prize, contact the Wolf Foundation at +972 (9) 955 7120 or visit their Web site at *www.aquanet.co.il/wolf/*.

1983
Ralph Erskine (Sweden)

1988
Fumihiko Maki (Japan)
Giancarlo de Carlo (Italy)

1992
Frank O. Gehry (US)
Jørn Utzon (Denmark)
Sir Denys Lasdun (UK)

1996
Frei Otto (Germany)
Aldo van Eyck (Holland)

2001
Alvaro Siza (Portugal)

Source: Wolf Foundation

Design is synergy of form and function, a coming together of these elements rather than a pulling apart.

**Richard Lambertson
and John Truex**

Wood Design Awards

The Wood Design Awards annually recognize excellence in wood architecture in the United States and Canada. Judging criteria include the creative, distinctive, and appropriate use of wood materials, though buildings do not need to be constructed entirely of wood. Entries may include residential and nonresidential buildings, new construction, or renovations. Honor, merit, and citation awards may be given in each category, at the discretion of the jury. Special awards issues of *Wood Design & Building* (US) and *Wood Le Bois* (Canada) magazines feature winning projects.

For project descriptions and photos, visit *www.woodmags.com/wda/* on the Internet.

2005 Recipients

Honor Awards
The Point House
Rural Montana
Bohlin Cywinski Jackson

Bigelow Chapel
New Brighton, MN
HGA

Conversation Piece
Toronto, ON, Canada
PLANT Architect Inc.

Merit Awards
Grace Episcopal Church
Bainbridge Island, WA
Cutler Anderson Architects

Madrona Residence
Seattle, WA
Vandeventer + Carlander Architects

Belmont Street Lofts
Portland, OR
Holst Architecture

Citation Awards
Surrey Central City
Surrey, BC, Canada
Bing Thom Architects

Naramata Residence
Naramata, BC, Canada
Florian Maurer Architect

Ghost 6 Research Laboratory
Upper Kingsburg, NS, Canada
MacKay-Lyons Sweetapple Architects Ltd.

Prototype Infill Housing
Dallas, TX
Edward M. Baum FAIA

Prince George Airport Expansion
Prince George, BC, Canada
McFarlane Green Architecture + Design

Jury
Margaret Helfand, Helfand Architecture
Bruce Kuwabara, Kuwabara Payne McKenna
    Blumberg Architects
Hsin-ming Fung, Hodgetts + Fung Design
    Associates

Source: Wood Design & Building *magazine and*
Wood Le Bois *magazine*

Young Architects Award

The Young Architects Award is presented annually by the American Institute of Architects to an architect in the early stages of his or her career who has made significant contributions to the profession. The competition is open to AIA members who have been licensed to practice for less than 10 years. The term "young architect" has no reference to the age of nominees.

For additional information about the Young Architects Award, visit the AIA online at *www.aia.org* or contact the AIA Honors and Awards Department at (202) 626-7586.

1993
Joan M. Soranno
Vicki L. Hooper
Thomas Somerville Howorth
Brett Keith Laurila

1995
William A. Blanski
Anne Tate

1996
Christopher W. Coe
George Thrush
Keith Moskow

1997
Robert S. Rothman
William J. Carpenter
Michael A. Fischer
Brad Simmons

1998
J. Windom Kimsey
Jose Luis Palacious
Karin M. Pitman
Charles Rose
Karl W. Stumpf
David Louis Swartz
Maryann Thompson
Randall C. Vaughn

1999
Father Terrence Curry
Victoria Tatna Jacobson
Michael Thomas Maltzan
David T. Nagahiro
Peter Steinbrueck

2000
Mary Katherine Lanzillotta
Andrew Travis Smith

2001
J. Scott Busby
P. Thomas M. Harboe
Jeffry Lee Kagermeier
Elizabeth Chu Richter
George A. Takoudes

2002
Randy G. Brown
Barbara Campagna
Mohammed Lawal
Joe Scott Sandlin

2003
Lisa M. Chronister
Paul D. Mankins
Paul Neuhaus
Ronald Todd Ray
Paul Woolford

Young Architects Award

2004
John Burse
David Y. Jameson
Donna Kacmar
Janis LaDouceur
Kevin G. Sneed

2005
F. Michael Ayles
Jeffrey DeGregorio
Miguel Rivera
Rick Harlan Schneider
Eric Strain

Source: American Institute of Architects

In addition to addressing the client's direct program needs, part of the architect's public responsibility is to look beyond the property line and address the relationship between the architecture and the broader public realm. If in designing the one you take into account the other, both benefit, as do the people who live, work, and recreate there.

B. Aaron Parker

Plate 2: Faculty of Philology Library, Free University, Berlin, Germany, Foster and Partners. Photo: Foster and Partners

Plates 3.1–3.2: Scottish Parliament Building, Edinburgh, Scotland, UK, EMBT/RMJM. Photos: © Roland Halbe Architectural Photography, www.rolandhalbe.com

Plate 4: Bayer Headquarters, Leverkusen, Germany, Murphy/Jahn, Inc. Architects.
Photo: © Roland Halbe Architectural Photography, www.rolandhalbe.com

Plates 5.1–5.3: Millennium Park, Chicago, IL. Plate 5.1 (left): Jay Pritzker Pavilion, Frank O. Gehry & Associates, Inc. (Photo: © Roland Halbe Architectural Photography, www.rolandhalbe.com); Plate 5.2 (top right): Lurie Garden by Gustafson Guthrie Nichol Ltd (Photo: Gustafson Guthrie Nichol Ltd); Plate 5.3 (bottom right): Cloud Gate by Anish Kapoor (Photo: City of Chicago/Chris McGuire)

Plate 7: United States Courthouse, Seattle, WA, NBBJ. Photo: Frank Ooms

Plates 8.1–8.3: Duffield Hall Nanotechnology Research Facility, Cornell University, Ithaca, NY, Zimmer Gunsul Frasca Partnership. Photos: Larry Falke

Plates 9.1–9.3: Seattle Central Library, Office for Metropolitan Architecture with LMN Architects and Bruce Mau Design. Photos courtesy of the Seattle Public Library.

Plates 10.1–10.2: Mirador Tower, Madrid, Spain, MVRDV. Photos: © Roland Halbe Architectural Photography, www.rolandhalbe.com

Plate 11: Central Building, BMW Plant, Leipzig, Germany, Zaha Hadid Architects. Photo: © Roland Halbe Architectural Photography, www.rolandhalbe.com

Plate 12: Turning Torso, Malmö, Sweden, Santiago Calatrava. Photo: courtesy of Santiago Calatrava SA

Plates 13.1–13.3: Walt Disney Concert Hall, Los Angeles, CA, Frank O. Gehry & Associates, Inc.
Photos © Roland Halbe Architectural Photography, www.rolandhalbe.com

Plates 14.1–14.3: Fornarina Mandalay Bay, Las Vegas, NV. Giorgio Buruso Design. Photos: Benny Chan.

Plate 15: Bigelow Chapel, United Theological Seminary, New Brighton, MN, Hammel, Green and Abrahamson, Inc.
Photo: © Paul Warchol

Plate 16: Haworth 2004 Chicago Showroom, Chicago, IL. Perkins+Will. Photo: Hedrich Blessing/Steve Hall

Plates 17.1–17.2: Burda Collection Museum, Baden-Baden, Germany, Richard Meier & Partners Architects.
Photos: © Roland Halbe Architectural Photography, www.rolandhalbe.com

Plates 18.1–18.2: Kreielsheimer Promenade at Marion O. McCaw Hall, Seattle, WA, Gustafson Guthrie Nichol Ltd.
Photos: Gustafson Guthrie Nichol Ltd

Plate 19: Agosta House, San Juan Island, WA, Patkau Architects. Photo: James Dow

Plate 21 (top): Gallery 37 Center for the Arts, Chicago, IL, Daniel P. Coffey & Associates, Ltd. Photo: Steinkamp/Ballogg

Plate 22 (left): Schaumburg Performing Arts Center, Schaumburg, IL, Daniel P. Coffey & Associates, Ltd. Photo: Daniel P. Coffey & Associates, Ltd.

Leadership
In Design

Induction as a fellow, honorary fellow, or honorary member, or serving as president of a professional organization, is an honor commonly bestowed upon the industry's preeminent leaders. This chapter lists those noteworthy individuals along with a number of other honorific titles. Names in bold indicate new inductees.

Architecture Critics

Below is a listing of the major US newspapers that regularly feature architectural writing and criticism. Some papers have a staff architecture critic while others have an art critic or critic-at-large that routinely covers architecture stories.

Arizona Republic
Richard Nilsen
Fine Arts Critic
200 East Van Buren Street
Phoenix, AZ 85004
(602) 444-8000
www.azcentral.com

Atlanta Journal-Constitution
Catherine Fox
Architecture Critic
72 Marietta Street NW
Atlanta, GA 30303
(404) 586-9650
www.ajc.com

Austin American-Statesman
Jeanne Claire van Ryzin
Arts Writer
305 South Congress Avenue
Austin, TX 78704
(512) 445-3500
www.statesman.com

Baltimore Sun
Edward Gunts
Architecture Critic
501 N. Calvert Street
Baltimore, MD 21202
(410) 332-6000
www.baltimoresun.com

Bergen Record
John Zeaman
Art Critic
150 River Street
Hackensack, NJ 07601
(201) 646-4000
www.bergen.com

Boston Globe
Robert Campbell
Architecture Critic
135 William T. Morrissey Boulevard
Boston, MA 02108
(617) 929-2200
www.boston.com

Boston Herald
David Eisen
Architecture Critic
One Herald Square
Boston, MA 02118
(617) 426-3000
www.bostonherald.com

Charleston Post and Courier
Robert Behre
Architecture & Preservation Critic
134 Columbus Street
Charleston, SC 29403
(843) 577-7111
www.charleston.net

Charlotte Observer
Allen Norwood
Home Editor
600 S. Tryon Street
Charlotte, NC 28202
(704) 358-5000
www.charlotte.com

Chicago Sun-Times
Kevin Nance
Architecture Critic
350 N. Orleans Street
Chicago, Il 60654
(312) 321-3000
www.suntimes.com

Architecture Critics

Chicago Tribune
Blair Kamin
Architecture Critic
435 N. Michigan Avenue
Chicago, IL 60611
(312) 222-3232
www.chicagotribune.com

Cleveland Plain Dealer
Steve Litt
Art & Architecture Critic
Plain Dealer Plaza
1801 Superior Avenue
Cleveland, OH 44114
(216) 999-5000
www.plaindealer.com

Dallas Morning News
David Dillon
Architecture Critic
508 Young Street
Dallas, TX 75202
(214) 977-8222
www.dallasnews.com

Dayton Daily News
Ronald Rollins
Critic-at-Large
45 S. Ludlow Street
Dayton, OH 45402
(937) 222-2000
www.daytondailynews.com

Denver Post
Kyle MacMillan
Critic-at-Large
1560 Broadway
Denver, CO 80202
(303) 820-1201
www.denverpost.com

Detroit Free Press
John Gallagher
Architecture Critic
600 West Fort
Detroit, MI 48226
(313) 222-6400
www.freep.com

Los Angeles Times
Christopher Hawthorne
Architecture Critic
202 West 1st Street
Los Angeles, CA 90012
(213) 237-5000
www.latimes.com

Louisville Courier-Journal
Diane Heilenman
Visual Arts Critic
525 W. Broadway
Louisville, KY 40202
(502) 582-4011
www.courier-journal.com

Milwaukee Journal Sentinel
Whitney Gould
Architecture Reporter
333 W. State Street
Milwaukee, WI 53203
(414) 225-5000
www.jsonline.com

Minneapolis Star-Tribune
Linda Mack
Architecture Critic
425 Portland Avenue
Minneapolis, MN 55488
(612) 673-4000
www.startribune.com

New York Times
Nicolai Ouroussoff
Architecture Critic
229 43rd Street
New York, NY 10036
(212) 556-1234
www.nytimes.com

New Yorker
Paul Goldberger
Architecture Critic
4 Times Square
New York, NY 10036
(212) 286-5400
www.newyorker.com

Architecture Critics

Newark Star-Ledger
Dan Bischoff
Art Critic
1 Star-Ledger Plaza
Newark, NJ 07102
(973) 392-4141
www.starledger.com

Newport News Daily Press
Mark Erickson
Critic-at-Large/Reporter
7505 Warwick Boulevard
Newport News, VA 23607
(757) 247-4600
www.dailypress.com

Philadelphia Inquirer
Inga Saffron
Architecture Critic
400 N. Broad Street
Philadelphia, PA 19103
(215) 854-2000
www.philly.com

Pittsburgh Post-Gazette
Patricia Lowry
Architecture Critic
34 Boulevard of the Allies
Pittsburgh, PA 15222
(412) 263-1100
www.post-gazette.com

Portland Oregonian
Randy Gragg
Architecture Critic
1320 SW Broadway
Portland, OR 97201
(503) 639-7233
www.oregonian.com

Providence Journal
Bill Van Siclen
Art Critic
75 Fountain Street
Providence, RI 02902
(401) 277-7000
www.projo.com

Raleigh News & Observer
Tommy Goldsmith
Features Editor
215 S. McDowell Street
Raleigh, NC 27602
(919) 829-4500
www.newsobserver.com

Rocky Mountain News
Mary Voelz Chandler
Art & Architecture Critic
100 Gene Amole Way
Denver, CO 80204
(303) 892-5000
www.rockymountainnews.com

San Antonio Express-News
Mike Greenberg
Arts & Entertainment Critic
400 Third Street
San Antonio, TX 78287
(210) 250-3000
www.mysanantonio.com

San Diego Union-Tribune
Ann Jarmusch
Architecture Critic
350 Camino De La Reina
San Diego, CA 92108
(619) 299-3131
www.signonsandiego.com

San Francisco Chronicle
John King
Architecture Writer
901 Mission Street
San Francisco, CA 94103
(415) 777-1111
www.sfgate.com

San Jose Mercury News
Alan Hess
Architecture Writer
750 Ridder Park Drive
San Jose, CA 95190
(408) 920-5000
www.mercurynews.com

Architecture Critics

Seattle Post-Intelligencer

Regina Hackett
Art & Architecture Columnist
101 Elliot Avenue West
Seattle, WA 98119
(206) 464-2121
http://seattlepi.nwsource.com

Seattle Times

Bill Ristow
Features Editor
1120 John Street
Seattle, WA 98109
(206) 464-2111
http://seattletimes.nwsource.com

South Florida Sun-Sentinel

Emma Trelles
Arts Writer
200 E. Las Olas Blvd
Fort Lauderdale, FL 33301
(954) 356-4000
www.sun-sentinel.com

St. Paul Pioneer Press

Heidi Raschke
Arts Editor
345 Cedar Street
St. Paul, MN 55101
(651) 222-1111
www.twincities.com

Wall Street Journal

Ada Louise Huxtable
Architecture Critic
200 Liberty Street
New York, NY 10281
(212) 416-2000
www.wsj.com

Washington Post

Ben Forgey
Architecture Critic
1150 15th Street NW
Washington, DC 20071
(202) 334-6000
www.washingtonpost.com

Source: DesignIntelligence

Chancellors of the American Institute of Architects' College of Fellows

Since the founding of the American Institute of Architects' College of Fellows in 1952, the chancellor is elected, now annually, by the fellows to preside over the college's investiture ceremonies and business affairs.

1952–53	Ralph Thomas Walker
1954–55	Alexander C. Robinson III
1956	Edgar I. Williams
1957–60	Roy F. Larson
1961–62	Morris Ketchum
1963–64	Paul Thiry
1965–66	George Holmes Perkins
1967–68	Norman J. Schlossman
1969–70	John Noble Richards
1971–72	Jefferson Roy Carroll Jr.
1973	Ulysses Floyd Rible
1974	Albert S. Golemon
1975	Robert S. Hutchins
1976	William Bachman
1977	Philip J. Meathe
1978	George Edward Kassabaum
1979	David Arthur Pugh
1980	Robert L. Durham
1981	Leslie N. Boney Jr.
1982	William Robert Jarratt
1983	William C. Muchow
1984	Bernard B. Rothschild
1985	Donald L. Hardison
1986	Vladimir Ossipoff
1987	S. Scott Ferebee Jr.
1988	C. William Brubaker
1989	Preston Morgan Bolton
1990	William A. Rose Jr.
1991	Robert B. Marquis
1992	L. Jane Hastings
1993	John A. Busby Jr.
1994	Thomas H. Teasdale
1995	Robert T. Coles
1996	Ellis W. Bullock Jr.
1997	Jack DeBartolo Jr.
1998	Harold L. Adams
1999	Jimmy D. Tittle
2000	Robert A. Odermatt
2001	Harold Roth
2002	C. James Lawler
2003	Sylvester Damianos
2004	Betsey Olenick Dougherty
2005	Lawrence J. Leis
2006	Ted P. Pappas

Source: American Institute of Architects

Did you know...

The American Institute of Architects' College of Fellows has awarded its 2005 Latrobe Fellowship, a grant of $100,000, to Chong Partners Architecture, Kaiser Permanente, and the University of California, Berkeley to examine the link between healthcare facility design and faster healing rates in patients.

Fellows of the American Academy of Arts and Sciences

Since its founding in 1780, the American Academy of Arts and Sciences has pursued its goal "To cultivate every art and science which may tend to advance the interest, honor, dignity, and happiness of a free, independent, and virtuous people." Throughout its history, the academy's diverse membership has included the best from the arts, science, business, scholarship, and public affairs. Nominations for new members are taken from existing fellows and evaluated by panels from each discipline and the membership at large.

Design Professionals

Christopher Alexander
Edward Larrabee Barnes
Herbert Lawrence Block
Robert Campbell
Henry Nichols Cobb
Peter D. Eisenman
Kenneth Frampton
James Ingo Freed
Frank Owen Gehry
Lawrence Halprin

Steven Holl
Robert S.F. Hughes
Ada Louise Huxtable
Philip Johnson
Gerhard Michael Kallmann
(Noel) Michael McKinnell
Maya Ying Lin
Richard Alan Meier
Henry Armand Millon
William Mitchell

I.M. Pei
James Polshek
Kevin Roche
Elizabeth Barlow Rogers
Robert Rosenblum
Moshe Safdie
Denise Scott Brown
Vincent J. Scully
Hugh Asher Stubbins
Robert Venturi

Foreign Honorary Members

Charles Correa (India)
Carl Theodor Dreyer
   (Denmark)
Norman Robert Foster (UK)
Phyllis Lambert (Canada)

Ricardo Legorreta (Mexico)
Fumihiko Maki (Japan)
José Rafael Moneo (Spain)
Oscar Niemeyer (Brazil)
Renzo Piano (UK)

Alvaro Siza (Portugal)
Kenzo Tange (Japan)

Source: American Academy of Arts and Sciences

Did you know...

At 97, Brazilian architect Oscar Niemeyer completed his latest building, the 840-seat concert hall in Sao Paolo, which opened in January 2005.

Fellows of the American Council of Engineering Companies

Fellowship in the American Council of Engineering Companies is open to any individual who has been a principal in a member firm for five or more years; has served ACEC as an officer, director, or active committee member or has served a member organization as an officer or director; and has notably contributed to the advancement of consulting engineering in administrative leadership, design, science, by literature, in education, or by service to the profession. The following individuals are current, active fellows of the ACEC.

Allen M. Acheson
A. George Adamson Jr.
William H. Addington
Vukoslav E. Aguirre
Frank E. Alderman
Harl P. Aldrich
Norman G. Almquist
Raymond G. Alvine
Al E. Anderson
Harry G. Anderson
Stephen C. Anderson
Peter N. Andrews
C. Adrian Arnold
Lindsey J. Aucoin
Frederick G. Aufiero
Quent Augspurger
Don Austin
Desmond A. Baker
John Baker
Charles L. Ballou
George Barnes
Bob Barnett
Michael Barrett
Robert T. Bates
Richard T. Baum
Clifton R. Baxter
Jon M. Beekman
James G. Bell
Theodore T. Bell
William I. Bigger
Wilson V. Binger
Harold F. Bishop
David K. Blake
Patrick E. Blayney
Robert C. Bogart
Ronald L. Bonar

Lewis A. Bosworth
Gary R. Bourne
Dwight A. Boyd
Gregg E. Brandow
Carlyle W. Briggs
Arthur N. Brooks
Jeffery M. Bross
Joseph L. Brown
Wayne H. Brown
Robert O. Bruton
Ross Bryan
Paul C. Bucknam Jr.
Dudley W. Budlong
Edmund Burke
Robert G. Burkhardt
R. Neal Campbell
Aubrey Caplan
James W. Carpenter
Charles D. Carr
Dominic B. Carrino
Daniel M. Carson
Hugh C. Carter
Robert J. Caton
M. Steve Cavanaugh Jr.
T.Z. Chastain
Fu Hua Chen
John H. Clark III
William A. Clevenger
James D. Cobb
Edward Cohen
William J. Collins Jr.
Paul E. Conrad
William H. Cooke Jr.
Philip M. Corlew
J. Richard Cottingham
Paul E. Cox

L. LeRoy Crandall
Ralph Crosby
Jeffrey M. Daggett
Henry Eugene Damon
David L. Davidson
Edward W. Davidson
G. Robert Davidson
Ansel L. Davis
Edward T. Davis
Ray H. Davis
Edwin K. Dedeaux
Kenneth L. Delap
Chris Demopulos
Daniel J. DeYoung
Fermin A. Diaz
H. Boyd Dickenson
Emery Domingue
Leo J. Dondanville
Wallace L. Donley
Stephen E. Dore
Albert A. Dorman
Cecil G. Doyle
J. Edward Doyle
Ronald J. Drnevich
James Duddlesten
James R. Duncan
Lamar Dunn
Howard C. Dutzi
Arthur A. Edwards
Carl Eiden
Stanley D. Elkerton
Gilbert L. Faison
Ben H. Faulkner
John R. Fee
Harry R. Feldman
Dean R. Felton

Fellows of the American Council of Engineering Companies

James F. Finn
David E. Fleming
James Ray Flemons Jr.
Eric L. Flicker
Harold E. Flight
Robert C. Flory
Michael E. Flynn
John H. Foster
Ronald D. Foster
William C. Freeman
E.M. Fucik
Lester Fukuda
David R. Fuller
Thomas D. Furman Jr.
Elliot H. Gage
E.B. (Bas) Gaither
F. Vreeland George Jr.
Frank B. Gianotti III
Ralph W. Gilbert Jr.
Bruce L. Gilmore
Albert B. Gipe
William J. Glover Jr.
Stephen G. Goddard
E. Jackson Going
Donald T. Goldberg
Luther Graef
Anthony J. Grasso
Brian L. Gray
Paul D. Guertin
John J. Guth Jr.
Wilton N. Hammond
Philip M. Hampton
Richard E. Hangen
Brian L. Hanson
Walter E. Hanson
Joseph E. Hardee
Thomas B. Harrell Jr.
Michael J. Hartigan
Arthur F. Hartung
Eugene C. Harvey
James M. Hastings
Donald Hattery
Amy J. Haugerud
Steve M. Hays
George Heck
Alfred Hedefine
Paul L. Heineman

Joseph E. Heney
John F. Hennessy III
Marble J. Hensley Sr.
Richard J. Hesse
Robert E. Hickman
Lyle F. Hird
Robert E. Hogan
A.W. Holland
Darrel V. Holmquist
Stephen A. Holt
W.N. Holway
Donald E. Houser
William S. Howard
Linda L. Huff
Harold E. Hughes
Dale L. Jacobs
Roger L. Jacobson
J. Edward Jenkins
Thomas L. Jester
Clifford W. Johnson
Derrell Johnson
Edmund G. Johnson
Melvin E. Jones
Ralph W. Junius Jr.
C. Hayden Kaiser Jr.
Dennis M. Kamber
John J. Kassner
D. Gary Kathol
Stanley K. Kawaguchi
Theodore S. Kawahigashi
Charles W. Keller
Chester C. Kelsey
David D. Kennedy
Todd J. Kenner
Frederick D. A. King Jr.
Edward B. Kinner
Jack Kinstlinger
George Kirgis
Gordon L. Kirjassoff
Robert C. Kirkpatrick
Donald F. Klebe
Donald H. Kline
Dag I. Knudsen
Kenneth J. Koch
James H. Konkel
Charles W. Kopplin
Emil Kordish

Michael E. Krannitz
James M. Kring Jr.
Donald R. LaRochelle
Jerry G. Lazenby
Calvin E. Levis
Raoul L. Levy
William D. Lewis
David H. Lillard
Frank L. Lincoln
Leon J. Lindbloom
James L. Linderholm
Howard D. Linders
Joseph Lipscomb
John L. Littrell
Bruce Livingstone
C. Richard Lortz
LeRoy D. Loy
Ray Lundgren
J.L. MacFarlane
Cline L. Mansur
Paul W. Masten
Richard E. Masters
Michael P. Matsumoto
David R. Matthews
Art Maxwell
Aubrey D. May
William (Skip) H. McCombs
H. Clay McEldowney
Robert McEldowney Jr.
James D. McFall
John C. McGlenn
Larry A. McKee
Robert W. McKenzie
Herbert P. McKim Jr.
Arthur W. McKinney
Raymond F. Messer
James P. Messmore
Gordon C. Meurer
Charles A. Meyer
Vernon F. Meyer
William J. Mielke
Raymond T. Miller
Robert H. Miller
Robert D. Mitchell
Thomas E. Mohler
Dayton Molzen
R. Duane Monical

Fellows of the American Council of Engineering Companies

Robert C. Moore
William W. Moore
Frederick K. Mosher
William A. Mossbarger
James (Bud) E. Moulder
Edward J. Mulcahy
Salim Najjar
Terry F. Neimeyer
Albert L. Nelson
Kenneth E. Nelson
Norman A. Neste
James R. Nichols
Frank Nicoladis
E.N. Nicolaides
George K. Nishimura
Lennox K. Nishimura
Judith Nitsch
Jack Noblitt
David Novick
Satoshi Oishi
Stephen M. Olko
Pedro J. Ortiz-Santiago
Paul Ostergaard
R. Stanton Over
J. Hambleton Palmer
Ralph J. Palmer
Stewart R. Palmer
Joseph P. Paoluccio
S.G. Papadopoulos
Andrew J. Parker Jr.
Charles A. Parthum
J.L. Patton
Donald D. Paxton
C.R. Pennoni
Leo F. Peters
Boyd W. Phelps
Emanuel Pisetzner
Richard Piske
Joe H. Pitts
William H. Plautz
Rex T. Pless
James M. Poché
Lester H. Poggemeyer
James W. Poirot
Allen G. Poppino
Richard Q. Praeger

Paul W. Prendiville
David G. Presnell
Daniel F. Prill
Richard E. Ragold
Stan L. Rankin
William R. Ratliff
Roccy J. Raymond
Frederick Reusswig
Robert B. Richards
Theodore J. Richards
G. Michael Ritchie
Cathy S. Ritter
William J. Rizzo Jr.
Robert F. Robertson
T.B. Robinson
Elmer Q. Rodes
Lawrence P. Rogoway
Sigmund Roos
Robert W. Rosene
Donald E. Ross
Donald K. Ross
David T. Rowe
John D. Rowland
Robert D. Rowland
George O. Sadler
Leo A. Santowasso
William H. Sayre
J. Gorman Schaffer Jr.
Charles E. Schaffner
Myron K. Scheibe
Harold A. Schlenger
Paul G. Scott
James F. Shivler Jr.
William E. Short
Wayne F. Shuler
Devindar S. Sidhu
James B. Siebkin
Donald J. Smally
Edwin E. Smith
Herman E. Smith
Lester H. Smith
Russell L. Smith Jr.
Scott Smith
E. Per Sorenson
William A. Sowers
James A. Speedie

Gerald E. Speitel
Arlo J. Spiess
Gary J. Spinkelink
Paul F. Sprehe
Richard H. Stanley
David R. Stewart
Henry A. Stikes
Roger G. Stroud
Douglas F. Suess
Billy T. Sumner
Anne C. Symonds
A.J. Szabo
John P. Talerico
Russell C. Taylor
Thomas J. Terrell
James R. Thomas Jr.
Gregs G. Thomopulos
Donald E. Thompson
Everett S. Thompson
Benedict Tiseo
T. Curtiss Torrance
Donald R. Trim
Jack K. Tuttle
John Urban
J. Howard Van Boerum
J.E. Van Dell
Charles O. Velzy
Donald Vick
Carlos C. Villarreal
Chester T. Vogel
Sam H. Wainwright
Robert A. Waitkus
Richard O. Walker Jr.
F. Spencer Weber
William W. Webster
Vernon M. Wegerer
Victor Weidmann
Richard Weingardt
John P. Weir
Robert D. Wesselink
Lewis H. West
Richard B. Wetzel
Brian R. Whiston
H. Kenneth White
Ronald R. White
Charles K. Whitescarver Jr.

215

Fellows of the American Council of Engineering Companies

Alexander Whitney Jr.
Eugene R. Wilkinson
Jerald A. Williams
Richard L. Williams
Harry M. Wilson
Arnold L. Windman
William J. Winiarski
Douglas G. Wolfangle
Riley D. Woodsen
Thomas D. Wosser
David L. Wright
Kenneth R. Wright
Robert G. Wright
Theodore E. Wynne
L. Carl Yates

Source: American Council of Engineering Companies

I have been privileged, or perhaps doomed, to eschew simpler, lighter burdens. Shaping man's surroundings entails a lot more than spatial, structural, mechanical, and other technical considerations—certainly a lot more than pontificating about matters of style. Our organic well-being is dependent on a wholesome, salubrious environment. Therefore exacting attention has to be paid to our intricate sensory world.

Richard Neutra

Fellows of the American Institute of Architects

The College of Fellows of the American Institute of Architects is composed of AIA members who have been elected to fellowship by a jury of their peers. Fellowship is granted for significant contributions to architecture and society and for achieving a high standard of professional excellence. Architect members who have been in good standing for at least 10 years may be nominated for fellowship. The following individuals are current active members of the AIA's College of Fellows.

A

Carlton S. Abbott, Williamsburg, VA
J. C. Abbott Jr., Sarasota, FL
James Abell, Tempe, AZ
Jan M. Abell, Tampa, FL
Stephen N. Abend, Kansas City, MO
Bruce A. Abrahamson, Minneapolis, MN
Max Abramovitz, Pound Ridge, NY
Fernando L. Abruña, San Juan, PR
Raymond C. Abst, Modesto, CA
Harold L. Adams, Baltimore, MD
William M. Adams, Venice, CA
William T. Adams, Dallas, TX
Michael Adlerstein, New York, NY
Antonin Aeck, Atlanta, GA
P. Aguirre Jr., Dallas, TX
Loren P. Ahles, Minneapolis, MN
Thomas R. Aidala, San Francisco, CA
Roula Alakiotou, Chicago, IL
Charles A. Albanese, Tucson, AZ
Richard K. Albyn, Pisgah Forest, NC
N. Sue Alden, Seattle, WA
Iris S. Alex, New York, NY
Cecil A. Alexander Jr., Atlanta, GA
Earle S. Alexander Jr., Houston, TX
Henry C. Alexander Jr., Coral Gables, FL
James G. Alexander, Boston, MA
A. Notley Alford, Englewood, FL
Stanley N. Allan, Chicago, IL
John William Allegretti, St. Joseph, MI
Maurice B. Allen Jr., Bloomfield Hills, MI
Ralph G. Allen, Chicago, IL
Rex W. Allen, Sonoma, CA
Robert E. Allen, San Francisco, CA
Robert K. Allen, Longview, TX
Susan Allen, Morgantown, IN
Gerald L. Allison, Newport Beach, CA
James V. Allred, Reston, VA
Killis P. Almond Jr., San Antonio, TX
Alfred S. Alschuler, Highland Park, IL
Ronald A. Altoon, Los Angeles, CA
Jesus E. Amaral, San Juan, Puerto Rico

Joseph Amisano, Atlanta, GA
Gregg D. Ander, Irwindale, CA
Dorman D. Anderson, Seattle, WA
Harry F. Anderson, Oakbrook, IL
J. Timothy Anderson, Cambridge, MA
John D. Anderson, Denver, CO
Richard Anderson, Tucson, AZ
Ross S. Anderson, New York, NY
Samuel A. Anderson, Charlottesville, VA
William L. Anderson, Des Moines, IA
J. Philip Andrews, Pittsburgh, PA
Lavone D. Andrews, Houston, TX
Martha P. Andrews, Portland, OR
Charles Angyal, San Diego, CA
George Anselevicius, Albuquerque, NM
James H. Anstis, West Palm Beach, FL
Natalye Appel, Houston, TX
Richard M. Archer, San Antonio, TX
Peter F. Arfaa, Philadelphia, PA
Bruce P. Arneill, Glastonbury, CT
Chris Arnold, Palo Alto, CA
Christopher C. Arnold, Commerce
    Township, MI
Robert V. Arrigoni, San Francisco, CA
J. Tom Ashley III, Lower Rio Grande,
    Mexico
Yvonne W. Asken, Portage, MI
Laurin B. Askew, Columbia, MD
Lee Hewlett Askew III, Memphis, TN
Neil L. Astle, Salt Lake City, UT
Louis D. Astorino, Pittsburgh, PA
Charles H. Atherton, Washington, DC
Tony Atkin, Philadelphia, PA
James B. Atkins, Dallas, TX
John L. Atkins, Research Triangle Park,
    NC
Eugene E. Aubry, Holmes Beach, FL
Seymour Auerbach, Chevy Chase, MD
Douglas H. Austin, San Diego, CA
Daniel Avchen, Minneapolis, MN
Donald C. Axon, Laguna Beach, CA
Alfred L. Aydelott, Carmel, CA

B

Howard J. Backen, Sausalito, CA
Edmund N. Bacon, Philadelphia, PA
David C. Baer, Houston, TX
Stuart Baesel, La Jolla, CA
Deon F. Bahr, Lincoln, NE
Jonathan Bailey, Dallas, TX
Ray B. Bailey, Houston, TX
William J. Bain Jr., Seattle, WA
Royden Stanley Bair, Houston, TX
Louis J. Bakanowsky, Cambridge, MA
David Baker, San Francisco, CA
Isham O. Baker, Washington, DC
Jack Sherman Baker, Champaign, IL
James Barnes Baker, London, England
Josiah (Jay) Baker, Houston, TX
Alan T. Baldwin Jr., Charlotte, NC
Gregory S. Baldwin, Portland, OR
Samuel T. Balen, Waldport, OR
Rex M. Ball, Tulsa, OK
Richard S. Banwell, Walnut Creek, CA
Shalom S. Baranes, Washington, DC
Robert A. Barclay, Cleveland, OH
Peter L. Bardwell, Columbus, OH
Paul H. Barkley, Falls Church, VA
John M. Barley, II, Jacksonville, FL
Charles C. Barlow, Jackson, MS
William Lewis Barlow IV, Marblehead, MA
Edward L. Barnes, Cambridge, MA
Linda Barnes, Portland, OR
Rebecca Barnes, Boston, MA
Jay William Barnes Jr., Austin, TX
Jonathan Barnett, Washington, DC
Carol R. Barney, Chicago, IL
Howard R. Barr, Austin, TX
Raj Barr-Kumar, Washington, DC
Nolan E. Barrick, Lubbock, TX
Errol Barron, New Orleans, LA
Richard E. Barrow, Birmingham, AL
Richard W. Bartholomew, Philadelphia, PA
Armand Bartos, New York, NY
Edward C. Bassett, Mill Valley, CA

Fellows of the American Institute of Architects

Fred Bassetti, Seattle, WA
Peter Batchelor, Raleigh, NC
Ronald J. Battaglia, Buffalo, NY
Jay S. Bauer, Newport Beach, CA
Edward Baum, Dallas, TX
Joseph D. Bavaro, Punta Gorda, FL
Samuel R. Bayne, Southfield, MI
John Craig Beale, Dallas, TX
Burtch W. Beall Jr., Salt Lake City, UT
Leroy E. Bean, Petaluma, CA
Alan J. Beard, Portland, OR
Lee P. Bearsch, Binghamton, NY
William H. Beaty, Memphis, TN
William B. Bechhoefer, Bethesda, MD
Lee Becker, Washington, DC
Rex L. Becker, St. Louis, MO
Robert M. Beckley, Ann Arbor, MI
Michael Bednar, Charlottesville, VA
Carmi Bee, New York, NY
David W. Beer, New York, NY
Edgar C. Beery, Springfield, VA
Ann M. Beha, Boston, MA
Byron Bell, New York, NY
Frederic Bell, Long Island City, NY
M. Wayne Bell, Austin, TX
John Belle, New York, NY
Anthony Belluschi, Chicago, IL
Ralph C. Bender, San Antonio, TX
Barry Benepe, New York, NY
Daniel D. Bennett, Fayetteville, AR
David J. Bennett, Minneapolis, MN
Carol Rusche Bentel, Locust Valley, NY
Frederick R. Bentel, Locust Valley, NY
Maria A. Bentel, Locust Valley, NY
Paul Louis Bentel, Locust Valley, NY
Kenneth E. Bentsen, Houston, TX
Frederick J. Bentz, Minneapolis, MN
Karl A. Berg, Denver, CO
Richard R. Bergmann, New Canaan, CT
Lloyd F. Bergquist, Bloomington, MN
Robert J. Berkebile, Kansas City, MO
Marlene J. Berkoff, San Rafael, CA
Anthony N. Bernheim, San Francisco, CA
Phillip Bernstein, New Haven, CT
K. Norman Berry, Louisville, KY
Richard J. Bertman, Boston, MA
Ronald P. Bertone, Middletown, NJ
Donald A. Bertram, Denver, CO
Frederic A. Bertram, Clearwater, FL
Hobart Betts, Sag Harbor, NY
William Bevins, Charleston, WV
John H. Beyer, New York, NY
William Beyer, Minneapolis, MN
James Biber, New York, NY

John H. Bickel, Louisville, KY
Frederick C. Biebesheimer III,
  Old Lyme, CT
T. J. Biggs, Jackson, MS
Rebecca L. Binder, Playa Del Rey, CA
James Binkley, Arlington, VA
Lance L. Bird, Pasadena, CA
John R. Birge, Omaha, NE
Gunnar Birkerts, Bloomfield Hills, MI
James A. Bishop, Bellville, TX
George Bissell, Newport Beach, CA
Georgia Bizios, Chapel Hill, NC
J. Sinclair Black, Austin, TX
Walter S. Blackburn, Indianapolis, IN
Leonard D. Blackford, Sacramento, CA
Bruce E. Blackmer, Spokane, WA
Craig Blackmon, Dallas, TX
Jan Gaede Blackmon, Dallas, TX
Boyd A. Blackner, Salt Lake City, UT
Peter Blake, Riverdale, NY
Frederick A. Bland, New York, NY
Wilfred E. Blessing, Oak Harbor, WA
Richard L. Blinder, New York, NY
Richard L. Bliss, Kirkwood, MO
Robert L. Bliss, Salt Lake City, UT
Ronald B. Blitch, New Orleans, LA
Timothy Brent Blonkvist, San Antonio, TX
John D. Bloodgood, Des Moines, IA
Martin Bloomenthal, Princeton, NJ
Sigmund F. Blum, Naples, FL
Joan Blumenfeld, New York, NY
Susan Blumentals, Brooklyn Center, MN
H. M. Blumer, Paradise Valley, AZ
Kirk V. Blunck, Des Moines, IA
William A. Blunden, Cleveland, OH
William E. Blurock, Newport Beach, CA
Thomas H. Blurock, Costa Mesa, CA
William Bobenhausen, Norwalk, CT
L. Kirkpatrick Bobo, Memphis, TN
Michael L. Bobrow, Los Angeles, CA
Bruce T. Bockstael, Hartford, CT
William N. Bodouva, New York, NY
Joe Boehning, Albuquerque, NM
Robert J. Boerema, Gainesville, FL
Joseph Boggs, Annapolis, MD
Walter F. Bogner, Larchmont, NY
Peter Bohlin, Wilkes Barre, PA
Friedrich K.M. Bohm, Columbus, OH
Mario H. Boiardi, Washington, DC
Stanley G. Boles, Portland, OR
Michael E. Bolinger, Baltimore, MD
Robert D. Bolling, Torrance, CA
Antonio R. Bologna, Memphis, TN
Preston M. Bolton, Houston, TX

James R. Bonar, Los Angeles, CA
J. Max Bond Jr., New York, NY
Charles Hussey Boney, Wilmington, NC
Paul D. Boney, Wilmington, NC
Dwight M. Bonham, Wichita, KS
Daniel Boone, Abilene, TX
David C. Boone, Santa Cruz, CA
Laurence O. Booth, Chicago, IL
Bill C. Booziotis, Dallas, TX
L. G. Borget, Houston, TX
Bernard Bortnick, Dallas, TX
Thomas L. Bosworth, Seattle, WA
Elmer Botsai, Honolulu, HI
Gary A. Bowden, Baltimore, MD
David M. Bowen, Fishers, IN
Gary Bowen, Omaha, NE
Ronald Gene Bowen, Middleton, WI
John A. Bower Jr., Philadelphia, PA
Paul D. Bowers Jr., Grand Rapids, MI
William A. Bowersox, St. Louis, MO
Chester Bowles Jr., San Francisco, CA
J. Donald Bowman, Bellevue, WA
John Harold Box, Austin, TX
Hugh A. Boyd, Montclair, NJ
Robert A. Boynton, Richmond, VA
John Bozalis, Oklahoma City, OK
James H. Bradburn, Denver, CO
David R. Braden, Dallas, TX
Richard H. Bradfield, Clearwater, FL
Thomas G. Bradley, Decatur, IL
Clyde A. Brady, III, Orlando, FL
Karen L. Braitmayer, Seattle, WA
Scott W. Braley, Atlanta, GA

Did you know...

The States with the most AIA fellows are:

California – 433
New York – 249
Texas – 235
Illinois – 146
Massachusetts – 129
Florida – 109
Washington – 108
Pennsylvania – 88
Virginia – 79
District of Columbia – 76
Michigan – 73

Source: DesignIntelligence

Fellows of the American Institute of Architects

Ronald M. Brame, Dallas, TX
Joel Brand, Houston, TX
Robert Brannen, Boston, MA
Charles S. Braun, Longwood, FL
Richard M. Brayton, San Francisco, CA
William E. Brazley Jr., Matteson, IL
Melvin Brecher, Broomhall, PA
William N. Breger, New York, NY
Simon Breines, Scarsdale, NY
John Michael Brendle, Denver, CO
Daniel R. Brents, Houston, TX
Adrienne G. Bresnan, New York, NY
Joseph Bresnan, New York, NY
Leon Bridges, Baltimore, MD
Stanford R. Britt, Washington, DC
Joseph M. Brocato Sr., Alexandria, LA
Myra M. Brocchini, Berkeley, CA
Ronald G. Brocchini, Berkeley, CA
Paul Broches, New York, NY
Raymond D. Brochstein, Houston, TX
William R. Brockway, Baton Rouge, LA
M. J. Brodie, Baltimore, MD
H. Gordon Brooks, II, Lafayette, LA
John W. Broome, Tualatin, OR
Robert C. Broshar, Clear Lake, IA
David J. Brotman, Los Angeles, CA
Charles E. Broudy, Philadelphia, PA
George D. Brown Jr., Peekskill, NY
Jennie Sue Brown, Seattle, WA
Kenneth F. Brown, Honolulu, HI
Lance Jay Brown, New York, NY
Paul B. Brown, Traverse City, MI
Peter Hoyt Brown, Houston, TX
Robert F. Brown Jr., Philadelphia, PA
Robert L. Brown Jr., Lithonia, GA
Terrance Brown, Albuquerque, NM
Woodlief Brown, Abilene, TX
Barry B. Bruce, Bellaire, TX
Van B. Bruner Jr., Haddonfield, NJ
Harry A. Bruno, Walnut Creek, CA
Larry S. Bruton, Portland, OR
Harvey Bryan, Belmont, MA
John H. Bryant, Stillwater, OK
Algimantas V. Bublys, Birmingham, MI
Bradley Scott Buchanan, Denver, CO
Marvin H. Buchanan, Berkeley, CA
Davis A. Buckley, Washington, DC
James W. Buckley, Greensboro, GA
Michael P. Buckley, New Haven, CT
Rick Buckley, Seattle, WA
Richard H. Buday, Houston, TX
Huber H. Buehrer, Maumee, OH
John B. Buenz, Chicago, IL
Glenn A. Buff, Miami, FL

Henrik H. Bull, San Francisco, CA
Ellis W. Bullock Jr., Pensacola, FL
Thomas A. Bullock Sr., Brenham, TX
W. Glenn Bullock, Knoxville, TN
Franklin S. Bunch, Sugar Land, TX
Richard S. Bundy, San Diego, CA
John H. Burgee, Montecito, CA
Charles E. Burgess, Houston, TX
J. Armand Burgun, Kitty Hawk, NC
Edward M. Burke, Austin, TX
James E. Burlage, Sausalito, CA
Robert Burley, Waitsfield, VT
Arthur L. Burns, Winter Haven, FL
John A. Burns, Alexandria, VA
Joseph G. Burns, Chicago, IL
Norma DeCamp Burns, Raleigh, NC
Robert P. Burns, Raleigh, NC
F. Andrus Burr, Williamstown, MA
Rodger E. Burson, Wimberley, TX
John A. Busby Jr., Atlanta, GA
C. Joe Buskuhl, Dallas, TX
H. Kennard Bussard, Des Moines, IA
Jerome R. Butler, Chicago, IL
Theodore R. Butler, Minneapolis, MN
Fred W. Butner, Winston Salem, NC
Thomas K. Butt, Point Richmond, CA
Harold Buttrick, New York, NY
Paul S. Byard, New York, NY
Brent Byers, Austin, TX
Jeanne Byrne, Pacific Grove, CA
Arne Bystrom, Seattle, WA

C

Burns Cadwalader, Oakland, CA
Timothy G. Cahill, Kansas City, MO
Harold Calhoun, Houston, TX
C. Robert Campbell, Albuquerque, NM
Robert Campbell, Cambridge, MA
Wendell J. Campbell, Chicago, IL
Jaime Canaves, Miami, FL
H. F. Candela, Coral Gables, FL
Robert H. Canizaro, Jackson, MS
William T. Cannady, Houston, TX
Jamie Cannon, Town & Country, MO
Roger Cannon, Raleigh, NC
Marvin J. Cantor, Fairfax, VA
Horace S. Cantrell Jr., Indianapolis, IN
Richard Scott Carde, Santa Monica, CA
Kenneth Harvey Cardwell, Berkeley, CA
Jean P. Carlhian, Boston, MA
William A. Carlisle, Columbia, SC
DeVon M. Carlson, Boulder, CO
Donald Edwin Carlson, Seattle, WA
Clyde R. Carpenter, Lexington, KY

Jack A. Carpenter, San Diego, CA
William J. Carpenter, Atlanta, GA
Edwin Winford Carroll, El Paso, TX
Marley Carroll, Charlotte, NC
W. T. Carry, Atlanta, GA
Chris Carson, San Antonio, TX
Donald K. Carter, Pittsburgh, PA
Virgil R. Carter, Newtown Square, PA
David R. Cartnal, San Jose, CA
Timothy A. Casai, Bloomfield Hills, MI
John Casbarian, Houston, TX
A. Cascieri, Lexington, MA
Donald W. Caskey, Irvine, CA
Heather W. Cass, Washington, DC
Joseph W. Casserly, Chicago, IL
John J. Castellana, Bloomfield Hills, MI
Stephan Castellanos, Stockton, CA
John H. Catlin, Boston, MA
Samuel J. Caudill, Aspen, CO
Giorgio Cavaglieri, New York, NY
Peter David Cavaluzzi, New York, NY
Lawrence Chaffin Jr., Koloa, HI
Ann R. Chaintreuil, Rochester, NY
Alfred V. Chaix, South Pasadena, CA
Michael Dale Chambers, Minneapolis, MN
Dean B. Chambliss, Denver, CO
Junius J. Champeaux, II, Lake Charles, LA
Lo-Yi Chan, Ashley Falls, MA
Wing T. Chao, Burbank, CA
L. William Chapin II, Alexandria, VA
Donald D. Chapman, Kula, HI
John S. Chase, Houston, TX
Walter F. Chatham, New York, NY
Peter Chermayeff, Boston, MA
Edith Cherry, Albuquerque, NM
Edward E. Cherry, Hamden, CT
Robert A. Chervenak, Mount Vernon, WA
Lugean L. Chilcote, Little Rock, AR
G. Cabell Childress, Castle Rock, CO
James C. Childress, Centerbrook, CT
David M. Childs, New York, NY
Maurice F. Childs, Boston, MA
Susan Chin, New York, NY
Robert E. Chisholm, Miami, FL
Gordon H. Chong, San Francisco, CA
Frederick L. Christensen, Salinas, CA
George W. Christensen, Scottsdale, AZ
James W. Christopher, Salt Lake City, UT
Daniel Chun, Honolulu, HI
Eric A. Chung, Radnor, PA
William C. Church, Portland, OR
Richard J. Chylinski, Los Angeles, CA
Mario J. Ciampi, Kentfield, CA
Robert L. Cioppa, New York, NY

Fellows of the American Institute of Architects

Eugene D. Cizek, New Orleans, LA
George L. Claflen, Philadelphia, PA
John M. Clancy, Boston, MA
James F. Clapp Jr., Cambridge, MA
Fred W. Clarke III, New Haven, CT
Gerald L. Clark, Havasu City, AZ
Roger H. Clark, Raleigh, NC
John P. Clarke, Trenton, NJ
Marshall F. Clarke, Greenville, SC
Charles Clary, Destin, FL
Thomas R. Clause, Des Moines, IA
Gregory Clement III, New York, NY
Jerry L. Clement, St. Louis, MO
Glen E. Cline, Boise, ID
Elizabeth Close, St. Paul, MN
Robert K. Clough, Chicago, IL
James A Clutts, Dallas, TX
Henry N. Cobb, New York, NY
R. F. Coffee, Austin, TX
Daniel P. Coffey, Chicago, IL
Adrian O. Cohen, Los Angeles, CA
Andrew P. Cohen, Santa Monica, CA
Andrew S. Cohen, Middlebury, CT
Jack C. Cohen, Bethesda, MD
Jonathan W. Cohen, Berkeley, CA
Martin H. Cohen, Armonk, NY
Stuart Cohen, Evanston, IL
Doris Cole, Concord, MA
Robert Traynham Coles, Buffalo, NY
David S. Collins, Cincinnati, OH
Donald Comstock, Sacramento, CA
William T. Conklin, Washington, DC
Richard T. Conrad, Sacramento, CA
W. M. Conrad, Kansas City, MO
John Conron, Santa Fe, NM
J. J. Conroy, Chicago, IL
Eugene E. Cook, Roselle, IL
Lawrence D. Cook, Falls Church, VA
Richard B. Cook, Chicago, IL
William H. Cook, Sonoita, AZ
Alexander Cooper, New York, NY
Jerome M. Cooper, Atlanta, GA
W. Kent Cooper, Washington, DC
Christopher Coover, Phoenix, AZ
Gerald M. Cope, Philadelphia, PA
Lee G. Copeland, Seattle, WA
C. Jack Corgan, Dallas, TX
Jack M. Corgan, Dallas, TX
William Corlett, Berkeley, CA
Araldo A. Cossutta, New York, NY
Walter H. Costa, Lafayette, CA
Anthony J. Costello, Muncie, IN
Leland Cott, Cambridge, MA
John O. Cotton, Marina Del Rey, CA
W. Philip Cotton Jr., St. Louis, MO

Tommy N. Cowan, Austin, TX
C. H. Cowell, Houston, TX
Page Ayres Cowley, New York City, NY
Dan C. Cowling, Little Rock, AR
David C. Cox, Washington, DC
Frederic H Cox, Richmond, VA
Warren J. Cox, Washington, DC
Whitson W. Cox, Carmichael, CA
William Allan Cox, Alexandria, VA
Bruce I. Crabtree Jr., Nashville, TN
Kirk R. Craig, Greenville, SC
Steade Craigo, Sacramento, CA
George M. Crandall, Portland, OR
David A. Crane, Tampa, FL
Steve H. Crane, Salt Lake City, UT
Ronald O. Crawford, Roanoke, VA
Martin W. Crennen, Helena, MT
Frank W. Crimp, Milton, MA
James H. Crissman, Watertown, MA
Edwin B. Crittenden, Anchorage, AK
K. C. Crocco, Chicago, IL
Charles B. Croft, Austin, TX
Edwin B. Cromwell, Little Rock, AR
Eason Cross Jr., Alexandria, VA
Samuel Crothers III, Radnor, PA
S. Fiske Crowell Jr., Boston, MA
R. L. Crowther, Denver, CO
Randolph R. Croxton, New York, NY
Metcalf Crump, Memphis, TN
Evan D. Cruthers, Honolulu, HI
Beatriz del Cueto, Guaynabo, Puerto Rico
John W. Cuningham, Minneapolis, MN
Ben Cunningham, St. Petersburg, FL
Gary M. Cunningham, Dallas, TX
Warren W. Cunningham, Philadelphia, PA
James L. Cutler, Bainbridge Is, WA
Bernard J. Cywinski, Havertown, PA

D

Charles E. Dagit Jr., Philadelphia, PA
Fernand W. Dahan, Rockville, MD
David A. Daileda, Springfield, VA
Todd Dalland, New York, NY
J. E. Dalton, Kent, OH
Leo A. Daly III, Washington, DC
Paul Damaz, East Hampton, NY
Sylvester Damianos, Pittsburgh, PA
Robert Damora, Bedford, NY
George E. Danforth, Chicago, IL
Arthur C. Danielian, Irvine, CA
George N. Daniels, Salt Lake City, UT
Stanley L. Daniels, Atlanta, GA
Doris Andrews Danna, St. Louis, MO
Robert F. Darby, Jacksonville, FL
Samuel N. Darby, Rockford, IL

Edwin S. Darden, Fresno, CA
Ben R. Darmer, Atlanta, GA
Richard Dattner, New York, NY
Theoharis L. David, New York, NY
D. G. Davidson, Washington, DC
David S. Davidson, Great Falls, MT
Robert I. Davidson, New York, NY
Albert J. Davis, Blacksburg, VA
Arthur Q. Davis, New Orleans, LA
Charles M. Davis, San Francisco, CA
Clark Davis, St. Louis, MO
Clark A. Davis, San Francisco, CA
Jerry A. Davis, New York, NY
John M. Davis, Austin, TX
Lewis Davis, New York, NY
Nicholas Davis, Auburn, AL
Steven M. Davis, New York, NY
W. T. Davis, Greenville, SC
Clare Henry Day, Redlands, CA
Frederic L. Day Jr., Concord, MA
Thomas DeAngelo, Minneapolis, MN
Natalie De Blois, San Antonio, TX
John Neff De Haas Jr., Bozeman, MT
Rey de la Reza, Houston, TX
Alfredo De Vido, New York, NY
Jack DeBartolo Jr., Phoenix, AZ
Rudolph V. DeChellis, Woodland Hills, CA
Vernon DeMars, Berkeley, CA
Kenneth DeMay, Watertown, MA
Louis DeMoll, Moylan, PA
Mary Werner DeNadai, Chadds Ford, PA
Dirk Denison, Chicago, IL
J. R. DeStefano, Chicago, IL
Panayotis E. DeVaris, South Orange, NJ
E. L. Deam, Highland Park, IL
Robert C. Dean, Boston, MA
C. M. Deasy, San Luis Obispo, CA
Howard S. Decker, Chicago, IL
Ward W. Deems, Solana Beach, CA
Allan J. Dehar, New Haven, CT
Jorge Del Rio, San Juan, Puerto Rico
Homer T. Delawie, San Diego, CA
Eugene A. Delmar, Olney, MD
Pamela J. Delphenich, New Haven, CT
Sidney L. Delson, East Hampton, NY
Olvia Demetriou, Washington, DC
William Deno, Boulder, CO
Jos. Robert Deshayes, Caldwell, TX
Gary L. Desmond, Denver, CO
John J. Desmond, Baton Rouge, LA
Gita Dev, Woodside, CA
Suzanne Di Geronimo, Paramus, NJ
Antonio Di Mambro, Boston, MA
A P. DiBenedetto, Portland, OR
Eugene L. DiLaura, Milan, MI

Fellows of the American Institute of Architects

Robert Diamant, Longboat Key, FL
J. J. Diamond, Jacksonville, FL
Katherine Diamond, Los Angeles, CA
Horacio Diaz, San Juan, Puerto Rico
James R. Diaz, San Francisco, CA
David R. Dibner, McLean, VA
Bruce Dicker, Portsmouth, NH
Gerald G. Diehl, Dearborn, MI
Paul E. Dietrich, Cambridge, MA
Robert H. Dietz, Apache Junction, AZ
William M. Dikis, Des Moines, IA
Frank Dimster, Los Angeles, CA
David D. Dixon, Boston, MA
F. Dail Dixon Jr., Chapel Hill, NC
John M. Dixon, Old Greenwich, CT
Michael A. Dixon, St. Charles, IL
Lawrence S. Doane, San Francisco, CA
Jim C. Doche, Amarillo, TX
Peter H. Dodge, San Francisco, CA
George S. Dolim, San Francisco, CA
Peter Hoyt Dominick Jr., Denver, CO
Milford W. Donaldson, San Diego, CA
Janet Donelson, Seattle, WA
Richard C. Donkervoet, Baltimore, MD
Paul J. Donnelly, St. Louis, MO
Kermit P. Dorius, Newport Beach, CA
Albert A. Dorman, Los Angeles, CA
Richard L. Dorman, Santa Fe, NM
Robert W. Dorsey, Cincinnati, OH
Darwin V. Doss, Salem, OR
Betsey O. Dougherty, Costa Mesa, CA
Brian P. Dougherty, Costa Mesa, CA
Frank F. Douglas, Houston, TX
John Douglas, Scottsdale , AZ
H. Robert Douglass, Missouri City, TX
C.R. George Dove, Washington, DC
Gerald A. Doyle, Phoenix, AZ
Peter G. Doyle, Houston, TX
Boris Dramov, San Francisco, CA
Helene Dreiling, Warrenton, VA
Roy M. Drew, San Diego, CA
Albert M. Dreyfuss, Sacramento, CA
Robert W. Drummond, Gainesville, FL
Andrés Duany, Miami, FL
Martin David Dubin, Highland Park, IL
George A. Dudley, Rensselaerville, NY
J. Paul Duffendack, Leawood, KS
Herbert E. Duncan, Kansas City, MO
Foster W. Dunwiddie, Henderson, NV
Eugene C. Dunwody, Macon, GA
William L. Duquette, Los Gatos, CA
Gabriel Durand-Hollis, San Antonio, TX
Almon J. Durkee, Traverse City, MI
William R. Dutcher, Berkeley, CA
Donald J. Dwore, Coral Gables, FL

Daniel L. Dworsky, Los Angeles, CA
Alan Dynerman, Washington, DC

E ───────────

Mary Jean Eastman, New York, NY
John P. Eberhard, Alexandria, VA
Jeremiah Eck, Boston, MA
Stanton Eckstut, New York, NY
Robert N. Eddy, Bakersfield, CA
Judith Edelman, New York, NY
David J. Edwards Jr., Columbia, SC
Jared I. Edwards, Hartford, CT
Albert Efron, Staten Island, NY
David L. Eggers, West Palm Beach, FL
John P. Ehrig, Merritt Island, FL
Joseph Ehrlich, Menlo Park, CA
Steven D. Ehrlich, Culver City, CA
Thomas N. Eichbaum, Washington, DC
John A. Eifler, Chicago, IL
Steven L. Einhorn, Albany, NY
Peter D. Eisenman, New York, NY
Sidney H. Eisenshtat, Los Angeles, CA
Richard Karl Eisner, Oakland, CA
Barry P. Elbasani, Berkeley, CA
Joseph L. Eldredge, Vineyard Haven, MA
Charles N. Eley, San Francisco, CA
James H. Eley, Jackson, MS
Howard F. Elkus, Boston, MA
Harry Ellenzweig, Cambridge, MA
Robin M. Ellerthorpe, Chicago, IL
Dale R. Ellickson, Great Falls, VA
Benjamin P. Elliott, Rockville, MD
Rand L. Elliott, Oklahoma City, OK
John M. Ellis, New York, NY
James E. Ellison, Washington, DC
Frank L. Elmer, Columbus, OH
James W. Elmore, Phoenix, AZ
Frederick E. Emmons, Bel Tiburon, CA
Terrel M. Emmons, Springfield, VA
William Eng, Champaign, IL
Douglas K. Engebretson,
    West Springfield, MA
Mark C. Engelbrecht, Des Moines, IA
Philip J. Enquist, Chicago, IL
William L. Ensign, Annapolis, MD
Lawrence Enyart, Phoenix, AZ
Herbert Epstein, Delray Beach, FL
Elizabeth S. Ericson, Boston, MA
Jerome R. Ernst, Seattle, WA
R. Allen Eskew, New Orleans, LA
Philip A. Esocoff, Washington, DC
Harold Lionel Esten, Silver Spring, MD
James Estes, Newport, RI
A. B. Etherington, Honolulu, HI
Deane M. Evans Jr., Arlington, VA

J. Handel Evans, Camarillo, CA
Ralph F. Evans, Salt Lake City, UT
Robert J. Evans, Marshall, CA
S. Michael Evans, Norfolk, VA
William S. Evans, Shreveport, LA
C. Richard Everett, Houston, TX
Gary Everton, Nashville, TN
Peter Exley, Chicago, IL
Thomas J. Eyerman, Chicago, IL

F ───────────

Otto Reichert Facilides, Philadelphia, PA
William H. Fain Jr., Los Angeles, CA
James Falick, Houston, TX
Kristine K. Fallon, Chicago, IL
Jay David Farbstein, San Luis Obispo, CA
Michael Farewell, Princeton, NJ
Richard T. Faricy, Saint Paul, MN
Mehrdad Farivar, Los Angeles, CA
Richard C. Farley, Denver, CO
Stephen J. Farneth, San Francisco, CA
Avery C. Faulkner, Delaplane, VA
Winthrop W. Faulkner, Chevy Chase, MD
James G. Fausett, Marietta, GA
Robert E. Fehlberg, Pleasanton, CA
Werner L. Feibes, Schenectady, NY
Daniel J. Feil, Washington, DC
Edward A. Feiner, Fairfax, VA
Jose Feito, Miami, FL
Curtis W. Fentress, Denver, CO
S. Scott Ferebee Jr., Charlotte, NC
Franklin T. Ferguson, Salt Lake City, UT
Richard E. Fernau, Berkeley, CA
Stephanie E. Ferrell, Tampa, FL
Miguel Ferrer, Santurce, Puerto Rico
Richard B. Ferrier, Arlington, TX
Robert D. Ferris, San Diego, CA
M. L. Ferro, Weare, NH
Donald E. Ferry, Springfield, IL
Michael T. Fickel, Kansas City, MO
H. H. Field, Shirley, MA
John L. Field, San Francisco, CA
Barbara Field, Asheville, NC
Edwin L. Fields, Los Angeles, CA
Robert A. Fielden, Las Vegas, NV
Michael M. Fieldman, New York, NY
Kenneth J. Filarski, Providence, RI
R. Jerome Filer, Miami, FL
Bob G. Fillpot, Norman, OK
Ronald C. Filson, New Orleans, LA
Curtis Finch, Lake Oswego, OR
James H. Finch, Alpharetta, GA
Robert A. Findlay, Ames, IA
Maurice N. Finegold, Boston, MA
Ira S. Fink, Berkeley, CA

Fellows of the American Institute of Architects

Jerry V. Finrow, Seattle, WA
A. Robert Fisher, Belvedere, CA
Benjamin P. Fisher, San Francisco, CA
James Herschel Fisher, Dallas, TX
John L. Fisher, Marysville, CA
Laura A. Horstman Fisher, Chicago, IL
Hollye C. Fisk, Dallas, TX
Michael A. Fitts, Nolensville, TN
Darrell A. Fitzgerald, Atlanta, GA
James T. Fitzgerald, Cincinnati, OH
Joseph F. Fitzgerald, Chicago, IL
Richard A. Fitzgerald, Houston, TX
Joseph H. Flad, Madison, WI
Earl Robert Flansburgh, Boston, MA
Ted Flato, San Antonio, TX
Joseph L. Fleischer, New York, NY
Richard J. Fleischman, Cleveland, OH
Norman C. Fletcher, Lexington, MA
David J. Flood, Santa Monica, CA
Colden R. Florance, Washington, DC
Luis Flores-Dumont, Santurce,
    Puerto Rico
J. Chadwick P. Floyd, Centerbrook, CT
Richard F. Floyd, Dallas, TX
W. Jeff Floyd Jr., Atlanta, GA
Ligon B. Flynn, Wilmington, NC
Michael Flynn, New York, NY
John W. Focke, Houston, TX
Bernd Foerster, Manhattan, KS
James Follett, Chicago, IL
Fred L. Foote, San Francisco, CA
Stephen M. Foote, Boston, MA
Peter Forbes, Boston, MA
Robert M. Ford, Starkville, MS
Russell Forester, La Jolla, CA
Bernardo Fort-Brescia, Miami, FL
James R. Foster, Fayetteville, AR
Richard Foster, Wilton, CT
Bruce S. Fowle, New York, NY
Bob J. Fowler, Pasadena, CA
Marion L. Fowlkes, Nashville, TN
Sheldon Fox, Stamford, CT
Harrison Fraker, Berkeley, CA
Edward D. Francis, Detroit, MI
Jay E. Frank, Dallas, TX
Morton Frank, Redwood City, CA
Richard C. Frank, Gregory, MI
Neil P. Frankel, Chicago, IL
James R. Franklin, San Luis Obispo, CA
Gregory Franta, Boulder, CO
John P. Franzen, Southport, CT
Ulrich J. Franzen, New York, NY
Robert J. Frasca, Portland, OR
James I. Freed, New York, NY

Philip G. Freelon, Research Triangle
    Park, NC
Beverly L. Freeman, Charlotte, NC
William W. Freeman, Burlington, VT
Jeffrey S. French, Philadelphia, PA
Thomas K. Fridstein, Chicago, IL
Stephen Friedlaender, Cambridge, MA
Daniel S. Friedman, Cincinnati, OH
Hans A. Friedman, Evanston, IL
Rodney F. Friedman, Belvedere, CA
Edward Friedrichs, Santa Monica, CA
Louis E. Fry, Washington, DC
Louis E. Fry Jr., Washington, DC
Richard E. Fry, Ann Arbor, MI
Lonn L. Frye, Chicago, IL
Randall K. Fujiki, Kailua, HI
Albert B. Fuller Jr., St. Louis, MO
Frank L. Fuller, IV, Oakland, CA
Duncan T. Fulton, Dallas, TX
David F. Furman, Charlotte, NC
James E. Furr, Houston, TX

G

Michael Gabellini, New York, NY
Robert C. Gaede, Cleveland, OH
Fulton G. Gale III, Seattle, WA
Carl Galioto, New York, NY
Herbert K. Gallagher, Boston, MA
Leslie M. Gallery-Dilworth, Philadelphia, PA
Harvey B. Gantt, Charlotte, NC
Theodore Garduque, Honolulu, HI
Robert D. Garland Jr., El Paso, TX
Douglas A. Garofalo, Chicago, IL
Charles E. Garrison, Diamondhead, MS
Truitt B. Garrison, Granbury, TX
Alan G. Gass, Denver, CO
Fred C. Gast Jr., Portland, OR
Kirk A. Gastinger, Kansas City, MO
James A. Gatsch, Princeton, NJ
Martha M. Gates, Pittsford, NY
Robert F. Gatje, New York, NY
James B. Gatton, Houston, TX
F. E. Gaulden, Greenville, SC
John C. Gaunt, Lawrence, KS
Robert Geddes, Princeton, NJ
Barbara L. Geddis, Stamford, CT
William J. Geddis, Chestnut Hill, MA
Robert J. Geering, San Francisco, CA
Frank O. Gehry, Santa Monica, CA
Carolyn D. Geise, Seattle, WA
Martin B. Gelber, Los Angeles, CA
M. Arthur Gensler Jr., San Francisco, CA
David W. George, Southlake, TX
Frank Dan George, Stamford, CT
Reagan W. George, Willow City, TX

Robert S. George, San Bruno, CA
Stephen A. George, Pittsburgh, PA
W. Eugene George, San Antonio, TX
Diane Georgopulos, Boston, MA
Preston M. Geren, Fort Worth, TX
Thomas B. Gerfen, San Francisco, CA
Phillip H. Gerou, Evergreen, CO
Mahmoud Gharachedaghi, Los Angeles, CA
Joe P. Giattina Jr., Birmingham, AL
James D. Gibans, Cleveland, OH
Dale L. Gibbs, Lincoln, NE
Donald H. Gibbs, Long Beach, CA
Randall C. Gideon, Fort Worth, TX
Sidney P. Gilbert, New York, NY
Victor C. Gilbertson, Minnetonka, MN
Wilmot G. Gilland, Eugene, OR
Norman M. Giller, Miami Beach, FL
W. Douglas Gilpin, Charlottesville, VA
James S. Gimpel, Chicago, IL
Raymond L. Gindroz, Pittsburgh, PA
David L. Ginsberg, New York, NY
Raymond Girvigian, South Pasadena, CA
Joseph Carl Giuliani, Washington, DC
Romaldo Giurgola, Australia
Richard E. Glaser, Cincinnati, OH
William R. Glass, Oakland, CA
David Evan Glasser, Fayetteville, AR
E. A. Glendening, Cincinnati, OH
Val Glitsch, Houston, TX
Richard J. Gluckman, New York, NY
Harold D. Glucksman, Union, NJ
James M. Glymph, Santa Monica, CA
Ronald V. Gobbell, Nashville, TN
H. Carleton Godsey Jr., Louisville, KY
James Goettsch, Chicago, IL
Lewis J. Goetz, Washington, DC
Alan E. Goldberg, New Canaan, CT
Steven M. Goldberg, New York, NY
M. H. Goldfinger, New York, NY
Ron Goldman, Malibu, CA
Nicholas Goldsmith, New York, NY
Roger Neal Goldstein, Boston, MA
Stanley J. Goldstein, West Orange, NJ
Harmon H. Goldstone, New York, NY
Harry A. Golemon, Houston, TX
Bennie M. Gonzales, Nogales, AZ
Armando L. Gonzalez, Pasadena, CA
Donald W. Y. Goo, Honolulu, HI
R. L. Good, Dallas, TX
Wayne L. Good, Annapolis, MD
D. B. Goodhue, Monterey, CA
Cary C. Goodman, Kansas City, MO
John P. Goodman, Manlius, NY
Michael K. Goodwin, Phoenix, AZ
Warren N. Goodwin, Brentwood, TN

Fellows of the American Institute of Architects

Joan E. Goody, Boston, MA
Ezra Gordon, Chicago, IL
Harry T. Gordon, Washington, DC
Alexander Gorlin, New York, NY
T.J. Gottesdiener, New York, NY
Amy L. Gould, Baltimore, MD
Robert E. Gould, Kansas City, MO
Ronald Gourley, Tucson, AZ
Brian Gracey, Knoxville, TN
Bernard J. Grad, Elberon, NJ
Bruce J. Graham, Hobe Sound, FL
Gary L. Graham, Boston, MA
Roy E. Graham, Washington, DC
Robert E. Gramann, Cincinnati, OH
Warren Wolf Gran, New York, NY
Charles P. Graves, Lexington, KY
Dean W. Graves, Kansas City, MO
Michael Graves, Princeton, NJ
Ann E. Gray, Los Angeles, CA
David Lawrence Gray, Santa Monica, CA
Thomas A. Gray, Little Rock, AR
Lyn E. Graziani, Miami, FL
Robert E. Greager, Pleasant Ridge, MI
Dennis W. Grebner, St. Paul, MN
Raymond D. Greco, Minneapolis, MN
Aaron G. Green, San Francisco, CA
Richard J. Green, Cambridge, MA
Thomas G. Green, Boston, MA
David B. Greenbaum, Washington, DC
Aubrey J. Greenberg, Chicago, IL
James A. Greene, Oviedo, FL
Sanford R. Greenfield, Westfield, NJ
Susan Greenwald, Chicago, IL
John O. Greer, Bryan, TX
Glenn H. Gregg, New Haven, CT
Nonya Grenader, Houston, TX
Raymond Grenald, Narberth, PA
James A. Gresham, Tucson, AZ
William C. Gridley, Washington, DC
L. Duane Grieve, Knoxville, TN
James R. Grieves, Baltimore, MD
Donald I. Grinberg, Boston, MA
Edward A. Grochowiak, San Diego, CA
Adam A. Gross, Baltimore, MD
Olindo Grossi, Manhasset, NY
William H. Grover, Centerbrook, CT
J. C. Grube, Portland, OR
Ernest A. Grunsfeld, Chicago, IL
Jordan L. Gruzen, New York, NY
John C. Guenther, St. Louis, MO
Francis A. Guffey II, Charleston, WV
Paul J. Gumbinger, San Mateo, CA
Graham Gund, Cambridge, MA
Brooks R. Gunsul, Portland, OR
Gerald Gurland, West Orange, NJ

Robert M. Gurney, Alexandria, VA
William R. Gustafson, Philadelphia, PA
Dean L. Gustavson, Salt Lake City, UT
Cabell Gwathmey, Harwood, MD
Charles Gwathmey, New York, NY
Willard E. Gwilliam, Hayes, VA

H

E. Keith Haag, Cuyahoga Falls, OH
Lester C. Haas, Shreveport, LA
Stanley A. Haas, Austin, TX
Wallace L. Haas Jr., Redding, CA
Thomas Owen Hacker, Portland, OR
Donald J. Hackl, Chicago, IL
John B. Hackler, Charlotte, NC
Stephen R. Hagan, Washington, DC
L.R. Hahnfeld, Fort Worth, TX
Frank S. Haines, Honolulu, HI
William H. Haire, Stillwater, OK
Imre Halasz, Boston, MA
Dennis J. Hall , Charlotte, NC
Gaines B. Hall, Downers Grove, IL
George Peyton Hall Jr., Hollywood, CA
Mark W. Hall, Toronto, ON
William A. Hall, New York, NY
Harry C. Hallenbeck, Sacramento, CA
Stanley I. Hallet, Washington, DC
Gerald Hallissy, Port Washington, NY
Anna M. Halpin, New York, NY
Frances Halsband, New York, NY
William Hamby, New York, NY
Robert L. Hamill Jr., Boise, ID
D.K. Hamilton, Bellaire, TX
E.G. Hamilton Jr., Dallas, TX
Robert P. Hammell, Arlington, VA
Theodore S. Hammer, New York, NY
Gerald S. Hammond, Cincinnati, OH
John Hyatt Hammond, Greensboro, NC
W. Easley Hamner, Cambridge, MA
Mark G. Hampton, Coconut Grove, FL
John Paul C. Hanbury, Norfolk, VA
Peter H. Hand, Atlanta, GA
J. Paul Hansen, Savannah, GA
Richard F. Hansen, Sanibel, FL
Robert E. Hansen, Hendersonville, NC
Alan M. Hantman, Washington, DC
Ernest H. Hara, Honolulu, HI
John M. Hara, Honolulu, HI
Dellas H. Harder, Columbus, OH
Paul A. Harding, Chicago, IL
Donald L. Hardison, El Cerrito, CA
Henry C. Hardnett, Seattle, WA
Hugh Hardy, New York, NY
John C. Harkness, Arlington, MA
Sarah P. Harkness, Lexington, MA

Frank Harmon, Raleigh, NC
Harry W. Harmon, Lake San Marcos, CA
John C. Haro, Scottsdale, AZ
Charles F. Harper, Wichita Falls, TX
David M. Harper, Coral Gables, FL
James W. Harrell, Cincinnati, OH
David A. Harris, Washington, DC
Edwin F. Harris Jr., Raleigh, NC
James Martin Harris, Tacoma, WA
Robert S. Harris, Los Angeles, CA
Robert V.M. Harrison, Jackson, MS
Roy P. Harrover, Memphis, TN
Craig W. Hartman, San Francisco, CA
Douglas C. Hartman, Dallas, TX
George E. Hartman, Washington, DC
Morton Hartman, Highland Park, IL
John F. Hartray Jr., Chicago, IL
Timothy Hartung, New York, NY
Wilbert R. Hasbrouck, Chicago, IL
Dennis E. Haskell, Seattle, WA
Albert L. Haskins Jr., Raleigh North, NC
Peter M. Hasselman, Orinda, CA
Sami Hassid, Pleasant Hill, CA
Herman A. Hassinger, Moorestown, NJ
George J. Hasslein, San Luis Obispo, CA
L. J. Hastings, Seattle, WA
Marvin Hatami, Denver, CO
Harold D. Hauf, Sun City, AZ
Robert O. Hausner, Santa Fe, NM
Daniel J. Havekost, Denver, CO
Perry A. Haviland, Oakland, CA
Velpeau E. Hawes Jr., Dallas, TX
H. Ralph Hawkins, Dallas, TX
Jasper Stillwell Hawkins, Phoenix, AZ
William J. Hawkins III, Portland, OR
William R. Hawley, E. Palo Alto, CA
Bruce A. Hawtin, Jackson, WY
Richard S. Hayden, New York, NY
J. F. Hayes, Cambridge, MA
John Freeman Hayes, Radnor, PA
Irving B. Haynes, Lincoln, RI
Edward H. Healey, Cedar Rapids, IA
Michael M. Hearn, San Francisco, CA
George T. Heery, Atlanta, GA
Clovis Heimsath, Austin, TX
Dan Heinfeld, Irvine, CA
Richard J. Heisenbottle, Coral Gables, FL
John Hejduk, Bronx, NY
Margaret Helfand, New York, NY
Barbara Heller, Washington, DC
Jeffrey Heller, San Francisco, CA
Maxwell Boone Hellmann, Cardiff
  by the Sea, CA
George F. Hellmuth, St. Louis, MO
A. C. Helman, Maitland, FL

Fellows of the American Institute of Architects

David P. Helpern, New York, NY
James C. Hemphill Jr., Charlotte, NC
Arn Henderson, Norman, OK
John D. Henderson, San Diego, CA
Philip C. Henderson, Dallas, TX
James L. Hendricks, Rockwall, TX
William R. Henry, Jackson, MS
Justin Henshell, Red Bank, NJ
Charles Herbert, Des Moines, IA
Robert G. Herman, San Francisco, CA
William W. Herrin, Huntsville, AL
Ricardo C. Herring, Washington, DC
Robert G. Hershberger, Tucson, AZ
Paul A. Hesson, San Antonio, TX
Charles R. Heuer, Charlottesville, VA
D. M. Hewitt, Seattle, WA
Warren Cummings Heylman, Spokane, WA
Mason S. Hicks, Fayetteville, NC
Charles C. Hight, Charlotte, NC
Dean F. Hilfinger, Bloomington, IL
Eric Hill, Detroit, MI
John W. Hill, Baltimore, MD
J. Robert Hillier, Princeton, NJ
Mark Hinshaw, Seattle, WA
Kem G. Hinton, Nashville, TN
Don M. Hisaka, Berkeley, CA
Jon D. Hlafter, Princeton, NJ
Gregory O. Hnedak, Memphis, TN
Paul S. Hoag, Bellevue, WA
Jack C. Hobbs, Boston, MA
Richard W. Hobbs, Washington, DC
Peter S. Hockaday, Seattle, WA
Murlin R. Hodgell, Norman, OK
Thomas H. Hodne, Minneapolis, MN
David C. Hoedemaker, Seattle, WA
August F. Hoenack, Bethesda, MD
David H. Hoffman, Evant, TX
David L. Hoffman, Wichita, KS
John J. Hoffmann, North Haven, CT
J. David Hoglund, Pittsburgh, PA
John A. Holabird, Chicago, IL
L. M. Holder, Austin, TX
Major L. Holland, Tuskegee, AL
Dwight E. Holmes, Tampa, FL
Jess Holmes, Henderson, NV
Nicholas H. Holmes Jr., Mobile, AL
Harry J. Holroyd, Columbus, OH
David A. Holtz, Potomac, MD
Michael J. Holtz, Boulder, CO
Malcolm Holzman, New York, NY
George W. Homsey, San Francisco, CA
Bobbie S. Hood, San Francisco, CA
Van D. Hooker, Albuquerque, NM
G. N. Hoover, Houston, TX
George Hoover, Denver, CO

Ray C. Hoover III, Atlanta, GA
Frank L. Hope Jr., San Diego, CA
Eugene Hopkins, Detroit, MI
Edward M. Hord, Baltimore, MD
Howard N. Horii, Newark, NJ
Gerald Horn, Chicago, IL
Mark Hornberger, San Francisco, CA
Patrick Horsbrugh, South Bend, IN
T. Horty, Minneapolis, MN
Reginald D. Hough, Larchmont, NY
Marvin C. Housworth, Atlanta, GA
David C. Hovey, Winnetka, IL
J. Murray Howard, Charlottesville, VA
John Howey, Tampa, FL
Thomas S. Howorth, Oxford, MS
Charles K. Hoyt, Old Lyme, CT
Michael M. Hricak Jr., Venice, CA
Robert Y. Hsiung, Boston, MA
Charles A. Hubbard, Cortez, CO
Jeffrey A. Huberman, Charlotte, NC
Daniel Huberty, Seattle, WA
Richard W. Huffman, Philadelphia, PA
Stanford Hughes, San Francisco, CA
Stephan S. Huh, Minneapolis, MN
Robert E. Hull, Seattle, WA
Charles F. Hummel, Boise, ID
Fred E. Hummel, Sacramento, CA
Harry J. Hunderman, Northbrook, IL
Gregory Hunt, Washington, DC
Walter A. Hunt Jr., New York, NY
Frances P. Huppert, New York, NY
Sam T. Hurst, Montecito, CA
Syed V. Husain, Kensington, CA
Mary Alice Hutchins, Portland, OR
Remmert W. Huygens, Wayland, MA
Fred J. Hynek, Parker, CO

I

Dean Illingworth, Indianapolis, IN
Nestor I. Infanzon, Dallas, TX
Elizabeth W. Ingraham, Colorado
  Springs, CO
William A. Isley, Bainbridge Island, WA
H. Curtis Ittner, St. Louis, MO
Robert A. Ivy Jr., New York, NY

J

Huson Jackson, Lexington, MA
Mike Jackson, Springfield, IL
R. G. Jackson, Houston, TX
Ralph T. Jackson, Boston, MA
Bernard Jacob, Minneapolis, MN
Harry M. Jacobs, Oakland, CA
Stephen B. Jacobs, New York, NY
Hugh N. Jacobsen, Washington, DC

Phillip L. Jacobson, Seattle, WA
J. P. Jacoby, Menomonee Falls, WI
Helmut Jahn, Chicago, IL
James C. Jankowski, Chicago, IL
Vincent James, Minneapolis, MN
Timm Jamieson, Roanoke, VA
William R. Jarratt, Ann Arbor, MI
Lloyd Jary, San Antonio, TX
Peter Jefferson, Highlands, NC
Jordan O. Jelks, Macon, GA
J. J. Jennewein, Tampa, FL
Richard W. Jennings, Austin, TX
Bruce H. Jensen, Salt Lake City, UT
David Jepson, Hartford, CT
Jon Adams Jerde, Venice, CA
John W. Jickling, Birmingham, MI
John M. Johansen, New York, NY
Anthony N. Johns Jr., Mt. Irvine,
  Trinidad and Tobago
Arthur D. Johnson, Omaha, NE
Danie Johnson, Asheville, NC
Edwin J. Johnson, Dallas, TX
Eric B. Johnson, Savannah, GA
Floyd E. Johnson, Scottsville, VA
James H. Johnson, Denver, CO
Jed V. Johnson, Wappingers Falls, NY
Mark Robert Johnson, Valley Forge, PA
Marvin R. Johnson, Raleigh, NC
Philip C. Johnson, New York, NY
Phillip Craig Johnson, Chicago, IL
Ralph E. Johnson, Chicago, IL
Scott Johnson, Los Angeles, CA
Walker C. Johnson, Chicago, IL
Yandell Johnson, Little Rock, AR
Norman J. Johnston, Seattle, WA
James O. Jonassen, Seattle, WA
Arthur E. Jones, Houston, TX
Bernard I. Jones, Carbondale, IL
J. Delaine Jones, Troy, NY
Jack B. Jones, Tamuning, Guam
Johnpaul Jones, Seattle, WA
Paul Duane Jones, Kailua, HI
Renis Jones, Montgomery, AL
Robert Lawton Jones, Tulsa, OK
Rudard Artaban Jones, Urbana, IL
Bendrew G. Jong, Orinda, CA
Joe J. Jordan, Philadelphia, PA
David A. Jordani, Minneapolis, MN
Roberta W. Jorgensen, Irvine, CA
Wendy Evans Joseph, New York, NY
Henri V. Jova, Atlanta, GA
Bruce D. Judd, San Francisco, CA
Yu Sing Jung, Boston, MA
Howard H. Juster, San Diego, CA

Fellows of the American Institute of Architects

K

Carl F. Kaelber Jr., Pittsford, NY
Richard E. Kaeyer, Mt. Kisco, NY
Gerald Kagan, New Haven, CT
David T. Kahler, Milwaukee, WI
Charles H. Kahn, Chapel Hill, NC
Eino O. Kainlauri, Ames, IA
Harry Kale, Conshohocken, PA
Mark Kalin, Newton Center, MA
G. M. Kallmann, Boston, MA
Stephen H. Kanner, Los Angeles, CA
Gary Y. Kaplan, Red Bank, NJ
Richard H. Kaplan, Cleveland, OH
Raymond L. Kappe, Pacific Palisades, CA
Bill Karst, Seattle, WA
Raymond John Kaskey, Washington, DC
Herbert A. Katz, Los Angeles, CA
Kirby M. Keahey, Houston, TX
Gustave R. Keane, Bradenton, FL
Jan Keane, New York, NY
Richard C. Keating, Marina Del Rey, CA
Allan Kehrt, Princeton, NJ
Douglas S. Kelbaugh, Ann Arbor, MI
Duane A. Kell, St. Paul, MN
John H. Kell, San Antonio, TX
Bernard Kellenyi, Red Bank, NJ
Larry J. Keller, Fairfax, VA
Emanuel Kelly, Philadelphia, PA
Frank S. Kelly, Houston, TX
Kevin A. Kelly, Houston, TX
F. L. Kelsey, Scottsdale, AZ
Diane Legge Kemp, Chicago, IL
William D. Kendall, Houston, TX
Robert N. Kennedy, Indianapolis, IN
Gertrude L. Kerbis, Chicago, IL
Thomas L. Kerns, Arlington, VA
Herbert A. Ketcham, Minneapolis, MN
Russell V. Keune, Arlington, VA
A.H. Keyes Jr., Washington, DC
James T. Kienle, Indianapolis, IN
Stephen J. Kieran, Philadelphia, PA
Leevi Kiil, New York, NY
Lee F. Kilbourn, Portland, OR
James R. Killebrew, Grapevine, TX
Tai Soo Kim, Hartford, CT
Jong S. Kimm, Seoul, South Korea
J. Windom Kimsey, Las Vegas, NV
David R. H. King, Washington, DC
Dennis M. King, Huntington Woods, MI
Donald King, Seattle, WA
Gordon L. King, Sacramento, CA
J. Bertram King, Asheville, NC
Sol King, Palm Beach, FL
M. Ray Kingston, Salt Lake City, UT
Judith Kinnard, Charlottesville, VA

Paul Kinnison Jr., San Antonio, TX
Ballard H. Kirk, Columbus, OH
D. W. Kirk Jr., Fort Worth, TX
Stephen J. Kirk, Grosse Pointe Park, MI
John M. Kirksey, Houston, TX
Peyton E. Kirven, Westlake Village, CA
Robert S. Kitchen, Ocean Hills, CA
William L. Kite Jr., Providence, RI
Henry Klein, Mount Vernon, WA
J. Arvid Klein, New York, NY
Robert M. Kliment, New York, NY
Stephen A. Kliment, New York, NY
Kenneth F. Klindtworth, Duck Key, FL
Lee B. Kline, Los Angeles, CA
Vincent G. Kling, Chester Springs, PA
Brian R. Klipp, Denver, CO
James F. Knight, Gunnison, CO
Roy F. Knight, Tallahassee, FL
William H. Knight, Santa Rosa, CA
Stuart Knoop, Chevy Chase, MD
Charles M. Kober, Long Beach, CA
Carl Koch, Cambridge, MA
Steven Y. Kodama, San Francisco, CA
Edward J. Kodet Jr., Minneapolis, MN
Alfred H. Koetter, Boston, MA
A. Eugene Kohn, New York, NY
Keith R. Kolb, Seattle, WA
Nathaniel K. Kolb Jr., Dallas, TX
Ronald Kolman, Savannah, GA
S. Richard Komatsu, El Cerrito, CA
Hendrik Koning, Santa Monica, CA
Norman L. Koonce, McLean, VA
James F. Kortan, Atlanta, GA
Panos G. Koulermos, La Crescenta, CA
Alexander Kouzmanoff, Rye Brook, NY
Gerhardt Kramer, Webster Groves, MO
Robert Kramer, Brookline, MA
Peter Krasnow, New York City, NY
M. Stanley Krause Jr., Newport News, VA
William Henry Kreager, Seattle, WA
Eugene Kremer, Manhattan, KS
J. Richard Kremer, Louisville, KY
Jerrily R. Kress, Washington, DC
John L. Kriken, San Francisco, CA
Robert N. Kronewitter, Denver, CO
Kenneth C. Kruger, Santa Barbara, CA
James O. Kruhly, Philadelphia, PA
Rod Kruse, Des Moines, IA
Denis G. Kuhn, New York, NY
Julian E. Kulski, Orlean, VA
Ernest J. Kump, Zurich, Switzerland
Moritz Kundig, Spokane, WA
Thomas Kundig, Seattle, WA
Theodore E. Kurz, Cleveland, OH
Peter Kuttner, Cambridge, MA

Sylvia P. Kwan, San Francisco, CA
Michael Kwartler, New York, NY

L

David N. LaBau, Bloomfield, CT
Ronald J. Labinski, Kansas City, MO
John W. Lackens Jr., Minneapolis, MN
Bill N. Lacy, Purchase, NY
Thomas Laging, Lincoln, NE
Henry J. Lagorio, Orinda, CA
Jerry Laiserin, Woodbury, NY
David C. Lake, San Antonio, TX
Charles E. Lamb, Annapolis, MD
James Lambeth, Fayetteville, AR
James I. Lammers, Chisago City, MN
Patricia Lancaster-Brown, New York, NY
Gregory W. Landahl, Chicago, IL
Peter H. Landon, Chicago, IL
D. E. Landry, Dallas, TX
Jane Landry, Dallas, TX
John M. Laping, West Amherst, NY
Arnold Les Larsen, Port Salerno, FL
Robert G. Larsen, New York City, NY
Dayl A. Larson, Denver, CO
William L. Larson, Omaha, NE
William N. Larson, Park Ridge, IL
C. James Lawler, West Hartford, CT
Charles E. Lawrence, Houston, TX
Jerry Lawrence, Tacoma, WA
Robert M. Lawrence, Oklahoma City, OK
David E. Lawson, Madison, WI
Elizabeth Lawson, Charlottesville, VA
William R. Lawson, Reston, VA
Franklin D. Lawyer, Houston, TX
William E. Leddy, San Francisco, CA
James P. Leggitt, Denver, CO
Robert LeMond, Fort Worth, TX
Glen S. LeRoy, Kansas City, MO
Angie Lee, Chicago, IL
Benjamin B. Lee, Honolulu, HI
Donald R. Lee, Charlotte, NC
Elizabeth B. Lee, Lumberton, NC
John Lee, New York, NY
Laura A. Lee, Pittsburgh, PA
M. David Lee, Boston, MA
Gene Leedy, Winter Haven, FL
James M. Leefe, Sausalito, CA
Andrea P. Leers, Boston, MA
Gillet Lefferts, Darien, CT
Michael B. Lehrer, Los Angeles, CA
Spencer A. Leineweber, Honolulu, HI
Lawrence J. Leis, Louisville, KY
Richard Leitch, South Laguna, CA
Herbert Lembcke, San Francisco, CA
James T. Lendrum, Phoenix, AZ

225

Fellows of the American Institute of Architects

Peter A. Lendrum, Phoenix, AZ
Jill N. Lerner, New York, NY
Ralph Lerner, Princeton, NJ
Nicholas Lesko, Cleveland, OH
Francis D. Lethbridge, Nantucket, MA
Conrad Levenson, New York, NY
Jonathan Levi, Boston, MA
Brenda A. Levin, Los Angeles, CA
Richard D. Levin, Longboat Key, FL
Alan G. Levy, Philadelphia, PA
Eugene P. Levy, Little Rock, AR
Herbert W. Levy, Spring House, PA
Max Levy, Dallas, TX
Morton L. Levy, Houston, TX
Toby S. Levy, San Francisco, CA
Anne McCutcheon Lewis, Washington, DC
Calvin F. Lewis, Des Moines, IA
David Lewis, Homestead, PA
George B. Lewis, Oklahoma City, OK
Howarth Lewis Jr., West Palm Beach, FL
Richard L. Lewis, Pebble Beach, CA
Roger K. Lewis, Washington, DC
Tom Lewis Jr., Kissimmee, FL
Walter H. Lewis, Champaign, IL
Merlin Lickhalter, Jacksonville, FL
Alan C. Liddle, Lakewood, WA
Frederick Liebhardt, La Jolla, CA
Theodore Liebman, New York, NY
Bernard J. Liff, Pittsburgh, PA
John H. Lind, Iowa City, IA
Winford Lindsay, Dacula, GA
David Lindsey, Seattle, WA
Gail A. Lindsey, Wake Forest, NC
Charles D. Linn, New York, NY
H. Mather Lippincott Jr., Moylan, PA
William H. Liskamm, San Rafael, CA
Robert A. Little, Cleveland, OH
Robert S. Livesey, Columbus, OH
Stanley C. Livingston, San Diego, CA
Thomas W. Livingston, Anchorage, AK
Walter R. Livingston Jr., Crum Lynne, PA
Peter Lizon, Knoxville, TN
W. Kirby Lockard, Tucson, AZ
James L. Loftis, Oklahoma City, OK
Vivian Loftness, Pittsburgh, PA
Donn Logan, Berkeley, CA
Dirk Lohan, Chicago, IL
Thomas E. Lollini, Berkeley, CA
Jerrold E. Lomax, Carmel Valley, CA
David W. Look, San Francisco, CA
J. Carson Looney, Memphis, TN
R. Nicholas Loope, Phoenix, AZ
Gabor Lorant, Phoenix, AZ
Larry Lord, Atlanta, GA
George H. Loschky, Seattle, WA

John C. Loss, Whitehall, MI
Rex Lotery, Montecito, CA
Avram Lothan, Chicago, IL
William C. Louie, New York, NY
William Love, Los Angeles, CA
Ivenue Love-Stanley, Atlanta, GA
Robert D. Loversidge Jr., Columbus, OH
Wendell H. Lovett, Seattle, WA
Frank E. Lucas, Charleston, SC
Thomas J. Lucas, Southfield, MI
Lenore M. Lucey, Washington, DC
Carl F. Luckenbach, Ann Arbor, MI
Lucinda Ludwig, Omaha, NE
Graham B. Luhn, Houston, TX
Anthony J. Lumsden, Los Angeles, CA
Frithjof Lunde, Center Valley, PA
Phillip Lundwall, Grand Rapids, MI
Victor A. Lundy, Bellaire, TX
Donald H. Lutes, Springfield, OR
Frederic P. Lyman, Sebeka, MN
Robert Dale Lynch, Pittsburgh, PA
Robert J. Lynch, Scottsdale, AZ
Donlyn Lyndon, Berkeley, CA
Maynard Lyndon, Kuessaberg, Germany

M

R. Doss Mabe, Los Angeles, CA
John E. MacAllister, San Francisco, CA
Donald MacDonald, San Francisco, CA
Virginia B. MacDonald, Kaneohe, HI
H. A. MacEwen, Tampa, FL
Ian MacKinlay, San Francisco, CA
Charles H. MacMahon, Deland, FL
Robert C. Mack, Minneapolis, MN
Eugene J. Mackey III, St. Louis, MO
John Macsai, Chicago, IL
Robert P. Madison, Cleveland, OH
Peter E. Madsen, Boston, MA
Theodore S. Maffitt Jr., Palestine, TX
Henry J. Magaziner, Philadelphia, PA
Gary Mahaffey, Minneapolis, MN
Victor C. Mahler, New York, NY
John E. Mahlum, Seattle, WA
C. R. Maiwald, Wilmington, NC
Marvin J. Malecha, Raleigh, NC
Stephanie Mallis, New York, NY
L. Vic Maloof, Atlanta, GA
Paul D. Mankins, Des Moines, IA
Arthur E. Mann, Irvine, CA
Michael Mann, Los Angeles, CA
Carter H. Manny Jr., Chicago, IL
Clark D. Manus, San Francisco, CA
Virginia S. March, Fairhope, AL
Roger W. Margerum, Detroit, MI
Phillip T. Markwood, Columbus, OH

Harvey V. Marmon Jr., San Antonio, TX
Jud R. Marquardt, Seattle, WA
Clinton Marr Jr., Riverside, CA
Mortimer M. Marshall Jr., Reston, VA
Richard C. Marshall, San Francisco, CA
Albert C. Martin, Los Angeles, CA
Christopher C. Martin, Los Angeles, CA
David C. Martin, Los Angeles, CA
Robert E. Martin, Toledo, OH
W. Mike Martin, Berkeley, CA
Walter B. Martinez, Miami, FL
Thomas S. Marvel, San Juan, Puerto Rico
Joseph V. Marzella, Wallingford, PA
Ronald L. Mason, Denver, CO
Thomas R. Mathison, Grand Rapids, MI
George Matsumoto, Oakland, CA
Charles Matta, Arlington, VA
Edward H. Matthei, Chicago, IL
Robert F. Mattox, Boston, MA
Frank J. Matzke, St. Augustine, FL
John M. Maudlin-Jeronimo, Bethesda, MD
Laurie M. Maurer, Brooklyn, NY
Susan A. Maxman, Philadelphia, PA
Murvan M. Maxwell, Metairie, LA
Arthur May, New York, NY
Kenneth D. Maynard, Anchorage, AK
Thom Mayne, Santa Monica, CA
Marsha Maytum, San Francisco, CA
Charles F. McAfee, Wichita, KS
Cheryl Lynn McAfee-Mitchell, Atlanta, GA
Charles McCafferty, Saint Clair Shores, MI
E. K. McCagg II, Kirkland, WA
Joe M. McCall, Dallas, TX
Ann K. McCallum, Williamstown, MA
John McCartney, Washington, DC
Bruce McCarty, Knoxville, TN
Wesley A. McClure, Raleigh, NC
Richard E. McCommons,
   Falls Church, VA
Robert E. McConnell, Tucson, AZ
Edward D. McCrary, Hillsborough, CA
M. Allen McCree, Austin, TX
Gerald M. McCue, Cambridge, MA
Grant G. McCullagh, Chicago, IL
James McCullar, New York, NY
Margaret McCurry, Chicago, IL
William A. McDonough,
   Charlottesville, VA
Stephen A. McDowell, Kansas City, MO
Connie S. McFarland, Tulsa, OK
A. S. McGaughan, Washington, DC
John M. McGinty, Houston, TX
Milton B. McGinty, Houston, TX
Richard A. McGinty, Hilton
   Head Island, SC

Fellows of the American Institute of Architects

John W. McGough, Spokane, WA
John Paul McGowan, Potomac, MD
James R. McGranahan, Lacey, WA
H. Thomas McGrath Jr., Frederick, MD
Mark McInturff, Bethesda, MD
Herbert P. McKim, Wrightsville Beach, NC
David A. McKinley, Seattle, WA
Noel M. McKinnell, Boston, MA
Thomas L. McKittrick, College Station, TX
H. Roll McLaughlin, Carmel, IN
C. Andrew McLean II, Atlanta, GA
James M. McManus, Glastonbury, CT
George A. McMath, Portland, OR
William G. McMinn, Coconut Grove, FL
E. Eean McNaughton Jr., New Orleans, LA
Carrell S. McNulty Jr., Cincinnati, OH
E. Keith McPheeters, Auburn, AL
John M. McRae, Starkville, MS
Charles B. McReynolds, Newport News, VA
Franklin Mead, Boston, MA
George C. Means Jr., Clemson, SC
David Meckel, San Francisco, CA
Henry G. Meier, Fishers, IN
Richard A. Meier, New York, NY
Carl R. Meinhardt, New York, NY
Roger C. Mellem, Port Republic, MD
R. A. Melting, New York, NY
Mark R. Mendell, Boston, MA
Mike Mense, Anchorage, AK
Francois de Menil, New York, NY
John O. Merrill, Tiburon, CA
William Dickey Merrill, Carmel, CA
James R. Merritt, Tacoma, WA
David R. Messersmith, Lubbock, TX
Robert C. Metcalf, Ann Arbor, MI
William H. Metcalf, McLean, VA
Andrew Metter, Evanston, IL
David Metzger, Washington, DC
C. Richard Meyer, Seattle, WA
Carl F. Meyer, El Segundo, CA
James H. Meyer, Richardson, TX
John T. Meyer, Saginaw, MI
Kurt W. Meyer, Los Angeles, CA
Richard C. Meyer, Philadelphia, PA
Marshall D. Meyers, Pasadena, CA
Nancy A. Miao, New York, NY
Linda H. Michael, Charlottesville, VA
Constantine E. Michaelides, St. Louis, MO
Valerius Leo Michelson, Minneapolis, MN
Andres Mignucci, San Juan, PR
Robert Miklos, Boston, MA
Arnold Mikon, Detroit, MI
Juanita M. Mildenberg, Bethesda, MD
Don C. Miles, Seattle, WA
Daniel R. Millen Jr., Cherry Hill, NJ

David E. Miller, Seattle, WA
Ewing H. Miller, Port Republic, MD
George H. Miller, New York, NY
Henry F. Miller, Orange, CT
Hugh C. Miller, Richmond, VA
James W. Miller, Madison, WI
John F. Miller, Cambridge, MA
Joseph Miller, Washington, DC
L. Kirk Miller, San Francisco, CA
Leroy B. Miller, Santa Monica, CA
Richard Miller, Nashville, TN
Robert L. Miller, Washington, DC
Steven Miller, Prague, Czechoslovakia
William C. Miller, Salt Lake City, UT
Edward I. Mills, New York, NY
Gordon E. Mills, Dubuque, IA
Michael Mills, Glen Ridge, NJ
Willis N. Mills Jr., Ponte Vedra Beach, FL
John D. Milner, Chadds Ford, PA
Lee Mindel, New York, NY
Adolfo E. Miralles, Altadena, CA
Henry D. Mirick, Fairless Hills, PA
Dan S. Mitchell, St. Louis, MO
Ehrman B. Mitchell Jr., Philadelphia, PA
Melvin L. Mitchell, Baltimore, MD
Richard R. Moger, Port Washington, NY
Ronald L. Moline, Bourbonnais, IL
Robert B. Molseed, Annandale, VA
Lynn H. Molzan, Indianapolis, IN
Frank Montana, Dade City, FL
Joseph D. Monticciolo, Woodbury, NY
Curtis J. Moody, Columbus, OH
Thomas B. Moon, Rancho
    Santa Margarita, CA
Arthur C. Moore, Washington, DC
Barry M. Moore, Houston, TX
Gerald L. Moorehead, Houston, TX
Jill K. Morelli, Columbus, OH
Jesse O. Morgan Jr., Shreveport, LA
Robert Lee Morgan, Port Townsend, WA
William N. Morgan, Jacksonville, FL
Howard H. Morgridge, Newport Beach, CA
Toshiko Mori, New York, NY
Lamberto G. Moris, San Francisco, CA
Seth I. Morris, Houston, TX
Lionel Morrison, Dallas, TX
Murdo D. Morrison, Redwood City, CA
John Morse, Seattle, WA
James R. Morter, Vail, CO
Allen D. Moses, Kirkland, WA
Robert Mosher, La Jolla, CA
Samuel Z. Moskowitz, Naples, FL
Eric O. Moss, Culver City, CA
G. Michael Mostoller, Princeton, NJ
Kenneth L. Motley, Roanoke, VA

John K. Mott, Alexandria, VA
Frederic D. Moyer, Northbrook, IL
Frank R. Mudano, Clearwater, FL
Theodore Mularz, Ashland, OR
Paul Muldawer, Atlanta, GA
Dale Mulfinger, Excelsior, MN
John W. Mullen III, Dallas, TX
Rosemary F. Muller, Oakland, CA
Harold C. Munger, Toledo, OH
Frank W. Munzer, Clinton Corners, NY
Charles F. Murphy, Mesa, AZ
Elizabeth Corbin Murphy, Akron, OH
Frank N. Murphy, Clayton, MO
David G. Murray, Tulsa, OK
Stephen A. Muse, Washington, DC
Robert C. Mutchler, Fargo, ND
John V. Mutlow, Los Angeles, CA
Donald B. Myer, Washington, DC
John R. Myer, Tamworth, NH
Barton Myers, Beverly Hills, CA
Hyman Myers, Philadelphia, PA
Ralph E. Myers, Prairie Village, KS

N ——————

Daniel J. Nacht, Fair Oaks, CA
Barbara Nadel, Forest Hills, NY
Herbert N. Nadel, Los Angeles, CA
Chester Emil Nagel, Colorado Springs, CO
James L. Nagle, Chicago, IL
Louis Naidorf, Burbank, CA
Noboru Nakamura, Orinda, CA
C. S. Nakata, Colorado Springs, CO
Daniel H. Nall, Princeton, NJ
Robert J. Nash, Oxon Hill, MD
Eric Christopher Naslund, San Diego, CA
Thomas M. Nathan, Memphis, TN
Kenneth H. Natkin Esq., San Francisco, CA
James A. Neal, Greenville, SC
Paul R. Neel, San Luis Obispo, CA
Ibsen Nelsen, Vashon, WA
Edward H. Nelson, Tucson, AZ
James Richard Nelson, Wilmington, DE
John H. Nelson, Chicago, IL
T. C. Nelson, Kansas City, MO
Ede I. Nemeti, Houston, TX
Marilys R. Nepomechie, Miami, FL
Donald E. Neptune, Newport Beach, CA
John F. Nesholm, Seattle, WA
Barbara Neski, New York, NY
Walter A. Netsch, Chicago, IL
Perry King Neubauer, Cambridge, MA
Kurt Neubek, Houston, TX
Roger L. Neuenschwander, Atlanta, GA
J. Victor Neuhaus III, Hunt, TX
William O. Neuhaus III, Houston, TX

Fellows of the American Institute of Architects

David J. Neuman, Palo Alto, CA
Hans Neumann, Las Vegas, NV
S. Kenneth Neumann, Beverly Hills, MI
Peter Newlin, Chestertown, MD
Herbert S. Newman, New Haven, CT
Michael Newman, Winston-Salem, NC
Robert L. Newsom, Los Angeles, CA
Chartier C. Newton, Austin, TX
Doreve Nicholaeff, Osterville, MA
Karen V. Nichols, Princeton, NJ
Michael H. Nicklas, Raleigh, NC
Robert Duncan Nicol, Oakland, CA
George Z. Nikolajevich, St. Louis, MO
Edward R. Niles, Malibu, CA
Christopher G. Nims, Denver, CO
Ivey L. Nix, Atlanta, GA
Robert J. Nixon, Port Angeles, WA
Dan H. Noble, Dallas, TX
Douglas Noble, Los Angeles, CA
George M. Notter Jr., Washington, DC
John M. Novack, Dallas, TX
Frederick Noyes, Boston, MA
Jimmie R. Nunn, Flagstaff, AZ
John Nyfeler, Austin, TX

O

James W. O'Brien, Minneapolis, MN
W. L. O'Brien Jr., Research
   Triangle Park, NC
Thomas O'Connor, Detroit, MI
L. J. O'Donnell, Chicago, IL
Arthur F. O'Leary, County Louth, Ireland
Paul Murff O'Neal Jr., Shreveport, LA
Charles W. Oakley, Pacific Palisades, CA
Gyo Obata, St. Louis, MO
Jeffrey K. Ochsner, Seattle, WA
Francis S. Oda, Honolulu, HI
Robert A. Odermatt, Berkeley, CA
Mary L. Oehrlein, Washington, DC
Rodney O'Hiser, Portland, PA
Rolf H. Ohlhausen, New York, NY
Richard M. Olcott, New York, NY
Edward A. Oldziey, Wyckoff, NJ
P. S. Oles, Newton, MA
H. B. Olin, Chicago, IL
Donald E. Olsen, Berkeley, CA
Carole J. Olshavsky, Columbus, OH
James W. Olson, Seattle, WA
Sheri Olson, Seattle, WA
Edmund W. Ong, San Francisco, CA
Herbert B. Oppenheimer, New York, NY
Joseph K. Oppermann, Winston-Salem, NC
Edward L. Oremen, San Diego, CA
Robert E. Oringdulph, Portland, OR
Wendy Ornelas, Manhattan, KS

Gordon D. Orr Jr., Madison, WI
Diane R.K. Osan, Houston, TX
David William Osler, Ann Arbor, MI
G. F. Ouedens, Chevy Chase, MD
Raymond C. Ovresat, Wilmette, IL
Kenneth Owens Jr., Birmingham, AL

P

C. J. Paderewski III, San Diego, CA
Elizabeth Seward Padjen, Marblehead, MA
Gregory Palermo, Des Moines, IA
Zoltan E. Pali, Los Angeles, CA
Joshua J. Pan, Taipei, Taiwan
Solomon Pan, Tucson, AZ
Lester C. Pancoast, Miami, FL
John R. Pangrazio, Seattle, WA
Donald H. Panushka, Salt Lake City, UT
Dennis A. Paoletti, San Francisco, CA
Tician Papachristou, New York, NY
Laszlo Papp, New Canaan, CT
George C. Pappageorge, Chicago, IL
Constantine George Pappas, Troy, MI
Nicholas A. Pappas, Richmond, VA
Ted P. Pappas, Jacksonville, FL
Charles J. Parise, Grosse Pointe Woods, MI
Ki Suh Park, Los Angeles, CA
Sharon C. Park, Arlington, VA
Alfred B. Parker, Gainesville, FL
Derek Parker, San Francisco, CA
Howard C. Parker, Dallas, TX
Leonard S. Parker, Minneapolis, MN
R. C. Parrott, Knoxville, TN
Steven A. Parshall, Houston, TX
Giovanni Pasanella, New York, NY
C. H. Paseur, Houston, TX
Joseph Passonneau, Washington, DC
Piero Patri, San Francisco, CA
Allen L. Patrick, Columbus, OH
S. Glen Paulsen, Ann Arbor, MI
Sherida Elizabeth Paulsen, New York, NY
Charles Harrison Pawley, Coral Gables, FL
Thomas M. Payette, Boston, MA
H. Morse Payne, Lincoln, MA
Richard W. Payne, Houston, TX
John Pearce, Durham, NC
Bryce Pearsall, Phoenix, AZ
Charles Almond Pearson Jr., Arlington, VA
Clarence W. Pearson Jr., Washington, DC
J. Norman Pease Jr., Charlotte, NC
John G. Pecsok, Indianapolis, IN
William Pedersen Jr., New York, NY
Katherine N. Peele, Raleigh, NC
Gerard W. Peer, Charlotte, NC
William R. Peery, Clearwater, FL
I. M. Pei, New York, NY

Maris Peika, Toluca Lake, CA
Norbert A. Peiker, Mansfield, OH
John W. Peirce, Topsfield, MA
Cesar Pelli, New Haven, CT
William M. Pena, Houston, TX
Thompson E. Penney, Charleston, SC
David L. Perkins, Lafayette, LA
L. Bradford Perkins, New York, NY
John Gray Perry, Portland, OR
Norman K. Perttula, Aurora, OH
Stuart K. Pertz, New York, NY
Robert W. Peters, Albuquerque, NM
Carolyn S. Peterson, San Antonio, TX
Guy W. Peterson, Sarasota, FL
Jesse Julius Peterson Jr., Wilmington, NC
Leonard A. Peterson, Chicago, IL
Randal L. Peterson, San Diego, CA
David Petta, Berkeley, CA
Jay S. Pettitt Jr., Beulah, MI
Mark A. Pfaller, Elm Grove, WI
Norman Pfeiffer, Los Angeles, CA
Peter L. Pfeiffer, Austin, TX
J. D. Pfluger, Austin, TX
Barton Phelps, Los Angeles, CA
Frederick F. Phillips, Chicago, IL
W. Irving Phillips Jr., Houston, TX
J. Almont Pierce, Falls Church, VA
John Allen Pierce, Dallas, TX
Walter S. Pierce, Lexington, WA
Raymond A. Pigozzi, Evanston, IL
George J. Pillorge, Oxford, MD
Robert J. Piper, Winnetka, IL
Carl W. Pirscher, Windsor, Canada
John W. Pitman, Santa Barbara, CA
Peter A. Piven, Philadelphia, PA
Elizabeth Plater-Zyberk, Miami, FL
Charles A. Platt, New York, NY
Kalvin J. Platt, Sausalito, CA
G. Gray Plosser Jr., Birmingham, AL
Jan Hird Pokorny, New York, NY
Lee A. Polisano, London, England
William M. Polk, Seattle, WA
Richard N. Pollack, San Francisco, CA
Wilson Pollock, Cambridge, MA
James Stewart Polshek, New York, NY
Donald P. Polsky, Omaha, NE
Ralph Pomerance, New York, NY
Leason F. Pomeroy, III, Santa Ana, CA
Lee H. Pomeroy, New York, NY
Lynn S. Pomeroy, Sacramento, CA
Gerrard S. Pook, Bronx, NY
Samuel D. Popkin, West Bloomfield, MI
William L. Porter, Cambridge, MA
John C. Portman Jr., Atlanta, GA
Penny H. Posedly, Phoenix, AZ

Fellows of the American Institute of Architects

Raymond G. Post Jr., Baton Rouge, LA
Louis R. Pounders, Memphis, TN
Boone Powell, San Antonio, TX
Peter Pran, Seattle, WA
James Pratt, Dallas, TX
Antoine Predock, Albuquerque, NM
Andy Pressman, Albuquerque, NM
Barbara Milan Price, Charlotte, NC
William T. Priestley, Lake Forest, IL
Michael L. Prifti, Philadelphia, PA
Kathryn Tyler Prigmore, Washington, DC
Arnold J. Prima Jr., Washington, DC
Harold E. Prinz, Dallas, TX
Theodore H.M. Prudon, New York, NY
Carroll Lee Pruitt, Keller, TX
Homer L. Puderbaugh, Lincoln, NE
David A. Pugh, Portland, OR
William L. Pulgram, Atlanta, GA
James G. Pulliam, Pasadena, CA
Joe T. Pursell, Jackson, MS
Michael Pyatok, Oakland, CA

Q

G. William Quatman, Kansas City, MO
Jerry L. Quebe, Chicago, IL
Robert W. Quigley, San Diego, CA
Marcel Quimby, Dallas, TX
Michael L. Quinn, Washington, DC
Richard W. Quinn, Avon, CT

R

Martin D. Raab, New York, NY
Bruce A. Race, Berkeley, CA
John A. Raeber, San Francisco, CA
Craig E. Rafferty, St. Paul, MN
George E. Rafferty, St. Paul, MN
Richard J. Rafferty, St. Paul, MN
Lemuel Ramos, Miami, FL
Linda M. Ramsay, Savannah, GA
Peter A. Rand, Minneapolis, MN
Terry Rankine, Cambridge, MA
Raymond R. Rapp, Galveston, TX
Ralph Rapson, Minneapolis, MN
Howard Terry Rasco, Little Rock, AR
Peter T. Rasmussen, Tacoma, WA
John K. Rauch Jr., Philadelphia, PA
John G. Rauma, Minneapolis, MN
William L. Rawn, Boston, MA
James T. Ream, San Francisco, CA
Suzane Reatig, Kensington, MD
Mark Reddington, Seattle, WA
Charles Redmon, Cambridge, MA
Daniel A. Redstone, Southfield, MI
Ronald Reed, Cleveland, OH
Vernon Reed, Liberty, MO

William R. Reed, Tacoma, WA
Henry S. Reeder Jr., Cambridge, MA
Frank Blair Reeves, Gainesville, FL
I.S.K. Reeves V, Winter Park, FL
Roscoe Reeves Jr., Chevy Chase, MD
Victor A. Regnier, Los Angeles, CA
Patrick C. Rehse, Phoenix, AZ
Pierce K. Reibsamen, Los Angeles, CA
Jerry Reich, Chicago, IL
Johnstone Reid Jr., Orlando, FL
Leonard H. Reinke, Oshkosh, WI
Stephan Reinke, London, UK
Ilmar Reinvald, Tacoma, WA
John Rex, Carpinteria, CA
John S. Reynolds, Eugene, OR
M. Garland Reynolds Jr., Gainesville, GA
David A. Rhodes, Memphis, TN
James W. Rhodes, New York, NY
Kenneth Ricci, New York, NY
Paul J. Ricciuti, Youngstown, OH
David E. Rice, San Diego, CA
Richard L. Rice, Raleigh, NC
James W. Rich, Tulsa, OK
Lisle F. Richards, San Jose, CA
Heidi A. Richardson, Sausalito, CA
Walter J. Richardson, Newport Beach, CA
Charles H. Richter Jr., Baltimore, MD
David R. Richter, Corpus Christi, TX
Elizabeth Chu Richter, Corpus Christi, TX
Hans Riecke, Haiku, HI
Juergen Riehm, New York, NY
James V. Righter, Boston, MA
Jorge Rigau, Rio Piedras, Puerto Rico
Jefferson B. Riley, Centerbrook, CT
Ronnette Riley, New York, NY
David N. Rinehart, La Jolla, CA
David Rinehart, Los Angeles, CA
M. Jack Rinehart Jr., Charlottesville, VA
Mark W. Rios, Los Angeles, CA
Darrel D. Rippeteau, Delray Beach, FL
P. Richard Rittelmann, Butler, PA
James W. Ritter, Alexandria, VA
Richard E. Ritz, Portland, OR
Rolando Rivas-Camp, Washington, DC
I. L. Roark, Lawrence, KS
Jack Robbins, Berkeley, CA
Darryl Roberson, San Francisco, CA
Jaquelin T. Robertson, New York, NY
C. David Robinson, San Francisco, CA
Harry G. Robinson III, Washington, DC
J. W. Robinson, Atlanta, GA
Kevin Roche, Hamden, CT
Garth Rockcastle, Minneapolis, MN
George T. Rockrise, Glen Ellen, CA
Burton L. Rockwell, San Francisco, CA

Kenneth A. Rodrigues, San Jose, CA
Susan T. Rodriguez, New York, NY
Carl D. Roehling, Detroit, MI
Chester E. Roemer, St. Louis, MO
Ralph J. Roesling II, San Diego, CA
R. G. Roessner, Austin, TX
Archibald C. Rogers, Baltimore, MD
James G. Rogers III, New York, NY
John B. Rogers, Denver, CO
John D. Rogers, Asheville, NC
Craig W. Roland, Santa Rosa, CA
B. F. Romanowitz, Lexington, KY
James G. Rome, Corpus Christi, TX
Benjamin T. Rook, Charlotte, NC
Robert W. Root, Denver, CO
Richard M. Rosan, Washington, DC
William A. Rose Jr., White Plains, NY
Alan Rosen, Palm Desert, CA
Alan R. Rosen, Lake Forest, IL
Manuel M. Rosen, La Jolla, CA
Arthur Rosenblatt, New York, NY
Norman Rosenfeld, New York, NY
Edgar B. Ross, Tiburon, CA
Ken L. Ross Jr., Houston, TX
James S. Rossant, New York, NY
Louis A. Rossetti, Birmingham, MI
Thomas J. Rossiter, Chicago, IL
Bill Rostenberg, San Francisco, CA
Harold Roth, New Haven, CT
Richard Roth Jr., Freeport, ME
Edward N. Rothe, Edison, NJ
Martha L. Rothman, Boston, MA
Richard Rothman, Rising Fawn, GA
Bernard B. Rothschild, Atlanta, GA
Bernard Rothzeid, New York, NY
Maurice Rotival, Paris, France
Michael Rotondi, Los Angeles, CA
Lauren L. Rottet, Los Angeles, CA
Judith L. Rowe, Oakland, CA
Daniel Rowen, New York, NY
Ralph T. Rowland, Cheshire, CT
Albert W. Rubeling Jr., Towson, MD
John Ruble, Santa Monica, CA
J. Ronald Rucker, Tyler, TX
J. W. Rudd, Knoxville, TN
Heinz K. Rudolf, Portland, OR
Gordon E. Ruehl, Spokane, WA
Evett J. Ruffcorn, Seattle, WA
John A. Ruffo, San Francisco, CA
Herman O. Ruhnau, Riverside, CA
Peter L. Rumpel, St. Augustine, FL
William W. Rupe, St. Louis, MO
T. T. Russell, Miami, FL
Walter A. Rutes, Scottsdale, AZ
H. Mark Ruth, Agana, Guam

Fellows of the American Institute of Architects

Harry R. Rutledge, York, PA
Roger N. Ryan, N. Canton, OH
James E. Rydeen, Rio Verde, AZ
Donald P. Ryder, New Rochelle, NY

S ─────────────

Werner Sabo, Chicago, IL
Harold G. Sadler, San Diego, CA
Moshe Safdie, Somerville, MA
Carol S. Sakata, Honolulu, HI
Raj Saksena, Bristol, RI
David D. Salmela, Duluth, MN
F. Cuthbert Salmon, Stillwater, OK
Nathaniel W. Sample, Madison, WI
Peter Samton, New York, NY
Danny Samuels, Houston, TX
Thomas Samuels, Chicago, IL
Gil A. Sanchez, Santa Cruz, CA
James J. Sanders, Seattle, WA
Kenneth D. Sanders, Portland, OR
Linda Sanders, Walnut, CA
Donald Sandy Jr., San Francisco, CA
Martin G. Santini, Englewood Cliffs, NJ
Adele N. Santos, San Francisco, CA
Carlos R. Sanz, Santurce, Puerto Rico
Charles M. Sappenfield, Sanibel, FL
Angel C. Saqui, Coral Gables, FL
Victor Saroki, Birmingham, MI
Louis Sauer, Pittsburgh, PA
Louis R. Saur, Clayton, MO
Robert W. Sawyer, Wilmington, NC
Peter M. Saylor, Philadelphia, PA
Sam Scaccia, Chicago, IL
Joseph J. Scalabrin, Columbus, OH
Mario L. Schack, Baltimore, MD
K. M. Schaefer, Kirkwood, MO
Robert J. Schaefer, Wichita, KS
Walter Schamu, Baltimore, MD
David Scheatzle, Tempe, AZ
James A. Scheeler, Reston, VA
Jeffrey Allen Scherer, Minneapolis, MN
David W. Schervish, Detroit, MI
G. G. Schierle, Los Angeles, CA
Arthur A. Schiller, Manhasset, NY
Don P. Schlegel, Albuquerque, NM
Frank Schlesinger, Washington, DC
Jon R. Schleuning, Portland, OR
Todd H. Schliemann, New York, NY
John I. Schlossman, Hubbard Woods, IL
Roger Schluntz, Albuquerque, NM
Mildred F. Schmertz, New York, NY
Fred C. Schmidt, Oklahoma City, OK
Wayne S. Schmidt, Indianapolis, IN
R. Christian Schmitt, Charleston, SC

Herbert W. Schneider, Scottsdale, AZ
Walter Scholer Jr., Fort Myers, FL
John P. Schooley, Columbus, OH
Barnett P. Schorr, Seattle, WA
Charles F. Schrader, San Rafael, CA
Stephen Schreiber, Tampa, FL
Douglas F. Schroeder, Chicago, IL
Kenneth A. Schroeder, Chicago, IL
John H. Schruben, North Bethesda, MD
George A. D. Schuett, Glendale, WI
Frederic Schwartz, New York, NY
Kenneth Schwartz, Charlottesville, VA
Kenneth E. Schwartz,
    San Luis Obispo, CA
Robert Schwartz, Washington, DC
Warren Schwartz, Boston, MA
Alan Schwartzman, Paris, France
Aaron B. Schwarz, New York, NY
Katherine L. Schwennsen, Ames, IA
Charles E. Schwing, Baton Rouge, LA
Alan D. Sclater, Seattle, WA
David M. Scott, Pullman, WA
William W. Scott, Taylors Falls, MN
Willard M. Scribner, Richmond, VA
Der Scutt, New York, NY
Jim W. Sealy, Dallas, TX
Linda Searl, Chicago, IL
Thomas J. Sedgewick, Clio, MI
Jonathan Segal, La Jolla, CA
Paul Segal, New York, NY
Lawrence P. Segrue, Visalia, CA
E. J. Seibert, Boca Grande, FL
Alexander Seidel, Belvedere, CA
Robert I. Selby, Champaign, IL
Larry D. Self, St. Louis, MO
Theodore Seligson, Kansas City, MO
Bruce M. Sellery, Marina Del Rey, CA
Dale E. Selzer, Dallas, TX
John C. Senhauser, Cincinnati, OH
Ronald S. Senseman, Silver Spring, MD
Jerome M. Seracuse, Colorado Springs, CO
Diane Serber, Old Chatham, NY
Phillip K. Settecase, Salem, OR
Betty Lee Seydler-Hepworth, Franklin, MI
Richard S. Sharpe, Norwich, CT
John A. Sharratt, Boston, MA
James L. Shay, San Rafael, CA
Leo G. Shea, Leland, MI
John P. Sheehy, Mill Valley, CA
George C. Sheldon, Portland, OR
W. Overton Shelmire, Dallas, TX
Carol Shen, Berkeley, CA
John V. Sheoris, Grosse Pointe, MI
Herschel E. Shepard, Atlantic Beach, FL

Hugh Shepley, Manchester, MA
Patricia C. Sherman, Concord, NH
Takashi Shida, Santa Monica, CA
Roger D. Shiels, Portland, OR
Dan Sidney Shipley, Dallas, TX
Edward H. Shirley, Atlanta, GA
Philip A. Shive, Charlotte, NC
William C. Shopsin, New York, NY
Evan H. Shu, Melrose, MA
George Whiteside Shupee, Arlington, TX
Jack T. Sidener, Shatin,
    New Territories, China
Paul G. Sieben, Toledo, OH
Henry I. Siegel, Emeryville, CA
Lloyd H. Siegel, Washington, DC
Robert H. Siegel, New York, NY
Charles M. Sieger, Miami, FL
Robert Silver, Boston, MA
Henry N. Silvestri, Corona Del Mar, CA
Brad Simmons, St. Louis, MO
Cathy J. Simon, San Francisco, CA
Mark Simon, Centerbrook, CT
Lawrence L. Simons, Santa Rosa, CA
Donal R. Simpson, Dallas, TX
Grant A. Simpson, Dallas, TX
Robert T. Simpson Jr., Berkeley, CA
Scott Simpson, Cambridge, MA
Howard F. Sims, Detroit, MI
Jerome J. Sincoff, St. Louis, MO
Donald I. Singer, Fort Lauderdale, FL
E. Crichton Singleton, Kansas City, MO
Charles S. Sink, Denver, CO
Lorri D. Sipes, Ann Arbor, MI
William H. Sippel Jr., Allison Park, PA
Michael M. Sizemore, Atlanta, GA
Ronald L. Skaggs, Dallas, TX
Norma M. Sklarek, Pacific Palisades, CA
Gary Skog, Southfield, MI
Lee H. Skolnick, New York, NY
Murray A. Slama, Walnut Creek, CA
Clifton M. Smart Jr., Fayetteville, AR
Saul C. Smiley, Minnetonka, MN
Adrian D. Smith, Chicago, IL
Arthur Smith, Southfield, MI
Bill D. Smith, Dallas, TX
Bruce H. Smith, Pontiac, MI
Christopher G. Smith, New York, NY
Christopher J. Smith, Honolulu, HI
Cole Smith, Dallas, TX
Colin L. M. Smith, Cambridge, MA
Darrell L. Smith, Eugene, OR
Edward Smith, Salt Lake City, UT
Fleming W. Smith Jr., Nashville, TN
Frank Folsom Smith, Sarasota, FL

Fellows of the American Institute of Architects

Hamilton P. Smith, Garden City, NY
Ivan H. Smith, Jacksonville, FL
John R. Smith, Ketchum, ID
Joseph N. Smith III, Atlanta, GA
Kenneth Smith, Jacksonville, FL
Macon S. Smith, Raleigh, NC
Michael E. Smith, Bellingham, WA
Stephen B. Smith, Salt Lake City, UT
T. Clayton Smith, Baton Rouge, LA
Tyler Smith, Hartford, CT
David I. Smotrich, New York, NY
Neil H. Smull, Boise, ID
Richard Snibbe, New York, NY
Sheila Snider, Indianapolis, IN
Julie V. Snow, Minneapolis, MN
Sam T. Snowdon Jr., Laurinburg, NC
William E. Snyder, Henderson, NV
Walter H. Sobel, Chicago, IL
Daniel Solomon, San Francisco, CA
Richard J. Solomon, Chicago, IL
Stuart B. Solomon, Watertown, MA
James Hamilton Somes Jr.,
    Portsmouth, NH
Hak Son, Santa Monica, CA
Suman Sorg, Washington, DC
John R. Sorrenti, Mineola, NY
Charles B. Soule, Montgomery
    Village, MD
Michael Southworth, Berkeley, CA
Edward A. Sovik, Northfield, MN
George S. Sowden, Fort Worth, TX
Marvin Sparn, Boulder, CO
Laurinda H. Spear, Miami, FL
Beverley Spears, Santa Fe, NM
Lawrence W. Speck, Austin, TX
Michael H. Spector, New Hyde Park, NY
John H. Spencer, Hampton, VA
Tomas H. Spiers Jr., Camp Hill, PA
Pat Y. Spillman, Dallas, TX
Robert A. Spillman, Bethlehem, PA
Donald E. Sporleder, South Bend, IN
Joseph G. Sprague, Dallas, TX
Kent Spreckelmeyer, Lawrence, KS
Paul D. Spreiregen, Washington, DC
Bernard P. Spring, Brookline, MA
Everett G. Spurling Jr., Bethesda, MD
Dennis W. Stacy, Dallas, TX
Alfred M. Staehli, Portland, OR
Richard P. Stahl, Springfield, MO
Raymond F. Stainback Jr., Atlanta, GA
Duffy B. Stanley, El Paso, TX
William J. Stanley III, Atlanta, GA
Jane M. Stansfeld, Austin, TX
Michael J. Stanton, San Francisco, CA

Stanley Stark, New York, NY
Earl M. Starnes, Cedar Key, FL
Frank A. Stasiowski, Newton, MA
Donald J. Stastny, Portland, OR
Russell L. Stecker, Montpelier, VT
Mark W. Steele, La Jolla, CA
John E. Stefany, Tampa, FL
Peter Steffian, Boston, MA
Charles W. Steger Jr., Blacksburg, VA
Douglas Steidl, Akron, OH
Carl Stein, New York, NY
Morris A. Stein, Phoenix, AZ
Goodwin B. Steinberg, San Jose, CA
Robert T. Steinberg, San Jose, CA
Ralph Steinglass, New York, NY
Henry Steinhardt, Mercer Island, WA
Douglas E. Steinman Jr., Beaumont, TX
James A. Stenhouse, Charlotte, NC
Donald J. Stephens, Berlin, NY
Michael J. Stepner, San Diego, CA
Robert A. M. Stern, New York, NY
William F. Stern, Houston, TX
Preston Stevens Jr., Atlanta, GA
James M. Stevenson, Highland Park, IL
W. Cecil Steward, Lincoln, NE
R. K. Stewart, San Francisco, CA
William W. Stewart, Clayton, MO
Sherwood Stockwell, Wolcott, CO
Claude Stoller, Berkeley, CA
Randall Paul Stout, Los Angeles, CA
Neal P. Stowe Salt Lake City, UT
H. T. Stowell, Western Springs, IL
Neil E. Strack, Champaign, IL
Ronald A. Straka, Denver, CO
Michael J. Stransky, Salt Lake City, UT
Frank Straub, Troy, MI
Mark E. Strauss, New York, NY
John R. Street Jr., Marietta, GA
Arthur V. Strock, Santa Ana, CA
Norman Strong, Seattle, WA
Hugh Asher Stubbins Jr., Cambridge, MA
Sidney W. Stubbs Jr., Mount Pleasant, SC
Donald L. Stull, Boston, MA
Robert S. Sturgis, Weston, MA
Erik Sueberkrop, San Francisco, CA
Marvin D. Suer, Willow Grove, PA
John W. Sugden, Park City, UT
Douglas R. Suisman, Santa Monica, CA
Edward Sullam, Honolulu, HI
John P. Sullivan, Valhalla, NY
Patrick M. Sullivan, Claremont, CA
Gene R. Summers, Cloverdale, CA
Alan R. Sumner, St. Louis, MO
Richard P. Sundberg, Seattle, WA

Donald R. Sunshine, Blacksburg, VA
Sarah Susanka, Raleigh, NC
Eugene L. Surber, Atlanta, GA
Sharon E. Sutton, Seattle, WA
George Suyama, Seattle, WA
Vernon D. Swaback, Scottsdale, AZ
Eugene C. Swager, Peoria, IL
Robert M. Swatt, San Francisco, CA
Earl Swensson, Nashville, TN
Richard Swett, Bow, NH
Stephen Swicegood, Decatur, GA
H. H. Swinburne, Philadelphia, PA
Don A. Swofford, Charlottesville, VA
John M. Syvertsen, Chicago, IL

T

Edgar Tafel, Venice, FL
Marvin Taff, Beverly Hills, CA
Edward K. Takahashi, Santa Monica, CA
Ray Takata, Sacramento, CA
Francis T. Taliaferro, Santa Monica, CA
R. H. Tan, Spokane, WA
Ted Tokio Tanaka, Marina Del Rey, CA
Virginia W. Tanzmann, Pasadena, CA
Charles R. Tapley, Houston, TX
A. Anthony Tappe, Boston, MA
John Tarantino, New York City, NY
H. Harold Tarleton, Greenville, SC
D. Coder Taylor, Glenview, IL
Marilyn J. Taylor, New York, NY
Richard L. Taylor Jr., Atlanta, GA

Did you know...

**The States with the least
AIA fellows are:**

Wyoming – 1
South Dakota – 1
North Dakota – 1
Delaware – 2
Maine – 2
West Virginia – 2
Montana – 3
Nevada – 4
Alaska – 5
Idaho – 5
New Hampshire – 7
Rhode Island – 7
Vermont – 7

Source: **DesignIntelligence**

Fellows of the American Institute of Architects

Walter Q. Taylor, Jacksonville, FL
Thomas H. Teasdale, Kirkwood, MO
Jerry R. Tepe, Hopkinton, NH
Clinton C. Ternstrom, Los Angeles, CA
Roland Terry, Mt. Vernon, WA
Robert L. Tessier, Yarmouth Port, MA
B. C. Tharp, Montgomery, TX
Dorwin A. J. Thomas, Boston, MA
James B. Thomas, Houston, TX
James L. Thomas, Spartanburg, SC
Joseph F. Thomas, Pasadena, CA
Val Thomas, Seattle, WA
David C. Thompson, San Diego, CA
Milo H. Thompson, Minneapolis, MN
Robert L. Thompson, Portland, OR
Warren D. Thompson, Fresno, CA
Charles B. Thomsen, Houston, TX
Duane Thorbeck, Minneapolis, MN
Karl Thorne, Gainesville, FL
Oswald H. Thorson, Marco, FL
George Thrush, Boston, MA
John P. Tice Jr., Pensacola, FL
Stanley Tigerman, Chicago, IL
Patrick Tillett, Portland, OR
James H. Timberlake, Philadelphia, PA
Robert H. Timme, Los Angeles, CA
Leslie D. Tincknell, Saginaw, MI
Glen A. Tipton, Baltimore, MD
James D. Tittle, Abilene, TX
Philip E. Tobey, Reston, VA
Calvin J. Tobin, Highland Park, IL
Logic Tobola II, El Campo, TX
Anderson Todd, Houston, TX
David F. M. Todd, New York, NY
Thomas A. Todd, Jamestown, RI
Lee Tollefson, Saint Paul, MN
John Tomassi, Chicago, IL
James E. Tomblinson, Flint, MI
Richard F. Tomlinson II, Chicago, IL
Frank Tomsick, San Francisco, CA
John Francis Torti, Silver Spring, MD
Mark Joseph Tortorich, Martinez, CA
Coulson Tough, The Woodlands, TX
Dennis T. Toyomura, Honolulu, HI
Jack Train, Chicago, IL
Jack Travis, New York, NY
Karl E. Treffinger Sr., West Linn, OR
Kenneth Treister, Coconut Grove, FL
Michael Tribble, Charlotte, NC
David M. Trigiani, Jackson, MS
William H. Trogdon, Olga, WA
Leroy Troyer, Mishawaka, IN
William H. Truex Jr., Burlington, VT
David Owen Tryba, Denver, CO
Chiu Lin Tse-Chan, San Francisco, CA

Charles N. Tseckares, Boston, MA
Edward T. M. Tsoi, Arlington, MA
Seab A. Tuck, III, Nashville, TN
Jack R. Tucker Jr., Memphis, TN
Thomas B. Tucker, San Diego, CA
Richard L. Tully, Columbus, OH
Emanuel N. Turano, Boca Raton, FL
John Gordon Turnbull, San Francisco, CA
Michael G. Turnbull, Manassas, VA
Ronald F. Turner, Los Angeles, CA
Thomas P. Turner Jr., Charlotte, NC
Wilbur H. Tusler Jr., Kentfield, CA
Ilene R. Tyler, Ann Arbor, MI
James L. Tyler, Pacific Palisades, CA
Robert Tyler, Tarzana, CA
Anne G. Tyng, Philadelphia, PA

U ————————————

Edward K. Uhlir, Chicago, IL
Kenneth A. Underwood, Philadelphia, PA
Dean F. Unger, Sacramento, CA
Roberta Marrano Unger, Atlanta, GA
Denorval Unthank Jr., Eugene, OR
Robert H. Uyeda, Los Angeles, CA

V ————————————

Joseph D. Vaccaro, Los Angeles, CA
Edward Vaivoda Jr., Portland, OR
William E. Valentine, San Francisco, CA
Joseph M. Valerio, Chicago, IL
William L. Van Alen, Wilmington, DE
Robert Van Deusen, Grand Junction, CO
Peter van Dijk, Cleveland, OH
George V. Van Fossen Schwab,
   Baltimore, MD
Thomas Van Housen, Minneapolis, MN
Harold F. VanDine Jr., Birmingham, MI
Johannes VanTilburg, Santa Monica, CA
Mitchell Vanbourg, Berkeley, CA
Harutun Vaporciyan, Huntington
   Woods, MI
Harold R. Varner, Berkley, MI
Andrew A. Vazzano, Detroit, MI
Leonard M. Veitzer, San Diego, CA
Thomas W. Ventulett, Atlanta, GA
Robert Venturi, Philadelphia, PA
Shirley J. Vernon, Philadelphia, PA
Kathryn C. Vernon-McKeen, Hartford, CT
William R. Vick, Sacramento, CA
Robert L. Vickery, Charlottesville, VA
Wilmont Vickrey, Chicago, IL
Frank Villalobos, Los Angeles, CA
Gregory D. Villanueva, Los Angeles, CA
John Vinci, Chicago, IL
Rafael Vinoly, New York, NY

Stephen Vogel, Detroit, MI
Leonard W. Volk II, Dallas, TX
A. R. Von Brock, Buchanan, VA
Robert J. Von Dohlen, West Hartford, CT
Richard L. Von Luhrte, Denver, CO
Thomas Vonier, Paris, France
Bartholome Voorsanger, New York, NY
R. Randall Vosbeck, Vail, CO
William F. Vosbeck, Alexandria, VA
Thomas R. Vreeland, Century City, CA
R. E. Vrooman, College Station, TX

W ————————————

Hobart D. Wagener, Coronado, CA
William J. Wagner, Dallas Center, IA
John G. Waite, Albany, NY
Lawrence G. Waldron, Mercer Island, WA
Bruce M. Walker, Spokane, WA
Kenneth H. Walker, New York, NY
David D. Wallace, Westport, MA
Donald Q. Wallace, Lexington, KY
Les Wallach, Seattle, WA
Charles G. Walsh, Los Angeles, CA
Lloyd G. Walter Jr., Winston Salem, NC
W. G. Wandelmaier, New York, NY
Sheldon D. Wander, New York, NY
R. J. Warburton, Coral Gables, FL
G. T. Ward, Fairfax, VA
Robertson Ward Jr., Boston, MA
C. E. Ware, Rockford, IL
John Carl Warnecke, San Francisco, CA
Charles H. Warner Jr., Nyack, NY
Clyde K. Warner Jr., Louisville, KY
James M. Warner, Manchester, NH
William D. Warner, Exeter, RI
Sharon F. Washburn, Bethesda, MD
Robert E. Washington, Richmond, VA
Barry L. Wasserman, Sacramento, CA
Joseph Wasserman, Southfield, MA
David H. Watkins, Bellaire, TX
Donald R. Watson, Trumbull, CT
Raymond L. Watson, Newport Beach, CA
William J. Watson, LaJolla, CA
John L. Webb, Ponchatoula, LA
P. R. Webber, Rutland, VT
Arthur M. Weber, Aiea, HI
Frederick S. Webster, Cazenovia, NY
C. R. Wedding, St. Petersburg, FL
Benjamin H. Weese, Chicago, IL
Cynthia Weese, Chicago, IL
Gary K. Weeter, Dallas, TX
Wesley Wei, Philadelphia, PA
Bryce Adair Weigand, Dallas, TX
Joe Neal Weilenman, Pago Pago,
   American Samoa

132

Fellows of the American Institute of Architects

Nicholas H. Weingarten, Chicago, IL
Amy Weinstein, Washington, DC
Edward Weinstein, Seattle, WA
Jane Weinzapfel, Boston, MA
Gerald G. Weisbach, San Francisco, CA
Sarelle T. Weisberg, New York, NY
Steven F. Weiss, Chicago, IL
Martha L. Welborne, Los Angeles, CA
Frank D. Welch, Dallas, TX
John A. Welch, Tuskegee, AL
Louis L. Weller, Albuquerque, NM
William P. Wenzler, Milwaukee, WI
Lester Wertheimer, Los Angeles, CA
Helge Westermann, Cambridge, MA
Merle T. Westlake, Lexington, MA
Paul E. Westlake Jr., Cleveland, OH
I. Donald Weston, Brooklyn, NY
Donald A. Wexler, Palm Springs, CA
Charles H. Wheatley, Charlotte, NC
C. Herbert Wheeler, State College, PA
Daniel H. Wheeler, Chicago, IL
James H. Wheeler Jr., Abilene, TX
Kenneth D. Wheeler, Lake Forest, IL
Richard H. Wheeler, Los Angeles, CA
Murray Whisnant, Charlotte, NC
Arthur B. White, Havertown, PA
Edward D. White Jr., Denver, CO
George M. White, Bethesda, MD
Janet Rothberg White, Bethesda, MD
Norval C. White, Salisbury, CT
Samuel G. White, New York, NY
Alison M. Whitelaw, San Diego, CA
Stephen Q. Whitney, Detroit, MI
Ward B. Whitwam, Sioux Falls, SD
Jay Wickersham, Boston, MA
Leonard S. Wicklund, Long Grove, IL
Christopher Widener, Springfield, OH
Chester A. Widom, Santa Monica, CA
William Wiese II, Shelburne, VT
E. D. Wilcox, Tyler, TX
Jerry Cooper Wilcox, Little Rock, AR
Gordon L. Wildermuth, Greeley, PA
James E. Wiley, Dallas, TX
Charles E. Wilkerson, Richmond, VA
Joseph A. Wilkes, Annapolis, MD
Michael B. Wilkes, San Diego, CA
Barbara E. Wilks, Baltimore, MD
Paul Willen, Yorktown Heights, NY
A. Richard Williams, Saint Ignace, MI
Allison G. Williams, San Francisco, CA
Daniel E. Williams, Coconut Grove, FL
Donald L. Williams, Houston, TX
E. Stewart Williams, Palm Springs, CA
F. Carter Williams, Raleigh, NC
Frank Williams, New York, NY

George Thomas Williams, Kitty Hawk, NC
Harold L. Williams, Los Angeles, CA
Homer L. Williams, Riverside, MO
John G. Williams, Fayetteville, AR
Lorenzo D. Williams, Minneapolis, MN
Mark F. Williams, Ambler, PA
Roger B. Williams, Seattle, WA
Terrance R. Williams, Washington, DC
Tod C. Williams, New York, NY
W. Gene Williams, The Woodlands, TX
Wayne R. Williams, Harmony, CA
James F. Williamson, Memphis, TN
Beverly A. Willis, New York, NY
Michael E. Willis, San Francisco, CA
John C. Wilmot, Damascus, MD
Bill T. Wilson II, Corpus Christi, TX
Carol A. Wilson, Falmouth, ME
Jeffrey Wilson, Anchorage, AK
John E. Wilson, Richmond, VA
John L. Wilson, Boston, MA
William D. Wilson, Bridgehampton, NY
Steven R. Winkel, Berkeley, CA
Jon Peter Winkelstein, San Francisco, CA
John H. Winkler, Verbank, NY
Paul D. Winslow, Phoenix, AZ
Arch R. Winter, Mobile, AL
Steven Winter, Norwalk, CT
Marjorie M. Wintermute,
    Lake Oswego, OR
Norman E. Wirkler, Denver, CO
Joseph J. Wisnewski, Alexandria, VA
Gayland B. Witherspoon, Pendleton, SC
Charles Witsell Jr., Little Rock, AR
Gordon G. Wittenberg, Little Rock, AR
Fritz Woehle, Birmingham, AL
Robert L. Wold, Hilton Head, SC
Harry C. Wolf III, Malibu, CA
Martin F. Wolf, Wilmette, IL
Richard Wolf, San Mateo, CA
Ronald E. Wommack, Dallas, TX
Gin D. Wong, Los Angeles, CA
Joseph O. Wong, San Diego, CA
Kellogg H. Wong, New York, NY
William Wong Jr., Taikooshing, PRC
Carolina Y. Woo, San Francisco, CA
George C. Woo, Dallas, TX
Kyu S. Woo, Cambridge, MA
H. A. Wood III, Boston, MA
John M. Woodbridge, Sonoma, CA
David Geoffrey Woodcock,
    College Station, TX
David Woodhouse, Chicago, IL
Robert S. Woodhurst III, Augusta, GA
Stanford Woodhurst Jr., Augusta, GA
Enrique Woodroffe, Tampa, FL

Thomas E. Woodward, Buena Vista, CO
David L. Wooley, Knoxville, TN
Evans Woollen, Indianapolis, IN
J. R. Wooten, Fort Worth, TX
John C. Worsley, Portland, OR
David H. Wright, Seattle, WA
George S. Wright, Fort Worth, TX
Henry L. Wright, Canby, OR
John L. Wright, Redmond, WA
Rodney H. Wright, Liberty, KY
Thomas W. D. Wright, Washington, DC
Hofu Wu, Pomona, CA
Cynthia Wuellner, Kansas City, MO
Scott W. Wyatt, Seattle, WA

Y

Jack R. Yardley, Dallas, TX
Barry David Yatt, Arlington, VA
John L. Yaw, Aspen, CO
Zeno Lanier Yeates, Memphis, TN
Raymond W. Yeh, Honolulu, HI
Ronald W. Yeo, Corona Del Mar, CA
David N. Yerkes, Washington, DC
William R. Yost, Portland, OR
Clayton Young, Seattle, WA
Joseph L. Young, Clemson, SC
Norbert Young Jr., New York, NY
Theodore J. Young, Greenwich, CT
Linda Yowell, New York City, NY
Hachiro Yuasa, Orleans, CA
Robert J. Yudell, Santa Monica, CA

Z

James Zahn, Chicago, IL
Saul Zaik, Portland, OR
H. Alan Zeigel, Denver, CO
J. Zemanek, Houston, TX
Golden J. Zenon Jr., Omaha, NE
Robert L. Ziegelman, Birmingham, MI
Raymond Ziegler, Altadena, CA
Rick Zieve, Seattle, WA
Frank Zilm, Kansas City, MO
John J. Zils, Chicago, IL
Bernard B. Zimmerman, Los Angeles, CA
Gary V. Zimmerman, Milwaukee, WI
Thomas A. Zimmerman, Rochester, NY
Hugh M. Zimmers, Philadelphia, PA
Joel P. Zingeser, Rockville, MD
Peter Jay Zweig, Houston, TX

Source: American Institute of Architects

Fellows of the American Institute of Certified Planners

Election as a fellow in the American Institute of Certified Planners is one of the highest honors the AICP can bestow upon a member. Fellowship is granted every two years to planners who have been a member of AICP and have achieved excellence in professional practice, teaching and mentoring, research, public/community service, and leadership.

Charles C. Allen	Nancy Benziger Brown	James B. Duncan
David J. Allor	Martin Bruno	Wilmer C. Dutton Jr.
Karen B. Alschuler	Raymond Burby	Michael V. Dyett
John E. Anderson	Bob Burke	V. Gail Easley
Richard T. Anderson	David Lee Callies	Joseph T. Edmiston
Uri P. Avin	Paulette Carolin	Robert C. Einsweiler
Edmund Bacon	Eugene E. Carr	Frank L. Elmer
Robert S. Baldwin	Sam Casella	Henry Eng
Tridib K. Banerjee	Anthony James Catanese	Leon S. Eplan
Mitzi Barker	Robert A. Catlin	John W. Epling
Jonathan Barnett	F. Stuart Chapin Jr.	Ernest Erber
Carol D. Barrett	George B. Chapman	Craig Farmer
Ernest R. Bartley	Jay Chatterjee	Hermann Haviland Field
Peter Batchelor	Hyung C. Chung	Frank Fish
Ralph E. Becker Jr.	Philip Hart Clark	David J. Forkenbrock
Robert W. Becker	Arnold Cogan	Clyde W. Forrest
Katherine Ford Beebe	Fred Collignon	Joe E. Frank Jr.
James R. Bell	Brad Collins	Ralph Gakenheimer
Teree L. Bergman	Arlan M. Colton	Joanne Garnett
Paul A. Bergmann	Thomas Cooke	Laurence Conway Gerckens
Richard C. Bernhardt	Connie B. Cooper	David R. Godschalk
James Bertram	Bob Cornish	Carl Goldschmidt
Dale F. Bertsch	Linda R. Cox	Dennis Andrew Gordon
Dave E. Bess	Paul C. Crawford	Sigurd Grava
Eugenie Ladner Birch	Betty Croly	Clifford W. Graves
Daniel Bird	John F. (Jack) Crowley	Sherman Griselle
Merle H. Bishop	Charles L. Crumpton	Albert Guttenberg
Alan Black	Samuel J. Cullers	Dianne Guzman
Lachlan F. Blair	James W. (Bill) Curtis	Besim S. Hakim
John A. Blayney	Patrick J. Cusick Jr.	Irving Hand
David Booher	C. Gregory Dale	Wes Hankins
Fred P. Bosselman	Wayne Daltry	Angela N. Harper
William W. Bowdy	Linda Lund Davis	Michael A. Harper
Melville C. Branch	Dennis E. Daye	Britton Harris
John E. Bridges	Lillian Frost Dean	William M. Harris Sr.
Jane S. Brooks	F. John Devaney	Michael S. Harrison
Michael P. Brooks	Tom Dinell	Roger K. Hedrick
David J. Brower	Boris Dramov	Edward Helfeld

Fellows of the American Institute of Certified Planners

Mary Lou Henry
Vernon G. Henry
Albert Herson
Jesus H. Hinojosa
Mark L. Hinshaw
John E. Hirten
Allan A. Hodges
Stanley R. Hoffman
Edward A. Holden
Lewis D. Hopkins
Patrick Horsbrugh
Deborah A. Howe
Robert P. Huefner
Robert Hunter
Fred Hurand
Edward J. Hustoles
Daniel S. Iacofano
David A. Johnson
Morris E. Johnson
Robert J. Juster
Vivian Kahn
Edward Kaiser
William G. Kane
Jerome L. Kauffman
Barbara Kautz
Lloyd Keefe
John Keller
Eric Damian Kelly
Paul B. Kelman
Oliver Kerr
Mary R. Kihl
Lawrence S. Kline
Bruce A. Knight
Kenneth M. Kreutziger
Bruce M. Kriviskey
Donald A. Krueckeberg
Norman Krumholz
Glenn Kumekawa
Steven K. Kurtz
Richard T. Lai
Bruce Laing
William Lamont Jr.
Floyd Lapp
Glen S. LeRoy
Anthony Lettieri
Julius S. Levine

Constance Lieder
Helen M. Olson Lightle
Richard R. Lillie
Barbara Lukermann
Robert H. Lurcott
Dean L. Macris
Marjorie Macris
George G. Mader
Howard R. Maier
Riad G. Mahayni
Alan Mallach
Daniel R. Mandelker
Lawrence Mann
George T. Marcou
Peter Marcuse
Richard May Jr.
Michael D. McAnelly
Heather McCartney
Bruce W. McClendon
Alan McClennen Jr.
Ron McConnell
Mike McCormick
Margarita P. McCoy
Bruce D. McDowell
Dorn Charles McGrath Jr.
Stuart Meck
Joy Mee
Dwight Merriman
John Merrill
Darrell C. Meyer
Martin Meyerson
Ronald P. Miller
J. Laurence Mintier
Vijay Mital
Terry Moore
Harvey Moskowitz
Louis Bert Muhly
John R. Mullin
Norman Murdoch
Arthur C. Nelson
Dick Netzer
Thomas P. Niederkorn
Perry Norton
Ki Suh Park
Jacqueline A. Parnell
Carl V. Patton

James Paulmann
Robert J. Paternoster
Gene Pearson
Phillip D. Peters
Robert J. Piper
Norbert J. Pointner
Leslie S. Pollock
Peter L. Pollock
Douglas R. Porter
David J. Portman
Roy Wilson Potter
Steven A. Preston
Rick Pruetz
David L. Pugh
Mary Joan Pugh
Ray Quay
Julianne R. Rankin
George Raymond
Robert E. Reiman
H. Randal Roark
Thomas H. Roberts
Harold Robertson
Gloria W. Robinson
Sergio Rodriguez
Wolfgang G. Roeseler
Joseph Lee Rodgers
Marsha Rood
Janet M. Ruggiero
Peter D. Salins
David S. Sawicki
Gary Schoennauer
Sue Schwartz
Paul H. Sedway
Ann Meriweather Shafor
Sumner Sharpe
Ronald Shiffman
Ronald N. Short
Donald Shoup
Martin H. Shukert
Marshall D. Slagle
Michael A. Slavney
Herbert H. Smith
Myles Greene Smith
Frank So
Lester Solin
Cheryl D. Soon

Fellows of the American Institute of Certified Planners

Jeff Soule
James A. Spencer
Marvin Springer
Earl M. Starnes
Donald J. Stastny
Jay M. Stein
Stuart W. Stein
Michael J. Stepner
Jill Brown Sterrett
Bruce Stiftel
Susan Stoddard
Israel Stollman
Robert L. Sturdivant
Kenneth E. Sulzer
Vernon Dale Swaback
Robert B. Teska
Carol J. Thomas
June Manning Thomas

Sidney F. Thomas Jr.
Michael P.C. Tillett
Anthony R. Tomazinis
Kenneth C. Topping
Nohad A. Toulan
Joseph W. Tovar
Frank F. Turner
Stuart Turner
Richard E. Tustian
Stephen D. Villavaso
Francis Violich
Alan M. Voorhees
Martin Wachs
Fritz Wagner
Robert Wagoner
Roger S. Waldon
D. William Wallace
Larry W. Watts

Robert Wegner Sr.
Frank B. Wein
Louis B. Wetmore
Sara Jane White
David Wilcox
Ronald A. Williamson
Dick Winchell
J.D. Wingfield
Mark Winogrond
Arch R. Winter
Benjamin Withers
Joel C. Wooldridge
Mark A. Wyckoff
Bruce T. Yoder
Paul Zucker

Source: American Institute of Certified Planners

In our civilization infrastructure is fundamental. Public spaces, avenues, bridges over rivers—these are what bring men together and condition our quality of life. But there are also needs which one cannot measure, which are more spiritual.

Sir Norman Foster

Fellows of the American Society of Interior Designers

The American Society of Interior Designers grants fellowships to those members who have made notable and substantial contributions to the profession and society. The following individuals are current, active fellows of the ASID.

Stanley Abercrombie
Dan Acito
Stephen W. Ackerman
Gail Adams
Joy E. Adcock
Estelle Alpert
Jerry R. Alsobrook
William F. Andrews
Ellen Angell
Robert A. Arehart
Warren G. Arnett
Anita Baltimore
David Barrett
Nancy Hoff Barsotti
Jeannine Bazer-Schwartz
Tamara A. Bazzle
Roy F. Beal
Marjorie A. Bedell
Frank Lee Berry
Hal F.B. Birchfield
Adriana Bitter
Joan Blutter
Penny Bonda
Joseph Daniel Bouligny
Blair S. Bowen
H. Don Bowden
William D. Bowden
Susan Bradford
Bruce J. Brigham
C. Dudley Brown
Everett Brown
R. Michael Brown
Mary A. Bryan
Eleanor Brydone
Joyce A. Burke-Jones
David M. Butler
Rosalyn Cama
Barbara J. Campbell
Orville V. Carr
Elizabeth M. Castleman
Juliana M. Catlin

Leslie Cheek
Carl E. Clark
Brian Clay Collins
Jim Colson
John P. Conron
Loverne C. Cordes
Herbert Cordier
Jini Costello
Virginia W. Courtenay
P.A. Dale
Hortense Davis
Robert John Dean
Ken Deck
Cheryl Donaho
Dede Draper
Hilda M. East
H. Gerard Ebert
Barbara Ebstein
Arlis Ede
Martin Elinoff
John Elmo
Joel M. Ergas
Sammye J. Erickson
Adele Faulkner
Jon J. Fields
Lyn Fontenot
John G. Ford
Deborah Lloyd Forrest
Dorothy L. Fowles
Thomas Frank
Sandra C. Friend
Charles D. Gandy
Marion Gardiner
Judy Girod
Milton Glaser
Suzan Globus
Diane Gote
Thomas C. Grabowski
Theodora Kim Graham
Stephen Greenberger
Jody Greenwald

Roberta S. Griffin
Rita C. Guest
David W. Hall
James M. Halverson
Shirley Hammond
A. Niolon Hampton
Marilyn Hansen
Patricia Harvey
Dennis Haworth
Dorothy G. Helmer
Albert E. Herbert
Fred B. Hershey
Luann Holmes
Joseph P. Horan
Elizabeth B. Howard
Nina Hughes
Dorian Hunter
H. Cliff Ivester
Barbara L. Jacobs
Sarah B. Jenkins
Charlotte Jensen
Connie Johannes
Wallace R. Jonason
Richard W. Jones
Henry Jordan
Henri V. Jova
Janet E. Kane
Donna Kirby
Mary V. Knackstedt
Binnie Kramer
Gayle Kreutzfeld
Karlyn Kuper
Hugh L. Latta
Drue Lawlor
Dennis W. Leczinski
Nila Leiserowitz
Robert S. Lindenthal
Boyd L. Loendorf
Michael Love
Odette Lueck
Ruth K. Lynford

Fellows of the American Society of Interior Designers

William M. Manly
Helen Masoner
Terri Maurer
Sandra McGowen
James E. McIntosh
Dennis McNabb
Constance Mercer
James Mezrano
John Richard Miller
Thomas H. Miller
Susan I. Mole
Kathy Ford Montgomery
Phyllis Moore
Mark Nelson
Roi C. Nevaril
Linda Newton
W.E. Noffke
Barbara Nugent
Jan Parker
Suzanne Patterson
Lawrence Peabody
Edward J. Perrault
B.J. Peterson
H. Albert Phibbs
Judith Pickett
Eugene Potente
Betty J. Purvis
Catharine G. Rawson
William Dunn Ray
Martha Garriott Rayle

Mary Jane Reeves
John Robinson
Pedro Rodriguez
Agnes H. Rogers
Jack G. Ruthazer
Chester F. Sagenkahn
Barbara A. Sauerbrey
Hollie Schick
Janet S. Schirn
Barbara Schlattman
Robin Schmidt
E. Williard Schurz
Irving D. Schwartz
Melinda K. Sechrist
Otho S. Shaw
Shelley Siegel
James L. Simpson
Theodore A. Simpson
Edna A. Smith
Fran Kellog Smith
James Merrick Smith
Linda Elliot Smith
Sandra H. Sober
Michael Souter
Beulah G. Spiers
Edward H. Springs
Rita St. Clair
Russell M. Stanley
Ed Starr
Karl L. Steinhauser

Deborah Steinmetz
C. Eugene Stephenson
Blanche F. Strater
Ann Sullivan
Michael Thomas
Caroline Torley
Doris Nash Upshur
Judith André Verges
Bernard Vinick
Donna Vining
G.F. Weber
Maurice Weir
Vicki Wenger
Gary E. Wheeler
Miriam Whelan
Michael Wiener
William L. Wilkoff
Frances E. Wilson
Gail Casey Winkler
Michael Wirtz
John B. Wisner
D.C. Witte
Edmund D. Wood
Alene Workman
Diane B. Worth
Robert Wright
Julie M. Wyatt

Source: American Society of Interior Designers

Beauty applies to us all. Ignore it at your peril.

Virginia Postrel

Fellows of the American Society of Landscape Architects

Fellows of the American Society of Landscape Architects are landscape architects of at least 10 years standing as full members of the ASLA elected to fellowship in honor of their outstanding contributions to the profession. Categories of election are works of landscape architecture, administrative work, knowledge, and service to the profession. The list below indicates current, active fellows of the ASLA.

B9

Calvin R. Abe
Howard G. Abel
Molly E. Feltham Adams
William Dwayne Adams Jr.
Jerry L. Adamson
Marvin I. Adleman
Russell A. Adsit
Timothy M. Agness
John F. Ahern
J. Robert Anderson
William Anglin Jr.
Domenico Annese
Ellis L. Antuñez
David E. Arbegast
David S. Armbruster
Henry F. Arnold
Sadik C. Artunc
Roy O. Ashley
D. Lyle Aten
Donald B. Austin
Kenneth J. Backman
Ted Baker
William H. Baker
Harry J. Baldwin
Edward B. Ballard
Thomas Balsley
Alton A. Barnes Jr.
Milton Baron
Cheryl Barton
James H. Bassett
Kenneth E. Bassett
Anthony M. Bauer
Clarence W. Baughman
Eldon W. Beck
Yoshiro Befu
Arthur G. Beggs
William A. Behnke
James R. Bell

Richard C. Bell
Vincent Bellafiore
Claire R. Bennett
Shary Page Berg
Karl Gilbert Berry
Charles A. Birnbaum
Calvin T. Bishop
David H. Blau
Kerry Blind
Alfred Bohling
Lloyd M. Bond
Thomas H. Bonnell
Norman K. Booth
Scott O. Bradley
Sheila Brady
W. Frank Brandt
J. Brooks Breeden
Michael Wayne Breedlove
Theodore W. Brickman Jr.
Samuel W. Bridgers
Don H. Brigham Jr.
Donald Carl Brinkerhoff
Mark K. Brinkley
Robert F. Bristol
Judy Byrd Brittenum
Frank Brower
Gary A. Brown
Joseph E. Brown
Jeffrey L. Bruce
Robert Owen Brush
Jackie Karl Bubenik
Alexander Budrevics
Robert S. Budz
Dennis R. Buettner
Wayne L. Buggenhagen
Troy L. Bunch
Frank Burggraf Jr.
James D. Burnett

Russell L. Butler II
Warren Turnbull Byrd Jr.
Willard C. Byrd
Raymond F. Cain
Malcolm D. Cairns
Robert A. Callans
William B. Callaway
Craig S. Campbell
Jeffrey Carbo
Dean Cardasis
Robert R. Cardoza
Charles Cares
Bryan D. Carlson
John Leslie Carman
John Paul Carman
Dennis B. Carmichael
Derr A. Carpenter
David B. Carruth
Donald R. Carter
Eugene H. Carter
Anthony B. Casendino
Carlos J. Cashio
Patrick W. Caughey
Craig Cawrse
Gordon Chappell
James E. Christman
Ann Christoph
Russell Y. J. Chung
Alan B. Clarke
Lewis J. Clarke
Roger D. Clemence
Franklin C. Clements
Sandra Clinton
Jack R. Cochran
Jon Charles Coe
Beatriz de Winthuysen Coffin
Laurence E. Coffin Jr.
Donald L. Collins

Fellows of the American Society of Landscape Architects

John F. Collins
Dennis C. Colliton
Richard Conant
Max Z. Conrad
George Glenn Cook
Charles Douglas Coolman
Fred J. Correale
James Robert Cothran
Kenneth R. Coulter
Van L. Cox
H. Kenneth Crasco
George E. Creed
Samuel G. Crozier
Joseph H. Crystal
George W. Curry
C. Edward Curtin
Jack Curtis
John E. Cutler
Jack R. Daft
Bernie Dahl
Peter Dangermond
Edward L. Daugherty
Stuart O. Dawson
Dennis J. Day
Francis H. Dean
Neil J. Dean
Roy H. DeBoer
Richard K. Dee
Robert B. Deering
Bruce Dees
C. Christopher Degenhardt
Dickson DeMarche
Alain deVergie
Roger DeWeese
P. Woodward Dike
F. Christopher Dimond
Nicholas T. Dines
Carlton T. Dodge
Dan W. Donelin
Jim Donovan
Thomas R. Dunbar
Robert W. Dyas
Robert P. Ealy
Garrett Eckbo
Allen R. Edmonson
John C. Ellsworth

Jon Stidger Emerson
Katherine G. Emery
Donald H. Ensign
Stephen Ervin
Steve Estrada
James Matthew Evans
Morgan Evans
L. Susan Everett
Julius Gy. Fabos
Barbara Faga
Oliver M. Fanning
Damon Farber
David Fasser
Rudy J. Favretti
Barbara V. Fealy
Bruce K. Ferguson
Donald L. Ferlow
John J. Fernholz
James C. Fetterman
Ian J. Firth
Charles Albert Flink
Phillip E. Flores
William L. Flournoy Jr.
Everett L. Fly
George E. Fogg
James Frederick Fondren
Donald Mark Fox
Kathleen M. Fox
Mark Francis
Carol L. Franklin
Rene Fransen
Robert L. Frazer
Jere S. French
John W. Frey
M. Paul Friedberg
John F. Furlong
Emily J. Gabel-Luddy
Kathleen A. Garcia
Paul Gardescu
Harry L. Garnham
Benjamin W. Gary Jr.
George G. Gentile
Richard George Gibbons
James E. Glavin
D. Newton Glick
Donald H. Godi

James B. Godwin
Ellin Goetz
Robert E. Goetz
Susan M. Goltsman
Sandra Gonzalez
Robert Wilson Good
Robert T. Gorman
J. Patrick Graham IV
Philip H. Graham Jr.
Leonard Grassli
James W. Gray Jr.
Bradford M. Greene
Isabelle Clara Greene
E. Robert Gregan
John N. Grissim
Clare A. Gunn
Anthony M. Guzzardo
Richard Haag
Frederick Edward Halback
John C. Hall
Lawrence Halprin
Craig C. Halvorson
Calvin S. Hamilton
Asa Hanamoto
Karen C. Hanna
Robert M. Hanna
Becca Hanson
Richard E. Hanson
Nancy M. Hardesty
George Hargreaves
Terence G. Harkness
Charles W. Harris
Robert R. Harvey
Susan M. Hatchell
Richard G. Hautau
William H. Havens
Richard S. Hawks
Robert Graham Heilig
Kenneth I. Helphand
Edith H. Henderson
Glenn O. Hendrix
Glendon M. Herbert Jr.
Randolph T. Hester
Gary R. Hilderbrand
Donald F. Hilderbrandt
Arthur W. Hills

Fellows of the American Society of Landscape Architects

James E. Hiss
Allen W. Hixon Jr.
Leonard J. Hopper
Mark Elison Hoversten
Perry Howard
Donovan E. Hower
Catherine M. Howett
Joseph Hudak
Sam L. Huddleston
Mary V. Hughes
Mark B. Hunner
Lester Hikoji Inouye
Alice R. Ireys
Wayne D. Iverson
Ronald M. Izumita
H. Rowland Jackson
Bernard Jacobs
Peter D.A. Jacobs
Susan L.B. Jacobson
Dale G.M. Jaeger
Frederick D. Jarvis
Leerie T. Jenkins Jr.
David R. Jensen
Linda Lee Jewell
Sonja Johansson
Guy Robert Johns
Carl D. Johnson
Carol R. Johnson
Dean A. Johnson
Mark W. Johnson
Todd D. Johnson
William J. Johnson
Daniel Jones
Grant R. Jones
Ilze Jones
Warren D. Jones
Dirk Jongejan
Gary E. Karner
Joseph P. Karr
Jean Stephans Kavanagh
Frank H. Kawasaki
James E. Keeter
Walter H. Kehm
Carl Kelemen
J. Timothy Keller
Leslie A. Kerr

Gary B. Kesler
Sidney R. Kime Jr.
Steven G. King
Masao Kinoshita
Charles L. Knight
Harold N. Kobayashi
Ken R. Krabbenhoft
Daniel Krall
Brian S. Kubota
William B. Kuhl
Ray O. Kusche
Alon Kvashny
Joseph J. Lalli
Joe W. Langran
Lucille Chenery Lanier
Mary Ann Lasch
William H. Laubmann
Warren E. Lauesen
Michael M. Laurie
Dennis L. Law
Richard K. Law
Jack E. Leaman
Donald Leary
Donald F. Lederer
Charles L. Leider
Donald W. Leslie
Aaron Levine
Philip H. Lewis Jr.
J. Roland Lieber
Mark S. Lindhult
Lloyd Lindley II
Karl Linn
J. Mack Little
Susan P. Little
Earl R. Littlejohn
R. Burton Litton Jr.
Thomas A. Lockett
David Eric Locke
Nimrod W.E. Long III
David O. Lose
Eldridge Lovelace
Paul C.K. Lu
J. Douglas Macy
A. Catherine Mahan
Michael H. Malyn
Cameron R. J. Man

Richard K. Marshall
Gerald Marston
Edward C. Martin Jr.
Roger B. Martin
Steve Martino
Robert M. Mattson
Lewis T. May
Richard E. Mayer
Carol Mayer-Reed
Earl Byron McCulley
Phillip McDade
Vincent C. McDermott
Roger B. McErlane
Mark E. McFarland
Ian McHarg
Kathryn E. McKnight-Thalden
David A. McNeal
Gary W. Meisner
Lauren Melendrez
Robert Melnick
Dee Merriam
Vincent N. Merrill
Elizabeth K. Meyer
Richard J. Meyers
Luciano Miceli
E. Lynn Miller
Patrick A. Miller
Ann Milvsoroff
Debra L. Mitchell
Michael T. Miyabara
Lawrence R. Moline
Donald J. Molnar
Lynn A. Moore
Patrick C. Moore
Richard A. Moore
Roger D. Moore
Margret Mori
Paul F. Morris
Darrel G. Morrison
Mark K. Morrison
Baker H. Morrow
Robert H. Mortensen
Margaret Ann Mullins
Robert K. Murase
Thomas A. Musiak
Kenneth S. Nakaba

241

Fellows of the American Society of Landscape Architects

Kenichi Nakano
Joan I. Nassauer
Darwina L. Neal
John A. Nelson
William R. Nelson Jr.
Joseph N. Nevius
Signe Nielsen
Thomas J. Nieman
Satoru Nishita
Robert L. O'Boyle
Patricia M. O'Donnell
William A. O'Leary
Cornelia A. Oberlander
Warren J. Oblinger
Neil Odenwald
Wolfgang W. Oehme
Laurie D. Olin
Peter J. Olin
Edward J. Olinger
Charles Oliver
Don H. Olson
Brian Orland
Thomas R. Oslund
Theodore Osmundson
Dennis Y. Otsuji
J. Steve Ownby
Michael Painter
James F. Palmer
Thomas P. Papandrew
Cary M. Parker
John G. Parsons
Tito Patri
Gerald D. Patten
Courtland P. Paul
Merlyn J. Paulson
Gerald Phillip Pearson
Robert Perron
Robert C. Perry Jr.
Karen A. Phillips
J. Edward Pinckney
Marjorie E. Pitz
Kenneth J. Polakowski
Peter M. Pollack
Harry W. Porter
Joe A. Porter
Neil H. Porterfield

Marion Pressley
William Pressley
Rae L. Price
Paul N. Procopio
Edward L. Pryce
Helen M. Quackenbush
Nicholas Quennell
F. Truitt Rabun Jr.
David C. Racker
John Rahenkamp
Geoffrey Lew Rausch
Michael Redd
Douglas Reed
Robert S. Reich
Grant W. Reid
Robert G. Reimann
John J. Reynolds
Elliot Rhodeside
John Paul Ribes
Artemas P. Richardson
Donald Richardson
Jane S. Ries
Robert B. Riley
Craig D. Ritland
James F. Ritzer
William H. Roberts
Gary O. Robinette
Jon Rodiek
Richard H. Rogers
Peter G. Rolland
Stephanie Rolley
Peter Rothschild
Clarence Roy
Harvey M. Rubenstein
Robert H. Rucker
Virginia Lockett Russell
Terry Warriner Ryan
Paul M. Saito
Charles S. Saladino II
Margaret Sand
William D. Sanders
George L. Sass
Terry W. Savage
Paul Scardina
Herbert R. Schaal
Horst Schach

Janice C. Schach
Sally Schauman
Mario G. Schjetnan
Arno S. Schmid
Glen Schmidt
Helmut Schmitz
Amy L. Schneckenburger
Gunter A. Schoch
Ollie Schrickel
Sunny Jung Scully
Bradford G. Sears
Jonathan G. Seymour
Bruce Sharky
Richard William Shaw
J. Patrick Shea Jr.
Juanita D. Shearer-Swink
Ruth P. Shellhorn
Hamid Shirvani
J. Kipp Shrack
Jeffrey L. Siegel
Peter Simone
Kenneth B. Simmons Jr.
John Ormsbee Simonds
John B. Slater
Gerald Smith
Herrick H. Smith
Robert W. Smith
Jerrold Soesbe
Randy Sorensen
Stanley V. Specht
Burton S. Sperber
Anne Whiston Spirn
Andrew J. Spurlock
James C. Stansbury
Barry W. Starke
Richard G. Stauffer
Robert Steenhagen
Achva Benzinberg Stein
Frederick R. Steiner
Stephen C. Stimson
John Goddfrey Stoddart
Edward D. Stone Jr.
Edward H. Stone II
Allen D. Stovall
Jan Striefel
Steven Strom

Fellows of the American Society of Landscape Architects

Rosheen Marie Styczinski
Doris Preisendorf Sullivan
Jack Sullivan
Rodney L. Swink
Lolly Tai
Austin Paul Tao
D. Rodney Tapp
James R. Taylor
Leslee A. Temple
Christine Ten Eyck
Barry R. Thalden
Robert Thayer Jr.
Michael Theilacker
J. William Thompson
Robert Tilson
William H. Tishler
Donald H. Tompkins
L. Azeo Torre
Shavaun Towers
Roger T. Trancik
Howard E. Troller
Peter J. Trowbridge
Stephen J. Trudnak
James R. Turner
Jerry Mitchell Turner
Suzanne Louise Turner
Ronald W. Tuttle
Ronald C. Tyne
Anthony Tyznik
Takeo Uesugi

James R. Urban
James Van Sweden
Michael R. Van Valkenburgh
Don Vaughan
E. Michael Vergason
Albert R. Veri
Keith J. Villere
Karl Von Bieberstein
Mark J. Von Wodtke
John Wacker
Lawrence L. Walker
Peter E. Walker
Theodore D. Walker
Victor J. Walker
Larry D. Walling
Thomas H. Wallis
Ronald M. Walters
Thomas C. Wang
Barry J. Warner
Kent E. Watson
Dwight W. Weatherford
E. Neal Weatherly Jr.
Katherine Weidel
Scott S. Weinberg
V. Michael Weinmayr
Roger Wells
William E. Wenk
Robert A. Weygand
James K. Wheat
Morgan Dix Wheelock

Carol A. Whipple
George W. Wickstead
Ron Wigginton
Sara Katherine Williams
Larry T. Wilson
Richard A. Wilson
William P. Winslow III
Theodore J. Wirth
Robert L. Woerner
J. Daniel Wojcik
John Wong
Perry L. Wood
Joan Woodward
David G. Wright
Patrick H. Wyss
Joseph Y. Yamada
Thomas F. Zarfoxx
Mark J. Zarillo
Floyd W. Zimmerman
Robert L. Zion
Robert W. Zolomij
Ervin H. Zube
Laurence W. Zuelke
Jack W. Zunino
K. Richard Zweifel

Source: American Society of Landscape Architects

143

Fellows of the Design Futures Council

Fellowship in the Design Futures Council is granted annually to an outstanding individual(s) who has provided noteworthy leadership to the advancement of design, design solutions, and/or the design professions. Senior fellows of the DFC are recognized for significant contributions toward the understanding of changing trends, new research, and applied knowledge leading to innovative design models that improve the built environment and the human condition. Any person world-wide may nominate candidates. Final selection of the senior fellows is made by the Senior Fellows Selection Committee.

Ray Anderson, Interface, Inc.
Rodrigo Arboleda, MIT Media Lab
Peter Beck, Beck Group
Robert J. Berkebile, BNIM Architects
Phil Bernstein, Autodesk
Friedl Bohm, NBBJ
John Seely Brown, Xerox Research PARC
Janine M. Benyus, author
Santiago Calatrava, architect
Robert Campbell, *Boston Globe*
James P. Cramer†, Greenway Group
Michael Crichton, author and film director
Sylvester Damianos, Damianosgroup
Williston (Bill) Dye, TSA, Inc.
Phil Enquist, Skidmore, Owings & Merrill
Richard Farson, Western Behavioral Sciences Institute
Edward Feiner, Skidmore, Owings & Merrill
Tom Fisher, University of Minnesota
Ed Friedrichs, Friedrichs Group
Steve Fiskum, HGA
Jim Follett, Gensler
Norman Foster, Foster and Partners
Harrison Fraker, University of California, Berkeley
Neil Frankel, Frankel + Coleman
R. Buckminster (Bucky) Fuller*, engineer, inventor, educator, and architectural innovator
Frank Gehry, Gehry Partners
Art Gensler, Gensler
Milton Glaser, graphic designer
Roger Godwin, architect and interior designer
Paul Goldberger, *The New Yorker*
David Gottfried, WorldBuild Technologies Inc.

Zaha Hadid, Zaha Hadid Architects
Jeremy Harris, Urban Strategy Institute
Paul Hawken, Natural Capital Institute
Jerry Hobbs, AC Neilson, vnu
Carl Hodges, Seaphire International
Jane Jacobs, author
Louis I. Kahn*, architect and educator
Tom Kelly, IDEO
A. Eugene Kohn, Kohn Pedersen Fox Associates
Norman Koonce, American Institute of Architects
Steve Jobs, Apple Computer, Inc. and Pixar Animation Studios
Lucinda Ludwig*, Leo A Daly
Chris Luebkeman, Arup
Janet Martin, Communication Arts, Inc.
William McDonough, William McDonough + Partners
Alisdair McGregor, Arup
Sandra Mendler, HOK
Raymond F. Messer, Walter P. Moore Engineers + Consultants
Doug Parker, architect
Alexander (Sandy) Pentland, MIT Media Lab
B. Joseph Pine II, Strategic Horizons LLP
Witold Rybczynski, University of Pennsylvania
Moshe Safdie, Moshe Safdie and Associates
Jonas Salk*, Salk Institute and architectural patron
Adele Santos, Massachusetts Institute of Technology
Peter Schwartz, Global Business Network
Kate Schwenssen, Iowa State University
Terrence J. Sejnowski, Salk Institute

Fellows of the Design Futures Council

Scott Simpson, The Stubbins Associates
Karen Stephenson, Harvard University and
    NetForm International
Cecil Steward, University of Nebraska–Lincoln
    and Joslyn Castle Institute
Sarah Susanka, Susanka Studios
Richard Swett, former US ambassador
    to Denmark
Jack Tanis, Steelcase
April Thornton, consultant
Alan Traugott, CJL Engineering
Robert Tucker, The Innovation Resource
John Carl Warnecke, architect
Jon Westling, Boston University
Gary Wheeler, Gensler
Arol Wolford, Tectonic
Richard Saul Wurman, author and architect

* Deceased
† Resident fellow and foresight advisor

Source: Design Futures Council

245

Architecture, unlike other arts, is not an escape from, but an acceptance of, the human condition, including its many frailties as well as the technical advances of its scientists and engineers. It may rise to great art if it achieves unity, order, and form by appropriate technical means, and if it meets its purposes with conviction. I suppose only then will we have achieved the Great Society. The great architect strives for comprehension, rather than originality for its own sake; a thorough study of a problem, made within the freedom that knowledge provides, is always the greatest source of originality.

Pietro Belluschi

Fellows of the Industrial Designers Society of America

Membership in the Industrial Designers Society of America's Academy of Fellows is conferred by a two-thirds majority vote of its board of directors. Fellows must be society members in good standing who have earned the special respect and affection of the membership through distinguished service to the society and to the profession as a whole. The following individuals are current, active fellows of the IDSA.

James M. Alexander
Wallace H. Appel
Alexander Bally
Betty Baugh
George Beck
Jack Beduhn
Robert I. Blaich
Mort Blumenfeld
William Bullock
Peter Bressler
Bruce Claxton
Tim Cunningham
Thomas David
Niels Diffrient
Mark Dziersk
Arden Farey
Vincent M. Foote
Roger Funk
Walter Furlani
Carroll M. Gantz
John S. Griswold
Olle Haggstrom
James G. Hansen
Stephen G. Hauser
Richard Hollerith
James L. Hvale

Charles L. Jones
Marnie Jones
Lorraine Justice
Steve Kaneko
Jim Kaufman
Ron Kemnitzer
Rudolph W. Krolopp
David Kusuma
LeRoy LaCelle
Richard S. Latham
Raymond Loewy
Peter Edward Lowe
Tucker Madawick
Pascal Malassigné
Joseph R. Mango
Katherine J. McCoy
Donald McFarland
Leon Gordon Miller
Patricia Moore
Charles Pelly
Nancy J. Perkins
James J. Pirkl
William Plumb
Carl Price
Robert E. Redmann
Deane W. Richardson

James M. Ryan
Clair A. Samhammer
Kenneth Schory
F. Eugene Smith
Robert G. Smith
Paul B. Specht
Darrell S. Staley
Budd Steinhilber
Philip H. Stevens
David D. Tompkins
Herbert H. Tyrnauer
Tucker Viemeister
Craig Vogel
Noland E. Vogt
Sandor Weisz
Stephen Wilcox
Arnold Wolf
Peter Wooding
Cooper C. Woodring
Edward Wormley
Edward J. Zagorski

Source: Industrial Designers Society of America

Fellows of the International Interior Design Association

Professional members of the International Interior Design Association are inducted into the IIDA College of Fellows by a two-thirds vote by its board of directors. This honor recognizes members who have demonstrated outstanding service to IIDA, the community, and the interior design profession. The following individuals are current, active fellows of the IIDA.

Luis Adolfo López Amaya
Marilyn Archer
Laura Bailey
Jeanne Baldwin
Anita Barnett
Louis M.S. Beal
Claude Berube
Charles Blumberg
Marla Bommarito-Crouch
Dan Bouligny
Michael Bourque
Bonnie Bruce
Richard Carlson
Particia Gutierrez Castellanos
Amarjeet Singh Chatrath
Susan Coleman
David F. Cooke
Eleanor Corkle
Michael H. Cushwa
Christine Dandan
Eugene M. Daniels
Carol Disrud
Jacqueline Duncan
Chip duPont
Cheryl Duvall
Hilda East
Eric Engstrom
Suzanne P. Fairly-Green
Marilyn Farrow
Dorothy L. Fowles
Neil P. Frankel
Angela Frey
Edward C. Friedrichs
Charles Gandy
Charles Gelber
M. Arthur Gensler Jr.
Lewis Goetz
Carol S. Graham
Karen Guenther
Beth Harmon-Vaughan

Olaf M. Harris
Judith Hastings
Jo S. Heinz
Edna Henner
John E. Herron
Frederick P. Hutchirs
David Immenschuh
Cary Johnson
Christina Johnson
Jan Johnson
Carol Jones
Margo Jones
Robert J. Kennedy
Tessa Kennedy
Robin Klehr Avia
Sooz Klinkhamer
Mary Knackstedt
Marjorie Kriebel
Michael Kroelinger
Robert Ledingham
Fola Lerner-Miller
Jack Levin
Neville Lewis
Pamela Light
John A. Lijewski
Nick Luzietti
Hiroko Machida
Candace MacKenzie
Richard Mazzucotelli
Jose T. Medrano
Ruth Mellergaard
Kenneth A. Muller
Peggy Noakes
Donald Parker
J. Derrell Parker
Janie E. Petkus
Paul Petrie
Richard N. Pollack
Mary Helen Pratte
Shirley Pritchard

Sandra Ragan
Charles A. Raymond
Patti Richards
Jane Rohde
Wayne Ruga
Joyce C. Saunders
Mitchell Sawasy
Allan Shaivitz
Donald Sherman
Rayne Sherman
Gail H. Shiel
Bernard Soep
Henrietta Spencer-Churchill
Andre Staffelbach
Andrew L. Stafford
William Stankiewicz
Deborah Steinmetz
Janice Stevenor-Dale
Donald Thomas
Joann A. Thompson
Betty McKee Treanor
Marcia Troyan
Robert Valentine
Margaret Velardo
Roen Viscovich
Gary Wheeler
Allison Carll White
Ron Whitney-Whyte
Glenda Wilcox
Frances E. Wilson
M. Judith Wilson
D. Geary Winstead
Michael H. Wirtz
Robert Lee Wolf
Minoru Yokoyama
Janice R. Young

Source: International Interior Design Association

Fellows of the Society of Architectural Historians

Fellowship in the Society of Architectural Historians is granted for "exceptional and distinguished service to the society." The following individuals are current, active fellows of the SAH.

H. Allen Brooks
Richard W. Howland
Carol Herselle Krinsky
Elisabeth Blair MacDougall
Carter H. Manny
Henry A. Millon
Osmund Overby
Seymour H. Persky
William H. Pierson Jr.
Damie Stillman
George B. Tatum

Source: Society of Architectural Historians

But watch out, the time has not come yet; another hundred years at least do we have to pretend to ourselves and to others, as the witches say in Macbeth, that beautiful is what is ugly, because that which is ugly is useful and that which is beautiful is not.

Lord Keynes (1930)

Honorary Fellows of the American Institute of Architects

The American Institute of Architects grants honorary fellowships to non-members, both architects and non-architects, who have made substantial contributions to the field of architecture.

Kurt H.C. Ackermann, Munich, Germany
Gunnel Adlercreutz, Helsinki, Finland
O.J. Aguilar, Lima, Peru
Hisham Albakri, Kuala Lumpur, Malaysia
William A. Allen, London, England
Alfred V. Alvares, Vancouver, Canada
Jose Alvarez, Lima, Peru
Mario R. Alvarez, Buenos Aires, Argentina
Tadao Ando, Osaka, Japan
John H. Andrews, Australia
Carlos D. Arguelles, Manila, Philippines
Gordon R. Arnott, Regina, Canada
Carl Aubock, Austria
Carlo Aymonino, Venice, Italy
George G. Baines, England
Juan Navarro Baldeweg, Madrid, Spain
W.D. Baldwin, Sterling, Canada
Shigeru Ban, Japan
W.K. Banadayga, Sterling, Canada
Essy Baniassad, Halifax, Canada
Nikolai B. Baranov, Moscow, Russia
Carlo Baumschlager, Austria
Geoffrey M. Bawa, Columbo, Sri Lanka
Eugene Beaudouin, France
Gerard Benoit, Paris, France
Jai R. Bhalla, New Delhi, India
Jacob Blegvad, Aalborg, Denmark
Ricardo L. Bofill, Barcelona, Spain
Oriol Bohigas, Barcelona, Spain
Irving D. Boigon, Richmond Hill, Canada
Ferenc Callmeyer, Telki, Hungary
Santiago A. Calvo, Lima, Peru
Felix Candela, Raleigh, North Carolina
Massimo Carmassi, Firenze, Italy
Rifat Chadirji, Surrey, England
Suk-Woong Chang, Seoul, Korea
Te L. Chang, Taipei, Taiwan
Jean Marie Charpentier, France
Bill Chomik, Calgary, Canada
Adolf Ciborowski, Warsaw, Poland
E. Gresley Cohen, Dalkeith, Australia

Charles M. Correa, Bombay, India
Philip S. Cox, Sydney, Australia
Charles H. Cullum, Newfoundland, Canada
Carlos E. Da Silva, Rizal, Philippines
John M. Davidson, Richmond, Australia
David Y. Davies, Surrey, England
Sara T. De Grinberg, Mexico
Rafael De La Hoz, Spain
S.D. De La Tour, Durville, France
Eduardo De Mello, Braga, Portugal
Costantin N. Decavalla, Greece
Ignacio M. Delmonte, Mexico City, Mexico
A.J. (Jack) Diamond, Toronto, Canada
Ignacio Diaz-Morales, Jalisco, Mexico
Balkrishna V. Doshi, Ahmedabad, India
Philip Dowson, London, England
Kiril Doytchev, Sofia, Bulgaria
G.M. Dubois, Toronto, Canada
Allan F. Duffus, Halifax, Canada
Werner Duttman, Lindenalle, Germany
Dietmar Eberle, Austria
David W. Edwards, Regina, Canada
Yehya M. Eid, Cairo, Egypt
Abdel W. El Wakil, Kent, England
Arthur C. Erickson, Vancouver, Canada
Lord Esher, England
Inger Exner, Denmark
Johannes Exner, Denmark
Tobias Faber, Copenhagen, Denmark
Francisco B. Fajardo, Philippines
Hassan Fathy, Egypt
Sverre Fehn, Oslo, Norway
Bernard M. Feilden, Norfolk, England
Ji Z. Feng, Shanghai, China
Angelina Munoz Fernandez de Madrid,
    Sonora, Mexico
A.I. Ferrier, Red Hill, Australia
Jozsef Finta, Budapest, Hungary
Antonio F. Flores, Mexico
Cesar X. Flores, Mexico DF, Mexico
Norman Foster, London, England

Honorary Fellows of the American Institute of Architects

Charles A. Fowler, Canada
Massimiliano Fuksas, Rome, Italy
Jorge Gamboa de Buen, Mexico DF, Mexico
Juan Gonzalez, Spain
Roderick P. Hackney, Cheshire, England
Zaha Hadid, London, England
H.H. Hallen, Australia
Shoji Hayashi, Tokyo, Japan
Mikko Heikkinen, Helsinki, Finland
Herman Hertzberger, Netherlands
Jacques Herzog, Switzerland
Tao Ho, North Point, Hong Kong, China
Barry J. Hobin, Ottawa, Canada
Hans Hollein, Vienna, Austria
Wilhelm Holzbauer, Vienna, Austria
Sir Michael Hopkins, London, England
Lady Patricia Hopkins, London, England
Thomas Howarth, Toronto, Canada
Nobuo Hozumi, Tokyo, Japan
Il-in Hwang, Korea
Paul Hyett, Woodford Green, UK
Arata Isozaki, Tokyo, Japan
Toyo Ito, Tokyo, Japan
Daryl Jackson, Melbourne, Australia
R.D. Jackson, Sydney, Australia
Alvaro Joaquim de Meio Siza, Porto, Portugal
Barry Johns, Edmonton, Canada
P.N. Johnson, Australia
Sumet Jumsai, Bangkok, Thailand
Achyut P. Kanvinde, New Dehli, India
Vladimir Karfik, Brno, Czech Republic
Kiyonori Kikutake, Tokyo, Japan
Reiichiro Kitadai, Tokyo, Japan
Azusa Kito, Tokyo, Japan
Josef P. Kleihues, Berlin, Germany
Markku Komonen, Helsinki, Finland
Rob Krier, Berlin, Germany
Dogan Kuban, Istanbul, Turkey
Alexandr P. Kudryavtsev, Moscow, Russia
Kisho Kurokawa, Tokyo, Japan
Colin Laird, Port of Spain, Trinidad and Tobago
Jean L. Lalonde, Canada
Phyllis Lambert, Canada
Henning Larsen, Denmark
Denys L. Lasdun, London, England
Kwang-Ro Lee, Seoul, Korea

Kyung-Hoi Lee, Seoul, Korea
Sang-Leem Lee, Seoul, Korea
Juha Ilmari Leiviskä, Helsinki, Finland
Sergio Lenci, Rome, Italy
Jaime Lerner, Parana, Brazil
Wu Liang Yong, Beijing, China
Kington Loo, Kuala Lumpur, Malaysia
Aldana E. Lorenzo, San Jeronimo, Mexico
Serapio P. Loza, Jalisco, Mexico
Kjell Lund, Oslo, Norway
Brian MacKay-Lyons, Halifax, Canada
Olufemi Majekodunmi, Gaborone, Botswana
Fumihiko Maki, Tokyo, Japan
Matti K. Makinen, Finland
Rutilo Malacara, Mexico DF, Mexico
Motlatsi Peter Malefane, Johannesburg,
  South Africa
Albert Mangones, Port Au Prince, Haiti
Yendo Masayoshi, New York, New York
Peter McIntyre, Victoria, Australia
Rodrigo Mejia-Andrion, Panama
Hector Mestre, Mexico DF, Mexico
Pierre de Meuron, Switzerland
Wladimir Mitrofanoff, Paris, France
Jose Raphael Moneo, Madrid, Spain
Raymond Moriyama, Toronto, Canada
Padraig Murray, Dublin, Ireland
Toshio Nakamura, Tokyo, Japan
Nikola I. Nikolov, Sofia, Bulgaria
Juan Bassegoda Nonell, Barcelona, Spain
Rafael Norma, Mexico DF, Mexico
Jean Nouvel, Paris, France
Carl J.A. Nyren, Stockholm, Sweden
ShinIchi Okada, Tokyo, Japan
Oluwole O. Olumyiwa, Lagos, Nigeria
Georgui M. Orlov, Moscow, Russia
Suha Ozkan, Switzerland
Juhani Pallasmaa, Helsinki, Finland
Gustav Peichl, Vienna, Austria
Raili Pietila, Helsinki, Finland
Methodi A. Pissarski, Sofia, Bulgaria
Ernst A. Plischke, Vienna, Austria
Paolo Portoghesi, Rome, Italy
Christian de Portzamparc, Paris, France
Ivor C. Prinsloo, Rondebosch, South Africa
Victor M. Prus, Montreal, Canada

Honorary Fellows of the American Institute of Architects

Luis M. Quesada, Lima, Peru
Hector M. Restat, Santiago, Chile
Jose F. Reygadas, Mexico DF, Mexico
Philippe Robert, Paris, France
Derry Menzies Robertson, Picton, Canada
Juan J. Rocco, Montevideo, Uruguay
Xavier Cortes Rocha, Coyoacan, Mexico
Aldo A. Rossi, Milano, Italy
Witold Rybczynski, Philadelphia, PA
Thomas J. Sanabria, Miami, FL
Alberto Sartoris, Cossonay Ville, Switzerland
Helmut C. Schulitz, Braunschweig, Germany
Michael Scott, Ireland
Harry Seidler, Australia
J. Francisco Serrano, Mexico DF, Mexico
Hchioh Sang Seung, Seoul, Korea
Vassilis C. Sgoutas, Athens, Greece
Haigo T.H. Shen, Taipei, Taiwan
Peter F. Shepheard, Philadelphia, PA
Tsutomu Shigemura, Kobe, Japan
Zheng Shiling, Shanghai, China
Kazuo Shinohara, Yokohama, Japan
Brian Sim, Vancouver, Canada
Antonio S. Sindiong, Rizal, Philippines
Heikki Siren, Helsinki, Finland
Kaija Siren, Helsinki, Finland
Nils Slaatto, Oslo, Norway
Vladimir Slapeta, Praha, Czech Republic
Inette L. Smith, Cornwall, England
J.M. Smith, Cornwall, England
Gin Su, Bethesda, MD
Michio Sugawara, Tokyo, Japan
Timo Suomalainen, Espoo, Finland
Minoru Takeyama, Littleton, CO
Yoshio Taniguchi, Tokyo, Japan
German Tellez, Bogota, Colombia
Anders Tengbom, Sweden
Paul-André Tétreault, Montreal, Canada
Alexandros N. Tombazis, Athens, Greece
Luben N. Tonev, Bulgaria
Marion Tournon-Branly, Paris, France
Shozo Uchii, Tokyo, Japan
Lennart Uhlin, Stockholm, Sweden
Jørn Utzon, Denmark
Pierre Vago, Noisy, France
Gino Valle, Udine, Italy

Marcelo E. Vargas, Lima, Peru
Pedro R. Vasquez, Mexico DF, Mexico
Eva Vecsei, Montreal, Canada
Jorge N. Verdugo, Mexico DF, Mexico
Tomas R. Vicuna, Santiago, Chile
Jean-Paul Viguier, Paris, France
Ricardo L. Vilchis, Mexico DF, Mexico
Eduardo O. Villacortaq, Lima, Peru
William Whitefield, London, England
Terence J. Williams, Victoria, Canada
Roy W. Willwerth, Halifax, Canada
C.A. Wunderlich, Guatemala City, Guatemala
Chung Soo Won, Seoul, Korea
Bernard Wood, Ottawa, Canada
Rutang Ye, Beijing, China
Richard Young, Sterling, Canada
Abraham Zabludovsky, Codesa, Mexico
Jose M. Zaragoza, Philippines
Moshe Zarhy, Israel
Eberhard Heinrich Zeidler, Toronto, Canada
Peter Zumthor, Switzerland

Source: American Institute of Architects

Did you know...

For the first time since opening her practice in London in 1979, Zaha Hadid has received a commission from her adopted county. Britain's Architecture Foundation selected Hadid's design for its new exhibition center in London, due to open in late 2006.

Honorary Fellows of the American Society of Interior Designers

Honorary fellowship is the highest honor that the American Society of Interior Designers can bestow on an individual who is not an interior designer by profession. It is granted to individuals who have shown achievements on a national or international level in areas related to design and those who have made noteworthy contributions to the advancement of the interior design profession. The following individuals are current honorary fellows of ASID.

Michael Alin
Robert H. Angle
Thomas Banks
Edwin Bitter
Daisy Houston Bond
Walton E. Brown
Murray Douglas
Francis J. Geck
Alexander Girard
Olga Gueft

Lawrence Halprin
William D. Hamilton
Buie Harwood
Robert Herring
Constantinos Doxiadis
Franklin S. Judson
Joseph LoVecchio
Anita M. Laird
Douglas Parker
Dianne H. Pilgrim

Norman Polsky
Wayne Ruga
Alan Siegel
Jerrold Sonet
Michael Sorrentino
Paul D. Spreiregen

Source: American Society of Interior Designers

When shapes are beautiful, they're timeless.

Jacques Garcia

Honorary Members of the American Institute of Architects

The American Institute of Architects grants honorary membership to individuals outside the architecture profession who are not otherwise eligible for membership in the institute. They are chosen for their distinguished service to architecture or the allied arts and sciences. Nominations may be submitted by the national AIA Board of Directors, a component, or a professional interest area. National and component staff with 10 years or more of service are also eligible for honorary membership.

Suzie Adams, Fort Worth, TX
Ava J. Abramowitz, Chevy Chase, MD
Joseph F. Addonizio, New Rochelle, NY
His Highness The Aga Khan
Joseph Ahearn, Littleton, CO
Michael L. Ainslie, New York, NY
R. Mayne Albright, Charlotte, NC
Barbara Allan, Seattle, WA
George A. Allen, Tallahassee, FL
Trudy Aron, Topeka, KS
Ludd Ashley, Washington, DC
Janice Axon, Laguna Niguel, CA
William M. Babcock, Madison, WI
Kermit Baker, Washington, DC
Mariana Barthold, Oklahoma City, OK
Augustus Baxter, Sr., Philadelphia, PA
Stephen M. Bennett, Columbus, OH
Leo L. Beranek, Cambridge, MA
Elaine Bergman, Tulsa, OK
James Biddle, Andalusia, PA
J. Bidwill, Chicago, IL
Sherry Birk, Washington, DC
Sherwood L. Boehlert, Utica, NY
Oriol Bohigas, Barcelona, Spain
Sara H. Boutelle, Santa Cruz, CA
A.S. Boyd, Washington, DC
Ann Marie Boyden, Arlington, VA
Eleanor K. Brassel, Bethesda, MD
John W. Braymer, Richmond, VA
David Brinkley, Chevy Chase, MD
Jack Brooks, Washington, DC
A.B. Brown, Providence, RI
Charlotte Vestal Brown, Raleigh, NC
J.N. Brown, Providence, RI
William A. Brown Sr., Washington, DC

William D. Browning, Snowmass, CO
John M. Bryan, Columbia, SC
Muriel Campaglia, Washington, DC
Donald Canty, Seattle, WA
Joan Capelin, New York, NY
Edward Carlough, Washington, DC
Charles M. Cawley, Wilmington, DE
Henry C. Chambers, Beaufort, SC
Mary Chapman-Smith, Mancelona, MI
William W. Chase, Alexandria, VA
Henry Cisneros, San Antonio, TX
F.J. Clark, Washington, DC
Grady Clay Jr., Louisville, KY
Ernest A. Connally, Alexandria, VA
S.B. Conroy, Washington, DC
Rolaine V. Copeland, Seattle, WA
Weld Coxe, Block Island, RI
Lois Craig, Cambridge, MA
James P. Cramer, Atlanta, GA
Alfonse M. D'Amato, Washington, DC
Kathleen L. Daileda, Washington, DC
Ann Davidson, North Canton, OH
Joan K. Davidson, New York, NY
Brent L. Davis, Tucson AZ
Mabel S. Day, Alexandria, VA
Fred R. Deluca, Washington, DC
Barbaralee Diamonstein-Spielvogel, New York, NY
Deborah Dietsch, Washington, DC
John A. DiNardo, Austin, TX
Carlos Diniz
Rae Dumke, Detroit, MI
M. Durning, Seattle, WA
J. Sprigg Duvall, Washington, DC
Linda J. Ebitz, Oakland, PA
Judy A. Edwards, New Haven, CT

Honorary Members of the American Institute of Architects

M.D. Egan, Anderson, SC
James R. Ellis, Seattle, WA
John D. Entenza, Santa Monica, CA
Marie L. Farrell, Belvedere, CA
Mary E. Fenelon, Reston, VA
Alan M. Fern, Chevy Chase, MD
Angelina Munoz Fernandez de Madrid, Sonora, Mexico
L.A. Ferre, San Juan, Puerto Rico
David W. Field, Columbus, OH
Harold B. Finger, Washington, DC
James M. Fitch, New York, NY
Louise H. (Polly) Flansburgh, Boston, MA
Sally Ann Fly, Austin, TX
Terrance R. Flynn, Wilmington, DE
J.D. Forbes, Charlottesville, VA
William S. Fort, Eugene, OR
Arthur J. Fox Jr., New York, NY
Doris C. Freedman, New York, NY
Mildred Friedman, New York, NY
Patsy L. Frost, Columbus, OH
Ruth Fuller, Houston, TX
Paul Gapp, Chicago, IL
D.E. Gardner, Delaware, OH
Paul Genecki, Kensington, MD
C.D. Gibson, Ogden, UT
Brendan Gill, New York, NY
Jorge Glusberg, Buenos Aires, Argentina
Tina M. Gobbel, Phoenix, AZ
Alfred Goldberg, Belvedere Tiburon, CA
Howard G. Goldberg Esq.
Paul Goldberger, New York, NY
Douglas E. Gordon, Washington, DC
H.B. Gores, Alpharetta, GA
D.R. Graham, Tallahassee, FL
Ginny W. Graves, Prairie Village, KS
Barbara Gray, Takoma Park, MD
Roberta Gratz
Cecil H. Green, Dallas, TX
Thomas Griffith, New York, NY
Roberta J. Guffey, Charleston, WV
Robert Gutman, Princeton, NJ
Richard Haag, Seattle, WA
Donald J. Hall, Kansas City, MO
William L. Hall, Eden Prairie, MN
Donalee Hallenbeck, Sacramento, CA

Charles E. Hamlin, Little Compton, RI
P. Hammer, Beverley Beach, MD
Marga Rose Hancock, Seattle, WA
Mayor Jeremy Harris, Honolulu, HI
Partrick K. Harrison, London, UK
F. Otto Hass, Philadelphia, PA
Arthur A. Hart, Boise, ID
Dianne Hart, California
Beverly E. Hauschild-Baron, Minneapolis, MN
A. Hecksher, New York, NY
Paul K. Heilstedt, Frankfort. IL
Andrew Heiskell, New York, NY
Brenda Henderson, Washington, DC
Amy Hershfang
Gerald D. Hines, Houston, TX
Charles L. Hite
David E. Hollowell, Newark, DE
William Houseman, Portland, ME
Thomas P. Hoving, New York, NY
Philip A. Hutchinson, Harwood, MD
Ada L. Huxtable, New York, NY
J. Michael Huey
Donald G. Iselin, Santa Barbara, CA
Kathy C. Jackson, Jackson, MS
J.B. Johnson, Watertown, NY
Joseph E. Johnson
Lady B. Johnson, Austin, TX
Gerre Jones, Albuquerque, NM
V. Jordan Jr., New York, NY
H.A. Judd, Beaverton, OR
Lloyd Kaiser, Oakmont, PA
Shelly Kappe
Robert J. Kapsch, Gaithersburg, MD
Suzanne Keller, Princeton, NJ
Dorothy Kender
Roger G. Kennedy, Alexandria, VA
Jonathan King, Houston, TX
R. Lawrence Kirkegaard, Downers Grove, IL
Suzanne C. Koonce, McLean, VA
Lee E. Koppelman, Stonybrook, NY
Pamela L. Kortan, Washington, DC
Peter H. Kostmayer, Washington, DC
Mabel Krank, Oklahoma City, OK
Florence C. Ladd, Cambridge, MA
Anita M. Laird, Cape May, NJ
David P. Lancaster, Austin, TX

Honorary Members of the American Institute of Architects

George Latimer, St. Paul, MN
Robert C. Lautman, Washington, DC
Robin Lee, Washington, DC
William J. Le Messurier, Cambridge, MA
Barry B. LePatner
Aaron Levine, Menlo Park, CA
E.H. Levitas, Washington, DC
Karen Lewand, Baltimore, MD
Lawrence Lewis Jr.
Ulrich M. Lindner, San Diego, CA
David Littlejohn, Kensington, CA
Weiming Lu, St. Paul, MN
Eugene Lupia, Washington, DC
Jane Maas, New York, NY
Diane Maddox, Washington, DC
Jon D. Magnusson, Seattle, WA
Randell Lee Makinson
Stanley Marcus, Dallas, TX
Louis L. Marines, Corte Madera, CA
Judy Marks, Washington, DC
Albert R. Marschall, Alexandria, VA
Maureen Marx, Springfield, VA
Mary Tyler Cheek McClenaham
F.M. McConihe, Potomac, MD
Robert McCoy
Terrence M. McDermott, Chicago, IL
Evelyn B. McGrath, Holiday, FL
Cheri C. Melillo, New York, NY
Paul Mellon, Upperville, VA
Betty H. Meyer
E.P. Mickel, Bethesda, MD
Martha P. Miller, Portland, OR
R. Miller, Sherman Oaks, CA
Richard B. Miller, Elmsford, NY
Roger Milliken, Spartanburg, SC
Hermine Mitchell, Philadelphia, PA
Richard Moe, Washington, DC
Martha Barber Montgomery
William B. Moore Jr., Kilmarnock, VA
John W. Morris, Arlington, VA
Philip A. Morris, Birmingham, AL
Terry B. Morton, Chevy Chase, MD
Woolridge Brown Morton III
Jean G. Muntz, Omaha, NE
Martha Murphree, Houston, TX
Maria Murray, Kensington, MD

Betty J. Musselman, Accokeek, MD
Raymond D. Nasher, Dallas, TX
Doreen Nelson, Los Angeles, CA
Shirley J. Norvell, Springfield, IL
Laurie D. Olin, Philadelphia, PA
Mary E. Osman, Columbia, SC
Lynn J. Osmond, Chicago, IL
Frank Pallone, Long Branch, NJ
Ronald J. Panciera, Bradenton, FL
R.B. Pease, Pittsburgh, PA
C. Ford Peatross, Washington, DC
Robert A. Peck Esq, Washington, DC
Claiborne Pell, Washington, DC
David Perdue, Silver Spring, MD
Michael D. Perry, Virginia Beach, VA
G.E. Pettengill, Arlington, VA
Janet D. Pike, Lexington, KY
Philip W. Pillsbury Jr., Washington, DC
Walter F. Pritchard II, Costa Mesa, CA
Jody Proppe, Portland, OR
Marvin Rand, Venice, CA
Sidney A. Rand, Minneapolis, MN
David P. Reynolds, Richmond, VA
William G. Reynolds Jr., Richmond, VA
Brenda Richards
Carolyn Richie
Raymond P. Rhinehart, Washington, DC
Joseph P. Riley, Charleston, SC
J.P. Robin, Pittsburgh, PA
Laurance Rockefeller, New York, NY
Barbara J. Rodriguez, Albany, NY
Gini Rountree, Sacramento, CA
Mario G. Salvadori, New York, NY
Stephen P. Sands
Carl M. Sapers, Boston, MA
William D. Schaefer, Baltimore, MD
Martin Schaum, Garden City, NY
Paul Schell, Seattle, WA
Vincent C. Schoemehl Jr., Clayton, MO
Philip Schreiner, Washington, DC
Rosemary Schroeder, Dallas, TX
Robert H. Schuller, Garden Grove, CA
Susan E. Schur
Frederick D. Schwengel
Suzanne K. Schwengels, Des Moines, IA
Rex Scouten, Washington, DC

255

Honorary Members of the American Institute of Architects

B. Sebastian, San Francisco, CA
James H. Semans, Durham, NC
Julian B. Serrill, Des Moines, IA
Elaine K. Sewell Jones, Los Angeles, CA
Polly E. Shackleton, Washington, DC
Julius Shulman, Los Angeles, CA
John R. Silber
Betty W. Silver, Raleigh, NC
Alice Sinkevitch, Chicago, IL
John B. Skilling, Seattle, WA
W.L. Slayton, Washington, DC
Eleanor McNamara Smith, Somerset, WI
Nancy Somerville, Washington, DC
S. Spencer, Washington, DC
Ann Stacy, Baltimore, MD
B. Carole Steadham
S. Steinborn, Seattle, WA
Saundra Stevens, Portland, OR
P.D. Stitt, Yreka, CA
Deborah Sussman, Culver City, CA
Anne J. Swager, Pittsburg, PA
Pipsan S. Swanson, Bloomfield, MI
G.B. Tatum, Chester, CT
Anne Taylor, Kansas City, MO
Richard Thevenot, Baton Rouge, LA
J.S. Thurmond, Washington, DC
Carolyn H. Toft, St. Louis, MO
Richard L. Tomasetti, New York, NY

Bernard Tomson, Voorheesville, NY
W.F. Traendly, Thetford Center, VT
R.E. Train, Washington, DC
Tallman Trask III, Durham, NC
Lloyd N. Unsell Jr., College Park, MD
Pierre Vago, Noisy, France
Mariana L. Verga, Edmond, OK
Wolf Von Eckardt, Washington, DC
Richard S. Vosko, Clifton Park, NY
Connie C. Wallace, Nashville, TN
Paul Weidlinger, New York, NY
Paul W. Welch, Jr. Sacramento, CA
Emmet L. Wemple, Los Angeles, CA
Katie Westby, Tulsa, OK
Frank J. Whalen Jr., Cheverly, MD
Richard Guy Wilson, Charlottesville, VA
Gloria Wise, Dallas, TX
Pete Wilson, Washington, DC
Arol Wolford, Atlanta, GA
Marilyn Wood, Santa Fe, NM
Tony P. Wrenn, Fredricksburg, VA
Sidney Yates, Washington, DC
Jill D. Yeomans, Santa Barbara, CA
John Zukowsky, Chicago, IL

Source: American Institute of Architects

Architecture, like the shaft of an axe, must beautifully and precisely symbolize its own good reasons for its necessary existence. Insight and sincerity will tell us which reasons are good.

Ralph Erskine

Honorary Members of the American Society of Landscape Architects

Honorary membership is granted by the board of directors of the American Society of Landscape Architects to persons, other than landscape architects, who have performed notable service to the profession of landscape architecture.

Edward H. Able Jr.
Randall Arendt
Philip J. Arnold
Douglas Bereuter
Charles Eliot Beveridge
Randall Biallas
Earl Blumenauer
Nancy Callister Buley
Dale Bumpers
James Earl Carter Jr.
Clarence (Buck) Chaffee
Grady Clay
Richard M. Daley
Russell E. Dickenson
Walter L. Doty
Marvin Durning
Carolyn B. Etter
Don D. Etter
Albert Fein
Edward A. Feiner
Charles E. Fraser
Marshall M. Fredericks
Gwen Frostic

Mary L. Hanson
Donald M. Harris
George B. Hartzog Jr.
Vance R. Hood
Patrick Horsbrugh
Thomas Hylton
Lyndon B. Johnson
Harley Jolley
Genevieve Pace Keller
Edward M. Kennedy
Barbara A. King
Peter A. Kirsch
Balthazar Korab
Norbert Kraich
Walter H. Lewis
Dr. Binyi Liu
John A. Love
Lee MacDonald
E. Bruce MacDougall
William C. Main
Charles C. McLaughlin
Ed McMahon
Bette Midler

Hugh C. Miller
Philip A. Morris
Tom Murphy
Frederick L. Noland
Gyo Obata
Ross D. Pallay
R. Max Peterson
William Phelps
Richard Pope, Sr.
Colin Powell
Peter H. Raven
Joseph P. Riley Jr.
Laurance S. Rockefeller
Martin J. Rosen
John Seiberling
Thomas D. Seifert
Ron Taven
Ralph J. Warburton

Source: American Society of Landscape Architects

Honorary Members of the Industrial Designers Society of America

The board of directors of the Industrial Designers Society of America grants honorary membership to individuals whose relationship to, involvement with, or special efforts on behalf of the design profession merit the recognition and gratitude of the society. Honorary membership is awarded by a three-quarters majority vote by the board of directors.

Florence Knoll Bassett
Ralph Caplan
Ray Eames
R. Buckminster Fuller
Edgar Kaufmann Jr.
Vicki Matranga
Bruce Nussbaum
Brian J. Wynne

Source: Industrial Designers Society of America

The most critical thing in design at this moment is to think of design as an evolutionary process. Even lines and elements of furniture can build upon themselves over time in an evolutionary way.

Luigi Ferrara

Honorary Members of the International Interior Design Association

The International Interior Design Association grants honorary membership to individuals who, although they are not interior designers, have made substantial contributions to the interior design profession. The following individuals are current honorary members of the IIDA.

Stanley Abercrombie
Clarellen Adams
George Baer
Shirley Black
Charles Blumberg
Chilton Brown
Margaret Buckingham
Dennis Cahill
Len Corlin
Christine Cralle
James P. Cramer

Tom Cramer
Cheryl Durst
Lori Graham
Dianne Jackman
Cynthia Leibrock
Paul Leonard
Viscount David Linley
Chris McKellar
Doug Parker
Norman Polsky
Lois Powers

John Sample
Thomas Sutton Jr.
Dean Thompson
Jan Toft
Jill Vanderfleet-Scott
John West

Source: International Interior Design Association

Did you know...

Salvador Dali collaborated with the famous Parisian interior designer Jean-Michel Frank on several projects, including the production of furniture as well as more mundane items such as handles and faucets.

Interior Design Hall of Fame

In 1985, *Interior Design* magazine established the Interior Design Hall of Fame to recognize individuals who have made significant contributions to the growth and prominence of the interior design profession. New inductees are presented every December at an awards ceremony in New York. This event also serves as a fundraising effort for the nonprofit Foundation for Interior Design Education Research and other charitable organizations supporting interior design educational initiatives.

Marvin. B Affrime
Kalef Alaton
Davis Allen
Stephen A. Apking
Pamela Babey
Benjamin Baldwin
Barbara Barry
Florence Knoll Bassett
Louis M.S. Beal
Ward Bennett
Maria Bergson
Deborah Berke
Bruce Bierman
Laura Bohn
Joseph Braswell
Robert Bray
Don Brinkmann
Thomas Britt
R. Scott Bromley
Mario Buatta
Richard A. Carlson
Arthur Casas
Francois Catroux
Steve Chase
Antonio Citterio
Clodagh
Celeste Cooper
Robert Currie
Barbara D'Arcy
Joseph P. D'Urso
Thierry W. Despont
Orlando Diaz-Azcuy
Angelo Donghia
Jaime Drake
Jack Dunbar
Tony Duquette
Melvin Dwork
David Anthony Easton
Henry End

Mica Ertegun
Edward A. Feiner
Bernardo Fort-Brescia
Billy W. Francis
Neil Frankel
Michael Gabellini
Frank Gehry
Arthur Gensler
Richard Gluckman
Mariette Himes Gomez
Jacques Grange
Michael Graves
Bruce Gregga
Charles Gwathmey
Albert Hadley
Victoria Hagan
Anthony Hail
Mel Hamilton
Mark Hampton
Antony Harbour
Hugh Hardy
Gisue Hariri
Mojgan Hariri
Kitty Hawks
David Hicks
Edith Mansfield Hills
Richard Himmel
Howard Hirsch
William Hodgins
Malcolm Holzman
Franklin D. Israel
Carolyn Iu
Eva Jiricna
Jed Johnson
Melanie Kahane
Ronette King
Robert Kleinschmidt
Ronald Krueck
Gary L. Lee

Sarah Tomerlin Lee
Naomi Leff
Debra Lehman-Smith
Joseph Lembo
Lawrence Lerner
Neville Lewis
Sally Sirkin Lewis
Christian Liaigre
Piero Lissoni
Eva Maddox
Stephen Mallory
Peter Marino
Patrick McConnell
Margaret McCurry
Zack McKown
Kevin McNamara
Robert Metzger
Lee Mindel
Juan Montoya
Frank Nicholson
James Northcuh
Dorothy May Kinnicutt Parish
John Pawson
Norman Pfeiffer
Charles Pfister
Warren Platner
Donald D. Powell
William Pulgram
Glenn Pushelberg
Andrée Putman
Chessy Rayner
David Rockwell
Lauren Rottet
John F. Saladino
Michael Schaible
Denise Scott Brown
Peter Shelton
Betty Sherrill
Julius Shulman

Interior Design Hall of Fame

Robert Siegel
Ethel Smith
William Sofield
Laurinda Spear
Jay Spectre
Andre Staffelbach
Rita St. Clair
Philippe Starck
Robert A.M. Stern
Rysia Suchecka
Louis Switzer
Rose Tarlow
Michael Taylor
Matteo Thun
Stanley Tigerman
Adam Tihany
Calvin Tsao
Billie Tsien
Carleton Varney

Robert Venturi
Lella Vignelli
Massimo Vignelli
Kenneth H. Walker
Margo Grant Walsh
Sally Walsh
Kevin Walz
Gary Wheeler
Clive Wilkinson
Bunny Williams
Tod Williams
Trisha Wilson
Vicente Wolf
George Yabu

Source: Interior Design *magazine*

Presidents of the American Council of Engineering Companies

1973–74	William N. Holway	1994–95	J. Les MacFarlane
1974–75	Malcolm M. Meurer	1995–96	Richard G. Weingardt
1975–76	Billy T. Sumner	1996–97	Stanley K. Kawaguchi
1976–77	Richard H. Stanley	1997–98	James R. Thomas Jr.
1977–78	William A. Clevenger	1998–99	Donald R. Trim
1978–79	R. Duane Monical	1999–00	Leo F. Peters
1979–80	George W. Barnes	2000–01	Arlo J. Spiess
1980–81	Everett S. Thompson	2001–02	Stephen G. Goddard
1981–82	William R. Ratliff	2002–03	Daniel J. DeYoung
1982–83	Russell L. Smith Jr.	2003–04	Eric L. Flicker
1983–84	Shelby K. Willis	2004–05	William S. Howard
1984–85	Clifford E. Evanson	2005–06	Edward J. Mulcany
1985–86	Arnold L. Windman	2006–07	Jeff M. Daggett
1986–87	Lester H. Poggemeyer		
1987–88	Lester H. Smith Jr.		
1988–89	Robert E. Hogan		
1989–90	James W. Poirot		
1990–91	William D. Lewis		
1991–92	Andrew J. Parker Jr.		
1992–93	John H. Foster		
1993–94	Paul F. Sprehe		

* In 2001, the title of president was changed to chairman.

Source: American Council of Engineering Companies

Did you know...

At 98 feet in length, TVSA's Omni/ CNN Center in Atlanta features the world's largest freestanding escalator.

Presidents of the American Institute of Architects

1857–76	Richard Upjohn
1877–87	Thomas U. Walter
1888–91	Richard M. Hunt
1892–93	Edward H. Kendall
1894–95	Daniel H. Burnham
1896–98	George B. Post
1899	Henry Van Brunt
1900–01	Robert S. Peabody
1902–03	Charles F. McKim
1904–05	William S. Eames
1906–07	Frank M. Day
1908–09	Cass Gilbert
1910–11	Irving K. Pond
1912–13	Walter Cook
1914–15	R. Clipston Sturgis
1916–18	John L. Mauran
1919–20	Thomas R. Kimball
1921–22	Henry H. Kendall
1923–24	William B. Faville
1925–26	Dan E. Waid
1927–28	Milton B. Medary
1929–30	Charles H. Hammond
1931–32	Robert D. Kohn
1933–34	Earnest J. Russell
1935–36	Stephen F. Voorhees
1937–38	Charles D. Maginnis
1939–40	Edwin Bergstrom
1941–42	Richmond H. Shreve
1943–44	Raymond J. Ashton
1945–46	James R. Edmunds Jr.
1947–48	Douglas W. Orr
1949–50	Ralph T. Walker
1951–52	A. Glenn Stanton
1953–54	Clair W. Ditchy
1955–56	George B. Cummings
1957–58	Leon Chatelain Jr.
1959–60	John Noble Richards
1961–62	Philip Will Jr.
1963	Henry L. Wright
1964	J. Roy Carroll Jr.
1965	A. Gould Odell Jr.
1966	Morris Ketchum Jr.
1967	Charles M. Nes Jr.
1968	Robert L. Durham
1969	George E. Kassabaum
1970	Rex W. Allen
1971	Robert F. Hastings
1972	Max O. Urbahn
1973	S. Scott Ferebee Jr.
1974	Archibald C. Rogers
1975	William (Chick) Marshall Jr.
1976	Louis DeMoll
1977	John M. McGinty
1978	Elmer E. Botsai
1979	Ehrman B. Mitchell Jr.
1980	Charles E. Schwing
1981	R. Randall Vosbeck
1982	Robert M. Lawrence
1983	Robert C. Broshar
1984	George M. Notter Jr.
1985	R. Bruce Patty
1986	John A. Busby Jr.
1987	Donald J. Hackl
1988	Ted P. Pappas
1989	Benjamin E. Brewer Jr.
1990	Sylvester Damianos
1991	C. James Lawler
1992	W. Cecil Steward
1993	Susan A. Maxman
1994	L. William Chapin Jr.
1995	Chester A. Widom
1996	Raymond G. (Skipper) Post Jr.
1997	Raj Barr-Kumar
1998	Ronald A. Altoon
1999	Michael J. Stanton
2000	Ronald Skaggs
2001	John D. Anderson
2002	Gordon Chong
2003	Thompson E. Penney
2004	Eugene C. Hopkins
2005	Douglas L. Steidl
2006	Katherine Lee Schwennsen

Source: American Institute of Architects

Presidents of the American Society of Interior Designers

1974–75	Norman DeHaan		1994–95	Gary Wheeler
1974–76	Richard Jones		1995–96	Penny Bonda
1977	H. Albert Phibbs		1996–97	Kathy Ford Montgomery
1978	Irving Schwartz		1997–98	Joyce Burke-Jones
1979	Rita St. Clair		1998–99	Rosalyn Cama
1980	Wallace Jonason		1999–00	Juliana M. Catlin
1981	Jack Lowery		2000–01	Terri Maurer
1982	Martin Ellinoff		2001–02	Barbara Nugent
1984	William Richard Waley		2002–03	H. Don Bowden
1985	Gail Adams		2003–04	Linda Elliot Smith
1986	Janet Schirn		2004–05	Anita Baltimore
1987	Joy Adcock		2005–06	Robert Wright
1988	Charles Gandy		2006–07	Suzan Globus
1989	Elizabeth Howard			
1990	Robert John Dean			
1991	Raymond Kennedy			
1992	Martha G. Rayle			
1993	B.J. Peterson			

Source: American Society of Interior Designers

Presidents of the American Society of Landscape Architects

1899–01	John C. Olmsted*	1979–80	Robert L. Woerner
1902	Samuel Parsons Jr.*	1980–81	William A. Behnke
1903	Nathan F. Barrett*	1981–82	Calvin T. Bishop
1904–05	John C. Olmsted*	1982–83	Theodore J. Wirth
1906–07	Samuel Parsons Jr.*	1983–84	Darwina L. Neal
1908–09	Frederick Law Olmsted Jr.*	1984–85	Robert H. Mortensen
1910–11	Charles N. Lowrie*	1985–86	John Wacker
1912	Harold A. Caparn	1986–87	Roger B. Martin
1913	Ossian C. Simonds*	1987–88	Cheryl L. Barton
1914	Warren H. Manning*	1988–89	Brian S. Kubota
1915–18	James Sturgis Pray	1989–90	Gerald D. Patten
1919–22	Frederick Law Olmsted Jr.*	1990–91	Claire R. Bennett
1923–27	James L. Greenleaf	1991–92	Cameron R.J. Man
1927–31	Arthur A. Shurcliff	1992–93	Debra L. Mitchell
1931–35	Henry Vincent Hubbard	1993–94	Thomas Papandrew
1935–41	Albert D. Taylor	1994–95	Dennis Y. Otsuji
1941–45	S. Herbert Hare	1995–96	Vincent Bellafiore
1945–49	Markley Stevenson	1996–97	Donald W. Leslie
1949–51	Gilmore D. Clarke	1997–98	Thomas R. Dunbar
1951–53	Lawrence G. Linnard	1998–99	Barry W. Starke
1953–57	Leon Zach	1999–00	Janice Cervelli Schach
1957–61	Norman T. Newton	2000–01	Leonard J. Hopper
1961–63	John I. Rogers	2001–02	Rodney Swink
1963–65	John Ormsbee Simonds	2002–03	Paul Morris
1965–67	Hubert B. Owens	2003–04	Susan L.B. Jacobson
1967–69	Theodore Osmundson	2004–05	Patrick A. Miller
1969–71	Campbell E. Miller	2005–06	Dennis B. Carmichael
1971–73	Raymond L. Freeman	2006–07	Patrick W. Caughey
1973–74	William G. Swain		
1974–75	Owen H. Peters		
1975–76	Edward H. Stone II		
1976–77	Benjamin W. Gary Jr.		
1977–78	Lane L. Marshall		
1978–79	Jot D. Carpenter		

*Charter member

Source: American Society of Landscape Architects

Make the plan fit the ground, and [don't] twist the ground to fit a plan.

Charles Sprague Sargent

Presidents of the Association of Collegiate Schools of Architecture

1912–21	Warren Laird University of Pennsylvania	1967–69	Robert Bliss University of Utah
1921–23	Emil Lorch University of Michigan	1969–71	Charles Burchard Virginia Polytechnic Institute
1923–25	William Emerson Massachusetts Institute of Technology	1971–72	Alan Taniguchi Rice University and University
1925–27	Francke Bosworth Jr. Cornell University		of Texas, Austin
1927–29	Goldwin Goldsmith University of Kansas	1972–73	Robert Harris University of Oregon
1929–31	Everett Meeks Yale University	1973–74	Sanford Greenfield Boston Architectural Center
1931–34	Ellis Lawrence University of Oregon	1974–75	Don Schlegal University of New Mexico
1934–36	Roy Childs Jones University of Minnesota	1975–76	Bertram Berenson University of Illinois at Chicago
1936–38	Sherely Morgan Princeton University	1976–77	Donlyn Lyndon Massachusetts Institute of Technology
1938–40	George Young Jr. Cornell University	1977–78	Dwayne Nuzum University of Colorado, Boulder
1940–42	Leopold Arnaud Columbia University	1978–79	William Turner Tulane University
1942–45	Wells Bennett University of Michigan	1979–80	Robert Burns North Carolina State University
1945–47	Loring Provine University of Illinois	1980–81	Richard Peters University of California, Berkeley
1947–49	Paul Weigel Kansas State College	1981–82	Eugene Kremer Kansas State University
1949–51	B. Kenneth Johnstone Carnegie Institute	1982–83	O. Jack Mitchell Rice University
1951–53	Thomas FitzPatrick Iowa State College	1983–84	Charles Hight University of North Carolina, Charlotte
1953–55	Lawrence Anderson Massachusetts Institute of Technology	1984–85	Wilmot Gilland University of Oregon
1955–57	Elliott Whitaker Ohio State University	1985–86	George Anselevicius University of New Mexico
1957–59	Buford Pickens Washington University	1986–87	Blanche Lemco van Ginkel University of Toronto
1959–61	Harlan McClure Clemson College	1987–88	J. Thomas Regan University of Miami
1961–63	Olindo Grossi Pratt Institute	1988–89	Robert Beckley University of Michigan
1963–65	Henry Kamphoefner North Carolina State College	1989–90	Marvin Malecha California State Polytechnic University, Pomona
1965–67	Walter Sanders University of Michigan	1990–91	John Meunier Arizona State University

Presidents of the Association of Collegiate Schools of Architecture

1991–92   Patrick Quinn
Rensselaer Polytechnic Institute

1992–93   James Barker
Clemson University

1993–94   Kent Hubbell
Cornell University

1994–95   Diane Ghirardo
University of Southern California

1995–96   Robert Greenstreet
University of Wisconsin–Milwaukee

1996–97   Linda W. Sanders
Calif. State Polytechnic University, Pomona

1997–98   John M. McRae
Mississippi State University

1998–99   R. Wayne Drummond
University of Florida

1999–00   Jerry Finrow
University of Washington

2000–01   Tony Schuman
New Jersey Institute of Technology

2001–02   Frances Bronet
Rensselaer Polytechnic Institute

2002–03   Bradford C. Grant
Hampton University

2003–04   Geraldine Forbes Isais
Woodbury University

2004–05   Rafael Longoria
University of Houston

2005–06   Stephen Schreiber
University of South Florida

2006–07   Theodore C. Landsmark
Boston Architectural Center

Source: Association of Collegiate Schools of Architecture

I want to see therefore I draw.

Carlo Scarpa

Presidents of the Council of Architectural Component Executives

The Council of Architectural Component Executives is comprised of the CEOs of the staffed chapters and components of the American Institute of Architects. There are more than 300 active chapters of the AIA, including those in cities, states, regions as well as nations outside the United States. CACE conducts educational programs, training, and mentorship for the executive staff to assist in their support of professional architects.

1971	Julian B. Serrill AIA Iowa	1991	Beverly Hauschild-Baron American Institute of Architects Minnesota
1972	Don Edward Legge Texas Society of Architects/AIA	1992	Eleanor McNamara AIA Georgia
1973–75	Fotis Karasoutis Florida Association of American Institute of Architects	1993	Martha Murphree AIA Houston
1976–77	Dan Sheridan American Institute of Architects Minnesota	1994	Paul Welch Jr. AIA California Council
1978–79	Des Taylor Texas Society of Architects/AIA	1995	John Braymer Virginia Society AIA
1980–81	Ann Stacy AIA Michigan	1996	Suzanne Schwengels AIA Iowa
1982	James P. Cramer American Institute of Architects Minnesota	1997	Connie Wallace AIA Tennessee
1983	Lowell Erickson Boston Society of Architects/AIA	1998	Peter Rand American Institute of Architects Minnesota
1984	Sandra Stickney AIA East Bay	1999	Gayle Krueger AIA Nebraska
1985	George Allen Florida Association of the American Institute of Architects	2000	Timothy D. Kent AIA North Carolina
1986	Brent Davis AIA Southern Arizona	2001	Janet D. Pike AIA Kentucky
1987	Barbara J. Rodriguez AIA New York State	2002	Karen Lewand AIA Baltimore
1988	Linda Young AIA Kansas City	2003	David Lancaster Texas Society of Architects/AIA
1989	Kathleen Davis AIA Orange County	2004	Saundra Stevens AIA Oregon/AIA Portland
1990	Rae Dumke AIA Michigan/AIA Detriot	2005	Elizabeth Mitchell AIA Utah/AIA Salt Lake
		2006	David A. Crawford AIA North Carolina

Source: American Institute of Architects

268

Presidents of the Industrial Designers Society of America

1965	Henry Dreyfuss
1966	Joseph Marshall Parriott
1967–68	Robert H. Hose
1969–70	Tucker Madawick
1971–72	William M. Goldsmith
1973–74	Arthur Jon Pulos
1975–76	James F. Fulton
1977–78	Richard Hollerith
1979–80	Carroll M. Gantz
1981–82	Robert G. Smith
1983–84	Katherine J. McCoy
1985–86	Cooper C. Woodring

1987–88	Peter H. Wooding
1989–90	Peter W. Bressler
1991–92	Charles Pelly
1993–94	David Tompkins
1995–96	James Ryan
1997–98	Craig Vogel
1999–00	Mark Dziersk
2001–02	Betty Baugh
2003–04	Bruce Claxton
2005–06	Ron B. Kemnitzer

Source: Industrial Designers Society of America

169

Design has an important task: to resolve problems, to offer better solutions, to save, and add value to our lives. Development of a new product should always "make sense" in these terms.

Kristiina Lassus

Presidents of the International Interior Design Association

1994–95	Marilyn Farrow
1995–96	Judith Hastings
1996–97	Beth Harmon-Vaughan
1997–98	Karen Guenther
1998–99	Neil Frankel
1999–00	Carol Jones
2000–01	Richard Pollack
2001–02	Cary D. Johnson
2002–03	Anita L. Barnett
2003–04	Lewis Goetz
2004–05	John Lijewski
2005–06	Eric Engstrom

Source: International Interior Design Association

Presidents of the International Union of Architects

1948–53 Sir Patrick Abercrombie (UK)
1953–57 Jean Tschumi (Switzerland)
1957–61 Hector Mardones-Restat (Chili)
1961–65 Sir Robert Matthew (UK)
1965–69 Eugène Beaudouin (France)
1969–72 Ramon Corona Martin (Mexico)
1972–75 Georgui Orlov (Russia)
1975–78 Jai Rattan Bhalla (India)
1978–81 Louis DeMoll (US)
1981–85 Rafael de la Hoz (Spain)
1985–87 Georgi Stoilov (Bulgaria)
1987–90 Rod Hackney (UK)
1990–93 Olufemi Majekodunmi (Nigeria)
1993–96 Jaime Duro Pifarré (Spain)
1996–99 Sara Topelson de Grinberg (Mexico)
1999–02 Vassilis Sgoutas (Greece)
2002–05 Jaime Lerner (Brazil)

Honorary Presidents

1948–53 Auguste Perret (France)
1953–57 Sir Patrick Abercrombie (UK)
1969–02 Pierre Vago (France)
2005–08 Gaétan Siew (Mauritius)

Source: International Union of Architects

271

The one thing in terms of good design that will never change is proportion. When you look at design ranging from Palladio to Mies van der Rohe, the one constant is the beautiful proportions. Ultimately we are all human, and there are natural reasons why these proportions feel right to us. So, however adventuresome our material or smart our designs become, the proportions will stay the same.

Lee Ledbetter

Presidents of the National Council of Architectural Registration Boards

1920–22	Emil Loch	1976	William C. Muchow
1923–24	Arthur Peabody	1977	Charles A. Blondheim Jr.
1925	Miller I. Kast	1978	Paul H. Graven
1926–27	W.H. Lord	1979	Lorenzo D. Williams
1928	George D. Mason	1980	John R. Ross
1929–30	Clarence W. Brazer	1981	Dwight M. Bonham
1931–32	James M. White	1982	Thomas H. Flesher Jr.
1933	A.L. Brockway	1983	Sid Frier
1933	A.M. Edelman	1984	Ballard H.T. Kirk
1934–35	Joseph W. Holman	1985	Robert E. Oringdulph
1936	Charles Butler	1986	Theodore L. Mularz
1938–39	William Perkins	1987	Robert L. Tessier
1940–41	Mellen C. Greeley	1988	Walter T. Carry
1942–44	Louis J. Gill	1989	George B. Terrien
1945–46	Solis Seiferth	1990	Herbert P. McKim
1947–49	Warren D. Miller	1991	Charles E. Garrison
1950	Clinton H. Cowgill	1992	Robert H. Burke Jr.
1951	Roger C. Kirchoff	1993	Harry G. Robinson III
1952–54	Charles E. Firestone		William Wiese II, *Honorary Past President*
1954–55	Fred L. Markham		
1956–58	Edgar H. Berners	1994	Robert A. Fielden
1959–60	Walter F. Martens	1995	Homer L. Williams
1961	A. Reinhold Melander	1996	Richard W. Quinn
1962	Chandler C. Cohagen	1997	Darrell L. Smith
1963	Paul W. Drake	1998	Ann R. Chaintreuil
1964	Ralph O. Mott	1999	Susan May Allen
1965	C.J. (Pat) Paderewski	2000	Joseph P. Giattina Jr.
1966	Earl L. Mathes	2001	William Bevins
1967	George F. Schatz	2002	C. Robert Campbell
1968–69	Howard T. Blanchard	2003	Robert A. Boynton
1970	Dean L. Gustavson	2004	Frank M. Guillot
1971	William J. Geddis	2005	H. Carleton Godsey Jr.
1972	Daniel Boone	2006	Robert E. Luke
1973	Thomas J. Sedgewick		
1974	E.G. Hamilton		
1975	John (Mel) O'Brien Jr.		

Source: National Council of Architectural Registration Boards

Presidents of the Royal Architectural Institute of Canada

1907–10	A.E. Dunlop
1910–12	E.S. Baker
1912–16	J.H.G. Russell
1916–18	J.P. Ouellet
1918–20	A. Frank Wickson
1920–22	David R. Brown
1922–24	Lewis H. Jordan
1924–26	John S. Archibald
1926–29	J.P. Hynes
1929–32	Percy E. Nobbs
1932–34	Gordon M. West
1934–36	W.S. Maxwell
1936–38	W.I. Somerville
1938–40	H.L. Fetherstonbaugh
1940–42	Burwell R. Coon
1942–44	Gordon McL. Pirts
1944–46	Forsey Page
1946–48	David Chas
1948–50	A.J. Hazelgrove
1950–52	J. Roxburgh Smith
1952–54	R. Scholfield Morris
1954–56	A.J.C. Paine
1956–58	D.F. Kertland
1958–60	Maurice Payette
1960–62	Harland Steele
1962–64	John I. Davies
1964–65	F. Bruce Brown
1965–66	Gérard Venne
1966–67	Charles A.E. Fowler
1967–68	James F. Searle
1968–69	Norman H. McMurrich
1969–70	Wm. G. Leithead
1970–71	Gordon R. Arnott
1971–72	Jean-Louis Lalonde
1972–73	C.F.T. Rounthwaite

1973–74	Allan F. Duffus
1974–75	Bernard Wood
1975–76	Fred T. Hollingsworth
1976–77	Charles H. Cullum
1977–78	W. Donald Baldwin
1978–79	Gilbert R. Beatson
1980–81	David H. Hambleton
1981–82	J. Douglass Miller
1982–83	G. Macy DuBois
1983–84	Patrick Blouin
1984–85	W. Kirk Banadyga
1985–86	Brian E. Eldred
1986–87	Rudy P. Ericsen
1987–88	Terence J. Williams
1988–89	Alfred C. Roberts
1989–90	Essy Baniassad
1990–91	Richard Young
1991–92	David W. Edwards
1992–93	Roy Willwerth
1993–94	J. Brian Sim
1994–95	Paul-André Tétreault
1995–97	Bill Chomik
1997–98	Barry J. Hobin
1998–99	Eva Matsuzaki
1999–00	Eliseo Temprano
2000–01	David Simpson
2001–02	Diarmuid Nash
2002–03	Ronald Keenberg
2003–04	Bonnie Maples
2004–05	Christopher Fillingham
2005–06	Yves Gosselin
2006–07	Vivian Manasc

Source: Royal Architectural Institute of Canada

Enchantment is a useless thought, but as indispensable as bread.

Gio Ponti

Presidents of the Royal Australian Institute of Architects

1929–30	Alfred Samuel Hook	1973–75	Peter McIntyre
1930–31	William Arthur Blackett	1975–76	Harold Bryce Mortlock
1931–32	Philip Rupert Claridge	1976–77	Blair Mansfield Wilson
1932–33	Lange Leopold Powell	1977–78	Eustace Gresley Cohen
1933–34	Charles Edward Serpell	1978–79	John Davidson
1934–35	Arthur William Anderson	1979–80	Geoffrey Lawrence
1935–36	Guy St. John Makin	1980–81	Alexander Ian Ferrier
1936–37	James Nangle	1981–82	Michael Laurence Peck
1937–38	Louis Laybourne-Smith	1982–83	Richard Norman Johnson
1938–39	Frederick Bruce Lucas	1983–84	David Alan Nutter
1939–40	Otto Abrecht Yuncken	1984–85	Richard Melville Young
1940–42	William Ronald Richardson	1985–86	Roland David Jackson
1942–44	John Francis Scarborough	1986–87	Graham Alan Hulme
1944–46	Roy Sharrington Smith	1987–88	Robert Darwin Hall
1946–48	William Rae Laurie	1988–89	Dudley Keith Wilde
1948–50	Jack Denyer Cheesman	1989–90	Ronald Barrie Bodycoat
1950–52	Cobden Parkes	1990–91	Robert Lindsay Caufield
1952–54	Robert Snowden Demaine	1991–92	Jamieson Sayer Allom
1954–56	Edward James Weller	1992–93	Robert Cheesman
1956–57	William Purves Godfrey	1993–94	James Taylor
1957–59	Wilfried Thomas Haslam	1994–95	Virginia Louise Cox
1959–60	Kenneth Charles Duncan	1995–96	Peter Robertson Gargett
1960–61	Thomas Brenan Gargett	1996–97	John Stanley Castles
1961–62	Henry Ingham Ashworth	1997–98	Eric Graham Butt
1962–63	James Campbell Irwin	1998–99	Graham Humphries
1963–64	Max Ernest Collard	1999–00	Nigel Warren Shaw
1964–65	Raymond Berg	2000–01	Edward Robert Haysom
1965–66	Gavin Walkley	2001–02	Graham Jahn
1966–67	Mervyn Henry Parry	2002–03	Caroline Pidcock
1967–68	Acheson Best Overend	2003–04	David Parken
1968–69	Jack Hobbs McConnell	2004–05	Warren Kerr
1969–70	John David Fisher	2005–06	Bob Nation
1970–71	Ronald Andrew Gilling		
1971–72	Kenneth William Shugg		
1972–73	Henry Jardine Parkinson		

Source: Royal Australian Institute of Architects

Presidents of the Royal Institute of British Architects

1835–59	Earl de Grey
1860	Charles Robert Cockerell
1861–63	Sir William Tite
1863–65	Thomas L. Donaldson
1865–67	A.J.B. Beresford Hope
1867–70	Sir William Tite
1870–73	Thomas Henry Wyatt
1873–76	Sir Gilbert G. Scott
1876–79	Charles Barry Jr.
1879–81	John Whichcord
1881	George Edmund Street
1882–84	Sir Horace Jones
1884–86	Ewan Christian
1886–87	Edward l'Anson
1888–91	Alfred Waterhouse
1891–94	J. Macvicar Anderson
1894–96	Francis C. Penrose
1896–99	George Aitchison
1899–02	Sir William Emerson
1902–04	Sir Aston Webb
1904–06	John Belcher
1906–08	Thomas Edward Collcutt
1908–10	Sir Ernest George
1910–12	Leonard Stokes
1912–14	Sir Reginald Blomfield
1914–17	Ernest Newton
1917–19	Henry Thomas Hare
1919–21	Sir John William Simpson
1921–23	Paul Waterhouse
1923–25	J. Alfred Gotch
1925–27	Sir Guy Dawber
1927–29	Sir Walter Tapper
1929–31	Sir Banister Fletcher
1931–33	Sir Raymond Unwin
1933–35	Sir Giles Gilbert Scott
1935–37	Sir Percy Thomas
1937–39	H.S. Goodhart-Rendel
1939–40	E. Stanley Hall
1940–43	W.H. Ansell
1943–46	Sir Percy Thomas
1946–48	Sir Lancelot Keay
1948–50	Michael T. Waterhouse
1950–52	A. Graham Henderson
1952–54	Sir Howard Robertson
1954–56	C.H. Aslin
1956–58	Kenneth M.B. Cross

1958–60	Sir Basil Spence
1960–62	The Lord Holford
1962–64	Sir Robert Matthew
1964–65	Sir Donald Gibson
1965–67	The Viscount Esher
1967–69	Sir Hugh Wilson
1969–71	Sir Peter Shepheard
1971–73	Sir Alex Gordon
1973–75	F.B. Pooley
1975–77	Eric Lyons
1977–79	Gordon Graham
1979–81	Bryan Jefferson
1981–83	Owen Luder
1983–85	Michael Manser
1985–87	Larry Rolland
1987–89	Rod Hackney
1989–91	Max Hutchinson
1991–93	Richard C. MacCormac
1993–95	Frank Duffy
1995–97	Owen Luder
1997–99	David Rock
1999–01	Marco Goldschmied
2002–03	Paul Hyett
2003–05	George Ferguson
2005–07	Jack Pringle

Source: Royal Institute of British Architects

275

Did you know...

Sir John Soane's tomb in London's Saint Pancras Churchyard is one of only two tombs in London designated with grade 1 status for its exceptional architectural importance, the highest distinction granted to structures on the UK's List of Buildings of Architectural or Historic Interest. The other is Karl Marx.

Presidents of the Society of Architectural Historians

1941–42	Turpin C. Bannister
1943–44	Rexford Newcomb
1945–47	Kenneth John Conant
1948–49	Carroll L.V. Meeks
1950	Buford L. Pickens
1951	Charles E. Peterson
1952–53	Henry-Russell Hitchcock
1954	Agnes Addison Gilchrist
1955–56	James G. Van Derpool
1957–58	Carroll L.V. Meeks
1959	Walter L. Creese
1960–61	Barbara Wriston
1962–63	John D. Forbes
1964–65	H. Allen Brooks
1966–67	George B. Tatum
1968–69	Henry A. Millon
1970–71	James F. O'Gorman
1972–74	Alan W. Gowans

1975–76	Spiro Kostof
1976–78	Marian C. Donnelly
1978–80	Adolph K. Placzek
1980–82	David S. Gebhard
1982–84	Damie Stillman
1984–86	Carol Herselle Krinsky
1986–88	Osmund Overby
1988–90	Richard J. Betts
1990–93	Elisabeth Blair MacDougall
1993–94	Franklin Toker
1994–96	Keith N. Morgan
1996–98	Patricia Waddy
1998–00	Richard Longstreth
2000–02	Christopher Mead
2002–04	Diane Favro
2004–06	Therese O'Malley

Source: Society of Architectural Historians

Did you know...

The sons of abolitionists and friends William Furness and James Miller McKim both became important architects: Frank Furness and Charles McKim.

Records, Rankings & Achievements

4

Aquariums, airports, sports stadiums, the world's tallest buildings, and a list of architecturally significant American art museums are just some of the notable accomplishments covered in this chapter. Numerous other rankings and ratings are available for professional reference and diversion. The results of the annual Most Popular Historic House Museums survey can be found in the Design & Historic Preservation chapter on page 449; the annual rankings of architecture, industrial design, interior design, and landscape architecture schools are located in the Design Education chapter on pages 491–495.

Airports: 1990–2005

Airports have evolved over the last century from small, utilitarian structures to sprawling, multi-purpose complexes, sometimes likened to small cities in and of themselves. Development in the airport sector has been multifaceted due to diverse factors such as the popularity of regional airlines, heightened security procedures, the need to accommodate larger jets, and expansion in Asia. Notable engineering challenges posed by recent airports include the need to construct artificial islands (Incheon, Hong Kong, Kansai) and building in a tropical jungle (Kuala Lumpur). Some contain signature details, such as the white-peaked, tented terminal roof of the Denver Airport, while some smaller airports, as in Bilbao, can also boast breathe-taking architecture. While not comprehensive, this list contains noteworthy airport terminals, in terms of their architecture and/or engineering, built since 1990.

Concourse A, Seattle-Tacoma International Airport. NBBJ transformed this undersized concourse into a stunning centerpiece for the Sea-Tac Airport. The arrival hall, comprised of a 70-ft. tall wall of glass, includes a scale replica of the Voyager, the first aircraft to fly around the world non-stop without refueling. The 14-gate airside concourse elicits a feeling of flight with an evocative butterfly-roof design. **Photo by Christian Richters.**

Airports: 1990–2005

Airport	Location	Architect	Opened
Terminal 3, Madrid Barajas International Airport (MAD)	Madrid, Spain	Richard Rogers Partnership with Estudio Antionio Lamela	2005
Central Terminal, Seattle-Tacoma International Airport (SEA)	Seattle, WA	Fentress Bradburn Architects	2005
South Terminal, Barcelona International Airport (BCN)	Barcelona, Spain	Taller de Arquitectura	2005
American Airlines Terminal, Phase 1, John F. Kennedy International Airport (JFK)	New York, NY	DMJM Aviation	2005
Chubu Centrair International Airport (NGO)	Tokoname City, Aichi Prefecture, Japan	Nikken Sekkei Ltd.; Azusa Sekkei Co. Ltd.; Hellmuth, Obata & Kassabaum; Arup	2005
Terminal D, Dallas-Ft. Worth International Airport (DFW)	Dallas/Fort Worth, TX	HNTB; HKS; Corgan Associates, Inc.	2005
Passenger Terminal, Astanta International Airport (KZT)	Astana, Kazakhstan	Kisho Kurokawa Architect and Associates	2005
Airside Centre, Zurich Airport (ZRH)	Zurich, Switzerland	Grimshaw with Itten+Brechbühl	2004
New Terminal 1, Lester B. Pearson International Airport (YYZ)	Toronto, Ontario	Skidmore, Owings & Merrill; Moshe Safdie and Associates; Adamson Associates Architects	2004
Concourse A, Seattle-Tacoma International Airport (SEA)	Seattle, WA	NBBJ	2004
Airside Complex, Ben Gurion Airport (TLV)	Tel Aviv, Israel	Moshe Safdie and Associates; TRA Consultants, Inc.— a joint venture	2004
Guangzhou Baiyun International Airport (CAN)	Guangdong, China	Parsons Brinckerhoff with URS Greiner	2004
Chongqing Jiangbei International Airport (CKG)	Chongqing, China	Llewelyn-Davies Ltd. with Arup	2004
International Terminal A-West, Philadelphia International Airport (PHL)	Philadelphia, PA	Kohn Pedersen Fox Associates	2003
Terminal 2, Munich International Airport (MUC)	Munich, Germany	Koch+Partner; Koch Drohn Schneider Voigt	2003
Terminal 2E, Charles de Gaulle Airport (CDG)	Paris, France	Aéroports de Paris	2003*
Dusseldorf International Airport (DUS)	Dusseldorf, Germany	JSK Architekten; Perkins & Will	2001–03
Landside Complex, Ben Gurion Airport (TLV)	Tel Aviv, Israel	Skidmore, Owings & Merrill; Karmi Associates; Lissar Eldar Architects—a joint venture	2002

* Since the partial collapse of Terminal 2E on May 23, 2004, the terminal has been closed while the remaining roof structure is demolished and rebuilt.

Airports: 1990–2005

Airport	Location	Architect	Opened
McNamara Terminal, Detroit Metropolitan Wayne County Airport (DTW)	Romulus, MI	SmithGroup	2002
Integrated Transportation Center, Incheon International Airport (ICN)	Seoul, South Korea	Terry Farrell and Partners	2002
Incheon International Airport (ICN)	Seoul, South Korea	Fentress Bradburn Architects with BHJW and Korean Architects Collaborative International	2001
Terminal 4, John F. Kennedy International Airport (JFK)	New York, NY	Skidmore, Owings & Merrill	2001
Domestic Terminal, Shenzhen Baoan International Airport (SZX)	Shenzhen, China	Llewelyn-Davies Ltd.	2001
Terminal 2, Cologne/Bonn Airport (CGN)	Cologne, Germany	Murphy/Jahn Architects	2000
Terminal Building, Bilbao Airport (BIO)	Bilbao Spain	Santiago Calatrava	2000
Terminal Access Program, Portland International Airport (PDX)	Portland, OR	Zimmer Gunsul Frasca Partnership	2000
International Terminal, San Francisco International Airport (SFO)	San Francisco, CA	Skidmore, Owings & Merrill with Del Campo & Maru and Michael Willis and Associates	2000
Domestic Terminal, Beihai Fucheng Airport (BHX)	Beihai, Guangxi, China	Llewelyn-Davies Ltd.	2000
Airside 2, Orlando International Airport (MCO)	Orlando, FL	Hellmuth, Obata & Kassabaum	2000
Learmonth International Airport (LEA)	Exeter, Australia	Jones Coulter Young Architects	1999
Shanghai Pudong International Airport (PVG)	Shanghai, China	Aéroports de Paris	1999
International Terminal, Fukuoka International Airport (FUK)	Hakata-ku, Fukuoka City, Japan	Hellmuth, Obata & Kassabaum; Azusa Sekkei; Mishima Architects; MHS Planners	1999
Airport Center, Munich International Airport (MUC)	Munich, Germany	Murphy/Jahn Architects	1999
Terminal 2F, Charles de Gaulle Airport (CDG)	Paris, France	Aéroports de Paris	1998
Kuala Lumpur International Airport (KUL)	Kuala Lumpur, Malaysia	Kisho Kurokawa Architect and Associates with Akitek Jururancang	1998
Satellite D, McCarran International Airport (LAS)	Las Vegas, NV	Leo A Daly; Tate & Snyder	1998
Terminal 1, John F. Kennedy International Airport (JFK)	New York, NY	William Nicholas Bodouva + Associates	1998

283

Airports: 1990–2005

Airport	Location	Architect	Opened
Chek Lap Kok International Airport (HKG)	Lantau Island, Hong Kong, China	Foster and Partners	1998
Sendai International Airport (SDJ)	Natori, Japan	Hellmuth, Obata & Kassabaum; Nikken Sekkei	1998
Gardermoen Airport (GEN)	Oslo, Norway	AVIAPLAN and Niels Torp Architects	1998
North Terminal, Ronald Reagan Washington National Airport (DCA)	Washington, DC	Cesar Pelli & Associates; Leo A Daly	1997
Passenger Terminal, Buffalo Niagara International Airport (BUF)	Cheektowaga, NY	Cannon Design, Inc.; William Nicholas Bodouva + Associates; and Kohn Pedersen Fox Associates—a joint venture	1997
Pointe à Pitre Le Raizet International (PTP)	Pointe à Pitre, Guadeloupe	Aéroports de Paris	1996
Denver International Airport (DEN)	Denver, CO	Fentress Bradburn Architects	1995
Kansai International Airport (KIA)	Osaka Bay, Japan	Renzo Piano Building Workshop; AEP	1994
Terminal 2, Haneda Airport (HND)	Tokyo, Japan	Cesar Pelli & Associates Architects; Jun Mitsui & Associates Inc. Architects	1994
Terminal 5, Chicago-O'Hare International Airport (ORD)	Chicago, IL	Perkins & Will, with Heard & Associates	1994
Terminal 2, Frankfurt Airport (FRA)	Frankfurt, Germany	Perkins & Will; JSK Architekten	1994
Passenger Terminal, Graz International Airport (GRZ)	Graz, Austria	Riegler Riewe Architekten	1994
Southampton Airport (SOU)	Southampton, UK	Manser Associates	1994
Pier 4A, Heathrow Airport (LHR)	London, UK	Nicholas Grimshaw & Partners	1993
San Pablo Airport (SVQ)	Seville, Spain	Rafael Moneo	1992
Munich International Airport (MUC)	Munich, Germany	Von Busse & Parterns	1992
Europier, Heathrow Airport (LHR)	London, UK	Richard Rogers Partnership	1992
Stansted Airport (STN)	London, UK	Foster and Partners	1991
Terminal 4, Hamburg Airport (HAM)	Hamburg, Germany	von Gerkan, Marg & Partner Architekten	1991

Source: DesignIntelligence

Aquariums

The opening of Boston's New England Aquarium in 1969 ushered in a new age for aquariums. It combined the traditional ideas found in the classic aquariums of the early 20th century with new technology and revised educational and research commitments. Some have called it the first modern public aquarium. Since that time, aquariums have proliferated across the United States. On the following pages is a list of the major free-standing aquariums currently operating in the United States along with their requisite architectural statistics.

Ocean Journey, Tennessee Aquarium. The Tennessee Aquarium's new $30-million Ocean Journey building is an extension of its popular Gulf of Mexico exhibit that will add 700,000 gallons of saltwater exhibits to what is currently the world's largest freshwater aquarium. **Photo courtesy of the Tennessee Aquarium.**

Aquariums

Aquarium	Location	Architect
Alaska SeaLife Center	Seward, AK	Cambridge Seven Associates with Livingston Slone
Aquarium of the Bay	San Francisco, CA	Esherick Homsey Dodge and Davis
Aquarium of the Pacific	Long Beach, CA	A joint venture of Hellmuth, Obata & Kassabaum and Esherick Homsey Dodge and Davis
Audubon Aquarium of Americas	New Orleans, LA	The Bienville Group: a joint venture of The Mathes Group, Eskew + Architects, Billes/Manning Architects, Hewitt & Washington, Concordia
Belle Isle Aquarium	Royal Oak, MI	Albert J. Kahn
Birch Aquarium at Scripps Institution of Oceanography, UCSD	La Jolla, CA	Wheeler Wimer Blackman & Associates
Colorado's Ocean Journey	Denver, CO	Odyssea: a joint venture of RNL Design and Anderson Mason Dale
Flint RiverQuarium	Albany, GA	Antoine Predock Architect with Robbins Bell Kreher Inc.
Florida Aquarium	Tampa, FL	Hellmuth, Obata & Kassabaum and Esherick Homsey Dodge and Davis
Georgia Aquarium	Atlanta, GA	Thompson, Ventulett Stainback & Associates
Great Lakes Aquarium	Duluth, MN	Hammel, Green and Abrahamson, Inc.
John G. Shedd Aquarium	Chicago, IL	Graham Anderson, Probst, and White (Lohan and Associates, 1991 addition)
Maritime Aquarium at Norwalk	Norwalk, CT	Graham Gund Architects (original building and 2001 addition)
Monterey Bay Aquarium	Monterey, CA	Esherick Homsey Dodge and Davis (original building and 1996 addition)
Mystic Aquarium	Mystic, CT	Flynn, Dalton and Van Dijk (Cesar Pelli & Associates, 1999 expansion)
National Aquarium	Washington, DC	York & Sawyer Architects
National Aquarium in Baltimore	Baltimore, MD	Cambridge Seven Associates (Grieves & Associates, 1990 addition; Chermayeff, Sollogub and Poole, Inc., 2005 addition)
New England Aquarium	Boston, MA	Cambridge Seven Associates (Schwartz/Silver Architects, 1998 addition; E. Verner Johnson and Associates, Inc., 2001 expansion)
New Jersey State Aquarium	Camden, NJ	The Hillier Group
New York Aquarium at Coney Island	Brooklyn, NY	n/a

Opened	Cost	Total square ft. (original/current)	Tank capacity (original/current, in gallons)
1998	$56 M	115,000	400,000
1996	$38 M	48,000	707,000
1998	$117 M	156,735	900,000
1990	$42 M	110,000	1.19 M
1904	$175,000	10,000	32,000
1992	$14 M	34,000	150,000
1999	$94 M	107,000	1 M
2004	$30 M	30,000	175,000
1994	$84 M	152,000	1 M
2005	$200 M	430,000	5 M
2000	$34 M	62,382	170,000
1930	$ 3.25 M ($45 M addition)	225,000/395,000	1.5 M/3 M
1988	$11.5 M ($9 M addition)	102,000/135,000	150,000
1984	$55 M ($57 M addition)	216,000/307,000	900,000/1.9 M
1973	$1.74 M ($52 M expansion)	76,000/137,000	1.6 M/2.3 M
1931	n/a	13,500	32,000
1981	$21.3 M ($35 M 1990 addition, $66 M 2005 addition)	209,000/324,000/389,400	1 M/1.5 M/1.578 M
1969	$8 M ($20.9 M 1998 addition; $19.3 M 2001 expansion)	75,000/1,082,400	1 M
1992	$52 M	120,000	1 M
1957	n/a	150,000	1.8 M

Aquariums

Aquarium	Location	Architect
Newport Aquarium	Newport, KY	GBBN Architects (original and 2005 expansion)
North Carolina Aquarium at Fort Fisher	Kure Beach, NC	Cambridge Seven Associates (BMS Architects, 2002 expansion)
North Carolina Aquarium on Roanoke Island	Manteo, NC	Lyles, Bissett, Carlisle and Wolff Associates of North Carolina Inc. with Cambridge Seven Associates (BMS Architects, 2002 expansion)
Oklahoma Aquarium	Tulsa, OK	SPARKS
Oregon Coast Aquarium	Newport, OR	SRG Architects
Ripley's Aquarium	Myrtle Beach, SC	Enartec
Ripley's Aquarium of the Smokies	Gatlinburg, TN	Helman Hurley Charvat Peacock Architects/Inc.
Seattle Aquarium	Seattle, WA	Fred Bassetti & Co.
South Carolina Aquarium	Charleston, SC	Eskew + Architects with Clark and Menefee Architects
Steinhart Aquarium	San Francisco, CA	Lewis P. Hobart
Tennessee Aquarium	Chattanooga, TN	Cambridge Seven Associates (Chermayeff, Sollogub & Poole, Inc., 2005 addition)
Texas State Aquarium	Corpus Christi, TX	Phelps, Bomberger, and Garza (Corpus Christi Design Associates, 2003 addition)
Virginia Aquarium & Marine Science Center	Virginia Beach, VA	E. Verner Johnson and Associates (original building and 1996 expansion)
Waikiki Aquarium	Honolulu, HI	Hart Wood and Edwin A. Weed with Ossipoff, Snyder, and Rowland
Wonders of Wildlife at the American National Fish and Wildlife Museum	Springfield, MO	Cambridge Seven Associates

Source: DesignIntelligence

Opened	Cost	Total square ft. (original/current)	Tank capacity (original/current, in gallons)
1999	$40 M ($4.5 M expansion)	100,000/121,200	1 M/1.01 M
1976	$1.5 M ($17.5 M expansion)	30,000/84,000	77,000/455,000
1976	$1.6 M ($16 M expansion)	34,000/68,000	5,000/400,000
2003	$15 M	71,600	500,000
1992	$25.5 M	51,000	1.4 M
1997	$40 M	87,000	1.3 M
2000	$49 M	115,000	1.3 M
1977	n/a	68,000	753,000
2000	$69 M	93,000	1 M
1923	n/a	22,566	300,000
1992	$45 M ($30 M addition)	130,000/190,000	400,000/1.1 M
1990	$31 M ($14 M addition)	43,000/73,800	325,000/725,000
1986	$7.5 M ($35 M expansion)	41,500/120,000	100,000/800,000
1955	$400,000	19,000	152,000
2001	$34 M	92,000	500,000

Firm Anniversaries

The following currently practicing architecture firms were founded in 1906, 1931, 1956, and 1981 respectively.

Firms Celebrating their 100th Anniversary

Calloway Johnson Moore & West, Winston Salem, NC
Ratcliff, Emeryville, CA
Swanke Hayden Connell Architects, New York, NY
Zimmerman Design Group, Milwaukee, WI

Firms Celebrating their 75th Anniversary

Solomon Cordwell Buenz & Associates, Chicago, IL

Firms Celebrating their 50th Anniversary

Buff Smith & Hensman Architects, Pasadena, CA
Edwards & Daniels, Inc., Salt Lake City, UT
Fischer-Fischer-Theis, Inc., Waukesha, WI
Glankler & Associates, Alexandria, LA
KZF Design, Cincinnati, OH
RNL Design, Denver, CO
Sakellar Associates Architects, Tucson, AZ
Shriver and Holland Associates, Norfolk, VA
WKWW, Inc., Charlotte, NC

Firms Celebrating their 25th Anniversary

AHSC Architects, Tarrytown, NY
Architecture + Design, Battle Creek, MI
Ashley McGraw Architects, Syracuse, NY
Bower Downing Partnership, Inc., Austin, TX
Bowie Gridley Architects, Washington, DC
Caro, Monroe & Liang Architects, Newport News, VA
Craiker Architects, San Rafael, CA
David C. Hughes Architects, Columbus, OH
Di Domenico + Partners, New York, NY
DMS Architects, Inc., Fort Worth, TX
Douglas Architecture & Planning, Scottsdale, AZ
Elbert M. Wheeler, Architect, Enid, OK
Francoise Bollack Architects, New York, NY

Frank H. Smith III, AIA, Architect, Atlanta, GA
Gastinger Walker Harden Architects, Kansas City, MO
Goldberg Group-Architects, St. Joseph, MO
Graham Design Associates, Clearwater, FL
Hayes Large Architects, Harrisburg, PA
Holland Lessard Group, Washington, DC
Holmes King, Kallquist & Associates, Syracuse, NY
ICON architecture/planning, Beaverton, OR
Ikemire Architect Inc., Dallas, TX
John Sawyer Architects, Wilmington, NC
Karkau & Associates, Brentwood, TN
Kendrick Design Group, Bakersfield, CA
Kenyon Architectural Group, Tempe, AZ
Koning Eizenberg Architecture, Inc., Santa Monica, CA
La Canada Design Group, Pasadena, CA
Lantz-Boggio-Architects, Englewood, CO
Leon E. Felus, Architect, Marina del Rey, CA
Liberstudio Architects Inc., Santa Monica, CA
LPA Group Incorporated, Columbia, SC
M+O+A Architectural Partnership, Denver, CO
MBAJ Architecture, Charlotte, NC
Meyer, Scherer & Rockcastle, Ltd., Minneapolis, MN
Michael Anthony D'Aconti Architects, Commack, NY
Milbrandt Architects, Inc., Bellevue, WA
Miranda Stauffer Architects, Fernandina Beach, FL
MRSA Architects & Planners, Chicago, IL
N.J. Cifaretto, AIA, Architect, Montville, NJ
Newport Collaborative Architects, Inc., Newport, RI
PC Architects, Inc., St. George, UT
Phillips Swager Associates, Inc., Dallas, TX
Prairie Wind Architecture, Lewistown, MT
Reynolds Group, Haddonfield, NJ
Richard L. Worley AIA Architect, Brevard, NC
River Architects, Inc., La Crosse, WI
Rubeling & Associates, Inc., Towson, MD
S/L/A/M Collaborative, Cambridge, MA

Firm Anniversaries

Shalom Baranes Associates, Washington, DC
Shope Reno Wharton, Greenwich, CT
Siebein Associates, Gainesville, FL
Skinner Vignola McLean, Inc., Gainesville, FL
Skip Shaputnic Architect, San Diego, CA
Smallwood, Reynolds, Stewart, Stewart Interiors,
     Inc., Atlanta, GA
Spears Architects, Santa Fe, NM
Steven P. Elkins Architects Inc., Bellevue, WA
Terry A. Cone, Architect, Fort Worth, TX
TGS Architects, Dallas, TX
Treanor Architects, Lawrence, KS
Trittipo Architecture & Planning,
     San Marcos, CA
Venezia and Associates, New Brunswick, NJ
Wallace Floyd Design Group, Boston, MA
Williams + Paddon, Architects + Planners, Inc.,
     Roseville, CA
Wronsky Architect, North Palm Beach, FL
Yeates and Yeates Architects, New Orleans, LA

Source: DesignIntelligence

Did you know...

Founded in 1906 by Walter H. Ratcliff, a key figure in the early development of Bay Area architecture, Ratcliff has been led by three generations of the Ratcliff family: Walter, 1881–1973; Robert, 1913–1998; and now Christopher.

Firm Statistics: Architecture

	Number of Establishments[1]	Annual Payroll ($1,000)	Paid Employees[2]
Alabama	236	76,522	1,593
Alaska	47	23,495	345
Arizona	559	186,101	3,806
Arkansas	154	45,884	1,082
California	3,440	1,576,783	26,685
Colorado	730	226,758	4,133
Connecticut	340	138,355	2,296
Delaware	38	12,731	254
District of Columbia	155	173,006	2,654
Florida	1,693	475,457	9,772
Georgia	615	308,532	5,642
Hawaii	188	60,366	1,097
Idaho	129	29,966	762
Illinois	1,169	469,517	8,644
Indiana	316	125,771	2,683
Iowa	121	41,619	851
Kansas	170	68,448	1,364
Kentucky	173	57,138	1,167
Louisiana	255	68,939	1,548
Maine	106	32,504	740
Maryland	419	175,695	3,152
Massachusetts	786	496,609	8,217
Michigan	595	263,281	5,130
Minnesota	437	247,750	4,580
Mississippi	109	31,426	718
Missouri	415	264,532	4,630
Montana	118	27,835	673
Nebraska	110	69,383	1,342
Nevada	157	75,292	1,465
New Hampshire	76	21,601	384
New Jersey	714	273,945	4,783
New Mexico	171	38,376	985

291

Firm Statistics: Architecture

	Number of Establishments[1]	Annual Payroll ($1,000)	Paid Employees[2]
New York	2,036	923,428	16,258
North Carolina	623	230,744	4,596
North Dakota	39	11,145	257
Ohio	690	318,286	6,324
Oklahoma	190	67,921	1,467
Oregon	343	121,578	2,548
Pennsylvania	737	428,276	8,106
Rhode Island	89	20,828	448
South Carolina	260	76,836	1,511
South Dakota	38	9,686	258
Tennessee	292	157,624	2,822
Texas	1,466	693,558	12,824
Utah	202	54,901	1,389
Vermont	89	22,467	478
Virginia	549	248,753	4,602
Washington	711	281,190	5,437
West Virginia	46	12,427	268
Wisconsin	295	124,824	2,638
Wyoming	50	9,432	241
US Total	**23,486**	**9,997,521**	**185,649**

[1] All numbers are 2002.
[2] Paid employees for the pay period including March 12.

Source: US Census Bureau

293

Firm Statistics

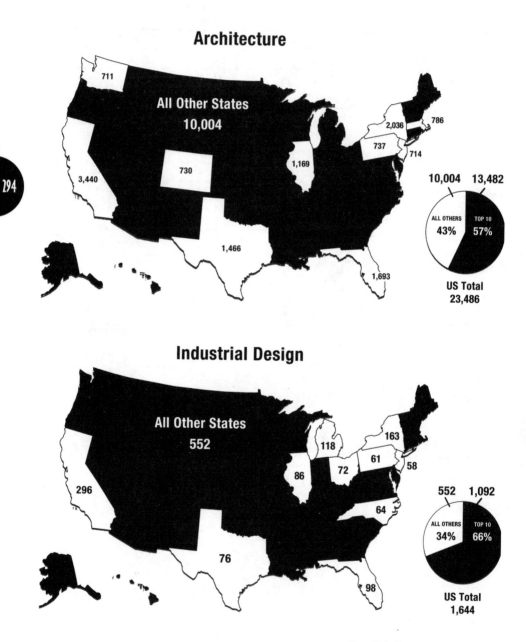

Architecture

711
All Other States
10,004
2,036
786
737
714
294
730
1,169
3,440
1,466
1,693

10,004   13,482
ALL OTHERS   TOP 10
43%   57%
US Total
23,486

Industrial Design

All Other States
552
163
118
61
58
86
72
296
64
76
98

552   1,092
ALL OTHERS   TOP 10
34%   66%
US Total
1,644

Source: DesignIntelligence

Firm Statistics: Industrial Design

	Number of Establishments[1]	Annual Payroll ($1,000)	Paid Employees[2]
Alabama	6	Withheld	0–19
Alaska	1	Withheld	0–19
Arizona	19	8,589	136
Arkansas	6	Withheld	0–19
California	296	116,687	1,932
Colorado	34	Withheld	100–249
Connecticut	23	8,049	151
Delaware	3	Withheld	100–249
District of Columbia	1	Withheld	0–19
Florida	98	8,477	273
Georgia	38	6,462	165
Hawaii	1	Withheld	0–19
Idaho	8	Withheld	20–99
Illinois	86	25,680	493
Indiana	21	8,646	162
Iowa	4	Withheld	20–99
Kansas	8	403	16
Kentucky	10	Withheld	20–99
Louisiana	7	543	20
Maine	5	Withheld	20–99
Maryland	28	Withheld	250–499
Massachusetts	54	Withheld	250–499
Michigan	118	64,922	1,153
Minnesota	39	18,122	332
Mississippi	1	Withheld	0–19
Missouri	15	3,572	107
Montana	2	Withheld	0–19
Nebraska	6	Withheld	0–19
Nevada	11	Withheld	0–19
New Hampshire	10	3,982	75
New Jersey	58	22,536	403
New Mexico	8	3,694	66

Firm Statistics: Industrial Design

	Number of Establishments[1]	Annual Payroll ($1,000)	Paid Employees[2]
New York	163	47,808	844
North Carolina	64	9,178	169
North Dakota	n/a	n/a	n/a
Ohio	72	32,069	706
Oklahoma	4	Withheld	20–99
Oregon	27	50,598	726
Pennsylvania	61	74,725	1,898
Rhode Island	13	2,878	64
South Carolina	13	Withheld	100–249
South Dakota	3	Withheld	0–19
Tennessee	20	7,035	177
Texas	76	25,395	530
Utah	12	Withheld	20–99
Vermont	2	Withheld	0–19
Virginia	20	Withheld	100–249
Washington	31	Withheld	100–249
West Virginia	4	Withheld	20–99
Wisconsin	31	Withheld	250–499
Wyoming	3	Withheld	20–99
US Total	**1,644**	**550,050**	**10,598**

[1] All numbers are 2002.
[2] Paid employees for the pay period including March 12.
 Data was withheld from certain fields to avoid disclosing data of individual companies.

Source: US Census Bureau

Firm Statistics: Interior Design

	Number of Establishments[1]	Annual Payroll ($1,000)	Paid Employees[2]
Alabama	104	6,474	298
Alaska	13	1,688	49
Arizona	228	25,681	716
Arkansas	46	3,530	134
California	1,451	261,906	6,286
Colorado	347	37,630	1,077
Connecticut	161	24,120	556
Delaware	34	4,867	124
District of Columbia	51	36,883	593
Florida	1,395	147,197	4,751
Georgia	439	63,345	1,635
Hawaii	33	5,337	112
Idaho	39	Withheld	100–249
Illinois	571	78,056	1,956
Indiana	191	15,604	535
Iowa	54	3,060	112
Kansas	54	4,481	213
Kentucky	96	9,044	338
Louisiana	105	7,892	302
Maine	23	Withheld	20–99
Maryland	223	Withheld	500–999
Massachusetts	269	42,819	966
Michigan	281	34,207	931
Minnesota	197	24,479	700
Mississippi	40	2,090	115
Missouri	166	17,036	566
Montana	28	Withheld	20–99
Nebraska	43	Withheld	100–249
Nevada	109	17,832	437
New Hampshire	35	2,249	94
New Jersey	357	36,073	1,055
New Mexico	31	2,111	73

Firm Statistics: Interior Design

	Number of Establishments[1]	Annual Payroll ($1,000)	Paid Employees[2]
New York	1,038	188,894	3,507
North Carolina	343	23,702	909
North Dakota	10	Withheld	20–99
Ohio	308	32,914	1,136
Oklahoma	91	Withheld	250–499
Oregon	116	12,027	331
Pennsylvania	291	43,866	1,191
Rhode Island	44	5,989	156
South Carolina	148	10,401	477
South Dakota	13	Withheld	20–99
Tennessee	149	14,706	436
Texas	699	107,290	2,592
Utah	87	6,490	260
Vermont	18	Withheld	100–249
Virginia	310	32,668	994
Washington	201	20,545	664
West Virginia	17	1,524	62
Wisconsin	109	10,641	402
Wyoming	11	Withheld	20–99
US Total	**11,217**	**1,427,348**	**37,841**

[1] All numbers are 2002.
[2] Paid employees for the pay period including March 12.
Data was withheld from certain fields to avoid disclosing data of individual companies.

Source: US Census Bureau

298

Firm Statistics

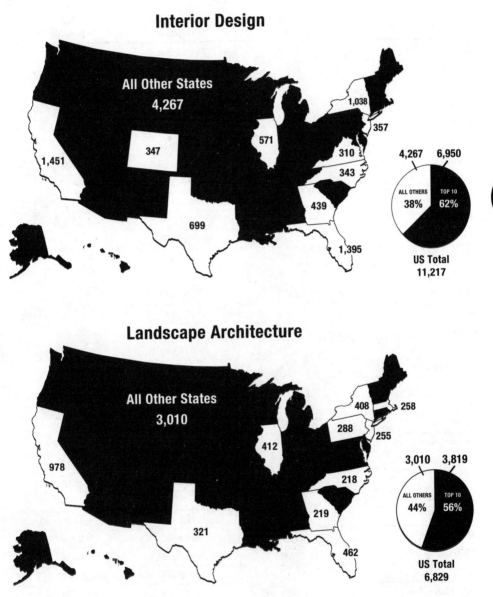

Interior Design

All Other States
4,267

1,038
357
571
347
310
343
1,451
439
699
1,395

4,267 6,950

ALL OTHERS TOP 10
38% 62%

299

US Total
11,217

Landscape Architecture

All Other States
3,010

408 258
288
255
412
978
218
219
321
462

3,010 3,819

ALL OTHERS TOP 10
44% 56%

US Total
6,829

Source: DesignIntelligence

Firm Statistics: Landscape Architecture

	Number of Establishments[1]	Annual Payroll ($1,000)	Paid Employees[2]
Alabama	63	12,306	517
Alaska	8	Withheld	20–99
Arizona	146	42,843	1,286
Arkansas	33	Withheld	100–249
California	978	322,274	9,419
Colorado	200	56,910	1,273
Connecticut	105	22,169	508
Delaware	27	4,313	146
District of Columbia	19	13,243	210
Florida	462	98,791	3,010
Georgia	219	43,694	1,448
Hawaii	37	16,152	434
Idaho	36	4,429	140
Illinois	412	93,543	1,872
Indiana	112	15,249	454
Iowa	50	9,216	239
Kansas	35	11,900	443
Kentucky	58	8,097	314
Louisiana	60	7,840	404
Maine	48	8,415	206
Maryland	145	29,621	841
Massachusetts	258	63,396	1,300
Michigan	213	57,311	1,118
Minnesota	99	18,676	457
Mississippi	43	8,073	334
Missouri	85	10,910	368
Montana	34	Withheld	20–99
Nebraska	32	Withheld	100–249
Nevada	49	12,639	417
New Hampshire	32	5,876	131
New Jersey	255	46,802	1,194
New Mexico	54	6,573	245

300

Firm Statistics: Landscape Architecture

	Number of Establishments[1]	Annual Payroll ($1,000)	Paid Employees[2]
New York	408	77,383	1,690
North Carolina	218	40,737	1,314
North Dakota	9	Withheld	0–19
Ohio	188	36,594	1,016
Oklahoma	54	6,966	283
Oregon	92	18,037	645
Pennsylvania	288	56,525	1,566
Rhode Island	35	Withheld	20–99
South Carolina	99	15,385	549
South Dakota	16	1,741	59
Tennessee	102	20,089	867
Texas	321	115,733	3,467
Utah	73	5,538	166
Vermont	34	2,815	62
Virginia	157	37,358	1,257
Washington	187	27,196	735
West Virginia	15	Withheld	20–99
Wisconsin	109	29,107	752
Wyoming	17	Withheld	20–99
US Total	**6,829**	**1,542,465**	**43,156**

[1] All numbers are 2002.
[2] Paid employees for the pay period including March 12.
 Data was withheld from certain fields to avoid disclosing data of individual companies.

Source: US Census Bureau

Dr. Pepper/Seven Up Ballpark. David M. Schwartz Architectural Services and HKS gave a residential feel to this award-winning ball field. An airy "park within a park" design was achieved using multiple, free-standing pavilions along the back of the concourse covered in Hardiplank siding, and welcoming garden-walk landscaping. **Photos** ©2005 by Joe Mock, BASEBALLPARKS.COM.

Minor League Ballparks

Minor league baseball's increasing popularity during the last two decades has spawned greater interest in its ballparks. Half of today's AAA ballparks were built within the last 10 years. Only six of the 30 were built before 1983. The other leagues have seen quite a bit of activity as well, with multiple parks opening each year. The design of these new parks has evolved along with the Majors, offering similar amenities on a smaller scale. Today's stadium offerings of brew pubs, suites and club seats, trademark scoreboards, and souvenir shops are a long way from the simplicity and straightforwardness of the park of old. Corporate naming rights is also a growing trend that has found its way to the Minors. The following charts contain a list of all the AAA ballparks, along with their requisite architectural statistics, as well as a list of non-AAA ballparks that have opened since 2000.

Whataburger Field. HKS incorporated two 1920-era cotton processing structures in the design of this facility. Timbers from an old cotton warehouse were also used in the construction of the picnic area. Photos ©2005 by Joe Mock, BASEBALLPARKS.COM.

AAA Ballparks: Pacific Coast League

Team Name	Major League Affiliation	Stadium Name	Location
Albuquerque Isotopes	Florida Marlins	Isotopes Park	Albuquerque, NM
Colorado Springs Sky Sox	Colorado Rockies	Security Services Field	Colorado Springs, CO
Fresno Grizzlies	San Francisco Giants	Grizzlies Stadium	Fresno, CA
Iowa Cubs	Chicago Cubs	Sec Taylor Stadium	Des Moines, IA
Las Vegas 51s	Los Angeles Dodgers	Cashman Field	Las Vegas, NV
Memphis Redbirds	St. Louis Cardinals	AutoZone Park	Memphis, TN
Nashville Sounds	Milwaukee Brewers	Herschel Greer Stadium	Nashville, TN
New Orleans Zephyrs	Washington Nationals	Zephyr Field	New Orleans, LA
Oklahoma RedHawks	Texas Rangers	SBC Bricktown Ballpark	Oklahoma City, OK
Omaha Royals	Kansas City Royals	Rosenblatt Stadium	Omaha, NE
Portland Beavers	San Diego Padres	PGE Park	Portland, OR
Round Rock Express	Houston Astros	Dell Diamond	Round Rock, TX
Sacramento River Cats	Oakland A's	Raley Field	Sacramento, CA
Salt Lake Stingers	Anaheim Angeles	Franklin Covey Field	Salt Lake City, UT
Security Services Field	Colorado Rockies	Sky Sox Stadium	Colorado Springs, CO
Tacoma Rainiers	Seattle Mariners	Cheney Stadium	Tacoma, WA
Tucson Sidewinders	Arizona Diamondbacks	Tucson Electric Park	Tuscon, AZ

* Although Isotopes Park was officially renovated in 2003, little of the original 1969 park remains aside from the original bowl structure, general park dimensions, and some of the service areas connecting the dugouts and clubhouses.

Opened	Architect (original)	Cost (original)	Capacity (current)	Naming Rights (amt. and expiration)
2003*	HOK Sport + Venue + Event	$25 M	11,075	
1988	HNTB Architecture	$3.7 M	8,500	$1.5 M (12 yrs.)
2002	HOK Sport + Venue + Event	$46 M	12,500	
1992	HOK Sports Facilities Group	$11.5 M	11,000	
1983	Tate and Snyder	$26 M	9,334	
2000	Looney Ricks Kiss Architects in Association with HOK Sports Facilities Group	$46 M	14,320	$4.5 M (15 yrs.)
1977	Stoll-Reed Architects Inc.	$1 M	10,130	
1997	HOK Sports Facilities Group	$25 M	10,000	
1998	Architectural Design Group	$32.4 M	13,066	Undisclosed
1948	Leo A Daly	$750,000	21,871	
1926	A.E. Doyle (Ellerbe Becket with Fletcher, Farr, Ayotte, PC, 2001 renovation)	$502,000 ($38.5 M) for 2001 renovation	18,000	$7.1 M (10 yrs.)
2002	HKS, Inc.	$25 M	9,816	$2.5 M (15 yrs.)
2000	HNTB Architecture	$40 M	11,092	$15 M (20 yrs.)
1994	HOK Sports Facilities Group	$22 M	15,500	$1.4 M (10 yrs.)
1988	HNTB Architecture	$3.7 M	8,500	$1.5 M (12 yrs.)
1960	E.L Mills & Associates	$940,000	9,600	
1998	HOK Sports Facilities Group	$37 M	11,000	$4 M (15 yrs.)

AAA Ballparks: International League

Team Name	Major League Affiliation	Stadium Name	Location
Buffalo Bisons	Cleveland Indians	Dunn Tire Park	Buffalo, NY
Charlotte Knights	Chicago White Sox	Knights Stadium	Fort Mill, SC
Columbus Clippers	New York Yankees	Cooper Stadium	Columbus, OH
Durham Bulls	Tampa Bay Devil Rays	Durham Bulls Athletic Park	Durham, NC
Indianapolis Indians	Pittsburgh Pirates	Victory Field	Indianapolis, IN
Louisville Bats	Cincinnati Reds	Louisville Slugger Field	Louisville, KY
Norfolk Tides	New York Mets	Harbor Park	Norfolk, VA
Ottawa Lynx	Baltimore Orioles	Lynx Stadium	Ottawa, ON, Canada
Pawtucket Red Sox	Boston Red Sox	McCoy Stadium	Pawtucket, RI
Richmond Braves	Atlanta Braves	The Diamond	Richmond, VA
Rochester Red Wings	Minnesota Twins	Frontier Field	Rochester, NY
Scranton-Wilkes Barre Red Barons	Philadelphia Phillies	Lackawanna County Stadium	Scranton, PA
Syracuse Sky Chiefs	Toronto Blue Jays	Alliance Bank Stadium	Syracuse, NY
Toledo Mud Hens	Detriot Tigers	Fifth Third Field	Toledo, OH

Opened	Architect (original)	Cost (original)	Capacity (current)	Naming Rights (amt. and expiration)
1988	HOK Sports Facilities Group	$40 M	21,050	$2.5 M (8 yrs.)
1990	Odell & Associates	$12 M	10,002	
1932	Osborn Engineering (Trautwein Associates, Architects and Planners, 1977 renovation)	450,000 ($6 M, 1977 renovation)	15,000	
1995	HOK Sports Facilities Group	$16 M	10,000	
1996	HOK Sports Facilities Group	$18 M	15,696	
2000	HNTB Architecture and K. Norman Berry & Associates	$26 M	13,131	
1993	HOK Sports Facilities Group	$16 M	12,067	
1993	Brian W. Dickey Architect	$17 M	10,332	
1942	Mark Linenthal and Thomas E. Harding (Heery International, 1999 renovation)	$1.2 M ($16 M, 1999 renovation)	10,031	
1985	Baskervill & Son, P.C.	$8 M	12,134	
1997	Ellerbe Beckett	$35.3 M	10,868	$3.5 M (20 yrs.)
1989	GSGS&B	$25 M	11,432	
1997	HOK Sports Facilities Group	$16 M	11,602	$2.8 M (20 yrs.)
2002	HNTB Architecture	$39.2 M	10,000	$5 M (15 yrs.)

Other New Minor League Ballparks: 2000–05

Team Name Level/League	Major League Affiliation	Stadium Name	Location
Corpus Christi Hooks Class AA/Texas League	Houston Astros	Whataburger Field	Corpus Christi, TX
Greensboro Grasshoppers Class A/Southern Atlantic League	Florida Marlins	First Horizon Park	Greenboro, SC
Lancaster Barnstormers Independent/Atlantic League	Independent	Clipper Magazine Stadium	Lancaster, PA
Mississippi Braves Class AA/Southern League	Atlanta Braves	Trustmark Park	Pearl, MS
New Hampshire Fisher Cats Class AA/Eastern League	Toronto Blue Jays	Fisher Cats Ballpark	Manchester, NH
Rockford RiverHawks Independent/Frontier League	Independent	RiverHawks Stadium	Rockford, IL
Stockton Ports Class A/California League	Oakland A's	Banner Island Ballpark	Stockton, CA
West Viginia Power Class A/Southern Atlantic League	Milwaukee Brewers	Appalachian Power Park	Charleston, WV
Clearwater Threshers Class A/Florida State League	Philadelphia Phillies	Bright House Networks Field	Clearwater, FL
Missoula Osprey Pioneer League	Arizona Diamondbacks	Missoula Civic Stadium	Missoula, MT
Montgomery Buscuits Class AA/Southern League	Tampa Bay Devil Rays	Montgomery Riverwalk Stadium	Montgomery, AL
Springfield Cardinals Class AA/Texas League	St. Louis Cardinals	Hammons Field	Springfield, MO
Frisco RoughRiders Class AA/Texas League	Texas Rangers	Dr. Pepper/Seven Up Ballpark	Frisco, TX
Gary Southshore RailCats Independent/Northern League	Independent	The Steel Yard	Gary, IN
Jacksonville Suns Class AA/Southern League	Los Angeles Dodgers	Baseball Grounds of Jacksonville	Jacksonville, FL
Kansas City T-Bones Independent/Northern League	Independent	CommunityAmerica Ballpark	Kansas City, KS
Lake County Captains Class A/South Atlantic	Cleveland Indians	Eastlake Stadium	Eastlake, OH
Rome Braves Class A/South Atlantic	Atlanta Braves	State Mutual Stadium	Rome, GA

Architect (original)	Opened	Cost (original)	Capacity (current)	Naming Rights (amt. and expiration)
HKS, Inc.	2005	$27.7 M	8,255	Undisclosed
Moser Mayer Phoenix Associates	2005	$20 M	5,021	$3 M (10 yrs.)
Tetra Tech, Inc.	2005	$23.4 M	6,500	$2.5 M (10 yrs.)
HOK Sport + Venue + Event with Dale and Associates Architects	2005	$25 M	7,062	$25 M (10 yrs.)
HNTB Architecture	2005	$20 M	7,000	
CSHQA	2005	$7 M	4,000	
HKS, Inc.	2005	$14.5 M	5,000	
HNTB Architecture	2005	$23 M	4,500	$1.25 M (10 yrs.)
HOK Sport + Venue + Event with EwingCole	2004	$32 M	7,000	$1.7 M (10 yrs.)
Heery International with CTA Architects	2004	$10.2 M	3,500	
HOK Sport + Venue + Event	2004	$26 M	7,000	
Pellham Phillips Hagerman	2004	$32 M	8,056	
David M. Schwarz Architectural Services with HKS, Inc.	2003	$28 M	10,600	Undisclosed
HNTB Architecture	2003	$45 M	6,000	$875,000 (10 yrs.)
HOK Sport + Venue + Event	2003	$34 M	10,000	
Heinlein Schrock Stearns	2003	$15 M	5,500	Undisclosed
DLR Group	2003	$19.5 M	7,273	
Brisbin Brook Benyon	2003	$14.8 M	6,100	Undisclosed

Other New Minor League Ballparks: 2000–05

Team Name Level/League	Major League Affiliation	Stadium Name	Location
Aberdeen IronBirds New York-Penn League	Baltimore Orioles	Ripken Stadium	Little Aberdeen, MD
Cedar Rapids Kernels Class A/Midwest League	Anaheim Angels	Veterans Memorial Stadium	Cedar Rapids, IA
Joliet Jackhammers Independent/Northern League	Independent	Silver Cross Field	Joliet, IL
Midland RockHounds Class AA/Texas League	Oakland A's	First American Bank Ballpark	Midland, TX
Tri-City ValleyCats New York-Penn League	Houston Astros	Joseph L. Bruno Stadium	Troy, NY
Brooklyn Cyclones New York-Penn League	New York Mets	KeySpan Park	Brooklyn, NY
Camden Riversharks Independent/Atlantic League	Independent	Campbell's Field	Camden, NJ
Casper Rockies Pioneer League	Colorado Rockies	Mike Lansing Field	Casper, WY
Lakewood BlueClaws Class A/South Atlantic	Philadelphia Phillies	First Energy Park	Lakewood, NJ
Lexington Legends Class A/Midwest League	Houston Astros	Applebee's Park	Lexington, KY
Lincoln Salt Dogs Independent/Northern League	Independent	Haymarket Park	Lincoln, NE
Staten Island Yankees New York-Penn League	New York Yankees	Richmond County Bank Ballpark at St. George	Staten Island, NY
Chattanooga Lookouts Class AA/Southern League	Cincinnati Reds	BellSouth Park	Chattanooga, TN
Dayton Dragons Class A/Midwest League	Cincinnati Reds	Fifth Third Field	Dayton, OH
Long Island Ducks Atlantic League (Independent)	Independent	Citibank Park	Central Islip, NY
Peoria Chiefs Class A/Midwest League	Chicago Cubs	O'Brien Field	Peoria, IL
Tennessee Smokies Class AA/Southern League	Arizona Diamondbacks	Smokies Park	Kodak, TN

Source: DesignIntelligence

Architect (original)	Opened	Cost (original)	Capacity (current)	Naming Rights (amt. and expiration)
Tetra Tech, Inc.	2002	$35 M	6,000	
"Heinlein Schrock Stearns"	2002	$14 M	6,100	
Sink Combs Dethlefs	2002	$27 M	6,915	$1.5 M (10 yrs.)
HOK Sport + Venue + Event	2002	$25 M	5,000	$2.1 M (25 yrs.)
DLR Group	2002	$14 M	4,500	
Jack L. Gordon Architects	2001	$35 M	8,000	
Clarke, Caton and Hintz	2001	$20.5 M	6,425	$3 M (10 yrs.)
GSG Architecture	2001	$4 M	2,500	
HNTB Architecture	2001	$20 M	6,588	$4.5 M (20 yrs.)
Brisbin Brook Benyon	2001	$13.5 M	6,994	$3 M (10 yrs.)
DLR Group	2001	$32 M	4,500	
HOK Sport + Venue + Event	2001	$34 M	6,886	Undisclosed
DLR Group with TWH Architects	2000	$10 M	6,157	$1 M (10 yrs.)
HNTB Architecture	2000	$22.7 M	7,250	Undisclosed
HNTB Architecture with Beatty Harvey Asociates	2000	$14 M	6,200	Undisclosed
HNTB Architecture	2000	$24 M	7,500	
HNTB Architecture	2000	$20 M	6,412	

311

Most Popular US Buildings

The following rankings provide a glimpse into the minds of architects (and, in one case, architecture critics) as they they reflected at various points in history on the question of what are America's best buildings.

1885 Poll conducted by the *American Architect & Building News*:

1. Trinity Church, Boston, MA
   H.H. Richardson, 1877
2. US Capitol, Washington, DC
   William Thornton, Benjamin Henry Latrobe,
   Charles Bulfinch, 1793–1829
3. Vanderbilt House, New York, NY
   Richard Morris Hunt, 1883
4. Trinity Church, New York, NY
   Richard Upjohn, 1846
5. Jefferson Market Courthouse, New York, NY
   Frederick Withers & Calvert Vaux, 1877
6. Connecticut State Capitol, Hartford, CT
   Richard Upjohn, 1879
7. City Hall, Albany, NY
   H.H. Richardson, 1883
8. Sever Hall, Harvard University, Cambridge, MA
   H.H. Richardson, 1880
9. New York State Capitol, Albany, NY
   H.H. Richardson, 1886
10. Town Hall, North Easton, MA
    H.H. Richardson, 1881

Source: American Architect & Building News

1986 Poll conducted by the American Institute of Architects:

1. Fallingwater, Mill Run, PA
   Frank Lloyd Wright, 1936
2. Seagram Building, New York, NY
   Ludwig Mies van der Rohe, 1954–58
3. Dulles Airport, Chantilly, VA
   Eero Saarinen, 1962
4. University of Virginia, Charlottesville, VA
   Thomas Jefferson, 1826
5. Robie House, Chicago, IL
   Frank Lloyd Wright, 1909
6. Trinity Church, Boston, MA
   H.H. Richardson, 1877
7. East Wing, National Gallery, Washington, DC
   I.M. Pei & Partners, 1978
8. Rockefeller Center, New York, NY
   Raymond Hood, 1940
9. S.C. Johnson & Son Admin. Building,
   Racine, WI
   Frank Lloyd Wright, 1936
10. Monticello, Charlottesville, VA
    Thomas Jefferson, 1769–84; 1796–1809

Source: American Institute of Architects

Did you know...

When the Frederick C. Robie House was threatened with demolition in 1957, architects and preservationists lobbied for the creation of the Commission on Chicago Landmarks, and subsequently, the Robie house became the commission's first building designated a Chicago landmark.

Most Popular US Buildings

2000 Building of the Century Poll conducted at the 2000 AIA Convention in Philadelphia:

1. Fallingwater, Mill Run, PA
   Frank Lloyd Wright,1936
2. Chrysler Building, New York, NY
   William Van Alen, 1930
3. Seagram Building, New York, NY
   Ludwig Mies van der Rohe, 1958
4. Thorncrown Chapel, Eureka, AR
   E. Fay Jones, 1980
5. Dulles Airport, Chantilly, VA
   Eero Saarinen, 1962
6. Salk Institute, La Jolla, CA
   Louis I. Kahn, 1966
7. Vietnam Veterans Memorial,
   Washington, DC
   Maya Lin, 1982
8. Robie House, Chicago, IL
   Frank Lloyd Wright, 1909
9. Guggenheim Museum, New York, NY
   Frank Lloyd Wright, 1959
10. East Wing, National Gallery, Washington, DC
    I.M. Pei, 1978
11. S.C. Johnson & Son Admin. Building,
    Racine, WI
    Frank Lloyd Wright, 1939

Source: American Institute of Architects

2001 Architecture Critics' Poll of the Top Rated Buildings:

1. Brooklyn Bridge, New York, NY
   John Augustus Roebling, 1883
2. Grand Central Station, New York, NY
   Warren & Wetmore, Reed & Stem, 1913
3. Chrysler Building, New York, NY
   William Van Alen, 1930
4. Monticello, Charlottesville, VA
   Thomas Jefferson, 1769–84; 1796–1809
5. University of Virginia, Charlottesville, VA
   Thomas Jefferson, 1826
6. Robie House, Chicago, IL
   Frank Lloyd Wright, 1909
7. Carson Pirie Scott Building, Chicago, IL
   Louis Sullivan, 1904

8. Empire State Building, New York, NY
   Shreve, Lamb & Harmon, 1931
9. S.C. Johnson & Son Admin. Building,
   Racine, WI
   Frank Lloyd Wright, 1939
10. Unity Temple, Oak Park, IL
    Frank Lloyd Wright, 1907

Source: The Architecture Critic, National Arts Journalism Program, Columbia University

Great Architectural Works of the 21st Century:

1. Rose Center for Earth and Space
   New York, NY
   Polshek Partnership Architects
2. Quadracci Pavilion, Milwaukee Art Museum
   Milwaukee, WI
   Santiago Calatrava with Kahler Slater Architects
3. Sandra Day O'Connor US Courthouse
   Phoenix, AZ
   Richard Meier & Partners
4. 3Com Midwest Headquarters
   Rolling Meadows, IL
   Valerio Dewalt Train
5. Westside Light Rail Corridor
   Portland, OR
   Zimmer Gunsul Frasca Partnership

Source: USA Weekend

National Historic Planning Landmarks

Every year the American Institute of Certified Planners, the American Planning Association's professional and educational arm, grants National Historic Planning Landmark status to up to three historically significant projects. To be eligible, projects must be 25 years old, have initiated a new direction in planning, made a significant contribution to the community, and be available for public use and viewing. Newly designated sites are indicated in bold.

For additional information about National Historic Planning Landmarks, contact the AICP at (202) 872-0611 or visit them on the Web at *www.planning.org*.

Arizona
The Salt River Project (1911)

California
Bay Conservation and Development Commission and Creation of the San Francisco Bay Plan (1965–69)
East Bay Regional Park District, San Francisco (1934)
Los Angeles Co. "Master Plan of Highways" (1940) and "Freeways for the Region" (1943)
Napa County Agricultural Preserve (1968)
Petaluma Plan (1971–72)
San Francisco Zoning Ordinance (1867)

Colorado
The Denver Parks and Parkway System (1906+)
Speer Boulevard, Denver

Connecticut
The Nine Square Plan of New Haven (1639)

District of Columbia
Euclid v. Ambler, US Supreme Court (1926)
Federal Housing Assistance "701" Program (Federal Housing Act of 1954)
First National Conference on City Planning (1909)
The McMillan Commission Plan for Washington, DC (1901)
National Resources Planning Board (1933–43)
Plan of Washington, DC (1791)

Georgia
Plan of Savannah (1733)

Hawaii
Hawaii's State Land Use Law (1961)

Illinois
The American Society of Planning Officials (ASPO, 1934)
The Chicago lakefront (1836–present)
"Local Planning Administration" (1941)
Merriam Center, Chicago (1930+)
Plan of Chicago (1909)
Plan of Park Forest (1948)
Plan of Riverside (1869)

Indiana
New Harmony (1814–27)

Kentucky
Lexington Urban Service Area (1958)

Louisiana
Plan of the Vieux Carre, New Orleans (1721)

Maryland
Columbia (1967+)
Greenbelt (A Greenbelt Town, 1935+)
Plan of Annapolis (1695)

National Historic Planning Landmarks

Massachusetts
Billerica Garden Suburb, Lowell (1914)
"Emerald Necklace" Parks, Boston (1875+)
Founding of the Harvard University Graduate
Planning Program (1929)

Michigan
Kalamazoo Mall (1956)

Missouri
Country Club Plaza, Kansas City (1922)
Founding of the American City Planning
Institute (ACPI, 1917)
Kansas City Parks Plan (1893)

Montana
Yellowstone National Park (1872)

New Jersey
"Radburn" at Fair Lawn (1928–29)
Society for the Establishment of Useful
Manufactures Plan for Paterson (1791–92)
Southern Burlington County NAACP v. Township
of Mount Laurel (1975)
Yorkship Village, Camden (1918)

New Mexico
The Laws of the Indies (1573; 1681)

New York
Bronx River Parkway and the Westchester County
Parkway System (1907+)
Central Park, New York City (1857)
First Houses, New York City (1935–36)
Forest Hills Gardens, Long Island (1911+)
Founding of the American City Planning
Institute (ACPI, 1917)
Grand Central Terminal, New York City
(1903–13)
Long Island Parkways (1885) and Parks (1920s)
New York City Zoning Code (1916)
New York State Adirondack Preserve & Park
New York State Commission on Housing and
Regional Planning (1923–26)
Niagara Reservation State Park (1885)
Regional Plan of New York & Environs (1929)

Second Regional Plan of the Regional Plan
Association of New York (1968)
Sunnyside Gardens, Long Island (1924+)
University Settlement House and the Settlement
House Movement (1886)

North Carolina
Blue Ridge Parkway (1935+)

Ohio
Cincinnati Plan of 1925
Cleveland Group Plan (1903)
Cleveland Policy Plan (1974)
Founding of Ohio Planning Conference (1919)
Greenhills (A Greenbelt Town, 1935+)
Miami Valley Region's Fair Share Housing
Plan of 1970
Plan of Mariemont (1922)

Oregon
Oregon's Statewide Program for Land Use
Planning (1973)

Pennsylvania
Plan of Philadelphia (1683)

Rhode Island
College Hill Demonstration of Historic Renewal,
Providence (1959)

South Carolina
First American Historic District,
Charleston (1931)

Tennessee
Plan of Metro Government, Nashville/
Davidson County (1956)
Tennessee Valley Authority (1933+)
Town of Norris (1933)

Texas
"A Greater Fort Worth Tomorrow" (1956)
Paseo del Rio, San Antonio (1939–41)

Utah
Plat of the City of Zion (1833)

315

National Historic Planning Landmarks

Virginia
Blue Ridge Parkway (1935+)
Jeffersonian Precinct, University of
    Virginia (1817)
Monument Avenue Historic District,
    Richmond (1888)
The New Town of Reston (1962)
Roanoke Plans (1907; 1928)

West Virginia
Appalachian Trail (1921+)

Wisconsin
Greendale (A Greenbelt Town, 1935+)
Wisconsin Planning Enabling Act (1909)

Wyoming
Yellowstone National Park (1872)

Source: American Institute of Certified Planners

Did you know...
Incorporated June 30, 1914, the Billerica Garden Suburb is the first US attempt to provide affordable homeownership to workers using Ebenezer Howard's garden city model. City planner Arthur C. Comey and landscape architect Warren H. Manning helped to develop this "workers' paradise," which is still recognizable today.

National Historic Planning Pioneers

Every year the American Institute of Certified Planners, the American Planning Association's professional and educational arm, selects up to three National Historic Planning Pioneers for significant contributions and innovation in American planning. Recipients have led planning practice, education, and/or theory on a national scale with long-term beneficial results. Their contributions must have occurred no less than 25 years ago. New inductees are indicated in bold.

For additional information about National Planning Pioneers, contact the American Institute of Certified Planners at (202) 872-0611 or visit them on the Internet at *www.planning.org*.

Charles Abrams
Frederick J. Adams
Thomas Adams
Sherry Arnstein
Edmund N. Bacon
Harland Bartholomew
Edward M. Bassett
Catherine (Wurster) Bauer
Edward H. Bennett
Alfred Bettman
Walter H. Blucher
Ernest John Bohn
Daniel Hudson Burnham
F. Stuart Chapin Jr.
Charles H. Cheney
Paul Davidoff
Frederic Adrian Delano
Earle S. Draper
Simon Eisner
Carl Feiss
George Burdett Ford
Paul Goodman
Percival Goodman
Aelred Joseph Gray
Frederick Gutheim
S. Herbert Hare
Sid J. Hare

Elisabeth Herlihy
John Tasker Howard
Henry Vincent Hubbard
Theodora Kimball Hubbard
Harlean James
T.J. Kent Jr.
George Edward Kessler
Pierre Charles L'Enfant
Kevin Lynch
Benton MacKaye
Ian Lennox McHarg
Albert Mayer
Harold V. Miller
Corwin R. Mocine
Arthur Ernest Morgan
Robert Moses
Lewis Mumford
Jesse Clyde Nichols
John Nolen Sr.
Charles Dyer Norton
Charles McKim Norton
Frederick Law Olmsted Sr.
Frederick Law Olmsted Jr.
Lawrence M. Orton
The Outdoor Circle
Harvey S. Perloff
Clarence Arthur Perry

Gifford Pinchot
Planners for Equal
    Opportunity, 1964–1974
John Reps
Jacob August Riis
Charles Mulford Robinson
James W. Rouse
Charlotte Rumbold
Mel Scott
Ladislas Segoe
Flavel Shurtleff
Mary K. Simkhovitch
Robert E. Simon Jr.
William E. Spangle
Clarence S. Stein
Telesis, 1939–1953
Rexford Guy Tugwell
Lawrence T. Veiller
Francis Violich
Charles Henry Wacker
Lillian Wald
Gordon Whitnall
Donald Wolbrink
Edith Elmer Wood
Henry Wright

Source: American Institute of Certified Planners

Number of Registered Architects by State

Registered architects in each state are divided into two categories: resident and reciprocal, or non-resident, registrants. Based on current population levels, the chart below also calculates the per capita number of resident architects in each state. The following information is from the National Council of Architectural Registration Boards' 2004 survey.

State	Resident Architects	Reciprocal Registrations	Total	Population[1]	Per capita # of Resident Architects (per 100,000)
Alabama	810	1,441	2,251	4,447,100	18
Alaska	217	141	358	626,932	35
Arizona	1,983	4,207	6,190	5,130,632	39
Arkansas	450	974	1,424	2,673,400	17
California	16,397	4,653	21,050	33,871,648	48
Colorado	2,869	3,329	6,198	4,301,261	67
Connecticut*	1,537	3,972	5,509	3,405,565	45
Delaware	100	1,000	1,100	783,600	13
D.C.	770	1,845	2,615	572,059	135
Florida	4,551	3,745	8,296	15,982,378	28
Georgia	2,406	3,008	5,414	8,186,453	29
Hawaii	922	1,040	1,962	1,211,537	76
Idaho	481	1,050	1,531	1,293,953	37
Illinois*	5,345	3,551	8,896	12,419,293	43
Indiana	955	2,312	3,267	6,080,485	16
Iowa	442	1,064	1,506	2,926,324	15
Kansas	963	1,519	2,482	2,688,418	36
Kentucky	657	1,608	2,265	4,041,769	16
Louisiana	1,083	1,550	2,633	4,468,976	24
Maine	375	965	1,340	1,274,923	29
Maryland	1,758	3,413	5,171	5,296,486	33
Massachusetts	4,287	5,534	9,821	6,349,097	68
Michigan	3,564	2,313	5,877	9,938,444	36
Minnesota	1,750	1,543	3,293	4,919,479	36
Mississippi	300	1,068	1,368	2,844,658	11
Missouri	1,830	2,554	4,384	5,595,211	33
Montana	374	886	1,260	902,195	41

Number of Registered Architects by State

State	Resident Architects	Reciprocal Registrations	Total	Population[1]	Per capita # of Resident Architects (per 100,000)
Nebraska	507	1,022	1,529	1,711,263	30
Nevada	522	1,987	2,509	1,998,257	26
New Hampshire	281	1,287	1,568	1,235,786	23
New Jersey	2,895	4,434	7,329	8,414,350	34
New Mexico	702	1,140	1,842	1,819,046	39
New York	8,257	5,274	13,531	18,976,457	44
North Carolina	2,003	2,785	4,788	8,049,313	25
North Dakota	127	468	595	642,200	20
Ohio	3,671	3,353	7,024	11,353,140	32
Oklahoma	778	1,163	1,941	3,450,654	23
Oregon	1,063	1,400	2,463	3,421,399	31
Pennsylvania	3,915	3,585	7,500	12,281,054	32
Rhode Island	243	1,027	1,270	1,048,319	23
South Carolina	949	2,267	3,216	4,012,012	24
South Dakota	102	522	624	754,844	14
Tennessee	1,369	1,968	3,337	5,689,283	24
Texas	6,803	2,964	9,767	20,851,820	33
Utah	689	1,359	2,048	2,233,169	31
Vermont	269	725	994	608,827	44
Virginia	2,501	3,790	6,291	7,078,515	35
Washington	3,521	1,911	5,432	5,894,121	60
West Virginia	116	987	1,103	1,808,344	6
Wisconsin	1,612	3,205	4,817	5,363,675	30
Wyoming	110	754	864	493,782	22
Totals	**100,181**	**109,662**	**209,843**	**281,421,906**	**36**

[1] 2000 Population Estimate from the US Census Bureau
* Counts are estimated based on data from prior years.

Source: National Council of Architectural Registration Boards

319

320

of Registered Architects
(Top 10 Shown)

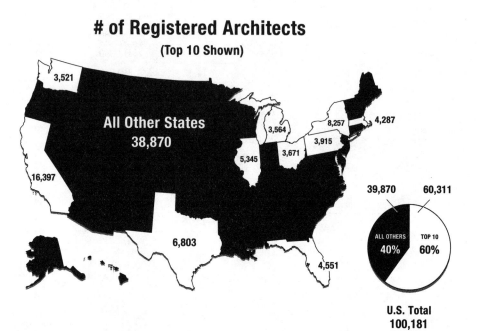

3,521

All Other States
38,870

3,564

8,257   4,287

3,915

5,345   3,671

16,397

6,803

4,551

39,870   60,311

ALL OTHERS   TOP 10
40%   **60%**

U.S. Total
100,181

Source: DesignIntelligence

Oldest Practicing Architecture Firms in North America

The following firms were founded prior to 1900 (their specific founding dates indicated below) and are still operational today.

1827
The Mason & Hanger
Group, Inc.
Lexington, KY

1832
Lockwood Greene
Spartanburg, SC

1853
Luckett & Farley Architects,
Engineers and Construction Managers, Inc.
Louisville, KY

1853
SmithGroup
Detroit, MI

1868
Jensen and Halstead Ltd.
Chicago, IL

1868
King & King Architects
Manlius, NY

1870
Harriman Associates
Auburn, ME

1871
Scholtz-Gowey-Gere-Marolf
Architects & Interior
Designers
Davenport, IA

1873
Graham Anderson Probst
& White
Chicago, IL

1873
River Bluffs Architects
St. Joseph, MO

1874
Shepley Bulfinch
Richardson and
Abbott, Inc.
Boston, MA

1878
The Austin Company
Kansas City, MO

1878
Ballinger
Philadelphia, PA

1880
Beatty Harvey & Associates,
Architects
New York, NY

1880
Green Nelson Weaver, Inc.
Minneapolis, MN

1880
Holabird & Root
Chicago, IL

1880
Zeidler Partnership
Architects
Toronto, Canada

1881
Keffer/Overton Architects
Des Moines, IA

1883
Ritterbush-Ellig-Hulsing
Bismarck, ND

1883
SMRT Architecture
Engineering Planning
Portland, ME

1885
Cromwell Architects
Engineers
Little Rock, AR

1885
HLW International
New York, NY

1887
Bradley & Bradley
Rockford, IL

1889
Architectural Design
West, Inc.
Salt Lake City, UT

1889
CSHQA Architects/
Engineers/Planners
Boise, ID

1889
MacLachlan, Cornelius
& Filoni, Inc.
Pittsburgh, PA

1889
Wank Adams Slavin
Associates
New York, NY

1890
Kendall, Taylor
& Company, Inc.
Billerica, MA

Oldest Practicing Architecture Firms in North America

1890
Mathes Brierre Architects
New Orleans, LA

1890
Plunkett Raysich Architects
Milwaukee, WI

1891
SSP Architectural Group
Somerville, NJ

1892
Bauer Stark +
  Lashbrook, Inc.
Toledo, OH

1892
FreemanWhite, Inc.
Raleigh, NC

1893
Foor & Associates
Elmira, NY

1894
Colgan Perry Lawler
  Architects
Nyack, NY

1894
Freese and Nichols, Inc.
Fort Worth, TX

1894
Parkinson Field Associates
Austin, TX

1895
Brooks Borg Skiles
  Architecture Engineering
Des Moines, IA

1895
Albert Kahn Associates, Inc.
Detroit, MI

1896
Hummel Architects
Boise, ID

1896
Kessels DiBoll Kessels
  & Associates
New Orleans, LA

1896
Lehman Architectural
Group
Fairfield, NJ

1897
Baskervill
Richmond, VA

1897
LHRS Architects, Inc.
Huntington, IN

1898
Beardsley Design Associates
Auburn, NY

1898
BSA, Inc.
Green Bay, WI

1898
Burns & McDonnell
Kansas City, MO

1898
Eckles Architecture
New Castle, PA

1898
Emery Roth & Sons
New York, NY

1898
Foss Associates
Fargo, ND & Moorhead, MN

1898
PageSoutherlandPage
Austin, TX

1899
William B. Ittner, Inc.
St. Louis, MO

Source: DesignIntelligence

100 American Art Museums and their Architects

It has been estimated that there are more than 16,000 different museums in the United States. While the collections they hold are often priceless, the facilities that contain them are also significant. A look at a list of US art museums reveals some of the century's finest buildings. A recent museum building and renovation boom led by world-class architects ensures that perhaps no other class of architecture, whether civil or public, similarly produces the quality of design. (Please note that some museums have had a nomadic history, and the buildings listed are not always the first ones they occupied. Information about significant additions and expansions is included. However, renovations and minor alterations are not included nor any additions that have been demolished.)

Walker Art Center. The Walker Art Center's new expansion by Pritzker Prize-winning architects Herzog & de Meuron has nearly doubled the museum's size, providing much-needed public spaces and adding an energetic, vibrant contrast to the original minimalist red brick building by Edward Larabee Barnes. **Photo courtesy of the Walker Art Center.**

100 American Art Museums and their Architects

Museum	Location	Originally Opened
Albright-Knox Art Gallery	Buffalo, NY	1905
Allen Memorial Art Museum	Oberlin, OH	1917
American Folk Art Museum	New York, NY	2001
Amon Carter Museum	Ft. Worth, TX	1961
Anchorage Museum of History and Art	Anchorage, AK	1968
Art Institute of Chicago	Chicago, IL	1893
Arthur M. Sackler Museum	Cambridge, MA	1985
Asian Art Museum	San Francisco, CA	2003
Baltimore Museum of Art	Baltimore, MD	1929
Barnes Foundation	Merion, PA	1925
Bass Museum of Art	Miami, FL	1964
Berkeley Art Museum + Pacific Film Archive	Berkeley, CA	1970
Birmingham Museum of Art	Birmingham, AL	1959
Brooklyn Museum of Art	Brooklyn, NY	1897-1927
Butler Institute of American Art	Youngstown, OH	1919
Cincinnati Art Museum	Cincinnati, OH	1886

Original Architect	Expansion/Addition Architects
Edward B. Green	Skidmore, Owings & Merrill, 1961 addition
Cass Gilbert	Venturi, Scott Brown, and Associates, 1977 addition
Tod Williams/Billie Tsien + Associates	
Philip Johnson	Johnson/Burgee, 1977 expansion; Philip Johnson/Alan Ritchie Architects, 2001 expansion
Kirk, Wallace, and McKinley with Schultz/Maynard Mitchell/Giurgola Architects with Maynard and Partch, 1986 addition	Kenneth Maynard Associates, 1974 addition;
Shepley, Rutan, and Coolidge	Skidmore, Owings & Merrill, 1977 Arthur Rubloff Building; Hammond, Beebe and Babka, 1988 Daniel F. and Ada L. Rice Building
James Stirling	
Gae Aulenti with HOK, LDA Architects, and Robert Wong Architects (adapted the 1917 main library by George Kelham)	
John Russell Pope	John Russell Pope, 1937 Jacobs Wing; Wrenn, Lewis & Jancks, 1950 May Wing, 1956 Woodward Wing and 1957 Cone Wing; Bower Lewis & Thrower Architects, 1994 West Wing for Contemporary Art
Paul Philippe Cret	
B. Robert Swartburg (adapted the 1930 Miami Beach Library by Russell Pancoast)	Arata Isozaki with Spillis Candela DMJM, 2002 expansion
Mario J. Ciampi & Associates	
Warren, Knight and Davis	Warren, Knight and Davis, 1965 west wing, 1967 east wing, 1974 expansion, 1979 addition, and 1980 expansion; Edward Larrabee Barnes, 1993 expansion
McKim, Mead, and White	Prentice & Chan, Ohlhausen, 1978 addition; Arata Isozaki & Associates and James Stewart Polshek & Partners, 1991 Iris and B. Gerald Cantor Auditorium; James Stewart Polshek & Partners, 2004 front entrance and public plaza addition
McKim, Mead and White	Paul Boucherie, 1931 north and south wings; C. Robert Buchanan & Associates, 1967 addition; Buchanan, Ricciuti & Associates, 1986 west wing addition
James McLaughlin	Daniel H. Burnham, 1907 Schmidlapp Wing; Garber and Woodward, 1910 Ropes Wing and 1930 Emery, Hanna & French Wings; Rendigs, Panzer and Martin, 1937 Alms Wing; Potter, Tyler, Martin and Roth, 1965 Adams-Emery Wing

315

100 American Art Museums and their Architects

Museum	Location	Originally Opened
Cleveland Museum of Art	Cleveland, OH	1916
Colorado Springs Fine Arts Center	Colorado Springs, CO	1936
Columbus Museum of Art	Columbus, OH	1931
Contemporary Art Museum St. Louis	St. Louis, MO	2003
Contemporary Arts Museum, Houston	Houston, TX	1972
Corcoran Gallery of Art	Washington, DC	1897
Cranbrook Art Museum	Cranbrook, MI	1941
Dallas Museum of Art	Dallas, TX	1984
Dayton Art Institute	Dayton, OH	1930
Denver Art Museum	Denver, CO	1971
Des Moines Art Center	Des Moines, IA	1948
Detroit Institute of Arts	Detroit, MI	1888
Elvehjem Museum of Art	Madison, WI	1970
Everson Museum of Art	Syracuse, NY	1968
Fogg Art Museum	Cambridge, MA	1927
Frances Lehman Loeb Art Center	Poughkeepsie, NY	1993
Frederick R. Weisman Art Museum	Minneapolis, MN	1993
Freer Gallery Art	Washington, DC	1923
Frist Center for the Visual Arts	Nashville, TN	2001
Frye Art Museum	Seattle, WA	1952
Herbert F. Johnson Museum of Art	Ithaca, NY	1973
High Museum of Art	Atlanta, GA	1983
Hirshhorn Museum and Sculpture Garden	Washington, DC	1974
Hood Museum of Art	Hanover, NH	1985
Indiana University Art Museum	Bloomington, IN	1982
Indianapolis Museum of Art	Indianapolis, IN	1970
Iris & B. Gerald Cantor Center for Visual Arts	Stanford, CA	1894

Original Architect	Expansion/Addition Architects
Benjamin Hubbell and W. Dominick Benes	J. Byers Hays and Paul C. Ruth, 1958 addition; Marcel Breuer and Hamilton Smith, 1971 addition; Dalton, van Dijk, Johnson & Partners, 1984 addition
John Gaw Meem	
Richards, McCarty and Bulford	Van Buren and Firestone, Architects, Inc., 1974 addition
Allied Works Architecture	
Gunnar Birkerts & Associates	
Ernest Flagg	Charles Adams Platt, 1927 expansion
Eliel Saarinen	Rafael Moneo, 2002 addition
Edward Larrabee Barnes	Edward Larrabee Barnes, 1985 decorative arts wing and 1991 Nancy and Jake L. Hamon Building
Edward B. Green	Levin Porter Associates, Inc., 1997 expansion
Gio Ponti with James Sudler Associates	
Eliel Saarinen	I.M. Pei & Associates, 1968 addition; Richard Meier & Partners, 1985 addition
James Balfour	Cret, Zantzinger, Borie and Medary, 1927 addition; Harley, Ellington, Cowin and Stirton, with Gunnar Birkerts, 1966 south wings; Harley, Ellington, Cowin and Stirton, 1966 north wing
Harry Weese	
I.M. Pei & Associates	
Coolidge, Shepley, Bulfinch, and Abbott	
Cesar Pelli & Associates	
Frank O. Gehry and Associates	
Charles Adams Platt	
Tuck Hinton Architects (adapted the 1934 US Post Office by Marr and Holman Architects)	
Paul Albert Thiry	Olson Sundberg Kundig Allen Architects, 1997 expansion
I.M. Pei & Partners	
Richard Meier & Partners	
Skidmore, Owings & Merrill	
Charles Moore and Centerbrook Architects	
I.M. Pei & Partners	
Richardson, Severns, Scheeler and Associates	Edward Larrabee Barnes and John M.Y. Lee, 1990 Mary Fendrich Hulman Pavilion
Percy & Hamilton Architects with Ernest J. Ransome	Polshek Partnership, 1999 addition

321

100 American Art Museums and their Architects

Museum	Location	Originally Opened
J. Paul Getty Museum	Los Angeles, CA	1997
Joslyn Art Museum	Omaha, NE	1931
Kemper Museum of Contemporary Art and Design	Kansas City, MO	1994
Kimbell Art Museum	Fort Worth, TX	1972
Kreeger Museum	Washington, DC	1967
Lois & Richard Rosenthal Center for Contemporary Art	Cincinnati, OH	2003
Mead Art Museum	Amherst, MA	1949
Memphis Brooks Museum of Art	Memphis, TN	1916
Menil Collection	Houston, TX	1987
Metropolitan Museum of Art	New York, NY	1880
Milwaukee Art Museum	Milwaukee, WI	1957
Minneapolis Institute of Arts	Minneapolis, MN	1915
Modern Art Museum of Ft. Worth	Ft. Worth, TX	2002
Munson-Williams-Proctor Arts Institute	Utica, NY	1960
Museum of Contemporary Art, Chicago	Chicago, IL	1996
Museum of Contemporary Art, Los Angeles (at California Plaza)	Los Angeles, CA	1986
Museum of Contemporary Art, San Diego	La Jolla, CA	1941
Museum of Fine Arts, Boston	Boston, MA	1909

Original Architect	Expansion/Addition Architects
Richard Meier	
John and Alan McDonald	Norman Foster, 1994 Walter and Suzanne Scott Pavilion
Gunnar Birkerts & Associates	
Louis I. Kahn	
Philip Johnson with Richard Foster	
Zaha Hadid Architects with KZF Design	
McKim, Mead and White	
James Gamble Rogers with Carl Gutherz	Walk Jones and Francis Mah, 1973 addition; Skidmore, Owings & Merrill with Askew, Nixon, Ferguson & Wolf, 1989 expansion
Renzo Piano with Richard Fitzgerald & Partners	
Calvert Vaux and J. Wrey Mould	Theodore Weston, 1888 SW wing; Richard Morris Hunt and Richard Howland Hunt, 1902 Central Fifth Avenue facade; McKim, Mead, and White, 1906, side wings along Fifth Avenue; Brown, Lawford & Forbes, 1965 Thomas J. Watson Library; Kevin Roche John Dinkeloo & Associates, 1975 Lehman Wing, 1979 Sackler Wing, 1980 American Wing, 1981 Michael C. Rockefeller Wing for Primitive Art, 1988 European Sculpture and Decorative Art Wing
Eero Saarinen with Maynard Meyer	Kahler, Fitzhugh and Scott, 1975 addition; Santiago Calatrava, 2001 Quadracci Pavilion
McKim, Mead and White	Kenzo Tange, 1974 addition
Tadao Ando	
Philip Johnson	Lund McGee Sharpe Architecture, 1995 Education Wing
Josef Paul Kleihues	
Arata Isozaki	
Irving Gill (originally designed as a residence in 1916)	Mosher & Drew, 1950 transition to museum; Mosher & Drew, 1959 Sherwood Auditorium; Venturi, Scott Brown and Associates, 1996 expansion and renovation
Guy Lowell	Guy Lowell, 1915 Robert Dawson Evans Wing and 1928 Decorative Arts Wing; Hugh Stubbins Associates, 1968 Forsyth Wickes Galleries and George Robert White Wing; I.M. Pei & Partners, 1981 West Wing

100 American Art Museums and their Architects

Museum	Location	Originally Opened
Museum of Fine Arts, Houston	Houston, TX	1924
Museum of Modern Art	New York, NY	1939
Nasher Sculpture Center	Dallas, TX	2003
National Gallery of Art, East Building	Washington, DC	1978
National Gallery of Art, West Building	Washington, DC	1941
National Portrait Gallery and American Art Museum	Washington, DC	1968
Nelson Fine Arts Center	Tempe, AZ	1989
Nelson-Atkins Museum of Art	Kansas City, MO	1933
Nevada Museum of Art	Reno, NV	2003
New Orleans Museum of Art	New Orleans, LA	1911
Oakland Museum of California	Oakland, CA	1969
Parrish Art Museum	Southampton, NY	1897
Pennsylvania Academy of the Fine Arts	Philadelphia, PA	1876
Philadelphia Museum of Art	Philadelphia, PA	1928
Phoenix Art Museum	Phoenix, AZ	1959
Portland Art Museum	Portland, OR	1932
Portland Museum of Art	Portland, ME	1911
Princeton University Art Museum	Princeton, NJ	1922
Pulitzer Foundation for the Arts	St. Louis, MO	2001
Renwick Gallery	Washington, DC	1859
Rodin Museum	Philadelphia, PA	1929

Original Architect	Expansion/Addition Architects
William Ward Watkin	William Ward Watkin, 1926 addition; Kenneth Franzheim, 1953 Robert Lee Blaffer Memorial Wing; Mies van der Rohe, 1958 Cullinan Hall and 1974 Brown Pavilion; Rafael Moneo, 2000 Audrey Jones Beck Building
Philip L. Goodwin and Edward Durrell Stone	Philip Johnson, 1964 east wing; Cesar Pelli, 1984 tower; Yoshio Taniguchi with Kohn Pedersen Fox Associates and Cooper, Robertson & Partners, 2004 expansion and renovation
Renzo Piano with Peter Walker	
I.M. Pei & Partners	
John Russell Pope	
Faulkner, Stenhouse, Fryer (adapted the 1836–67 Old Patent Office Building by Robert Mills)	
Antoine Predock	
Wight and Wight	
Will Bruder	
Samuel Marx	August Perez with Arthur Feitel, 1971 Wisner Education Wing, City Wing, and Stern Auditorium; Eskew Filson Architects with Billes/Manning Architects, 1993 expansion
Kevin Roche John Dinkeloo & Associates	
Grosvenor Atterbury	Grosvenor Atterbury, 1902 and 1913 wings
Frank Furness and George W. Hewitt	
Horace Trumbauer with Zantzinger, Borie, and Medary	
Alden B. Dow	Alden B. Dow, 1965 east wing; Tod Williams/Billie Tsien + Associates, 1996 expansion
Pietro Belluschi	Pietro Belluschi, 1939 Hirsch Wing; Pietro Belluschi, with Wolff, Zimmer, Gunsul, Frasca, and Ritter, 1970 Hoffman Wing; Ann Beha Associates, 2000 expansion
John Calvin Stevens	I.M. Pei & Partners, 1983 Charles Shipman Payson Building
Ralph Adams Cram	Steinman and Cain, 1966 expansion; Mitchell/Giurgola Architects, 1989 Mitchell Wolfson Jr. Wing
Tadao Ando	
James Renwick Jr.	John Carl Warnecke and Hugh Newell Jacobsen, 1971 restoration
Paul Philippe Cret and Jacques Gréber	

331

100 American Art Museums and their Architects

Museum	Location	Originally Opened
Saint Louis Art Museum	St. Louis, MO	1903
San Diego Museum of Art	San Diego, CA	1926
San Francisco Museum of Modern Art	San Francisco, CA	1995
Santa Barbara Museum of Art	Santa Barbara, CA	1941
Seattle Art Museum	Seattle, WA	1991
Sheldon Memorial Art Gallery	Lincoln, NE	1963
Solomon R. Guggenheim Museum	New York, NY	1959
Speed Art Museum	Louisville, KY	1927
Tacoma Art Museum	Tacoma, WA	2003
Terra Museum of American Art	Chicago, IL	1987
Toledo Museum of Art	Toledo, OH	1912
UCLA Hammer Museum of Art	Los Angeles, CA	1990
Wadsworth Atheneum Museum of Art	Hartford, CT	1844
Walker Art Center	Minneapolis, MN	1971
Wexner Center for the Arts	Columbus, OH	1989
Whitney Museum of American Art	New York, NY	1966
Yale University Art Gallery	New Haven, CT	1953

Source: DesignIntelligence

Original Architect	Expansion/Addition Architects
Cass Gilbert	
William Templeton Johnson with Robert W. Snyder	Robert Mosher & Roy Drew, Architects, 1966 west wing; Mosher, Drew, Watson & Associates with William Ferguson, 1974 east wing
Mario Botta	
David Adler (adapted the 1914 Old Post Office designed by Francis Wilson)	Chester Carjola, 1942 Katherine Dexter McCormick Wing; Arendt/Mosher/Grants Architects, 1961 Preston Morton Wing and 1962 Sterling Morton Wing; Paul Gray, 1985 Alice Keck Park Wing; Edwards & Pitman, 1998 Peck Wing
Venturi, Scott Brown and Associates	
Philip Johnson	
Frank Lloyd Wright	Gwathmey Siegel & Associates, 1992 addition
Arthur Loomis	Nevin and Morgan, 1954 Preston Pope Satterwhite Wing; Brenner, Danforth, and Rockwell, 1973 north wing; Robert Geddes, 1983 South wing
Antoine Predock with Olson Sundberg Kundig Allen	
Booth Hansen Associates	
Green & Wicks with Harry W. Wachter	Edward B. Green and Sons, 1926 wing and 1933 expansion; Frank O. Gehry and Associates, 1992 Center for the Visual Arts addition
Edward Larrabee Barnes	
Ithiel Town and Alexander Jackson Davis	Benjamin Wistar Morris, 1910 Colt Memorial and 1915 Morgan Memorial; Morris & O'Connor, 1934 Avery Memorial; Huntington, Darbee & Dollard, Architects, 1969 Goodwin Wing
Edward Larrabee Barnes	Herzog & de Meuron with Hammel, Green and Abrahamson, Inc., 2005 expansion
Peter Eisenman	
Marcel Breuer	Gluckman Mayner Architects, 1998 expansion
Louis I. Kahn	

333

334

Pathways in American Planning History: A Thematic Chronology: 1785–2000

American planning is not simply a profession, it is a also a broad movement embracing many fields of social and economic action. The movement gave rise to the profession but is not identical with it. Therefore, this chronology reaches outside the limits of the history of professional planning, drawing pertinent items from many areas—in the histories of housing, agriculture, ecology, and so on. To present these events in both their temporal and topical context, a series of symbols is used at the end of each entry to indicate the theme(s) it represents (Landmark Publication, LP; Housing and Community Planning, HPC; Conservation and Environment, CE; History of the Planning Profession, HPP; Regional Planning, RP; Landmark Laws and Administrative Acts, LL; Economic Development and Redevelopment, ED). Comments and suggestions for future revisions can be sent to the author, Albert Guttenberg, at *a-gutten@uiuc.edu.*

This chronology is adapted with permission from a fully interactive version available online at *www.planning.org/pathways/.*

> *From the beginning of our national life, various forms of planning have been in evidence…The Constitution itself was an economic-political plan on a grand scale…The Constitutional Convention was…a large-scale planning board.*
>
> —Final Report of the National Planning Board, 1934

1785 The Ordinance of 1785 provides for the rectangular land survey of the Old Northwest, which has been called "the largest single act of national planning in our history and…the most significant in terms of continuing impact on the body politic." (Daniel Elazar). **LL** **ED**

1791 In his *Report on Manufactures,* US Secretary of the Treasury Alexander Hamilton argues for protective tariffs for manufacturing industry as a means of promoting industrial development in the young republic. **ED** **LP**

1818 In a speech before Congress, Henry Clay proposes a plan (called the American System) to allocate federal funds to promote the development of the national economy by combining tariffs with internal improvements, such as roads, canals, and other waterways. **ED**

1825 The Erie Canal is completed. This artificial waterway connects the northeastern states with the newly settled areas of what was then the West, facilitating the economic development of both regions. **ED** **RP**

1839 The National Road terminates in Vandalia, IL. Begun in 1811 in Cumberland, MD, it helps open the Ohio Valley to settlement. **ED**

Pathways in American Planning History
A Thematic Chronology: 1785–2000

1855 The first model tenement is built in Manhattan. **HCP**

1862 The Homestead Act opens the public domain lands to settlers for a nominal fee and a five-year residency requirement. **LL** **ED** **HCP**

1862 With the Morrill Act, Congress authorizes land grants from the public domain to the states. Proceeds from the sale are to be used to found colleges offering instruction in agriculture, engineering, and other practical arts. **ED** **LL**

1864 The New York City Council of Hygiene of the Citizens Association mounts a campaign to raise housing and sanitary standards. **HPC**

1868 Frederick Law Olmsted and Calvert Vaux begin the planning of Riverside, IL, a planned suburban community stressing rural as opposed to urban amenities. **HCP**

1869 The Union Pacific and the Central Pacific railroads meet at Promontory Point, UT, on May 10 to complete the first transcontinental railroad. **ED**

1878 John Wesley Powell's *Report on the Lands of the Arid Region of the United States* is published. It includes a proposed regional plan that would both foster settlement of the arid west and conserve scarce water resources. **CE** **RP** **ED** **LP**

1879 In his influential book *Progress and Poverty*, Henry George presents an argument for diminishing extremes of national wealth and poverty by means of a single tax (on land) that would capture the "unearned increment" of national development for public uses. **LP**

The Dumbbell Tenement, so called because of its shape, debuts. It is a form of multifamily housing widely built in New York until the end of the century and notorious for the poor living conditions (lack of light, air, and space) it imposed on its inhabitants. **HCP**

The US Geological Survey is established to survey and classify all public domain lands. **ED** **CE**

1884 Pullman, IL, a model industrial town by George Pullman for his workers, is completed. **HCP**

1890 *How the Other Half Lives*, by Jacob Riis, is published and becomes a powerful stimulus to housing and neighborhood reform. **LP** **HCP**

1891 The General Land Law Revision Act gives the President the power to create forest preserves by proclamation. **CE** **LL**

1892 The Sierra Club is founded to promote the protection and preservation of the natural environment. John Muir, a Scottish-American naturalist and a major figure in the history of American environmentalism, is the leading founder. **CE**

KEY

LL	Landmark Laws and Administrative Acts	**RP**	Regional Planning
ED	Economic Development and Redevelopment	**HPP**	History of the Planning Profession
LP	Landmark Publication	**CE**	Conservation and Environment
		HCP	Housing and Community Planning

Pathways in American Planning History
A Thematic Chronology: 1785–2000

1893 The World's Columbian Exposition in Chicago commemorating the 400th anniversary of the discovery of the New World is a source of the City Beautiful Movement and the urban planning profession. **HPP**

1896 In the first significant legal case concerning historic preservation, the *United States v. Gettysburg Electric Railway Co.*, the US Supreme Court rules that the acquisition of the national battlefield at Gettysburg serves a valid public purpose. **CE** **LL**

1897 Under the Forest Management Act, Congress authorizes some control by the Secretary of the Interior over the use and occupancy of forest preserves. **CE** **LL**

1898 *Tomorrow: A Peaceful Path to Real Reform* by Ebenezer Howard, a source of the Garden City Movement, is published. It is reissued in 1902 as *Garden Cities of Tomorrow.* **LP** **HCP**

Gifford Pinchot becomes the Chief Forester of the United States in the Department of Agriculture. From this position he publicizes the cause of forest conservation. **CE**

1901 The New York State Tenement House Law is the legislative basis for the revision of city codes that outlaw tenements such as the Dumbbell Tenement. Lawrence Veiller is the leading reformer. **HCP** **LL**

1902 The US Reclamation Act creates a fund from the sale of public land in the arid states in order to supply water to that region through the construction of water storage and irrigation works. **RP** **CE** **LL** **ED**

1903 Letchworth is constructed. It is the first English Garden City and a stimulus to the New Town movement in America (e.g. Greenbelt Towns, Columbia, MD). **HCP**

President Theodore Roosevelt appoints a Public Lands Commission to propose rules for orderly land development and management in the west. **RP** **CE** **LL**

1906 The Antiquities Act of 1906 is the first law to institute federal protection for preserving archaeological sites. It provides for the designation as National Monuments areas already in the public domain that contain "historic landmarks, historic and prehistoric structures, and objects of historic or scientific interest." **CE** **LL**

1907 The founding of the New York Committee on the Congestion of Population, led by its secretary, Benjamin Marsh, fosters the movement to decentralize New York's dense population. **HCP**

President Roosevelt establishes an Inland Waterway Commission to encourage multipurpose planning in waterway development: navigation, power, irrigation, flood control, water supply. **CE** **LL**

1908 State governors, federal officials, and leading scientists assemble for the White House Conservation Conference to deliberate about the conservation of natural resources. **CE**

1909 The first National Conference on City Planning is held in Washington, DC. **HPP**

Daniel Burnham's Plan of Chicago is published. It is the first metropolitan plan in the United States. (Key figures in its creation include Frederick A. Delano, Charles Wacker, and Charles Dyer Norton.) **RP**

Possibly the first course in city planning to be offered in the United States is inaugurated in Harvard College's Landscape Architecture Department. It is taught by James Sturgis Pray. **HPP**

Pathways in American Planning History
A Thematic Chronology: 1785–2000

1911 Frederick Winslow Taylor publishes *The Principles of Scientific Management*, a fountainhead of the efficiency movements in this country, including efficiency in city government. **LP**

1912 Walter D. Moody's *Wacker's Manual of the Plan of Chicago* is adopted as an eigth-grade textbook on city planning by the Chicago Board of Education. This is possibly the first formal instruction in city planning below the college level. **LP** **HPP**

1913 A chair in civic design, the first of its kind in the United States, is created in the University of Illinois' Department of Horticulture for Charles Mulford Robinson, one of the principal promoters of the World's Columbian Exposition. **HPP**

1914 Flavel Shurtleff writes *Carrying Out the City Plan*, the first major textbook on city planning. **LP** **HPP**

The Panama Canal is completed and opened to world commerce. **ED**

Harland Bartholomew, later the country's best-known planning consultant, becomes the first full-time employee of a city planning commission (Newark, NJ). **HPP**

1915 Scottish biologist Patrick Geddes, known as the father of regional planning and the mentor of Lewis Mumford, publishes *Cities in Evolution*. **LP** **RP**

1916 Nelson P. Lewis publishes *Planning of the Modern City*. **LP** **HPP**

The nation's first comprehensive zoning resolution is adopted by the New York City Board of Estimates under the leadership of George McAneny and Edward Bassett, known as the father of zoning. **HCP** **LL**

The National Park Service is established with sole responsibility for conserving and preserving resources of special value. **CE** **LL**

1917 Frederick Law Olmsted Jr. becomes the first president of the newly founded American City Planning Institute, a forerunner of the American Institute of Planners and American Institute of Certified Planners. **HPP**

1918 The US Housing Corporation and Emergency Fleet Corporation are established and operate at major shipping centers to provide housing for World War I workers. They influence later endeavors in public housing. **HCP** **LL**

1919 Three early unifunctional regional authorities, the Metropolitan Sewerage Commission, the Metropolitan Water Board, and the Metropolitan Park Commission, are combined to form the Boston Metropolitan District Commission. **RP**

1921 New Orleans designates the Vieux Carre Commission, the first historic preservation commission in the United States. **CE**

KEY

LL	Landmark Laws and Administrative Acts	**RP**	Regional Planning
ED	Economic Development and Redevelopment	**HPP**	History of the Planning Profession
		CE	Conservation and Environment
LP	Landmark Publication	**HCP**	Housing and Community Planning

Pathways in American Planning History
A Thematic Chronology: 1785–2000

1922 The Los Angeles County Regional
Planning Commission, the first of its kind
in the United States, is created. (Hugh
Pomeroy is head of staff.) **HPP** **RP**

The Regional Plan of New York is inaugurated under Thomas Adams. **RP**

1922 *In Pennsylvania Coal Co. v. Mahon*, the first
decision to hold that a land-use restriction
constitutes a taking, the US Supreme
Court notes "property may be regulated to
a certain extent, [but] if regulation goes
too far it will be recognized as a taking,"
thus acknowledging the principle of a regulatory taking. **LL**

1923 Ground is broken for construction of
Mariemont, OH, in suburban Cincinnati.
Some of its features (short blocks, mixture
of rental, and owner-occupied housing)
foreshadow the contemporary New
Urbanism movement. Mary Emery is its
founder and benefactor; John Nolen is the
planner. **HCP**

1924 The US Department of Commerce under
Secretary Herbert Hoover issues a
Standard State Zoning Enabling Act. **LL**

Work begins on Sunnyside Gardens, a
planned neighborhood designed by
Clarence Stein and Henry Wright and built
by the City Housing Corporation under
Alexander Bing, in Queens, NY. **HCP**

1925 The "Regional Plan" issue of *Survey Graphic*
is published containing influential essays
on regional planning by Lewis Mumford
and other members of the Regional
Planning Association of America (e.g.,
Catherine Bauer). **LP** **RP**

Cincinnati, OH, becomes the first major
American city officially to endorse a comprehensive plan. **HPP**

Ernest Burgess's Concentric Zone model of
urban structure and land use is published
in *The City*. **LP**

In April, the American City Planning
Institute and the National Conference on
City Planning publish Vol. 1, No. 1 of *City
Planning*, the ancestor of the present-day
Journal of the American Planning Association.
LP **HPP**

1926 In the *Village of Euclid v. Ambler Realty* the
constitutionality of zoning is upheld by the
US Supreme Court. (The case is argued
by Alfred Bettman.) **LL**

1928 The US Department of Commerce under
Secretary Herbert Hoover issues a
Standard City Planning Enabling Act.
LL **HPP**

Robert Murray Haig's monograph "Major
Economic Factors in Metropolitan Growth
and Arrangement" is published in volume I
of *The Regional Survey of New York and Its
Environs*. It views land use as a function of
accessibility. **LP** **RP**

Construction of Radburn, NJ, is begun.
This planned community designed by
Clarence Stein and Henry Wright, a forerunner of the New Deal's Greenbelt towns,
is inspired by Howard's Garden City concept. **HCP**

Benton MacKaye, known as the father of
the Appalachian Trail, publishes *The New
Exploration*. In this book, he proposes plans
for defending an earlier, more gentle form
of New England urbanism from the spread
of a rampant metropolitanism emanating
mainly from Boston. **LP** **CE**

1929 Clarence Perry's monograph on the
Neighborhood Unit is published in
Volume VII of *The Regional Survey of
New York and Its Environs*. **LP** **HCP**

Pathways in American Planning History
A Thematic Chronology: 1785–2000

In the first instance of rural zoning, Wisconsin law authorizes county boards "to regulate, restrict, and determine the areas within which agriculture, forestry, and recreation may be conducted." `LL`

The Stock market crash in October ushers in the Great Depression and fosters ideas of public planning on a national scale. `ED`

1931 The National Land Utilization Conference convenes in Chicago. Three hundred agricultural experts deliberate on rural recovery programs and natural resource conservation. `CE` `ED`

1932 The Federal Home Loan Bank System is established to shore up shaky home financing institutions. `HCP`

The Reconstruction Finance Corporation is established at the outset of the Great Depression to revive economic activity by extending financial aid to failing financial, industrial, and agricultural institutions. `ED`

1933 President Franklin Delano Roosevelt is inaugurated. The New Deal begins with a spate of counter-depression measures. `ED`

The Home Owners Loan Corporation is established to save homeowners facing loss through foreclosure. `HCP`

The National Planning Board is established in the Department of the Interior to assist in the preparation of a comprehensive plan for public works under the direction of Frederick Delano, Charles Merriam, and

Wesley Mitchell. Its last successor agency, the National Resources Planning Board, will be abolished in 1943. `CE` `ED` `HPP`

The Civilian Conservation Corps is established to provide work for unemployed youth and to conserve the nation's natural resources. `CE`

The Federal Emergency Relief Administration is set up under the leadership of Harry Hopkins to organize relief work in urban and rural areas. `LL`

The Tennessee Valley Authority is created to provide for unified and multipurpose rehabilitation and redevelopment of the Tennessee Valley, America's most famous experiment in river-basin planning. Senator George Norris of Nebraska fathers the idea, and David Lilienthal is its most effective implementer. `CE` `ED` `RP` `LL`

The Agricultural Adjustment Act is passed to regulate agricultural trade practices, production, prices, and supply areas (and therefore land use) as a recovery measure. `ED`

1934 The American Society of Planning Officials, an organization for planners, planning commissioners, and planning-related public officials, is founded. `HPP`

The National Housing Act establishes the Federal Savings and Loan Insurance Corporation for insuring savings deposits and the Federal Housing Administration for insuring individual home mortgages. `HCP` `LL`

339

KEY

`LL`	Landmark Laws and Administrative Acts
`ED`	Economic Development and Redevelopment
`LP`	Landmark Publication
`RP`	Regional Planning
`HPP`	History of the Planning Profession
`CE`	Conservation and Environment
`HCP`	Housing and Community Planning

Pathways in American Planning History
A Thematic Chronology: 1785–2000

The Taylor Grazing Act is passed to regulate the use of the range in the West for conservation purposes. CE RP LL

The "Final Report" by the National Planning Board on its first year of existence includes a section entitled "A Plan for Planning" and an account of the "Historical Development of Planning in the United States." The latter views American planning history in the context of US political and economic history. LP

1935 The Resettlement Administration is established under Rexford Tugwell, a Roosevelt "braintruster," to carry out experiments in land reform and population resettlement. This agency built the three Greenbelt towns (Greenbelt, MD; Greendale, WI; and Greenhills, OH), forerunners of the present-day New Towns, Columbia, MD, and Reston, VA. HCP LL

The National Resources Committee publishes *Regional Factors in National Planning*, a landmark in regional planning literature. LP CE RP

With the Soil Conservation Act, Congress moves to make prevention of soil erosion a national responsibility. CE LL

The Historic Sites, Buildings and Antiquities Act, a predecessor of the National Historic Preservation Act, is passed. It requires the secretary of the interior to identify, acquire, and restore qualifying historic sites and properties and calls upon federal agencies to consider preservation needs in their programs and plans. CE LL

The Social Security Act is passed to create a safety net for the elderly. Frances Perkins, the secretary of labor and the first woman Cabinet member, is a principal promoter. LL

Congress authorizes the construction of the Grande Coulee Dam on the Columbia River in central Washington state. Finished in 1941, it is the largest concrete structure in the United States and the heart of the Columbia Basin Project, a regional plan comparable in its scope to the TVA. The project's purposes are irrigation, electric power generation, and flood control in the Pacific Northwest. ED RP

1936 The Hoover Dam on the Colorado River is completed. It creates and sustains population growth and industrial development in Nevada, California, and Arizona. ED RP

1937 *Our Cities: Their Role in the National Economy*, a landmark report by the Urbanism Committee of the National Resources Committee, is published. (Ladislas Segoe heads the research staff.) LP HPP

The 1937 US Housing Act (Wagner-Steagall bill) sets the stage for future government aid by appropriating $500 million in loans for low-cost housing. It ties slum clearance to public housing . HCP LL

The Farm Security Administration, successor to the Resettlement Administration, is established to administer many programs to aid the rural poor. LL

1938 The American Institute of Planners (formerly the American City Planning Institute), states as its purpose "...the planning of the unified development of urban communities and their environs, and of states, regions and the nation, as expressed through determination of the comprehensive arrangement of land uses and land occupancy and the regulation thereof." HPP

1939 Homer Hoyt's influential sector theory of urban growth appears in his monograph *The Structure and Growth of Residential Neighborhoods in American Cities*. LP HCP

Pathways in American Planning History
A Thematic Chronology: 1785–2000

1941 *Local Planning Administration* by Ladislas Segoe, first of the Green Book series, appears. **LP** **HPP**

Robert Walker's *Planning Function in Urban Government* is published. The author advocated making the planning staff an arm of the city government rather than of a citizens planning board or commission. **LP** **HPP**

1944 Under the Bretton Woods (N.H.) Agreement, the United States and allies meet to establish the International Bank for Reconstruction and Development (also known as the World Bank). **ED**

The Serviceman's Readjustment Act (the GI bill) guarantees loans for homes to veterans under favorable terms, thereby accelerating the growth of suburbs. **HCP** **LL**

1947 The Housing and Home Financing Agency (predecessor of HUD) is created to coordinate the federal government's various housing programs. **HCP** **LL**

Construction of Park Forest, IL, and Levittown, NY, is begun. Park Forest is "the first post-World War II suburb to include a shopping center." **HCP**

US Secretary of State George C. Marshall uses his Harvard College commencement address to propose the Marshall Plan for the reconstruction of postwar Europe. **ED** **RP**

Communitas is published. This classic text by Paul and Percival Goodman explores three community paradigms and their possible physical-spatial forms. **LP** **HCP**

1949 The 1949 Housing Act (the Wagner-Ellender-Taft bill), the first US comprehensive housing legislation, is aimed to construct about 800,000 units. It also inaugurates the urban redevelopment program. **HCP** **LL**

The National Trust for Historic Preservation is created and chartered by Congress. **CE**

1954 In *Berman v. Parker*, the US Supreme Court upholds right of the Washington, DC, Redevelopment Land Agency to condemn properties that are unsightly, though non-deteriorated, if required to achieve the objectives of a duly established area redevelopment plan. **LL** **CE**

In *Brown v. Board of Education* (Topeka, KS), the US Supreme Court upholds school integration. **LL**

The Housing Act of 1954 stresses slum prevention and urban renewal rather than slum clearance and urban redevelopment as in the 1949 Housing Act. It also stimulates general planning for cities with a population under 25,000 by providing funds under Section 701 of the act, which is later extended by legislative amendments to foster statewide, interstate, and substate regional planning. **HPP** **RP** **LL** **HCP**

341

KEY

LL	Landmark Laws and Administrative Acts	**RP**	Regional Planning
ED	Economic Development and Redevelopment	**HPP**	History of the Planning Profession
LP	Landmark Publication	**CE**	Conservation and Environment
		HCP	Housing and Community Planning

Pathways in American Planning History
A Thematic Chronology: 1785–2000

The Council of Government movement begins in the Detroit area with the formation of a Supervisors' Inter-County Committee, composed of representatives from each county in southeastern Michigan for the purpose of confronting areawide problems. This movement soon spreads nationwide. **RP**

1956 Congress passes the multibillion-dollar Federal Aid Highway Act to create an interstate highway system linking all state capitals and most cities with a population of 50,000 or more. **LL** **ED**

1957 F. Stuart Chapin publishes *Urban Land Use Planning.* **LP**

Education for Planning, a seminal, book-length inquiry by Harvey S. Perloff into the "appropriate intellectual, practical and 'philosophical' basis for the education of city and regional planners...," is published. **HPP**

1959 "A Multiple Land Use Classification System" (A. Guttenberg) appears in *The Journal of the American Institute of Planners.* It advances the understanding of land use, a key planning concept by defining and classifying its major dimensions. **LP**

Congress establishes the Advisory Commission on Intergovernmental Relations with members drawn from various branches of government. It serves primarily as a research agency and think tank in the area of intergovernmental relations. **LL** **RP**

The St. Lawrence Seaway is completed. This joint US-Canada project creates, in effect, a fourth North American seacoast, opening the American heartland to seagoing vessels. **ED** **RP**

1960 *The Image of the City* by Kevin Lynch defines basic elements of a city's "imageability" (paths, edges, nodes, etc.). **LP**

1961 *The Death and Life of Great American Cities,* by Jane Jacobs, includes a critique of planning and planners. **LP** **HPP**

Richard Hedman and Fred Bair publish *And On the Eighth Day,* a book of cartoons poking fun at the planning profession by two of its own. **LP** **HPP**

Hawaii becomes the first state to institute statewide zoning. **LL**

A Delaware River Basin Commission representing the states of New York, New Jersey, and Pennsylvania is created to foster joint management of the river's water resources. **RP**

1962 The urban growth simulation model emerges in the Penn-Jersey Transportation Study. **RP**

"A Choice Theory of Planning," a seminal article in the *Journal of American Institute of Planners* by Paul Davidoff and Thomas Reiner, lays the basis for an advocacy planning concept. **LP**

Rachel Carson's book *Silent Spring* is published and wakes the nation to the deleterious effects of pesticides on animal, plant, and human life. **LP** **CE**

The Fairfax County Board of Supervisors establishes Virginia's first residential planned community zone, clearing the way for the creation of Reston, a full-scale, self-contained New Town 18 miles from Washington, DC. **HCP**

Lewis Mumford, an internationally renowned social critic and the American planning professions' leading intellectual, wins the National Book Award for his *The City in History.* **LP**

Pathways in American Planning History
A Thematic Chronology: 1785–2000

1963 Construction of Columbia, MD, a New Town, is begun at a site about halfway between Washington, DC, and Baltimore. It will feature some class integration and the neighborhood principle. **HCP**

1964 T.J. Kent publishes *The Urban General Plan.* **LP** **HPP**

The Civil Rights Act outlaws discrimination based on race, creed, and national origin in places of public accommodation. **LL**

The Federal Bulldozer by Martin Anderson indicts the then current urban renewal program as counterproductive to its professed aims of increased low- and middle-income housing supply. With Herbert Gans's *The Urban Villagers* (1962), a study of the consequences of urban renewal for community life in a Boston West End Italian-American community, it contributes to a change in urban policy. **LP** **HCP**

In a commencement speech at the University of Michigan, President Lyndon Johnson declares war on poverty and urges congressional authorization of many remedial programs plus the establishment of a Cabinet-level Department of Housing and Community Development. **ED** **HCP**

1965 A White House Conference on Natural Beauty in America is convened on May 24, owing much to the interest and advocacy of the First Lady, Lady Bird Johnson. **CE**

Housing and urban policy achieve Cabinet status when the Housing and Home Finance Agency is succeeded by the Department of Housing and Urban Development. Robert Weaver becomes HUD's first secretary and the nation's first African-American Cabinet member. **HCP** **LL**

Congress passes the Water Resources Management Act authorizing federal multi-state river basin commissions. **LL** **RP**

The Public Work and Economic Development Act passes Congress. It establishes the Economic Development Administration to extend coordinated, multifaceted aid to lagging regions to foster their redevelopment **ED** **LL** **RP**

The Appalachian Regional Planning Act establishes a region comprising all of West Virginia and parts of 12 other states plus a planning commission with the power to frame plans and allocate resources. **ED** **LL** **RP**

John Reps publishes *The Making of Urban America,* the first comprehensive history of American urban planning beginning with colonial times. **LP**

1966 The Demonstration Cities and Metropolitan Development Act launches the "model cities" program, an interdisciplinary attack on urban blight and poverty. It is a centerpiece of President Lyndon Johnson's "Great Society" program. **HCP** **LL**

343

KEY

LL	Landmark Laws and Administrative Acts
ED	Economic Development and Redevelopment
LP	Landmark Publication

RP	Regional Planning
HPP	History of the Planning Profession
CE	Conservation and Environment
HCP	Housing and Community Planning

Pathways in American Planning History
A Thematic Chronology: 1785–2000

344

1966 *With Heritage So Rich,* a seminal historic preservation book, is published. `CE` `LP`

The National Historic Preservation Act is passed. It establishes the National Register of Historic Places and provides, through its Section 106, for the protection of preservation-worthy sites and properties threatened by federal activities. This act also creates the national Advisory Council on Historic Preservation and directs that each state appoint a State Historic Preservation Officer. `CE` `LL`

Section 4(f) of the Department of Transportation Act provides protection to parkland, wildlife refuges, and other preservation-worthy resources in building national roads. `CE` `LL`

1967 The (Louis B.) Wetmore Amendment drops the final phrase in the 1938 American Institute of Planners' declaration of purpose, which ties it to the comprehensive arrangement and regulation of land use. The effect is to broaden the scope and membership of the profession by including social planners as well as physical planners. `HPP`

The planning profession marks its 50th anniversary with a celebratory conference in Washington, DC. For the occasion, Russell Van Nest Black prepares a monograph entitled *Planning and the Planning Profession 1917–1967.* `HPP` `LP`

1968 To implement the Intergovernmental Relations Act of 1968, the Office of Management and Budget issues Circular A-95 requiring state and substate regional clearinghouses to review and comment on federally assisted projects to facilitate coordination among the three levels of government. `LL` `RP`

1969 Ian McHarg publishes *Design with Nature,* tying planning to the natural environment. `CE` `LP`

The National Environmental Policy Act requires an "environmental impact statement" for every federal or federally-aided state or local major action that might significantly harm the environment. `CE` `LL`

Mel Scott publishes *American City Planning Since 1890,* which is reissued in 1995 by the American Planning Association. `LP` `HPP`

1970 The First Earth Day is celebrated on January 1. `CE`

The Federal Environment Protection Agency is established to administer the main provisions of the 1970 Clean Air Act. `CE` `LL` `RP`

The Miami Valley (Ohio) Regional Planning Commission Housing Plan is adopted, the first such plan in the nation to allocate low- and moderate-income housing on a "fair share" basis. `HCP` `RP`

1971 The American Institute of Planners adopts a Code of Ethics for professional planners. `HPP`

1972 The Coastal Zone Management Act is adopted. `CE` `RP` `LL`

General revenue sharing is inaugurated under the US State and Local Fiscal Assistance Act. `LL`

In *Golden v. Planning Board of Ramapo,* the New York high court allows the use of performance criteria as a means of slowing community growth. `LL`

Pathways in American Planning History
A Thematic Chronology: 1785–2000

Demolition of St. Louis' notorious Pruitt-Igoe low-income housing project symbolizes a nationwide move away from massive, isolating, high-rise structures to a more humane form of public housing architecture: low-rise, less isolated, dispersed. **HCP**

1973 The Endangered Species Act authorizes federal assistance to state and local jurisdictions to establish conservation programs for endangered plant and animal species. **CE** **LL**

1974 The Housing and Community Development Act replaces the categorical grant with the block grant as the principal form of federal aid for local community development. **LL** **HCP**

1975 The Cleveland Policy Plan Report shifts emphasis from traditional land-use planning to advocacy planning. **LP** **HPP**

1976 The Historic Preservation Fund is established. **CE**

1977 The first exam for American Institute of Planners membership is conducted. **HPP**

1978 In *Penn Central Transportation Co. v. City of New York*, the US Supreme Court upholds New York City's Landmark Preservation Law as applied to Grand Central Terminal. In this landmark decision, the Court finds that barring some development of air rights is not a taking when the interior of the property could be put to lucrative use. **LL** **CE**

The American Institute of Planners and the American Society of Planning Officials merge to become the American Planning Association. **HPP**

1979 John Reps becomes the second member of the planning profession (Lewis Mumford was the first) to win the National Book Award, with his *Cities of the American West.* **LP** **HPP**

1980 The Reagan Revolution begins, and the planning profession is challenged to adapt to a new (counter-New Deal) policy environment: reduced federal domestic spending, privatization, deregulation, and a phase-out of some earlier planning aids (e.g., sewer grants) and planning programs (e.g., Title V Regions).

The Superfund Bill (Comprehensive Response, Compensation and Liability Act) is passed by Congress, creating a liability for persons discharging hazardous waste into the environment. By taxing polluting industries, a trust fund is established for the cleanup of polluted sites in cases where individual responsibility is not ascertainable. **CE** **LL**

The Associated Collegiate Schools of Planning is established to represent the academic branch of the planning profession. **HPP**

1981 The ACSP issues Volume 1, Number 1 of *The Journal of Education and Planning Research.* **LP** **HPP**

345

KEY

LL	Landmark Laws and Administrative Acts
ED	Economic Development and Redevelopment
LP	Landmark Publication

RP	Regional Planning
HPP	History of the Planning Profession
CE	Conservation and Environment
HCP	Housing and Community Planning

Pathways in American Planning History
A Thematic Chronology: 1785–2000

1983 In a case focusing on Mt. Laurel, NJ, the New Jersey Supreme Court rules that all 567 municipalities in the state must build their "fair share" of affordable housing, a precedent-setting blow against racial segregation. LL HCP RP

1984 Construction begins on Seaside, FL, one of the earliest examples of New Urbanism (designed by Andres Duany and Elizabeth Plater-Zyberk). Unlike most earlier planned communities, New Urbanism emphasizes urban features—compactness, walkability, mixed use—and promotes a nostalgic architectural style reminiscent of the traditional urban neighborhood. The movement has links to the anti-sprawl, smart growth movement. HCP

1986 The First National Conference on American Planning History is convened in Columbus, OH, and leads to the founding of the Society of American City and Regional Planning History the following year. HPP

1987 In *First English Evangelical Lutheran Church v. County of Los Angeles*, the US Supreme Court finds that even a temporary taking requires compensation. In *Nollan v. California Coastal Commission*, it finds that land-use restrictions, to be valid, must be tied directly to a specific public purpose. LL

1989 The Planning Accreditation Board is recognized by the Washington-based Council on Post Secondary Education to be the sole accrediting agency in the field of professional planning education. HPP

1991 Passage of the Intermodal Surface Transportation Efficiency Act includes provisions for a National Scenic Byways Program and for transportation enhancements, each of which includes a historic preservation component. CE LL

1992 In *Lucas v. South Carolina Coastal Council*, the US Supreme Court limits local and state governments' ability to restrict private property without compensation. LL

1993 The Enterprise Zone/Empowerment Community proposal is signed into law. It aims tax incentives, wage tax credits, special deductions, and low-interest financing to a limited number of impoverished urban and rural communities to jumpstart their economic and social recovery. ED

1994 In *Dolan v. City of Tigard*, the US Supreme Court rules that a jurisdiction must show that there is a "rough proportionality" between the adverse impacts of a proposed development and the exactions it wishes to impose on the developer. LL

The North American Free Trade Agreement between the United States, Canada, and Mexico begins on Jan. 1 with the purpose of fostering trade and investment among the three nations by removing or lowering non-tariff as well as tariff barriers. ED LL RP

1999 The American Institute of Certified Planners inaugurates a College of Fellows to recognize distinguished individual contributions by longer-term AICP members. HPP

2000 President Clinton creates eight new national monuments in five western states: Canyons of the Ancients (CO); Cascade-Siskiyou (OR); Hanford Reach (WA); Ironwood Forest, Grand Canyon-Parashant, Agua Fria (AZ); Grand Sequoia, California Coastal (CA). He also expands one existing national monument in California (Pinnacles). CE

Source: Albert Guttenberg, FAICP. © Albert Guttenberg.
Reprinted with permission.

Sports Stadiums

From classic ballparks to cutting-edge arenas and stadiums, the following charts provide major statistics and architectural information for all major-league baseball, basketball, football, and hockey venues in the United States. All cost and architectural information refers to the stadiums as they were originally built and does not include any subsequent additions, renovations, or expansions. Capacity figures are the current numbers for the respective sports.

Petco Park. HOK and designer Antoine Predock incorporated the 95-year-old Metal Supply Company building and two multi-function executive-suite light towers into the unique design of this park. Patrons can enjoy a game and picnic lunch in a 2.7-acre "park in the park," which features a kid-sized ball field and a welcoming picnic hill. Photo ©2005 by Joe Mock, BASEBALLPARKS.COM.

Sports Stadiums: Baseball

AMERICAN LEAGUE	Stadium Name	Location	Opened
Anaheim Angels	Angel Stadium of Anaheim	Anaheim, CA	1966
Baltimore Orioles	Oriole Park at Camden Yards	Baltimore, MD	1992
Boston Red Sox	Fenway Park	Boston, MA	1912
Chicago White Sox	US Cellular Field	Chicago, IL	1991
Cleveland Indians	Jacobs Field	Cleveland, OH	1994
Detroit Tigers	Comerica Park	Detroit, MI	2000
Kansas City Royals	Kauffman Stadium	Kansas City, MO	1973
Minnesota Twins	Hubert H. Humphrey Metrodome	Minneapolis, MN	1982
New York Yankees	Yankee Stadium	Bronx, NY	1923
Oakland Athletics	McAfee Coliseum	Oakland, CA	1966
Seattle Mariners	Safeco Field	Seattle, WA	1999
Tampa Bay Devil Rays	Tropicana Field	St. Petersburg, FL	1990
Texas Rangers	Ameriquest Field in Arlington	Arlington, TX	1994
Toronto Blue Jays	Rogers Centre	Toronto, ON, Canada	1989

Architect (original)	Cost (original)	Capacity (current)	Roof Type	Surface	Naming Rights (amt. and expiration)
Robert A.M. Stern Architects	$25 M	45,050	Open-Air	Bluegrass	
HOK Sports Facilities Group with RTKL	$210 M	48,876	Open-Air	Grass	
Osborn Engineering	$365,000	33,871	Open-Air	Bluegrass	
HOK Sports Facilities Group	$150 M	44,321	Open-Air	Bluegrass	$68 M (20 yrs.)
HOK Sports Facilities Group	$173 M	43,345	Open-Air	Kentucky Bluegrass	$13.9 M (20 yrs.)
HOK Sports Facilities Group; SHG Inc.	$300 M	40,637	Open-Air	Grass	$66 M (30 yrs.)
HNTB	$50.45 M	40,625	Open-Air	Grass	
Skidmore, Owings & Merrill	$75 M	55,883	Dome	Astroturf	
Osborne Engineering Company	$3.1 M	57,545	Open-Air	Merion Bluegrass	
Skidmore, Owings & Merrill	$25.5 M	48,219	Open-Air	Bluegrass	$6 M (5 yrs.)
NBBJ	$517.6 M	46,621	Retractable	Grass	$40 M (20 yrs.)
HOK Sports Facilities Group; Lescher & Mahoney Sports; Criswell, Blizzard & Blouin Architects	$138 M	45,360	Dome	FieldTurf with dirt infield	$30 M (30 yrs.)
David M. Schwarz Architectural Services, Inc.; HKS, Inc.	$190 M	49,115	Open-Air	Bermuda Tifway 419 Grass	$75 M (30 yrs.)
Rod Robbie and Michael Allen	C$500 M	50,516	Retractable	Astroturf	C$20 M (10 yrs.)

Sports Stadiums: Baseball

NATIONAL LEAGUE	Stadium Name	Location	Opened
Arizona Diamondbacks	Bank One Ballpark	Phoenix, AZ	1998
Atlanta Braves	Turner Field	Atlanta, GA	1997
Chicago Cubs	Wrigley Field	Chicago, IL	1914
Cincinnati Reds	Great American Ball Park	Cincinnati, OH	2003
Colorado Rockies	Coors Field	Denver, CO	1995
Florida Marlins	Dolphins Stadium	Miami, FL	1987
Houston Astros	Minute Maid Park	Houston, TX	2000
Los Angeles Dodgers	Dodger Stadium	Los Angeles, CA	1962
Milwaukee Brewers	Miller Park	Milwaukee, WI	2001
New York Mets	Shea Stadium	Flushing, NY	1964
Philadelphia Phillies	Citizens Bank Park	Philadelphia, PA	2004
Pittsburgh Pirates	PNC Park	Pittsburgh, PA	2001
San Diego Padres	Petco Park	San Diego, CA	2004
San Francisco Giants	SBC Park	San Francisco, CA	2000
St. Louis Cardinals	Busch Stadium	St. Louis, MO	1966
Washington Nationals	RFK Stadium	Washington, DC	1961

Architect (original)	Cost (original)	Capacity (current)	Roof Type	Surface	Naming Rights (amt. and expiration)
Ellerbe Becket with Bill Johnson	$355 M	49,033	Convertible	Kentucky Bluegrass	$33.1 M (30 yrs.)
Heery International, Inc.; Williams-Russell and Johnson, Inc.; and Ellerbe Becket	$250 M	49,831	Open-Air	GN-1 Bermuda Grass	Undisclosed
Zachary Taylor Davis	$250,000	38,765	Open-Air	Merion Bluegrass and Clover	
HOK Sport + Venue + Event	$290 M	42,053	Open-Air	Grass	$75 M (30 yrs.
HOK Sports Facilities Group	$215 M	50,445	Open-Air	Grass	$15 M (indefinite)
HOK Sports Facilities Group	$125 M	47,662	Open-Air	Tifway 419 Bermuda Grass	
HOK Sports Facilities Group	$248.1 M	40,950	Retractable	Grass	$170 M (28 yrs.)
Emil Praeger	$24.47 M	56,000	Open-Air	Santa Ana Bermuda Grass	Undisclosed
HKS with NBBJ and Eppstein Uhen Architects	$399.4 M	42,500	Retractable	Grass	$41 M (20 yrs.)
Praeger-Kavanaugh-Waterbury	$24 M	55,601	Open-Air	Bluegrass	
EwingCole with HOK Sport + Venue + Event	$346 M	43,000	Open-Air	Grass	$57.5 M (25 yrs.)
HOK Sport + Venue + Event; L.D. Astorino Companies	$262 M	38,000	Open-Air	Grass	$30 M (20 yrs.)
Antoine Predock Architect with HOK Sport + Venue + Event	$453 M	46,000	Open-Air	Grass	$60 M (22 yrs.)
HOK Sports Facilities Group	$345 M	40,800	Open-Air	Sports Turf	$50 M (24 yrs.)
Sverdrup & Parcel and Associates; Edward Durell Stone, Schwarz & Van Hoefen, Associated	$24 M	49,676	Open-Air	Grass	Undisclosed
Osborn Engineering	$24 M	56,692	Open-Air	Grass	

Sports Stadiums: Basketball

EASTERN CONFERENCE	Stadium Name	Location	Opened
ATLANTIC			
Boston Celtics	Fleet Center	Boston, MA	1995
New Jersey Nets	Continental Airlines Arena	East Rutherford, NJ	1981
New York Knicks	Madison Square Garden	New York, NY	1968
Philadelphia 76ers	Wachovia Center	Philadelphia, PA	1996
Toronto Raptors	Air Canada Centre	Toronto, ON, Canada	1999
CENTRAL			
Chicago Bulls	United Center	Chicago, IL	1994
Cleveland Cavaliers	Gund Arena	Cleveland, OH	1994
Detroit Pistons	Palace of Auburn Hills	Auburn Hills, MI	1988
Indiana Pacers	Conseco Fieldhouse	Indianapolis, IN	1999
Milwaukee Bucks	Bradley Center	Milwaukee, WI	1988
SOUTHEAST			
Atlanta Hawks	Philips Arena	Atlanta, GA	1999
Charlotte Bobcats	Charlotte Coliseum	Charlotte, NC	1988
Miami Heat	American Airlines Arena	Miami, FL	1998
Orlando Magic	TD Waterhouse Centre	Orlando, FL	1989
Washington Wizards	MCI Center	Washington, DC	1997

Architect (original)	Capacity (original)	Cost (current)	Naming Rights (amt. and expiration)
Ellerbe Becket	18,624	$160 M	$30 M (15 yrs.)
Grad Partnership; DiLullo, Clauss, Ostroski & Partners	19,040	$85 M	$29 M (12 yrs.)
Charles Luckman	19,763	$116 M	
Ellerbe Becket	20,444	$206 M	$40 M (29 yrs.)
HOK Sports Facilities Group; Brisbin, Brook and Benyon	19,800	C$265 M	C$40 M (20 yrs.)
HOK Sports Facilities Group; Marmon Mok; W.E. Simpson Company	21,711	$175 M	$25 M (20 yrs.)
Ellerbe Becket	20,562	$152 M	$14 M (20 yrs.)
Rossetti Associates/Architects Planners	21,454	$70 M	
Ellerbe Becket	18,345	$183 M	$40 M (20 yrs.)
HOK Sports Facilities Group	18,717	$90 M	
HOK Sports Facilities Group; Arquitectonica	20,300	$213.5 M	$180 M (20 yrs.)
Odell & Associates	24,000	$52 M	
Arquitectonica	19,600	$175 M	$42 M (20 yrs.)
Lloyd Jones Philpot; Cambridge Seven	17,248	$98 M	$7.8 M (5 yrs.)
Ellerbe Becket	20,674	$260 M	$44 M (13 years)

Sports Stadiums: Basketball

WESTERN CONFERENCE	Stadium Name	Location	Opened
NORTHWEST			
Denver Nuggets	Pepsi Center	Denver, CO	1999
Minnesota Timberwolves	Target Center	Minneapolis, MN	1990
Portland Trail Blazers	Rose Garden	Portland, OR	1995
Utah Jazz	Delta Center	Salt Lake City, UT	1991
Seattle SuperSonics	Key Arena	Seattle, WA	1983
PACIFIC			
Golden State Warriors	Arena in Oakland	Oakland, CA	1966
Los Angeles Clippers	Staples Center	Los Angeles, CA	1999
Los Angeles Lakers	Staples Center	Los Angeles, CA	1999
Phoenix Suns	America West Arena	Phoenix, AZ	1992
Sacramento Kings	Arco Arena	Sacramento, CA	1988
SOUTHWEST			
Dallas Mavericks	American Airlines Center	Dallas, TX	2001
Houston Rockets	Toyota Center	Houston, TX	2003
Memphis Grizzlies	FedEx Forum	Memphis, TN	2004
New Orleans Hornets	New Orleans Arena	New Orleans, LA	1999
San Antonio Spurs	SBC Center	San Antonio, TX	2002

Architect (original)	Capacity (original)	Cost (current)	Naming Rights (amt. and expiration)
HOK Sports Facilities Group	19,309	$160 M	$68 M (20 yrs.)
KMR Architects	19,006	$104 M	$18.75 M (15 yrs.)
Ellerbe Becket	21,538	$262 M	
FFKR Architecture	19,911	$94 M	$25 M (20 yrs.)
NBBJ	17,072	$67 M	$15.1 M (15 yrs.)
HNTB Architecture	19,200	n/a	
NBBJ	20,000	$330 M	$100 M (20 yrs.)
NBBJ	20,000	$330 M	$100 M (20 yrs.)
Ellerbe Becket	19,023	$90 M	$26 M (30 yrs.)
Rann Haight Architect	17,317	$40 M	$7 M (10 yrs.)
David M. Schwarz Architectural Services, Inc. with HKS, Inc.	19,200	$420 M	$40 M (20 yrs.)
HOK Sport + Venue + Event	18,300	$175 M	Undisclosed
Ellerbe Becket with Looney Ricks Kiss	18,165	$250 M	$90 M (20 yrs.)
Arthur Q. Davis, FAIA & Partners	18,500	$112 M	
Ellerbe Becket with Lake/Flato Architects and Kelly Munoz	18,500	$86 M	$85 M (20 yrs.)

355

Sports Stadiums: Football

AFC	Stadium Name	Location	Opened	Cost (original)
EAST				
Buffalo Bills	Ralph Wilson Stadium	Orchard Park, NY	1973	$22 M
Miami Dolphins	Dolphins Stadium	Miami, FL	1987	$125 M
New England Patriots	Gillette Stadium	Foxboro, MA	2002	$325 M
New York Jets	Giants Stadium	E. Rutherford, NJ	1976	$75 M
NORTH				
Baltimore Ravens	M&T Bank Stadium	Baltimore, MD	1998	$220 M
Cincinnati Bengals	Paul Brown Stadium	Cincinnati, OH	2000	$400 M
Cleveland Browns	Cleveland Browns Stadium	Cleveland, OH	1999	$283 M
Pittsburgh Steelers	Heinz Field	Pittsburgh, PA	2001	$281 M
SOUTH				
Houston Texans	Reliant Stadium	Houston, TX	2002	$325 M
Indianapolis Colts	RCA Dome	Indianapolis, IN	1984	$82 M
Jacksonville Jaguars	Alltel Stadium	Jacksonville, FL	1995	$138 M
Tennessee Titans	The Coliseum	Nashville, TN	1999	$290 M
WEST				
Denver Broncos	Invesco Field at Mile High Stadium	Denver, CO	2001	$400.8 M
Kansas City Chiefs	Arrowhead Stadium	Kansas City, MO	1972	$43 M
Oakland Raiders	Network Associates Coliseum	Oakland, CA	1966	$25.5 M
San Diego Chargers	QUALCOMM Stadium	San Diego, CA	1967	$27 M

Architect (original)	Capacity (current)	Roof Type	Surface	Naming Rights (amt. and expiration)
HNTB Architecture	73,800	Open-Air	AstroTurf-12	
HOK Sports Facilities Group	74,916	Open-Air	Grass	
HOK Sport + Venue + Event	68,000	Open-Air	Grass	Undisclosed
HOK Sports Facilities Group	79,670	Open-Air	Grass	
HOK Sports Facilities Group	69,084	Open-Air	Grass	$75 M (15 yrs.)
NBBJ	65,535	Open-Air	Grass	Undisclosed
HOK Sports Facilities Group	73,200	Open-Air	Grass	
HOK Sport + Venue + Event with WTW Architects	64,440	Open-Air	Bluegrass blend	$58 M (20 yrs.)
HOK Sport + Venue + Event	69,500	Retractable	Grass	$300 M (30 yrs.)
HNTB Architecture	60,127	Dome	AstroTurf-12	$10 M (10 yrs.)
HOK Sports Facilities Group	73,000	Open-Air	Grass	$6.2 M (10 yrs.)
HOK Sports Facilities Group	67,000	Open-Air	Grass	
HNTB Architecture with Fentress Bradburn Architects and Bertram A. Burton and Associates	76,125	Open-Air	Grass	$120 M (20 yrs.)
Kivett and Meyers	79,409	Open-Air	Grass	
Skidmore, Owings & Merrill	62,026	Suspension (fixed)	Bluegrass	$6 M (5 yrs.)
Frank L. Hope and Associates	71,294	Open-Air	Grass	$18 M (20 yrs.)

Sports Stadiums: Football

NFC	Stadium Name	Location	Opened	Cost (original)
EAST				
Dallas Cowboys	Texas Stadium	Irving, TX	1971	$35 M
New York Giants	Giants Stadium	E. Rutherford, NJ	1976	$75 M
Philadelphia Eagles	Lincoln Financial Field	Philadelphia, PA	2003	$320 M
Washington Redskins	FedEx Field	Landover, MD	1996	$250.5 M
NORTH				
Chicago Bears	Soldier Field	Chicago, IL	2003	$365 M
Detroit Lions	Ford Field	Allen Park, MI	2002	$500 M
Green Bay Packers	Lambeau Field	Green Bay, WI	1957	$960,000
Minnesota Vikings	Hubert H. Humphrey Metrodome	Minneapolis, MN	1982	$55 M
SOUTH				
Atlanta Falcons	Georgia Dome	Atlanta, GA	1992	$214 M
Carolina Panthers	Bank of America Stadium	Charlotte, NC	1996	$248 M
New Orleans Saints	Louisiana Superdome	New Orleans, LA	1975	$134 M
Tampa Bay Buccaneers	Raymond James Stadium	Tampa, FL	1998	$168.5 M
WEST				
Arizona Cardinals	Sun Devil Stadium	Tempe, AZ	1958	$1 M
San Francisco 49ers	Monster Park	San Francisco, CA	1960	$24.6 M
Seattle Seahawks	Qwest Field	Seattle, WA	2002	$360 M
St. Louis Rams	Edward Jones Dome	St. Louis, MO	1995	$280 M

Architect (original)	Capacity (current)	Roof Type	Surface	Naming Rights (amt. and expiration)
Warren Morey	65,846	Partial Roof	Artificial	
HOK Sports Facilities Group	79,670	Open-Air	Grass	
NBBJ	66,000	Open-Air	Grass	$139.6 M (20 yrs.)
HOK Sports Facilities Group	80,116	Open-Air	Grass	$205 M (27 yrs.)
Wood + Zapata, Inc. with Lohan Caprile Goettsch	62,000			
SmithGroup	64,355	Dome	FieldTurf	$40 M (40 yrs.)
John Somerville	60,890	Open-Air	Grass	
Skidmore, Owings & Merrill	64,121	Dome	Artificial Turf	
Heery International	71,149	Dome	Artificial Turf	
HOK Sports Facilities Group	73,258	Open-Air	Grass	Undisclosed
Curtis & Davis Architects	69,065	Dome	Artificial Turf	
HOK Sports Facilities Group	66,000	Open-Air	Grass	$32.5 M (13 yrs.)
Edward L. Varney	74,186	Open-Air	Grass	
John & Bolles	69,843	Open-Air	Grass	$6 M (4 yrs.)
Ellerbe Becket with Loschky Marquardt & Nesholm	67,000	Partial Roof	FieldTurf	$75.27 M (15 yrs.)
HOK Sports Facilities Group	66,000	Dome	Astroturf	$31.8 M (12 yrs.)

359

Sports Stadiums: Hockey

EASTERN CONFERENCE	Stadium Name	Location	Opened
ATLANTIC DIVISION			
New Jersey Devils	Continental Airlines Arena	East Rutherford, NJ	1981
New York Islanders	Nassau Veterans Memorial Coliseum	Uniondale, NY	1972
New York Rangers	Madison Square Garden	New York, NY	1968
Philadelphia Flyers	Wachovia Center	Philadelphia, PA	1996
Pittsburgh Penguins	Mellon Arena	Pittsburgh, PA	1961
NORTHEAST DIVISION			
Boston Bruins	Fleet Center	Boston, MA	1995
Buffalo Sabres	HSBC Arena	Buffalo, NY	1996
Montreal Canadiens	Bell Center	Montreal, QC, Canada	1996
Ottawa Senators	Corel Centre	Kanata, ON, Canada	1996
Toronto Maple Leafs	Air Canada Centre	Toronto, ON, Canada	1999
SOUTHEAST DIVISION			
Atlanta Thrashers	Philips Arena	Atlanta, GA	1999
Carolina Hurricanes	RBC Center	Raleigh, NC	1999
Florida Panthers	Office Depot Center	Sunrise, FL	1998
Tampa Bay Lightning	St. Pete Times Forum	Tampa, FL	1996
Washington Capitals	MCI Center	Washington, DC	1997

Architect (original)	Capacity (current)	Cost (original)	Naming Rights (amt. and expiration)
Grad Partnership; DiLullo, Clauss, Ostroski & Partners	19,040	$85 M	$29 M (12 yrs.)
Welton Becket	16,297	$31 M	
Charles Luckman	18,200	$116 M	
Ellerbe Becket	18,168	$206 M	$40 M (29 yrs.)
Mitchell and Ritchie	17,323	$22 M	$18 M (10 yrs.)
Ellerbe Becket	17,565	$160 M	$30 M (15 yrs.)
Ellerbe Becket	18,595	$127.5 M	$24 M (30 yrs.)
Consortium of Quebec Architects	21,273	C$280 M	$100 M (20 yrs.)
Rossetti Associates Architects	18,500	C$200 M	C$26 M (20 yrs.)
HOK Sports Facilities Group; Brisbin, Brook and Benyon	18,800	C$265 M	C$40 M (20 yrs.)
HOK Sports Facilities Group; Arquitectonica	18,750	$213.5 M	$180 M (20 yrs.)
Odell & Associates	18,176	$158 M	$80 M (20 yrs.)
Ellerbe Becket	19,452	$212 M	$14 M (10 yrs.)
Ellerbe Becket	19,500	$139 M	$25 M (12 yrs.)
Ellerbe Becket	19,700	$260 M	$44 M (13 yrs.)

Sports Stadiums: Hockey

WESTERN CONFERENCE	Stadium Name	Location	Opened
CENTRAL DIVISION			
Chicago Blackhawks	United Center	Chicago, IL	1994
Columbus Blue Jackets	Nationwide Arena	Columbus, OH	2000
Detroit Red Wings	Joe Louis Arena	Detroit, MI	1979
Nashville Predators	Gaylord Entertainment Center	Nashville, TN	1997
St. Louis Blues	Savvis Center	St. Louis, MO	1994
NORTHWEST DIVISION			
Calgary Flames	Pengrowth Saddledome	Calgary, AB, Canada	1983
Colorado Avalanche	Pepsi Center	Denver, CO	1999
Edmonton Oilers	Rexall Place	Edmonton, AB, Canada	1974
Minnesota Wild	Xcel Energy Center	Saint Paul, MN	2000
Vancouver Canucks	General Motors Place	Vancouver, BC, Canada	1995
PACIFIC DIVISION			
Anaheim Mighty Ducks	Arrowhead Pond of Anaheim	Anaheim, CA	1993
Dallas Stars	American Airlines Center	Dallas, TX	2001
Los Angeles Kings	Staples Center	Los Angeles, CA	1999
Phoenix Coyotes	Glendale Arena	Phoenix, AZ	2003
San Jose Sharks	HP Pavilion	San Jose, CA	1993

Source: DesignIntelligence

Architect (original)	Capacity (current)	Cost (original)	Naming Rights (amt. and expiration)
HOK Sports Facilities Group; Marmon Mok; W.E. Simpson Company	20,500	$175 M	$25 M (20 yrs.)
Heinlein Schrock Stearns; NBBJ	18,500	$150 M	$135 M (indefinite)
Smith, Hinchmen and Grylls Associates	18,785	$57 M	
HOK Sports Facilities Group	17,500	$144 M	$80 M (20 yrs.)
Ellerbe Becket	19,260	$170 M	$70 M (20 yrs.)
Graham Edmunds/Graham McCourt	20,140	C$176 M	C$20 M (20 yrs.)
HOK Sports Facilities Group	18,129	$160 M	$68 M (20 yrs.)
Phillips, Barrett, Hillier, Jones & Partners w/ Wynn, Forbes, Lord, Feldberg & Schmidt	16,900	C$22.5 M	Undisclosed
HOK Sports Facilities Group	18,064	$130 M	$75 M (25 yrs.)
Brisbin, Brook and Beynon	18,422	C$160 M	C$18.5 M (20 yrs.)
HOK Sports Facilities Group	17,174	$120 M	$15 M (10 yrs.)
David M. Schwarz Architectural Services, Inc. with HKS, Inc.	18,000	$420 M	$40 M (20 yrs.)
NBBJ	18,500	$330 M	$100 M (20 yrs.)
HOK Sport + Venue + Event	17,653	$220 M	
Sink Combs Dethlefs	17,483	$162.5 M	$55.8 M (18 yrs.)

State Capitols

The architect(s) of each US state capitol, as well as the national Capitol, is listed below. When available, the contractor(s) is also listed immediately below the architect in italics.

Alabama
Montgomery, 1851
Barachias Holt

Alaska
Juneau, 1931
Treasury Department architects with James
    A. Wetmore, supervising architect
N.P. Severin Company

Arizona
Phoenix, 1900
James Riley Gordon
Tom Lovell

Arkansas
Little Rock, 1911–1915
George R. Mann; Cass Gilbert
Caldwell and Drake; William Miller & Sons

California
Sacramento, 1874
Miner F. Butler; Ruben Clark and
    G. Parker Cummings

Colorado
Denver, 1894–1908
Elijah E. Myers, Frank E. Edbrooke

Connecticut
Hartford, 1779
Richard M. Upjohn
James G. Batterson

Delaware
Dover, 1933
William Martin

Florida
Tallahassee, 1977
Edward Durell Stone with Reynolds,
    Smith and Hills

Georgia
Atlanta, 1889
Edbrooke & Burnham
Miles and Horne

Hawaii
Honolulu, 1969
John Carl Warnecke with Belt, Lemman and Lo
Reed and Martin

Idaho
Boise, 1912–1920
John E. Tourtellotte
*Stewart and Company with Herbert Quigley,
    construction supervisor*

Illinois
Springfield, 1877–87
J. C. Cochrane with Alfred H. Piquenard;
    W. W. Boyington

Indiana
Indianapolis, 1888
Edwin May; Adolf Scherrer
*Kanmacher and Dengi; Elias F. Gobel and
    Columbus Cummings*

Iowa
Des Moines, 1884–86
J. C. Cochrane and Alfred H. Piquenard;
    M.E. Bell and W. F. Hackney

Kansas
Topeka, 1873–1906
John G. Haskell; E.T. Carr and George Ropes
*D. J. Silver & Son; Bogart and Babcock; William
    Tweeddale and Company*

Kentucky
Frankfort, 1910
Frank Mills Andrews

State Capitols

Louisiana
Baton Rouge, 1931
Weiss, Dryfous and Seiferth
Kenneth McDonald

Maine
Augusta, 1832
Charles Bulfinch; John C. Spofford, 1891 rear
  wing addition; G. Henri Desmond, 1911
  expansion

Maryland
Annapolis, 1779
Joseph Horatio Anderson and Joseph Clark,
  interior architect; Baldwin and Pennington,
  1905 rear annex
Charles Wallace; Thomas Wallace

Massachusetts
Boston, 1798
Charles Bulfinch; Charles Brigham, 1895 rear
  addition; R. Clipson, William Chapman, and
  Robert Agnew, 1917 side wing additions

Michigan
Lansing, 1878–79
Elijah E. Myers
N. Osborne & Co.

Minnesota
St. Paul, 1905
Cass Gilbert

Mississippi
Jackson, 1903
Theodore C. Link; George R. Mann, dome
Wells Brothers Company

Missouri
Jefferson City, 1917
Tracy and Swartwout
*T.H. Johnson; A. Anderson & Company;
  John Gill & Sons*

Montana
Helena, 1902
Bell and Kent; Frank Mills Andrews and Link &
  Hare, 1912 east and west wing addition

Nebraska
Lincoln, 1932
Bertram Grosvenor Goodhue
*W.J. Assenmacher Company; J.H. Wiese Company;
  Peter Kewittand Sons; Metz Construction Co.*

Nevada
Carson City, 1871
Joseph Gosling; Frederic J. Delongchamps and
  C.G. Sellman, 1913 addition
Peter Cavanough and Son

New Hampshire
Concord, 1819
Stuart James Park; Gridley J. F. Bryant and David
  Bryce, 1866 addition; Peabody and Stearns,
  1909 addition

New Jersey
Trenton, 1792
Jonathan Doane; John Notman, 1845 expansion
  and renovation; Samuel Sloan, 1872 expansion; Lewis Broome and James Moylan, c.1885
  renovations; Karr Poole and Lum, 1900
  expansion; Arnold Moses, 1903 Senate wing
  renovations

New Mexico
Santa Fe, 1966
W. C. Kruger & Associates with John Gaw Meem,
  design consultant
Robert E. McKee General Contractor, Inc.

New York
Albany, 1879–99
Thomas Fuller; Leopold Eidlitz, Frederick Law
  Olmsted, Henry Hobson Richardson;
  Isaac G. Perry

North Carolina
Raleigh, 1840
Town and Davis, David Paton

North Dakota
Bismarck, 1934
Holabird & Root with Joseph B. DeRemer and
  William F. Kirke
Lundoff and Bicknell

365

State Capitols

Ohio
Columbus, 1857–1861
Henry Walter; William R. West; Nathan B. Kelly

Oklahoma
Oklahoma City, 1917
Layton and Smith

Oregon
Salem, 1938
Francis Keally of Trowbridge and Livingston

Pennsylvania
Harrisburg, 1906
Joseph M. Huston
George F. Payne Company

Rhode Island
Providence, 1904
McKim, Mead and White
Norcross Brothers Construction

South Carolina
Columbia, 1854–1907
John Rudolph Niernsee, 1854–85; J. Crawford
    Neilson, 1885–88; Frank Niernsee, 1888–91;
    Frank P. Milburn, 1900–04; Charles Coker
    Wilson, 1904–07

South Dakota
Pierre, 1911
C.E. Bell and M.S. Detwiler
*O.H. Olsen with Samuel H. Lea, state engineer
    and construction supervisor*

Tennessee
Nashville, 1859
William Strickland
A.G. Payne

Texas
Austin, 1888
Elijah E. Myers
*Mattheas Schnell; Taylor, Babcock & Co.
    with Abner Taylore*

Utah
Salt Lake City, 1915–16
Richard K. A. Kletting
James Stewart & Company

Vermont
Montpelier, 1859
Thomas W. Silloway; Joseph R. Richards

Virginia
Richmond, 1789
Thomas Jefferson with Charles-Louis Clérisseau;
    J. Kevin Peebles, Frye & Chesterman,
    1906 wings

Washington
Olympia, 1928
Walter R. Wilder and Harry K. White

West Virginia
Charleston, 1932
Cass Gilbert
George H. Fuller Company; James Baird Company

Wisconsin
Madison, 1909–1915
George B. Post & Sons

Wyoming
Cheyenne, 1890
David W. Gibbs; William Dubois, 1915 extension
*Adam Feick & Brother; Moses P. Keefe, 1890 wings;
    John W. Howard, 1915 extension*

US Capitol
Washington, DC, 1800–1829
William Thornton, 1793; Benjamin Henry
    Latrobe, 1803–11, 1815–17; Charles Bulfinch,
    1818–29; Thomas Ustick Walter, 1851–65;
    Edward Clark, 1865–1902; Elliot Woods,
    1902–23; David Lynn, 1923–54; J. George
    Stewart, 1954–70; George Malcolm White,
    FAIA, 1971–95; Alan M. Hantman, AIA,
    1997–present

Source: DesignIntelligence

Tallest Buildings in the World

The following list ranks the world's 100 tallest buildings. Each building's architect, number of stories, height, location, and completion year are also provided. Buildings that have reached their full height but are still under construction are deemed eligible and are indicated with a UC in the year category along with the anticipated completion date, if known. For the purposes of this list, heights are rounded to the nearest full unit of measurement.

For additional resources about tall buildings, visit the Council on Tall Buildings and Urban Habitat on the Internet at *www.ctbuh.org*, as well as *www.skyscrapers.com*.

Rank	Building	Completed	City/Country	Height (ft./m.)	Height (no. stories)	Architect
1	Taipei 101	2004	Taipei, Taiwan	1670/509	101	C.Y. Lee and Partners
2	Petronas Tower 1	1998	Kuala Lumpur, Malaysia	1483/452	88	Cesar Pelli & Associates
3	Petronas Tower 2	1998	Kuala Lumpur, Malaysia	1483/452	88	Cesar Pelli & Associates
4	Sears Tower	1974	Chicago, US	1450/442	110	Skidmore, Owings & Merrill
5	Jin Mao Building	1999	Shanghai, China	1381/421	88	Skidmore, Owings & Merrill
6	Two International Finance Center	2003	Hong Kong, China	1362/415	88	Cesar Pelli & Associates
7	CITIC Plaza	1996	Guangzhou, China	1283/391	80	Dennis Lau & Ng Chun Man & Associates
8	Shun Hing Square	1996	Shenzhen, China	1260/384	69	K.Y. Cheung Design Associates
9	Empire State Building	1931	New York, US	1250/381	102	Shreve, Lamb & Harmon
10	Central Plaza	1992	Hong Kong, China	1227/374	78	Ng Chun Man & Associates
11	Bank of China	1989	Hong Kong, China	1209/369	72	Pei Cobb Freed & Partners
12	Emirates Tower One	1999	Dubai, UAE	1165/355	54	Norr Group Consultants
13	Tuntex Sky Tower	1997	Kaohsiung, Taiwan	1140/348	85	C.Y. Lee/Hellmuth, Obata & Kassabaum
14	Aon Centre	1973	Chicago, US	1136/346	80	Edward D. Stone
15	The Center	1998	Hong Kong, China	1135/345	73	Dennis Lau & Ng Chun Man & Associates
16	John Hancock Center	1969	Chicago, US	1127/344	100	Skidmore, Owings & Merrill
17	Wuhan International Securities Building	UC	Wuhan, China	1087/331	68	n/a

Tallest Buildings in the World

Rank	Building	Completed	City/Country	Height (ft./m.)	Height (no. stories)	Architect
18	Shimao International Plaza	UC	Shanghai, China	1087/331	60	Ingenhoven Overdiek und Partner; East China Architecture and Design Institute
19	Ryugyong Hotel	1995	Pyongyang, North Korea	1083/330	105	Baikdoosan Architects & Engineers
20	Q1 Tower	UC	Gold Coast, Australia	1058/323	78	n/a
21	Burj al Arab Hotel	1999	Dubai, UAE	1053/321	60	WS Atkins & Partners
22	Nina Tower I	UC	Hong Kong, China	1046/319	80	n/a
23	Chrysler Building	1930	New York, US	1046/319	77	William van Alen
24	Bank of America Plaza	1993	Atlanta, US	1023/312	55	Kevin Roche, John Dinkeloo & Associates
25	US Bank Tower	1990	Los Angeles, US	1018/310	73	Pei Cobb Freed & Partners
26	Menara Telekom Headquarters	1999	Kuala Lumpur, Malaysia	1017/310	55	Daewoo & Partners
27	Emirates Tower Two	2000	Dubai, UAE	1014/309	56	Norr Group Consultants
28	AT&T Corporate Center	1989	Chicago, US	1007/307	60	Skidmore, Owings & Merrill
29	JP Morgan Chase Tower	1982	Houston, US	1002/305	75	I.M. Pei & Partners
30	Baiyoke Tower II	1997	Bangkok, Thailand	997/304	85	Plan Architects Co.
31	Two Prudential Plaza	1990	Chicago, US	995/303	64	Leobl Schlossman Dart & Hackl
32	Kingdom Centre	2002	Riyadh, Saudi Arabia	992/302	41	Ellerbe Becket and Omrania
33	First Canadian Place	1975	Toronto, Canada	978/298	72	Bregman + Hamann Architects
34	Eureka Tower	UC	Melbourne, Australia	975/297	91	Fender Katsalidis Architects
35	Wells Fargo Plaza	1983	Houston, US	972/296	71	Skidmore, Owings & Merrill
36	Landmark Tower	1993	Yokohama, Japan	971/296	70	Stubbins Associates
37	311 South Wacker Drive	1990	Chicago, US	961/293	65	Kohn Pedersen Fox Associates
38	SEG Plaza	2000	Shenzen, China	957/292	71	Hua Yi Design
39	American International Building	1932	New York, US	952/290	67	Clinton & Russell
40	Key Tower	1991	Cleveland, US	947/289	57	Cesar Pelli & Associates

Tallest Buildings in the World

Rank	Building	Completed	City/Country	Height (ft./m.)	Height (no. stories)	Architect
41	Plaza 66	2001	Shanghai, China	945/288	66	Kohn Pedersen Fox Associates with East China Architecture and Design Institute (ECADI) and Frank C. Y. Feng Architects & Associates
42	One Liberty Place	1987	Philadelphia, US	945/288	61	Murphy/Jahn
43	Sunjoy Tomorrow Square	2003	Shanghai, China	934/285	55	John Portman and Associates
44	Bank of America Center	1984	Seattle, US	933/284	76	Chester Lindsey Architects
45	Cheung Kong Centre	1999	Hong Kong, China	929/283	63	Cesar Pelli & Associates, Leo A Daly
46	Chongqing World Trade Center	UC	Chongqing, China	929/283	60	Haines Lundberg Waehler
47	The Trump Building	1930	New York, US	927/283	71	H. Craig Severance
48	Bank of America Plaza	1985	Dallas, US	921/281	72	JPJ Architects
49	United Overseas Bank Plaza	1992	Singapore	919/280	66	Kenzo Tange Associates
50	Republic Plaza	1995	Singapore	919/280	66	Kisho Kurokawa
51	Overseas Union Bank Center	1986	Singapore	919/280	63	Kenzo Tange Associates
52	Citigroup Center	1977	New York, US	915/279	59	The Stubbins Associates
53	Hong Kong New World Tower	2002	Shanghai, China	913/278	61	Bregman + Hamann Architects
54	Scotia Plaza	1989	Toronto, Canada	902/275	68	The Webb Zerafa Menkes Housden Partnership
55	Williams Tower	1983	Houston, US	901/275	64	Johnson/Burgee Architects
56	Wuhan World Trade Tower	1998	Wuhan, China	896/273	60	n/a
57	Renaissance Tower	1975	Dallas, US	886/270	56	Skidmore, Owings & Merrill
58	Dapeng International Plaza	UC	Guangzhou, China	883/269	56	Guangzhou Design Institute
59	21st Century Tower	2003	Dubai, UAE	883/269	55	WS Atkins & Partners
60	Al Faisaliah Center	2000	Riyadh, Saudi Arabia	876/267	30	Foster and Partners
61	900 North Michigan Avenue	1989	Chicago, US	871/265	66	Kohn Pedersen Fox Associates

Tallest Buildings in the World

Rank	Building	Completed	City/Country	Height (ft./m.)	Height (no. stories)	Architect
62	Bank of America Corporate Center	1992	Charlotte, US	871/265	60	Cesar Pelli & Associates
63	SunTrust Plaza	1992	Atlanta, US	871/265	60	John Portman & Associates
64	Triumph Palace	UC	Moscow, Russia	866/264	61	n/a
65	Shenzhen Special Zone Daily Tower	1998	Shenzhen, China	866/264	42	n/a
66	Tower Palace Three, Tower G	2004	Seoul, South Korea	865/264	73	Skidmore, Owings & Merrill
67	Trump World Tower	2001	New York, US	861/262	72	Costas Kondylis & Partners LLC Architects
68	Water Tower Place	1976	Chicago, US	859/262	74	Loebl Schlossman Dart & Hackl
69	Aon Center	1974	Los Angeles, US	858/262	62	Charles Luckman & Associates
70	BCE Place-Canada Trust Tower	1990	Toronto, Canada	856/261	53	Skidmore, Owings & Merrill; Bregman + Hamann
71	Post & Telecommunication Hub	2002	Guangzhou, China	853/260	66	n/a
72	Transamerica Pyramid	1972	San Francisco, US	853/260	48	William Pereira
73	GE Building, Rockefeller Center	1933	New York, US	850/259	70	Raymond Hood
74	Bank One Plaza	1969	Chicago, US	850/259	60	C.F. Murphy
75	Commerzbank Zentrale	1997	Frankfurt, Germany	850/259	56	Foster and Partners
76	Two Liberty Place	1990	Philadelphia, US	848/258	58	Murphy/Jahn
77	Philippine Bank of Communications	2000	Makati, Philippines	848/258	55	Skidmore, Owings & Merrill, G.F. & Partners
78	Park Tower	2000	Chicago, US	844/257	67	Lucien Lagrange Architects; HKS, Inc.
79	Messeturm	1990	Frankfurt, Germany	843/257	64	Murphy/Jahn
80	Sorrento 1	2003	Hong Kong, China	841/256	75	Wong & Ouyang (HK) Ltd.
81	US Steel Tower	1970	Pittsburgh, US	841/256	64	Harrison & Abramovitz
82	Mokdong Hyperion Tower A	2003	Seoul, South Korea	840/256	69	n/a
83	Rinku Gate Tower	1996	Izumisano, Japan	840/256	56	Nikken Sekkei; Yasui Architects & Engineers, Inc.

Tallest Buildings in the World

Rank	Building	Completed	City/Country	Height (ft./m.)	Height (no. stories)	Architect
84	The Harbourside	2003	Hong Kong, China	837/255	74	P & T Architects and Engineers Ltd.
85	Langham Place Office Tower	UC	Hong Kong, China	837/255	59	Wong & Ouyang Ltd.
86	Capital Tower	2000	Singapore	833/254	52	RSP Architects Planners & Engineers (Pte) Ltd.
87	Highcliff	2003	Hong Kong, China	831/253	73	DLN Architects & Engineers
88	Osaka World Trade Center	1995	Osaka, Japan	827/252	55	Nikken Sekkei
89	Bank of Shanghai Headquarters	UC	Shanghai, China	827/252	46	Kenzo Tange Associates
90	Jiali Plaza	1997	Wuhan, China	824/251	61	WMKY Ltd
91	Rialto Tower	1985	Melbourne, Australia	823/251	63	Gerard de Preu & Partners
92	One Atlantic Center	1987	Atlanta, US	820/250	50	Johnson/Burgee Architects
93	Chelsea Tower	2005	Dubai, UAE	820/250	49	WS Atkins & Partners
94	Wisma 46	1995	Jakarta, Indonesia	820/250	46	Zeidler Roberts Partnership with DP Architects
95	Korea Life Insurance Company	1985	Seoul, South Korea	817/249	60	C.M. Park with Skidmore, Owings and Merrill
96	CitySpire	1989	New York, US	814/248	75	Murphy/Jahn
97	One Chase Manhattan Plaza	1961	New York, US	813/248	60	Skidmore, Owings & Merrill
98	State Tower	2001	Bangkok, Thailand	811/247	68	Rangsan Architecture Co., Ltd.
99	Bank One Tower	1989	Indianapolis, US	811/247	48	The Stubbins Associates
100	Conde Nast Building	1999	New York, US	809/247	48	Fox & Fowle Architects

Source: © Council on Tall Buildings and Urban Habitat

371

Women in Architecture Timeline

While women still comprise less than 25 percent of practicing US architects, the road to attain that level of participation in the field has been bravely and most ably traversed by some genuine trailblazers. Since the late 1800s, women interested in design have been encouraged to work on domestic projects, including interior design, but to leave architecture, and particularly commercial work, to men. Less than 50 years ago, the dean of MIT's school of architecture advised women against entering the profession due to "great obstacles." Facing strong adversity, women have persevered, establishing their own firms and designing landmark buildings even while raising families. The timeline below illustrates highlights in the continuing struggle for women in the practice and to lead in the field of architecture. For the sake of continuity, the context line is limited to the United States.

1865 The Massachusetts Institute of Technology is founded and along with it the United States' first architecture program, which is only open to men.

1869 Harriet Beecher Stowe (1811–1896) and her sister, domestic economist Catherine Beecher (1800–1878,) write the seminal domestic tome *The American Woman's Home.* A central theme in Catherine's other publications as well, the book asserts the domestic superiority of women and celebrates their capacity for self-sacrifice. She includes designs for homes conducive to family life.

1869 Charlotte, North Carolina's Harriet Irwin (1828–1897) is the first woman to patent a dwelling plan. Although she had no formal architectural training, she will design and build at least two more houses.

1876 Mary Nolan (*dates unknown*) of Missouri exhibits a prototype house of interlocking bricks at the Philadelphia Centennial for which she won an award.

1878 Mary L. Page (*dates unknown*) graduates from the School of Architecture at the University of Illinois, Urbana–Champaign. She is the first woman to earn a degree in architecture from an American university.

1880 Margaret Hicks' (1858–1883) is the first female graduate of Cornell University's architecture program. Two years prior, her sketch of a Workman's Cottage was the first by a woman to appear in an American architectural journal.

1881 At age 25, Louise Blanchard (1856–1913) sets up architectural shop in Buffalo, NY, with Robert Bethune. Seven years later (now married) Louise Blanchard Bethune becomes the first woman to be voted a member of the American Institute of Architects. She becomes the AIA's first female fellow the following year when all members of the Western Association of Architects are made AIA fellows.

1890 Sophia Hayden (1868–1953) is the first woman to graduate from the Massachusetts Institute of Technology with a four-year degree in architecture (with honors). Born in Chile, Hayden moved to the United States with her parents when she was six.

1891 Sophia Hayden wins a competition to design the Woman's Building for the 1893 World's Columbian Exposition in Chicago. She is selected for the project by the all-female Board of Lady Managers, who opened the competition to women only. Despite accolades from Richard Morris

Women in Architecture Timeline

Hunt and Daniel Burnham, Hayden suffers a nervous breakdown following an arduous two-year construction process and leaves the profession.

1894 Julia Morgan (1872–1957) is one of the first women to receive a degree in civil engineering from the University of California, Berkeley. The program now bears her name.

1894 Marion Mahoney Griffin (1871–1961) is the second woman to graduate with a four-year degree from Massachusetts Institute of Technology's architecture program. She will become the first woman licensed to practice in the state of Illinois and will work from 1895–1909 in Frank Lloyd Wright's Oak Park office, becoming his chief draftsperson. When Wright departs for Europe in 1909, Hermann von Holst agrees to take over the Oak Park office only if Marion Mahoney will join him as a designer. Though she often acts as chief designer, most architectural drawings read "Hermann von Holst, Architect, Marion Mahoney, Associate." In 1911 she marries architect Walter Burley Griffin and dedicates herself to furthering his career, providing support and collaboration.

To date, only eight women in the United States are known to have completed four-year programs in architecture.

After two years of tests, Julia Morgan becomes the first woman in the world accepted to L'Ecole des Beaux Arts in Paris. In 1902 at the age of 29, she wins four the Ecole des Beaux Arts certification medals and becomes the first woman in the world to graduate from this prestigious institution.

1895 Pittsburgh, Pa., architect Elice Mercur (*dates unknown*) is awarded the commission for the Woman's Building at the Cotton States and International Exposition in Atlanta, GA, by its Board of Women Managers.

1900 By 1900, 39 female graduates are known to have completed formal four-year architectural training programs in the Unites States.

1901 The Fred Harvey Company, a vendor of hospitality services in the Southwest, including the National Parks, hires teacher and California School of Design graduate Mary Jane Colter (1869–1958). A high school graduate at the age of 14, she becomes the company's chief architect and over the course of her 40-year career. She is noted for her eye for detail and careful study of Native American architecture. Among her notable hotel, gift shop, and park designs are the Watchtower, Hopi House, and Hermit's Rest at the Grand Canyon National Park in Arizona. She also serves as architect and decorator for the Santa Fe Railway.

1903 Mary Rockwell Hook (1877–1978) is the first woman to enroll in the Chicago Art Institute's architecture department. In 1905, she departs for study in Paris. Upon completing her final examinations at the Atelier Auburtin, a studio of the Ecole des Beaux Arts, she is doused with buckets of water by French male students. She returns home to Kansas City where her father purchases lots around town for her to design houses on, including the city's first home with an attached garage, the first with a swimming pool, and the first using cast-in-place concrete walls.

1909 Theodate Pope Riddle (1868–1946) designs Middlebury, CT's Westover School. Cass Gilbert writes that it is "the most beautifully planned and designed…girls' school in the country."

1910 In one of the first known female partnerships, Ida Annah Ryan (1883–1960, MIT

Women in Architecture Timeline

class of 1905) asks Florence Luscomb (1887–1985, MIT class of 1908) to join her Waltham, MA, practice. Luscomb remains in the practice until 1917 after which she devotes the rest of her life to social and political activism.

Half of the architecture programs in the United States still deny entry to women.

1911 Anna Wagner Keichline (1889–1943) graduates from Cornell University's architecture program and becomes the first registered woman architect in Pennsylvania. She will later patent seven inventions, including an improved combined sink and washtub design, a kitchen design that includes sloped countertops and glass-doored cabinets, and K Brick, a hollow fireproof clay brick that was a precursor to the modern concrete block. The American Ceramic Society honored her for this invention in 1937.

1913 Lois Lilly Howe (1864–1964, MIT class of 1890) and Eleanor Manning (1884–1973, MIT class of 1906) form Howe & Manning, the first architecture firm founded by women in Boston and the second in the nation. Mary Almy (1883–1967, MIT class of 1922) joined the firm in 1926. They specialized in domestic architecture and championed the cause of urban and low-income housing. Manning designed the first public, low-income housing in Boston, and Howe focused on small, affordable housing in the suburbs. The firm dissolved in 1937 as a result of the Depression.

Mary Rockwell Hook (*dates unknown*) is selected to design the Pine Mountain Settlement School in Harlan County, KY. Serving students in the isolated Appalachian mountains of Eastern Kentucky, the Pine Mountain School includes natural elements, such as boulders, in its designs. With no mill nearby, native, chestnut, oak, and poplar trees

were cut, dried, and sawn onsite. Today the school serves as an environmental education facility.

1915 Harvard School of Architecture instructor Henry Frost and landscape architect Bremer Pond open the Cambridge School of Architecture and Landscape Architecture in Massachusetts, the first and only program of its kind exclusively for women. Frost had originally been tapped by the head of Harvard Univeristy's Landscape School, James Sturgis Pray, to tutor a woman who wanted to study drafting since Harvard did not accept women into its program. The number of women requesting lessons grew quickly, and so the Cambridge School was born. As of 1930, 83 percent of its graduates will be professionally active.

1919 William Randolph Hearst inherits a quarter million acres in San Simeon, CA, overlooking the Pacific Ocean. His alleged conversation with Julia Morgan begins, "Miss Morgan, we are tired of camping out in the open at the ranch in San Simeon, and I would like to build a little something…" Twenty years later, the Hearst Castle is done. Between 1919–1939, Morgan travels via train to the site more than 550 times for weekend work sessions. Her fee is estimated at $70,755.

1921 Elizabeth Martini (*dates unknown*) forms the Chicago Drafting Club, later the Women's Architectural Club. The group organizes displays for the Woman's World Fairs of 1927 and 1928 and sponsors an International Exhibition of Women in Architecture and the Allied Arts at Chicago's 1933 World's Fair.

1923 Alberta Pfeiffer (1899–1994) graduates first in her class from the School of Architecture at the University of Illinois, Urbana–Champaign and is the first woman to win the American Institute of Architects' School

Women in Architecture Timeline

Medal (now the Henry Adams medal). She works several years in New York before establishing a practice with her husband in Hadlyme, CT. She continues to work into the mid-1970s.

1934 Housing reformer Catherine Bauer's (1905–1964) book, *Modern Housing*, espouses European social philosophies of architecture, particularly as related to low-income housing. She later helps develop the US Housing Act of 1937, which provides federal funding for low-income housing.

1938 The Cambridge School of Architecture and Landscape Architecture becomes part of Smith College.

1941 *The Octagon* publishes a landmark report on public housing, prepared by Massachusetts Institute of Technology architecture program graduate Elizabeth Coit (1892–1987) from 1938–1940 under a Langley Fellowship from the American Institute of Architects. The report is revised and published in 1942 in *Architectural Record* as "Housing from the Tenant's Viewpoint." She goes on to spend her career working in public housing, including as principal project planner for the New York City Housing Authority from 1948 to 1962.

1942 Due to budgetary constraints, Smith College shuts down the Cambridge School of Architecture and Landscape Architecture. By this time, female architecture students can now attend Harvard University, and many transfer there.

1944 At age 25, Natalie de Blois (*dates unknown*) graduates from the Columbia University School of Architecture and joins Skidmore, Owings & Merrill's New York office. Following a break when she is awarded a Fullbright Fellowship to the L'Ecole des Beaux-Arts in the 1950s, she returns to SOM and works directly with Gordon

Bunshaft as a senior designer. After more than 20 years in the position, she is promoted to the level of associate. She never becomes a partner.

1945 Sarah Pillsbury Harkness (*dates unknown*), a 1940 graduate of the Smith College Graduate School of Architecture, becomes a founding member, with Walter Gropius and others, of the Architects Collaborative in Cambridge, MA.

1946 Florence Knoll (1917–) and her husband Hans form Knoll Associates (now Knoll International), offering modern furniture by well-known designers. Knoll studied closely under Eliel Saarinen at the Cranbrook Academy of Art, then at the Architectural Association in London and the Illinois Institute of Technology under Mies van der Rohe. She also revolutionized the look and function of American office interiors, ideas that were revolutionary in the 1950s but are still widely used today. Florence Knoll Bassett was awarded the National Medal of Arts in 2002 for "profoundly influence[ing] post-World War II design."

1948 *Architectural Record* runs a two-part article entitled "A Thousand Women in Architecture." At that time, the magazine profiled 18 of the 1,119 women trained to practice architecture, according to research by the Women's Architectural Association and the deans of architecture schools across the United States.

Eleanor Raymond (1888–1989), an early graduate of the Cambridge School of Architecture and Landscape Architecture and a colleague of the school's founder, Henry Atherton Frost, from 1919 to 1935, designs the Dover Sun House in Dover, MA. It is the first occupied solar-powered house in the United States. Her career will span more that 50 years; in 1961 she is elected to the American Institute of Architects' College of Fellows.

375

Women in Architecture Timeline

1952 As Julia Morgan retires, she destroys her office records. During her lengthy career Morgan designed more than 800 buildings.

1955 Pietro Belluschi, the dean of the Massachusett's School of Architecture writes in an essay entitled "The Exceptional One": *"I know some women who have done well at it, but the obstacles are so great that it takes an exceptional girl to make a go of it. If she insisted upon becoming an architect I would try to dissuade her. If then she was still determined, I would give her my blessing that she could be that exceptional one."*

Jane Hall Johnson (1919–2001) graduates from Harvard with a bachelor's degree in architecture. She receives a degree in civil engineering in 1941 from the Missouri School of Mines and works as a structural engineer before deciding to return to school. She later receives her MArch degree from Harvard University. In 1970 she forms the firm of Jane C. Hall, Architect in St. Louis with her engineer husband, Benjamin Johnson. She retires in 1997.

1956 Lutah Maria Riggs (1896–1984), the first licensed female architect in California and the first woman in the state to be elected to the American Institute of Architect's College of Fellows, produces her most famous work, Santa Barbara's Vedanta Temple. She is a 1919 graduate of the University of California, Berkeley.

1958 An architect named Rose Connor (*dates unknown*), combs the records of the Architecture Examining Boards of all the states and finds a total of 320 registered women architects. This represents one percent of the total number of registered architects in the United States at this time. No women are registered in seven states.

1960 Beverly A. Willis (1928–), a native of Oklahoma whose parents left her and a

brother in an orphanage during the Depression, establishes Willis and Associates in San Francisco. Though she began her career as a designer in 1954, Willis never attends architecture school and does not become a licensed architect until 1966. Still, she produces many significant architecture and design projects in that city, beginning with retail store design and including many residences, community planning projects, the San Francisco Ballet Building, a master plan for the University of California at San Francisco, and the design and master planning for Yerba Buena Gardens, a 24-acre mixed-use development. She also designs the Aliamanu Valley Community for the Army Corps of Engineers, housing 11,500 people in Hawaii. In the early 1970s, her firm becomes a pioneer in the use of computer-aided design and planning.

Joan Edelman Goody (1935–) marries fellow architect Marvin E. Goody, and they become partners in the Boston firm Goody, Clancy and Associates. In a 1998 interview with the *Boston Globe Magazine*, Goody says the 60+ member firm is "probably half women now. I was lucky. I married a very supportive architect husband, and I had wonderful partners."

1961 Senior editor of *Architectural Forum* magazine from 1952 to 1962, Jane Jacobs's seminal work *The Life & Death of Great American Cities* is published.

1962 Jane Jacobs (1916–) organizes the Committee to Save the West Village and succeeds in defeating an urban renewal plan for New York's historic Greenwich Village. Many such groups were formed in the 1960s as two pieces of legislation, the Housing Act of 1949 and the Highway Trust Act of 1956, triggered an aggressive alteration of the urban landscape. The Housing Act, promising "a decent house and suitable living environment for every

Women in Architecture Timeline

American Family," also contained a provision allowing the exercise of eminent domain, allowing states to seize private property for "the public benefit." The Highway Trust Act provided 90 percent federal funding to states for their portion of the interstate highway system. As urban areas are razed for highways and developer's projects, many organizations and advocacy groups formed to challenge the institutions behind urban renewal.

1963 Ada Louise Huxtable (1921–) is named the architecture critic of *The New York Times*, the first such staff position at any US newspaper. Huxtable will receive the Pulitzer Prize for distinguished criticism in 1970.

1972 Denise Scott Brown (1931–) turns down the deanship of the School of Art and Architecture at Yale University to continue her work with the firm of Venturi & Rauch, now Venturi, Scott Brown & Associates, Inc. With Robert Venturi and Steven Izenour she writes *Learning from Las Vegas*, one of the seminal texts of postmodernism. It celebrates the American commercial strip and encourages architects to broaden their acceptance of the tastes and values of ordinary people and everyday landscapes.

The American Institute of Architects establishes the Whitney M. Young Jr. Award, awarded to an individual or organization that demonstrates an outstanding commitment to expanding the profession. In 1960, Whitney M. Young Jr. was the executive director of the Urban League and urged the profession to reach out to women and minorities in an address at the AIA's national convention.

1973 Architect Beverly Willis becomes the first woman to chair the Federal Construction Council of the National Academy of Science. The council is comprised of directors of all construction departments within the federal government and is charged with overseeing joint agency cooperation. In 1976 she will be one of two architects selected as a member of the US Delegation to the United Nations Habitat One in Vancouver, Canada.

Sharon Sutton (1941–), a classically trained French horn player with a bachelor's degree in music, receives her MArch degree from the Columbia University Graduate School of Architecture and Planning. She will go on to become the first African-American woman to become a full professor in an accredited architecture professional degree program. Sutton pursues a distinguished career of writing and researching and in 1996 is presented with the Association of Collegiate Schools of Architecture Distinguished Professor Award.

1977 Miami native Laurinda Spear (1951–) forms the modernist architecture firm Arquitectonica in that city with Bernardo Fort-Brescia. Today, the firm has expanded to New York, Los Angeles, Paris, Hong Kong, Shanghai, Manila, Lima, Buenos Aires, and San Paulo. A fellow of the American Institute of Architects, she is the winner of the Rome Prize in Architecture and a member of the Interior Design Hall of Fame, among other honors.

Iraqi-born Zaha Hadid (1950–) graduates from London's Architectural Association, the winner of its Diploma Prize, and joins Rem Koolhaas and Elia Zenghelis at the Office for Metropolitan Architecture. She opens her own office in 1979 and goes on to become one of the world's great architectural theorists. In addition to teaching, Hadid enters a multitude of research-based competitions and designs a host of theoretical projects, most unbuilt. Her varied projects include exhibits of her paintings and drawings, furniture design, stage set design (including the Pet Shop Boys World Tour 1999/2000), and museum exhibition design.

Women in Architecture Timeline

1980 M. Rosaria Piomelli (1937–) becomes the first woman dean of a US architecture school when she is named to head the College of Architecture of the City College of New York. Before forming her own New York City firm in 1974, she worked for several firms, including I.M. Pei and Partners.

Elizabeth Plater-Zyberk (1950–) and Andrés Duany found the Miami practice Duany Plater-Zyberk & Company and quickly establish themselves as unparalleled experts in New Urbanism and town planning, which they pioneered with their now-famous town of Seaside, FL.

1981 Two surveys (1974 and 1981) of women in architecture firms by the American Institute of Architects reveal a majority experience discriminatory practices in school and later at work. Despite these negative responses, seven out of 10 say they would choose architecture again if they had the option of changing careers.

While still an undergraduate at Yale University, architecture student Maya Lin (1959–) wins a competition to design the Vietnam Veterans Memorial on the Mall in Washington, DC. She is 21 years old.

Illinois architect Carol Ross Barney (1949–) founds Carol Ross Barney Architects (now Ross Barney + Jankowski Architects). Aimed squarely at the commercial market, the firm insinuates itself into the fabric of Chicago and becomes one of the city's largest female-owned practices. In 2003, its Web site notes: "The makeup of our staff is a reflection of our belief that diversity is a desirable element in the design studio. Women compose 50 percent of our employees, ethnic minorities are approximately 30 percent (the remainder are very sensitive modern males)."

1983 The American Institute of Architects begins collecting data on the gender and race of its members.

1985 The International Archive of Women in Architecture is established as a joint program of the College of Architecture and Urban Studies and the University Libraries at Virginia Tech. The collection acquires, preserves, and stores the professional papers of women architects, landscape architects, designers, architectural historians, critics, and urban planners and the records of women's architectural organizations from around the world (http://spec.lib.vt.edu/iawa/).

Norma Merrick Sklarek (1928–) becomes the first African-American woman in the United States to form her own firm, Siegel–Sklarek-Diamond. She is also the first African-American woman in the country to become a licensed architect and to be inducted as a fellow of the American Institute of Architects. She is a graduate of Barnard College and the Columbia University School of Architecture.

1986 Collaborating since 1977, Billie Tsien and Tod Williams officially establish Tod Williams Billie Tsien & Associates in New York City. The firm will go to on to produce a body of high-profile, highly regarded projects, including Feinberg Hall at Princeton University, the Whitney Museum of American Art Downtown Branch in New York City, the Neurosciences Institute in La Jolla, CA, and the Museum of Folk Art in New York City. With a fine arts degree from Yale and a MArch from UCLA, Tsien is a design innovator, producing work that marries art and architecture in unique ways.

1987 Skidmore, Owings & Merrill elects Marilyn Jordan Taylor a partner of the firm. She joined SOM in 1971 working on urban design and transportation projects. From 1978 to 1985 Taylor served as director of design for the Stations Program of the Northeast Corridor Improvement Project, a $25-million, federally-funded project investing in intercity rail stations between

Women in Architecture Timeline

Washington, DC, and Boston. In 1985 she assumed leadership of an expanded urban design and planning practice within the firm, which includes billions of dollars of rail, airport, waterfront, subway, ferry, and land-use projects. She is twice named to *Crain's* list of Most Influential Women in New York. At the time of this writing, Taylor is the only current female partner at SOM.

1991 In Washington, DC, architects Debra Lehman-Smith and James McLeish form Lehman-Smith + McLeish (LSM). The firm will grow to more than 40 staff members with services in strategic planning, master planning, architectural design, interior design, and product design. By the end of the decade, *Contract Design* magazine will name LSM as one of the 20 Best Interior Design firms from 1975 to 1999.

1992 The American Institute of Architect's president Cecil Steward convenes a Task Force on Diversity.

L. Jane Hastings becomes the first woman Chancellor of the American Institute of Architects' College of Fellows.

1993 Susan Maxman becomes the first female president of the American Institute of Architects.

Elizabeth Plater-Zyberk, is named dean of Florida's University of Miami School of Architecture. She establishes a master of architecture program in suburb and town design.

1995 Chicago architect Sally Lynn Levine's multi-media exhibit "ALICE (Architecture Lets in Chicks, Except) Through the Glass Ceiling," opens in San Francisco, exploring the status of women in the field of architecture. A cofounder of CARY (Chicks in Architecture Refuse to Yield), a Chicago women architects group, Levine's teaching credits include architecture, design, drawing, digital design, and animation at the

School of the Art Institute of Chicago, Massachusetts College of Art, and University of Wisconsin–Milwaukee.

1998 Ann R. Chaintreuil becomes the first female president of the National Council of Architectural Registration Boards.

Heralded as a "cultural visionary," Minneapolis architect Sarah Susanka writes the bestseller *The Not So Big House*. Espousing a philosophy of better, not bigger, residential architecture, she is a guest on television shows, a popular speaker, and the subject of numerous magazine and newspaper articles. *US News & World Report* pronounces her an "innovator in American culture" upon the book's publication. Susanka will go on to write many more similarly themed books. In 2001, *Fast Company* magazine names her to their list of "Fast 50" innovators whose achievements have helped change society, following *Newsweek* magazine's 2000 selection of Susanka as a "top newsmaker" for the year.

2000 An *Architectural Record* editorial by Robert Ivy reveals that in 1997, women comprised around 9 percent of the American Institute of Architects' membership roster, and approximately 10 percent of licensed architects were women.

2001 According to the National Architectural Accrediting Board's annually survey, of the 1,038 tenured architecture school faculty members, 16 percent are female and 8 percent are ethnic minorities. Females comprise 37 percent of the architecture students, with ethnic minorities accounting for 15 percent. Of the architecture graduates, 34 percent are female and 20 percent are ethnic minorities.

Cornell University's College of Architecture, Art and Planning announces the appointment of Nasrine Seraji-Bozorgzad as chair of its Department of Architecture. Born in Tehran and trained

Women in Architecture Timeline

in London, Seraji is the principal of Paris' Atelier Seraji. In addition to visiting professorships in the United States, exhibitions, and lectures, she is a professor at Vienna's Akademie der Bildenden Künste. She is the first woman to head a department of architecture in the Ivy League.

Following the terrorist attacks of 9/11, architect Beverly Willis and *Metropolis* magazine editor-in-chief Susan Szenasy form Rebuild Downtown Our Town (R.Dot). Concerned with communicating a vision for the disaster site to the media, the public, and decision makers, the group is comprised of architects, lower Manhattan residents, businesses, community associations, and public officials and appointees.

Architect Sandra Mendler, vice president and sustainable design principal at HOK, is named the first recipient of the Sustainable Design Leadership Awards for her leadership and commitment to environmental issues in the design profession.

2002 Of the 102,002 licensed architects in the United States, 13 percent are women and 8 percent are ethnic minorities, according to the 2000–2002 AIA Firm Survey. Roughly 16 percent of full-time architectural faculty in US colleges and universities are women. Women continue to make up 9 percent of the total AIA membership.

MIT employs 154 women on its architecture department faculty. This equates to 16 percent of the total architecture faculty of 956 members. Over the same period, the proportion of female undergraduates has risen rapidly to 42 percent.

Maya Lin is named an alumni fellow of the Yale Corporation. She is the first artist to serve on the Yale Corporation and the first Asian-American woman trustee in Yale University's history.

Toshiko Mori is named chair of the Harvard Graduate School of Design's Department of Architecture. She studied under John Hejduk at Cooper Union and later received her MArch from Harvard, working first for Edward Larrabee Barnes and then opening her own practice, Toshiko Mori Architect, in 1981. She began teaching at Cooper Union in 1980 and joined the GSD staff in 1995.

2003 The 2003 AIA Firm Survey (reporting data from 2002) concludes that despite a period of economic weakness, women and minorities made significant gains over previous studies. The number of female registered architects rose to 20 percent from under 14 percent in 1999; racial and ethnic minorities comprised more than 11 percent, up from 6 percent.

The first woman ever to design an American museum, Zaha Hadid's Contemporary Arts Center in Cincinnati opens to great acclaim.

New Urbanists Elizabeth Plater-Zyberk and Andrés Duany announce the launch of the Fund for New Urbanism LLC, a real estate development company. The goal of the enterprise is to assist municipalities seeking alternatives to suburban sprawl. Partner Andrés Duany says the fund will option and permit at least 10 New Urbanist projects within 30 months.

2004 Zaha Hadid wins the Pritzker Architecture Prize, considered the Nobel Prize of architecture. She is the first female recipient in the award's 27-year history and only one of two female architects to be granted a major architecture prize. (Gae Aulenti was the 1991 recipient of the Praemium Imperiale.) To date no female has received the AIA Gold Medal or the RIBA Royal Gold Medal.

Source: DesignIntelligence

World's Best Skylines

This list ranks the impressiveness of the world's skylines by measuring the density and height of the skyscrapers in each city. Each building greater than 295 feet (90 meters) tall contributes points to its home city's score equal to the number of feet it exceeds this benchmark height.

An explanation of how the ranking is calculated and a ranking of more than 100 skylines can be found at *http://homepages.ipact.nl/~egram/skylines.htm.*

Ranking	Points	City/Country	# Buildings over 295 feet/90 meters
1	108,672	Hong Kong, China	3596
2	35,319	New York, US (incl. Jersey City, Guttenberg)	866
3	16,784	Tokyo, Japan	523
4	14,843	Shanghai, China	428
5	14,579	Chicago, US	327
6	11,889	Bangkok, Thailand	410
7	11,781	Dubai, UAE	177
8	8,027	Seoul, South Korea	356
9	7,692	Singapore	295
10	7,343	Kuala Lumpur, Malaysia	202
11	6,778	Shenzhen, China	184
12	6,445	Chongqing, China	235
13	6,163	Guangzhou, China	155
14	5,940	Manila, Philippines (incl. metro area)	174
15	5,531	Toronto, Canada (incl. Mississauga)	241
16	4,609	Houston, US	107
17	4,599	Sydney, Australia (incl. N. Sydney, Chatswood, Bondi Junction)	134
18	4,536	Osaka, Japan (incl. Izumisano)	112
19	4,460	Moscow, Russia	124
20	4,170	Miami, US (incl. Miami Beach)	103
21	3,887	Jakarta, Indonesia	118
22	3,604	Los Angeles, US	82
23	3,554	Nanjing, China	72
24	3,545	Melbourne, Australia	95
25	3,495	Beijing, China	140

Source: Egbert Gramsbergen and Paul Kazmierczak

Sustainable/ Green Design

Sustainable design is a philosophy that is increasingly becoming part of mainstream practice. Our built environment's profound impact on our natural environment, economy, health, and productivity makes attention to sustainable design imperative. Recent winners of sustainable design awards (buildings, products, and leaders), organizations devoted to developing and promoting green design guiding principles, and a timeline of the movement can be found in this chapter.

BSA Sustainable Design Awards

Every two years, the Boston Society of Architects' Urban Design Committee and AIA New York's Zoning and Urban Design Committee present the Sustainable Design Awards. Designers and projects from around the world are eligible with the primary criterion being that they "contribute to the creation of a sustainable world."

For more information, visit the Boston Society of Architects on the Internet at *www.architects.org* or contact them at (617) 951-1433.

2005 Winners

Awards for Design
Artists' Studios and Gallery
Boston, MA
Arrowstreet

Felician Sisters Convent and High School
Coraopolis, PA
Perkins Eastman

Citation for Design
60 Oxford Street
Cambridge, MA
Perry Dean Rogers Partners Architects;
    Einhorn Yaffee Prescott

Unified Science Center, Swarthmore College
Swarthmore, PA
Einhorn Yaffee Prescott with Helfand
    Architecture

National Association of Realtors Headquarters
Washington, DC
Gund Partnership; SMB Architects

Boarding School
Southwest France
Pierre Tourre Architecte

Jury
Dan Arons, Architerra
Hillary Brown, New Civic Works
Lynne Deninger, Sasaki Associates
Bruce Fowle, Fox & Fowle Architects
Kevin Settlemyre, The Green Roundtable

Source: Boston Society of Architects

385

Did you know...

The Swiss Re Headquarters, London's first ecologically progressive skyscraper, unanimously won the Sterling Prize for the first time in the award's history for the building that has made the greatest contribution to British architecture in the past year.

Building with Trees Awards of Excellence

Through the Building with Trees Awards of Excellence, the National Arbor Day Foundation (in cooperation with the National Association of Home Builders and Firewise Communities) recognizes builders and developers who save trees during construction and land development. A jury of developers and urban forestry professionals judge the entries on criteria such as creativity and attention to protecting trees during planning, design, and construction; planting trees and implementing long-term care procedures; demonstrating a commitment to tree protection by including a certified tree-care professional on the development team; taking an inventory of existing trees and striving to preserve trees; and adherence to tree protection goals throughout the construction process.

For additional information, visit the National Arbor Day Foundation online at *www.arborday.org*.

2005 Winners

Residential Development, 26–100 Lots
Brookside Development
Westfield, IN
Langston Development Company

Residential Development, 101–500 Lots
Grande Dunes, Phase 1
Myrtle Beach, SC
Grande Dunes Development Company, LLC

Residential Development, 501 or More Lots
Serrano
El Dorado Hills, CA
Parker Development

Woodlands Edge
West Little Rock, AR
Rocket Properties

Nonresidential
Wal-Mart Supercenter
Oldsmar, FL
Wal-Mart Stores, Inc.

Jury
Steve Pearson, National Arbor Day Foundation
Daniel Green, The Green Company
Mark S. Jordan, Mark S. Jordan Companies
Ed Tombari, National Association of Home Builders

Source: National Arbor Day Foundation

The possession of charming natural scenery is a form of wealth as practical . . . as that of sewers, aqueducts, and pavements.

Frederick Law Olmsted

Cradle to Cradle Design Protocol

In 2002, McDonough Braungart Design Chemistry, the private sustainable product and process design consultancy cofounded by American architect William McDonough and German chemist Michael Braungart, formed a nonprofit organization called GreenBlue to disseminate its Cradle to Cradle Design Framework. As opposed to traditional cradle-to-grave production processes in which materials eventually are landfilled or incinerated, Cradle to Cradle (C2C) is a model of sustainable production in which all waste materials are productively reincorporated into new production and use phases, or closed loops. This eco-effective method of production seeks to solve rather than to merely manage the problems currently created by industry.

The Cradle to Cradle Design Protocol assesses materials used in products and processes based on the Intelligent Products System, designed by Michael Braungart and colleagues at the Environmental Protection Encouragement Agency. Materials in products are inventoried and evaluated and finally placed in one of four categories—green, yellow, orange, or red—based on human health and environmental relevance criteria.

Green: Little or no risk. The chemical is acceptable.

Yellow: Low to moderate risk. The chemical is acceptable for use in the desired application until a green alternative is found.

Orange: No indication of a high-risk chemical. However, a complete assessment is not possible due to lack of information.

Red: High risk. Red chemicals should be phased out as soon as possible and include all known or suspected carcinogens, endocrine disruptors, mutagens, reproductive toxins, and teratogens.

Following assessment, the materials in a product are optimized by selecting green category replacements for the red category substances as they become available.

More information about protocol and other Cradle to Cradle initiatives, including the Chemical Profiles Knowledge Base, can be obtained through GreenBlue at *www.greenblue.org* or (434) 817-1425.

Source: GreenBlue

Declaration of Interdependence for a Sustainable Future

Adopted by the International Union of Architects (UIA) at their 1993 World Congress of Architects, the Declaration of Interdependence for a Sustainable Future was developed over the course of the event by a core group of architects, with input from the thousands of design professionals in attendance. The theme of the Congress was "Architecture at the Crossroads: Designing for a Sustainable Future." The Declaration is a statement of commitment on behalf of design professionals worldwide to "place environmental and social sustainability at the core of our practice..." with an affirmation that these professionals "adopt a worldview which embraces individual and collective interdependence with the local and global environment as the basis of a New Design Paradigm of Environmental Interdependence." The declaration was signed by both the presidents of the UIA and the American Institute of Architects, Olufemi Majekodunmi and Susan A. Maxman. To promote the realization of the declaration's ideas, a set of principles (included below) and practices was also drafted as a supplement to the document.

The complete text of the declaration can be found on the UIA's Web site at *www.uia-architectes.org.*

Principles

Principle 1
Individually and collectively the members of the Architecture Profession will advise their clients and assist with the education of the broader community on the environmental implications of development trends, strategies, and policies.

Principle 2
The Architecture Profession will engage with local communities in formulating appropriate strategies and design guidelines for sustainable human settlement, which are economically and environmentally appropriate to their particular culture and place.

Principle 3
Architects will, through their work, seek to give full expression to a culture of interdependence with the environment.

Principle 4
Architects will advance ecologically sustainable development by contributing to and supporting appropriate designs, products, services and technologies.

Principle 5
Architects should promote the development of an ecologically sustainable future for the planet and ensure that development strategies, design concepts, and innovations which are consistent with, or improve the prospect of, ecological sustainability are made available globally, including to disadvantaged groups and nations, with appropriate mechanism to protect intellectual property.

Declaration of Interdependence
for a Sustainable Future

Principle 6

In developing ecologically sustainable building and settlement practices all sources of relevant knowledge and methods, including those of indigenous people, should be considered.

Principle 7

Architects should promote healthy and environmentally responsible living and behavioral patterns and develop designs and technologies in support of such lifestyles.

Principle 8

Architects will promote development strategies and projects which anticipate the needs and recognize the rights of present and future generations.

Principle 9

Architects will, through their practices, implement the International Conventions and Agreements for protection of the rights and well being of the earth and its peoples; the integrity and diversity of the Cultural Heritage, Monuments, and Sites; and the biodiversity, integrity, and sustainability of the global ecosystem.

Principle 10

The initial education and Continuing Professional Development of Architects should recognize the need for a wide range of knowledge and insights from the arts, culture and humanities, the natural and social sciences, and the technologies as a basis for understanding the behavior and management of ecological systems, and for creating ecologically sustainable forms of production, development, and settlement.

Source: International Union of Architects

389

Architecture is not millinery. Fashions pass by, buildings remain to become grim reminders of transient enthusiasms.

Edward Durell Stone

Dubai International Award for Best Practices in Improving the Living Environment

The United Nations' Human Settlements Programme (UN-HABITAT), in conjunction with the Municipality of Dubai, UAE, biennially awards the Dubai International Award for Best Practices in Improving the Living Environment to initiatives that have made outstanding contributions to improving the quality of life in cities and communities worldwide. The first Best Practices Award was presented in 1996 following an international conference on best practices held in Dubai. Each project is reviewed for its compliance with the three criteria for best practice: impact, partnership, and sustainability. The award is open to all organizations, including governments and public and private groups. Winners receive a $30,000 prize, trophy, and certificate. In addition, all entries are listed in a best practices database at *www.bestpractices.org* that contains more than 1,100 solutions to the common social, economic, and environmental problems of an urbanizing world.

For additional information, contact HABITAT at (212) 963-4200 or on the Internet at *www.bestpractices.org*.

2004 Winners

Urban Agriculture Programme
Rosario, Argentina

Tomorrow's Seeds, Human Development
and Urban Poverty Reduction
Aurá, Brazil

First Nations Community Planning project
Canada

Brownfield Remediation of the Tangshan
Southern Coal Mining Area
China

A Green Path to Sustainable Development
of Marginal Drylands
Iran

Sand dams for water for semi-arid lands
Kitui District, Kenya

IT4Youth
Palestine

The Alba-Ter Consortium: an inter-jurisdictional
commitment to sustainable development of
the River Ter Basin
Spain

Business development to reduce poverty and
unemployment
Togo

Poverty reduction among women through
vocational training and micro-credit
Uzbekistan

Dubai International Award for Best Practices in Improving the Living Environment

Special Commendation
Association for Forest Development
    and Conservation
Lebanon

Flying Circus
Mexico

Jury
Rod Hackney, chair (UK)
Pedro Alejandro Florian Borbon (Colombia)
Hussein Lootah (UAE)
Nie Meisheng (China)
Marie Claire Cordonier Segger (Canada)

Source: United Nations Human Settlements Programme

391

Did you know...

The Green Communities Initiative, a $500-million effort, will provide 8,500 green houses to low-income families across the United States by offering financial incentives and technical assistance to developers and working with local community-based building groups to build the homes.

ED+C Excellence in Design Awards

Environmental Design + Construction's Excellence in Design Awards celebrates buildings that demonstrate a commitment to green building and sustainable design. Any architect, interior designer, contractor, building owner, or engineer is eligible to submit projects completed within the previous two years. A jury of professionals reviews each entry for features such as energy efficiency, indoor air quality, water conservation, sustainable or recycled materials, site selection, and other green design features.

For additional information, visit ED+C on the Web at *www.edcmag.com*.

2005 Winners

Commercial, Office, Industrial, Multiuse or Corporate
Alberici Group Corporate Headquarters
Overland, MO
Mackey Mitchell Associates

Runners Up
Nusta Spa
Washington, DC
Envision

Stewart's Building
Baltimore, MD
Design Collective, Inc.

Interface Showroom and Offices
Atlanta, GA
TVS Interiors, Inc.

RadioShack Corporate Campus
Forth Worth, TX
HKS, Inc.

Institutional, Nonprofit, Educational, or Healthcare
Richard J. Lacks Sr. Cancer Center, Saint Mary's
  Health Care
Grand Rapids, MI
Trinity Design

Runners Up
Seminar II Building, Evergreen State College
Olympia, WA
Mahlum Architects

Artists for Humanity EpiCenter
Boston, MA
Arrowstreet Inc.

Urban Ecology Center
Milwaukee, WI
Kubala Washatko Architects, Inc.

Ramapo College Student Housing, Phase VIII
Mahwah, NJ
Paulus, Sokolowski, and Sartor

ED+C Excellence in Design Awards

Government
Southeast Regional Office Building,
Pennsylvania Department of Environmental
Protection
Norristown, PA
L. Robert Kimball & Associates

Runners Up
Carl T. Curtis Midwest Regional Headquarters
Building
Omaha, NE
Leo A Daly

Cambridge City Hall Annex
Cambridge, MA
HKT Architects Inc.

City of Seattle Police Support Facility
Seattle, WA
Donald King Architects; Turner Construction
Company

Sweetgrass–Coutts Port of Entry
Sweetgrass, MT–Coutts, AB, Canada
Kasian Architecture Interior Design and
Planning Ltd.

Multiuse Residential
Eastern Village Cohousing Condominium
Silver Spring, MD
Eco Housing Corp.; EDG Architects

Single-Family Residential Home
Eastern Sierra Residence for Suzanne Johnson
Douglas County, NV
Arkin Tilt Architects

Runners Up
Hatfield Residence
Gearhart, OR
Dick Baty, Inc.

Solar Umbrella
Venice, CA
Pugh and Scarpa Architects and Engineers

Courtyard Residence
Austin, TX
Antenora Architects

Xanterra Parks and Resorts, Yellowstone
National Park
Gardiner, MT
Xanterra Parks and Resorts

Jury
Michael Arny, Leonardo Academy
Rick Fedrizzi, USGBC
Robert B. Prud'homme, Robert B. Prud'homme
Design
Steven Winter, Steven Winter Associates, Inc.
Jerry Yudelson, Interface Engineering, Inc.
Diana Brown, *ED+C*
Michelle Clark Hucal, *ED+C*
Heather Jenkins, *ED+C*
Amanda Knox, *ED+C*
Elizabeth Obloy, *ED+C*

Source: Environmental Design + Construction

393

Environmental Stewardship Award

The Construction Specifications Institute multifaceted mission includes being "an integrating force in creating and sustaining the built environment and providing a gateway to education and training resources and the development and exchange of knowledge by: advancing the tools and practices of specifying and document-ing design and construction information; promoting education and certification of specifications and information management practitioners; expanding CSI's presence in the industry through cooperative alliances that advance construction documentation systems and processes." One way CSI addresses its mission is with the Environmental Stewardship Award. This award, (previously known as the Environmental Sensitivity Award) is presented to an individual, team, chapter, region, firm, or organization for demonstrating environmental stewardship by promoting environmental awareness in the construction industry, practicing sus-tainable environmental design, or educating others in the advantages of design-ing for sustainability.

394

For additional information about the Environmental Stewardship Award, visit CSI on the Web at *www.csinet.org*.

1996	BSW Green Team
1997	Ross G. Spiegel
1998	Sandra Mendler
1999	Paolo Soleri
2000	City of Scottsdale's Green Building Program
2001	LHB Engineers & Architects, Inc.
2002	Jonathan M. Miller
2003	Lord, Aeck, and Sargent, Inc. Sarah Nettleton Architects
2004	Cheryl C. Walker
2005	Mike Leonard

Source: Construction Specifications Institute

I believe that architects should design gardens to be used, as much as the houses they build, to develop a sense of beauty and the taste and inclination toward the fine arts and other spiritual values.

Luis Barragán

Green Building Leadership Awards

The US Green Building Council's Green Building Leadership Awards are presented in multiple categories that can include the Green Business Award to honor an individual or company that has advanced the green building market through innovation; the Green Public Service Award for significant contributions in advancing green building through changes in policies, codes, and other means by an individual or organization; the USGBC Leadership Award to recognize a leader in the USGBC and the industry for advancing the mission of the council; and the Local/Regional Leadership Award. The leading US coalition for the advancement of buildings that are environmentally responsible, profitable, and healthy, the US Green Building Council offers a variety of services including the industry-standard LEED Green Building Rating System™ (see page 402). Nominations for the Leadership Awards are made in August; awards are presented in November at the International Green Building Conference and Exposition.

For additional information, visit the US Green Building Council's Web site at *www.usgbc.org*.

395

2004 Winners

Local/Regional Leadership Award
Mithun Architects + Designers + Planners

Green Building Business Award
Herman Miller

Green Public Service Award— Government
Edward A. Feiner
US General Services Administration

USGBC Leadership Award
William D. Browning
Green Development Services,
    Rocky Mountain Institute

Source: US Green Building Council

Did you know...
Atlanta's 171 17th Street building, located in the urban Brownfield redevelopment project Atlanta Station, is the first LEED silver-certified high-rise office building in the world.

Green Roof Awards of Excellence

Green Roofs for Healthy Cities established the Green Roof Awards of Excellence to recognize green roof projects that exhibit extraordinary leadership in integrated design and implementation. The awards also increase general awareness of green roof infrastructure and the associated public and private benefits while recognizing the valuable contributions of green roof design professionals. Awards are granted in six categories, which apply to all types of buildings and installed green roof designs. In addition, the Green Roof Civic Award of Excellence honors a public servant for their outstanding contribution to their community and the development of the green roof industry.

For additional information, visit the Green Roofs for Healthy Cities' Web site at *www.greenroofs.org.*

2005 Winners

Extensive Residential
Yorktown Square Condominiums
Falls Church, VA
Building Logics, Inc.

Extensive Institutional
Evergreen State College
Olympia, WA
The Garland Company, Inc.; Mahlum Architects;
    Mark Cork and Brent Compton

Extensive Industrial/Commercial
Heinz 57 Center
Pittsburgh, PA
Roofscapes, Inc.; Burt Hill Kozar
    Rittlemann Associates

Intensive Residential
North Beach Place
San Francisco, CA
PGAdesigninc Landscape Architects;
    Barnhart Associates Architect

Intensive Institutional
Schwab Rehabilitation Hospital
Chicago, IL
American Hydrotech, Inc.; Stephen Rankin
    Associates; Douglas Hills Associates Inc.

Intensive Industrial/Commercial
Millennium Park
Chicago, IL
Terry Guen Design Associates, Inc.

Green Roof Civic Award of Excellence
Karen Moyer

Jury
Jeffrey L. Bruce, Jeffrey L. Bruce & Company
Paul Farmer, American Planning Association
Michael F. Gibbons, Architectural Systems, Inc.
Monica Kuhn, OAA Architect
Steven Peck, Green Roofs for Healthy Cities
Ed Snodgrass, Green Roof Plants
Bill Thompson, *Landscape Architecture* magazine

Source: Green Roofs for Healthy Cities

Green Roof Awards of Excellence

North Beach Place (above). The success of this new, mixed-use development rests on its two-acre green roof, which is comprised of courtyards of various sizes and shapes that provide stimulating outdoor opportunities for community gathering and relaxation. Photo courtesy of Green Roofs for Healthy Cities and PGAdesigninc Landscape Architects.

Heinz 57 Center (left). This project has demonstrated how green roofs can reduce the heat island effect and improve the habitability of urban office space in downtown Pittsburgh. Citing this flagship example, the mayor has been encouraged to introduce incentives for more urban green roof projects in the city. Photo courtesy of Green Roofs for Healthy Cities and Roofscapes Inc.

GreenBlue

GreenBlue began as a nexus of projects at McDonough Braungart Design Chemistry, the private sustainable product and process design consultancy cofounded by American architect William McDonough and German chemist Michael Braungart in 1995. MBDC developed the Cradle to Cradle Design Protocol (see page 387), and established the nonprofit GreenBlue in 2002 to disseminate Cradle to Cradle information and resources. Cradle to Cradle (C2C) promotes eco-effective production, where all products are constructed from nutrients that replenish the earth (biological nutrients) or nutrients that can be infinitely recycled (technical nutrients). The name GreenBlue refers to these two types of building blocks: biological nutrients (green) and technical nutrients (blue). In addition to developing the Cradle to Cradle Design Framework, MBDC has produced C2CSpec, the Chemical Profiles Knowledge Base, and the C2C Training Module. GreenBlue has made the C2C protocol available for general use.

Address —————————————————————
600 East Water Street, Suite C
Charlottesville, VA 22901
(434) 817-1424
www.greenblue.org

Mission Statement

GreenBlue's mission is to inspire a transformation in the design of human industry based on principles found in the productive systems of nature, making commercial activity an ecological and socially regenerative force.

Hannover Principles

After being selected to host the 2000 World's Fair "Humanity, Nature, and Technology," the city of Hannover, Germany commissioned renowned sustainable design leader William McDonough to develop a set of guiding design principles for the event. In conjunction with Michael Braungart and the Environmental Protection Encouragement Agency in Hamburg, Germany, William McDonough Architects produced a list of issues inherent to sustainable design that has become a fundamental primer in its philosophy and practice. Universally recognized as a seminal expression on environmentally intelligent design, the Hannover Principles have inspired and influenced a wide array of works and documents, ranging from the International Union of Architects' Declaration of Interdependence to the US General Services Administration's Guidelines for Sustainability.

The principles conclude with the statement: "The Hannover Principles should be seen as a living document committed to the transformation and growth in the understanding of our interdependence with nature, so that they may adapt as our knowledge of the world evolves."

To read the full text of the principles, go to *www.mcdonough.com/principles.pdf.*

Principles

1. **Insist on rights of humanity and nature to co-exist** in a healthy, supportive, diverse, and sustainable condition.

2. **Recognize interdependence.** The elements of human design interact with and depend upon the natural world, with broad and diverse implications at every scale. Expand design considerations to recognize even distant effects.

3. **Respect relationships between spirit and matter.** Consider all aspects of human settlement including community, dwelling, industry, and trade in terms of existing and evolving connections between spiritual and material consciousness.

4. **Accept responsibility for the consequences of design,** decisions upon human well-being, the viability of natural systems, and their right to co-exist.

5. **Create safe objects of long-term value.** Do not burden future generations with requirements for maintenance or vigilant administration of potential design due to the careless creation of products, processes, or standards.

6. **Eliminate the concept of waste.** Evaluate and optimize the full life-cycle of products and processes to approach the state of natural systems, in which there is no waste.

Hannover Principles

7. Rely on natural energy flows. Human designs should, like the living world, derive their creative forces from perpetual solar income. Incorporate this energy efficiently and safely or responsible use.

8. Understand the limitations of design. No human creation lasts forever, and design does not solve all problems. Those who create and plan should practice humility in the face of nature. Treat nature as a model or mentor, not as an inconvenience to be evaded or controlled.

9. Seek constant improvement by the sharing of knowledge. Encourage direct and open communication between colleagues, patrons, manufacturers, and users to link long-term sustainable considerations with ethical responsibility, and re-establish the integral relationship between natural processes and human activity.

Source: William McDonough + Partners

400

In a world in which we are the irresponsible stewards of nature, it is our own nature, rather than the wildest extremity of the natural world, that is the frontier where the civilizing has to begin.

Suzannah Lessard

Joslyn Castle Institute for Sustainable Communities

Housed in the historic 1902 Joslyn Castle in Omaha, NE, the Joslyn Castle Institute for Sustainable Communities is a partnership among Nebraska state government, the Joslyn Art Museum, the University of Nebraska College of Architecture, and other public and private organizations. The institute focuses on promoting sustainable development through outreach and educational programs and research. Its goal is to encourage communities to develop by balancing economic, social, and environmental needs. The institute is one of 18 centers worldwide in partnership with the United Nations Centre for Human Settlement in its Best Practices in Local Leadership Program.

Address
3902 Davenport Street
Omaha, NE 68131
(402) 595-1902
www.ecospheres.org

401

Mission Statement

The Joslyn Castle's mission is to search for connections and relationships among issues of land, water, populations and culture, technology, and the environment; to promote an integrated approach to sustainability through dialogue, visioning, partnership, and coordination; to bring a design approach not only to improving the living environment but also to an integrated decision-making process; to promote public participation to create and work toward a shared vision for the future; to facilitate learning from and the transfer of best practices for improving the living environment; and to develop indicators of sustainability and to monitor our progress.

LEED™ Green Building Rating System

The LEED (Leadership in Energy and Environmental Design) Green Building Rating System™ is a voluntary national standard for developing sustainable buildings that was developed by members of the US Green Building Council. The system establishes a common set of measurements for green building and provides a framework for assessing building performance and meeting sustainability goals. LEED emphasizes state-of-the-art strategies for sustainable site development, water conservation, energy efficiency, materials selection, and indoor environmental quality. Project certification, professional accreditation, training, and resources are all a part of the LEED program. LEED standards are currently available or under development for new construction, major renovation projects, existing building operations, commercial interiors projects, core and shell projects, homes, and neighborhood development.

For more information on the LEED program, visit the USGBC's Web site at *www.usgbc.org* or call (202) 828-7422.

402

Did you know...

On April 8, 2005, the Washington state governor signed a law requiring the use of the LEED rating system for state-funded projects larger than 5,000 square feet and for major renovations. Although Washington is the first to pass such a law, several other states, counties, and municipalities currently have policies that require or encourage the use of LEED, and a number of states are currently drafting similar legislation.

Nantucket Principles: A Policy Agenda for Architecture and Design Firms on Green and Sustainable Design

Sept. 28–30, 2002, 85 design firm professionals and A/E/C leaders gathered in Nantucket, MA, for the Design Futures Council's Architects' Environment Summit. The think-tank session focused on analyzing, discussing, and debating the trends and issues that will influence green building and sustainable design over the next three years. During the event, participants developed an action agenda to equip firms and organizations of all sizes with a recommended strategy to facilitate the successful movement forward in green and sustainable design.

What follows was authored and unanimously agreed upon by the delegates of the Design Futures Council at the Architects' Environment Summit, Nantucket, MA, September 2002.

Current practices in the design and construction of the built environment are contributing to our accelerating environmental crises. The architecture, engineering, and interior design professions and their clients are a critical part of the solutions–solutions that point to a bright, alternative future. Recognizing the fragility of our environment, design firms and clients should redefine themselves

- to engage,
- to listen,
- to learn,
- to educate, and
- to act toward a strong sustainable model.

It is time to operate under a new paradigm, a new set of values, a new set of ethics, and with new awareness of the impact of design.

Under these Nantucket Principles, design and construction organizations commit to the principles of sustainable development, including:

- environmental awareness,
- social/cultural equity,
- economic fitness,
- public policy, and
- technological ingenuity.

Design excellence shall incorporate, by definition, the meeting of sustainable principles. We believe that there is no conflict between sustainability and the art of architecture and design.

Our future and our solutions start here...today.
- It is time to redefine our conscience and look toward expansion.
- We must expand our view of the client to include tomorrow's child.
- We must expand our obligations to include the health of the public environment and the planet.
- We must expand our consideration of the community, site, and space to always include the larger systems and influences.

We will integrate these models of sustainability in our future work:

- Sustainable Development is that which meets all the needs of the present without compromising the ability of future generations to meet their own needs.*
- Design for Sustainability requires awareness of the full short- and long-term consequences of any transformation of the environment. Sustainable design is the conception and realization of environmentally sensitive and

Nantucket Principles

responsible expression as a part of the evolving matrix of nature.[†]

An action agenda...the next steps for architecture and design professionals and firms:

- Lead with vision and integrity.
- Hold a sustainable conference in your office to educate and empower your employees.
- Develop a plan of action for your firm's sustainable agenda.
- Mandate firm and staff accountability toward sustainable action.
- Empower internal champions to mentor staff and external champions to guide the firm to day-to-day sustainable action.
- Build a Knowledge Base on sustainability within your firm.
- Encourage your staff and fellow principals to actively participate in organizations that support green values.
- Identify measurements of success: life cycles, issues, user success, durability, connection to the larger community.

Broaden the profession:

- Become a more responsible professional and adopt the role of sustainable design educator within your firm, with your clients, and in your community.
- Engage with design schools and listen to student perspectives about sustainability.
- Communicate the benefits of sustainability to the client and community at large, including research, shared knowledge, and case studies.
- Connect with fellow design professionals, schools, and other contributors to the industry to plan future directions toward sustainability.
- Develop a process which points to a holistic approach to sustainability that involves all disciplines (i.e. community, public sector) and seemingly unrelated or unexpected disciplines that can add value.

Redefine success goals in terms of service:

- To the users.
- To the community.
- To your clients.

Collaborate with leaders in your region to align larger development strategies that are more in line with sustainable principles, including:

- Transit/development solutions.
- Preservation of larger natural eco-systems.
- Commitment to existing urban centers.
- Reducing dependence on fossil fuel.
- Promote the development and use of ecological sustainable building products and components.

Envision your future victory and celebrate each increment of success. Sustainability is now clearly an ethical issue for us as professionals. It shall be reflected in all of our future work.

Authored and unanimously agreed upon by the delegates of the Design Futures Council at the Architects' Environment Summit, Nantucket, MA, September 2002.

[*] From the U.N. Brundtland Commission, 1987.
[†] Part of the Hannover Principles, 1992.

Source: Design Futures Council

404

National Award for Smart Growth Achievement

Through the National Award for Smart Growth Achievement, the US Environmental Protection Agency recognizes public entities that promote and achieve smart growth, thus creating better places, bringing about direct and indirect environmental benefits. Smart growth development practices support national environmental goals by preserving open spaces (including parkland) and protecting critical habitat; improving transportation choices (including walking, bicycling, and transit), which reduces automobile emissions; promoting brownfield redevelopment; and reducing impervious surfaces, which improves water quality. The competition is open to local and state governments and other public-sector entities. Nonprofit or private organizations or individuals are not eligible for the award; however, their participation will be acknowledged when collaborating with a governmental or public-sector entity.

For additional information about the National Award for Smart Growth Achievement, contact the EPA at (202) 272-0167 or visit their Web site at *www.epa.gov.*

405

2004 Awards

Overall Excellence in Smart Growth
Town of Davidson
Town of Davidson Planning Department
Davidson, NC

Built Projects
Southside Neighborhood
City of Greensboro, Department of Housing
    and Community Development
Greensboro, NC

Policies and Regulations
Accessory Dwelling Unit Program
City of Santa Cruz, Department of Housing
    and Community Development
Santa Cruz, CA

Community Outreach and Education
Sacramento Region Blueprint:
    Transportation/Land Use Study
Sacramento Area Council of Governments
Sacramento Region, CA

Small Communities
San Juan Pueblo Master Plan
San Juan Pueblo Office of the Governor
San Juan, NM

Source: US Environmental Protection Agency

National Green Building Awards

The National Association of Home Builders presents the annual Green Building Awards in conjunction with the annual National Green Building Conference. The awards recognize leaders in the advancement of the green-home building industry and showcase resource-efficient designs. A jury of industry professions selects the winning entries except the Outstanding Green Product Award, which is selected by conference attendees as the project that has had the greatest impact on advancing the cause of resource-efficient home construction.

For more information about the National Green Building Awards or the National Green Building Conference, call the NAHB conference line at (888) 602-4663 or visit their Web site at *www.nahb.org*.

2005 Recipients

406

Green Advocate of the Year: Builder
Pam Sessions
Hedgewood Properties

Green Advocate of the Year: Group/Organization
Building America program,
    US Department of Energy

Green Advocate of the Year: Individual
Mark Kelly
Building Science Engineering

Green Advocate of the Year: Remodeling
Carl Seville
Sawhorse Construction

Green Project of the Year: Affordable Multifamily
Felician Sisters Convent and School
Coraopolis, PA
Perkins Eastman Architects

Green Project of the Year: Custom
Cannon Beach Cottage
Cannon Beach, OR
Nathan Good with Rich Elstrom Construction

Green Project of the Year: Luxury Multifamily
Eastern Village Cohousing Condominiums
Silver Springs, MD
Eco Housing Corporation with Poretsky Builders

Green Project of the Year: Production
Veridian Homes
Madison, WI

Green Project of the Year: Remodeling
Historic 1915 home
Dallas, TX
RS Lawrence Construction

Green Program of the Year
California Green Builder

Outstanding Green Marketing Award
Venetian Golf and River Club
WCI Communities
Bonita Springs, FL

Source: National Association of Home Builders

Phoenix Awards

The Phoenix Award was created in 1997 to recognize excellence in brownfield redevelopment by honoring individuals and groups who are working to solve the critical environmental challenge of transforming abandoned industrial sites into productive new uses. One winner is selected from each of the Environmental Protection Agency's 10 regions. Additional special winners may also be selected, including projects that have had a significant impact on small communities. Winners receive a crystal trophy handcrafted by a Steuben Glass-trained artisan, in addition to international publicity. The awards are open to any individual, group, company, organization, government body, or agency. Criteria for the award include the magnitude of the project, innovative techniques, solutions to regulatory issues, and impact upon the community.

For more information on the Phoenix Awards, visit *www.phoenixawards.org* or contact the Phoenix Awards team at (717) 761-0544.

407

2005 Winners

Region 1
Save the Bay Project
Providence, RI

Region 2
Rheingold Brewery
Redevelopment Project
Brooklyn, NY

Region 3
Chester Waterfront
Redevelopment Project
Chester, PA

Region 4
Johnnie Ruth-Clarke Health
Center
St. Petersburg, FL

Region 5
Phalen Corridor
St. Paul, MN

Region 6
Pinnacle Park Redevelopment
Project
Dallas, TX

Region 7
Port of Dubuque
Dubuque, IA

Region 8
Platt River Commons and Salt
Creek Heights Business
Center
Casper, WY

Region 9
Petco Park and East Village
Redevelopment Project
San Diego, CA

Region 10
Rainier Court
Seattle, WA

Community Impact
Mountain Pine Pressure
Treating Site
Plainview, AR

Community Impact
Chesterfield Square
Los Angeles, CA

**Community Impact –
UST Winner**
Rosalia Visitor Resource and
Interpretive Center
Rosalia, WA

**Community Impact–
Mine Scarred Lands**
ARD&Art Project
Johnstown, PA

Source: Phoenix Award

SBIC Awards

The Sustainable Buildings Industry Council Awards have been granted annually since 2001 in two categories. The Best Sustainable Practice Award, open to all SBIC members, honors the exceptional contributions SBIC members are making to sustainability across the United States. The Exemplary Sustainable Building Award recognizes institutional, residential, and government buildings that demonstrate the successful application of the whole-building design approach. Each winning project offers valuable lessons, fostering the movement toward more sustainable buildings. All building design professionals, including SBIC members and non-members, are eligible to compete in this category.

For more information, visit the SBIC on the Internet at *www.sbicouncil.org* or contact them at (202) 628-7400.

2004 Best Sustainable Practice Awards Recipients

Sustainable Policy/Program Initiatives
Massachusetts Technology Collaborative

Sustainable Research, Development,
   Construction Process, and Demonstration
The Trane Company

Educational Initiatives
CTG Energetics, Inc.

Special Achievement in Communications
Environmental Design + Construction magazine

Honorable Mention
Stimulating Demand through Increased
   Consumer Awareness
Yuma Proving Ground, U.S. Army

2004 Exemplary Building Awards Recipients

First Place
Center for Neighborhood Technology
Chicago, IL
Farr Associates Architecture and Urban Design

Second Place
Clearview Elementary School
Hanover, PA
L. Robert Kimball and Associates

Third Place
Herman Miller MarketPlace
Zeeland, MI
Integrated Architecture

Honorable Mentions
Michael E. Capuano Early Childhood Center
Somerville, MA
HMFH Architects

Blach and Egan Schools Joint-Use Gymnasiums
Los Alto, CA
Gelfand RNP Architects

Jury
Cathy Barranger, EDAW, Inc.
Greg Crawford, Cool Metal Roofing Coalition
Alex Wilson, BuildingGreen Inc.
Mark Zoeteman, Fishbeck, Thompson, Carr & Huber, Inc.

Source: Sustainable Buildings Industry Council

Sustainable Buildings Industry Council

Since its founding in 1980 by the major building trade associations, the Sustainable Buildings Industry Council (originally named the Passive Solar Industries Council) has provided answers to the sustainability needs of its members, which include organizations, agencies, and individuals such as design professionals, home builders, utilities, consultants, product and material manufacturers and suppliers, universities, academics, students, as well as many other practicing professions and interested individuals. While still remaining a strong supporter of passive solar strategies and technology-driven building solutions, SBIC focuses on whole-building design committed to strategies that are both environmentally responsible (e.g. low-energy, climate-responsive, and using minimal fossil fuels and cleaner, renewable energy) while meeting other design objectives related to aesthetics, accessibility, cost effectiveness, flexibility, high productivity, and security.

Address
1112 16th Street NW, Suite 240
Washington, DC 20036
(202) 628-7400
www.sbicouncil.org

409

Mission Statement

The Sustainable Buildings Industry Council is an independent, nonprofit organization whose mission is to advance the design, affordability, energy performance, and environmental soundness of America's buildings.

Sustainable Design Leadership Awards

The annual Sustainable Design Leadership Awards are presented jointly by the International Interior Design Association, the American Institute of Architects' Interiors Committee, and CoreNet Global. The first award category honors an individual or firm who has demonstrated a commitment to environmental issues in the design profession; the second category recognizes a corporation(s) or organization(s) that has established sustainable business operations and practices, which include architecture and interior design. Companies servicing the interior design and furnishings industry are not eligible.

Additional information is available on the IIDA's Web site at *www.iida.org*.

2001
Sandra F. Mendler
Ford Motor Company

2002
Penny S. Bonda
Verizon Communications

2003
Mithun Architects + Designers + Planners
Toyota Motor Sales
Primary Industries and Resources

Special Commendation
Hellmuth, Obata & Kassabaum
Fox & Fowle Architects

2004
Environmental Home Center, Seattle
Hugh L. Carey Battery Park City Authority
BNIM Architects
ABN AMRO

Source: International Interior Design Association

We should learn from the snail: it has devised a home that is both exquisite and functional.

Frank Lloyd Wright

410

Sustainable/Green Design Timeline

As the effects of industrialized society are increasingly blamed for erosion of the planet's health and the quality of life for its inhabitants, the green movement in the A/E/C industry continues to gain momentum. The following timeline traces the significant moments in the development of sustainable/green design.

1871 The Chicago Fire stimulates uniform municipal building codes and ordinances.

1890s William T. Love purchases land in New York for a proposed hydroelectric power project; a century later Love Canal becomes the poster child for hazardous waste cleanup.

1892 The Sierra Club is founded on May 28.

1893 The Colombian Exposition (Chicago World's Fair) celebrates the dawn of the Industrial Revolution.

1916 New York City passes the first ordinance for separation of land-use zones.

1936 Frank Lloyd Wright develops his concept of Broad Acres to accommodate the automobile.

The Urban Land Institute is founded.

1939 Shell Oil and General Motors exhibit their "City of Tomorrow" at the New York World's Fair.

1946 Henry Dreyfus exhibits his "unlimited growth" plan for Toledo, OH.

1947 The Levitt brothers open the first development of subdivision housing built for speculation.

1956 The US Interstate Highway system is opened, justified on the basis of national defense.

1960 The Organization of the Petroleum Exporting Countries (OPEC) is formed by Iran, Iraq, Kuwait, Saudi Arabia, and Venezuela.

The Pruitt Igo public housing in St. Louis, MO, is razed after winning architectural awards.

1962 Rachel Carson publishes *Silent Spring*.

1969 The Apollo Space Program provides distant images of the whole Earth.

1970s Robert Davis inherits 80 acres of Gulf-front Florida Panhandle property from his grandfather that will eventually become Seaside.

1970 The First Earth Day is celebrated on April 22.

The Nixon administration forms the Environmental Protection Agency.

The Clean Air Act establishes emission standards.

1972 The first United Nations Conference on the Human Environment is held in Stockholm, Sweden.

1973 The Endangered Species Act protects plant and animal environments.

1977 President Jimmy Carter calls energy conservation "the moral equivalent of war," calling the United States "the most wasteful nation on Earth."

The Clean Water Act is passed.

411

Sustainable/Green Design Timeline

1978 The Love Canal contamination is discovered; 11 years of cleanup later, the land is declared habitable again.

1979 Portland, OR, establishes an urban growth boundary to prevent the "ravenous rampage of suburbia."

1980 The Superfund is established.

1982 The Energy and Environmental Building Association is formed.

1985 A team of British scientists report that there is a hole in the ozone layer over the Antarctic.

1988 The AIA Committee on the Environment is formed.

1989 The Exxon Valdez spills 11 million gallons of crude oil, resulting in a $1-billion criminal penalty.

1990 The Washington State Growth Management Act requires fast-growing areas to create comprehensive, coordinated plans for future development.

1991 Austin, TX, starts the first organized green building program.

1992 Wendy E. Brawer creates the Green Apple Map for New York City, and global effort follows (www.greenmap.org).

Environmental Building News publishes its first issue.

The US Department of Energy publishes a rating system (0–100) for home energy efficiency, with 100 being a home that is completely energy self-sufficient.

1993 The US Green Building Council is formed.

The Rural Studio begins designing and building houses under the direction of Auburn University professors Samuel Mockbee and Dennis K. Ruth.

The Declaration of Interdependence for a Sustainable Future is signed by Olufemi Majekodunmi and Susan A. Maxman, presidents of the International Union of Architects and the American Institute of Architects.

1994 The EPA launches its Brownfields reclamation program.

Seattle announces a 20-year urban growth plan to limit sprawl.

1996 General Motors unveils its battery-powered EV-1 electric car.

The United Nations stages the second Habitat Conference in Istanbul and launches the global Best Practices Program for Sustainable Communities; it concurrently establishes the biennial Dubai Award.

William McDonough receives the Presidential Award for Sustainable Development.

The University of Virginia launches the Institute of Sustainable Design.

The Kyoto Protocol limits emissions of greenhouse gases from industrialized countries.

Architect John Hermannsson publishes the *Green Building Resource Guide* with cost comparison for choosing a green vs. conventional products.

The American Planning Association publishes *Best Development Practices: Doing the Right Thing and Making Money at the Same Time.*

412

Sustainable/Green Design Timeline

1998 The Energy Star Commercial Buildings program begins.

The AIA Committee on the Environment grants it first annual Top 10 Green Projects awards.

The Sierra Club releases *The Dark Side of the American Dream*, listing the 20 cities most endangered by sprawl.

2000 New York becomes the first state to promote green building through tax credits.

The SmithGroup's Phillip Merrill Environmental Center for the Chesapeake Bay Foundation (Annapolis, MD) is the first project to achieve platinum status in the LEED Green Building Rating System™.

2001 The IIDA awards first annual Sustainable Design Leadership Award.

2002 The UN World Summit on Sustainable Development is held in Johannesburg, South Africa.

R.S. Means publishes the first estimating handbook for Green Building.

2003 William McDonough launches the GreenBlue organization as a means to openly share his accumulated knowledge on sustainable design.

Source: DesignIntelligence

413

Did you know...

With a $20,000 grant from the Chesapeake Bay Foundation, the American Society of Landscape Architects is installing a green roof on its Washington, DC, headquarters to emphasize the positive ecological and environmental impacts of green-roof technology and encourage green-roof installations throughout the city.

Top Green Projects

The Top Green Projects are selected by the American Institute of Architects' Committee on the Environment to highlight viable architectural design solutions that protect and enhance the environment. COTE represents architects who are committed to making environmental considerations and sustainable design integral to their practice. The following projects address one or more significant environmental challenges such as energy and water conservation, use of recycled construction materials, and designs that improve indoor air quality. Responsible use of building materials, use of daylight over artificial lighting, designs that produce efficiency in heating or cooling, and overall sensitivity to local environmental issues were some of the reasons COTE selected these projects.

To view photographs and descriptions, visit *www.aiatopten.org* on the Internet.

2005 Green Projects

Eastern Sierra Residence
Gardnerville, NV
Arkin Tilt Architects

The Barn at Fallingwater
Mill Run, PA
Bohlin Cywinski Jackson

Rinker Hall at the University of Florida
Gainesville, FL
Croxton Collaborative Architects and
    Gould Evans Associates

Pittsburgh Glass Center
Pittsburgh, PA
Davis Gardner Gannon Pope Architecture
    and Bruce Lindsey

Austin Resource Center for the Homeless
Austin, TX
LZT Architects

Seminar II Building, Evergreen State College
Olympia, WA
Mahlum Architects

Monika A. and Charles A. Heimbold Jr. Visual
    Arts Center, Sarah Lawrence College
Bronxville, NY
Polshek Partnership Architects

Leslie Shao-ming Sun Field Station
Woodside, CA
Rob Wellington Quigley

Special Commendation
Lloyd Crossing Sustainable Urban Design Plan
Portland, OR
Mithun Architects + Designers + Planners

Jury
Robert Berkebile, BNIM Architects
Susan A. Maxman, Susan Maxman & Partners,
    Architects
Daniel H. Nall, Flack + Kurtz, Inc.
Henry I. Siegel, Siegel & Strain Architects
Deborah Snoonian, *Architectural Record*

Source: American Institute of Architects

Top 10 Green Building Products of the Year

BuildingGreen, publisher of the *GreenSpec Directory* and *Environmental Building News*, annually presents the Top 10 Green Building Products of the Year award. The award recognizes outstanding products added to the *GreenSpec Directory* during the past year. With more than 250 new products appearing each year in the 1,700-plus product directory, these prize winners represent a wide range of materials, products, and equipment that can help reduce the environmental impact of a building. Products are selected for inclusion in the directory by the editors of *Environmental Building News* based on criteria the panel have developed over nearly a decade. Manufacturers do not pay to be listed in *GreenSpec,* and neither *GreenSpec* nor *Environmental Building News* carries advertising. Winners are announced each year at the Green Building Council conference and trade show.

For additional information about the awards, visit BuildingGreen on the Internet at *www.buildinggreen.com* or call (802) 257-7300.

415

2004 Winners

ECO™ I Paver
EP Henry

TimberSIL Nontoxic Pressure-treated Wood
Timber Treatment Technologies

FSC-Certified Framing Lumber and Plywood
Potlatch Corporation

Ethos Carpet-Cushion Backing
Tandus/C&A Floorcoverings

EcoVeil TPO Interior Shade Screening
MechoShade Systems, Inc.

Photovol Glass PV Glazing Panels
MSK Corporation

Winston Series CPC Solar Water Heating
    Collector
Solargenix

EcoSpace Elevator
KONE

FlushMate IV Pressure-Assist Toilet Flush
    Mechanism
Sloan Valve Company

Cold Climate Heat Pump
Nyle Special Products

Source: BuildingGreen

Respect is an important matter regarding quality of design. Always keep the user aspects in mind.

Björn Dahlström

US Green Building Council

The US Green Building Council was formed in 1993 to integrate, educate, and provide leadership for building industry leaders, environmental groups, designers, retailers, and building owners as they strive to develop and market products and services that are environmentally progressive and responsible. The council includes more than 4,000 worldwide organizations with a common interest in green building practices, technologies, policies, and standards. Their most visible program, the LEED™ Green Building Rating System, is a voluntary, consensus-based rating system for commercial buildings to provide a national standard on what constitutes a green building and market incentives to build green.

Address ————————————————

1015 18th Street NW, Suite 805
Washington, DC 20036
(202) 828-7422
www.usgbc.org

416

Mission Statement

The US Green Building Council is the nation's foremost coalition of leaders from across the building industry working to promote buildings that are environmentally responsible, profitable, and healthy places to live and work.

Design & Historic Preservation

This chapter highlights many of the organizations that assist individuals, communities, and professionals in their preservation efforts as well as advocacy programs that alert the public to historic resources in imminent danger of being lost. Preservation award programs and their current winners are also included, along with the results of the annual Most Popular Historic House Museums ranking.

Abbott Lowell Cummings Award

The Abbott Lowell Cummings Award is presented annually by the Vernacular Architecture Forum to honor outstanding books published about North American vernacular architecture and landscapes. A review committee prioritizes submissions based on new information, the role of fieldwork in research, critical approach, and the model provided in writing and research methods. A founder of the VAF, Abbott Lowell Cummings was a prolific researcher and writer, best known for his magnum opus *The Framed Houses of Massachusetts Bay, 1625-1725* (1979).

For more information, visit VAF online at *www.vernaculararchitectureforum.org*.

1983

"'In a Manner and Fashion Suitable to Their Degree': An Investigation of the Material Culture of Early Rural Pennsylvania," in *Working Papers from the Regional Economic History Research Center, Vol. 5 No. 1*, by Jack Michel

1984

No award granted

1985

Big House, Little House, Back House, Barn: The Connected Farm Buildings of New England by Thomas Hubka (University Press of New England)

1986

Hollybush by Charles Martin (University of Tennessee Press)

1987

Holy Things and Profane: Anglican Parish Churches in Colonial Virginia by Dell Upton (Architectural History Foundation)

1988

Architecture and Rural Life in Central Delaware, 1700–1900 by Bernard L. Herman (University of Tennessee Press)

1989

Study Report for Slave Quarters Reconstruction at Carter's Grove by the Colonial Williamsburg Foundation

Study Report for the Bixby House Restoration by Old Sturbridge Village

1990

Manhattan for Rent, 1785–1850 by Elizabeth Blackmar (Cornell University Press)

Building the Octagon by Orlando Rideout (American Institute of Architects Press)

1991

Architects and Builders in North Carolina by Catherine Bishir, Charlotte Brown, Carl Lounsbury, and Ernest Wood, III (University of North Carolina Press)

1992

Alone Together: A History of New York's Early Apartments by Elizabeth Cromley (Cornell University Press)

A Place to Belong, Community, Order and Everyday Space in Calvert, Newfoundland by Gerald Pocius (University of Georgia Press)

421

Abbott Lowell Cummings Award

1993

Homeplace: The Social Use and Meaning of the Folk Dwelling in Southwestern North Carolina by Michael Ann Williams (University of Georgia Press)

The Park and the People: A History of Central Park by Roy Rosenzweig and Elizabeth Blackmar (Cornell University Press)

1994

The Stolen House by Bernard L. Herman (University Press of Virginia)

1995

Living Downtown: The History of Residential Hotels in the United States by Paul Groth (University of California Press)

1996

An Illustrated Glossary of Early Southern Architecture and Landscape by Carl Lounsbury (Oxford University Press)

1997

Unplanned Suburbs: Toronto's American Tragedy, 1900–1950 by Richard Harris (Johns Hopkins University Press)

1998

City Center to Regional Mall: Architecture, the Automobile, and Retailing in Los Angeles, 1920–1950 by Richard Longstreth (MIT Press)

1999

The Myth of Santa Fe: Creating a Modern Regional Tradition by Chris Wilson (University of New Mexico Press)

Architecture of the United States by Dell Upton (Oxford University Press)

2000

Delta Sugar: Louisiana's Vanishing Plantation Landscape by John B. Rehder (Johns Hopkins University Press)

Honorable Mention

Cheap, Quick & Easy: Imitative Architectural Materials, 1870–1930 by Pamela H. Simpson (University of Tennessee Press)

Building Community, Keeping the Faith: German Catholic Vernacular Architecture in a Rural Minnesota Parish by Fred W. Peterson (Minnesota Historical Society Press)

2001

Vernacular Architecture by Henry Glassie (Indiana University Press)

2002

The Patina of Place: The Cultural Weathering of a New England Landscape by Kingston William Heath (University of Tennessee Press)

2003

Theaters of Conversion: Religious Architecture and Indian Artisans in Colonial Mexico by Samuel Y. Edgerton (University of New Mexico Press)

2004

A River and Its City: The Nature of Landscape in New Orleans by Ari Kelman (University of California Press)

2005

Temple of Grace: The Material Transformation of Connecticut's Churches, 1790–1840 by Gretchen Buggeln (University Press of New England

Source: Vernacular Architecture Forum

America's 11 Most Endangered Historic Places

Every June the National Trust for Historic Preservation, in conjunction with the History Channel, compiles a list of the 11 most threatened historic sites in the United States. Since 1988, the 11 Most Endangered List has highlighted more than 175 historic buildings, sites, and landscapes threatened by neglect, deterioration, insufficient funds, inappropriate development, or insensitive public policy. While being listed does not guarantee protection or financial support, in the past the attention generated by the program has brought a broader awareness to the country's diminishing historic resources and generated local support for the threatened sites.

For photos and a history of each site, visit the National Trust's Web site at *www.nationaltrust.org/11most/*.

2005 America's 11 Most Endangered Historic Places

Belleview Biltmore Hotel
Belleair, FL

Camp Security
York County, PA

Daniel Webster Farm
Franklin, NH

Eleutherian College
Madison, IN

Ennis-Brown House
Los Angeles, CA

Finca Vigía (Ernest Hemingway House)
San Francisco de Paula, Cuba

Historic Buildings of Downtown Detroit
Detroit, MI

Historic Catholic Churches of Greater Boston
Boston, MA

King Island
Alaska

National Landscape Conservation System
Alaska, Arizona, California, Colorado, Idaho,
   Montana, Nevada, New Mexico, Oregon,
   Utah, Washington, Wyoming

The Journey Through Hallowed Ground
   Corridor
Maryland, Pennsylvania, Virginia

4B

Did you know...

Listed on the 2000 Most Endangered Places List, the exterior of Lincoln Cottage in Washington, DC, the most significant historic site directly linked to the Lincoln presidency other than the White House, recently underwent a complete restoration.

Antoinette Forrester Downing Book Award

The Society of Architectural Historians annually grants the Antoinette Forrester Downing Book Award to an author for an outstanding publication in the field of historic preservation. Works published in the two years prior to the award are eligible.

For more information contact the SAH at (312) 573-1365 or visit their Web site at *www.sah.org.*

1987

Providence, A Citywide Survey of Historic Resources by William McKenzie Woodward and Edward F. Sanderson (Rhode Island Historic Preservation Commission)

1990

East Cambridge: A Survey of Architectural History in Cambridge by Susan E. Maycock (MIT Press)

1991

Somerset: An Architectural History by Paul Baker Touart (Maryland Historical Trust and Somerset County Historical Trust)

1994

The Buried Past: An Archaeological History of Philadelphia by John L. Cotter (University of Pennsylvania Press)

1995

Along the Seaboard Side: the Architectural History of Worcester County, Maryland by Paul Baker Touart (Worcester County)

1996

The Historic Architecture of Wake County, North Carolina by Kelly A. Lally (Wake County Government)

1997

A Guide to the National Road and The National Road by Karl B. Raitz (Johns Hopkins University Press)

1998

A Guide to the Historic Architecture of Eastern North Carolina by Catherine W. Bishir & Michael T. Southern (University of North Carolina Press)

1999

No award granted

2000

Boston's Changeful Times by Michael Holleran (Johns Hopkins University Press)

2001

Preserving Cultural Landscapes in America by Arnold R. Alanen and Robert Z. Melnick, editors (John Hopkins University Press)

2002

A Building History of Northern New England by James Garvin (University Press of New England)

2003

No award granted

2004

Restoring Women's History Through Historic Preservation by Gail Lee Dubrow and Jennifer B. Goodman, eds. (Johns Hopkins University Press and New Hampshire Preservation Alliance)

2005

A Richer Heritage: Historic Preservation in the Twenty-First Century by Robert E. Stipe (North Carolina University Press)

Source: Society for Architectural Historians

Crowninshield Award

The National Trust for Historic Preservation's highest honor, the Louise DuPont Crowninshield Award, recognizes an individual or organization who has demonstrated extraordinary lifetime achievement in the preservation of America's heritage. Winners are selected by the Preservation Committee of the National Trust's board of trustees.

For more information, contact the National Trust at (800) 944-6847 or visit their Web site at *www.nationaltrust.org*.

1960	The Mount Vernon Ladies Association
1961	Henry Francis DuPont
1962	Katherine Prentis Murphy
1963	Martha Gilmore Robinson
1964	Mr. and Mrs. Bertram R. Little
1965	Charles E. Peterson
1966	Ima Hogg
	Mary Gordon Latham Kellenberger
1967	*No award granted*
1968	St. Clair Wright
1969	Mr. and Mrs. Henry N. Flynt
1970	Frank L. Horton
1971	Frances R. Edmunds
1972	Alice Winchester
1973	Ricardo E. Alegria
1974	Mr. and Mrs. Jacob H. Morrison
1975	*No award granted*
1976	Katherine U. Warren
1977	San Antonio Conservation Society
1978	Helen Duprey Bullock
1979	Old Post Office Landmark Committee
1980	William J. Murtagh
	Ernest Allen Connally
1981	Gordon C. Gray
1982	Helen Abell
1983	Historic American Buildings Survey of the National Park Service, US Department of the Interior, in cooperation with the American Institute of Architects and the Library of Congress, Washington, DC

1984	Leopold Adler II
1985	James Marston Fitch
1986	Antoinette Downing
1987	Frank Blair Reeves
1988	Robert Stipe
1989	Fred Rath
	Association of Junior Leagues
1990	Frederick Gutheim
1991	Robert Garvey
1992	Joan Bacchus Maynard
1993	Carl B. Westmoreland
	Arthur P. Ziegler Jr.
1994	Walter Beinecke Jr.
1995	Dana Crawford
1996	Richard H. Jenrette
1997	Marguerite Neel Williams
1998	Frederick Williamson
	Anice Barber Read
1999	Daniel Patrick Moynihan
2000	National Park Service
2001	George and Cynthia Mitchell
2002	John F. Seiberling
2003	Walter Nold Mathis
2004	Nancy Campbell
2005	J. Reid Williamson Jr.

Source: National Trust for Historic Preservation

415

DOCOMOMO

DOCOMOMO (Documentation and Conservation of Buildings, Sites, and Neighborhoods of the Modern Movement) International is headquartered in France, with working parties in 40 countries. Founded in 1988, membership consists of architects, engineers, historians, and others dedicated to preserving the architectural heritage of the Modern movement through documentation and conservation. They are also organized into specialist committees that concentrate on issues relative to registers, technology, education and theory, urbanism and landscapes, and publications. They also produce the *DOCOMOMO Journal*, published twice a year, with thematic articles and news from the individual chapters. Their technical publications focus on conservation issues related to Modern structures.

Address

DOCOMOMO International
Institute Français d'Architecture
Palais de la Porte Dorée
273, avenue Daumesnil
F-75012 Paris, France
+33 1 58 51 52 65
www.docomomo.com

DOCOMOMO US
PO Box 230977
New York, NY 10023
www.docomomo-us.org

Mission Statement

DOCOMOMO's mission is to act as watchdog when important modern movement buildings anywhere are under threat; to exchange ideas relating to conservation technology, history, and education; to foster interest in the ideas and heritage of the modern movement; and to elicit responsibility towards this recent architectural inheritance.

Great American Main Street Awards

Each year, the National Trust for Historic Preservation's National Main Street Center selects five communities that have demonstrated considerable success with preservation- based revitalization. These towns have all generated broad-based support from its residents and business leaders, drawn financial assistance from both public and private sources, and created innovative solutions for their unique situations. Winners receive $5,000 to be used toward further revitalization efforts, a bronze plaque, road signs, and a certificate. Since its inception, the Main Street Center has helped more than 1,650 communities, which has resulted in an average of $40 in new downtown investments for every dollar spent on revitalization efforts.

For more information, visit the Main Street Center's Web site at *www.mainstreet.org* or contact them at (202) 588-6219.

411

1995
Clarksville, MO
Dubuque, IA
Franklin, TN
Sheboygan Falls, WI
Old Pasadena, CA

1996
Bonaparte, IA
Chippewa Falls, WI
East Carson Street Business District,
   Pittsburgh, PA
Saratoga Springs, NY
Wooster, OH

1997
Burlington, VT
DeLand, FL
Georgetown, TX
Holland, MI
Libertyville, IL

1998
Corning, IA
Lanesboro, MN
Morgantown, WV
Thomasville, GA
York, PA

1999
Bay City, MI
Cordell, OK
Denton, TX
Lafayette, IN
San Luis Obispo, CA

2000
Coronado, CA
Keokuk, IA
Newkirk, OK
Port Townsend, WA
St. Charles, IL

2001
Danville, KY
Elkader, IA
Enid, OK
Mansfield, OH
Walla Walla, WA

2002
Cedar Falls, IA
La Crosse, WI
Milford, NH
Okmulgee, OK
Staunton, VA

Great American Main Street Awards

2003

Greenville, SC
Littleton, NH
Manassas, VA
Rome, GA
Wenatchee, WA

2004

Burlington, IA
Encinitas, CA
Paso Robles, CA
Rogers, AR
Westfield, NJ

2005

Barracks Row, Washington, DC
Emporia, KS
Frederick, MD
New Iberia, LA
Washington Gateway, Boston, MA

Source: National Trust Main Street Center

Did you know...

The national Main Street program celebrated its 25th anniversary in 2005. Since its inception, the collective economic impact of local Main Street programs to date has yielded $18.3 billion in total reinvestment, 244,545 net gain in new jobs, the creation of 60,500 businesses, and the rehabilitation of 96,283 buildings.

Guidelines for Architectural Historians Testifying on the Historical Significance of Properties

The following guidelines were adopted by the Society of Architectural Historians in 1986 to enhance professional standards in the preservation review process. In developing the guidelines, the SAH established a framework of acceptable conduct for those testifying as members of the discipline. The document was intended for wide circulation, to be used by the staffs and members of review bodies at the state and local levels and by all others concerned with the integrity of the review process.

Guidelines

Architectural historians engage in research into, and the dissemination of knowledge about, the evolution of the art and craft of architecture and its place in the history of civilization. The knowledge which they perpetuate, acquire, and spread is central to understanding human growth, for the buildings of any age reflect not only the visions of their designers and clients, but also the values of their era. Architectural historians have a special responsibility to the past, for their judgments as to the value of its artifacts often figure large in public and private decisions about what to preserve and what to destroy. That which is preserved nurtures the culture whose past it represents. That which is destroyed is lost forever.

Thus, the architectural historian has an awesome burden when called upon to speak to the value of a building, group of buildings, and other components of the man-made environment. It is essential to the integrity of the discipline that the architectural historian's testimony be based on sound scholarship, be an honest appraisal of all the pertinent circumstances, and be given with due regard for the gravity of its consequences.

Architectural historians testifying on the significance of historic properties before a duly constituted review board, commission, council, legislative committee, or court of law should:

— Make objective and truthful statements and eschew dissemination of untrue, unfair, or exaggerated statements regarding the significance of any property or properties;

— Assess the significance of the property or properties in question according to applicable local, state, and/or federal criteria;

— Express their professional opinion only when it is founded upon adequate knowledge of the facts, upon expertise in pertinent areas of scholarship, and upon honest conviction;

— State specifically the circumstances under which they are presenting testimony, including whether they are taking, or at any time have taken, a fee for work related to the case in question; and

— Issue no statements on behalf of interested parties unless they indicate on whose behalf those statements are being made, the nature of any compensation related to the case, and any personal interest in the property or properties in question or in property which would be affected by the disposition of the property or properties in question.

Credentials

An individual who intends to testify as an expert on matters pertaining to architectural history before a duly constituted review board, commission, council, legislative committee, or court of law must have a demonstrated record of achievement in that discipline.

A full set of credentials applicable, directly and indirectly, to the case should be presented in writing for the public record.

As credentials, it is appropriate to cite institutions attended, degrees earned, research conduct-

Guidelines for Architectural Historians Testifying

ed, scholarly work published, pertinent consulting projects completed or in progress, and past and present employment. Professional affiliations, offices, committees, and similar forms of service related to the discipline may be included, but it must be made explicit that all testimony presented reflects solely that individual's opinion unless he or she has been duly authorized by an organization, agency, or firm to speak on its behalf.

All parties involved in a given case should understand that architectural historians are not certified, registered, or licensed according to a uniform set of standards comparable to those employed in professions such as law, medicine, or architecture. Moreover, it should be understood that no one form of academic program is acknowledged to be the sole means by which an individual can become an architectural historian. Advanced degrees in art and architectural history form the primary bases for entering the discipline; nevertheless, comparable preparation in other fields such as American history, American studies, geography, archaeology, and folk-life also may provide expertise in assessing aspects of the built environment in their historic context. Furthermore, architects, landscape architects, and others practicing in professional design and planning fields may have expertise in facets of architectural history. Finally, it is possible for a person to acquire such expertise with little or no formal education in the field.

From a legal standpoint, expert testimony must be based on specialized knowledge of a particular subject, surpassing that which might be acquired by the average, well-informed layperson. Therefore, in all the above cases, a demonstrated record of achievement related to the historical subjects in question, rather than training or professional practice per se, should be considered the essential basis for one's qualifications to testify as an expert on matters pertaining to architectural history in a given case. Moreover, simply having an interest in old buildings or being involved with efforts to preserve them should not be considered an adequate basis for such testimony.

In presenting qualifications, architectural historians should be specific in enumerating their areas of expertise with respect to the case. Working in architectural history, or even in the sphere of North American architecture, does not always render an individual fully qualified to address all pertinent topical areas with authority. For example, a scholar of 18th-century North American architecture may not necessarily be well equipped to assess the significance of properties dating from later periods. Moreover, it is doubtful whether someone who knows little or nothing about the architecture of a given locale is in a good position to assess the local significance of a property or properties in that place.

Research

A foremost responsibility of an architectural historian intending to testify on the significance of a property or properties is to familiarize himself or herself with that work to the fullest extent possible. Under all circumstances, this effort should include onsite study. Interiors also should be examined whenever feasible and must be scrutinized when all or a portion of them are being considered in the case.

Furthermore, the architectural historian intending to testify should gain familiarity with as much additional information as possible concerning the property or properties. Of at least equal importance is knowledge of the context within which the property's significance may be evaluated. Such contextual frameworks include, but are not necessarily limited to: other work of the period(s), type(s), and designer(s) involved; work employing similar materials, construction techniques, or systems; work commissioned by the same or comparable clients, occupied by the same or comparable clients, or occupied by the same or analogous groups; and the physical setting in both its historic and current dimensions. In cases involving one or more properties within a designated historic district, or a precinct that has the potential to become a historic district, the full nature of the contribution of the property or properties to that district should be carefully considered.

In some instances, the necessary research may already have been conducted for a case. The

Guidelines for Architectural Historians Testifying

architectural historian intending to testify then has the responsibility to examine this material carefully, making sure that it is complete and accurate prior to preparing his or her scholarly evaluation. In other instances, additional research may be needed, and the architectural historian intending to testify either should undertake this work or wait until it is completed by another responsible party before preparing an assessment. Whenever possible, architectural historians intending to testify should also seek consultation from colleagues known for their research in specialized subject areas pertinent to the case.

It should be realized that many such subject areas have received little or no scholarly attention and that the absence of this research should not necessarily preclude responsible efforts to save significant properties. It further should be recognized that many cases cannot be researched in a definitive manner when such an undertaking would require far more time than can be allocated even under favorable circumstances. Nevertheless, in all cases, an architectural historian intending to testify should exercise his or her best professional judgment in determining whether adequate information is available and determining that no available information is being concealed from consideration.

Moreover, the architectural historian offering testimony should be explicit regarding the degree to which his or her statements are based on his or her own research or on the work of others. Under no circumstances should an architectural historian convey the impression that an assessment is his or her own when it has in fact been wholly or substantially prepared by another party.

Criteria for Evaluation

Architectural historians intending to testify should be thoroughly familiar with applicable local, state, and federal criteria for evaluation and gain a full understanding of the issues relating to significance that the testimony is intended to resolve. The criteria for the National Register of Historic Places and for most, if not all, local landmark and historic district ordinances specify that properties may be designated on the basis of local significance as well as by virtue of their significance to a state or the nation.

However, the concept of local significance is often ignored or distorted in testimony and thus deserves special consideration here. A given work may not rank among the finest designed by a distinguished architect, for example, but this does not necessarily undermine its significance for the locality in question. Similarly, comparative analysis of examples of a building type in different geographic regions does not necessarily provide insight on the local significance of examples in any one of those regions.

Furthermore, local significance should not be interpreted as meaning only the earliest, oldest surviving, best, or most unusual examples unless the applicable criteria for evaluation so state. The objective of national preservation legislation and most local ordinances is to foster a comprehensive plan for protecting historic properties. Indeed, significance often may be fully understood only after it is studied in relation to the local context. Failure to assess a property's or properties' significance in any of the above ways will undermine the credibility of the testimony and run counter to the intent of the national historic preservation program.

Fees

Taking a fee for testimony is legal under most circumstances and should not, in itself, be construed as diminishing the value of testimony. At the same time, an architectural historian who even unintentionally conveys the impression that his or her testimony is in any way affected by monetary compensation or personal reasons contrary to those of sound scholarship blemishes both preservation efforts and the discipline's integrity. Indeed, the entire basis for scholarship, along with its public reputation, rests on its independence.

Therefore, architectural historians should make every reasonable effort to demonstrate that their testimony is motivated solely by honest conviction, understanding of all relevant material, and scholarly expertise. In every instance, architectural historians testifying should state explicit-

483

Guidelines for Architectural Historians Testifying

ly whether they are taking a fee for that testimony; whether they are taking, or at any time have taken, a fee for work related to the case; and the source or sources for same fees. They should further explicitly state all the circumstances under which they are presenting testimony in that case. In contractual agreements, which will, or may at some later date, include testimony, that agreement should stipulate that the underlying aim of the architectural historian's work is to arrive at an objective evaluation of the significance of the property or properties in question. The contracted fee should be structured according to the nature of the work undertaken for research, analysis, and preparation of findings in a report or other appropriate form and not according to the real or potential monetary value of the property or properties in question. Under some circumstances, it may be prudent to perform such work incrementally; that is, prepare preliminary findings, and, should the contracting parties so agree, then proceed with an in-depth study.

The contractual agreement should specifically preclude the contractor's later excerpting portions of the study in a manner that distorts the overall findings of that study. Furthermore, architectural historians should never agree "for monetary compensation or otherwise" to prepare a study that merely makes an argument pro or con without weighing all pertinent information and performing a full scholarly assessment.

No uniform set of standards should be established for such studies any more than for other forms of scholarly endeavor. Architectural historians should be guided by the same standards that are considered exemplary for other work in their discipline. A study too quickly prepared, lacking careful consideration of all aspects contributing to complete historical analysis, should be viewed as a serious breach of personal and professional integrity.

Summary

Architectural historians should regard testimony as a public service and as a constructive means of advocating the retention of significant components of the man-made environment in accordance with applicable local, state, and federal laws. All work done to prepare for testimony, as well as the testimony itself, also should reflect high scholarly standards and should not suggest personal gain of any sort acquired at the expense of these objectives.

The Society of Architectural Historians is the leading scholarly organization that promotes the study and preservation of the built environment world wide. For more information about the society, please visit their Web site at www.sah.org.

Source: © Society of Architectural Historians. Reprinted with permission.

Guidelines for the Treatment of Cultural Landscapes

The secretary of the interior is responsible for establishing professional standards and providing advice on the preservation of cultural resources listed or eligible for listing in the National Register of Historic Places. As the definition and scope of preservation has continued to broaden, the secretary of the interior developed the Guidelines for the Treatment of Cultural Landscapes to provide expert guidance when planning and implementing work involving cultural landscapes. A cultural landscape is defined as "a geographic area, including both cultural and natural resources and the wildlife or domestic animals therein, associated with a historic event, activity, or person or exhibiting other cultural or aesthetic values."

For more information about cultural landscapes and their preservation, visit the National Park Service's Web site at *www2.cr.nps.gov/hli/introguid.htm.*

1. Before undertaking project work, research of a cultural landscape is essential. Research findings help to identify a landscape's historic period(s) of ownership, occupancy, and development and bring greater understanding of the associations that make them significant. Research findings also provide a foundation to make educated decisions for project treatment and can guide management, maintenance, and interpretation. In addition, research findings may be useful in satisfying compliance reviews (e.g. Section 106 of the National Historic Preservation Act as amended).

2. Although there is no single way to inventory a landscape, the goal of documentation is to provide a record of the landscape as it exists at the present time, thus providing a baseline from which to operate. All component landscapes and features (see definitions below) that contribute to the landscape's historic character should be recorded. The level of documentation needed depends on the nature and the significance of the resource.

For example, plant material documentation may ideally include botanical name or species, common name, and size. To ensure full representation of existing herbaceous plants, care should be taken to document the landscape in different seasons. This level of research may most often be the ideal goal for smaller properties but may prove impractical for large, vernacular landscapes.

3. Assessing a landscape as a continuum through history is critical in assessing cultural and historic value. By analyzing the landscape changes over time—the chronological and physical "layers" of the landscape—can be understood. Based on analysis, individual features may be attributed to a discrete period of introduction, their presence or absence substantiated to a given date and therefore the landscape's significance and integrity evaluated. In addition, analysis allows the property to be viewed within the context of other cultural landscapes.

43

Guidelines for the Treatment of Cultural Landscapes

4. In order for the landscape to be considered significant, character-defining features that convey its significance in history must not only be present, but they also must possess historic integrity. Location, setting, design, materials, workmanship, feeling, and association should be considered in determining whether a landscape and its character-defining features possess historic integrity.

5. Preservation planning for cultural landscapes involves a broad array of dynamic variables. Adopting comprehensive treatment and management plans, in concert with a preservation maintenance strategy, acknowledges a cultural landscape's ever-changing nature and the interrelationship of treatment, management, and maintenance.

Source: National Park Service

Did you know...

Restoration of the house and gardens at Garland Farm on Mount Desert Island, ME, the final home of Beatrix Farrand, one of the country's premier landscape gardeners, is underway. Formed specifically to save this historic site, the Beatrix Farrand Society's plan includes the establishment of an educational center for design and horticulture.

Historic American Buildings Survey

The Historic American Buildings Survey, operating as part of the National Park Service, is dedicated to recording America's historic buildings through measured drawings, written histories, and large-format photographs. The program was started in 1933 as a Civil Works Administration project using unemployed architects to make permanent records of historic American architecture. Following a dropoff in activity after World War II, the program was restored in the early 1950s with student architects providing the research, a practice that continues to the present day. In 1969, the Historic American Engineering Record was established as a companion program focusing on America's technological heritage. Records of the more than 37,000 historic structures and sites are available to the public through the Prints and Photographs Division of the Library of Congress.

Address

HABS/HAER Division
National Park Service
Department of the Interior
1849 C Street, NW, 2270
Washington, DC 20240
(202) 354-2135
www.cr.nps.gov/habshaer/

For information on the HABS/HAER archives, contact:
Prints and Photographs Reading Room
Library of Congress
101 Independence Avenue, SE
Washington, DC 20540-4730
(202) 707-6394
www.loc.gov/rr/print/

435

Did you know...

HABS/HAER documents are some of the most requested materials at the Prints & Photographs Division of the Library of Congress. Only the Civil War photographs and Farm Security Administration records are more popular.

Historic Landscape Initiative

The Historic Landscape Initiative promotes responsible preservation practices to protect America's irreplaceable cultural landscapes, which leads to an improved quality of life, a sense of place, and identity for future generations as well as scenic, economic, ecological, recreational, social, and educational opportunities. As with historic properties, America's historic landscapes are threatened by loss and change through inappropriate uses, insensitive development, vandalism, and natural forces. The initiative provides guidance on sound preservation practices for a variety of landscapes, including parks, gardens, rural villages, industrial sites, and agricultural landscapes. Through their workshops, publications, technical assistance, and national policy advisement, the initiative serves as a clearinghouse for information related to cultural landscapes and their preservation.

Address

Heritage Preservation Services
National Park Service
1201 Eye Street NW, 2255
Washington, DC 20005
(202) 354-2076
www2.cr.nps.gov/hli/

Mission Statement

The National Park Service's Historic Landscape Initiative promotes responsible preservation practices that protect our nation's irreplaceable legacy—designed landscapes such as parks and gardens, as well as vernacular historic landscapes such as farms and industrial sites.

Historic Preservation Book Prize

Sponsored by the Center for Historic Preservation at the University Mary Washington in Fredericksburg, VA, the Historic Preservation Book Prize yearly honors a book judged to have made the most significant contribution to the field of historic preservation in the United States. A jury of preservation professionals from the university and other organizations focuses on books that break new ground or contribute to the intellectual vitality of the preservation movement. Entries are accepted from any discipline that relates to the theory or practice of historic preservation. Nominations may come from any source. Winners receive a $500 cash prize and are invited to lecture at the school.

More information is available on the Center for Historic Preservation Web site, *www.umw.edu/cas_mwc/chp/* or by calling (540) 654-1356.

1989
The Past is a Foreign Country by David Lowenthal (Cambridge University Press)

1990
Saving America's Countryside: A Guide to Rural Conservation by Samuel N. Stokes and A. Elizabeth Watson, et al. (Johns Hopkins University Press)

Imagining the Past: East Hampton Histories by T. H. Breen (University of Georgia Press)

1991
Architects and Builders in North Carolina: A History of the Practice of Building by Catherine W. Bishir, Charlotte V. Brown, Carl R. Lounsbury and Ernest H. Wood (University of North Carolina Press)

1992
Constructing Chicago by Daniel Bluestone (Yale University Press)

1993
The Park and the People: A History of Central Park by Roy Rosenzweig and Elizabeth Blackmar (Cornell University Press)

1994
The Politics of Public Memory: Tourism, History, and Ethnicity in Monterey, California by Martha K. Norkunas (State University of New York Press)

1995
An Illustrated Glossary of Early Southern Architecture and Landscape by Carl R. Lounsbury (Oxford University Press)

1996
Gender, Class, and Shelter: Perspectives in Vernacular Architecture by Elizabeth Collins Cromley and Carter Hudgins (University of Tennessee Press)

1997
Mickey Mouse History and Other Essays on American Memory by Mike Wallace (Temple Univ. Press)

1998
Shadowed Ground: America's Landscapes of Violence and Tragedy by Kenneth E. Foote (University of Texas Press)

Historic Preservation Book Prize

1999

The Presence of the Past: Popular Uses of History in American Life by Roy R. Rosenzweig (Columbia University Press)

2000

The Drive-In, The Supermarket, and The Transformation of Commercial Space in Los Angeles, 1914-1941 by Richard Longstreth (MIT Press)

2001

Houses from Books: Treatises, Pattern Books, and Catalogs in American Architecture, 1738–1950 by Daniel Reiff (Pennsylvania State University Press)

2002

From Cottage to Bungalow: Houses and the Working Class in Metropolitan Chicago 1869–1929 by Joseph C. Bigott (University of Chicago Press)

2003

A Modern Arcadia: Frederick Law Olmsted Jr. and the Plan for Forest Hills Gardens by Susan L. Klaus (University of Massachusetts Press)

2004

Gaining Ground: A History of Landmaking in Boston by Nancy S. Seasholes (MIT Press)

2005

Downtown America: A History of the Place and the People Who Made It by Alison Isenberg (University of Chicago Press)

Source: *Center for Historic Preservation*

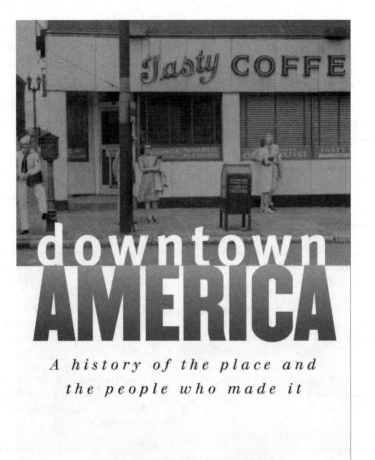

439

Downtown America. Alison Isenberg cuts beneath the archetypal story of
downtown's rise and fall to offer a dynamic new story of urban development in the United States. The book demonstrates that downtown's tra-
jectory was not dictated by inevitable free market forces or natural life-
and-death cycles but, instead, by a host of people such as retailers, developers, government leaders, architects, planners, political activists, con-
sumers, civic clubs, real estate appraisers, and more. Photo courtesy of the
University of Chicago Press.

Historic Preservation Timeline

Evolving from isolated, private initiatives to a full-scale national movement, the history of preservation in the United States is comprised of grassroots efforts, landmark court cases, and numerous laws and economic incentives. This timeline marks some of those moments, as the heroic efforts of pioneers has led to an organized and mature movement. Today, even the concept of endangered places has broadened to include not only historic buildings but entire neighborhoods, landscapes, and vernacular buildings.

1791 The Massachusetts Historical Society, the first statewide organization to collect and preserve resources for the study of American history, is established.

1812 The first national historical organization, the American Antiquarian Society, is founded in Worcester, MA.

1816 Considered one of the first acts of preservation, Philadelphia purchases Independence Hall (the Philadelphia State House, 1732) to rescue it from demolition.

1828 The Touro Synagogue (1765) in Newport, RI, is the nation's first recorded restoration.

1850 The New York legislature purchases the Hasbrouck House (1750), George Washington's headquarters in Newburgh, and opens it to the public as the nation's first historic house museum.

1853 Ann Pamela Cunningham founds the Mount Vernon Ladies' Association of the Union, the first private preservation organization of any kind in the United States, to save George Washington's Mount Vernon from eventual destruction by neglect.

1857 Philadelphia's Carpenter's Hall (1744), site of the First Continental Congress, is restored and presented to the public as the first privately-owned American building that is also a historic monument.

1872 Congress sets aside Yellowstone as a national park, the first such designation in America and the world.

1876 One of the first instances of preservation in an urban setting, Boston's Old South Meeting House (1729) is rescued from demolition.

1889 The Association for the Preservation of Virginia Antiquities is formed as the nation's first statewide preservation organization.

Congress provides $2,000 for preservation of the Casa Grande ruin in Arizona, the first instance of federal spending on preservation.

1890 Congress passes the first piece of legislation to authorize the preservation of an American battlefield—the Chickamauga and Chattanooga Battlefield in Georgia and Tennessee.

1896 In *US v. Gettysburg Electric Railway Company*, the first preservation case to go before the US Supreme Court, the condemnation of private property for a national memorial is upheld.

1906 The Antiquities Act, the first major federal preservation legislation, is passed, granting the President the power to designate national monuments and enacting penalties for destroying historic and cultural resources on federal land.

Historic Preservation Timeline

1910 The incorporation of the Society for the Preservation of New England Antiquities, America's first regional preservation organization, marks a broadening in preservation theory from preserving buildings with heroic associations to buildings that are "architecturally beautiful or unique."

1916 President Woodrow Wilson approves legislation establishing the National Park Service within the US Department of the Interior as the administrative agency responsible for sites designated as national park areas.

1925 The Vieux Carre Commission, the first historic preservation commission in the United States, is established to protect New Orleans' historic French Quarter, laid out in 1721. However, it is not until a 1936 state constitutional amendment passes that the commission is granted true enforcement powers.

1926 Henry Ford begins assembling old buildings and artifacts, which trace 300 years of technological and cultural history, at his Dearborn, MI, Greenfield Village.

John D. Rockefeller Jr. begins funding the restoration and reconstruction of Williamsburg, VA, the first attempt to restore an entire community.

1931 America's first municipal preservation ordinance to establish a historic district with regulatory control is passed in Charleston, SC, to protect the city's quickly vanishing heritage.

1933 Charles E. Peterson establishes the Historic American Buildings Survey to document historic buildings through measured drawings, photographs, and written descriptions.

1935 Congress passes the National Historic Sites Act, the first law to establish historic preservation as a national policy, and with it creates the National Historic Landmarks program.

1944 *This Is Charleston* is published in Charleston, SC, the country's first citywide inventory of public buildings.

1946 Robert Moses proposes the Vieux Carre Expressway, an elevated riverfront highway passing through the architecturally significant historic French Quarter in New Orleans. The proposal is finally defeated in 1969.

1947 The National Council for Historic Sites and Buildings, the first nationwide private preservation organization and predecessor of the National Trust for Historic Preservation (into which it merges in 1954), is formed.

The first US preservation conference is held in Washington, DC.

1949 Congress charters the National Trust for Historic Preservation to lead private-sector preservation efforts.

1951 Woodlawn Plantation (1805) in Alexandria, VA, becomes the first of 25 historic properties currently operated by the National Trust for Historic Preservation.

1952 *Historic Preservation* (now *Preservation*), the nation's first nationwide preservation magazine, is launched.

1959 The first urban renewal study to address preservation concerns, *College Hill, A Demonstration Study of Historic Area Renewal for Providence, RI,* becomes a national model for using historic preservation as a means of community renewal.

441

Historic Preservation Timeline

1959 President Dwight Eisenhower approves a six-year, $650 million urban renewal appropriation that removes rather than rehabilitates old buildings and leaves a legacy of torn neighborhoods and discontinuity.

1960 The Mount Vernon Ladies' Association of the Union is named the first recipient of the National Trust's Crowninshield Award, which honors a lifetime of achievement in the field of historic preservation.

1961 Jane Jacobs publishes *The Death and Life of Great American Cities,* a commentary on the increasing demise of America's urban environments that remains is relevant to today's issues of sprawl and the legacy of urban renewal.

1962 At their invitation, architect John Carl Warnecke meets with President John F. Kennedy and the First Lady to save Washington, DC's historic Lafayette Square from demolition, a collaboration that restores the square's 19th-century townhouses and the Renwick Gallery (1859). Warnecke also utilizes a pioneering context-sensitive approach in his design of the required federal buildings, which he inserts behind the restored townhouses.

1963 Despite widespread public outcry, the demolition of New York's Pennsylvania Station begins, a loss that galvanizes the preservation movement.

1964 Columbia University's School of Architecture offers the first graduate-level course in historic preservation.

William Matson Roth purchases the 1893 Ghirardelli Square, a former San Francisco chocolate factory, to save it from demolition. He restores the building and turns it into a retail center, one of the first successful adaptive-use projects in the country.

1965 The International Council on Monuments and Sites is created to establish international standards for the preservation, restoration, and management of the cultural environment.

1966 *With Heritage So Rich* is published, a seminal historic preservation book documenting American cultural resources and chronicling the preservation movement.

Congress passes the National Historic Preservation Act, a watershed for the preservation movement. It establishes the National Register of Historic Places and an Advisory Council on Historic Places; calls for broader federal funding of preservation activities and individual state historic preservation programs; encourages the creation of local historic districts; and provides, through its Section 106, for the protection of preservation-worthy sites and properties threatened by federal activities.

The Department of Transportation Act prohibits the destruction or adverse use of historic sites (as well as parklands) by transportation projects unless there is no feasible and prudent alternative.

1967 The first state historic preservation officers and the first keeper of the National Register are appointed.

1968 The Association for Preservation Technology is founded as an interdisciplinary clearinghouse for information and research about preservation techniques for historic structures.

New York City enacts the nation's first ordinance allowing the transfer of development rights, providing a tool to assist in the preservation of historic buildings.

1969 The National Environmental Policy Act requires federal agencies to prepare impact statements for projects that may affect cultural, as well as natural, resources.

Historic Preservation Timeline

The Historic American Engineering Record is established as a sister program to HABS to document and record engineering and industrial sites.

1971 Executive Order 11593 requires federal agencies to inventory their lands for cultural and historic sites and to nominate places to the National Register.

The National Trust for Historic Preservation begins its annual Preservation Honor Awards program to recognize individuals, organizations and projects that represent the best in preservation.

1972 Through the Surplus Real Property Act, Congress authorizes the transfer of surplus historic federal property to local public agencies for preservation.

The World Heritage List is founded by UNESCO to record cultural and natural properties with outstanding universal value.

1973 *Old House Journal* is launched as a newsletter for Brooklyn brownstoners and quickly expands its editorial and readership nationwide. By 2003, it has more than 130,000 readers.

The first National Historic Preservation Week is celebrated, an annual event held in May.

The city of New York amends its Landmarks Preservation Law to authorize the Landmarks Commission to designate interior landmarks.

1974 Preservation Action is formed and to date is the only national preservation lobby in the United States.

1976 The Tax Reform Act of 1976 provides the first major preservation tax incentives for the rehabilitation of certified historic income-producing properties in the form of a 60-month amortization of rehabilitation costs.

The Public Buildings Cooperative Use Act encourages restoration and adaptive use of historic buildings for federal use by requiring federal government to obtain and rehabilitate, where possible, historic buildings for use as federal office space.

The Historic Preservation Fund, funded by Outer Continental Shelf mineral receipts, is established to provide preservation grants to the states.

1977 The National Trust's Main Street Project, forerunner of today's National Main Street Center, is launched in Galesburg, IL; Hot Springs, SD; and Madison, IN; to demonstrate the value of preservation as a tool for downtown revitalization. Twenty-five years later the program boasts the participation of more than 1,650 communities, a total reinvestment in these communities of $16 billion, the creation of 226,900 new jobs and 88,700 building rehabilitation projects.

1978 In *Penn Central Transportation Co. v. City of New York*, one of preservation's landmark rulings, the US Supreme Court upholds the right of the city to block construction over Grand Central Terminal, thus affirming the legitimacy of preservation ordinances and local governments' power to enforce such ordinances.

The Secretary of the Interior's Standards for Historic Preservation are released as the first professional standards for work on historic resources.

The Revenue Act of 1978 creates a 10 percent tax credit for the rehabilitation of older commercial properties.

443

Historic Preservation Timeline

1978 Eero Saarinen's Dulles International Airport Terminal (Loudon County, VA) is deemed eligible for the National Register in 1978, only 16 years after its construction, breaking the Register's typical 50-year rule.

1979 With the largest concentration of 1920s and 1930s resort architecture in the United States, Miami Beach becomes the first National Register Historic District comprised entirely of 20th-century buildings.

This Old House debuts on Boston Public Television and will eventually become one of the most popular PBS and home improvement shows in history, reaching more than 3.9 million viewers weekly.

1980 Amendments to the National Historic Preservation Act are passed that direct federal agencies to nominate and protect historic federal properties, broaden participation of local governments,and require owner consent for National Register listing.

The Vernacular Architecture Forum is founded to encourage the study and preservation of traditional structures and landscapes.

1981 The Economic Recovery Tax Act expands the rehabilitation tax credit program, offering a 25 percent credit for renovating certified historic properties, and prompts a surge in rehab nationwide. It also abolishes the tax incentive for demolishing historic properties.

1982 The zero preservation funding proposed by the Reagan administration is fought, and funding is restored after an intensive nationwide campaign.

1983 After a zealous preservation protest, Congress approves a $48-million plan to restore the west front of the US Capitol rather than the planned $73-million addition that would have obscured the historic facade.

1985 McDonald's announces plans to restore the first roadside stand built by Ray Kroc in 1955 in Des Plaines, IL.

1986 After a nationwide campaign to save the rehabilitation tax credits, the Tax Reform Act of 1986 is passed, although the credits are reduced from the 1981 level.

1988 Manassas National Battlefield Park in Virginia is saved from a 1.2 million-square-foot shopping mall development. The park will face another battle in 1993 when Disney proposes a historic theme park, Disney's America, three miles from the Battlefield Park. After tremendous national outcry over concerns about the effect of the associated sprawl on the battlefield, Disney withdraws its proposal.

The National Trust issues its first 11 Most Endangered Historic Places List to bring attention to threatened historic sites and to generate local support. In 15 years, only one of the more than 160 listed sites has been destroyed.

DOCOMOMO (Documentation and Conservation of Buildings, Sites, Neighborhoods of the Modern Movement) is founded in the Netherlands in response to the increasing demolition of Modern architecture, documenting and advocating the preservation of the Modern heritage.

1991 The passage of the Intermodal Surface Transportation Efficiency Act provides a significant source of federal funding for preservation projects.

1995 The World Monuments Fund establishes its biennial World Monuments Watch list of 100 worldwide cultural sites in urgent need of intervention.

Historic Preservation Timeline

1996 In response to looming development, the National Trust purchases the land directly across the Ashley River from its 1738 Drayton Hall plantation (Charleston, SC) in order to preserve the site's natural vistas and historic character.

1997 The state of Texas becomes a pioneer in the digitizing of preservation records with its launch of the Texas Historic Sites Atlas (http://atlas.thc.state.tx.us/), an online database of 238,000 historic and archeological site records documenting Texas history with integrated mapping software for locating the resources.

1998 Save America's Treasures, a public-private partnership, is founded to identify and rescue the enduring symbols of America and raise public awareness and support for their preservation.

The first 20th-century vernacular structure less than 50 years old, the 1959 Ralph Sr. and Sunny Wilson House in Temple, TX, built for the founder of Wilsonart International, is listed in the National Register of Historic Places.

The 1966 appropriation providing federal funding for the National Trust is terminated. The Trust has since relied on private-sector contributions.

1998 Arapahoe Acres in Englewood, CO, is the first post-World War II residential subdivision listed as a historic district in the National Register of Historic Places.

2001 By 2001, historic buildings provide approximately one-fourth of The General Services Administration's federally-owned space.

2003 The National Trust is the first nonprofit group to receive the National Humanities Medal.

New York City passes contextual zoning regulations in a number of neighborhoods to encourage sympathetically-scaled new buildings within historic districts.

2004 In a vigorous fund-raising campaign, preservationists purchase Mies van der Rohe's landmark Farnsworth House (Plano, IL, 1951), considered by many a masterpiece of modernism and one of the most important residential designs of the 20th century, ensuring not just its survival but the context in which it was originally designed.

Source: DesignIntelligence

445

International Centre for the Study of the Preservation and Restoration of Cultural Property

Founded by the United Nations' Educational, Scientific, and Cultural Organization in 1956, the International Centre for the Study of the Preservation and Restoration of Cultural Property is an intergovernmental organization dedicated to the conservation of heritage of all types. It is funded by contributions from its more than 100 member states plus donors and sponsors. ICCROM provides members with information, publications, and training; offers technical assistance and sponsors workshops; performs ongoing research and archives findings; and serves as an advocate for preservation. The group also maintains one of the largest conservation libraries in the world.

Address
Via di San Michele 13
I-00153 Rome, Italy
+39 06 585531
www.iccrom.org

446

Mission Statement

ICCROM aims at improving the quality of conservation practice as well as raising awareness about the importance of preserving cultural heritage.

International Council on Monuments and Sites

Dedicated to the conservation of the world's historic monuments and sites, the International Council on Monuments and Sites is an international, non-governmental organization with national committees in more than 107 countries. The group is the United Nations' Educational, Scientific, and Cultural Organization's principal advisor on matters concerning the conservation of monuments and sites. With the World Conservation Union, ICOMOS advises the World Heritage Committee and UNESCO on the nomination of new sites to the World Heritage List. The group also works to establish international standards for the preservation, restoration, and management of the cultural environment. ICOMOS members are professional architects, archaeologists, urban planners, engineers, heritage administrators, art historians, and archivists. All members join ICOMOS through the national committee of their respective countries.

Address
49-51 rue de la Fédération
75015 Paris, France
+33 (0) 1 45 67 67 70
www.icomos.org

441

Mission Statement

The International Council on Monuments and Sites is an international non-governmental organization of professionals dedicated to the conservation of the world's historic monuments and sites. ICOMOS provides a forum for professional dialogue and a vehicle for the collection, evaluation, and dissemination of information on conservation principles, techniques, and policies.

Landslide Landscapes

The Cultural Landscape Foundation compiles a biennial thematic list of endangered cultural landscapes to rally public support at the local, state, and national level for the preservation of these important parts of our national heritage. Nominations for the list are accepted from local groups or individuals, professionals, government officials, and other interested parties. The 2002 Landslide Landscapes list focused on masterworks of landscape architecture designed within the past 250 years. The 2004 program is concerned with working landscapes, endangered historic rural or vernacular landscapes where people worked the land: farms and ranches, shipyards, logging camps, railroad yards, fishing villages, etc.

For photos, site histories, biographies, and status updates, visit the CLF Web site at *www.tclf.org/landslide/*.

2004 Landslide Landscapes: Working Landscapes

Acoma Pueblo
Acoma, NM

Agate Bay
Two Harbors, MN

Buckland Farm
Buckland, VT

Cienega Corridor
Vail, CO

Orson Adams House
Harrisburg, UT

Ridgewood Ranch
Willits, CT

Whitney Farm
Sherborn, MA

Source: Cultural Landscape Foundation

Most Popular Historic House Museums 2006

Every year *DesignIntelligence*, in conjunction with the *Almanac of Architecture & Design*, polls America's historic house museums to determine which are the most popular destinations. For the purposes of this study, a house museum is defined as a historic house that is currently exhibited and interpreted as a dwelling place.

1. Mount Vernon, Mount Vernon, VA
   George Washington, 1785-86
2. Biltmore Estate, Asheville, NC
   Richard Morris Hunt, 1895
3. Hearst Castle, San Simeon, CA
   Julia Morgan, 1927-1947
4. Graceland, Memphis, TN
   Furbringer & Ehrman, 1939
5. Arlington House, The Robert E. Lee
   Memorial, Arlington, VA
   George Hadfield, 1817
6. Monticello, Home of Thomas Jefferson,
   Charlottesville, VA
   Thomas Jefferson, 1768–79, 1793–1809
7. Vanderbilt Mansion, Hyde Park, NY
   McKim, Mead and White, 1898
8. The Breakers, Newport, RI
   Richard Morris Hunt, 1895
9. Betsy Ross House, Philadelphia, PA
   Architect unknown, 1740
10. The Edison and Ford Winter Estates,
    Fort Myers, FL
    Thomas Edison, 1886 (Edison home)
    Architect unknown, 1911 (Ford home)
11. Paul Revere House, Boston, MA
    Architect unknown, c.1680
12. Lincoln Home, Springfield, IL
    Architect unknown, 1839
13. The Hermitage, Home of President Andrew
    Jackson, Nashville, TN
    Architect unknown, 1819–1821; David
    Morrison, 1831–32; Joseph Reiff and William
    Hume; 1835–37

14. Boldt Castle, Alexandria Bay, NY
    Hewitt, Stevens & Paist, 1900–04
15. Fairlane—The Henry Ford Estate,
    Dearborn, MI
    William H. Van Tine, 1915
16. Vizcaya, Miami, FL
    Burrall Hoffman, 1916
17. Marble House, Newport, RI
    Richard Morris Hunt, 1892
18. Laura: A Creole Plantation, Vacherie, LA
    Architect unknown, 1805
19. Taliesen West, Scottsdale, AZ
    Frank Lloyd Wright, 1937
20. Fallingwater, Mill Run, PA
    Frank Lloyd Wright, 1939
21. House of the Seven Gables, Salem, MA
    Architect unknown, 1668
22. The Elms, Newport, RI
    Horace Trumbauer, 1901
23. George Eastman House, Rochester, NY
    J. Foster Warner, 1905
24. Rosecliff, Newport, RI
    Stanford White, 1902
25. Franklin D. Roosevelt Cottage, Lubec, ME
    William T. Sears, 1897

Note: Carter's Grove, which often appears on this list, is temporarily closed.

Source: DesignIntelligence

449

National Center for Preservation Technology & Training

The National Center for Preservation Technology & Training promotes and enhances the preservation and conservation of prehistoric and historic resources in the United States through the advancement and dissemination of preservation technology and training. Created by Congress, the NCPTT is an interdisciplinary program of the National Park Service intended to advance the art, craft, and science of historic preservation in the fields of archeology, historic architecture, historic landscapes, objects, materials conservation, and interpretation through research, education, and information management. The center also administers the Preservation Technology and Training Grants Program, one of the few preservation and conservation grants programs devoted to training, technology, and basic research issues.

Address
645 University Parkway
Natchitoches, LA 71457
(318) 356-7444
www. ncptt.nps.gov

450

Mission Statement

The National Center for Preservation Technology & Training advances the use of science and technology in historic preservation. Working in the fields of archeology, architecture, landscape architecture, and materials conservation, the center accomplishes its mission through training, education, research, technology transfer, and partnerships.

National Main Street Leadership Awards

The National Trust for Historic Preservation's National Main Street Leadership Awards identify and honor key leaders in the commercial district revitalization movement. In conjunction with its Main Street Awards, the National Trust annually recognizes exceptional accomplishments in the revitalization of America's downtowns and neighborhood commercial districts. The National Main Street Leadership Awards are presented in three categories: the Civic Leadership Award recognizing an elected official, government staff person, public agency, or nonprofit organization; the Business Leadership award recognizing a small business, an industry, or a corporation; and the Main Street Heroes Award for outstanding contribution by an individual toward the revitalization of a commercial district.

Applications, past winners, and eligibility requirements are available online at *www.mainstreet.org*.

2005

Civic Leadership Award
Institute for Local Self-Reliance for their
    New Rules Project
www.newrules.org

Business Leadership Award
Robert Brueck
Brueck Construction
Burlington, IA

Main Street Heroes Award
William King Jr.
Bath, ME

Source: National Trust for Historic Preservation

451

Preservation is about beautiful, everyday structures that create civilized communities.

Paul Goldberger

National Preservation Awards

The National Trust for Historic Preservation annually recognizes citizens, organizations, and public and private entities for their high level of dedication and support of the ideals and benefits of historic preservation through its National Preservation Awards program. A jury of preservation professionals and representatives selects winners based on their positive effect on the community, pioneering nature, quality, and degree of difficulty. Special interest is also placed on those undertakings that use historic preservation as a method of revitalization.

For more information, contact the National Trust at (800) 944-6847 or visit their Web site at *www.nationaltrust.org.*

2005 Winners

Bosco-Milligan Foundation
Portland, OR

Carnegie Library
Savannah, GA

Council of Educational Facility Planners
    International, Center for Preservation
    Technology and Training, and Environmental
    Protection Agency
Washington, DC

Essex County Courthouse
Newark, NJ

Grain Belt Brewhouse
Minneapolis, MN

Heimann Building and AVANCE, Inc.
San Antonio, TX

Linn Schoolhouse and Merle and
    Oliver Hamilton
Marion County, OH

Missouri River Programmatic Agreement
Missouri

Monroe School
Topeka, KS

Oregon Department of Transportation/
    Historic Bridge Preservation Program
Portland, OR

Beverly Rich and the San Juan County
    Historical Society
Silverton, CO

Ships Tavern Mews
Wilmington, DE

Stone Barns Center for Food and Agriculture
Pocantico Hills, NY

Tennessee Theatre
Knoxville, TN

Verizon Central Office Building/
    Barclay-Vesey Building
New York, NY

Yale Building
Chicago, IL

Source: National Trust for Historic Preservation

2005 National Preservation Award winners. Beverly Rich's leadership as chair of the San Juan County Historical Society has resulted in the preservation of many historic structures in the old mining town of Silverton, CO, including the Shenandoah Dives Mill (top). Originally built in 1933 for the Rockefeller family as a working farm near their home in Kykuit, NY, this magnificent Normandy style farm barn complex was completely restored and dedicated as the Stone Barns Center for Food and Agriculture in 2004 (middle). The newly restored grand 1928 movie palace, Knoxville's Tennessee Theater, with its Spanish-Moorish theme was originally designed by Graven & Mayger for Paramount Studios. Photos courtesy of the National Trust for Historic Preservation.

453

National Preservation Institute

The National Preservation Institute is a nonprofit organization dedicated to the management, development, and preservation of historic, cultural, and environmental resources. Toward this end, NPI offers specialized information, continuing education, and, upon request, professional training tailored to the sponsor's needs. Many preservation-related services are available from NPI, including authentication of historic reproductions and historic real estate. NPI is also registered with the American Institute of Architects' continuing education program.

Address
PO Box 1702
Alexandria, VA 22313
(703) 765-0100
www.npi.org

Mission Statement

Founded in 1980 as a nonprofit organization, the National Preservation Institute offers seminars in historic preservation and cultural resource management. NPI is proud to serve a broad spectrum of professionals from both the government and private sectors by providing preservation information, knowledge, and the skills to train and guide the stewards of this nation's historic and cultural places.

National Trust for Historic Preservation

Since its founding in 1949, the National Trust for Historic Preservation has worked to preserve historic buildings and neighborhoods. Through educational programs, publications, financial assistance, and government advocacy, the National Trust has been successful in revitalizing communities across the country. This private, non-profit organization operates six regional offices and 25 historic sites, publishes the award winning *Preservation* magazine, hosts the nation's largest annual preservation conference, and works with thousands of local community groups nationwide to preserve their history and buildings.

Address
1785 Massachusetts Avenue, NW
Washington, DC 20036
(202) 588-6000
www.nationaltrust.org

455

Mission Statement

The National Trust for Historic Preservation is a privately funded, nonprofit organization that provides leadership, education, advocacy, and resources to save America's diverse historic places and revitalize our communities.

NTHP/HUD Secretary's Award for Excellence in Historic Preservation

Each year, as part of its Preservation Conference, the National Trust for Historic Preservation confers several awards for preservation, including the HUD Secretary's Award for Excellence in Historic Preservation. This award specifically honors preservation projects that also provide affordable housing and/or expanded economic opportunities for low- and moderate-income families and individuals. The criteria for the award include the project's impact on the community, quality and degree of difficulty, unusual or pioneering nature, affordable housing/economic development opportunities, and ability to fit into an overall community redevelopment plan.

For additional information and to request an application, call HUD at (800) 245-2691, or visit the HUD Web site at *www.huduser.org/research/secaward.html*.

1998
A.T. Lewis and Rio Grande Lofts
Denver, CO

1999
Belle Shore Apartments
Chicago, IL

2000
The city of Covington (KY)

2001
Notre Dame Academy
Cleveland, OH

2002
Hamilton Hotel
Laredo, TX

2003
Ziegler Estate/La Casita Verde
Los Angeles, CA

2004
The Reviviendo Family Housing project
Lawrence, MA

2005
Umpqua Community Development
Corporation
Roseburg, OR

Source: National Trust for Historic Preservation

Preserve America Presidential Awards

The Preserve America Presidential Awards honor organizations, businesses, government entities, and individuals in order to encourage and support community efforts for the preservation and enjoyment of the cultural and natural heritage of the United States. Recipients are chosen for exemplary accomplishment in the sustainable use and preservation of America's cultural or national heritage; the interpretation and integration of this heritage into contemporary community life; and innovative, creative, and responsible approaches to showcasing historic resources within the community. In order to be eligible, the nominated activity must have been completed within the past three years.

For additional information about the award program, visit *www.preserveamerica.gov* on the Internet.

2005 Winners

Heritage Tourism
Restoration of The Mount
Edith Wharton Restoration, Inc.
Lenox, MA

Texas Heritage Trails Program
Texas Historical Commission

Private Preservation
Louis Bolduc House, Agatha Bolduc-LeMeilleur
    House, and Gemien Beauvaus/Linden House
Bolduc Historic Properties
Sainte Genevieve, MO

Isaiah Davenport House Museum
Savannah, GA

Source: Preserve America

457

Did you know...

The 48-block Old Louisville (KY) neighborhood is the third-largest national preservation district and the largest Victorian district in the United States.

Presidents of the National Trust for Historic Preservation

1949–56	Frederick L. Rath Jr.
1956–60	Richard H. Howland
1960–67	Robert R. Garvey Jr.
1968–80	James Biddle
1980–84	Michael L. Ainslie
1984–92	J. Jackson Walter
1992–	Richard Moe

Source: National Trust for Historic Preservation

Did you know...

The National Trust's Preservation Library Collection (now owned by and housed at the University of Maryland) contains 14,000 books, 25,000 photographs, and 18,500 postcards, as well as numerous films, manuscripts, serials, and memorabilia.

Save America's Treasures

Launched in May 1998, Save America's Treasures is a public-private initiative between the White House Millennium Council and the National Trust for Historic Preservation dedicated to identifying and rescuing the enduring symbols of America and to raising public awareness and support for their preservation. This national effort to protect America's threatened cultural treasures includes significant documents, works of art, maps, journals, and historic structures that document and illuminate the history and culture of the United States. Applications to be designated an official project are accepted on an ongoing basis from nonprofit organizations and federal, state, and local agencies that are involved in the preservation, restoration, or conservation of historic buildings, sites, documents, artifacts, objects, or related educational activities. Becoming an official project is the first step toward eligibility for Save America's Treasures grants and, in and of itself, often generates local support. In the two years since its founding, Save America's Treasures has designated more than 1,000 official projects (a list is available on their Web site) and raised more than $242 million in public-private funds to support preservation efforts.

Address

1785 Massachusetts Avenue, NW
Washington, DC 20036
(202) 588-6202
www.saveamericastreasures.org

459

Mission Statement

Save America's Treasures is dedicated to identifying and rescuing the enduring symbols of the American tradition that define us as a nation.

Secretary of the Interior's Standards for Rehabilitation

The Secretary of the Interior's Standards for Rehabilitation were developed to help protect our nation's irreplaceable cultural resources by promoting consistent preservation practices. The standards recognize the need to alter or add to a historic property in order to meet continuing or changing uses. Following the standards helps to preserve the distinctive character of a historic building and its site while accommodating new uses. The standards (36 CFR Part 67) apply to historic buildings of all periods, styles, types, materials, and sizes, as well as to both the exterior and the interior of historic buildings. The standards also encompass related landscape features and the building's site and environment as well as attached, adjacent, or related new construction. In addition, in order for a rehabilitation project to be eligible for the 20 percent rehabilitation tax credit, the standards must be followed.

For more information about how to apply these standards to restoration projects and tax credits, visit the National Park Service's Web site at *www2.cr.nps.gov/tps/tax/rehabstandards.htm.*

460

1. A property shall be used for its historic purpose or be placed in a new use that requires minimal change to the defining characteristics of the building and its site and environment.

2. The historic character of a property shall be retained and preserved. The removal of historic materials or alteration of features and spaces that characterize a property shall be avoided.

3. Each property shall be recognized as a physical record of its time, place, and use. Changes that create a false sense of historical development, such as adding conjectural features or architectural elements from other buildings, shall not be undertaken.

4. Most properties change over time; those changes that have acquired historic significance in their own right shall be retained and preserved.

5. Distinctive features, finishes, and construction techniques or examples of craftsmanship that characterize a historic property shall be preserved.

6. Deteriorated historic features shall be repaired rather than replaced. Where the severity of deterioration requires replacement of a distinctive feature, the new feature shall match the old in design, color, texture, and other visual qualities and, where possible, materials. Replacement of missing features shall be substantiated by documentary, physical, or pictorial evidence.

7. Chemical or physical treatments, such as sandblasting, that cause damage to historic materials shall not be used. The surface cleaning of structures, if appropriate, shall be undertaken using the gentlest means possible.

Secretary of the Interior's Standards for Rehabilitation

8. Significant archeological resources affected by a project shall be protected and preserved. If such resources must be disturbed, mitigation measures shall be undertaken.

9. New additions, exterior alterations, or related new construction shall not destroy historic materials that characterize the property. The new work shall be differentiated from the old and shall be compatible with the massing, size, scale, and architectural features to protect the historic integrity of the property and its environment.

10. New additions and adjacent or related new construction shall be undertaken in such a manner that if removed in the future, the essential form and integrity of the historic property and its environment would be unimpaired.

Source: National Park Service

Threatened National Historic Landmarks

National Historic Landmarks are buildings, sites, districts, structures, and objects determined by the Secretary of the Interior to possess national significance to American history and culture and are deemed worthy of preservation. Every two years, out of the almost 2,500 National Historic Landmarks, the National Park Service compiles a list of those that are in eminent danger of destruction due to deterioration, incompatible new construction, demolition, erosion, vandalism, and looting. The purpose of this list is to alert the Federal government and Americans to this potential loss of their heritage.

For additional information about the National Historic Landmarks program or the Threatened List, visit the National Park's web site at *www.cr.nps.gov/landmarks.htm* or contact Heritage Preservation Services at (202) 343-9583.

2004 Threatened Buildings and Historic Districts

Alaska
Alaska Native Brotherhood Hall, Sitka
Chilkoot Trail and Dyea Site, Skagway
Dutch Harbor Naval Operating Base and Fort Mears, US Army, Unalaska
Holy Assumption Orthodox Church, Kenai
Japanese Occupation Site, Kiska Island, Aleutian Islands
Seal Island Historic District, Pribilof Islands

American Samoa
Government House, Utelei

Arizona
Grand Canyon Depot, Grand Canyon
Old Oraibi, Oraibi
Tombstone Historic District, Tombstone

Arkansas
Bathhouse Row, Hot Springs
Rohwer Relocation Center Cemetery, Rohwer

California
Harada House, Riverside
Mare Island Naval Shipyard, Vallejo
Warner's Ranch, Warner Springs

Colorado
Central City/Black Hawk Historic District, Central City
Cripple Creek Historic District, Cripple Creek

District of Columbia
Mary Church Terrell House

Florida
Cape Canaveral Air Force Station, Cocoa
Pensacola Naval Air Station Historic District, Pensacola

Georgia
Savannah Historic District, Savannah

Hawaii
Kalaupapa Leprosy Settlement, Kalaupapa Peninsula, Moloka'i Island
United States Naval Base, Pearl Harbor, Pearl City

Indiana
Joseph Bailly Homestead, Porter County

Threatened National Historic Landmarks

Massachusetts
Boston Naval Shipyard, Boston
Lowell Locks & Canals Historic District, Lowell
King's Chapel, Boston
Nantucket Historic District, Nantucket
Springfield Armory, Springfield

Michigan
Calumet Historic District, Calumet
Highland Park Ford Plant, Highland Park
Quincy Mining Company Historic District,
    Hancock

Mississippi
Champion Hill Battlefield, Bolton
Siege and Battle of Corinth Sites, Corinth

Missouri
Mutual Musicians Association Building,
    Kansas City

Montana
Butte Historic District, Butte
Great Northern Railway Buildings, Glacier
    National Park
Virginia City Historic District, Virginia City

Nevada
Virginia City Historic District, Virginia City

New Jersey
Monmouth Battlefield, Freehold
Walt Whitman House, Camden

New Mexico
Blackwater Draw (formerly Anderson Basin),
    Clovis
Kit Carson House, Taos
El Santuario De Chimayo, Chimayo

New York
Adams Power Plant Transformer House,
    Niagara Falls
Hudson River State Hospital, Main Building,
    Poughkeepsie
New York State Inebriate Asylum, Binghamton
Gerrit Smith Estate, Peterboro

Ohio
Colonel Charles Young House, Wilberforce
Ohio and Erie Canal, Valley View Village
Stan Hywet Hall, Akron
William McKinley Tomb, Canton

Oklahoma
Fort Gibson, Fort Gibson
Wheelock Academy, Millerton

Pennsylvania
Albert Gallatin House, Point Marion
Gruber Wagon Works, Reading
Harrisburg Station and Train Shed, Harrisburg
Pearl S. Buck House, Perkasie
United States Naval Asylum, Philadelphia

Tennessee
Beale Street Historic District, Memphis

Texas
Dealey Plaza Historic District, Dallas
Spanish Governor's Palace, San Antonio

Virginia
Cedar Creek Battlefield and Belle Grove
    Plantation, Middletown
Hampton Institute, Hampton
    (Independent City)

Wisconsin
Taliesin East, Spring Green

Source: National Park Service

463

UNESCO Asia-Pacific Heritage Awards for Culture Heritage Conservation

As a part of the United Nations' Educational, Scientific, and Cultural Organization's culture heritage program in Asia and the Pacific, the Awards for Culture Heritage Conservation are presented each year to individuals and organizations within the private sector for superior conservation and restoration of structures more than 50 years old. The projects must have been restored within the past 10 years and must also be privately leased or owned. In addition, the Jury Commendation for Innovation award recognizes newly built structures that demonstrate outstanding standards for contemporary architectural design that are well integrated into historic contexts.

Regulations and entry forms, along with photos and descriptions of the winners, can be found online at *www.unescobkk.org/culture/heritageawards/*.

2005 Recipients

Award of Excellence
Houkeng Timber-Arched Corridor Bridge
Qingyuan County, Zhejiang Province, China

Dr. Bhau Daji Lad Museum
Mumbai, India

Award of Distinction
Sideng Market Square and Theatre (Shaxi
   Rehabilitation Project)
Yunnan Province, China

Mehrangarh Fort
Rajasthan, India

Award of Merit
St. Joseph's Chapel
Hong Kong, China

Tung Wah Coffin Home
Hong Kong, China

Amburiq Mosque
Skardu, Baltistan, Pakistan

Dutch Reformed Church
Galle, Sri Lanka

Ayuguthi Sattal
Lalitpur, Kathmandu, Nepal

Honorable Mention
Pingjiang Historic Block
Suzhou, Jiangsu Province, China

Zhaoxiang Huang Ancestral Hall
Foshan, Guangdong Province, China

Zain-ad-din Karavansara
Yazd, Iran

Far Eastern University
Manila, Philippines

Tamnak Yai, Devavesm Palace
Bangkok, Thailand

UNESCO Asia-Pacific Heritage Awards for Culture Heritage Conservation

Jury Commendation for Innovation

Meridian Gate Exhibition Hall of the Palace
    Museum
Beijing, China

Yuhu Primary School and Community Center
Lijiang, Yunnan Province, China.

*Source: United Nations' Educational, Scientific and Cultural
    Organization*

Vernacular Architecture Forum

Devoted to the ordinary architecture of North America, the Vernacular Architecture Forum was formed in 1980 to encourage the study and preservation of traditional structures and landscapes. These include agricultural buildings, industrial and commercial structures, 20th-century suburban houses, settlement patterns and cultural landscapes, and areas historically overlooked by scholars. The VAF embraces multidisciplinary interaction. Historians, designers, archaeologists, folklorists, architectural historians, geographers, museum curators, and historic preservationists contribute to the organization. The VAF holds its conference every spring with part of the agenda focusing on the vernacular architecture of that region. Every few years, papers are selected from past conferences and published in the series *Perspectives in Vernacular Architecture,* now in its ninth volume. The VAF presents two annual awards: the Abbott Lowell Cummings Award for the best book published on North American vernacular architecture and cultural landscapes and the Paul E. Buchanan Award for the best non-published work on North American vernacular architecture.

Address —————————————————————————
PO Box 1511
Harrisonburg, VA 22803-1511
www.vernaculararchitectureforum.org

Mission Statement

During the past 25 years, interest in the ordinary architecture of North America has grown rapidly and in diverse directions. Scholars and field professionals now apply the term vernacular architecture to traditional domestic and agricultural buildings, industrial and commercial structures, 20-century suburban houses, settlement patterns, and cultural landscapes. The Vernacular Architecture Forum was formed in 1980 to encourage the study and preservation of these informative and valuable material resources.

World Heritage List

Since 1972, the World Heritage Committee has placed more than 750 properties in 125 countries on the World Heritage List. Established under terms of the Convention Concerning the Protection of the World Cultural and Natural Heritage, the World Heritage List was adopted in November 1972 at the 17th General Conference of the United Nations Educational, Scientific, and Cultural Organization. The Convention states that a World Heritage Committee "will establish, keep up-to-date and publish" a World Heritage List of cultural and natural properties submitted by the states parties and considered to be of outstanding universal value. One of the main responsibilities of this committee is to provide technical cooperation under the World Heritage Fund for the safeguarding of World Heritage properties to states parties whose resources are insufficient. Assistance with the nomination process, training, grants, and loans are also available.

For a complete listing of all the World Heritage properties with detailed descriptions and photographs, visit their Web site at *www.unesco.org/whc.*

Historic Cities and Towns

Albania
Museum-City of Gjirokastra

Algeria
Kasbah of Algiers
M'Zab Valley

Austria
City of Graz – Historic Centre
Hallstatt-Dachstein Salzkammergut Cultural
    Landscape
Historic Centre of the City of Salzburg
Historic Centre of Vienna

Azerbaijan
Walled City of Baku with the Shirvanshah's
    Palace and Maiden Tower*

Belarus
Architectural, Residential and Cultural Complex
    of the Radziwill Family at Nesvizh

Belgium
Grand-Place, Brussels
Historic Centre of Brugge

Bolivia
City of Potosi
Historic City of Sucre

Bosnia and Herzegovina
Old Bridge Area of the Old City of Mostar

Brazil
Brasilia
Historic Centre of Salvador de Bahia
Historic Centre of São Luis
Historic Centre of the Town of Diamantina
Historic Centre of the Town of Goiás
Historic Centre of the Town of Olinda
Historic Town of Ouro Preto

Bulgaria
Ancient City of Nessebar

461

World Heritage List

Canada
Lunenburg Old Town
Quebec (Historic Area)

China
Ancient City of Ping Yao
Historic Centre of Macao
Old Town of Lijiang

Colombia
Historic Centre of Santa Cruz de Mompox
Port, Fortresses and Group of Monuments,
    Cartagena

Croatia
Historic City of Trogir
Historical Complex of Split with the Palace
    of Diocletian
Old City of Dubrovnik

Cuba
Old Havana and its Fortifications
Trinidad and the Valley de los Ingenios
Urban Historic Centre of Cienfuegos

Czech Republic
Cathedral of Our Lady at Sedlec
Historic Centre of Cesky Krumlov
Historic Centre of Prague
Historic Centre of Telc
Holasovice Historical Village Reservation
Kutná Hora: Historical Town Centre with the
    Church of St Barbara and the Cathedral of
    Our Lady at Sedlec

Dominican Republic
Colonial City of Santo Domingo

Ecuador
City of Quito
Historic Centre of Santa Ana de los Ríos de
    Cuenca

Egypt
Abu Mena*
Islamic Cairo

Estonia
Historic Centre (Old Town) of Tallinn

Finland
Old Rauma

Former Yugoslav Republic of Macedonia
Ohrid Region with its Cultural and Historical
    Aspect and its Natural Environment

France
Historic Centre of Avignon
Historic Fortified City of Carcassonne
Historic Site of Lyons
Le Havre, the City Rebuilt by Auguste Perret
Mont-Saint-Michel and its Bay
Paris, Banks of the Seine
Place Stanislas, Place de la Carrière and Place
    d'Alliance in Nancy
Provins, Town of Medieval Fairs
Roman and Romanesque Monuments of Arles
Grande Ile, Strasbourg

Germany
Classical Weimar
Collegiate Church, Castle, and Old Town
    of Quedlinburg
Hanseatic City of Lübeck
Historic Centres of Stralsund and Wismar
Mines of Rammelsberg and Historic Town
    of Goslar
Palaces and Parks of Potsdam and Berlin
Town of Bamberg

Greece
Historic Centre (Chorá) with the Monastery
    of Saint John "the Theologian" and the Cave
    of the Apocalypse on the Island of Pátmos
Medieval City of Rhodes

Guatemala
Antigua Guatemala

Holy See
Vatican City

World Heritage List

Holy See/Italy
Historic Centre of Rome, the Properties of the
Holy See in that City Enjoying Extraterritorial
Rights and San Paolo Fuori le Mura

Hungary
Budapest, the Banks of the Danube and the
Buda Castle Quarter
Iran
Meidan Emam, Esfahan

Israel
Old City of Acre

Italy
Assisi, the Basilica of San Francesco and Other
Franciscan Sites
Cathedral, Torre Civica and Piazza Grande,
Modena
City of Verona
City of Vicenza and the Palladian Villas of the
Veneto
Costiera Amalfitana
Crespi d'Adda
Ferrara, City of the Renaissance and its Po Delta
Historic Centre of the City of Pienza
Historic Centre of Florence
Historic Centre of Naples
Historic Centre of San Gimignano
Historic Centre of Siena
Historic Centre of Urbino
I Sassi di Matera
Late Baroque Towns of the Val di Noto
(South-Eastern Sicily)
Portovenere, Cinque Terre, and the Islands
(Palmaria, Tino and Tinetto)
Syracuse and the Rocky Necropolis of Pantalica
Venice and its Lagoon

Japan
Historic Monuments of Ancient Kyoto (Kyoto,
Uji and Otsu Cities)
Historic Monuments of Ancient Nara
Historic Villages of Shirakawa-go and Gokayama

Jerusalem
Old City of Jerusalem and its Walls*

Lao People's Democratic Republic
Town of Luang Prabang

Latvia
Historic Centre of Riga

Lebanon
Byblos

Libyan Arab Jamahiriya
Old Town of Ghadames

Lithuania
Vilnius Historic Centre

Luxembourg
City of Luxembourg: its Old Quarters and
Fortifications

Mali
Old Towns of Djenné
Timbuktu

Malta
City of Valletta

Mauritania
Ancient Ksour of Ouadane, Chinguetti,
Tichitt and Oualata

Mexico
Historic Centre of Mexico City and Xochimilco
Historic Centre of Morelia
Historic Centre of Oaxaca and Archaeological
Site of Monte Alban
Historic Centre of Puebla
Historic Centre of Zacatecas
Historic Fortified Town of Campeche
Historic Monuments Zone of Querétaro
Historic Monuments Zone of Tlacotalpan
Historic Town of Guanajuato and Adjacent Mines

469

World Heritage List

Morocco
Historic City of Meknes
Ksar of Ait-Ben-Haddou
Medina of Essaouira (formerly Mogador)
Medina of Fez
Medina of Marrakesh
Medina of Tétouan (formerly known as Titawin)
Portuguese City of Mazagan (El Jadida)

Mozambique
Island of Mozambique

Nepal
Kathmandu Valley*

Netherlands
Historic Area of Willemstad, Inner City and
   Harbour, Netherlands Antilles
Droogmakerij de Beemster (Beemster Polder)

Norway
Bryggen
Røros

Oman
Frankincense Trail

Panama
Historic District of Panamá, with the Salón
   Bolivar

Peru
City of Cuzco
Historic Centre of Lima
Historical Centre of the City of Arequipa

Philippines
Historic Town of Vigan

Poland
Cracow's Historic Centre
Historic Centre of Warsaw
Medieval Town of Torun
Old City of Zamosc

Portugal
Central Zone of the Town of Angra do Heroismo
   in the Azores
Cultural Landscape of Sintra
Historic Centre of Evora
Historic Centre of Guimarães
Historic Centre of Oporto

Republic of Korea
Kyongju Historic Areas

Romania
Historic Centre of Sighisoara
Villages with Fortified Churches in Transylvania

Russian Federation
Historic and Architectural Complex of the
   Kazan Kremlin
Historic Centre of Saint Petersburg and Related
   Groups of Monuments
Historical Centre of the City of Yaroslavl
Historic Monuments of Novgorod and
   Surroundings
Kremlin and Red Square, Moscow

Senegal
Island of Saint-Louis

Slovakia
Banska Stiavnica
Bardejov Town Conservation Reserve

Spain
Alhambra, Generalife and Albayzin, Granada
Archaeological Ensemble of Mérida
Historic Centre of Cordoba
Historic City of Toledo
Historic Walled Town of Cuenca
Ibiza, biodiversity and culture
Monuments of Oviedo and the Kingdom
   of the Asturias
Old City of Salamanca
Old Town of Avila with its Extra-Muros Churches
Old Town of Caceres
Old Town of Segovia and its Aqueduct
San Cristóbal de La Laguna
Santiago de Compostela (Old town)
University and Historic Precinct of Alcalá de
   Henares

World Heritage List

Sri Lanka
Old Town of Galle and its Fortifications
Sacred City of Kandy

Suriname
Historic Inner City of Paramaribo
Sweden
Church Village of Gammelstad, Luleå
Hanseatic Town of Visby
Naval Port of Karlskrona

Switzerland
Old City of Berne

Syrian Arab Republic
Ancient City of Aleppo
Ancient City of Bosra
Ancient City of Damascus

Tunisia
Kairouan
Medina of Sousse
Medina of Tunis

Turkey
City of Safranbolu
Historic Areas of Istanbul

Turkmenistan
Kunya-Urgench

Ukraine
L'viv – the Ensemble of the Historic Centre

United Kingdom of Great Britain and Northern Ireland
City of Bath
Historic Town of St George and Related
    Fortifications, Bermuda
Liverpool – Maritime Mercantile City
New Lanark
Old and New Towns of Edinburgh
Saltaire

United Republic of Tanzania
Stone Town of Zanzibar

United States of America
La Fortaleza and San Juan Historic Site in
    Puerto Rico

Uruguay
Historic Quarter of the City of Colonia del
    Sacramento

Uzbekistan
Itchan Kala
Historic Centre of Bukhara
Historic Centre of Shakhrisyabz
Samarkand – Crossroads of Culture

Venezuela
Coro and its Port

Vietnam
Complex of Hué Monuments
Hoi An Ancient Town

Yemen
Historic Town of Zabid*
Old City of Sana'a
Old Walled City of Shibam

Yugoslavia
Natural and Culturo-Historical Region of Kotor

* Indicates the site is also on the World Heritage in Danger list as
  determined by the World Heritage Committee.

Source: UNESCO, World Heritage Committee

411

World's 100 Most Endangered Sites

The World Monuments Fund's biennial list of the 100 Most Endangered Sites contains those cultural sites most in danger of destruction, either by natural or manmade causes. For many sites, inclusion on this list is their only hope for survival. Initial nominations are solicited from governments, heritage conservation organizations, and concerned individuals. Each site must have the support of a sponsoring institution, substantial cultural significance, an urgent need for intervention, and a viable intervention plan. The final selection committee is comprised of a panel of international experts. Limited financial support is also available from the World Monuments Watch Fund and is awarded on a competitive basis to selected sites. The World Monuments Fund is a private, nonprofit organization created in 1965 with the purpose of fostering a greater awareness of the world's cultural, artistic, and historic resources; facilitating preservation and conservation efforts; and generating private financial assistance.

For information and photos of each site, visit the World Monuments Fund's Web site at *www.wmf.org* or contact them at (646) 424-9594.

2006 Most Endangered Sites

Afghanistan
Haji Piyada Mosque, Balkh

Antarctica
Sir Ernest Shackleton's Expedition Hut, Cape Royds, Ross Island

Australia
Dampier Rock Art Complex, Dampier, Burrup Peninsula

Bangladesh
Sonargaon-Panam City, Sonargaon

Bosnia/Herzegovina
Mehmed-Pasha Sokolovic Bridge, Visegrad

Brazil
Convent of San Francisco and Historic Olinda, Olinda, Pernambuco

Cameroon
Bafut Palace, Bafut

Cape Verde
Tarrafal Concentration Camp, Tarrafal

Chile
Tulor Village, Antofagasta
Cerros Pintados, Tarapaca

China
Cockcrow Post Town, Cockcrow Post, Huailai
Lu Mansion, Dong Yang
Qikou Town, Shanxi Province
Stone Towers of Southwest China, Various
Tianshui Traditional Houses, Tianshui, Qincheng, Gansu
Tuanshan Historical Village, Yunnan Province

Croatia
Novi Dvori Castle, Zapresic, Croatia
Saint Blaise Church, Dubrovnik

World's 100 Most Endangered Sites

Cuba
Finca Vigia (Hemingway's House), San Francisco
de Paula

Egypt
Sabil Ruqayya Dudu, Cairo
Tarabay al-Sharify, Cairo
West Bank, Luxor

El Salvador
San Miguel Arcangel, Panchimalco, and Santa
Cruz de Roma, Huizucar

Eritrea
Asmara Historic City Center and Theater,
Asmara
Kidane-Mehret Church, Senafe
Massawa Historic Town, Massawa

Finland
Helsinki-Malmi Airport, Helsinki

Georgia
Jvari Monastery, Mtshekta

Greece
Helike Archaeological Site, Rizomylos and Eliki,
Achaia

Guatemala
Naranjo, El Petén

India
Dalhousie Square, Calcutta
Dhangkar Gompa, Himachal Pradesh
Guru Lhakhang and Sumda Chung Temples,
Sumda Chung
Watson's Hotel, Mumbai

Indonesia
Omo Hada, Nias Island

Iran
Bam, Bam

Iraq
Cultural Heritage Sites, Countrywide

Ireland
Wonderful Barn, Kildare

Italy
Academy of Hadrian's Villa, Tivoli
Cimitero Acattolico, Rome
Civita di Bagnoregio, Bagnoregio
Murgia dei Trulli, Murgia dei Trulli
Portici Royal Palace, Naples
Santa Maria in Stelle Hypogeum, Verona
Temple of Portunus, Rome

Kenya
Mtwapa Heritage Site, Kilifi, Mtwapa

Laos
Chom Phet Cultural Landscape, Luang Prabang

Latvia
Riga Cathedral, Riga

Lebanon
Chehabi Citadel, Hasbaya
International Fairground at Tripoli, Tripoli

Macedonia
Treskavec Monastery and Church, Treskavec

Mauritania
Chinguetti Mosque, Chinguetti

Mexico
Chalcatzingo, Morelos
Mexico City Historic Center, Mexico City
Pimería Alta Missions, Sonora
San Juan Bautista Cuauhtinchan, Puebla
San Nicolás Obispo, Morelia, Michoacán

Nepal
Patan Royal Palace Complex, Patan

Nigeria
Benin City Earthworks, Edo State

Norway
Sandviken Bay, Bergen

413

World's 100 Most Endangered Sites

Pakistan
Mian Nasir Mohamad Graveyard, Dadu District
Thatta Monuments, Thatta

Palestinian Territories
Tell Balatah (Shechem or Ancient Nablus),
    Nablus, West Bank

Panama
Panama Canal Area, Panama Canal area

Peru
Cajamarquilla, Lima
Presbítero Maestro Cemetery, Lima
Quinta Heeren, Lima
Revash Funerary Complex, Santo Tomas
    de Quillay
Túcume Archaeological Site, Lambayeque

Poland
Jerusalem Hospital of the Teutonic Order,
    Malborka
Mausoleum of Karol Scheibler, Lodz

Portugal
Teatro Capitolio, Lisbon

Romania
Oradea Fortress, Oradea

Russia
Melnikov's House Studio, Moscow
Narkomfin Building, Moscow
Semenovskoe-Otrada, Moscow Region

Samoa
Pulemelei Mound, Palauli, Letolo Plantation

Serbia/Montenegro
Prizren Historic Center, Prizren
Subotica Synagogue, Subotica

Sierre Leone
Old Fourah Bay College, Freetown

Slovakia
Lednicke-Rovne Historical Park, Lednické-Rovne

South Africa
Richtersveld Cultural Landscape, Northern
    Cape Province

Spain
Segovia Aqueduct, Segovia

Sudan
Suakin, Suakin Island

Syria
Amrit Archaeological Site, Amrit
Shayzar Castle, Shayzar
Tell Mozan (Ancient Urkesh)

Turkey
Aphrodisias, Aphrodisias
Little Hagia Sophia, Istanbul

United Kingdom
Saint Mary's Stow Church, Stow, Lincolnshire
Saint Vincent's Street Church, Glasgow, Scotland

United States
2 Columbus Circle, New York, NY
Bluegrass Cultural Landscape of Kentucky,
    Central Kentucky
Cyclorama Center, Gettysburg, PA
Dutch Reformed Church, Newbergh, NY
Ellis Island Baggage and Dormitory Building,
    New York, NY
Ennis Brown House, Los Angeles, CA
Hanging Flume, Montrose County, CO
Mount Lebanon Shaker Village,
    New Lebanon, NY

Venezuela
La Guaira Historic City, Vargas

Source: World Monument Fund

World's 100 Most Endangered Sites

Clockwise from the top: The recently renovated World Bank Office, originally a villa built in 1938, Asmara Historic City Center, Eritrea (photo: Edward Denison); Huang'en Residence, Tuanshan Historical Village, China (photo: Ralph Feiner); and a view of the Mqbara of Jan Nizam al-Din from the west, Thatta Monuments, Pakistan (photo: Heritage Foundation Pakistan). All photos courtesy of the World Monument Fund.

1

Design
Education

Current and prospective design students will find
this chapter of particular interest and use, with
entries ranging from student award programs and
associations to a comprehensive listing of design
degree programs and rankings of the best schools for
architecture, industrial design, interior design, and
landscape architecture. Of related interest are
award-winning student essays found in the Speeches
& Essays chapter beginning on page 1.

ACSA Distinguished Professor Award

The Association of Collegiate Schools of Architecture's Distinguished Professor Award is presented annually for "sustained creative achievement" in the field of architectural education, whether through teaching, design, scholarship, research, or service. Eligible candidates must be living faculty of an ACSA member school for a minimum of 10 years or be otherwise allied with architectural education at an ACSA member school. Students or faculty of an ACSA member school may make nominations. Each year, the awards committee recommends a maximum of five candidates to the ACSA board. Winners are entitled to use the title "ACSA Distinguished Professor" for life.

For additional information about the ACSA Distinguished Professor Award, contact the association at (202) 785-2324, or visit their Web site at *www.acsa-arch.org*.

1984–85
Alfred Caldwell, Illinois Institute of Technology
Robert S. Harris, Univ. of Southern California
Fay Jones, University of Arkansas
Charles Moore, University of Texas at Austin
Ralph Rapson, University of Minnesota

1985–86
James Marston Fitch, Columbia University
Leslie J. Laskey, Washington University
Harlan McClure, Clemson University
Edward Romieniec, Texas A&M University
Richard A. Williams, University of Illinois,
     Urbana–Champaign

1986–87
Christopher Alexander, University of California,
     Berkeley
Harwell Hamilton Harris, North Carolina
     State University
Stanislawa Nowicki, University of Pennsylvania
Douglas Shadbolt, University of British Columbia
Jerzy Soltan, Harvard University

1987–88
Harold Cooledge Jr., Clemson University
Bernd Foerster, Kansas State University
Romaldo Giurgola, Columbia University
Joseph Passonneau, Washington University
John G. Willams, University of Arkansas

1988–89
Peter R. Lee Jr., Clemson University
E. Keith McPheeters, Auburn University
Stanley Salzman, Pratt Institute
Calvin C. Straub, Arizona State University
Blanche Lemco van Ginkel, University of
     Toronto

1989–90
Gunnar Birkerts, University of Michigan
Olivio C. Ferrari, Virginia Polytechnic Institute
     and State University
George C. Means Jr., Clemson University
Malcolm Quantrill, Texas A&M University

1990–91
Denise Scott Brown, University of Pennsylvania
Panos Koulermos, Univ. of Southern California
William McMinn, Cornell University
Forrest Wilson, Catholic University of America
David Woodcock, Texas A&M University

1991–92
M. David Egan, Clemson University
Robert D. Dripps, University of Virginia
Richard C. Peters, University of California,
     Berkeley
David L. Niland, University of Cincinnati

419

ACSA Distinguished Professor Award

1992–93
Stanley W. Crawley, University of Utah
Don P. Schlegel, University of New Mexico
Thomas L. Schumacher, University of Maryland

1993–94
George Anselevicius, University of New Mexico
John Harold (Hal) Box, Univ. of Texas at Austin
Peter McCleary, University of Pennsylvania
Douglas Rhyn, Univ. of Wisconsin–Milwaukee
Alan Stacell, Texas A&M University

1994–95
Blake Alexander, University of Texas at Austin
Robert Burns, North Carolina State University
Robert Heck, Louisiana State University
Ralph Knowles, University of Southern California

1995–96
James Barker, Clemson University
Mui Ho, University of California, Berkley
Patricia O'Leary, University of Colorado
Sharon Sutton, University of Minnesota
Peter Waldman, University of Virginia

1996–97
Colin H. Davidson, Université de Montréal
Michael Fazio, Mississippi State University
Ben J. Refuerzo, Univ. of California, Los Angeles
Max Underwood, Arizona State University
J. Stroud Watson, University of Tennessee

1997–98
Roger H. Clark, North Carolina State University
Bob E. Heatly, Oklahoma State University
John S. Reynolds, University of Oregon
Marvin E. Rosenman, Ball State University
Anne Taylor, University of New Mexico

1998–99
Ralph Bennett, University of Maryland
Diane Ghirardo, University of Southern
    California
Robert Greenstreet, University of
    Wisconsin–Milwaukee
Thomas Kass, University of Utah
Norbert Schoenauer, McGill University
Jan Wampler, Massachusetts Inst. of Technology

1999–2000
Maelee Thomson Foster, University of Florida
Louis Inserra, Pennsylvania State University
Henry Sanoff, North Carolina State University

2000–01
Ikhlas Sabouni, Prairie View A&M University
Raymond J. Cole, University of British Columbia

2001–02
Steven Paul Badanes, University of Washington
Raymond Lifchez, Univ. of California, Berkeley
Marvin John Malecha, North Carolina State Univ.
Enrique Vivoni Farage, Universidad de Puerto Rico
James P. Warfield, University of Illinois,
    Urbana–Champaign

2002–03
Sherry Ahrentzen, Univ. of Wisconsin–Milwaukee
Lance Jay Brown, City College of New York, CUNY
David Crane, University of South Florida
Lars Lerup, Rice University
Edward Steinfeld, University at Buffalo, SUNY

2003–04
Michael Benedikt, University of Texas at Austin
Georgia Bizios, North Carolina State University
William C. Miller, University of Utah

2004–05
Stephen Verderber, Tulane University

Source: Association of Collegiate Schools of Architecture

480

ACSP Distinguished Educator Award

The ACSP Distinguished Educator Award is presented by the Association of Collegiate Schools of Planning in appreciation for distinguished service to planning education and practice. Nominations are welcomed from chairs and faculty members of ACSP member schools and are reviewed by the award committee. Recipients are chosen for scholarly contributions, teaching excellence, service to the profession, and significant contributions to planning education and/or practice.

For additional information about the Distinguished Educator Award, visit ACSP's Web site at *www.acsp.org.*

1983	Harvey Perloff
	University of California, Los Angeles
1984	John Reps
	Cornell University
1985	*No award granted*
1986	F. Stuart Chapin Jr.
	University of North Carolina at
	Chapel Hill
1987	John Friedmann
	University of California, Los Angeles
1988	*No award granted*
1989	John Dyckman
	Johns Hopkins University
1990	Barclay Gibbs Jones
	Cornell University
1991	Britton Harris
	University of Pennsylvania
1992	Melville Branch
	University of Southern California
1993	Ann Strong
	University of Pennsylvania
1994	John A. Parker
	University of North Carolina at
	Chapel Hill
1995	Alan Feldt
	University of Michigan
1996	Martin Meyerson
	University of Pennsylvania
1997	Lloyd Rodwin
	Massachusetts Institute of Technology
1998	Michael Teitz
	University of California, Berkeley
1999	Lisa Redfield Peattie
	Massachusetts Institute of Technology

2000	Melvin M. Webber
	University of California, Berkeley
2001	*No award granted*
2002	David R. Godschalk
	University of North Carolina at
	Chapel Hill
2003	Paul Niebanck
	University of Washington
2004	Susan Fainstein
	Rutgers, The State University
	of New Jersey
2005	Lawrence E. Susskind
	Massachusetts Institute of Technology

Source: Association of Collegiate Schools of Planning

481

AIA Education Honor Awards

The annual American Institute of Architects' Education Honor Awards program is designed to recognize the achievement of outstanding teachers and to increase awareness of educational excellence in the classroom, laboratory, studio, or community-based educational environment. An independent jury selects the winners based on their development of exceptional, innovative, and intellectually challenging courses that address broad issues and contribute to the advancement of architectural education and practice.

For more information, contact the AIA at (202) 626-7417 or visit their Web site at *www.aia.org.*

2005 Winners

Honor Award

"Finding the Social in Big Box Retail:
  Typological Investigations of a Wal-Mart
  Store"
Aaron Gabriel, Stephen Luoni
University of Arkansas

"(drawing [machines) drawing]"
Rebecca O'Neal Dagg, Bruce Lindsey,
  Rusty Smith
Auburn University

Honorable Mention

"Cal Poly Downtown Community Design Studio
  for Affordable Housing"
Alice Alison Mueller
California Polytechnic State University,
  San Luis Obispo

"Urban Acupuncture: Neighborhood Design-
  Build Studio"
Steve Badanes, Damon Smith
University of Washington

Jury

John Cary (chair)
Kathryn Prigmore
Robert Selby
Trinity Simons
Paul Taylor

Source: American Institute of Architects

482

Did you know...

Cesar Pelli has returned to his alma mater, the University of Illinois at Urbana–Champaign, to design his first building for the school—the new College of Business, slated to open in 2008.

AIA Education Honor Awards

Finding the Social in Big Box Retail: The goal of the Big Box Studio at the University of Arkansas is to develop community-based design solutions that are ecologically, socially, and economically responsive within big-box urbanism. "Finding the Social in Big Box Retail" explored design and planning scenarios for a typical Wal-Mart supercenter project that would enhance the connections between community and large discount retail development. **Images courtesy of the University of Arkansas Community Design Center.**

AICP Outstanding Student Award

The American Institute of Certified Planners each year presents its Outstanding Student Awards to recognize outstanding graduating students in accredited university planning programs, both at the undergraduate and graduate levels. Awarded students have been selected for the honor by their school's department head and colleagues who establish criteria with an emphasis on quality of work in the students' courses in planning and likelihood of success as a professional planner.

Additional information can be found on the American Planning Association's Web site at *www.planning.org* or by calling the Washington, DC, office of the APA at (202) 872-0611.

2005 Winners

Bachelor's Degree

Amber Gray, Alabama A&M University
Brian Glodney, California Polytechnic State University, San Luis Obispo
Brian P. Hanson, University of Cincinnati
Nathan O. Scramlin, Michigan State University
Crezia Tano, California State Polytechnic University, Pomona
Aaron L. Todd, Iowa State University
Shannon Margaret Yadsko, University of Virginia

Master's Degree

Ryan A. Bland, Iowa State University
Tokey Boswell, University of Iowa
Halle Butvin, Ohio State University
Jeremiah J. Christopher, Virginia Commonwealth University
Joanna Cucch, California State Polytechnic University, Pomona
Joshua Curtis, University of Washington
Jennifer Deitrich, University of Arizona
Darci Dore, University of Michigan
Carlos Finkley, Alabama A&M University
Brian P. Hanson, University of Cincinnati
Ikroop Kaur, Georgia Institute of Technology
Dana LeWinter, Tufts University
Travea Leveene Ghee, Morgan State University
Matt Mantell, University of Oklahoma
Jane Meconi, Pratt Institute

Barbara Sutton Mora, University of Memphis
Gavin Moynahan, San Jose State University
Ashon Nesbitt, University of Florida
Andrew Nothstine, University of Pennsylvania
Sean O'Hagan, Cleveland State University
Allyson Phelps, Florida State University
Page Phillips, University of Oregon
Justin J. Price, Clemson University
Christopher Riale, Rutgers, The State University of New Jersey
Susan Robinson, Hunter College, CUNY
Leigh Katharine Rosen, University of Virginia
Corinne Rosenblum, California Polytechnic State University, San Luis Obispo
Allen Serkin, University of North Carolina
Elizabeth Shoemaker, University of Kansas
Joshua Tootoo, University of Rhode Island
Kristina Wamstad-Evans, University of Nebraska–Lincoln
Landon T. Weisswasser Bartley, Michigan State University
John Robert Zeanah, University of Memphis
Danielle Rae Zeigler, Kansas State University
Valentina Zuin, Massachusetts Institute of Technology

Source: American Institute of Certified Planners

AICP Outstanding Student Project Award

Recognizing outstanding achievements that contribute to advances in the field of planning, the American Institute of Certified Planners presents the Outstanding Student Project Award each year at the National Planning Conference. Students or groups of students in an accredited planning curriculum may enter a paper or class project; no more than three awards will be given. Award categories include the project that best demonstrates the contribution of planning to contemporary issues and the project best applying the planning process.

For Student Project Award nomination packets, call (202) 872-0611.

2005 Winners

Applied Research
"Conservation and Landscape Planning Heritage Trail, featuring Historic Places in Massachusetts"
Ann Chapman
University of Massachusetts Amherst

Demonstrating the Contribution of Planning to Contemporary Issues
"Food for Growth: A Community Food System Plan for Buffalo's West Side"
Tangerine Almeida, Mark Bostaph, Mikaela Engert, Samuel Gold, Jeanne Leccese, Jordana Maisel, Anjali Malhotra, Joanna Rogalski, Tatiana Vejar, Keigo Yokoyama, Lesley Zlatev, Samina Raja (adviser), Diane Picard (adviser)
University at Buffalo, SUNY

Applying the Planning Process
"San Miguel 2025: Draft Community Plan"
Brian Alee, Sandra Code, Michael Conger, William Hellper, Cornelius Kempenaar, Brian Leveille, Eric Muzzy, Mandi Raike, Jason Rogers, Santiago Simon, David Stanfield, Fred Thacker, Zeljka Pavlovich Howard (adviser)
California Polytechnic State University, San Luis Obispo

Source: American Institute of Certified Planners

485

Alpha Rho Chi

Alpha Rho Chi is a national coeducational professional fraternity for students and professionals of architecture and the allied arts, founded in 1914 when the Arcus Society of the University of Illinois and Sigma Upsilon of the University of Michigan united. The organization remains dedicated to "promoting the artistic, scientific, and practical proficiency of its membership and the profession." For membership information, contact the local Alpha Rho Chi chapter.

Contact

Additional information about Alpha Rho Chi,
including a list of chapters and their contacts,
can be found online at *www.alpharhochi.org.*

Mission Statement

Alpha Rho Chi was established to encourage closer fellowship and a greater interest in the study of architecture and the allied arts.

Alpha Rho Chi Bronze Medal

Alpha Rho Chi, a national professional coeducational fraternity for students in architecture and the allied arts, selects its annual Bronze Medal recipients from more than 100 schools of architecture. The award was established in 1931 by the Grand Council of Alpha Rho Chi to "encourage professional leadership by regarding student accomplishment, promote the ideals of professional service by acknowledging distinctive individual contributions to social life, and stimulate professional merit by commending qualities in the student not necessarily pertaining to scholarship." Winners, selected by each schools' faculty, are graduating seniors who best exemplify the aforementioned qualities.

Additional information may be found on the fraternity's Web site: *www.alpharhochi.org.*

2005 Recipients

Andrews University
Eric W. Zaddock

Arizona State University
Catherine E. Britt

Auburn University
Alan Keeth Stevenson

Boston Architectural Center
Scott Ellyson Culley

California College of the Arts
Kazuko Anne Kimura

California State Polytechnic University—Pomona
William L Mauer Jr.

Carlton University
Sara Amber Salach

Carnegie Mellon University
Lynne Riesselman

Catholic University of America
Sharneise L. Turpin

City College of New York, CUNY
Venesa Alicea

Clemson University
Sean Clifford Raboin

Columbia University
Craig Intinarelli

Cooper Union
Amir S. Shahrokhi

Dalhousie University
Charlotte Dunfield

Drexel University
Robert M. Piasecki

Drury University
Lacey Bridget Thurman

Florida A&M University
Niasha Ross

Florida Atlantic University
Albert M. Caroccio

Georgia Institute of Technology
Megan C. Duttenhofer

Hampton University
Fredrick Davis

Harvard University
Brian Price
Jonathan Lott

Howard University
Kristopher Vernandez

Illinois Institute of Technology
Uriel Ortega

Iowa State University
Carl R. Clark

Kansas State University
Craig M. Van Dyke

487

Alpha Rho Chi Bronze Medal

Kent State University
Lauren M. Merski

Louisiana State University
Hunter Alan Brown

Louisiana Tech University
Jason Henson

Massachusetts Institute of Technology
Carl Solander

McGill University
Vanessa Fong

Miami University
Ellissa Van Houtte

Mississippi State University
Robyn Clary

Montana State University
Michael Patterson

New Jersey Institute of Technology
Antonietta Alberto
Joanne Viania

NewSchool of Architecture & Design
Derek J. Boldt

North Carolina State University
Adam Brakenbury

North Dakota State University
Andrew E. Koedam

Norwich University
David Pereira

Ohio State University
Luke Daniel Kautz

Parsons School of Design
W. Brooks McDaniel
Bronwyn Breitner

Pennsylvania State University
Andrew J. Swartzell

Pratt Institute
Karri Beth Lacourciere

Princeton University
Ian Oakley Smith

Rensselaer Polytechnic Institute
David Fannon
Shefali Sanghvi

Rhode Island School of Design
Geraldo Dannemann

Rice University
Frank Davis Niendorff

Roger Williams University
Brynnemarie Theresa Lanciotti

Savannah College of Art and Design
Franyel Zelaya
Brandie Kochan

Southern California Institute of Architecture
Eric Yin Cheong

Syracuse University
Emily A. Santilli

Temple University
Ronald Ames Moss II

Texas A&M University
Joshua Guerra

Texas Tech University
Bryce Adrian Hamels

Tulane University
Rebecca Leigh Jeanes

Universite Laval
Isabelle-Amelie Chauvin

University at Buffalo, SUNY
David P. Marcoux

University of Arizona
John Richard Kuchen

University of Arkansas
Stephen M. Faber

University of British Columbia
Ian Ross McDonald

University of California, Berkeley
Yasmin D. Vobis

University of California, Los Angeles
Amalia Gonzales

University of Colorado
Heather Gayle Thigpen

University of Detroit Mercy
Eric Hornik

Alpha Rho Chi Bronze Medal

University of Florida
Shannon Shirah

University of Houston
Johnny Kousparis

University of Idaho
Eric M. Roberts

University of Illinois at Chicago
Steven Smutny

University of Kansas
Robert Brandon Tobias

University of Louisiana at Lafayette
Kyle C. Libersat

University of Manitoba
Kessa Kathleen Edwards

University of Maryland
Matthew J. Fitzsimmons

University of Memphis
Theresa C. Crampton

University of Miami
Matthew Anders
Janet Rumble

University of Michigan
Amanda R. Christianson

University of Minnesota
Megan Persohn

University of Nebraska—Lincoln
Kurt A. Cisar

University of North Carolina—Charlotte
Leslie M. Phipps
Christopher M. Johnson

University of Notre Dame
Joseph Nickol

University of Pennsylvania
Stephanie C. Feldman

University of South Florida
Beverly Lee Frank

University of Tennessee, Knoxville
Melissa Sue Watkins

University of Texas at Arlington
Bradley James Sliva
Ronnie George Parsons

University of Texas at Austin
Joseph C. Rippole
Wenny Huai Wen Hsu

University of Texas at San Antonio
David C Matiella

University of Toronto
Megan Elizabeth Torza

University of Utah
Preston Dean

University of Virginia
Lewis Maverick McNeel

University of Washington
Ian Frazier Means

University of Waterloo
Daniel Hall

University of Wisconsin—Milwaukee
Kristi Jacobs

Washington University
Brian Randall Molski

Wentworth Institute of Technology
Scott Thomas Waddell

Woodbury University
Sylvie T. Nguyen

Yale University
David Charles Hecht

Source: Alpha Rho Chi

489

American Institute of Architecture Students

The American Institute of Architecture Students is a nonprofit, independent, student-run organization that seeks to promote excellence in architecture education, training, and practice, as well as to organize architecture students and promote the study of architecture. The AIAS was formed in 1956 and today serves more than 7,500 undergraduate and graduate architecture students. More than 150 chapters at US and Canadian colleges and universities support members with professional development seminars, community projects, curriculum advisory committees, guest speakers, and many other programs.

Address

1735 New York Avenue, NW
Washington, DC 20006
(202) 626-7472
www.aias.org

Mission Statement

The mission of the American Institute of Architecture Students is to promote excellence in architecture education, training, and practice; to foster an appreciation of architecture and related disciplines; to meet students and professionals with common interests and to interact with some of today's leading architects and designers; to enrich communities in a spirit of collaboration; and to organize students and combine their efforts to advance the art and science of architecture.

America's Best Architecture Schools 2006

Since 2000, the *Almanac of Architecture & Design,* in conjunction with *DesignIntelligence,* has conducted annual research to determine the best NAAB-accredited (National Architectural Accrediting Board) architecture schools in the United States. This study captures the unique perspective of practitioners, the constituency most qualified to comment on how recent graduates from these schools fare in the marketplace. These professionals are asked to consider their firms' hiring practices during the past five years and indicate which schools have produced the graduates best prepared for real-world practice. While these rankings can be helpful to current and prospective architecture students, they are only one of many factors to consider: What is a school's job placement record? Focus of study? Faculty reputation and areas of specialization? Availability and caliber of internship program?

An in-depth analysis of the rankings, including additional rankings by region and information about the survey methodology, can be found in *America's Best Architecture & Design Schools 2006,* available at *www.di.net.*

Undergraduate Programs

1. Cornell University
2. University of Texas at Austin
3. California Polytechnic State University, San Luis Obispo (tie)
   Rice University (tie)
5. Kansas State University (tie)
   Rhode Island School of Design (tie)
7. Syracuse University (tie)
   Virginia Polytechnic Institute and State University (tie)
9. Carnegie Mellon University
10. Pennsylvania State University (tie)
    Pratt Institute (tie)
12. University of Notre Dame
13. Iowa State University (tie)
    University of Kansas (tie)
15. Auburn University (tie)
    University of Oregon (tie)

491

Graduate Programs

1. Harvard University
2. University of Cincinnati
3. University of Virginia
4. Columbia University (tie)
   University of Pennsylvania (tie)
6. University of Texas at Austin
7. Rice University
8. Massachusetts Institute of Technology (tie)
   Yale University (tie)
10. University of Illinois at Urbana–Champaign (tie)
    Washington University in St. Louis (tie)
12. Syracuse University
13. Clemson University (tie)
    University of California, Berkeley (tie)
15. Princeton University (tie)
    Texas A&M University (tie)

Source: DesignIntelligence

America's Best Industrial Design Schools 2006

To complement its annual rankings of architecture, interior design, and landscape architecture schools, the *Almanac of Architecture & Design*, in conjunction with *DesignIntelligence*, has expanded its research to include industrial design schools. Based on their hiring practices during the past five years, leading US industrial design firms have selected the best industrial design programs—the programs these firms say best prepare graduates for real-world practice. While these rankings can be helpful to current and prospective industrial design students, they are intended as only one of many factors influencing the decision-making process. Schools should be analyzed from different perspectives: What is their job placement record? Focus of study? Faculty reputation and areas of specialization? Availability and caliber of internship program?

An in-depth analysis of the rankings, including information about the survey methodology, can be found in *America's Best Architecture & Design Schools 2006*, available at *www.di.net*.

Undergraduate Programs

1. Art Center College of Design
2. University of Cincinnati
3. Pratt Institute
4. College for Creative Studies (tie)
   Rhode Island School of Design (tie)
6. Carnegie Mellon University
7. Cleveland Institute of Art
8. University of Illinois–Urbana Champaign
9. Syracuse University
10. California College of the Arts

Graduate Programs

1. Art Center College of Design
2. Pratt Institute
3. Cranbrook Academy of Art
4. Illinois Institute of Technology
5. Stanford University
6. Rhode Island School of Design
7. Ohio State University
8. University of Illinois–Urbana Champaign
9. Syracuse University
10. Arizona State University (tie)
    Georgia Institute of Technology (tie)
    North Carolina State University (tie)

Source: DesignIntelligence

America's Best Interior Design Schools 2006

The following list of US interior design schools reflects the view of practitioners who hire and work with new graduates on a daily basis. This annual survey is conducted in conjunction with *DesignIntelligence*, the monthly newsletter of the Design Futures Council. These professionals were asked to consider how prepared for the rigors of real-world practice the graduates they've hired within the past five years have been and to indicate from which schools the best prepared have hailed. While this unique perspective can be helpful to current and prospective design students, there are other important considerations to note: What is the job placement record of a particular program? Focus of study? Faculty reputation and areas of specialization? Availability and caliber of internship program?

An in-depth analysis of the ranking, including information about the survey methodology and a historical breakdown of past rankings, can be found in *America's Best Architecture & Design Schools 2006*, available at *www.di.net*.

Undergraduate Programs

1. University of Cincinnati
2. Pratt Institute
3. Cornell University
4. Kansas State University*
5. Arizona State University

6. University of Texas at Austin
7. Auburn University* (tie)
   Iowa State University (tie)
   Syracuse University (tie)
10. Louisiana State University

Graduate Programs

1. Rhode Island School of Design
2. Pratt Institute
3. Cornell University
4. Savannah College of Art and Design
5. Syracuse University

6. Arizona State University (tie)
   Texas Tech University (tie)
8. University of Oregon† (tie)
9. Oklahoma State University (tie)
   Virginia Polytechnic Institute and
   State University (tie)

* Kansas State University offers two programs—interior architecture in the College of Architecture, Planning & Design and interior design in the College of Human Ecology (both FIDER-accredited)—which have been combined for the purposes of this study. Auburn University's two programs—interior design in the College of Human Sciences (FIDER-accredited) and interior architecture in the School of Architecture (non-FIDER-accredited)—have also been combined.

† FIDER (Foundation for Interior Design Education Research) is the accrediting body for first-professional interior design degrees. All the undergraduate programs are FIDER-accredited. The University of Oregon's first-professional master's program is also accredited by FIDER. In addition, the university also offers a post-professional master's degree, which does not fall under FIDER's accreditation purview.

Source: DesignIntelligence

America's Best Landscape Architecture Schools 2006

The *Almanac of Architecture & Design,* in conjunction with *DesignIntelligence,* conducts an annual study to determine the best LAAB-accredited (Landscape Architectural Accrediting Board) landscape architecture schools in the United States. Based on the hiring practices of leading US landscape architecture firms during the past five years, the following list represents what these firms say are the schools that produce the graduates best prepared for real-world practice. While these rankings can be helpful to current and prospective landscape architecture students, they are intended as only one of many factors influencing the decision-making process. Schools should be analyzed from different perspectives: What is their job placement record? Focus of study? Faculty reputation and areas of specialization? Availability and caliber of internship program?

An in-depth analysis of the rankings, including additional rankings by region and information about the survey methodology, can be found in *America's Best Architecture & Design Schools 2006,* available at *www.di.net.*

Undergraduate Programs

1. University of Georgia
2. Purdue University
3. Louisiana State University
4. Pennsylvania State University
5. Kansas State University
6. California Polytechnic State University, San Luis Obispo
7. Ohio State University
8. Virginia Polytechnic Institute and State University
9. College of Environmental Science and Forestry, SUNY (tie)
   Cornell University (tie)
11. Ball State University (tie)
    Texas A&M University (tie)
13. California State Polytechnic University, Pomona (tie)
    University of Florida (tie)
    West Virginia University (tie)

America's Best Landscape Architecture Schools 2006

Graduate Programs

1. Harvard University
2. University of Pennsylvania
3. University of Georgia
4. Louisiana State University
5. University of Virginia
6. Kansas State University
7. Cornell University (tie)
   University of California, Berkeley (tie)
9. California State Polytechnic University,
   Pomona (tie)
   Ohio State University (tie)
11. University of Michigan

12. North Carolina State University (tie)
    Texas A&M University (tie)
14. College of Environmental Science and
    Forestry, SUNY (tie)
    University of Florida (tie)
    Utah State University (tie)
    Virginia Polytechnic Institute and
    State University (tie)

Source: DesignIntelligence

Architecture Student Demographics

The following statistics are collected annually by the National Architectural Accrediting Board for all NAAB-accredited architecture degree programs at US colleges and universities. Because the study is undergoing a revision, statistics for the 2004/05 year are not available.

	1995/96	1996/97	1997/98	1998/99	1999/00	2000/01	2001/02*	2003/04
Pre-professional Undergraduate Programs								
Full-time students	9,655	12,130	11,789	12,062	13,391	13,610	12,824	15,498
Part-time students	1,494	1,602	1,524	1,386	1,782	1,856	1,651	1,168
Women students	3,432	4,317	4,419	4,495	5,314	5,836	5,094	6,233
African-American students	496	660	682	641	789	830	842	1,135
American Indian students	80	62	67	78	77	135	87	392
Asian/Pacific Isle students	807	1,112	1,065	1,042	1,106	1,079	855	1,069
Hispanic students	750	991	955	929	1,368	1,337	1,514	2,413
Total Graduates	2,154	2,324	2,199	2,397	2,716	2,791	2,191	2,509
Women graduates	603	746	807	774	1,044	1,127	761	921
African-American graduates	74	83	81	85	96	91	74	116
American Indian graduates	6	10	9	12	11	36	54	14
Asian/Pacific Isle graduates	198	225	233	226	244	272	301	166
Hispanic graduates	101	157	162	157	229	215	205	230
Accredited B. Arch Programs								
Full-time students	16,424	16,025	16,423	15,312	14,792	16,211	13,476	14,081
Part-time students	1,364	1,178	1,377	1,606	1,568	2,196	1,667	1,412
Women students	5,155	5,046	5,413	5,201	5,789	6,302	5,212	5,596
African-American students	1,247	1,122	1,165	1,243	1,342	1,156	923	1,069
American Indian students	195	163	138	151	129	116	99	96
Asian/Pacific Isle students	1,665	1,591	1,497	1,425	1,552	1,670	1,187	1,156
Hispanic students	1,436	1,340	1,249	1,184	1,400	2,090	1,797	1,426
Total Graduates	2,948	3,028	2,710	2,617	2,825	2,773	2,253	2,483
Women graduates	742	849	762	754	749	910	779	793
African-American graduates	148	131	111	131	137	153	129	116
American Indian graduates	14	14	8	13	19	26	43	25
Asian/Pacific Isle graduates	276	307	294	239	276	276	240	243
Hispanic graduates	215	223	222	198	212	206	147	186

Architecture Student Demographics

B. Arch Demographics, 2001-2002

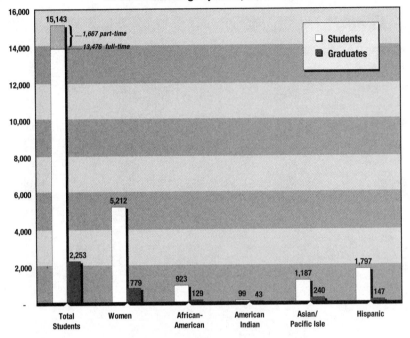

Legend: Students, Graduates

- Total Students: 15,143 (1,667 part-time, 13,476 full-time) students; 2,253 graduates
- Women: 5,212 students; 779 graduates
- African-American: 923 students; 129 graduates
- American Indian: 99 students; 43 graduates
- Asian/Pacific Isle: 1,187 students; 240 graduates
- Hispanic: 1,797 students; 147 graduates

M. Arch Demographics, 2001-2002

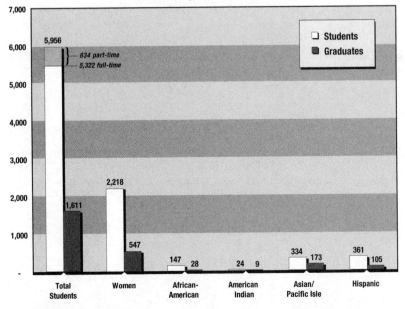

Legend: Students, Graduates

- Total Students: 5,956 (634 part-time, 5,322 full-time) students; 1,611 graduates
- Women: 2,218 students; 547 graduates
- African-American: 147 students; 28 graduates
- American Indian: 24 students; 9 graduates
- Asian/Pacific Isle: 334 students; 173 graduates
- Hispanic: 361 students; 105 graduates

Source: DesignIntelligence

49

Architecture Student Demographics

	1995/96	1996/97	1997/98	1998/99	1999/00	2000/01	2001/02*	2003/04
Pre-professional MArch Programs								
Full-time students	5,196	5,252	5,461	5,769	6,302	6,524	5,322	7,026
Part-time students	724	533	677	689	772	796	634	701
Women students	2,164	2,143	2,273	2,210	2,414	2,072	2,218	2,946
African-American students	142	133	133	119	160	143	147	199
American Indian students	21	17	20	42	16	30	24	30
Asian/Pacific Isle students	540	522	550	607	709	584	334	572
Hispanic students	267	302	301	427	595	380	361	451
Total Graduates	1,676	1,645	1,799	2,002	1,998	1,750	1,611	2,159
Women graduates	558	580	747	744	643	672	547	803
African-American graduates	26	45	32	40	41	49	28	40
American Indian graduates	5	3	9	10	4	5	9	8
Asian/Pacific Isle graduates	140	156	164	197	252	219	173	214
Hispanic graduates	83	82	92	104	113	116	105	157

* Not all schools participated in the 2001/02 survey.

Source: National Architectural Accrediting Board

ArchVoices

ArchVoices is a nonprofit organization and think tank focused on young professionals and the future of architecture. In addition to publishing news, resources, and editorials in its weekly e-mail newsletter, ArchVoices maintains multiple interactive Web sites to facilitate communication within and about the architecture profession. It also compiles data on architecture and other licensed professions through surveys and research. Finally, ArchVoices hosts regular conferences and an annual essay competition focusing on architectural internship and registration.

Address
1014 Curtis Street
Albany, CA 94706
(510) 757-6213
www.archvoices.org

Mission Statement

ArchVoices is an independent, non-profit organization and think tank on architectural education, internship, and licensure. It exists to foster a culture of communication through the collection and dissemination of information and research.

ArchVoices Essay Competition

Intended to encourage, promote, and reward critical thinking and writing, the ArchVoices Essay Competition was developed specifically for young architecture professionals. ArchVoices is an independent, nonprofit think tank on architectural education and internships. The competition is open to interns, non-registered architects, recent architecture school graduates, and graduating students. Entrants initially prepare a 500-word essay proposal reflecting on their daily experiences as interns. Selected semi-finalists further explore their ideas from their first submission, developing a 2,500-word essay. A jury of educators and professionals vote on the finalists, conferring multiple honors, including a first prize, second prize, and honorable mentions.

The competition is conducted online at *www.archvoices.org/competition*. The Web site contains additional information on eligibility, submission guidelines, the competition calendar, frequently asked questions, and writing resources. For more information, contact ArchVoices by e-mail at *info@archvoices.org* or call (510) 757-6213. To read this year's first-prize essay, see page 21.

2005 Winners

500

First Prize
"Engaging the Everyday"
Hannah Teicher (Canada)
University of British Columbia

Second Prize
"Foundations of Understanding"
Melissa Woehr (US)
Charles R. Myer and Partners

Honorable Mention
"A Revolution is Not a Dinner Party"
Sevra Davis (UK)
Architectural Association

"Listening to Learn, Learning to Lead"
Crystal Bowman (US)

"Of Wine and Parking Lots"
Kisha Patterson (US)

Jury
Maurice Cox, RBGC Architecture, Research,
  & Urbanism
Jessica Farrar, Texas House of Representatives
Richard Nelson Swett, Swett Associates
Jess Wendover, Urban Ecology

Source: ArchVoices

ASLA National Student Design Competition

The American Society of Landscape Architects annually conducts a competition to identify and recognize outstanding works of design and research from landscape architecture students. Any landscape architecture student in the United States or Canada is eligible to enter. Awards are granted by the jury at their discretion. Winning students and professors are honored at ASLA's annual conference.

For additional information about the competition, contact the ASLA at (202) 898-2444 or *www.asla.org*.

2005 General Design Winners

Award of Excellence
"Vivero Metropolitano: A Productive Nursery Landscape for Monterrey, Mexico"
Kate Kennen, Leland D. Cott (adviser), and Mario Schjetnan (adviser)
Harvard University

Award of Honor
"Revealed Resilience: An Extension of Roberto Burle Marx's Parque del Este"
Sarah Weidner and Anita Berrizbetia (adviser)
University of Pennsylvania

"Pike Place Park/Structure: Toward A Hybrid Morphology of Architecture, Landscape, and Urban Infrastructure"
Shoji Kaneko, Julie Johnson (adviser), and Jeff Hou (adviser)
University of Washington

"smartPARK"
Kira Appelhans, Maura Rockcastle, Keith Kaseman (adviser)
University of Pennsylvania

2005 Analysis & Planning Winners

Award of Honor
"Sustainable Milwaukee"
Ruth Stafford, Jennifer Strauss Hendricks, Veronica Meacham, David Kovacic (adviser), and Matthew Tucker (adviser)
University of Illinois at Urbana–Champaign

"Urban Infrastructure Strategy: Phased Neighborhood Retrofit"
Sky Allen and Gale Fulton (adviser)
University of Adelaide

"Bear River Greenway Master Plan/Bear Rive Ecological Corridor Restoration"
Lori Porreca, Sara Sevy, Kris Kvarfordt, Susan Buffler, Chad Kennedy, Laura McCoy, Peter Kumble (adviser), and Craig Johnson (adviser)
Utah State University

"X Zone"
Meredith Schildwachter, Kyle Hebel, Leila Tolderlund, (adviser) and Anthony Mazzeo (adviser)
University of Colorado at Denver

501

ASLA National Student Design Competition

2005 Research Winners

Award of Honor

"Phytoremediation: A New Avenue For
  Landscape Architecture"
Pamela Brown and Joan M. Safford (adviser)
California State Polytechnic University, Pomona

"Women as Force in Landscape Architecture,
  1893–1942"
Thaisa Way, Leonard Mirin (adviser), Daniel
  Krall (adviser), and Herbert Gottfried
  (adviser)
Cornell University

"Fool's Gold: Audubon International
  Certification as a Predictor of Foraging
  Habitat Suitability for Wading Birds,
  A Case Study"
Robert G. Collins and Susan J. Mulley (adviser)
Mississippi State University

2005 Communications Winners

Award of Excellence

"Site Unseen"
Allen Compton, Joan Woodward (adviser), and
  Jeff Juarez (adviser)
California State Polytechnic University, Pomona

2005 Community Service Winners

Award of Honor

"Community Studio"
A Collaborative of Volunteer Designers, Patrick
  Condon (adviser), Cynthia Girling (adviser),
  and Doug Paterson (adviser)
University of British Columbia

2005 Student Collaboration Winners

Award of Excellence

"Building Green for the Future: Case Studies of
  Sustainable Development in Michigan"
Allyson Pumphrey, Peter Acuff, and Larissa
  Larsen (adviser)
University of Michigan

Award of Honor

"The Spill: Utilizing the Active Method to
  Combat the Growing Combined Sewer
  Overflow Epidemic"
Morgan A. Burke, Allison Harness, Yi Hong, Kim
  Wilson (adviser), and Loring Nies (adviser)
Purdue University

"Alternative Futures for Tepotzotlán, Mexico"
Liat Margolis, Alex Robinson, Patrick Curran,
  Carl Steinitz (adviser), Victoria Wiley (advis-
  er), and Alexander Wiley (adviser)
Harvard University

Jury

Frederick R. Steiner, University of Texas at Austin
F. Christopher Dimond, HNTB Corporation
Ilze Jones, Jones & Jones Architects and
  Landscape Architects, Ltd.
Mikyoung Kim, Mikyoung Kim Design and
  Rhode Island School of Design
M. Ann Mullins, University of Colorado at
  Boulder
Kenneth W. Smith, Ken Smith Landscape
  Architect
Susan S. Szenasy, *Metropolis*

Source: *American Society of Landscape Architects*

Association Student Chapters

The following national design associations offer student memberships, often at reduced rates, and maintain student chapters at many US colleges and universities. Student newsletters, leadership opportunities, networking, job postings, discounts, and many other member benefits are typically available. More information about specific benefits and a current listing of the active student chapters are available from the organizations and their Web sites. Profiles of the associations can be found in the Organizations chapter beginning on page 559. As the American Institute of Architecture Students is independent of any association (although partially funded by the American Institute of Architects), detailed information about its programs and benefits can be found on page 490.

American Planning Association
www.planning.org/students/

**American Society of
Interior Designers**
www.asid.org/students/benefits.asp

**American Society of
Landscape Architects**
www.asla.org/nonmembers/student_news.html

**International Interior
Design Association**
www.iida.org

**Industrial Designers Society
of America**
www.idsa.org

503

Architecture is not a game of perfect. There's no right way; you're always practicing. Golf is that way, too. It's like Ben Hogan said: "I find the more I practice, the luckier I get." The more you practice architecture, the better you get. As in golf, there's a sort of discipline to it. You have to concentrate and relax at the same time. Architecture and golf—you don't do either of them casually.

Michael Graves

Berkeley Prize Essay Competition

The Berkeley Undergraduate Prize for Architectural Design Excellence, an annual online essay competition and the centerpiece of the Berkeley Prize Endowment, was established in 1996 at the Department of Architecture, University of California, Berkeley. The Endowment aspires to encourage students to embrace social ideals as fundamental to making buildings of worth and to recognize, through the lessons of past examples, how contemporary architecture may serve social needs. Each year, students submit essays in response to a question developed around the theme of architecture as a social art. Submissions are encouraged from undergraduate architecture students from around the world, but must be written in English.

For further information, including a history of the Berkeley Prize, past winning entries, or details about entering, visit *www.berkeleyprize.org* on the Internet. To read one of this year's winning essays, see page 9.

2005 Recipients

This year's competition asked students to answer the following question: What makes a place truly public? Go out into a community that you know well and find an exceptional, built example of one such place. In most likelihood, among other attributes, this place will embody the traditions of local culture and be a reflection of the world at large. Describe this place in a way that makes it a compelling demonstration of how other places might remain similarly vital to their own communities. Be both evocative and specific in your tribute to this place.

First Prize
"The Belmont Tunnel and Toluca Yard"
Brian Knight (US)
Southern California Institute of Architecture

Second Prize
"Granville Island: Urban Oasis Amidst a
    Metropolis"
Sarah Schaefer (Canada)
Dalhousie University

"People, place and events"
Kamana Dhakhwa and Swasti Bhattarai (Nepal)
Institute of Engineering

Third Prize
"Iceland > Reykjavik > Laugavegur: City within a
    City"
Andri Haflidason (UK)
University of Strathclyde

Jury
Lesley Naa Norle Lokko, University of London
    (Ghana)
Donlyn Lyndon, University of California,
    Berkeley (US)
Rahul Mehrotra, Rahul Mehrotra Associates
    (India)
Giles Oliver, Penoyre & Prasad (UK)

Source: The Berkeley Prize Endowment

504

Charles E. Peterson Prize

A student competition of measured drawings, the Charles E. Peterson Prize is presented jointly by the Historic American Buildings Survey of the National Park Service, Athenaeum of Philadelphia, and American Institute of Architects. The annual competition honors Charles E. Peterson, founder of the HABS program, and is intended to heighten awareness about US historic buildings and to add to the permanent HABS collection of measured drawings at the Library of Congress. In addition to generating more than 4,000 drawings for the collection to date, the competition presents awards totaling $7,000 to winning students each year. These have included those studying architecture, architectural history, interior design, and American studies. Drawings must be of a building that has not been recorded by HABS through measured drawings or be an addendum to existing HABS drawings that makes a substantial contribution to the understanding of the significant features of the building.

Additional information is available on the Internet at *www.cr.nps.gov/habshaer/joco/pete/*.

2005 Winners

First Place
Samuel G. Wiener House
Shreveport, LA
Stephanie Boyles, Natasha Dufrene, Valerie Fontentot, Jason Henson, Yomi Oluwole, Aaron Sanderson, Lenora Schilling, Dylan Towe, and Guy W. Carwile (professor)
Louisiana Tech University

Second Place
Montezuma Castle National Monument
Camp Verde, AZ
Rima Al-Ajlouni, Eric Blauert, Jose del Castillo, Jeff Dehaven, Charles P. Kolarick, Ji-Hyun Lee, Ashley Miller, Fatima Al-Nammari, Kristen Ramsey, Luke Scott, Robert B. Warden (professor), and David Woodcock (professor)
Texas A&M University

Third Place
Charles H. Bugbee and Harold Dow Bugbee Ranch House
Clarendon, TX
Samantha Hurst, Nathan Schneider, Jeremy Vincik, Melissa Wilson, and John P. White (professor)
Texas Tech University

Fourth Place
Thomas Farm Outbuildings
Monocacy National Battlefield, Frederick County, MD
William Applegate, Michael Bossman, Patricia Ceglia, Megan Cullen, Scott Doyle, Stephen Gray, Richard L. Green, Patricia Fisher-Olsen, Mirka John, Carla Loughlin, Leo Shane, Vanessa Zeoli, and Kathryn Auerbach (professor)
Bucks County Community College

505

Charles E. Peterson Prize

Honorable Mention
Charles Goodnight Ranch House
Goodnight, TX
Matthew Brinkman, William K. Harkness III,
    Jonathan Oltman, Trela Turnbough, Wei
    Xiong, and John P. White (professor)
Texas Tech University

Thalia Hall
Chicago, IL
Breanna Boulton, Theodore Dunn, Ann
    Halbrook, Katherine Jeffries, Beth Johnson,
    Benjamin Leech, Tisha Logan, Elisabeth
    Logman, Lauren Oswalt, Hema Pandya,
    Maura Pilcher, Tracy Slorupski, Saleh Van
    Erem, Nelson White, and Charles Pipal
    (professor)
Art Institute of Chicago

Source: Historic American Buildings Survey

The land has witnessed and survived the advent of man and the ephemeral episodes of his purposive adventure. And since the many differences in the form of the land...set limits to human effort, these must be the historian's concern.

W. Gordon East

Design Degree Programs

The following chart outlines the schools across the United States that offer design and design–related degrees, including associate (A), certificate (C), professional (P), bachelor's (B), and master's (M). All the architecture, interior design, landscape architecture and planning programs indicated below are accredited by the disciplines' respective accrediting bodies: National Architectural Accrediting Board, Foundation for Interior Design Education Research, Landscape Architectural Accrediting Board, and Planning Accreditation Board. For degree programs not listed or accredited by other bodies, consult the individual schools. For students seeking PhD programs, refer to the listing of doctorate programs on page 520.

School	City	Web Address	Architecture	Architecture History	Historic Preservation	Industrial Design	Interior Design	Landscape Architecture	Planning
ALABAMA									
Alabama A&M University	Normal	aamu.edu							B M
Auburn University	Auburn	auburn.edu	B			B M	B	M	M
Samford International University	Birmingham	samford.edu					B		
Tuskegee University	Tuskegee	tuskegee.edu	B						
University of Alabama	Tuscaloosa	ua.edu					B		
ARIZONA									
Arizona State University	Tempe	asu.edu	M			B M	B	B	B M
Art Center Design College	Tucson	theartcenter.edu					B		
Frank Lloyd Wright School of Architecture	Scottsdale	taliesin.edu	M						
Scottsdale Community College	Scottsdale	sc.maricopa.edu					A C		
University of Arizona	Tucson	arizona.edu	B					M	M
ARKANSAS									
University of Arkansas	Fayetteville	uark.edu	B				B	B	
CALIFORNIA									
Academy of Art University	San Francisco	academyart.edu	M¹			B M	B		
American InterContinental University	Los Angeles	aiula.edu					B		
Art Center College of Design	Pasadena	artcenter.edu				B M			
Brooks College	Long Beach	brookscollege.edu					A		

507

Design Degree Programs

School	City	Web Address	Architecture	Architecture History	Historic Preservation	Industrial Design	Interior Design	Landscape Architecture	Planning
California College of the Arts	Oakland and San Francisco	cca.edu	B			B M	B		
California Polytechnic State University	San Luis Obispo	calpoly.edu	B					B	B M
California State Polytechnic University	Pomona	csupomona.edu	B M					B M	B M
California State University, Fresno	Fresno	csufresno.edu					B		
California State University, Long Beach	Long Beach	csulb.edu				B M			
California State University, Northridge	Northridge	csun.edu					B		
California State University, Sacramento	Sacramento	csus.edu					B		
Design Institute of San Diego	San Diego	disd.edu					B		
Interior Designers Institute	Newport Beach	idi.edu					B		
NewSchool of Architecture and Design	San Diego	newschoolarch.edu	B M						
San Francisco State University	San Francisco	sfsu.edu				B M			
San Jose State University	San Jose	sjsu.edu				B			M
San Diego State University	San Diego	sdsu.edu					B		
Southern California Institute of Architecture	Los Angeles	sciarc.edu	B M						
University of California, Berkeley	Berkeley	berkeley.edu	M	M				M	
University of California, Berkeley Extension	Berkeley	unex.berkeley.edu					C		
University of California, Davis	Davis	ucdavis.edu						B	
University of California, Irvine	Irvine	uci.edu							M
University of California, Los Angeles	Los Angeles	ucla.edu	M	M					M
University of California, Los Angeles Extension	Los Angeles	uclaextension.edu					P		

Design Degree Programs

School	City	Web Address	Architecture	Architecture History	Historic Preservation	Industrial Design	Interior Design	Landscape Architecture	Planning
University of Southern California	Los Angeles	usc.edu	B M						M
West Valley College	Saratoga	westvalley.edu					C		
Woodbury University	Burbank	woodbury.edu	B				B		
COLORADO									
Art Institute of Colorado	Denver	cia.aii.edu				B	B		
Colorado State University	Fort Collins	colostate.edu					B	B	
Metropolitan State College of Denver	Denver	mscd.edu				B			
Rocky Mountain College of Art + Design	Lakewood	rmcad.edu					B		
University of Colorado at Denver	Denver	cudenver.edu	M					M	M
CONNECTICUT									
University of Bridgeport	Bridgeport	bridgeport.edu				B			
University of Connecticut	Storrs	uconn.edu						B	
University of Hartford	West Hartford	hartford.edu	M[1]						
Yale University	New Haven	yale.edu	M						
DELAWARE									
University of Delaware	Newark	udel.edu		M					
DISTRICT OF COLUMBIA									
Catholic University of America	Washington	cua.edu	M						
George Washington University	Washington	gwu.edu		M			B M		
Howard University	Washington	howard.edu	B						
FLORIDA									
Art Institute of Fort Lauderdale	Fort Lauderdale	aifl.edu				B			
Florida A&M University	Tallahassee	famu.edu	B M					M	
Florida Atlantic University	Fort Lauderdale	fau.edu	B						M
Florida International University	Miami	fiu.edu	M					M	
Florida State University	Tallahassee	fsu.edu		M			B		M

509

Design Degree Programs

School	City	Web Address	Architecture	Architecture History	Historic Preservation	Industrial Design	Interior Design	Landscape Architecture	Planning
International Academy of Design & Technology–Tampa	Tampa	academy.edu					B		
Miami International University of Art & Design	Miami	ifac.edu					B		
Ringling School of Art and Design	Sarasota	rsad.edu					B		
University of Florida	Gainesville	ufl.edu	M				B	B M	M
University of Miami	Miami	miami.edu	B M						
University of South Florida	Tampa	usf.edu	M						
GEORGIA									
American InterContinental University	Atlanta	aiubuckhead.com					B		
Art Institute of Atlanta	Dunwoody	aia.artinstitutes.edu					B		
Brenau University	Gainesville	brenau.edu					B		
Georgia Institute of Technology	Atlanta	gatech.edu	M	M		B M			M
Georgia Southern University	Statesboro	georgia southern.edu					B		
Georgia State University	Atlanta	gsu.edu			M				
Savannah College of Art and Design	Savannah	scad.edu	M	M	C B M				
Southern Polytechnic State University	Marietta	spsu.edu	B						
University of Georgia	Athens	uga.edu			C M		B	B M	
HAWAII									
University of Hawaii at Manoa	Honolulu	hawaii.edu							M
IDAHO									
Brigham Young University–Idaho	Rexburg	byui.edu					B		
University of Idaho	Moscow	uidaho.edu	M					B	
ILLINOIS									
Columbia College Chicago	Chicago	colum.edu					B		

Design Degree Programs

School	City	Web Address	Architecture	Architecture History	Historic Preservation	Industrial Design	Interior Design	Landscape Architecture	Planning
Harrington College of Design	Chicago	interiordesign.edu					B		
Illinois Institute of Art–Chicago	Chicago	ilic.artinstitutes.edu					B		
Illinois Institute of Art–Schaumburg	Schaumburg	ilis.artinstitutes.edu					B		
Illinois Institute of Technology	Chicago	iit.edu	B M						
Illinois State University	Normal	ilstu.edu					B		
International Academy of Design & Technology–Chicago	Chicago	iadtchicago.edu					B		
Judson College	Elgin	judson-il.edu	M						
School of the Art Institute of Chicago	Chicago	artic.edu/saic			M				
Southern Illinois University	Carbondale	siu.edu				B	B		
University of Chicago	Chicago	uchicago.edu		M					
University of Illinois at Chicago	Chicago	uic.edu	M	M		B M			M
University of Illinois at Urbana–Champaign	Urbana-Champaign	uiuc.edu	M	M		B M		B M	B M
INDIANA									
Ball State University	Muncie	bsu.edu	M		M			B M	B M
Indiana State University	Terre Haute	indstate.edu					B		
Indiana University	Bloomington	indiana.edu					B		
Purdue University	Lafayette	purdue.edu				B M	B	B	
University of Notre Dame	South Bend	nd.edu	B M				B M		
IOWA									
Iowa State University	Ames	iastate.edu	B M				B	B	B M
University of Iowa	Iowa City	uiowa.edu		M					M
KANSAS									
Kansas State University	Manhattan	ksu.edu	B				B	B M	M
University of Kansas	Lawrence	ku.edu	B M			B M			M

511

Design Degree Programs

School	City	Web Address	Architecture	Architecture History	Historic Preservation	Industrial Design	Interior Design	Landscape Architecture	Planning
KENTUCKY									
University of Kentucky	Lexington	uky.edu	B		M		B	B	
University of Louisville	Louisville	louisville.edu		M			B		
LOUISIANA									
Louisiana State University	Baton Rouge	lsu.edu	B M				B	B M	
Louisiana Tech University	Ruston	latech.edu	B				B		
Southern University and A&M College	Baton Rouge	subr.edu	B						
Tulane University	New Orleans	tulane.edu	M		C M				
University of Louisiana at Lafayette	Lafayette	louisiana.edu	B			B	B		
University of New Orleans	New Orleans	uno.edu							M
MARYLAND									
Goucher College	Baltimore	goucher.edu			B M				
Morgan State University	Baltimore	morgan.edu	M					M	M
University of Maryland	College Park	umd.edu	M		C M			B	M
MASSACHUSETTS									
Boston Architectural Center	Boston	the-bac.edu	B M				B M		
Boston University	Boston	bu.edu		M	M				
Endicott College	Beverly	endicott.edu					B		
Harvard University	Cambridge	harvard.edu	M					M	M
Massachusetts College of Art	Boston	massart.edu				B			
Massachusetts Institute of Technology	Cambridge	mit.edu	M	M					M
Mount Ida College	Newton	mountida.edu					B		
Newbury College	Brookline	newbury.edu					B		
New England School of Art & Design at Suffolk University	Boston	suffolk.edu/nesad					B M		
Northeastern University	Boston	northeastern.edu	M						
Tufts University	Medford	tufts.edu							M
University of Massachusetts Amherst	Amherst	umass.edu	M[1]					B M	M

Design Degree Programs

School	City	Web Address	Architecture	Architecture History	Historic Preservation	Industrial Design	Interior Design	Landscape Architecture	Planning
Wentworth Institute of Technology	Boston	wit.edu	B			B	B		
MICHIGAN									
Andrews University	Berrien Springs	andrews.edu	B						
College for Creative Studies	Detriot	ccscad.edu				B			
Cranbrook Academy of Art	Bloomfield Hills	cranbrookart.edu				M			
Eastern Michigan University	Ypsilanti	emich.edu				C M	B		B
Kendall College of Art and Design	Grand Rapids	kcad.edu				B	B		
Lawrence Technological University	Southfield	ltu.edu	M				B		
Michigan State University	East Lansing	msu.edu					B	B	B M
University of Detroit Mercy	Detroit	udmercy.edu	M						
University of Michigan	Ann Arbor	umich.edu	M			B M		M	M
Wayne State University	Detriot	wayne.edu							M
Western Michigan University	Kalamazoo	wmich.edu				B	B		
MINNESOTA									
Dakota County Technical College	Rosemount	dctc.mnscu.edu					A		
University of Minnesota	St. Paul/Mpls.	umn.edu	M				B	M	M
MISSISSIPPI									
Mississippi State University	Mississippi State	msstate.edu	B				B	B	
University of Southern Mississippi	Hattiesburg	usm.edu					B		
MISSOURI									
Drury University	Springfield	drury.edu	B						
Maryville University	St. Louis	maryville.edu					B		
Southeast Missouri State University	Cape Girardeau	semo.edu			B M				

Design Degree Programs

School	City	Web Address	Architecture	Architecture History	Historic Preservation	Industrial Design	Interior Design	Landscape Architecture	Planning
Southwestern Missouri State University	Springfield	smsu.edu							B
University of Missouri–Columbia	Columbia	missouri.edu		M			B		
Washington University in St. Louis	St. Louis	wustl.edu	M						
MONTANA									
Montana State University	Bozeman	montana.edu	M						
NEBRASKA									
University of Nebraska–Lincoln	Lincoln	unl.edu	M				B		M
NEVADA									
University of Nevada, Las Vegas	Las Vegas	unlv.edu	M				B	B	
NEW JERSEY									
Kean University	Union	kean.edu				B	B		
New Jersey Institute of Technology	Newark	njit.edu	B M						
Princeton University	Princeton	princeton.edu	M						
Rutgers, The State University of New Jersey	New Brunswick	rutgers.edu		M				B	M
NEW MEXICO									
University of New Mexico	Albuquerque	unm.edu	M	M				M	M
NEW YORK									
Binghamton University, SUNY	Binghamton	binghamton.edu		M					
Buffalo State College, SUNY	Buffalo	buffalostate.edu					B		
City College of New York, CUNY	New York	ccny.cuny.edu	B					B	
College of Environmental Science and Forestry, SUNY	Syracuse	esf.edu						B M	
Columbia University	New York	columbia.edu	M	M	M				M
Cooper Union	New York	cooper.edu	B						

Design Degree Programs

School	City	Web Address	Architecture	Architecture History	Historic Preservation	Industrial Design	Interior Design	Landscape Architecture	Planning
Cornell University	Ithaca	cornell.edu	B M[1]	M	M		B	B M	M
Fashion Institute of Technology, SUNY	New York	fitnyc.edu					B		
Hunter College, CUNY	New York	hunter.cuny.edu							M
New York Institute of Technology	various	nyit.edu	B				B		
New York School of Interior Design	New York	nysid.edu					B		
New York University	New York	nyu.edu		M					M
Parsons School of Design	New York	parsons.edu	M			B			
Pratt Institute	Brooklyn	pratt.edu	B M		M	B M	B		M
Rensselaer Polytechnic Institute	Troy	rpi.edu	B M						
Rochester Institute of Technology	Rochester	rit.edu				B M	B		
School of Visual Arts	New York	schoolofvisualarts.edu					B		
Syracuse University	Syracuse	syr.edu	B M	M		B M	B		
University at Albany, SUNY	Albany	albany.edu							M
University at Buffalo, SUNY	Buffalo	buffalo.edu	M						M
NORTH CAROLINA									
East Carolina University	Greenville	ecu.edu					B		B
Meredith College	Raleigh	meredith.edu					B		
North Carolina A&T State University	Greensboro	ncat.edu						B	
North Carolina State University	Raleigh	ncsu.edu	B M			B M		B M	
University of North Carolina at Chapel Hill	Chapel Hill	unc.edu							M
University of North Carolina at Charlotte	Charlotte	uncc.edu	B M						
University of North Carolina at Greensboro	Greensboro	uncg.edu					B		

Design Degree Programs

School	City	Web Address	Architecture	Architecture History	Historic Preservation	Industrial Design	Interior Design	Landscape Architecture	Planning
Western Carolina University	Cullowhee	wcu.edu					B		
NORTH DAKOTA									
North Dakota State University	Fargo	ndsu.edu	B				B	B	
OHIO									
Belmont Technical College	St. Clairsville	btc.edu			A				
Cleveland Institute of Art	Cleveland	cia.edu				B			
Cleveland State University	Cleveland	csuohio.edu							M
Columbus College of Art & Design	Columbus	ccad.edu				B	B		
Kent State University	Kent	kent.edu	M				B		
Miami University	Oxford	muohio.edu	M				B		
Ohio State University	Columbus	osu.edu	M	M		B M	B	B M	M
Ohio University	Athens	ohiou.edu					B		
University of Akron	Akron	uakron.edu					B		
University of Cincinnati	Cincinnati	uc.edu	M			B	B		B M
Ursuline College	Pepper Pike	ursuline.edu			B				
OKLAHOMA									
Oklahoma State University	Stillwater	okstate.edu	B				B	B	
University of Central Oklahoma	Edmund	ucok.edu					B		
University of Oklahoma	Norman	ou.edu	B M				B	M	M
OREGON									
Portland State University	Portland	pdx.edu							M
University of Oregon	Eugene	uoregon.edu	B M	M	M		B M	B	M
PENNSYLVANIA									
Bucks County Community College	Newtown	bucks.edu			C				
Carnegie Mellon University	Pittsburgh	cmu.edu	B			B			
Drexel University	Philadelphia	drexel.edu	B				B		
La Roche College	Pittsburgh	laroche.edu					B		
Moore College of Art & Design	Philadelphia	moore.edu					B		

Design Degree Programs

School	City	Web Address	Architecture	Architecture History	Historic Preservation	Industrial Design	Interior Design	Landscape Architecture	Planning
Pennsylvania State University	State College	psu.edu	B	M				B	
Philadelphia University	Philadelphia	philau.edu	B			B	B		
Temple University	Philadelphia	temple.edu	B					B	
University of Pennsylvania	Philadelphia	upenn.edu	M	M	C M			M	M
University of Pittsburgh	Pittsburgh	pitt.edu		M					
University of the Arts	Philadelphia	uarts.edu				B M			
RHODE ISLAND									
Brown University	Providence	brown.edu		M					
Rhode Island School of Design	Providence	risd.edu	B M			B M		M	
Roger Williams University	Bristol	rwu.edu	M		B				
Salve Regina University	Newport	salve.edu			B				
University of Rhode Island	Kingston	uri.edu						B	M
SOUTH CAROLINA									
Clemson University	Clemson	clemson.edu	M					B	M
College of Charleston	Charleston	cofc.edu			B				
Winthrop University	Rock Hill	winthrop.edu					B		
TENNESSEE									
Middle Tennessee State University	Murfreesboro	mtsu.edu			M		B		
O'More College of Design	Franklin	omorecollege.edu					B		
University of Memphis	Memphis	memphis.edu					B		M
University of Tennessee at Chattanooga	Chattanooga	utc.edu					B		
University of Tennessee, Knoxville	Knoxville	utk.edu	B M				B		
Watkins College of Art & Design	Nashville	watkins.edu					B		
TEXAS									
Abilene Christian University	Abilene	acu.edu					B		
Art Institute of Dallas	Dallas	aid.edu					B		
Art Institute of Houston	Houston	aii.edu					B		
Baylor University	Waco	baylor.edu					B		

Design Degree Programs

School	City	Web Address	Architecture	Architecture History	Historic Preservation	Industrial Design	Interior Design	Landscape Architecture	Planning
El Centro College	Dallas	ecc.dcccd.edu					C		
Prairie View A&M University	Prairie View	pvamu.edu	M						
Rice University	Houston	rice.edu	B M						
Stephen F. Austin State University	Nacogdoches	sfasu.edu					B		
Texas A&M University	College Station	tamu.edu	M					B M	M
Texas Christian University	Fort Worth	tcu.edu					B		
Texas State University–San Marcos	San Marcos	txstate.edu					B		
Texas Tech University	Lubbock	ttu.edu	M				B	B	
University of Houston	Houston	uh.edu	B M						
University of North Texas	Denton	unt.edu					B		
University of Texas at Arlington	Arlington	uta.edu	M				B	M	M
University of Texas at Austin	Austin	utexas.edu	B M	M	C M		B		M
University of Texas at San Antonio	San Antonio	utsa.edu	M				B		
UTAH									
Brigham Young University	Provo	byu.edu				B			
University of Utah	Salt Lake City	utah.edu	M						
Utah State University	Logan	usu.edu					B	B M	
VERMONT									
Norwich University	Northfield	norwich.edu	M						
University of Vermont	Burlington	uvm.edu			M				
VIRGINIA									
Hampton University	Hampton	hamptonu.edu	M						
James Madison University	Harrisonburg	jmu.edu					B		
Marymount University	Arlington	marymount.edu					B M		
University of Mary Washington	Fredericksburg	umw.edu			B				
University of Virginia	Charlottesville	virginia.edu	M	M				M	B M
Virginia Commonwealth University	Richmond	vcu.edu		M			B		M

Design Degree Programs

School	City	Web Address	Architecture	Architecture History	Historic Preservation	Industrial Design	Interior Design	Landscape Architecture	Planning
Virginia Polytechnic Institute and State University	Blacksburg	vt.edu	B M			B	B	B M	M
WASHINGTON									
Eastern Washington University	Spokane	ewu.edu							B M
Washington State University	Pullman	wsu.edu	M				B	B	
Western Washington University	Bellingham	wwu.edu				B			
University of Washington	Seattle	washington.edu	M	M				B M	M
WEST VIRGINIA									
West Virginia University	Morgantown	wvu.edu					B	B	
WISCONSIN									
Milwaukee Institute of Art & Design	Milwaukee	miad.edu				B			
Mount Mary College	Milwaukee	mtmary.edu					B		
University of Wisconsin–Madison	Madison	wisc.edu		M			B	B	M
University of Wisconsin–Milwaukee	Milwaukee	uwm.edu	M						M
University of Wisconsin–Stevens Point	Stevens Point	uwsp.edu					B		
University of Wisconsin–Stout	Menomonie	uwstout.edu					B	B	

519

¹ This program is currently in candidate status for National Architectural Accreditation Board accreditation.

Note: There are some accredited BArch programs that do not appear on the above list because they are no longer accepting new students and will be phased out once the currently enrolled BArch students have graduated.

Source: Foundation for Interior Design Education Research, Industrial Designers Society of America, Landscape Architectural Accrediting Board, National Architectural Accrediting Board, National Council for Preservation Education, Planning Accreditation Board, and Society of Architectural Historians

Doctorate Programs in Architecture and Design

The following US schools offer doctorate and PhD degrees in architecture and design. Detailed information about entrance requirements and the programs' field of study is available from the individual schools.

Architecture

Arizona State University (Tempe)
Carnegie Mellon University (Pittsburgh, PA)
Columbia University (New York, NY)
Cornell University (Ithaca, NY)
Georgia Institute of Technology (Atlanta)
Harvard University (Cambridge, MA)
Illinois Institute of Technology (Chicago)
Massachusetts Institute of Technology
   (Cambridge)
North Carolina State University (Raleigh)
Princeton University (Princeton, NJ)
Rice University (Houston, TX)
Texas A&M University (College Station)
Texas Tech University (Lubbock)

University of California, Berkeley
University of California, Los Angeles
University of Colorado (Denver)
University of Florida (Gainesville)
University of Hawaii (Manoa)
University of Illinois at Urbana–Champaign
University of Michigan (Ann Arbor)
University of Nebraska–Lincoln
University of Pennsylvania (Philadelphia)
University of Texas at Austin
University of Wisconsin–Milwaukee
Virginia Polytechnic Institute and State
   University (Blacksburg)

Architectural History

The Society of Architectural Historians' Web site, www.sah.org, in addition to the individual schools, offers detailed information about each program, including their areas of focus, faculty data, and statistics.

Binghamton University, SUNY
Boston University (MA)
Brown University (Providence, RI)
City University of New York (New York)
Columbia University (New York, NY)
Cornell University (Ithaca, NY)
Florida State University (Tallahassee)
George Washington University (Washington, DC)
Georgia Institute of Technology (Atlanta)
Harvard University (Cambridge, MA)
Massachusetts Institute of Technology
   (Cambridge)
New York University (New York)
Northwestern University (Evanston, IL)
Ohio State University (Columbus)
Pennsylvania State University (State College)
Princeton University (Princeton, NJ)
Rutgers, The State University of New Jersey
   (New Brunswick)
Stanford University (Stanford, CA)
University of California, Berkeley

University of California, Los Angeles
University of California, Santa Barbara
University of Chicago (IL)
University of Delaware (Newark)
University of Illinois at Chicago
University of Illinois at Urbana–Champaign
University of Iowa (Iowa City)
University of Louisville (KY)
University of Missouri–Columbia
University of New Mexico (Albuquerque)
University of Oregon (Eugene)
University of Pennsylvania (Philadelphia)
University of Pittsburgh (PA)
University of Texas at Austin
University of Virginia (Charlottesville)
University of Washington (Seattle)
University of Wisconsin–Madison
North Carolina State University (Raleigh)
Virginia Commonwealth University (Richmond)
Yale University (New Haven, CT)

Doctorate Programs in Architecture and Design

Historic Preservation

Cornell University (Ithaca, NY)
Tulane University (New Orleans, LA)

University of Texas at Austin

Industrial Design

Arizona State University (Temple)
Carnegie Mellon University (Pittsburgh, PA)

North Carolina State University (Raleigh)

Interior Design

Arizona State University (Tempe)
Bard Graduate Center for Studies in the
    Decorative Arts, Design and Culture
    (New York, NY)
Michigan State University (East Lansing)
North Carolina State University (Raleigh)

Oregon State University (Eugene)
Texas Tech University (Lubbock)
Virginia Polytechnic Institute and State
    University (Blacksburg)
University of Minnesota (St. Paul/Minneapolis)
University of Missouri–Columbia

Landscape Architecture

In addition to landscape architecture, other schools offer related PhD degrees that may be of interest with such titles as environmental design and land-use planning.

Harvard University (Cambridge, MA)
North Carolina State University (Raleigh)

University of Illinois at Urbana–Champaign
University of Michigan (Ann Arbor)

Planning

Arizona State University (Tempe)
Cleveland State University (OH)
Columbia University (New York, NY)
Cornell University (Ithaca, NY)
Florida State University (Tallahassee)
Georgia Institute of Technology (Atlanta)
Harvard University (Cambridge, MA)
Massachusetts Institute of Technology
    (Cambridge)
Ohio State University (Columbus)
Portland State University (OR)
Princeton University (Princeton, NJ)
Rutgers, The State University of New Jersey
    (New Brunswick)
Texas A&M University (College Station)
University of Akron (OH)
University of California, Berkeley
University of California, Irvine
University of California, Los Angeles
University of Cincinnati (OH)

University of Colorado (Boulder)
University of Illinois at Chicago
University of Illinois at Urbana–Champaign
University of Maryland (College Park)
University of Massachusetts (Amherst)
University of Michigan (Ann Arbor)
University of New Orleans (LA)
University of North Carolina at Chapel Hill
University of Pennsylvania (Philadelphia)
University of Southern California (Los Angeles)
University of Texas at Austin
University of Washington (Seattle)
University of Wisconsin–Madison
Virginia Polytechnic Institute and State
    University (Blacksburg)
Washington State University (Pullman)

521

Source: Association of Collegiate Schools of Architecture; Society of Architectural Historians; National Council for Preservation Education; Industrial Designers Society of America; Interior Design Educators Council; Association of Collegiate Schools of Planning; American Society of Landscape Architects

Educational Resources

In addition to the individuals schools, the following organizations can provide information about design education.

ARCHITECTURE

Association of Collegiate Schools of Architecture
1735 New York Avenue NW
3rd Floor
Washington, DC 20006
(202) 785-2324
www.acsa-arch.org

National Architectural Accrediting Board
1735 New York Avenue NW
Washington, DC 20006
(202) 783-2007
www.naab.org

ARCHITECTURE HISTORY

Society of Architectural Historians
1365 North Astor Street
Chicago, Illinois 60610
(312) 573-1365
www.sah.org

HISTORIC PRESERVATION

National Council for Preservation Education
www.uvm.edu/histpres/ncpe/

INDUSTRIAL DESIGN

Industrial Designers Society of America
45195 Business Center #250
Dulles, VA 20166
(703) 707-6000
www.idsa.org

INTERIOR DESIGN

Foundation for Interior Design Education Research
146 Monroe Center NW, Suite 1318
Grand Rapids, MI 49503-2822
(616) 458-0400
www.fider.org

Interior Design Educators Council
7150 Winton Drive, Suite #300
Indianapolis, IN 46268
(317) 328-4437
www.idec.org

LANDSCAPE ARCHITECTURE

Council of Educators in Landscape Architecture
PO Box 7506
Edmond, OK 73083
(405) 341-3631
www.ssc.msu.edu/~la/cela/

Landscape Architectural Accreditation Board
www.asla.org/nonmembers/
accredited_programs.cfm

PLANNING

Association of Collegiate Schools of Planning
6311 Mallard Trace
Tallahassee, FL 32312
(850) 385-2054
www.acsp.org

Planning Accreditation Board
Merle Hay Tower, Suite 302
3850 Merle Hay Road
Des Moines, IA 50310
(515) 252-0729
http://showcase.netins.net/web/pab_fi66/

Source: DesignIntelligence

Educator of Distinction

The American Society of Interior Designers' Educator of Distinction Award recognizes an individual, institution, or research project that has made lasting and significant contributions to the interior design profession. It is granted on an annual basis as merited. Recipients are selected by a jury of professionals and are presented with an engraved crystal award.

For additional information, visit ASID on the Web at *www.asid.org.*

2003	Buie Harwood
	Virginia Commonwealth University
2004	Dianne Jackman
	University of Manitoba

Source: American Society of Interior Designers

> The pursuit of design is not about the way things appear but rather about the way things have meaning and how these things add or detract from the human experience.
>
> **Rob Forbes**

Eye for Why Student Design Competition

The Eye for Why Student Design Competition is sponsored by Dyson, Inc. and the Industrial Designers Society of America. The goal is to encourage students to take everyday household objects and reinvent them to reflect the Dyson philosophy: a commitment to intelligent and function-first design. (James Dyson, the British industrial engineer, invented the innovative, patented Dyson DC07 bagless vacuum cleaner, which is in the permanent collections of leading museums such as the San Francisco Museum of Modern Art, the Metropolitan Museum of Modern Art, and the Victoria and Albert Museum in London.) This competition is open to undergraduate and graduate industrial design students enrolled in a degree program in a school accredited by the National Association of Schools of Art & Design or individual student members of IDSA enrolled in an undergraduate or graduate program. Awards are granted at three levels: first place, $5,000; second place, $2,000; third place, $1,000; as well as $2,000 for the faculty adviser of the first-place winner. In addition, the first-place winner and faculty adviser will also receive a paid trip to New York to attend the prize announcement.

For more information, visit IDSA on the Internet at *www.idsa.org*.

2005 Winners

First Place
Apples & Oranges
Brandon Warren
California College of the Arts

Second Place
Moisture Keeper
Isamu Yoda
California College of the Arts

Third Place
ACORN Manual Coffee Grinder
Christine Miller
California College of the Arts

Booie
Jennifer Olson
California College of the Arts

CutKit
Arthur Hamling
Cleveland Institute of the Arts

Vacurake
Josh Aukema, Matt Cavalier, Joe McCurry
Philadelphia University

Honorable Mention
Re-Bag
Brad Jolitz
Notre Dame University

Jury
Michael Carey, Kenmore Fabric Care,
   Whirlpool Corp.
Jerome Caruso, Jerome Caruso Design
Mark Dziersk, Herbst LaZar Bell, Inc.
Emma Jane Heatley, Dyson, Inc.
Michael McCoy, Jerome Caruso Design
Janet Villano, Rockwell Group

Source: Industrial Designers Society of America

Gerald D. Hines Student Urban Design Competition

The Urban Land Institute established the Gerald D. Hines Student Urban Design Competition to honor the legacy of urban development pioneer Gerald D. Hines, chairman of the Hines real estate organization. This two-stage competition is open to multidisciplinary groups of graduate students enrolled in North American colleges and universities. The first stage, an 11-day charrette, requires the proposal of an urban development solution to a problem that is not revealed until the first day of the charrette. Four finalist teams are chosen to advance to the second stage, which is a refinement of the first stage problem with more detail and focus on such issues as phasing, existing and future infrastructure, environment, sustainability, and financial feasibility. A $50,000 prize is awarded to the winning team; the other three finalist teams share $30,000 in additional prize money.

Further information is available from the Urban Land Institute on their Web site at *www.udcompetition.uli.org.*

2005 Recipients

This year's competition involved plans for the redevelopment of one of two sites in Magna Township, Salt Lake Valley, UT: Magna includes developable and undevelopable areas, and the Northwest Planning Area is a completely undeveloped site.

First Prize

"Emergence Magna"
Thomas Magloczki (team leader), Nathan Abbott, Blake Belanger, Blake Church, Chip Radebaugh, Tom Thibodeau (adviser), Curtis Fentress (adviser)
University of Colorado at Denver

Runners-Up

"Tail's End"
Elliott Cohen, Melissa Dittmer, Alejandro Guerrero, Kleber Salas, Date Scott, Andrea Kahn (adviser), Richard Bass (adviser)
Columbia University

"Seeden"
Russell Constantine, Megan Cummins, Daniel Forster, Ommeed Sathe, Adam Semel, James Stockard (adviser), Sam Lasky (adviser)
Harvard University

"Magna Township: Community, Culture, Conservation"
Catherine Craig, Theodore Dykoski, Brian Richey, Justin Sabatini, Daniel Sharp, Dean Almy (adviser), Dave Knoll (adviser)
University of Texas at Austin

Honorable Mention

"Sustainable Roots"
Jimmy Amichandwala, Chirayu Bhatt, Sean Brady, Huzefa Rangwala, Jeffrey Williams, Richard Dagenhart (adviser), Brian Leary (adviser)
Georgia Institute of Technology

"Trading Places"
Genevieve Bantle, Jill Dau, Kate Kennen, Cory Schreier, Audrey Tendell, John Beardsley (adviser), Richard Reynolds (adviser)
Harvard University

Gerald D. Hines Student Urban Design Competition

"Reclaiming the Edge"
Misty Boykin, Matthew Cunningham, Mitali Ganguly, Sarah Cowles Gerhan, Cody Thornton, Janine S. Clifford (adviser)
Harvard University

"New Magna"
Jeffrey Fugate, Il-Joong Kim, Jeremy Shaw, Ritesh Warade, Jacob Wegmann, Eran Ben-Joseph (adviser), Lisa Davis (adviser)
Massachusetts Institute of Technology

Jury
Joseph E. Brown, EDAW, Inc. (chair)
Denise Gammon, Forest City Stapleton
Con Howe, City of Los Angeles, Planning
Charles R. Kendrick Jr., Clarion Ventures
A. Eugene Kohn, Kohn Pedersen Fox Associates
Todd W. Mansfield, Crosland Inc.
Patrick L. Phillips, Economics Research Associates
Marilyn Taylor, Skidmore, Owings & Merrill

Source: Urban Land Institute

Buildings of superior quality and architectural merit backed by responsive, professional management attract better tenants; command higher rents; and retain their value longer despite the ups and downs of real estate cycles.

Gerald D. Hines

Gerckens Prize

The Society for American City and Regional Planning History awards its Gerckens Prize to an educator who has demonstrated sustained excellence in teaching planning history. The prize is granted biennially at the National Conference on Planning History and is named after its first recipient, Professor Emeritus Laurence C. Gerckens, who not only helped define city planning history as a discipline but also inspired a generation of students and colleagues to study planning through a crafted historical lens. He was also a founder of SACRPH at the first National Conference on American Planning History in Columbus, OH, in 1986.

More information about SACRPH and the Gerckens Prize is available online at *www.urban.uiuc.edu/sacrph/*.

2001	Laurence C. Gerckens
	Ohio State University
2003	David Schuyler
	Franklin & Marshall College

Source: Society for American City and Regional Planning History

Cities depend on streets more than buildings.

Paul Goldberger

Henry Adams Medal

Each year the American Institute of Architects and the American Architectural Foundation award an engraved medal and certificate of merit to the top-ranking graduating student from each architecture program accredited by the National Architectural Accrediting Board. A certificate of merit is also awarded to the second-ranking graduating student. Recipients are chosen by the architecture faculty at each school based on their scholastic standings. Graduating students in bachelor's and master's programs are eligible. Formerly called "The School Medal," the program began in 1914 and eventually evolved into the Henry Adams Medal, named after the noted historian and journalist Henry Adams who was a supporter of the program. The top-ranking student(s) is listed below first, followed by the second-ranked student(s). Not all schools participate each year; nor do they always honor a second-ranked student.

For more information about the medal, contact the individual schools' architecture department or Mary Felber at the American Architectural Foundation at (202) 626-7511.

2005 BArch Recipients

Andrews University
Isaac Smith
Paul Weber

Auburn University
Carl Dereck Aplin
Amy Marie Green

Boston Architectural Center
Don H. Kim
Ari Segal

California College of the Arts
Stephanie Ressel
Mariah Nielson

California Polytechnic State University, San Luis Obispo
Carl R. Black
Kelly M. Jarrell

California State Polytechnic University, Pomona
Steven Key
Oliver Inauen

Carnegie Mellon University
Yu Hsien Chhia
Michael S. Baker

City College of New York, CUNY
Ayat Fadaifard
Jaroslaw Krawczyk

Cooper Union
Yeon Wha Hong
Laila Seewang

Cornell University
Ina Wong
Sean Baumes

Drexel University
Timothy Cock
Benjamin Garvin

Drury University
Bonnie Kathleen Schlett
Julie Ann Romig

Florida A&M University
Joshua Ward
Niasha Ross

Hampton University
Sandra Kay
Donald Martin

Illinois Institute of Technology
Uriel Ortega
Jihye Park

Iowa State University
John-Paul Gabrielson
Andrew Steffen

Henry Adams Medal

Kansas State University
Tessa Noel Reist
Christopher Robert Ricke

Louisiana State University
Sarah Guthrie
John Taylor Batey

Louisiana Tech University
Sara Kathyn Bruce
Lenora Schilling

Mississippi State University
Richard A. Webre
Justin JaHue Taylor

New Jersey Institute of Technology
Catherine Large
John Phillip Murphey

New York Institute of Technology
Joseph Zappulla
Brad Pettyjohn

NewSchool of Architecture & Design
David E. Grass
Derek J. Boldt

North Carolina State University
Robert Harkey
Catherine Wakeford

Ohio State University
Jane E. Gooding
Stephenie K. Strogney

Oklahoma State University
Charisse Bennett
Andrew Parli

Parsons School of Design
Ian M. Keough
Johan Christian Chung

Pennsylvania State University
Sally J. Gimbert
Christopher Conner

Philadelphia University
Christian Jordan
Josh Rider

Pratt Institute
Mary Jane Starks
Rachel Valerie Gunnard

Rensselaer Polytechnic Institute
Michael Blancato
Travis Frankel

Rice University
Jason Cook
Emily Clanahan

Southern California School of Architecture
Brian Frederick Knight
Richard Cagasca

Syracuse University
Jesse G. Hilgenberg
Whitney Izor

Temple University
Andrew Hart
Jessica S. Ruben

University of Arizona
Michael P. Anglin
Ryan P. Meeks; Laura Allison
    Carr

University of Arkansas
Emily Baker
Christopher Thomas

University of British Columbia
Shamus Sachs

University of Detroit Mercy
Jonathan Wehri
Chapin Cornillaud

University of Houston
Johnny Kousparis
Leticia Murray; Sonia Hong
    Siang Siaw

University of Idaho
Pamela Suzanne Overholtzer
Alexis Marie Elliott

University of Kansas
Eman S. Ismaiel
Adam Edward Beck

University of Louisiana at Lafayette
Abdulaziz J. Al-Najjar
Waleed K. Almershad

University of Miami
Leticia Acosta
Becky J. Fromm

University of Montreal
Isabelle Beauchamp
Eve Lamarre-Biebuyck

University of Nebraska
Andrew Charles Peterson
Jeffrey O'Neil Scott

University of North Carolina at Charlotte
William Garry Algiere Jr.
Elena B. Pupillo

University of Notre Dame
Christina Belmonte
Allison Michels

Henry Adams Medal

University of South Florida
Aimee Font-Sanborn

University of Tennessee, Knoxville
Jennifer Lynn Gildea
Patrick Carl Hazari

University of Texas at Austin
Sharon Deborah Steiner
Vicki Dewey Yuan

University of Waterloo
Pascale Dionne

Woodbury University
Amirbabak Eshraghi
Sylvie Nguyen

2005 MArch Recipients

Arizona State University
Michael Braun
Sophia Meger

Boston Architectural Center
Gabriel Bergeron
Andrew T. Claar

California State Polytechnic University, Pomona
Thomas Weitzel
Dag Compeau

Carleton University
Michael Marcel Simon
Dominique Robin Seydoux

Catholic University of America
Hakim Zeidan; Yazmany
  Arboleda; Carissa A. Rubini;
  Joseph M. Siewers
Juan P. Zavala; Simona Rossi;
  Jeremy E. Mack; Patrick S.
  Finucan

Clemson University
Steven Roberts Grogan
Lindsey Anne Sabo

Dalhousie University
Jeffrey Skinner
Stephanie Lam

Florida A&M University
Azizi Arrington-Bey
Lifaite Alcime

Illinois Institute of Technology
Ananth Robert Sampathkumar
Shabbir Yusuf Chandabhai

Iowa State University
JaDee Goehring
Darleen Gluck

Louisiana State University
Shelby Lewis
Amy Dimm

Massachusetts Institute of Technology
Danny C. Chan
Elizabeth K. Burow

McGill University
Lisa Hasan
Barbora Vokac

Miami University
Pradnya Madkaikar
Nathan England

Montana State University
Cari Critelli; Jessica Jellison
Lindsay Schack; Marie Folgert

Morgan State University
Utku Akbulut
Janean McCalla

New Jersey Institute of Technology
Masumo Nagano
Siro Prisco Tarquinio

NewSchool of Architecture & Design
Todd S. Lukas
Eliana M. Abu-Hamdi

Norwich University
Brian Paul Baril; Nathan Lee
  Rittgarn

Princeton University
Carolyn Y. Yerkes
William R. Hartzog

Rensselaer Polytechnic Institute
Joshua Emig
Francis Spataro III

Roger Williams University
Joshua Paul Vacca
Jeffrey David Massey

Savannah College of Art and Design
Ashley Lauren Silvernell
Ryan Fraser Simpson

Henry Adams Medal

Southern California Institute of Architecture
Elizabeth Keslacy
Margaret Jee-Hee Haar Farris

Syracuse University
Katherine M. Hogan
Adriana L. Zarillo

Texas A&M University
Shivani Kumar
Gaurav Khadse

Texas Tech University
Bryce Adrian Hamels
Han Nan Beh

Tulane University
Meredith Jean Gaglio; David Yakar Fuchs
Catherine Mamrie Sckerl; Laura Kay Flannery

University at Buffalo, SUNY
Jana Kasikova
Jose L. Chang

University of Calgary
Jerry Hacker
Yvonne Harper

University of California, Berkeley
Alexis Burch
Cy Keener

University of California, Los Angeles
Carmen Cham
Andrew Holder

University of Colorado at Denver
Selma Catovic
Robert Scott Mech

University of Florida
Erica Nelles
David Crabtree

University of Houston
Jeremy Clay Phillips
Melissa Elaine Campbell

University of Illinois at Chicago
Aleksandra Otwinowska
Andrew Dribin

University of Illinois at Urbana–Champaign
Anthony P. Corso
Glenn Christians

University of Kansas
Amy Ann Stecklein
Michael J. Gonos

University of Laval
Emmanuelle Champagne
Erick Rivard

University of Louisiana at Lafayette
Matthew H. Baker; Kevin R. Stewart

University of Manitoba
John Melo
Charlie Chuong Hoang

University of Maryland
Juan Gabriel Benavides
Seonhee Kim

University of Miami
Janet Rumble
Matthew Anders

University of Michigan
Mary Louise Johnson
Jessica Noelle Van Houzen

University of Nebraska
Andrew Charles Peterson
Jeffrey O'Neil Scott

University of New Mexico
Scott Stoll
Malia Orell

University of North Carolina at Charlotte
Lauren Pryor Wise
Jeremy Wayne Fisher

University of Pennsylvania
Jenny E. Sabin
Carmen A. McKee

University of South Florida
Aimee Font-Sandborn

University of Tennessee, Knoxville
Myles N. Trudell; Melissa Anne Ruff
Stephen E. Collins

University of Texas at Arlington
Jayson Kabala
Julian Power

University of Texas at Austin
Anthony Lee Yoder; Kelly Noelle Rittenhouse
Laura Caffrey

University of Texas at San Antonio
Consuelo A. Acevedo
Jason M. Winn

University of Toronto
Patrick Joseph Wheeler
Megan Elizabeth Torza

Henry Adams Medal

University of Utah
Joshua Hansen
Shane Trump

University of Virginia
Y-Vi Nam Nguyen
Rebecca Ann Yurek

University of Washington
Laura Lenns
Katherine Cudney

University of Waterloo
Andrea Kordos

University of Wisconsin–Milwaukee
Andrew S. Zimmer
Teresa M. Mattke

Yale University
Emily Alice Atwood
Michael Alan Rey

Source: American Architectural Foundation

The past was devoted to answers; the modern period confines itself to questions.

Irving Howe

IDP Outstanding Firm Award

Since 1991, the American Institute of Architects has granted the IDP Outstanding Firm Award to those firms that exhibit an exemplary commitment to the professional development of interns. Firms must give outstanding support to interns by providing comprehensive training opportunities, promoting mentorship and participation as IDP (Internship Development Program) advisers, and encouraging supplementary education activities. Beginning in 2003, awards are granted in three categories based on the number of employees—small firm (seven or fewer), medium firm (eight to 49), and large firm (50 or more)—with an overall winner chosen from the finalists. The awards are presented at the National Associates Committee Awards Reception at the AIA National Convention.

For additional information, visit the AIA at *www.aia.org* or contact them at (202) 626-7300.

1991
Askew Nixon Ferguson, Memphis, TN
Clark Nexsen Owen Barberi Gibson, Norfolk, VA
Gilley–Hinkel Architects, Bristol, CT
Kekst Architecture, Cleveland, OH
RTKL, Baltimore, MD

1992
HKS Architects, Dallas, TX
Luey Architects, Tigard, OR

1993
Jeffrey S. Conrad, Architect, Oxnard, CA
CUH2A, Princeton, NJ
Earl Swensson Associates, Nashville, TN
Western Michigan University, Kalamazoo, MI

1994
Albert Kahn Associates, Detroit, MI
Cynthia Easton, Sacramento, CA
Johnson, Laffen, Meland, Grand Forks, ND
Klipp Colussy Jenks DuBois, Denver, CO

1995
BSW International, Tulsa, OK
Einhorn Yaffee Prescott, Washington, DC
Naval Facilities Engineering Command,
    Alexandria, VA

1996
Collins Rimer & Gordon, Cleveland, OH
Schmidt Associates, Inc., Indianapolis, IN
Watkins Hamilton Ross Architects, Bellaire, TX

1997
Giattina Fisher Aycock Architects,
    Birmingham, AL

1998
Everton Oglesby Askew, Nashville, TN
Loebl Schlossman & Hackl/Hague Richards,
    Chicago, IL

Honorable Mention
BWBR Architects, St. Paul, MN
Caldwell Architects, Marina del Rey, CA
RTKL Associates, Baltimore, MD

1999
NBBJ, Columbus, OH

Honorable Mention
The Hillier Group, Princeton, NJ

2000
No awards granted

IDP Outstanding Firm Award

2001

Gorman Richardson Architects, Inc.,
  Hopkinton, MA

Honorable Mention
Kling-Lindquist, Philadelphia, PA

2002
Payette Associates, Boston, MA

Honorable Mention
Flad & Associates, Madison, WI

2003
James, Harwick + Partners, Dallas, TX

Finalist, Small Firm
TTV Architects, Jacksonville, FL

Finalist, Large Firm
FreemanWhite, Inc., Charlotte, NC

2004
InVision Architecture, Sioux City, IA

FEH Associates, Sioux City, IA

Finalist, Large Firm
KKE Architects, Inc., Minneapolis, MN

2005
Stahl Architects, Fargo, ND

Finalist, Medium Firm
Caldwell Architects, Marina del Ray, CA

Finalist, Large Firm
Torti Gallas and Partners, Silver Springs, MD

Source: American Institute of Architects

We desire to enter into and inhabit any great and original work of art—to possess it and allow it to possess us, be it literature, painting, music, or architecture. This is why architecture is such a powerful art: we can inhabit it physically as well as spiritually in time and space. Someday perhaps it will, like music, become less earth-bound, more flexible and athletic, more ever-changing and free.

Bruce Goff

IDSA Education Award

The Industrial Designers Society of America grants the Education Award to recognize excellence in industrial design education. Educators are presented this award in honor of significant and distinguished contributions.

For additional information, visit IDSA on the Internet at *www.idsa.org.*

1988	Arthur J. Pulos
	Syracuse University
1989	Robert Lepper
	Carnegie Mellon University
1990	Edward Zagorski
	University of Illinois at Urbana–
	Champaign
1991	James M. Alexander
	Art Center College of Design
1992	Strother MacMinn
	Art Center College of Design
	Robert Redmann
	University of Bridgeport
1993	Vincent Foote
	North Carolina State University
	Herbert Tyrnauer
	California State University, Long Beach
1994	Hin Bredendieck
	Georgia Institute of Technology
	Joseph Koncelik
	Ohio State University
1996	Toby Thompson
	Rochester Institute of Technology

1997	Marc Harrison
	Rhode Island School of Design
1998	Bruce Hannah
	Pratt Institute
1999	Michael Nielsen
	Arizona State University
2000	Katherine McCoy
	Illinois Institute of Technology
	Michael McCoy
	Illinois Institute of Technology
2001	Jim Pirkl
	Syracuse University
2002	Steven Skov Holt
	California College of the Arts
2003	*No award granted*
2004	Joe Ballay
	Carnegie Mellon University
2005	Carl Garant
	Columbus College of Art & Design

Source: Industrial Designers Society of America

Avoiding mistakes is one of the strongest points that designers can bring into this world.

Ron Nabarro

Interior Design and Related Graduate Programs

For those interested in interior design education beyond a bachelor's degree, a number of schools offer graduate-level programs. Compiled in August 2004 by the Interior Design Educators Council, which is dedicated to the advancement of education and research in interior design, this list contains first-professional, post-professional, and other related degree programs. (First-professional programs (FP) are directed at students who hold a degree in an unrelated discipline, such as nursing or business, while post-professional programs (PP) are designed for students with an bachelor's degree in interior design or a closely related field.) The programs below offer a wide variety of degree types (e.g. MFA, MS, PhD) in a diverse range of interior design and related specialties. Note that although FIDER does accredit some first-professional master's degrees (a list can be found beginning on page 507), FIDER does not accredit post-professional graduate programs.

This list is also available online from IDEC, *www.idec.org*, containing additional information about each program, such as thesis and credit hour requirements, enrollment statistics, program length, and detailed contact information.

School	City	Web Address	Degree Type	Program Emphasis	First/Post Professional
ALABAMA					
University of Alabama	Tuscaloosa	ua.edu	MS	Interior design	PP
ARIZONA					
Arizona State University	Tempe	asu.edu	MSD	Human factors; Facilities planning and management; Design methodology, theory, criticism; Visual communications design	PP
			PhD	Design; Planning; History, theory and criticism	PP
CALIFORNIA					
Academy of Art University	San Francisco	academyart.edu	MFA	Residential/Commercial	—
California State University, Northridge	Northridge	csun.edu	MS	Interior design	PP
San Diego State University	San Diego	sdsu.edu	MA MFA	Individualized	FP PP
COLORADO					
Colorado State University	Fort Collins	colostate.edu	MS	Interior design	FP PP

Interior Design and Related Graduate Programs

School	City	Web Address	Degree Type	Program Emphasis	First/Post Professional
DISTRICT OF COLUMBIA					
George Washington University at Mount Vernon College	Washington	mvc.gwu.edu	MFA	Interior design	FP
FLORIDA					
Florida State University	Tallahassee	fsu.edu	MS MA MFA	Individual; Design research; Diverse areas of expertise available	FP PP
University of Florida	Gainesville	ufl.edu	MID	Research degree with emphasis in design specialties, historic preservation, environment and behavior	PP
GEORGIA					
Georgia State University	Atlanta	gsu.edu	MFA	Individualized	PP
Savannah College of Art and Design	Savannah	scad.edu	MA	Design; Theory and criticism; Technology and electronic design	FP
			MFA	Design, theory and criticism; Environmental — issues; Technology and electronic design; Professional development	
University of Georgia	Athens	uga.edu	MFA	Interior design	PP
ILLINOIS					
Columbia College	Chicago	colum.edu	MFA	Interior architecture; Architectural studies—	
Illinois State University	Normal	ilstu.edu	MA	Interior and environmental design	PP
			MS	Individualized	PP
INDIANA					
Indiana State University	Terre Haute	indstate.edu	MS	Individualized	PP
Indiana University	Bloomington	indina.edu	MS	Individualized	FP PP
Purdue University	West Lafayette	purdue.edu	MA	Interior design	PP
IOWA					
Iowa State University	Ames	iastate.edu	MA MFA	Individualized	PP
KENTUCKY					
University of Kentucky	Lexington	uky.edu	MA MS	Individualized	PP
LOUISIANA					
Louisiana Tech University	Ruston	latech.edu	MFA	Accessibility/Universal design	PP

Interior Design and Related Graduate Programs

School	City	Web Address	Degree Type	Program Emphasis	First/Post Professional
MASSACHUSETTS					
Boston Architectural Center	Boston	the-bac.edu	MID	Concurrent practice and academic education	FP
New England School of Art & Design at Suffolk University	Boston	suffolk.edu/ nesad	MA	Interior design with commercial, healthcare/institutional, hospitality/ retail and residential tracks	FP
University of Massachusetts	Amherst	umass.edu	MS	Individualized; Interior architecture	FP
			MS	Exposure to building and material science, cultural, historical and environmental perspectives (Interdepartmental program)	—
MICHIGAN					
Eastern Michigan University	Ypsilanti	emich.edu	MS	Individualized	FP PP
Lawrence Technological University	Southfield	ltu.edu	MID	Interior architecture	FP PP
Michigan State	East Lansing	msu.edu	MA	Human shelter; Interior design Preservationand conservation	PP
			PhD	Human environment; Design and management	PP
MINNESOTA					
University of Minnesota	St. Paul	umn.edu	MA MS PhD	Design research; Sustainable design; Culture and design, Learning styles; Sacred geometry	PP
MISSOURI					
University of Missouri– Columbia	Columbia	missouri.edu	MA	Environmental and behavior studies; Design with digital media (onsite and online)	FP PP
			PhD	Environmental and behavior studies; Design with digital media (onsite and online)	—
NEBRASKA					
University of Nebraska–Lincoln	Lincoln	unl.edu	MS	Architecture with specialization in interior design (research based, blending theory and practice)	PP
NEW YORK					
Bard Graduate Center for Studies in the Decorative Arts, Design and Culture	New York	bgc.bard.edu	MA PhD	American design and culture	—

Interior Design and Related Graduate Programs

School	City	Web Address	Degree Type	Program Emphasis		First/Post Professional
Cornell University	Ithaca	cornell.edu	MA	Interior design		PP
			MA MS	Interior design; Human environmental relations		
New York School of Interior Design	New York	nysid.edu	MFA	Advanced studio; History and theory		PP
Pratt Institute	Brooklyn	pratt.edu	MS	Professional practice		PP
Syracuse University	Syracuse	syr.edu	MFA	Interior design research; Human interiors; Sustainability		FP
NORTH CAROLINA						
University of North Carolina at Greensboro	Greensboro	uncg.edu	MS	Interior architecture with concentrations in lighting, historic preservation, design for special populations, design technology and individualized topics		PP
			MS	Environmental design; Interior product design; Digital design, Historic preservation and museum studies		PP
OHIO						
Ohio State University	Columbus	osu.edu	MA MFA	Design development; Design management; Planning design education		—
			MS PhD	Consumer; Textiles; Interiors; Aging specialization		—
OKLAHOMA						
Oklahoma State University	Stillwater	okstate.edu	MS	Environmental design		PP
University of Central Oklahoma	Edmond	ucok.edu	MFA	Interior design; Graphic design; Design education		—
OREGON						
Oregon State University	Corvallis	oregonstate.edu	MA MS	Merchandising, management, design in the near environment; Cultural/Historic aspects of the near environment; Human behavior and the near environment		PP
			PhD	Human behavior; Cultural/Historic aspects of the near environment		PP
University of Oregon	Eugene	uoregon.edu	MIA	Interior architecture		PP
PENNSYLVANIA						
Drexel University	Philadelphia	drexel.edu	MS	Individualized; Professional practice		FP
TENNESSEE						
University of Memphis	Memphis	memphis.edu	MFA	Individualized; Professional practice		PP

Interior Design and Related Graduate Programs

School	City	Web Address	Degree Type	Program Emphasis	First/Post Professional
TEXAS					
Texas Tech University	Lubbock	ttu.edu	MS PhD	Environmental design	PP
University of Houston	Houston	uh.edu	MFA	Concept and theory	FP PP
University of North Texas	Denton	unt.edu	MFA	Individualized	PP
UTAH					
Utah State University	Logan	usu.edu	MS	Various	PP
VIRGINIA					
Marymount University	Arlington	marymount.edu	MA	General	FP
			MA	Individualized; Historic preservation/History	PP
Virginia Commonwealth University	Richmond	vcu.edu	MFA	Design	PP
Virginia Polytechnic Institute and State University	Blacksburg	vt.edu	MS PhD	Design research; Design for aging; History of interiors; Behavioral aspects of design	PP
WASHINGTON					
Washington State University at Pullman	Pullman	wsu.edu	MA	Post professional research; Accelerated studies for professional preparation	PP
Washington State University at Spokane (Interdisciplinary Design Institute)	Spokane	spokane.wsu. edu	MA	Post professional research; Accelerated studies for professional preparation	PP
WISCONSIN					
University of Wisconsin-Madison	Madison	wisc.edu	MS MFA PhD	Human ecology; Design studies	PP

Source: Interior Design Educators Council, Inc.

Joel Polsky Academic Achievement Award

In order to recognize outstanding design research or a thesis project by an undergraduate or graduate student, the American Society of Interior Designers presents the ASID Educational Foundation/Joel Polsky Academic Achievement Award. Winning entries should address the needs of the public, designers, and students on topics related to design business, education, process, research, behavioral science, theory, or other technical subjects. Recipients receive a $1,000 prize.

More information is available on ASID's Web site, *www.asid.org*, or by calling the ASID Educational Foundation at (202) 546-3480.

1988
"Open Office Programming: Assessment of the Workstation Game," Nancy C. Canestaro

1989
"Restroom Usage in Selected Public Buildings and Facilities: A Comparison of Males and Females," Sandra K. Rawls

1990
"Preference, Mystery and Visual Attributes of Interiors: A Study of Relationships," Suzanne Benedict Scott

1991
"The History of the Railroad of New Jersey Maritime Terminal in Jersey City, New Jersey, Commemorating its Centennial 1889-1989," Sharon K. Sommerlad Keenan

1992
"Design for a Residential Facility for the Elderly in Combination with a Child Care Facility," Marida A. Stearns

1993
"View to Nature: Effects on Attentional Capacity," Carolyn Marie Gilker

1994
"WAYFINDING – You are Here/You are There," Jacqueline Gommel

1995
"Home Builders' and Remodelers' Role in the Adoption and Diffusion of Universally Designed Housing," Beatriz E. Blanco

Honorable Mention
"Impact on the Campus Physical Environment on Older Adult Learners," Maurine Moore

1996
"Impact of Interior Design on the Dining Disabilities of the Elderly Residents in Assisted Living and Nursing Homes," Elizabeth Rylan

Honorable Mention
"Computers in the Design Process: Comparing Creativity Ratings of Interior Design Solutions Using Pencil Based Design Methods in Schematic Development," Lynn Brandon

1997
"A Comparison of Spatial Interpretations of NASA's Payload Operations Control Center, Marshall Space Flight Center, Using Real World and Virtual Reality Observations," Patricia F. Lindsey

"La Bottega D'Artigianato Regionale in the Palazzo Massimo alle Colonne, Rome, Italy: A Story of Adaptive Reuse," Cigdem T. Bulut

Joel Polsky Academic Achievement Award

1998

"Residential Interior Environments of Retired Government Employees in Thailand," Benjamas Kutintara

"Physical and Social Attributes Influencing Mobile Workers' Sense of Place," Jacquelyn Purintan

1999

"Interior Design for Alzheimer Care Facilities: Investigating Established Design Recommendations," Kathleen L. Cackowski

"Graduate Education Research and the Interior Design Profession," Patti Lawlor

2000

"A Comparison of Career Preparation and Development Between Two-year and Four-Year Interior Design Graduates," Barbara Marini

2001

"Universal Design Standards for Single-Family Housing," Nancy L. Wolford

2002

"Environmental Quality and Healing Environments: A Study of Flooring Materials In a Healthcare Telemetry Unit," Debra Harris

2003

"An Exploration of Critical Factors for Accessibility and Wayfinding for Adults with Mental Retardation," Patricia Salmi

Honorable Mention
"Bridging the Gap Between Graduation and Registered Professional Practice in Interior Design," Sooz Klinkhamer

2004

"The Interrelation of Art and Space: An Investigation of late Nineteenth- and Early Twentieth-Century European Painting and Interior Space," Devin Fitzpatrick

Honorable Mention
"Shades of Green: A Sustainable Resource Guide for Interior Designers, Architects, Students and Educators Committed to Making a Difference," Maureen Norman

Source: American Society of Interior Designers

Jot D. Carpenter Medal

The American Society of Landscape Architects bestows the Jot D. Carpenter Prize and Medal upon a university educator who has made a sustained and significant teaching contribution to a landscape architecture program at a school with an official ASLA Student Chapter. The award, consisting of a medal and a cash prize, began in 2000 to honor the memory of Ohio State University professor Jot D. Carpenter and his significant contributions to landscape architecture education and the profession. Nominations for the award may be made by an ASLA member or an ASLA student chapter member.

For additional information, call (202) 216-2338 or visit *www.asla.org* on the Web.

2000	Roy H. DeBoer
	Rutgers, The State Univ. of New Jersey
2002	Alton A. Barnes Jr.
	Kansas State University
2003	Craig W. Johnson
	Utah State University
2004	Marvin I. Adleman
	Cornell University
2005	Robert S. (Doc) Reich
	Louisiana State University

Source: American Society of Landscape Architects

Jot D. Carpenter Medal

Robert S. Reich. Robert Reich led the landscape architecture program at Louisiana State University from its inception in 1946 until his retirement in 1983. In a film about Reich's life, produced by the Louisiana chapter of ASLA, he is asked what he considers to be his biggest contribution to the profession. His reply was, "developing a corps of disciples, who go out with the same philosophy and do great things...a lot greater than I've done."

Michael Tatum Educator of the Year Award

The Michael Tatum Excellence in Education Award was created by the International Interior Design Association to honor outstanding interior design educators. The award also celebrates the life and career of Michael Tatum, an outstanding educator and IIDA member who passed away in 1998. When reviewing the nominations, the awards committee considers excellence in teaching, innovative teaching techniques, student mentoring, contributions to the profession, creative scholarship (including the publication of scholarly research), and leadership in interior design education within the community. Nominees must be full-time faculty at FIDER-accredited schools. Recipients are awarded a $5,500 cash prize and are invited to present a scholarly paper to the IIDA membership.

For more information about the Tatum Award, contact IIDA at (312) 467-1950 or visit them on the Internet at *www.iida.org*.

1999	Joy Dohr
	University of Wisconsin–Madison
2000	Henry P. Hildebrandt
	University of Cincinnati
2001	Stephen Marc Klein
	Pratt Institute
2002	Denise Guerin
	University of Minnesota
	JoAnn Asher Thompson
	Washington State University
2003	*No award granted*
2004	*No award granted*

Source: International Interior Design Association

545

Subversion is very important—we must be modern rebels and reinvent the rules for the next generation, which we hope to call the moral market. Companies must have a duty to give something honest to people.

Philippe Starck

NCARB Prize for Creative Integration of Practice and Education in the Academy

The National Council of Architectural Registration Boards presents its annual NCARB Prize for Creative Integration of Practice and Education in the Academy to recognize accredited academic programs that best emphasize the continuum between practice and education. A jury consisting of the five members of the NCARB Practice Education Task Force and one dean from a school in each of the six NCARB regions selects the winners. Six cash awards are presented: one grand prize award of $25,000 and five awards of $7,500 each. The prize was inspired by the 1996 Carnegie Foundation report, *Building Community: A New Future for Architectural Education and Practice,* by Lee D. Mitgang and the late Ernest L. Boyer.

For additional information or to request an entry packet, contact NCARB at (202) 879-0535, or visit its Web site at *www.ncarb.org.*

2005 Winners

Grand Prize
"West Side Streetscape/Small Built Works Project"
University at Buffalo, SUNY

Prize Winners
"The Alumni Traveling Studio"
Miami University

"The Big Box Studio in the Community Design Center"
University of Arkansas

"Bridging: The Links Between Practice and Education in the Academy"
University of Florida

"Chicago Studio"
Virginia Polytechnic Institute and State University

"Organic Farm Market: A Collaborative Studio"
University of Illinois at Chicago

Honorable Mentions
"Making Connections | Building Knowledge: An Assessment of Construction Management at Risk"
North Carolina State University

"designbuildBLUFF"
University of Utah

Jury
Robert A. Boynton, Boynton Rothschild Rowland Architects
C. Robert Campbell, BDA Architecture
Brian Carter, University at Buffalo, SUNY
David Chasco, University of Illinois at Urbana-Champaign
Karen L. W. Harris, Architecture Matters
Bob Mugerauer, University of Washington
Stephen Schreiber, University of South Florida
J. Randall Seitsinger, Oklahoma State University
Barbara Sestak, Portland State University
Jeff J. Stein, Director, Boston Architectural Center
John C. Wyle, Rosser International

Source: National Council of Architectural Registration Boards

Presidents of the American Institute of Architecture Students

1956–57	James R. Barry Rice University		1978–79	John Maudlin-Jeronimo University of Miami
1957–58	Robert Harris Princeton University		1979–80	Richard Martini Boston Architectural Center
1958–59	Paul Ricciutti Case Western Reserve University		1980–81	Alejandro Barbarena University of Houston
1959–60	Charles Jones University of Arizona		1981–82	Bill Plimpton University of California, Berkeley
1960–61	Ray Gaio University of Notre Dame		1982–83	Robert Klancher University of Cincinnati
1961–62	Donald Williams Univ. of Illinois at Urbana–Champaign		1983–84	Robert Fox Temple University
1962–63	Carl Schubert California State Polytechnic University		1984–85	Thomas Fowler IV New York Inst. of Tech.–Old Westbury
1964–65	Joseph Morse Howard University		1985–86	Scott Norberg University of Nebraska–Lincoln
1965–66	Kenneth Alexander Pratt Institute		1986–87	Scott Norberg University of Nebraska–Lincoln
1966–67	Jack Worth III Georgia Institute of Technology		1987–88	Kent Davidson University of Nebraska–Lincoln
1967–68	Morten Awes University of Idaho		1988–89	Matthew W. Gilbertson University of Minnesota
1968–69	Edward Mathes University of Southwestern Louisiana		1989–90	Douglas A. Bailey Montana State University
1969–70	Taylor Culver Howard University		1990–91	Alan D.S. Paradis Roger Williams College
1970–71	Michael Interbartolo Boston Architectural Center		1991–92	Lynn N. Simon University of Washington
1971–72	Joseph Siff Rice University		1992–93	Courtney E. Miller University of Maryland
1972–73	Fay D'Avignon Boston Architectural Center		1993–94	Garen D. Miller Drury College
1973–74	Fay D'Avignon Boston Architectural Center		1994–95	Dee Christy Briggs City College of New York, CUNY
1974–75	Patric Davis Boston Architectural Center		1995–96	Robert J. Rowan Washington State University
1975–76	Ella Hall North Carolina State University		1996–97	Raymond H. Dehn University of Minnesota
1976–77	Jerry Compton Southern California Inst. of Arch.		1997–98	Robert L. Morgan Clemson University
1977–78	Charles Guerin University of Houston		1998–99	Jay M. Palu University of Nebraska–Lincoln

Presidents of the American Institute of Architecture Students

1999–00 Melissa Mileff
University of Oklahoma
2000–01 Scott Baldermann
University of Nebraska–Lincoln
2001–02 Matt Herb
University of Maryland
2002–03 Lawrence Fabbroni
Carnegie Mellon University
2003–04 Wayne Mortenson
University of Nebraska–Lincoln
2004–05 Jacob Day
University of Maryland
2005–06 Eric Zaddock
Andrews University

Source: American Institute of Architects Students

Truly memorable buildings exploit the tension between the sensuous and the intellectual, strive for the balance of the poetic and the pragmatic, and search for elusive qualities both timely and timeless.

Will Bruder

Rotch Travelling Scholarship

Established in 1883 by the sons and daughters of Benjamin Smith Rotch, an active arts patron, the Rotch Travelling Scholarship affirms the value of foreign travel through firsthand acquaintance with the great buildings of the past to stimulate the creative imagination of young architects and to enrich their cultural knowledge. The oldest scholarship of its kind in America, many of the country's most distinguished architects have been awarded this honor. The winner receives $35,000 for a minimum of eight months travel and study abroad and a payment of $3,500 upon the completion of the scholar's travel journal, which is on permanent file for the general public at the Massachusetts Institute of Technology.

For more information about the Rotch Travelling Scholarship visit their Web site at *www.rotchscholarship.org.*

1884	Clarence Howard Blackall	1913	William Leo Smith
1885	Samuel Walker Mead	1914	Ralph Johnson Batchelder
1886	George Frederick Newton	1915	Frederick Roy Witton
1887	Edgar A. Josselyn	1916	Ralph Thomas Walker
1888	Austin Willard Lord	1917	James Newhall Holden
1889	Henry Bacon	1918	*No award granted*
1890	William Thomas Partridge	1919	*No award granted*
1891	Robert Closon Spenser	1920	Robert Murray Blackall
1892	John Watrous Case	1921	Frank Somerville Carson
1893	Walter Harrington Kilham	1922	Wallace Kirkman Harrison
1894	Harold Van Bruen Manonigle	1923	Isidor Richmond
1895	Will Stein Aldrich	1924	Eugene Francis Kennedy
1896	Louis Holmes Boynton	1925	Walter F. Bogner
1897	Henry Bodge Pennell	1926	Louis Skidmore
1898	Louis Chapel Newhall	1927	Edward D. Stone
1899	Louis Warren Pulsifer	1928	Ralph E. Winslow
1900	William Leslie Welton	1929	Charles St. George Pope
1901	William Luther Mowll	1930	Barnett Sumner Gruzen
1902	James Ford Clapp	1931	Carney Goldberg
1903	Edward T. Foulkes	1932	Carroll Coletti
1904	Frederick Charles Hirons	1933	George Stephen Lewis
1905	William DeForrest Crowell	1934	Newbhard N. Culin
1906	Leroy Pearls Burnham	1935	Gordon Bunshaft
1907	Otto Faelten	1936	Leon Hyzen
1908	Isreal P. Lord	1937	John A. Valtz
1909	Horace G. Simpson	1938	Malcolm C. Robb
1910	Joseph McGinniss	1939	William E. Hartmann
1911	Niels Hjalmar Larsen	1940	George R. McClellan
1912	Charles Cameron Clark	1941	J. Martin Rosse

Rotch Travelling Scholarship

1942	*No award granted*	1975	Philip Dangerfield
1943	*No award granted*	1976	Duane E. Kell
1944	*No award granted*	1977	Patrick M. Sullivan
1945	*No award granted*	1978	Ernest F. Cirangle
1946	Melvern Coates Ensign	1979	Glenn Matsumoto
1947	Dale C. Byrd	1980	Marvin J. Malecha
1948	Victor A. Lundy	1981	William A. McGee
1949	Eduard H. Bullerjahn	1982	John M. Reimnitz
1950	Robert Lewis Bliss	1983	John K. McLaughlin Jr.
1951	Bruce A. Abrahamson	1984	Eric Liebmann
1952	Norman M. Klein	1985	Thomas M. Walsh
1953	Richard C. Brigham Jr.	1986	J. Scott Kilbourne
1954	Paul J. Corrol	1987	Mark A. Engberg
1955	Robert T. Coles	1988	Thomas Carlson-Reddig
1956	James Stageberg	1989	Joseph Mamavek
1957	John I. Schlossman	1990	Mark Moeller
1958	W. Byron Ireland	1991	Joslin Stewart
1959	Gardner Ertman	1992	Debi L. McDonald
1960	Jack Chun	1993	David T. Nagahiro
1961	John O. Cotton	1994	Craig Mutter
1962	Thomas N. Larson	1995	Jose Sama
1963	James T. Flynn	1996	Nicholas Isaak
1964	Harry F. Eagan	1997	Andrew James Davis
1965	John Wilson Cuningham	1998	Julia Holmes McMorrough
1966	Dennis Walsh	1999	Robert Linn
1967	William E. Roesner	2000	Patricia Anahory
1968	James Sandell	2001	Lorenzo Mattii
1969	Michael Buckley	2002	Kari Silloway
1970	Gary Lowe	2003	Bradley Shanks
1971	John Sheehy	2004	Aaron Follett
1972	Valdis Smits	2005	Zachary Hinchliffe
1972	Richard Green		
1973	Craig D. Roney		
1974	Nelson Scott Smith		

Source: Rotch Travelling Scholarship

Everything is looking like everywhere,
and everywhere is nowhere.

Meg Maguire

SOM Foundation Traveling Fellowship Program

Each year, the Skidmore, Owings & Merrill Foundation invites accredited schools of architecture, design, engineering, and urban design to nominate their most promising students for traveling fellowships. The SOM Foundation Traveling Fellowship Program fulfills the foundation's mission to help young architects broaden their education and take an enlightened view of society's need to improve the built and natural environments. The program recognizes the importance of travel to a designer's education—immersion in another place and culture can transform an architect's work and, ultimately, the field itself. The programs of the SOM Foundation, created in 1980, are funded by an endowment established by the partners of Skidmore, Owings & Merrill.

For more information, visit the SOM Foundation on the Internet at *www.somfoundation.som.com.*

2005 Recipients

Master of Architecture Fellowship
Kevin Fennell
University of Pennsylvania

Bachelor of Architecture Fellowship
Brian Knight
Southern California Institute of Architecture

Design Fellowship
Jungsoo Kim
School of the Art Institute of Chicago

Structural Engineering Fellowship
Annè Kountz
University of Washington

Urban Design Fellowship
Jason Frantzen
Harvard University

Source: SOM Foundation

Student Sustainable Design Competition

The International Interior Design Association and DuPont™ Antron® partner to present the annual Student Sustainable Design Competition. Inaugurated in 2003, the contest recognizes outstanding sustainable design by students enrolled in post-secondary interior design programs. Designs are judged for innovative character of overall design, responsible use of materials, practical application, visual comfort, and sustainable material application. Projects should be between 1,000 and 30,000 square feet. Award prizes include: $3,500 (grand prize); $1,500 (first prize); and a gift certificate for the honorable mention.

Additional information and entry forms are available online at *www.iida.org* or by contacting the IIDA at (312) 467-1950.

2005 Winners

Grand Prize
"Lux Electronics"
Nicole Kelln
Washington State University

First Prize
"eco-efficient campus"
Lynda Duray, Joelle Epstein, Laura Radebaugh
Mount Ida College

Honorable Mention
"The Sanctuary"
Raine Heidenberg
Pratt Institute

Source: International Interior Design Association

Man has too long forgotten that the world was given to him for usufruct alone, not for consumption, still less for profligate waste.

George Perkins Marsh

Tau Sigma Delta

Formed in 1913 at the University of Michigan, Tau Sigma Delta is an honor society for architecture and the allied arts. University juniors and seniors who are majoring in architecture, architectural engineering, architectural design, landscape architecture, painting, sculpting, planning, decorative design, interior design, and all allied arts are eligible for membership. To date. more than 65 chapters have been organized at schools across the United States, each administered by the universities' of architecture schools. In addition, each year the society presents a gold medal (see page 183) to honor a professional's outstanding contributions to architecture, landscape architecture, or an allied field.

Contact

Additional information about Tau Sigma Delta, including a list of chapters and their contacts, can be found online at *www.tausigmadelta.org*

Mission Statement

Tau Sigma Delta was established to provide a national collegiate honor society open to students of all American colleges and universities wherein an accredited program of architecture, landscape architecture, or the allied arts is established. Its prime objective is to celebrate excellence in scholarship, to stimulate mental achievement, and to award those students who attain high scholastic standing in architecture, landscape architecture, and allied arts of design by the rewards of membership in an honor society.

TOPAZ Medallion

The TOPAZ Medallion is awarded jointly by the American Institute of Architects and the American Collegiate Schools of Architecture to honor individuals who have made an outstanding contribution to the field of architectural education. Candidates may be nominated by colleagues, students, and former students. Recipients have made a significant impact on the field of architecture, expanded into fields beyond their specialty, and had a lasting impact on their students.

For additional information about this award program, visit the AIA's Web site at *www.aia.org*.

1976	Jean Labatut Princeton University	1992	Spiro Kostof* University of California, Berkeley
1977	Henry Kamphoefner North Carolina State University	1993	Mario Salvadori Columbia University
1978	Lawrence Anderson Massachusetts Institute of Technology	1994	Harlan E. McClure Clemson University
1979	G. Holmes Perkins University of Pennsylvania	1995	Henry N. Cobb Harvard University
1980	Serge Chermayeff Yale University	1996	Denise Scott Brown University of Pennsylvania
1981	Marcel Breuer Harvard University	1997	Donlyn Lyndon University of California, Berkeley
1982	Joseph Esherick University of California, Berkeley	1998	Werner Seligmann Syracuse University
1983	Charles E. Burchard Virginia Polytechnic Institue and State University	1999	W. Cecil Steward University of Nebraska–Lincoln
1984	Robert Geddes Princeton University	2000	Alan H. Balfour Rensselaer Polytechnic Institute
1985	Colin Rowe Cornell University	2001	Lee G. Copeland Washington College and University of Pennsylvania
1986	Vincent Scully Jr. Yale University	2002	Jerzy Soltan Harvard University
1987	Ralph Rapson University of Minnesota	2003	Marvin J. Malecha North Carolina State University
1988	John Hejduk Cooper Union	2004	Stanford Anderson Massachusetts Institute of Technology
1989	Charles Moore University of California, Berkeley	2005	Edward Allen University of Oregon
1990	Raymond L. Kappe Southern California Institute of Arch.		* Honored posthumously
1991	Kenneth B. Frampton Columbia University		

Source: American Institute of Architects

TOPAZ Medallion

555

Edward Allen. In his nomination letter, Christine Theodoropoulos, head of the Department of Architecture at the University of Oregon, described Edward Allen's impact, "In his teaching and his writing, Ed's message is clear. He believes that buildings that are successful architecturally must also be successful technically, and his love and enthusiasm for the craft of making buildings is extremely contagious. Ed has the extraordinary ability to eliminate the gap between building technology and architectural achievement that is often such a struggle for novice designers."

Organizations

The history, purpose, and membership benefits of major national and international design associations can be found in this chapter, along with a summary listing of numerous design and building-related organizations and government agencies. Other organizations related to sustainable design, historic preservation, and design education can be found in their respective chapters.

American Architectural Foundation

AAF

Headquartered in America's oldest museum devoted to architecture, Washington, DC's Octagon, the American Architectural Foundation is dedicated to furthering the public's understanding of the relationship between architecture and the human experience. The nonprofit AAF sponsors education and outreach programs that foster public participation in the design process, encourage public stewardship of America's architectural heritage, and promote alliances between architects and their communities. It is also home to a growing architectural archive of more than 60,000 drawings and 30,000 photographs.

Address
1799 New York Avenue NW
Washington, DC 20006
(202) 626-7318
www.archfoundation.org

Mission Statement

The American Architectural Foundation is a national resource for those who want our communities to be centers of civilization and our children to inherit a wholesome physical environment that uplifts the spirit. The AAF is a national resource that seeks to educate people about the value of architecture and design as a resource to enrich lives and transform communities.

American Council of Engineering Companies

ACEC

The American Council of Engineering Companies represents private engineering firms in the United States by promoting their interests and providing educational opportunities to members. Specifically, the goals of the group are to help members achieve higher business standards, serve as an information clearinghouse, advise on legislation, and to support the advancement of engineering. The ACEC was formed by the union of the American Institute of Consulting Engineers and the Consulting Engineers Council in 1973. Today it is the largest national organization of consulting engineers. Fifty-one state and regional member organizations represent more than 5,800 engineering firms. These firms employ more than 309,000 engineers, architects, land surveyors, scientists, technicians, and other professionals who design approximately $100 billion of private and public works annually.

Address
1015 15th Street NW, 8th Floor
Washington, DC 20005
(202) 347-7474
www.acec.org

Mission Statement

The American Council of Engineering Companies is the business association of America's engineering industry, representing approximately 6,000 independent engineering companies throughout the United States engaged in the development of America's transportation, environmental, industrial, and other infrastructure. Founded in 1910 and headquartered in Washington, DC, ACEC is a national federation of 51 state and regional organizations.

American Institute of Architects

AIA

Representing the professional interests of America's architects since 1857, the American Institute of Architects provides education, government advocacy, community redevelopment, and public outreach activities with and for its 62,000 members. With more than 300 local and state AIA organizations, the institute closely monitors legislative and regulatory actions at all levels of government. It provides professional development opportunities, industry standard contract documents, information services, and a comprehensive awards program.

Address

1735 New York Avenue NW
Washington, DC 20006
(202) 626-7300
www.aia.org

56

Mission Statement

The American Institute of Architects is the voice of the architecture profession dedicated to serving its members, advancing their value, and improving the quality of the built environment.

American Institute of Graphic Arts

AIGA

Billing itself as the oldest and largest membership association for professionals engaged in the discipline, practice, and culture of visual communication and graphic design, the American Institute of Graphic Arts was founded in 1914 and now represents more than 15,000 designers. Members of AIGA include professional designers, educators, and students engaged in type and book design, editorial design, communications and corporate design, posters, interface and Web design, and new media and motion graphics design. AIGA serves as a hub of information and activity within the design community through conferences, competitions, exhibitions, publications, educational activities, and its Web site.

Address ————————————————————————————
164 Fifth Avenue
New York, NY 10010
(212) 807-1990
www.aiga.org

562

Mission Statement

The purpose of the American Institute of Graphic Arts is to further excellence in communication design as a broadly defined discipline, strategic tool for business, and cultural force. AIGA is the place design professionals turn to first to exchange ideas and information, participate in critical analysis and research, and advance education and ethical practice.

American Planning Association

APA

The American Planning Association represents 30,000 planners, officials, and citizens involved with urban and rural planning issues. Sixty-five percent of APA's members are employed by state and local government agencies. The mission of the organization is to encourage planning that will contribute to public well-being by developing communities and environments that meet the needs of people and society more effectively. APA is headquartered in Washington, DC, and operates local chapters across the country. The American Institute of Certified Planners is APA's professional and educational arm, certifying planners who meet specific criteria. The group also has research, publications, conference, and education components.

Address

122 S. Michigan Avenue, Suite 1600
Chicago, IL 60603
(312) 431-9100
www. planning.org

1776 Massachusetts Avenue NW
Washington, DC 20036
(202) 872-0611
www.planning.org

563

Mission Statement

The American Planning Association is a nonprofit public interest and research organization committed to urban, suburban, regional, and rural planning. APA and its professional institute, the American Institute of Certified Planners, advance the art and science of planning to meet the needs of people and society.

American Society of Interior Designers

ASID

The American Society of Interior Designers was formed in 1975 by the consolidation of the American Institute of Designers and the National Society of Interior Designers. It serves more than 30,000 members with continuing education and government affairs departments, conferences, publications, online services, and more. Members include residential and commercial designers; 1,700 manufacturers of design-related products and services, also known as industry partners; and 9,500 interior design students. ASID operates 48 local chapters throughout the United States.

Address

608 Massachusetts Avenue NE
Washington, DC 20002-6006
(202) 546-3480
www.asid.org

Mission Statement

The mission of the American Society of Interior Designers is to advance the interior design profession through knowledge generation and sharing, advocacy of interior designers' right to practice, professional and public education, and expansion of interior design markets.

American Society of Landscape Architects

ASLA

Representing the landscape architecture profession in the United States since 1899, the American Society of Landscape Architects currently serves more than 15,000 members through 48 chapters across the country. The ASLA's goal is to advance knowledge, education, and skill in the art and science of landscape architecture. The benefits of membership include a national annual meeting, *Landscape Architecture* magazine, continuing education credits, seminars and workshops, professional interest groups, government advocacy, and award programs. In addition, the US Department of Education has authorized the Landscape Architectural Accreditation Board of the ASLA as the accrediting agency for landscape architecture programs at US colleges and universities.

Address ——————————————————————————
636 Eye Street NW
Washington, DC 20001
(202) 898-2444
www.asla.org

Mission Statement
The mission of the American Society of Landscape Architects is to lead, to educate, and to participate in the careful stewardship, wise planning, and artful design of our cultural and natural environments.

Design Futures Council

DFC

The Design Futures Council is a think tank of design and building industry leaders who collaborate through a series of regular meetings, summits, and *DesignIntelligence*, a monthly newsletter. The group shares information among its members on best practices and new trends in the design community in order to help member organizations anticipate change and increase competitive fitness. Recent summit topics have included sustainable/green design and creativity (with the Salk Institute). Members include leading architecture and design firms; dynamic manufacturers; service providers; and small, forward-thinking A/E/C companies taking an active interest in their future.

Address ———————————————————————————
30 Technology Parkway South, Suite 200
Atlanta, GA 30092
(800) 726-8603
www.di.net

Mission Statement

The Design Futures Council is a think tank with the mission to explore trends, changes, and new opportunities in design, architecture, engineering, and building technology for the purpose of fostering innovation and improving the performance of member organizations.

Industrial Designers Society of America

IDSA

Founded in 1965, the Industrial Designers Society of America is a professional association of industrial designers, educators, and students dedicated to the promotion of the profession. By fostering innovation and high standards of design, IDSA communicates the value of design to the public and mentors young designers in their professional career development. IDSA serves its constituency through the professional journal *Innovation*, award programs, an annual conference, research sponsorship and collection, networking opportunities, and promotion of the practice at all levels of government.

Address ———————————————————————————

45195 Business Court, Suite 250
Dulles, VA 20166
(703) 707-6000
www.idsa.org

561

Mission Statement

The Industrial Designers Society of America is dedicated to communicating the value of industrial design to society, business and government. IDSA provides leadership to and promotes dialogue between practice and education. As a professional association, it serves its diverse membership by recognizing excellence, promoting the exchange of information, and fostering innovation.

International Interior Design Association

IIDA

The International Interior Design Association provides a variety of services and benefits to its more than 10,000 members through eight specialty forums, nine regions, and more than 30 chapters around the world. This professional networking and educational association promotes the interior design practice to the public and serves its members as a clearinghouse for industry information. IIDA was founded in 1994 as the result of a merger of the Institute of Business Designers, the International Society of Interior Designers, and the Council of Federal Interior Designers. The goal of the merger was to create an international association with a united mission that would represent interior designers worldwide.

Address
13-500 Merchandise Mart
Chicago, IL 60654
(312) 467-1950
www.iida.org

Mission Statement

The International Interior Design Association is committed to enhancing the quality of life through excellence in interior design and advancing interior design through knowledge. IIDA advocates for interior design excellence, provides superior industry information, nurtures a global interior design community, maintains educational standards, and responds to trends in business and design.

Society of Architectural Historians

SAH

Since its founding in 1940, the Society of Architectural Historians has sought to promote the history of architecture. The membership of SAH ranges from professionals, such as architects, planners, preservationists, and academics, to those simply interested in architecture. The society produces a quarterly journal and monthly newsletter and organizes study tours and an annual conference. There are also a number of associated, although independent, local chapters. The SAH's national headquarters is located in Chicago's architecturally significant Charnley-Persky House, which was designed in 1891 by the firm of Dankmar Adler and Louis Sullivan. Guided tours of the house are offered.

Address

1365 North Astor Street
Chicago, IL 60610
(312) 573-1365
www.sah.org

Mission Statement

The mission of the Society of Architectural Historians is to advance knowledge and understanding of the history of architecture, design, landscape, and urbanism worldwide.

Society for Environmental Graphic Design

SEGD

The Society for Environmental Graphic Design is a non-profit organization formed in 1973 to promote public awareness of and professional development in environmental graphic design. This interdisciplinary field encompasses the talents of many design professionals, including graphic designers, architects, landscape architects, product designers, planners, interior designers, and exhibition designers in the planning and design of graphic elements that shape our built and natural environments. Practitioners in this field design graphic elements to help identify, direct, inform, interpret, and visually enhance our surroundings. From wayfinding systems and mapping to exhibit design and themed environments, environmental graphic design impacts our experiences everywhere. SEGD offers its members an interdisciplinary network to support and enhance their efforts in this growing discipline, a bi-monthly newsletter, an annual conference, a design award program, technical bulletins, job bank listings, and many other formal and informal resources.

Address

1000 Vermont Avenue, Suite 400
Washington, DC 20005
(202) 638-5555
www. segd.org

Mission Statement

The Society for Environmental Graphic Design is an international nonprofit educational organization providing resources for design specialists in the field of environmental graphic design, architecture, and landscape, interior, and industrial design.

Urban Land Institute

ULI

Formed in 1936 as a research arm of the National Association of Real Estate Boards (now the National Association of Realtors), the Urban Land Institute is an independent organization for those engaged in the entrepreneurial and collaborative process of real estate development and land-use policymaking. ULI has 22,000 members working in the public and private sectors, a staff of 100 in Washington, DC, and a $27-million operating budget. ULI members are the people that plan, develop, and redevelop neighborhoods, business districts, and communities across the United States and around the world, working in private enterprise and public service. The institute's activities include research, forums and task forces, awards, education, and publishing.

Address ─────────────────────────────────
1025 Thomas Jefferson Street NW
Suite 500 West
Washington, DC 20007
(202) 624-7000
www.uli.org

Mission Statement

The mission of the Urban Land Institute is to provide responsible leadership in the use of land in order to enhance the total environment. ULI's strategic direction is to extend its industry leadership to bring together the people able to influence the outcome of important issues related to land use and the built environment, communicate who we are and what we— our members and our Institute—have learned about land use to increase ULI's influence on land use policy and practice, and continue to provide relevant and current information about land use and real estate development to all our members and stakeholders.

Design & Building-Related Organizations

The following associations, organizations, and government agencies offer a variety of information and support for the design and construction industry.

Associations & Organizations

Acoustical Society of America
2 Huntington Quadrangle, Suite 1NO1
Melville, NY 11747
(516) 576-2360
http://asa.aip.org

Air-Conditioning & Refrigeration Institute
4100 North Fairfax Drive, Suite 200
Arlington, VA 22203
(703) 524-8800
www.ari.org

Air Conditioning Contractors of America
2800 Shirlington Road, Suite 300
Arlington, VA 22206
(703) 575-4477
www.acca.org

Alliance to Save Energy
1200 18th Street NW, Suite 900
Washington, DC 20036
(202) 857-0666
www.ase.org

American Arbitration Association
335 Madison Avenue, 10th Floor
New York, NY 10017
(212) 716-5800
www.adr.org

American Architectural Manufacturers Association
1827 Walden Office Square, Suite 550
Schaumburg, IL 60173
(847) 303-5664
www.aamanet.org

American Concrete Institute
38800 Country Club Drive
Farmington Hills, MI 48331
(248) 848-3700
www.aci-int.org

American Forest Foundation
1111 19th Street NW, Suite 780
Washington, DC 20036
(202) 463-2462
www.affoundation.org

American Gas Association
400 North Capitol Street NW, Suite 450
Washington, DC 20001
(202) 824-7000
www.aga.org

American Hardware Manufacturers Association
801 North Plaza Drive
Schaumburg, IL 60173
(847) 605-1025
www.ahma.org

American Horticultural Society
7931 East Boulevard Drive
Alexandria, VA 22308
(703) 768-5700
www.ahs.org

American Institute of Building Design
2505 Main Street, Suite 209-B
Stratford, CT 06615
(800) 366-2423
www.aibd.org

American Institute of Steel Construction
One East Wacker Drive, Suite 700
Chicago, IL 60601-1802
(312) 670-2400
www.aisc.org

American Lighting Association
PO Box 420288
Dallas, TX 75342
(800) 274-4484
www.americanlightingassoc.com

Design & Building-Related Organizations

American National Standards Institute
1819 L Street NW, Sixth Floor
Washington, DC 20036
(202) 293-8020
www.ansi.org

American Nursery & Landscape Association
1000 Vermont Avenue NW, Suite 300
Washington, DC 20005
(202) 789-2900
www.anla.org

American Resort Development Association
1201 15th Street NW, Suite 400
Washington, DC 20005
(202) 371-6700
www.arda.org

American Society for Horticulture Science
113 South West Street, Suite 200
Alexandria, VA 22314
(703) 836-4606
www.ashs.org

American Society for Testing & Materials
100 Barr Harbor Drive
PO Box C700
West Conshohocken, PA 19428
(610) 832-9500
www.astm.org

American Society of Civil Engineers
1801 Alexander Bell Drive
Reston, VA 20191
(800) 548-2723
www.asce.org

American Society of Consulting Arborists
15245 Shady Grove Road, Suite 130
Rockville, MD 20850
(301) 947-0483
www. asca-consultants.org

American Society of Golf Course Architects
125 North Executive Drive, Suite 106
Brookfield, WI 53005
(262) 786-5960
www.asgca.org

American Society of Heating, Refrigerating & Air-Conditioning Engineers
1791 Tullie Circle NE
Atlanta, GA 30329
(404) 636-8400
www.ashrae.org

American Society of Mechanical Engineers
Three Park Avenue
New York, NY 10016
(212) 591-7722
www.asme.org

American Society of Plumbing Engineers
8614 W. Catalpa Avenue, Suite 1007
Chicago, IL 60656
(773) 693-2773
www.aspe.org

American Society of Professional Estimators
2525 Perimeter Place Drive, Suite 103
Nashville, TN 37214
(615) 316-9200
www.aspenational.com

American Subcontractors Association, Inc.
1004 Duke Street
Alexandria, VA 22314
(703) 684-3450
www.asaonline.com

American Textile Manufacturers Institute
1130 Connecticut Avenue NW
Washington, DC 20036
(202) 862-0500
www.textileweb.com

APA – The Engineered Wood Association
7011 South 19th Street
Tacoma, WA 98466
(253) 565-6600
www.apawood.org

Architectural Woodwork Institute
1952 Isaac Newton Square West
Reston, VA 20190
(703) 733-0600
www.awinet.org

Design & Building-Related Organizations

ASFE
8811 Colesville Road, Suite G106
Silver Spring, MD 20910
(301) 565-2733
www.asfe.org

Asphalt Roofing Manufacturers Association
1156 15th Street NW, Suite 900
Washington, DC 20005
(202) 207-0917
www.asphaltroofing.org

Associated Builders & Contractors
4250 North Fairfax Drive, 9th Floor
Arlington, VA 22203
(703) 812-2000
www.abc.org

Associated General Contractors of America
333 John Carlyle Street, Suite 200
Alexandria, VA 22314
(703) 548-3118
www.agc.org

Associated Owners & Developers
PO Box 4163
McLean, VA 22103
(703) 734-2397
www.constructionchannel.net/aod

Association for Contract Textiles
PO Box 101981
Fort Worth, TX 76185
(817) 924-8048
www.contract-textiles.com

Association for Facilities Engineering
8160 Corporate Park Drive, Suite 125
Cincinnati, OH 45242
(513) 489-2473
www.afe.org

Association for the Advancement of Cost Engineering
209 Prairie Avenue, Suite 100
Morgantown, WV 26501
(304) 296-8444
www.aacei.org

Association of Energy Engineers
4025 Pleasantdale Road, Suite 420
Atlanta, GA 30340
(770) 447-5083
www.aeecenter.org

Association of Higher Education Facilities Officers
1643 Prince Street
Alexandria, VA 22314
(703) 684-1446
www.appa.org

Association of Pool and Spa Professionals
2111 Eisenhower Avenue
Alexandria, VA 22314
(703) 838-0083
www.theapsp.org

Association of the Wall & Ceiling Industry
803 West Broad Street, Suite 600
Falls Church, VA 22046
(703) 534-8300
www.awci.org

Brick Industry Association
11490 Commerce Park Drive
Reston, VA 20191
(703) 620-0010
www.bia.org

Building Codes Assistance Project
241 Angell Street
Providence, RI 02906
(402) 273-0263
www.bcap-energy.org

Building Futures Council
333 John Carlyle Street, Suite 200
Alexandria, VA 22314
(703) 837-5323
www.thebfc.com

Building Owners & Managers Association International
1201 New York Avenue NW, Suite 300
Washington, DC 20005
(202) 408-2662
www.boma.org

Design & Building-Related Organizations

Building Stone Institute
300 Park Boulevard, Suite 335
Itasca, IL 60143
(630) 775-9130
www.buildingstone.org

California Redwood Association
405 Enfrente Drive, Suite 200
Novato, CA 94949
(415) 382-0662
www.calredwood.org

Carpet and Rug Institute
PO Box 2048
Dalton, GA 30722
(706) 278-3176
www.carpet-rug.com

Cedar Shake and Shingle Bureau
PO Box 1178
Sumas, WA 98295
(604) 820-7700
www.cedarbureau.org

Center for Health Design
1850 Gateway Boulevard, Suite 1083
Concord, CA 94520
(925) 521-9404
www.healthdesign.org

Color Association of the United States
315 West 39th Street, Studio 507
New York, NY 10018
(212) 947-7774
www.colorassociation.com

Composite Panel Association/
Composite Wood Council
18922 Premiere Court
Gaithersburg, MD 20879
(301) 670-0604
www.pbmdf.com

Construction Management Association
of America
7918 Jones Branch Drive, Suite 540
McLean, VA 22102
(703) 356-2622
www.cmaanet.org

Construction Specifications Institute
99 Canal Center Plaza, Suite 300
Alexandria, VA 22314
(703) 684-0300
www.csinet.org

Copper Development Association
260 Madison Avenue, 16th Floor
New York, NY 10016
(212) 251-7200
www.copper.org

Council of Professional Surveyors
1015 15th Street NW, 8th Floor
Washington, DC 20005
(202) 347-7474
www.acec.org/about/cops.cfm

Council on Tall Buildings and Urban Habitat
Illinois Institute of Technology
S.R. Crown Hall
3360 South State Street
Chicago, IL 60616
(312) 909-0253
www.ctbuh.org

Deep Foundations Institute
326 Lafayette Avenue
Hawthorne, NJ 07506
(973) 423-4030
www.dfi.org

Design-Build Institute of America
1100 H Street NW, Suite 500
Washington, DC 20005
(202) 682-0110
www.dbia.org

Design Management Institute
29 Temple Place, 2nd Floor
Boston, MA 02111
(617) 338-6380
www.dmi.org

Door & Hardware Institute
14150 Newbrook Drive, Suite 200
Chantilly, VA 20151
(703) 222-2010
www.dhi.org

575

Design & Building-Related Organizations

Edison Electric Institute
701 Pennsylvania Avenue NW
Washington, DC 20004
(202) 508-5000
www.eei.org

EIFS Industry Members Association
3000 Corporate Center Drive, Suite 270
Morrow, GA 30260
(770) 968-7945
www.eima.com

Electrical Power Research Institute
3420 Hillview Avenue
Palo Alto, CA 94304
(800) 313-3774
www.epri.com

Gas Technology Institute
1700 South Mount Prospect Road
Des Plaines, IL 60018
(847) 768-0500
www.gastechnology.org

Glass Association of North America
2945 SW Wanamaker Drive, Suite A
Topeka, KS 66614
(785) 271-0208
www.glasswebsite.com

Hardwood Plywood & Veneer Association
PO Box 2789
Reston, VA 20195
(703) 435-2900
www.hpva.org

Hearth, Patio & Barbecue Association
1601 North Kent Street, Suite 1001
Arlington, VA 22209
(703) 522-0086
www.hpba.org

Human Factors and Ergonomics Society
PO Box 1369
Santa Monica, CA 90406
(310) 394-1811
www.hfes.org

**Illuminating Engineering Society
of North America**
120 Wall Street, 17th Floor
New York, NY 10005
(212) 248-5000
www.iesna.org

**Institute of Electrical & Electronics
Engineers, Inc.**
3 Park Avenue, 17th Floor
New York, NY 10016
(212) 419-7900
www.ieee.org

Institute of Store Planners
25 North Broadway
Tarrytown, NY 10591
(800) 379-9912
www.ispo.org

International Association of Lighting Designers
The Merchandise Mart
200 World Trade Center, Suite 9-104
Chicago, IL 60654
(312) 527-3677
www.iald.org

International Code Council
5203 Leesburg Pike, Suite 600
Falls Church, VA 22041
(888) 422-7233
www.iccsafe.org

International Facility Management Association
1 East Greenway Plaza, Suite 1100
Houston, TX 77046
(713) 623-4362
www.ifma.org

International Furnishings and Design Association
191 Clarksville Road
Princeton Junction, NJ 08550
(609) 799-3423
www.ifda.com

Design & Building-Related Organizations

International Society of Arboriculture
PO Box 3129
Champaign, IL 61826
(217) 355-9411
www.isa-arbor.com

International Wood Products Association
4214 King Street, West
Alexandria, VA 22302
(703) 820-6696
www.iwpawood.org

Irrigation Association
6540 Arlington Boulevard
Falls Church, VA 22042
(703) 536-7080
www.irrigation.org

ISA–The Instrumentation, Systems, and Automation Society
67 Alexander Drive
Research Triangle Park, NC 27709
(919) 549-8411
www.isa.org

Light Gauge Steel Engineers Association
1201 15th Street NW, Suite 320
Washington, DC 20005
(202) 263-4488
www.lgsea.com

Maple Flooring Manufacturers Association
60 Revere Drive, Suite 500
Northbrook, IL 60062
(847) 480-9138
www.maplefloor.org

Marble Institute of America
28901 Clemens Road, Suite 100
Westlake, OH 44145
(440) 250-9222
www.marble-institute.com

Metal Building Manufacturers Association
1300 Sumner Avenue
Cleveland, OH 44115
(216) 241-7333
www.mbma.com

National Association of Environmental Professionals
PO Box 2086
Bowie, MD 20718
(301) 860-1140
www.naep.org

National Association of Home Builders
1201 15th Street NW
Washington, DC 20005
(202) 266-8200
www.nahb.org

National Clearinghouse for Educational Facilities
1090 Vermont Avenue NW, Suite 700
Washington, DC 20005
(202) 289-7800
www.edfacilities.org

National Concrete Masonry Association
13750 Sunrise Valley Drive
Herndon, VA 20171
(703) 713-1900
www.ncma.org

National Conference of States on Building Codes & Standards
505 Huntmar Park Drive, Suite 210
Herndon, VA 20170
(703) 437-0100
www.ncsbcs.org

National Council of Acoustical Consultants
66 Morris Avenue, Suite 1A
Springfield, NJ 07081
(973) 564-5859
www.ncac.com

National Electrical Contractors Association
3 Bethesda Metro Center, Suite 1100
Bethesda, MD 20814
(301) 657-3110
www.necanet.org

National Electrical Manufacturers Association
1300 North 17th Street, Suite 1847
Rosslyn, VA 22209
(703) 841-3200
www.nema.org

Design & Building-Related Organizations

National Fire Protection Association
1 Batterymarch Park
Quincy, MA 02169
(617) 770-3000
www.nfpa.org

National Fire Sprinkler Association
PO Box 1000
Patterson, NY 12563
(845) 878-4200
www.nfsa.org

National Glass Association
8200 Greensboro Drive, Suite 302
McLean, VA 22102
(866) 342-5642
www.glass.org

National Institute of Building Sciences
1090 Vermont Avenue NW, Suite 700
Washington, DC 20005
(202) 289-7800
www.nibs.org

National Lighting Bureau
8811 Colesville Road, Suite G106
Silver Spring, MD 20910
(301) 587-9572
www.nlb.org

National Kitchen & Bath Association
687 Willow Grove Street
Hackettstown, NJ 07840
(800) 843-6522
www.nkba.org

National Organization of Minority Architects
c/o School of Architecture and Design
College of Engineering, Architecture
and Computer Sciences
Howard University
2366 6th Street NW, Room 100
Washington, DC 20059
(202) 686-2780
www.noma.net

National Paint & Coatings Association
1500 Rhode Island Avenue NW
Washington, DC 20005
(202) 462-6272
www.paint.org

National Society of Professional Engineers
1420 King Street
Alexandria, VA 22314
(703) 684-2800
www.nspe.org

National Sunroom Association
2945 SW Wanamaker Drive, Suite A
Topeka, KS 66614
(785) 271-0208
www.nationalsunroom.org

National Wood Flooring Association
111 Chesterfield Industrial Boulevard
Chesterfield, MO 63005
(800) 422-4556
www.woodfloors.org

New Buildings Institute, Inc.
PO Box 653
142 East Jewett Boulevard
White Salmon, WA 98672
(509) 493-4468
www.newbuildings.org

NOFMA: The Wood Flooring Manufacturers Association
PO Box 3009
Memphis, TN 38173
(901) 526-5016
www.nofma.org

North American Insulation Manufacturers Association
44 Canal Center Plaza, Suite 310
Alexandria, VA 22314
(703) 684-0084
www.naima.org

Design & Building-Related Organizations

North American Steel Framing Alliance
1201 15th Street NW, Suite 320
Washington, DC 20005
(202) 785-2022
www.steelframingalliance.com

NSSN: A National Resource for Global Standards/American National Standards Institute
25 West 43rd Street
New York, NY 10036
(212) 642-4980
www.nssn.org

Plumbing Manufacturers Institute
1340 Remington Road, Suite A
Schaumburg, IL 60173
(847) 884-9764
www.pmihome.org

Portland Cement Association
5420 Old Orchard Road
Skokie, IL 60077
(847) 966-6200
www.cement.org

Precast/Prestressed Concrete Institute
209 West Jackson Boulevard
Chicago, IL 60606
(312) 786-0300
www.pci.org

Preservation Trades Network, Inc.
PO Box 10236
Rockville, MD 20849
(866) 853-9335
www.ptn.org

Professional Construction Estimators Association of America
PO Box 680336
Charlotte, NC 28216
(704) 987-9978
www.pcea.org

Professional Landcare Network (PLANET)
950 Herndon Parkway, Suite 450
Herndon, VA 20170
(703) 736-9666
www.landcarenetwork.org

Rocky Mountain Institute
1739 Snowmass Creek Road
Snowmass, CO 81654
(970) 927-3851
www.rmi.org

Society of Fire Protection Engineers
7315 Wisconsin Avenue, Suite 620E
Bethesda, MD 20814
(301) 718-2910
www.sfpe.org

Society for Marketing Professional Services
99 Canal Center Plaza, Suite 330
Alexandria, VA 22314
(800) 292-7677
www.smps.org

Tile Council of America, Inc.
100 Clemson Research Boulevard
Anderson, SC 29625
(864) 646-8453
www.tileusa.com

Tree Care Industry Association
3 Perimeter Road, Unit 1
Manchester, NH 03103
(603) 314-5380
www.treecareindustry.org

Underwriters Laboratories Inc.
333 Pfingsten Road
Northbrook, IL 60062
(847) 272-8800
www.ul.com

United Nations Human Settlements Programme
PO Box 30030
Nairobi, Kenya
(254-20) 623120
www.unchs.org

Design & Building-Related Organizations

Vinyl Institute
1300 Wilson Boulevard, Suite 800
Arlington, VA 22209
(703) 741-5670
www.vinylinfo.org

Waterfront Center
1622 Wisconsin Avenue NW
Washington, DC 20007
(202) 337-0356
www.waterfrontcenter.org

Western Red Cedar Lumber Association
1501-700 West Pender Street
Pender Place 1, Business Building
Vancouver BC
Canada V6C 1G8
(604) 684-0266
www.wrcla.org

Window & Door Manufacturers Association
1400 East Touhy Avenue, Suite 470
Des Plaines, IL 60018
(847) 299-5200
www.wdma.org

Government Agencies

Army Corps of Engineers
441 G Street NW
Washington, DC 20314
(202) 761-0011
www.usace.army.mil

Bureau of Land Management
Office of Public Affairs
1849 C Street, Room 406-LS
Washington, DC 20240
(202) 452-5125
www.blm.gov

Census Bureau Manufacturing, Mining, and Construction Statistics
US Census Bureau
Manufacturing and Construction Division
Washington, DC 20233
(301) 763-5160
www.census.gov/const/www

Department of Agriculture
1400 Independence Avenue SW
Washington, DC 20250
(202) 720-2791
www.usda.gov

Department of Energy
Forrestal Building
1000 Independence Avenue SW
Washington, DC 20585
(800) 342-5363
www.energy.gov

Department of Labor
Frances Perkins Building
200 Constitution Avenue NW
Washington, DC 20210
(866) 487-2365
www.dol.gov

Department of the Interior
1849 C Street NW
Washington, DC 20240
(202) 208-3100
www.doi.gov

Department of Transportation
400 7th Street SW
Washington, DC 20590
(202) 366-4000
www.dot.gov

Environmental Protection Agency
Ariel Rios Building
1200 Pennsylvania Avenue NW
Washington, DC 20460
(202) 272-0167
www.epa.gov

Federal Emergency Management Agency
500 C Street SW
Washington, DC 20472
(202) 566-1600
www.fema.gov

Design & Building-Related Organizations

General Services Administration
1800 F Street NW
Washington, DC 20405
(800) 333-4636
www.gsa.gov

National Institute of Standards & Technology
100 Bureau Drive, Stop 1070
Gaithersburg, MD 20899
(301) 975-6478
www.nist.gov

United States Access Board
1331 F Street NW, Suite 1000
Washington, DC 20004
(202) 272-0080
www.access-board.gov

International Organizations

Architects' Council of Europe
Rue Paul Emile Janson, 29
Brussels 1050
Belgium
+32 2 543 11 40
www.ace-cae.org

Architecture Institute of Japan
26-20, Shiba 5-chome, Minato-ku
Tokyo 108-8414
Japan
+81-3-3456-2051
www.aij.or.jp

International Council of Societies of Industrial Design
ICSID Secretariat
455 St-Antoine West, Suite SS10
Montreal, Quebec H2Z 1J1
Canada
(514) 488-4949
www.icsid.org

International Federation of Interior Architects/Designers
(IFI Interim Secretariat)
Suite 209, Namsan Mansion
726-24, Hannam-dong, Yongsan-gu
Seoul 140-21
Korea
+82 2 710 9968
www.ifiworld.org

International Federation of Landscape Architects
4 rue Hardy
Versailles 78009
France
+33 1 39 51 84 39
www.iflaonline.org

International Union of Architects
51, rue Raynouard
Paris 75016
France
33 (1) 45 24 36 88
www.uia-architectes.org

Japan Institute of Architects
Kenchikuka Kaikan
2-3-18, Jingumae
Shibuya-ku, Tokyo 150-0001
Japan
+81-3-3408-7125
www.jia.or.jp

Royal Architectural Institute of Canada
330-55 Murray Street
Ottawa, Ontario K1N 5M3
Canada
(613) 241-3600
www.raic.org

581

Design & Building-Related Organizations

Royal Australian Institute of Architects
2a Mugga Way
Red Hill ACT 2603
Australia
(02) 6273 1548
www.architecture.com.au

Royal Institute of British Architects
66 Portland Place
London W1B 1AD
UK
+44 (0)20 7580 5533
www.riba.org

Source: DesignIntelligence

9

Design
Resources

This chapter contains a variety of concise, informative entries, from the fully updated Salary and Compensation Guide, registration and licensure laws, guidelines for hiring an architect or interior designer, to lists of design-oriented bookstores, journals and magazines, and museums.

Bookstores

The following is a list of US architecture and design bookstores, including rare and out-of-print dealers that specialize in design titles.

ARIZONA
Builder's Book Depot
1001 E. Jefferson, Suite 5
Phoenix, AZ 85034
(800) 284-3434
www.buildersbookdepot.com

CALIFORNIA
Builders Booksource
1817 Fourth Street
Berkeley, CA 94710
(800) 843-2028
www.buildersbooksource.com

J.B. Muns Fine Arts Books
1162 Shattuck Avenue
Berkeley, CA 94707
(510) 525-2420

Moe's Books
2476 Telegraph Avenue
Berkeley, CA 94704
(510) 849-2133
www.moesbooks.com

Builder's Book Inc. Bookstore
8001 Canoga Avenue
Canoga Park, CA 91304
(800) 273-7375
www.buildersbook.com

Builders Booksource
Ghirardelli Square
900 North Point
San Francisco, CA 94109
(415) 440-5773
www.buildersbooksource.com

William Stout Architectural Books
804 Montgomery Street
San Francisco, CA 94133
(415) 391-6757
www.stoutbooks.com

Sullivan Goss, Ltd.
7 E. Anapamu Street
Santa Barbara, CA 93101
(805) 730-1460
www.sullivangoss.com

Hennessey + Ingalls Art + Architecture Books
214 Wilshire Boulevard
Santa Monica, CA 90401
(310) 458-9074
www.hennesseyingalls.com

COLORADO
Tattered Cover Bookstore
Historic LoDo
1628 16th Street
Denver, CO 80202
(303) 436-1070
www.tatteredcover.com

Tattered Cover Bookstore
2955 East First Avenue
Denver, CO 80206
(303) 322-7727
www.tatteredcover.com

DISTRICT OF COLUMBIA
AIA Bookstore
American Institute
of Architects
1735 New York Avenue NW
Washington, DC 20006
(202) 626-7475
www.aia.org/books

Franz Bader Bookstore
1911 I Street NW
Washington, DC 20001
(202) 337-5440

National Building Museum Shop
401 F Street NW
Washington, DC 20001
(202) 272-7706
www.nbm.org/shop

ILLINOIS
Chicago Architecture Foundation Bookstore
224 S. Michigan Avenue
Chicago, IL 60604
(312) 922-3432
www.architecture.org

Prairie Avenue Bookshop
418 S. Wabash Avenue
Chicago, IL 60605
(800) 474-2724
www.pabook.com

INDIANA
Architectural Center Bookstore
Indiana Society of Architects
47 S. Pennsylvania Street,
Suite 110
Indianapolis, IN 46204
(317) 634-3871

MASSACHUSETTS
Ars Libri
500 Harrison Avenue
Boston, MA 02118
(617) 357-5212
www.arslibri.com

Cambridge Architectural Books
12 Bow Street
Cambridge, MA 02138
(617) 354-5300

587

Bookstores

**Charles B. Wood III
Antiquarian Booksellers**
PO Box 2369
Cambridge, MA 02238
(617) 868-1711

F.A. Bernett
144 Lincoln Street
Boston, MA 02111
(617) 350-7778
www.fabernett.com

MARYLAND
Baltimore AIA Bookstore
11 1/2 West Chase Street
Baltimore, MD 21201
(410) 625-2585
www.aiabalt.com

MISSOURI
St. Louis AIA Bookstore
911 Washington Avenue
Suite 100
St. Louis, MO 63101
(314) 621-3484
www.aia-stlouis.org

NEW YORK
Argosy Bookstore
116 E. 59th Street
New York, NY 10022
(212) 753-4455
www.argosybooks.com

**Cooper-Hewitt Museum
Bookstore**
2 East 91st Street
New York, NY 10128
(212) 849-8355
www.ndm.si.edu/shop/

Hacker/Strand Art Books
45 West 57th Street, 5th Floor
New York, NY 10019
(212) 688-7600
www.strandbooks.com

Perimeter Books
21 Cleveland Place
New York, NY 10012
(212) 334-6559

Potterton Books
D & D Building
Lobby Level
979 Third Avenue
New York, NY 10022
(212) 644-2292
www.pottertonbooks.co.uk

Rizzoli Bookstore
31 West 57th Street
New York, NY 10019
(212) 759-2424
www.rizzoliusa.com

Royoung Bookseller
564 Ashford Avenue
Ardsley, NY 10502
(914) 693-6116
www.royoung.com

Strand Book Store
828 Broadway
New York, NY 10003
(212) 473-1452
www.strandbooks.com

Urban Center Books
457 Madison Avenue
New York, NY 10022
(212) 935-3592
www.urbancenterbooks.com

Ursus Books
981 Madison Avenue
New York, NY 10021
(212) 772-8787
www.ursusbooks.com

OHIO
Wexner Center Bookstore
1871 N. High Street
Columbus, OH 43210
(614) 292-1807

OREGON
Powell's City of Books
1005 W. Burnside
Portland, OR 97209
(503) 228-4651
www.powells.com

David Morrison Books
530 NW 12th Street
Portland, OR 97209
(503) 295-6882

PENNSYLVANIA
**AIA Bookstore &
Design Center**
117 South 17th Street
Philadelphia, PA 19103
(215) 569-3188
www.aiaphila.org

TEXAS
Brazos Bookstore
2421 Bissonnet Street
Houston, TX 77005
(713) 523-0701
www.brazosbookstore.com

WASHINGTON
AIA Spokane Bookstore
335 West Sprague Avenue
Spokane, WA 99201
(509) 747-5498
www.aiaspokane.org

**Peter Miller Architecture and
Design Books**
1930 First Avenue
Seattle, WA 98101
(206) 441-4114
www.petermiller.com

Source: DesignIntelligence

How to Hire an Architect

The information provided below was prepared by the American Institute of Architects to assist the public with the architect selection process. The AIA Web site contains a wealth of information about the profession and additional resources to guide you through the process of selecting an architect. This includes a list of 20 suggested questions to ask an architect during the interview process and an online searchable database of architects, all available at *www.aia.org*.

Finding an Architect

Each architect has an individual style, approach to design, and a method of work, so, it's important to find an architect who is compatible with your style and needs.

Ask around. Find out who designed projects in your community that you like. Get recommendations from friends, relatives, and acquaintances who have worked with architects. Check to see if the architect is a member of the American Institute of Architects. Membership in the AIA means that the architect subscribes to a high professional purpose to advance standards of practice and service to society. This includes having a code of ethics and access to a variety of professional and technical resources.

The Architect Finder (*www.aia.org/consumer/ profile/profile_search.asp*), available on the AIA's Web site, can help you find AIA architects interested in your type of project. Call your local AIA chapter for details on firms that interest you, or to see examples of the firms' work. Many AIA chapters have directories containing details of local architecture firms and photos of completed projects.

Call each firm on your short list and describe your project. Ask if they are available to accomplish it, and if so, request literature that outlines the firm's qualifications and experience. If the office is unable to handle your project, ask if they can recommend another firm. Interviewing a firm gives you a chance to meet the people who will design your project and to learn if the chemistry between you is right. Allow at least an hour for the interview, preferably at the architect's office where you can see where the work

will be done. Some architects charge for the interview; ask if there is a fee.

During the interview, ask questions. How busy is the firm? Does it have the capacity to take on your work? Who will handle the job? Insist on meeting the person who will actually design your project. What is the firm's design philosophy? Talk about a project budget and the range of fees that the architect anticipates for your project. Before you select an architect, ask to be taken to at least one completed project. Also, ask for references from past clients. These are invaluable. In addition, obtain an Architect's Qualification Statement (B431) from your local AIA chapter. This standardized document may be used to verify an architect's credentials and other information prior to selecting an architect for a project. The right architect will be the one who can provide the judgment, technical expertise, and creative skills—at a reasonable cost—to help you realize a project that fits your practical needs as well as your dreams.

Why an AIA Architect?

Like doctors and lawyers, architects are licensed professionals. The title "Architect" may be used only by an individual who possesses a state license to practice architecture. They are ethically bound to represent you, the building owner.

Professional qualifications generally include:

- College degree from an accredited school of architecture
- Three years of internship under the supervision of licensed architects
- Passage of a rigorous five-day examination

589

How to Hire an Architect

Only those professionals who have fulfilled these requirements, or other requirements as stipulated by each individual state, may legally call themselves architects and practice architecture in the jurisdiction granting the license.

Look for the AIA initials after the name of any architect you consider for your project. AIA architects remain current with professional standards through continuing education and subscribe to a code of ethics and professional conduct that assure clients, the public and colleagues of their dedication to high standards in professional practice.

The Architect's Fee

There is no set fee arrangement for a particular type of project. Fees are established in a number of ways, depending on the type of project plus the extent and nature of services required from an architect.

Common methods of compensation include: hourly rates, a stipulated sum based on the architect's compensation proposal, a stipulated sum per unit of what's to be built (i.e., the number of square feet or rooms), a percentage of construction costs, or a combination of these methods. Your architect will explain how a fee is to be established. Then, the basis for the fee, the amount, and the payment schedule are issues for you and your architect to work out together.

The 1998 Means Square Footage Cost Data survey indicates that fees for architectural services on a custom house can range from 5 to 15 percent of the total cost of construction. Factors that affect the fees include the scope of the project, the level of quality and detail, and economic conditions. The architect's fee is usually a relatively small part of the cost of the entire building project, including the estimated construction cost (on which the fee is computed), the furnishings and equipment, and the interest paid on the mortgage.

Get It in Writing: AIA Contract Documents

The AIA Contract Documents Program, the oldest and most comprehensive program of its kind in the world, develops standardized contract forms and administrative procedures for the building industry. AIA contract documents provide the basis for nationwide uniformity for contractual relationships in the design and construction process. They represent the state of the law regarding construction industry practices and new legal developments. Most important they assure fairness to all parties—owners, architects, engineers, builders, and contractors—and contribute to successful projects.

Any project will benefit from the use of AIA contract documents. Contact your local AIA chapter, or discuss AIA contract documents with an AIA architect.

Source: © 2003 by the American Institute of Architects. Reprinted with permission of American Institute of Architects, 1735 New York Avenue, Washington, DC 20006.

How to Hire an Interior Designer

The following information has been prepared by the American Society of Interior Designers to assist the public in making an informed choice about hiring and working with an interior designer. More information about the interior design profession is available from ASID on the Web at *www.asid.org*. An online searchable database of interior designers can be found at *www.interiors.org*.

What Is My Role In the Design Process?

Before contacting an interior designer, take some time to think about what you want and what you need. **The first step in this process** is to consider some questions that an interior designer will ask regarding your project:

- For whom is the space being designed?
- What activities will take place there?
- How long do you plan to occupy the space?
- What is your time frame?
- What is your budget?

If you're feeling overwhelmed, don't worry. Your interior designer will lead you through the process. Keep in mind the more information you provide, the more successful your designer will be in meeting your needs and expectations. You may want to reference other visual images (photos, postcards, corporate logos, magazine photographs) or environments that reflect your aesthetic and functional criteria.

The second step is to interview designers. Interview several designers to become familiar with differences in personality, style and business methods. Take this opportunity to acquaint the designer with your project ideas. Ask to see the designer's portfolio and request a list of relevant experience and client references. During an interview, you may want to:

- Inquire about the designer's education, experience, and other credentials.
- Ask about other services the designer can provide.
- Ask what can be done to help you optimize your understanding of the cost of the project.
- Discuss project duration or deadlines.
- Establish parameters for ongoing communication between you and the interior designer.
- Discuss the designer's fee structure.

The third step is to hire the designer. Once you've interviewed several designers, take time to compare their estimates. Don't base your decision on price alone. Keep in mind that differences in each proposal reflect variables such as level of service and quality of merchandise. After the designer is hired, you need to address specific project needs and goals. You will share ideas and the designer will lend insights and observations to your ideas to identify the overall scope of the project. During this process, your design professional will:

- Communicate concepts and help you understand the design process.
- Articulate your ideas, and help you to visualize the finished product.

Are Contracts Important?

Contracts are very important because they allow both you and the designer to define the scope of your project. A contract allows you to specify who will be responsible for what, how long the project will last and what the budget limits will be. It is in your best interest to have a signed contract before any work begins or any money is exchanged.

How Much Is This Going to Cost?

It depends on what you want. There are many variables including the size of the project (one room or whole house?), quality of products selected (custom or prefabricated cabinets?), and the timeframe in which the project needs to be completed (two weeks or two months?). Developing the budget is a partnership between the client and the designer. A professional designer assesses your needs and helps you determine where to spend and where to save, prioritiz-

How to Hire an Interior Designer

ing expenses while creating an interior that is within your budget. Also, remember that not everything has to be completed at once. Your designer can develop a long-range plan, consult with you to establish a list of priorities and determine a time line for accomplishing your project.

How Interior Designers Charge for Their Services

Designers work with a variety of fee structures, and as with other professions, base their fees on variables such as complexity of the project, its geographical location, and the expertise of the designer. Most designers will work in one of the following methods, or combine methods to suit a client's particular needs:

Fixed fee (or flat fee)—The designer identifies a specific sum to cover costs, exclusive of reimbursement for expenses. One total fee applies to the complete range of services, from conceptual development through layouts, specifications and final installation.

Hourly fee—Compensation is based on actual time expended by the designer on a project or specific service.

Percentage fee—Compensation is computed as a percentage of construction/ project costs.

Cost plus—A designer purchases materials, furnishings, and services (e.g., carpentry, drapery workrooms, picture framing, etc.) at cost and sells to the client at the designer's cost plus a specified percentage agreed to with the client.

Retail—The designer sells furnishings, furniture, and all other goods to the client at retail rates to cover the designer's fee and services. This is most applicable to retail establishments offering design services.

Per square foot—The designer charges fees based on the area of the project as might be calculated for large commercial properties.

In addition to the fee structures outlined above, designers may require a retainer before beginning a design project. A retainer is an amount of money paid by the client to the designer and applied to the balance due at the termination of the project. The retainer is customarily paid upon signing the contractual agreement in advance of design services.

Source: ©2003 by the American Society of Interior Designers. Reprinted with permission.

Journals & Magazines

The following is a list of major architecture and design journals and magazines from around the world, ranging from the most popular to the cutting edge. Whether looking for periodicals that take a less-traditional approach or for exposure to the most recent projects and design news, this list is intended to provide an opportunity to explore new ideas and perspectives about design and expand your knowledge about the profession.

US Publications

The Architect's Newspaper
PO Box 937
New York, NY 10013
(212) 966-0630
www.archpaper.com
Published bimonthly.

Architectural Digest
6300 Wilshire Boulevard
Los Angeles, CA 90048
(800) 365-8032
www.archdigest.com
Published monthly by Condé Nast
Publications, Inc.

Architectural Record
Two Penn Plaza
New York, NY 10121
(212) 904-2594
www.architecturalrecord.com
The official magazine of the AIA, published
monthly by the McGraw-Hill Companies.

Architecture
770 Broadway, 4th Floor
New York, NY 10003
(646) 654-5766
www.architecturemag.com
Published monthly by VNU Business
Publications, USA, Inc.

ASID ICON
608 Massachusetts Avenue NE
Washington, DC 20002
(202) 546-3480
www.asid.org
The magazine of the American Society of
Interior Designers, published quarterly.

Contract
770 Broadway, 4th Floor
New York, NY 10003
(646) 654-5447
www.contractmagazine.com
Published monthly by VNU Business
Publications, USA, Inc.

Common Ground
1849 C Street, NW
Washington, DC 20240
(202) 354-2272
http://commonground.cr.nps.gov/
Published quarterly by the National Park Service
for the heritage community.

Communication Arts
110 Constitution Drive
Menlo Park, CA 94025
(650) 326-6040
www.commarts.com/ca
Published eight times per year.

Journals & Magazines

Dwell
99 Osgood Place
San Francisco, CA 94133
(415) 743-9990
www.dwellmag.com
Published eight times per year by
Pixie Communications.

Engineering News Record
Two Penn Plaza, 9th Floor
New York, NY 10121
(212) 512-2000
www.enr.com
Published by McGraw-Hill Companies.

Faith & Form
4742 42nd Avenue SW
Seattle, WA 98116
(206) 938-6202
www.faithnform.com
The journal of the Interfaith Forum on Religion,
Art and Architecture (IFRAA), a professional
interest area of the AIA, published three times
a year.

Fine Homebuilding
Taunton Press
63 S. Main Street
Newtown, CT 06470
(203) 426-8171
www.taunton.com/fh/
Published bimonthly by Taunton Press.

Harvard Design Magazine
48 Quincy Street
Cambridge, MA 02138
(617) 495-7814
www.gsd.harvard.edu/research/publications/hdm/
Published twice a year by the Harvard University
Graduate School of Design.

I.D.
38 East 29th Street, Floor 3
New York, NY 10016
(212) 447-1400
www.idonline.com
Published eight times per year.

Innovation
45195 Business Court
Suite 250
Dulles, VA 20166
(703) 707-6000
www.innovationjournal.org
Quarterly journal of the Industrial Designers
Society of America.

Interior Design
360 Park Avenue South
New York, NY 10010
(646) 746-6400
www.interiordesign.net
Published 15 times a year by Reed Business
Information.

Interiors & Sources
840 US Highway One, Suite 330
North Palm Beach, FL 33408
(561) 627-3393
www.isdesignet.com
Published nine times a year by L.C. Clark
Publishing Co.

Journal of Architectural Education
Association of Collegiate Schools of Architecture
1735 New York Avenue, NW
Washington, DC 20006
(213) 821-3092
www.jaeonline.ws
Published quarterly by MIT Press for the ACSA.

Journal of Interior Design
Interior Design Educators Council, Inc.
7150 Winton Drive, Suite 300
Indianapolis, IN 46268
(317) 328-4437
www.ejid.org
Published biannually by the Interior Design
Educators Council.

Journals & Magazines

Journal of the American Planning Association
122 S. Michigan Avenue
Suite 1600
Chicago, IL 60603
(312) 431-9100
www.planning.org
Published quarterly by the American Planning
Association.

Journal of the Society of Architectural Historians
1365 N. Astor Street
Chicago, IL 60610
(312) 573-1365
www.sah.org
Published quarterly by the Society of
Architectural Historians.

Landscape Architecture
636 Eye Street NW
Washington, DC 20001
(202) 898-2444
www.asla.org
Published monthly by the American Society of
Landscape Architects.

Metropolis
61 W. 23rd Street, 4th Floor
New York, NY 10010
(212) 627-9977
www.metropolismag.com
Published 11 times a year.

Old House Journal
1000 Potomac Street NW
Suite 102
Washington, DC 20007
(202) 399-0744
www.oldhousejournal.com
Published bimonthly.

Perspective
13-500 Merchandise Mart
Chicago, IL 60654
(888) 799-4432
www.iida.org
Published quarterly by the International Interior
Design Association.

Places
Center for Environmental Design Research
University of California, Berkeley
College of Environmental Design
390 Wurster Hall, #1839
Berkeley, CA 94720
(510) 642-2896
www.cedr.berkeley.edu
Published three times a year by the Design
History Foundation.

Preservation
1785 Massachusetts Avenue NW
Washington, DC 20036
(202) 588-6000
www.nationaltrust.org
Published bimonthly by the National Trust
for Historic Preservation.

International Publications

Abitare
Via Ventura, 5
Milano, 20134
Italy
+39 022 1058 1
www.abitare.it
Monthly magazine in Italian and English.

AD (Architectural Design)
1 Oaklands Way
Bognor Regis
West Sussex 22 9 SA
United Kingdom
+44 01243 843 272
Published bi-monthly by Wiley-Academy.

Journals & Magazines

AJ (Architects' Journal)
151 Rosebery Avenue
London, EC1R 4GB
United Kingdom
+44 020 7505 6700
www.ajplus.co.uk
Published by EMAP Construct.

l'Arca
Via Valcava 6
Milano, 20155
Italy
+39 02 325246
www.arcadata.com
Published 11 times a year.

Archis
Stichting Archis
Distelweg 90
1031 HH Amsterdam
Netherlands
31 20 3203926
www.archis.org
Bilingual magazine published six times each year
by Stichting Archis in association with the
Netherlands Architecture Institute.

**Architectural History: The Journal of the Society
of Architectural Historians of Great Britain**
Pixham Mill, Pixham Lane
Dorking, Surrey, RH14 1PQ
United Kingdom
www.sahgb.org.uk
Published annually.

Architectural Review
151 Rosebery Avenue
London, EC1R 4GB
United Kingdom
+44 020 7505 6622
www.arplus.com
Published by EMAP Construct.

Architecture Australia
4 Princes Street
Level 3
Port Melbourne, Victoria 3207
Australia
+61 (03) 9646 4760
www.archaust.com/aa/
Official magazine of the RAIA.

l'Architecture d'Aujourd'hui
6, rue Lhomond
Paris, F-75005
France
+33 1 44320590
www.architecture-aujourdhui.presse.fr
Published six times a year in French and English.

Arkitektur
Box 4296
SE 66 Stockholm
Sweden
+46 8 702 7850
www.arkitektur.se
Published eight times yearly; with English
summaries.

a+u magazine
2-31-2 Yushima, Bunkyo-ku
Tokyo, 113-0034
Japan
+81 33816-2935
www.japan-architect.co.jp
Published monthly in Japanese and English
by A+U Publishing Co., Ltd.

Blueprint
Roseberry House
41 Springfield Road
Chelmsford Essex CM2 6JJ
United Kingdom
+44 01245 4917 17
www.blueprintmagazine.co.uk
Published monthly by ETP Ltd.

Journals & Magazines

Canadian Architect
12 Concord Place, Suite 800
Toronto, ON, M3C 4J2
Canada
(416) 510-6854
www.canadianarchitect.com
Published monthly by Business Information
Group, a division of Hollinger Canadian
Newspapers, LP

Casabella
D. Trentacoste 7
Milan, 20134
Italy
+39 02 66 21 56 31
Published monthly in Italian with an English
summary.

El Croquis
Avda de los Reyes Catolicos 9
Madrid, 28280 El Escorial
Spain
+34 91 8969410
www.elcroquis.es
Published five times a year in Spanish and
English.

Domus
Via Achille Grandi 5/7
Rozzano
Milan, 20089
Italy
+39 0282472276
www.domusweb.it
Published monthly in Italian and English.

Hinge
2/F West, Sincere Insurance Building
6 Hennessy Road
Wanchai
Hong Kong, China
+852 2520 2468
www.hingenet.com
Published monthly.

Japan Architect
2-31-2 Yushima, Bunkyo-ku
Tokyo, 113-0034
Japan
+81 3 3816-2532
www.japan-architect.co.jp
Published quarterly in Japanese and English.

Journal of Architecture
4 Park Square
Milton Park
Abingdon
Oxfordshire OX14 4RN
United Kingdom
+44 20 7017 6000
www.tandf.co.uk/journals/routledge/
Published four times a year by Taylor & Francis
Journals for the RIBA.

Journal of Urban Design
Institute of Urban Planning
University of Nottingham
University Park
Nottingham, NG7 2RD
United Kingdom
+44 115 951 4873
Published three times a year by Carfax
Publishing Limited for the Institute of Urban
Planning.

Ottagono
Via Stalingrado, 97/2
Bologna, 40128
Italy
+39 051 3540 111
www.ottagono.com
Published bimonthly in Italian and English.

Wallpaper
Brettenham House
Lancaster Place
London, WC2E 7TL
United Kingdom
+44 20 7322 1177
www.wallpaper.com
Published 10 times a year.

Source: DesignIntelligence

Museums

There are many museums around the world devoted solely to architecture and design, and many major museums that maintain strong design collections and regularly host architecture and design related exhibits. Below is a listing of those museums, along with their contact information.

US Museums

A+D Architecture and Design Museum
8560 W. Sunset Boulevard
Ground Floor
West Hollywood, CA 90069
(310) 659-2445
www.aplusd.org

Art Institute of Chicago
111 South Michigan Avenue
Chicago, IL 60603
(312) 443-3949
www.artic.edu/aic/

Athenaeum of Philadelphia
219 South Sixth Street
Philadelphia, PA 19106
(215) 925-2688
www.PhilaAthenaeum.org

Center for Architecture
536 LaGuardia Place
New York, NY 10012
(212) 683-0023
www.aiany.org/centerforarchitecture/

Chicago Architecture Foundation
224 South Michigan Avenue
Chicago, IL 60604
(312) 922-3432
www.architecture.org

Cooper-Hewitt, National Design Museum, Smithsonian Institution
2 East 91st Street
New York, NY 10128
(212) 849-8400
www.ndm.si.edu

Heinz Architectural Center, Carnegie Museum of Art
4400 Forbes Avenue
Pittsburgh, PA 15213
(412) 622-3131
www.cmoa.org

MAK Center for Art & Architecture LA
Schindler House
835 North Kings Road
West Hollywood, CA 90069
(323) 651-1510
www.makcenter.org

Museum of Arts & Design
40 West 53rd Street
New York, NY 10019
(212) 956-3535
www.madmuseum.org

Museum of Contemporary Art, Los Angeles
MOCA at California Plaza
250 South Grand Avenue
Los Angeles, CA 90012
(213) 626-6222
www.moca-la.org

Museum of Design
Marquis II Office Tower
285 Peachtree Center Avenue
Atlanta, GA 30303-1229
(404) 688-2467
www.museumofdesign.org

Museums

Museum of Modern Art
11 West 53rd Street
New York, NY 10019
(212) 708-9400
www.moma.org

National Building Museum
401 F Street NW
Washington, DC 20001
(202) 272-2448
www.nbm.org

The Octagon
1799 New York Avenue, NW
Washington, DC 20006
(202) 638-3221
www.theoctagon.org

San Francisco Museum of Craft + Design
555 Sutter Street
San Francisco, CA 94102
(415) 773-0303
www.sfmcd.org

San Francisco Museum of Modern Art
151 Third Street
San Francisco, CA 94103
(415) 357-4000
www.sfmoma.org

Skyscraper Museum
39 Battery Place
New York, NY 10280
(212) 968-1961
www.skyscraper.org

Van Alen Institute
30 West 22 Street
New York, NY 10010
(212) 924-7000
www.vanalen.org

Virginia Center for Architecture
2501 Monument Avenue
Richmond, VA 23220
(804) 644-3041
www.virginiaarchitecture.org

International Museums

Alvar Aalto Museum
(Alvar Aalto Museo)
Alver Aallon katu 7
Jyväskylä, Finland
+358 14 624 809
www.alvaraalto.fi

Architectural Museum, Basel
(Architekturmuseum Basel)
Steinenberg 7
Postfach 911
CH-4001 Basel
Switzerland
+41 61 261 1413
www.architekturmuseum.ch

Architecture Center of Vienna
(Architekturzentrum Wien)
Museumsplatz 1, im MQ
A-1070 Vienna
Austria
+43 522 3115
www.azw.at

Bauhaus Archive/Museum of Design
(Bauhaus-Archiv/Museum für Gestaltung)
Klingelhöferstraße 14
10785 Berlin
Germany
+49 30 254 00 20
www.bauhaus.de

Museums

Canadian Centre for Architecture
1920 Baile Street
Montreal, Quebec
Canada H3H 2S6
(514) 939-7026
www.cca.qc.ca

Danish Architecture Center
(Dansk Arkitektur Center)
Strandgade 27B
1401 Copenhagen K
Denmark
+45 32 57 19 30
www.dac.dk

Danish Design Center
(Dansk Design Center)
H C Andersens Boulevard 27
1553 Copenhagen V
Denmark
+45 33 69 33 69
www.ddc.dk

Design Museum, Finland
(Designmuseo)
Korkeavuorenkatu 23
00130 Helsinki
Finland
+35 89 622 0540
www.designmuseum.fi

Design Museum, London
28 Shad Thames
London SE1 2YD
United Kingdom
+44 87 0833 9955
www.designmuseum.org

Design Museum at the Cultural Center of Belém
(Museu do Design, Centro Cultural de Belém)
Praça do Império
1499-003 Lisbon
Portugal
+351 213 612 400
www.ccb.pt

German Centre for Architecture
(Deutsches Architektur Zentrum)
Direktorin Kristien Ring
Köpenicker Straße 48/49 Aufgang A
10179 Berlin
Germany
+49 30 278799-28
www.daz.de

German Architecture Museum
(Deutsches Architektur Museum)
Schaumainkai 43
60596 Frankfurt am Main
Germany
+49 69-212 38844
www.dam-online.de

The Lighthouse: Scotland's Centre for Architecture, Design & the City
11 Mitchell Lane
Glasgow, G1 3NU
United Kingdom
+44 141 221 6362
www.thelighthouse.co.uk

Museum of Finnish Architecture
(Suomen Rakennustaiteen Museo)
Kasarmikatu 24, 00130
Helsinki, Finland
+358 9 8567 5100
www.mfa.fi

Netherlands Architecture Institute
(Nederlands Architectuurinstituut)
Mueumpark 25
3015 CB Rotterdam
Netherlands
+3110-4401200
www.nai.nl

National Museum of Art, Architecture and Design
(Nasjonalmuseet for Kunst, Arkitektur og Design)
Kristian Augusts gate 23
Oslo, Norway
+47 21 98 20 00
www.nationalmuseum.no

Museums

RIBA Architecture Gallery
66 Portland Square
London W1B 1AD
United Kingdom
+44 20 7580 5533
www.architecture.com

Röhsska Museum of Design and Applied Art
(Röhsska Museet för Konsthantverk och Design)
Vasagatan 37-39
SE-400 15 Göteborg
Sweden
+46 31-61 38 50
www.designmuseum.se

Swedish Museum of Architecture
(Arkitekturmuseet)
Skeppsholmen
SE-111 49 Stockholm
Sweden
+46 8 587 270 00
www.arkitekturmuseet.se

Victoria and Albert Museum
Cromwell Road
London SW7 2RL
United Kingdom
+44 20 7942 2000
www.vam.ac.uk

Vitra Design Museum
Charles-Eames-Str. 1
D-79576 Weil am Rhein
Germany
+49 7621 702 32 00
www.design-museum.de

Zurich Museum of Design
(Museum für Gestaltung Zürich)
Ausstellungsstrasse 60
CH-8005 Zürich
Switzerland
+41 43 446 67 67
www.museum-gestaltung.ch

Source: DesignIntelligence

Public Architecture

Public Architecture is a nonprofit organization that puts the resources of architecture in the service of the public interest. It identifies and solves practical problems of human interaction in the built environment and acts as a catalyst for public discourse through education, advocacy, and the design of public spaces and amenities. Rather than wait for commissions, Public Architecture encourages all architecture professionals to proactively identify significant problems of broad relevance that require innovative research and design. The goal is to address needs and desires that are palpable, if poorly defined, in circumstances where both clients and financing must be imagined, sought, and secured in new ways. Public Architecture's national "1% Solution" program, through which design professionals pledge a portion of their time to the common good, aims to mainstream public interest and *pro bono* practice.

Address

1126 Folsom Street, No. 3
San Francisco, CA 94103
(415) 861-8200
www.publicarchitecture.org

Registration Laws: Architecture

The following information provides a brief overview of the major components of initial licensure requirements for architects, including work experience, degree requirements, and the Architectural Registration Exam. Complete information regarding registration requirements, renewal procedures, interstate registration, and corporate practice guidelines is available from the individual state boards at the phone numbers listed below. Due to the complex and changing nature of the requirements, it is recommended that the state licensing board(s) be contacted to receive the most up-to-date information. The National Council of Architectural Registration Boards (NCARB) also maintains information about registration on its Web site at *www.ncarb.org*.

States and State Boards		Type of Law		Initial Requirements			Ongoing Requirements
		Title Act	Practice Act	College Degree Required	Internship Required	ARE Exam Required	Continuing Education Required
Alabama	(334) 242-4179	O	O	O	O	O	O
Alaska	(907) 465-1676	O	O	O	O	O	
Arizona	(602) 364-4937	O	O		CB	O	
Arkansas	(501) 682-3171	O	O	O	O	O	O
California	(916) 445-3394	O	O		O	O	
Colorado	(303) 894-7784	O	O		CB	O	
Connecticut	(860) 713-6145	O	O	O	O	O	
Delaware	(302) 744-4505	O	O	O	O	O	O
District of Columbia	(202) 442-4461	O	O	O	O	O	
Florida	(850) 487-1395	O	O	O	O	O	O
Georgia	(478) 207-1401	O	O		O	O	O
Hawaii	(808) 586-2702	O	O		O	O	
Idaho	(208) 334-3233	O	O		O	O	O
Illinois	(217) 524-3211	O	O	O	O	O	O
Indiana	(317) 234-3048	O	O	O	O	O	O
Iowa	(515) 281-7362	O	O	O	O	O	O
Kansas	(785) 296-3053	O	O	O	O	O	O
Kentucky	(859) 246-2069	O	O	O	O	O	O
Louisiana	(225) 925-4802	O	O	O	O	O	O
Maine	(207) 624-8520	O	O		O	O	

603

Registration Laws: Architecture

States and State Boards		Type of Law		Initial Requirements			Ongoing Requirements
		Title Act	Practice Act	College Degree Required	Internship Required	ARE Exam Required	Continuing Education Required
Maryland	(410) 230-6262	O	O		CB	O	O
Massachusetts	(617) 727-3072	O	O	O	O	O	O
Michigan	(517) 241-9253	O	O	O	O	O	
Minnesota	(651) 296-2388	O	O	O	O	O	O
Mississippi	(601) 899-9071	O	O	O	O	O	
Missouri	(573) 751-0047	O	O	O	O	O	
Montana	(406) 841-2367	O	O	O	O	O	
Nebraska	(402) 471-2021	O	O	O	O	O	O
Nevada	(702) 486-7300	O	O	O	O	O	
New Hampshire	(603) 271-2219	O	O		O	O	
New Jersey	(973) 504-6385	O	O	O	O	O	O
New Mexico	(505) 476-1103	O	O	O	O	O	O
New York	(518) 474-3817	O	O		O	O	O
North Carolina	(919) 733-9544	O	O	O	O	O	O
North Dakota	(701) 223-3540	O	O	O	O	O	
Ohio	(614) 466-2316	O	O	O	O	O	
Oklahoma	(405) 949-2383	O	O	O	O	O	O
Oregon	(503) 763-0662	O	O	O	O	O	O
Pennsylvania	(717) 783-3397	O	O	O	O	O	
Rhode Island	(401) 222-2565	O	O	O	O	O	O
South Carolina	(803) 896-4412	O	O	O	O	O	O
South Dakota	(605) 394-2510	O	O	O	O	O	
Tennessee	(615) 741-3221	O	O	O	O	O	O
Texas	(512) 305-8535	O	O	O	O	O	O
Utah	(801) 530-6720	O	O	O	O	O	
Vermont	(802) 828-2373	O	O		O	O	O
Virginia	(804) 367-8512	O	O	O	O	O	
Washington	(360) 664-1388	O	O		O	O	
West Virginia	(304) 528-5825	O	O	O	O	O	O
Wisconsin	(608) 261-4486	O	O		O	O	
Wyoming	(307) 777-7788	O	O	O	O	O	O

CB: Contact Board

Source: National Council of Architectural Registration Boards

Registration Laws: Interior Design

The following information provides a brief overview of the major components of initial registration requirements for interior designers, including work experience, degree requirements, and the National Council for Interior Design Qualification exam. More specific details about these requirements are available from the individual state boards reachable at the phone numbers listed below. Due to the complex and changing nature of registration laws, it is recommended that the state licensing board(s) be contacted for the most up-to-date information. The American Society of Interior Designers also maintains information about registration on their Web site at *www.asid.org*. Note that not all states regulate the interior design profession.

States and State Boards		Type of Law		Initial Requirements			Ongoing Requirements
		Title Act	Practice Act	College Degree Required	Internship Required	NCIDQ Exam Required	Continuing Education Required
Alabama	(205) 879-6785	O	O	O	O	O	O
Arkansas	(870) 226-6875	O		O	O	O	O
California	(760) 761-4734	*			O	O	O
Colorado	(303) 894-7784	†		‡	O	O	
Connecticut	(860) 713-6135	O		O	O	O	
District of Columbia	(202) 442-4461	O	O	‡	O	O	O
Florida	(850) 487-1395	O	O	‡	O	O	O
Georgia	(478) 207-1400	O		O		O	O
Illinois	(217) 785-0813	O		‡	O	O	
Iowa	(515) 281-7362	O		‡	O	O	O
Kentucky	(859) 246-2069	O		O	O	O	O
Louisiana	(225) 298-1283	O	O	‡	O	O	O
Maine	(207) 624-8603	O		O	O	O	
Maryland	(410) 230-6322	O		O	O	O	O
Minnesota	(651) 296-2388	O		CB	O	O	O
Missouri	(573) 522-4683	O		‡	O	O	O
Nevada	(702) 486-7300	O	O	‡	O	O	
New Jersey	(973) 504-6385	O		‡	O	O	O
New Mexico	(505) 476-4865	O		‡	O	O	O
New York	(518) 474-3846	O		‡	O	O	

605

Registration Laws: Interior Design

States and State Boards		Type of Law		Initial Requirements			Ongoing Requirements
		Title Act	Practice Act	College Degree Required	Internship Required	NCIDQ Exam Required	Continuing Education Required
Tennessee	(615) 741-3221	O		‡	O	O	O
Texas	(512) 305-8539	O		‡	O	O	O
Virginia	(804) 367-8512	O		O	O	O	
Wisconsin	(608) 266-5439	O		‡	O	O	O

* Self-certification act

† Permitting statute

‡ Two years post-high school education required

Source: American Society of Interior Designers

Registration Laws: Landscape Architecture

The following matrix provides a brief overview of the major components of initial licensure for landscape architects. Complete information is available from the individual state boards at the phone numbers listed below. Due to the complex and changing nature of the regulations, it is recommended that the state licensing board(s) be contacted for the latest information. The Council of Landscape Architectural Registration Boards and the American Society of Landscape Architects also maintain information about licensure on their Web sites at *www.clarb.org* and *www.asla.org*, respectively. Note that not all states regulate the landscape architecture profession.

States and State Boards		Type of Law		Initial Requirements				Ongoing Requirements
		Title Act	Practice Act	Non-LAAB Accredited Degree Accepted	Non-LA Degree with Exp. Accepted	Experience Only Accepted	LARE Exam Required	Continuing Education Required
Alabama	(334) 262-1351		O	O	O	O	O	O
Alaska	(907) 465-1681		O	O	CB	O	O	
Arizona	(602) 364-4930		O	O	O	O	O	
Arkansas	(501) 682-3112		O	O	O	O	O	O
California	(916) 445-4954		O	O			O	
Connecticut	(860) 713-6145		O			O	O	O
Delaware	(302) 744-4530		O				O	O
Florida	(850) 487-1395		O			O	O	O
Georgia	(478) 207-1400		O				O	O
Hawaii	(808) 586-2702		O	O	O	O	O	
Idaho	(208) 334-3233		O			O	O	
Illinois	(217) 782-8556	O					O	
Indiana	(317) 232-2980		O				O	O
Iowa	(515) 281-7393		O	O	O	O	O	O
Kansas	(785) 296-3053		O				O	O
Kentucky	(859) 246-2753		O				O	O
Louisiana	(225) 952-8100		O		O	O	O	
Maine	(207) 624-8522	O		CB	CB	CB	O	
Maryland	(410) 230-6322		O			O	O	
Massachusetts	(617) 727-3074	O				O	O	O
Michigan	(517) 241-9201	O				O	O	

Registration Laws: Landscape Architecture

States and State Boards	Type of Law		Initial Requirements				Ongoing Requirements
	Title Act	Practice Act	Non-LAAB Accredited Degree Accepted	Non-LA Degree with Exp. Accepted	Experience Only Accepted	LARE Exam Required	Continuing Education Required
Minnesota (651) 296-2388		○	○	○	○	○	○
Mississippi (601) 899-9071		○	○	○	○	○	○
Missouri (573) 751-0047		○				○	
Montana (406) 841-2329		○				○	
Nebraska (402) 471-2407		○			○	○	○
Nevada (775) 688-1316		○	○	○	○	○	
New Jersey (973) 504-6385	○		CB			○	○
New Mexico (505) 476-7078		○	○	○		○	○
New York (518) 474-3817		○	○	○		○	
North Carolina (919) 850-9088		○	○	○		○	○
North Dakota (701) 223-3540		○	○	○	○	○	
Ohio (614) 466-2316		○				○	
Oklahoma (405) 949-2383		○				○	○
Oregon (503) 589-0093		○	○	○	○	○	○
Pennsylvania (717) 772-8528		○			○	○	○
Rhode Island (401) 222-2565		○	CB	CB	○	○	
South Carolina (803) 734-9131		○			○	○	
South Dakota (605) 394-2510		○				○	○
Tennessee (615) 741-3221		○				○	○
Texas (512) 305-9000		○				○	○
Utah (801) 530-6628		○			○	○	
Virginia (804) 367-8514	○		○	○	○	○	
Washington (360) 664-1388	○		○	○	○	○	
West Virginia (304) 727-5501	○					○	○
Wisconsin (608) 266-5511	○		CB			○	
Wyoming (307) 777-7788		○			○	○	○

CB: Contact board
LAAB: Landscape Architecture Accrediting Board

Source: Council of Landscape Architectural Registration Boards and American Society of Landscape Architects

Salary and Compensation Guide

Each year as part of its ongoing research agenda, *DesignIntelligence*, the monthly journal of the Design Futures Council, tracks the hiring of design professionals and reviews compensation packages This study includes information about what architects earn, managing the future of compensation and benefits, and insight into whether you are getting paid what you're worth. Below is an executive brief from the 2005 study about salary compensation for a select category of positions for different firm profiles. Please use caution in drawing conclusions from this summary as there can be significant variations depending upon geographic location and micro-economic fluctuations within certain professions and building types.

Salary ranges for additional firm types and a variety compensation-related information can be found in the annual *Compensation Survey of Architecture and Design Firms* available from *www.di.net.*

Composite Midsize Professional Practice–Regional Focus

Intern Architect
$39,500–$50,500

Technical Staff–Grades 10–15 (A)
$35,600–$61,000

Technical Staff–Grades 15–30 (AA)
$42,750–71,200

Technical Staff–Grades 30–50 (AAA)
$58,000–135,000

Administrative
$28,000–140,000

Technology
$34,000–95,000

Marketing
$36,000–88,000

Associate Principal
$56,000–102,500

Principal
$80,000–155,000

Partner
$140,000–220,000

Partner (C Level, Managing Partner)
$150,000–350,00

Salary and Compensation Guide

Composite Large Professional Practice–Multiple Offices, National Focus

Intern Architect
$35,000–50,000

Interior Designer
$48,000–92,000
Landscape Architect
$48,000–102,000

Project Manager
$70,000–110,000

Administrative
$32,000–55,000

Technology
$60,000–70,000

Marketing
$47,000–85,000

Associate Principal
$85,000–110,000 (pre-incentive, pre bonus)

Principal/Partner
$140,000–175,000 (pre-incentive, pre bonus)

CEO
$225,000 (pre-incentive, pre bonus)

Note: In the United States, the increases in base salaries from 2004 to 2005 were moderate (typically 2.5 to 3.5 percent). However, many best-of-class firms offer significantly higher incentive compensation, ranging from relatively small amounts to several times base salary for equity partners. Most all practices now include retirement plans such as 401(k) plans and SEP IRAs. Typical retirement-plan contributions range from 3 to 6 percent of base salary, and profit sharing is now included in all best practices. All firms include health and life insurance.

Source: DesignIntelligence

10

Obituaries

This chapter is in memory of the design and preservation leaders and patrons who died between Sept. 1, 2004, and July 31, 2005.

Robert Abele, 83

A leading designer of shopping malls, Robert Abele, died Nov. 19, 2004. A partner in one of the largest Miami architectural firms during the 1960s, Robert Weed and Associates (which later evolved into Herbert H. Johnson and Associates and then finally Abele and Forfar), Abele designed numerous malls throughout the country, including the 1.5-million-square-foot Burlington Mall in Boston and the Seneca Mall in Buffalo, NY. Abele also designed many malls in southern Florida, including the Bal Harbour Shoppes, and the Hollywood and West Palm Beach malls. Born in Memphis, TN, Abele moved to Miami Beach as a child, and following World War II completed his bachelor's degree at the University of Florida. Abele also designed US consulate buildings in the Congo and Nigeria, the Unger Computer Center and Calder Medical Library at the University of Miami, and more than 100 local banks, office buildings, churches, and educational buildings. In the 1980s, his firm oversaw the planning and design of the new construction at the Miami International Airport.

Max Abramovitz, 96

A significant contributor to postwar modernist architecture and the deputy director of planning for the United Nations complex, Max Abramovitz, died Sept. 12, 2004. Abramovitz was born in Chicago, earned his BA in architectural engineering in 1929 from the University of Illinois at Urbana–Champaign, then received a prestigious fellowship to spend two years studying architecture at the Ecole des Beaux-Arts in Paris. Subsequently settling in New York City, he became acquainted with Wallace K. Harrison. Joining Harrison's firm as an associate in 1935, Abramovitz quickly became a partner and collaborated with Harrison on a number of well-known Manhattan buildings, including ones for Time & Life, McGraw-Hill, and Exxon; the Celanese on the Avenue of the Americas; and the controversial Avery Fisher Hall at Lincoln Center. In addition to designing US embassies in Havana and Rio de Janeiro and more than 100 other buildings, Abramovitz served as the master planner for Brandeis University. A self-admitted workaholic (He once commented, "I'm just a working fool."), Abramovitz collected art and sculpture as his main hobby.

Frederick H. Bair Jr., 89

Planning pioneer and accomplished author Frederick H. Bair Jr., died Feb. 14, 2005. "Few planners have influenced the practice of planning to the degree that Fred Bair has," said fellow planner Dennis Andrew Gordon. "His pioneering work helped to define the relational, progressive, humane side of planning that so many members of our profession aspire to implement." Bair enjoyed a varied career in government and private practice in his firm Bair, Abernathy and Associates, founded in 1953, and served as executive secretary of the Florida Planning and Zoning Association and editor of the *Florida Planning and Development* magazine, which he edited for 17 years. His three editions of *The Text of a Model Zoning Ordinance* guided several decades of planners. For 30 years, Bair worked as a reporter and editorial board member for *Zoning Digest*, where his commentaries helped advance sound zoning practices before a national audience. One of his important zoning innovations was the refinement of the land-use intensity system. Bair cited his work with two New Deal agencies (after graduating from the University of Chicago in 1935 with a sociology degree), the Works Progress Administration and the Soil Conservation Service, as providing him with valuable road experience for his later career.

Edward Larrabee Barnes, 89

Edward Larrabee Barnes, a diehard modernist who remained true to the cause of simplicity and functionalism in architecture, died Sept. 21, 2004. Trained at Harvard University in the 1940s under Walter Gropius, Barnes was part of the second generation of American modernists that included Philip Johnson, I.M. Pei, Paul Rudolph, and John Carl Warnecke. One of his most beloved works was his 1961 Haystack Mountain School of Crafts in Deer Isle, ME, an assemblage of shingled cottages linked by a grid of wooden decks leading to a spectacular ocean view. Winning the Twenty-five Year Award from the American Institute of Architects in 1994, the jury cited it as an "early and profound example of the fruitful and liberating fusion of the vernacular building tradition with the rationality and discipline of Modern architecture." Speaking of Haystack in 1989, Barnes told *Architecture* magazine: "I've always been drawn to making things as simple as possible, if you can do that without making them inhuman or dull or oppressive." Barnes admitted that his style was influenced by a visit in the late 1950s to Mykonos Island in Greece, whose style also inspired Le Corbusier's volumetric, three-dimensional forms. These pure forms were so characteristic of Barnes' style that the *International Dictionary of Architects and Architecture* wrote in 1993, "Barnes' office towers are the embodiment of the late Modern development of the thin-skinned office tower as a taut technological membrane." Throughout the 45-year lifespan of his Manhattan firm, nearly 500 architects, many of them prominent, worked for Barnes. "Like his Harvard mentor Walter Gropius, Barnes may be remembered by future generations as much for the architects he helped train as for the buildings he created," wrote Lester Korzilius, one of those architects, in a glowing review in *Oculus* magazine of Barnes' book, *Edward Larrabee Barnes: Architect*, which he published in 1994 at the time of his retirement.

James Biddle, 75

James Biddle, former president of the National Trust for Historic Preservation and a member of Philadelphia's "first family," died March 10, 2005. Biddle's family included William Biddle, a 17th-century acquaintance of William Penn; Nicholas Biddle, founder of the Second Bank of the United States; Francis Biddle, Franklin Roosevelt's attorney general; and painter George Biddle. Andalusia, the family's sprawling estate and mansion in Bensalem, PA, is one of the finest examples of Greek Revival domestic architecture in the United States. It was begun in 1797 and expanded in 1806 and 1835 by two of America's most acclaimed architects: Benjamin H. Latrobe and Thomas U. Walter. James Biddle was a 1951 graduate of Princeton where he studied art and archaeology and joined the staff of New York's Metropolitan Museum of Art in 1955. There he was the curator of the American Wing prior to serving as president of the National Trust of Historic Preservation from 1968 to 1980. Under his leadership, the Trust grew from 5,000 to 150,000 members and many of the organization's significant initiatives were implemented, including the Main Street program, the Preservation Honor Awards, and National Preservation Week. Biddle also devoted himself to the preservation of Andalusia, which he inherited from his father. He hosted public concerts on the grounds, and eventually moved into "The Cottage," an eight-bedroom mansion on the estate grounds, in order to open the "Big House" to the public in 1975. Biddle left the estate in the hands of the Andalusia Foundation to be preserved and maintained. He also served on Jacqueline Kennedy's Fine Arts Committee, was a past chair of the National Preservation Institute, a non-profit educational consulting firm, and chaired the historical portion of the nation's 1976 Bicentennial celebration.

Bruce A. Bolt, 75

Seismologist and building safety advocate Bruce A. Bolt died July 21, 2005. A native of Australia, Bolt spent his career working to more accurately predict how different areas would react to strong earthquakes. As a researcher, he used synchronized seismographs to measure movement along fault lines as well as records of seismic wave activity and geological patterns in able to better understand why some areas fare better than others after heavy shaking. A lecturer, author, public policy advocate, and educator at University of California, Berkeley, Bolt felt that trying to predict when a big quake might strike was futile, and he instead worked toward preparedness. In 1963 Bolt arrived in United States to head what is now known as the Berkeley Seismological Laboratory after teaching math at the University of Sydney from 1954 to 1962. He had received his bachelor's, master's, and PhD at that institution. Bolt's work led to stronger building codes, and as a former chair of the California Seismic Safety Commission, he worked to disseminate information that would keep safety on the minds of the public and policy makers. He advocated for legislation requiring earthquake reinforcement for schools, hospitals, mobile homes, and unreinforced masonry buildings. Both the Southern California and Bay Area Earthquake Preparedness Projects and the California Earthquake Education Project developed as a result of legislation Bolt helped initiate. A former trustee and board president of the Academy of Sciences in San Francisco's Golden Gate Park, Bolt helped design an exhibit on earthquake preparedness that was installed there. As a consultant, Bolt contributed to the construction of Egypt's Aswan High Dam, the Trans-Alaska Pipeline, and many California projects, including the Pacific Gas & Electric's Diablo Canyon nuclear power plant. He stepped down as head of the Berkeley Seismological Laboratory in 1993 but continued to consult and lecture.

Alexander C. Bonutti, 53

Alexander C. Bonutti, a community-building San Francisco Bay Area architect, died Feb. 5, 2005. As executive vice president of Anshen + Allen Architects, Bonutti melded his knowledge of architecture with his sensitivity toward people's needs to develop a model for mental health facility design based on the residents' daily cycles of live/work activities. Bonutti also pioneered a model for long-term care-unit design that organized groups of family/neighborhood clusters. After receiving his master's degree in architecture and urban design from Columbia University in 1978 and his bachelor's degree in architecture from the Illinois Institute of Technology in 1974, Bonutti held leadership positions at HOK and KMD, in addition to managing his own firm. While serving as 1990 president of AIA San Francisco, Bonutti was influential in the initiative to remove the Embarcadero Freeway following the Loma Prieta earthquake. While chairing the Urban Design Committee, Bonutti was involved in revising zoning in the South of Market and the Embarcadero Corridor Study (which received a national AIA Urban Design Award). Bonutti's leadership also helped create the Architectural Foundation of San Francisco, whose valuable mission is to introduce primary and secondary school students to architecture.

Charles I. Bryant, 76

Washington, DC, architect Charles I. Bryant, died June 7, 2005. He was the surviving principal of the firm Bryant & Bryant (now Bryant Bryant Williams), which earned more than 1,000 commissions under his leadership and was one of the oldest African-

American owned firms in the United States. He formed the firm in 1969 with his younger brother Robert; both men were graduates of the architecture program at Howard University. With projects ranging from office buildings and shopping centers to industrial plants, schools, and hospitals, the firm had been the architect of record to the University of the District of Columbia for more than 20 years. They designed the Potomac Mills Mall in Woodbridge, VA, and in DC the Stadium Armory Metro Station, Howard University's Cancer Research Center, and the award-winning Washington Design Center. The firm handled master-planning projects in Guyana, South Africa and served as architects and planners on the Fort Lincoln New Town project in northeast DC. The US Commission of Fine Arts cited the firm's design for Dunbar Senior High School in DC for its innovative design. A graduate of Armstrong Technical High School in DC, Bryant received his degree from Howard University in 1954 and served in the Air Force before returning to the city. He worked for the Veterans Administration and the General Services Administration until leaving to practice on his own in 1965. A teacher and lecturer in the architecture schools at Howard University, Morgan State University, and the University of DC, he is remembered as a mentor to scores of young architects, many of whom now head their own firms. He was a past president of DC's Architects Registration Board and served on the boards of many civic organizations including the DC Private Industry Council. In 1976, when the firm employed 50 people, it was cited in *Black Enterprise Magazine* as the largest African American-owed firm in the United States and one of the top-revenue generators among all black-owned businesses in the country. Bryant's son Charles Bryant II, also an architect, will continue to run the firm.

Richard G. Buckley, 51

Richard G. Buckley, managing partner and partner-in-charge of design at NBBJ in Seattle, died Jan. 1, 2005. With overall responsibility for design quality, he contributed to a multitude of the firm's projects, many honored with awards from the American Institute of Architects. Buckley received the Arthur Spayd Brook Memorial Gold Medal in Design from the University of Pennsylvania where he received a master's degree in architecture. Following graduation in 1982, he joined the staff of Venturi, Rauch and Scott Brown in Philadelphia. He earned his undergraduate degree from the University of Washington and returned to the state in 1984 to take a position with NBBJ. He was a guest lecturer, at the University of Washington, Cornell University, Columbia University, and the University of Pennsylvania. He also served as a judge for the 1998 International Architectural Forum at the University of Kyung Pook in South Korea.

Willard C. Byrd, 85

Willard C. Byrd, a fellow of the American Society of Landscape Architects and the American Society of Golf Course Architects died Dec. 18, 2004. Born in 1919 in North Carolina, Byrd served aboard a minesweeper in World War II before earning a degree in landscape architecture (with an emphasis on land planning) from North Carolina State University in 1948. After working for seven years as a city planner for the Federal Housing Administration in the early 1950s, during the heyday of suburban growth, Byrd founded his Atlanta-based firm, Willard C. Byrd & Associates, in 1956 and within a few years began designing residential golf course developments. Although Byrd is cited as the architect of record for the award-winning courses of the Country Club of North Carolina in Pinehurst and the Atlanta Country Club, the names of more famous designers, (acting more as minor consultants than overall designers) such as Ellis Maples and Joe Finger, are generally credited with those respective designs. Byrd was often mistakenly viewed as a neophyte and not given the proper recognition. Byrd's firm also designed Heather Glen Golf Links and Wild Wing Plantation in Myrtle Beach, SC; Lockwood Folly Country Club in Holden Beach, NC; and Willow Creek Golf Club in Boone NC.

Maurice F. Childs, 72

Architect and preservationist Maurice F. Childs died March 3, 2005. He was a founding partner of Boston's CBT/Childs Bertman Tseckares, Inc. with Richard Bertman and Charles Tseckares. The 182-person firm has a large portfolio of public and private projects in the Northeast, the Bahamas, Puerto Rico, Australia, Argentina. and China. Childs served as the principal architect on the restoration of the historic John Adams Courthouse in Boston. His other projects include the Morntshire Museum of Science in Norwich, VT; the Shirley and Alex Aidekman Arts Center at Tufts University in Medford, MA; several Harvard University building renovations, including the restoration of the Memorial Hall Tower Spire; and several Massachusetts Bay Transit Authority subway stations. An avid preservationist, Childs recently served as chair of the private group Preservation Massachusetts. Under his leadership, the group spearheaded passage of the 2000 State Community Preservation Act, helping communities preserve landmarks. Following a bachelor's degree from Amherst College and service during World War II, Childs studied architecture at the Massachusetts Institute of Technology, completing a master's degree in 1959. For a year, he worked as an architect in Denmark then returned to join Sasaki Associates Inc. in Watertown, MA. It was there that he met his partners, and they formed CBT in 1967. Childs was named a fellow of the American Institute of Architects in 1996.

H. David Dalquist, 86

H. David Dalquist, inventor of the now ubiquitous aluminum Bundt cake pan, died Jan. 2, 2005. A metallurgist before forming the kitchenware company Nordic Ware with his wife Dorothy in the late 1940s, Dalquist was asked by the Jewish women's volunteer group Hadassah to design a metal pan similar to a ceramic style dish they used for baking kugels. He made some small changes to the design including the many folds which make it easy to slice the perfect size piece, and patented it. He added a "t" to the German word for gathering, "bund," and trademarked the name. Sales were laggard until Ella Helfrich of Texas placed second in the 1966 Pillsbury Bake-Off with her Tunnel of Fudge cake, baked in a Bundt pan. Demand soared and Nordic Ware switched to round-the-clock production, manufacturing 30,000 pans a day. Though the Nordic Ware line has grown to include many kitchen products, the company still sells more than 1 million Bundt cake pans each year. To show his gratitude to Hadassah, Dalquist donated his production seconds to them, and through fundraisers the group has used the proceeds to build schools and hospitals in Israel. In addition to the cake pan, Dalquist introduced the Micro-Go-Round, a rotating glass carousel for the microwave oven, and many cooking containers and utensils for microwave cooking. A native of Minnesota, Dalquist earned his bachelor's degree in chemical engineering from the University of Minnesota before working two years for US Steel and then serving on a destroyer during World War II. He was inducted into the Minnesota Business Hall of Fame in 1987 and the Entrepreneur's Hall of Fame in Boston.

Vernon DeMars, 97

Vernon DeMars, an architect and University of California, Berkeley professor, died April 29, 2005. He taught nearly 30 years at the school, joining the faculty in 1949, and was a professor emeritus in the College of Environmental Design. Upon his 1975 retirement, he received the school's highest honor, the Berkeley Citation. He had also served as the chair of the architecture department there. While on the staff, he designed the Berkeley student center complex, including 1961 Sproul Plaza that was a frequent site of political rallies and demonstrations. That same year he was part of a team, which included noted architect William Wurster, that designed the highly visible Golden Gateway residential towers in San Francisco, an attempt to bring living opportunities to the heart of the city. DeMars began his career in the 1930s designing homes for migrant farmers in California's Central Valley. He taught at the Massachusetts Institute of Technology before joining UC Berkeley. In San Francisco he advocated for submerging the roadway through downtown near Market Street to create a large public plaza, instead of elevating the Embarcadero freeway in front of the landmark Ferry Building. He worked with Carl Maletic to present a plan that would run the road underground following its damage in the 1989 Loma Prieta earthquake.

George Dudley, 90

Architect George Dudley, who worked with Walter K. Harrison designing such New York landmarks as the United Nations Headquarters, Rockefeller Center, and Lincoln Center as well as the Empire State Plaza in Albany, NY, died Feb. 7, 2005. He was the former dean of architecture at Rensselaer Polytechnic Institute before departing in 1963 to establish the School of Architecture and Urban Planning at the University of California, Los Angeles. He spent the 1950s developing low-cost housing in developing countries. In 1941, he put together the first master's of fine arts program in urban planning at Yale University, his alma mater and also where his father, Samuel William Dudley, had been head of the mechanical engineering department.

John Ebstein, 92

Raymond Loewy collaborator John Ebstein died Feb. 18, 2005. From 1938 until 1963, Ebstein worked with the Loewy on the design of space capsules for NASA, locomotives for the Pennsylvania Railroad, and Air Force One for President Kennedy. But Ebstein is best known for his work on the Avanti sports car for the Studebaker-Packard Corporation. In just two weeks, Loewy's design team, led by Ebstein, took Loewy's preliminary drawings and came up with an overall initial design. Ebstein completed the airbrushed renderings of the Avanti, and Loewy presented them to Studebaker. Though sales of the Avanti were not strong enough to save the ailing automaker, the car remains a highly regarded and highly collectible classic. Manufactured for two years, in 1963 and 1964, the Avanti did away with the front grill, was long and shapely, and had an aircraft-inspired dashboard. Fleeing to Europe from his native Germany where he left on his motorcycle in 1933 as Hitler came to power, Ebstein studied in Paris and Prague, earning an architectural degree. He moved to the United States in 1938 and joined Raymond Loewy Associates. When he departed in 1963, Ebstein became chief designer for Gabriel Industries and patented many toys and sporting goods. He retired in 1977. The Florida chapter of the Avanti Owners Association International named its chapter after him.

Pierre El-Khoury, 75

Lebanese architect Pierre El-Khoury died July 4, 2005. Educated in the West, he returned to his native Lebanon in the late 1950s and founded Pierre El-Khoury and Partners, having completed more than 165 commissions, largely in the Middle East.

He earned worldwide renown for his modern, vernacular designs and is credited with adding icons to the Beirut skyline. He also collaborated with many of the biggest names in the profession, including Alvar Aalto, Kenzo Tange, and Ricardo Bofill. His father, Fouad El-Khoury, was an architect in Lebanon and worked closely with French architect Andre Leconte during his time in the country. Pierre attended the Ecole des Beaux Arts in Paris, graduating in 1957. Upon returning to Lebanon, his career escalated quickly, as his own 1959 home was noted for its Frank Lloyd Wright-like elements and excellent siting in a wooded area. His first commission in 1960 for the Clarisses Sisters Convent in Yarze, Lebanon, and his second shortly after for a monastery close to Jezzine, Lebanon, were both award-winners. His talent at siting structures, both residential and commercial, became a tenent of his work. He is perhaps best known in Lebanon for the Basilica of Our Lady of Harissa, designed with Noel Abouhamad, which features 60 concrete shells varying in height from 90 to 165 feet. Among El-Khoury's many notable projects were the 1963 Lebanese Pavilion at the New York World's Fair with Assem Salam and Michel Harmouch, the Sabbagh Center in Lebanon with Alvar Aalto and Alfred Roth, and the Banque du Liban et d'Outre-Mer (BLOM) building in Beirut. He also worked to preserve many of his country's historic buildings and was a founder of the Association pour la Préservation des Anciennes Demeures (Association for Protecting Natural Sites and Old Buildings). El-Khoury served as the Lebanese minister of public works, transport, and agriculture from 1982 until 1984. He was a professor at the American University of Beirut, Université du St. Esprit Kaslik (Lebanon), and the Lebanese University.

Ralph Erskine, 91

Ralph Erskine, a British-born and educated architect who practiced most of his career in Sweden, died March 16, 2005. His work is characterized by a strong sense of design with a social purpose, with projects ranging from the redevelopment of a Victorian slum in the UK, to schools, office buildings, and town plans. Competing against 400 others, he won a 1997 competition to design Millennium Village in Greenwich, a housing project for workers and visitors to London's Millennium Dome. Raised by educated parents who were drawn to socialism, Erskine attended a Quaker school, and there he formed strong ideas about society, community, and humanism. A graduate of Regent Street Polytechnic in London, he worked for a firm in the city and studied town planning at night before setting off for Sweden on his bicycle in 1939. There social architecture and modernist design were more than ideas and experiments—they were tools being implemented on a wide scale to transform the country. Erskine approached his early commissions there with the philosophy that the climate and function of a building should determine its form. He was creative in his use of materials, often incorporating pre-fab elements into his public housing projects, which had become a substantial portion of his work. He sited towns for limited exposure to the elements, designed balconies that could be removed from buildings during harsh winters, and creasted office buildings with expansive views and natural light. His library and student union for Stockholm University included a pulpit built into a staircase so that speeches could be made in the event of a student revolt. He also placed reading balconies outside the building, facing the south. In the UK, Erskine worked from 1969 to 1982 on the housing scheme at Byker in Newcastle-upon-Tyne, producing a complete plan for colorful vernacular, low-cost housing, landscaping, streetscapes, and even a wall over a kilometer long to protect the neighborhood from highway noise. (He built a similar wall at Millennium Village to block a strong north wind.) With his colleague, Aage Rosenvold, Erskine would only accept housing projects in conjunction with other community buildings, whether a shop, church, or school. He is remembered for his commitment to designing positive, uplifting spaces and for his belief that the built environment should work to improve society. Erskine won the RIBA Gold Medal in 1987.

Winthrop W. Faulkner, 73

Washington, DC, architect and leading modernist residential designer Winthrop W. Faulkner died Oct. 19, 2004. A number of his noteworthy houses are located in the city's Cleveland Park neighborhood, including three detached townhouses that he designed in 1977 on a 10-acre parcel owned by his grandfather, Avery Coonley, featuring volumetric shapes and solar collectors on the roofs. Some of his notable residential designs include a house for heiress Lucy Rockefeller Waletzky in Tarrytown, NY; the renovation of the Richard England house in Washington, DC, originally designed by Walter Gropius; and US Embassy housing in Jakarta, Indonesia. At the National Zoo he designed the Great Ape House and Crocodile Pavilion. An advocate of universal design to better serve those with physical disabilities, his projects won many local and national design awards and were featured in periodicals including *Architectural Record, Architectural Digest, Metropolitan Home, The New York Times,* and *The Washington Post.* His father, Waldron Faulkner, had also been a Washington architect, with commissions including the Brookings Institution and the original campus of Madeira School. His mother, the former Elizabeth Coonley, had been raised in a Frank Lloyd Wright house, the Coonley house of Riverside, IL, which her father commissioned. A graduate of Trinity College in Hartford, CT, Faulkner served two years in the Army and then attended Yale University, receiving a graduate architecture degree in 1959. With Joseph Wilkes he founded Wilkes & Faulkner in 1961 (later

Wilkes, Faulkner, Jenkins & Bass and then Winthrop Faulkner & Partners). He retired in 2001 and started a custom contemporary furniture business, Architectural Furniture. In recent years Faulkner lectured about his furniture at the Corcoran Gallery of Art and the National Building Museum. He was elected to the American Institute of Architects' College of Fellows in 1983 and served as chair of the Octagon Museum's board of trustees.

Richard Feilden, 54

British architect Richard Feilden died Jan. 3, 2005. Passionate about the environment and led by a sense of social responsibility, Feilden and his partner Peter Clegg had grown their Bath, England, storefront practice, now called Feilden Clegg Bradley, into a 110-person firm with a second office in London and a growing list of projects in that city. The firm was named the *Building Design*'s Architect of the Year in December 2004. The firm designed such award-winning projects as the RAF Museums at Cosford and Hendon, a new student village at the University of London, and urban renewal plans for Bristol and Gloucester. Advocates for sustainability and environmentally friendly designs, the firm was awarded commissions for a Greenpeace headquarters in Islington, the New Environmental Office for the Building Research Establishment, and the National Trust's new headquarters in Swinton. Awarded the Order of the British Empire in 1999, Feilden was a founding commissioner of the Commission for Architecture and the Built Environment, an advisory committee on planning issues to the British government.

John L. Fisher, 83

Longtime Skidmore, Owings & Merrill associate John L. Fisher died May 13, 2005. He was a fire protection expert and had been a member of the AIA Codes and Standards Committee for many years. For more than 30 years, Fisher operated from SOM's San Francisco office, working closely with founding partner Nathanial Owings on many of the firm's most prominent projects, including the Sears Tower in Chicago; Federal Reserve Building, Bank of America World Headquarters, and Metropolitan Life Building, all in San Francisco; and the Air Force Academy in Colorado Springs. Following service in the Navy during World War II, Fisher worked in electrical engineering, developing an aptitude and interest in mechanical systems and life safety. He became one of the great innovators in the designs of these systems. He was also a charter member in the Architects, Engineers and Building Officials Section of the National Fire Protection Association. The American Institute of Architects named him a fellow 1983.

Joseph H. Flad, 82

Joseph H. Flad, an architect who helped shape the skyline of Madison, WI, died Dec. 26, 2004. Flad joined his father's Madison firm of John J. Flad & Associates after serving in World War II and earning an architectural degree from Iowa State University. After his father retired in the 1960s, Joseph H. Flad became the firm's president, expanding its focus to include the newly-emerging building types of hospitals, schools, and research laboratories. Under his leadership, the firm is credited with designing buildings at the University of Wisconsin–Madison, including the Wisconsin Alumni Research Foundation Building, as well as that city's La Follette High School and St. Maria Goretti Catholic Church. Flad's managers thrived under his hands-off management style, contends Ralph Jackson, president of the company from 1993 to 2000, stating that "his philosophy was to hire the best and brightest and then let them do whatever they thought was best." Flad's legacy endures in the dual entities spawned by the original firm: Flad & Associates, one of the nation's largest architectural practices, and Affiliated Engineers, Inc., one of the nation's largest engineering firms. Combined they employ more than 800 people in eight states, serving clients such as Eli Lilly, the Centers for Disease Control, NASA, and other large biotechnical companies.

Helen Liu Fong, 78

Helen Liu Fong, a Los Angeles architect who helped pioneer the Googie style (named after an eponymous 1949 restaurant designed by John Lautner) of futuristic modern architecture for coffee shops in the city, died April 17, 2005. As a key member of the design staff for Armet & Davis in Los Angeles, Fong led the team as it produced glass-fronted, sweeping, zig-zagging restaurants for Denny's, Bob's Big Boy, Norms, and many others. With their signature mid-century upswept roofs, geometric patterns, and biomorphic boomerang shapes, many of these projects were demolished before the late 1980s modernist preservation movement took hold in Southern California. Of Fong's projects, the Johnie's coffee shop on Wilshire Boulevard, a portion of the Holiday Bowl on Crenshaw Boulevard, and Pann's coffee shop near Westchester are still standing. Fong designed the interiors of many of these structures and is credited with making them so modern and particularly warm and inviting. Meticulous space planning, plentiful, yet soft, lighting, and indoor planters were hallmarks of Fong's work. A 1949 graduate of the University of California, Berkeley with a degree in city planning, Fong's first architecture job was as a secretary for the office of Eugene Choy. In 1951 she joined Louis Armet and Eldon Davis and was soon running many functions of the firm, from the drafting and interior design departments to day-to-day office management. She retired in the late 1970s.

Edward Frank, 87

Southern California furniture retailer Edward Frank died March 21, 2005. The store he owned with his brother Maurice—Frank Brothers in Long Beach, CA—introduced many in the area to modern designs by Charles and Ray Eames, Marcel Breuer, Ludwig Mies van der Rohe, and others. The store quickly became a favorite of design aficionados. Frank Brothers also imported Scandinavian designs. Edward traveled frequently to the region, as well as Milan, and around the United States, meeting with the Eames' and other designers in their showrooms. *Arts & Architecture* magazine editor John Entenza selected the Frank Brothers to furnish the model houses for his Case Study House program. Modernist architect Edward Killingsworth, whom Frank had known since high school, redesigned the firm's showroom in 1961 and built Frank a home, Case Study House No. 25 in Long Beach. Following his brother's death, Frank moved to New York for several years, working for furniture importer DUX. He returned to Long Beach in the late 1980s.

C. Britton Harris, 90

C. Britton Harris, professor emeritus of city and regional planning at Pennsylvania State University, died Feb. 8, 2005. During his 35-year career at the school Harris was the UPS Professor of Planning, Transportation, and Public Policy, had served as chair of the Department of City and Regional Planning, and was dean of the former School of Public and Urban Policy. Upon his retirement in 1984 he continued to write and lecture and spent a year at Stanford University as a visiting professor. During his career at Penn, Harris contributed to the Penn Jersey Transportation Study, which resulted in a special May 1965 issue of the *Journal of the American Institute of Planning* and a conference on transportation planning. This conference was published as *Special Report No. 97* by the Highway Research Board in Washington, DC. Harris is credited with innovating new methods in planning including the advanced use of computer technology and modeling. Harris received his bachelor's degree from Wesleyan University and his master's degree from the planning program at the University of Chicago. He worked for the Chicago Housing Authority and the government of Puerto Rico before joining the Penn staff in 1972. In 1991, the Association of Collegiate Schools of Planning awarded Harris its Distinguished Educator Award. He was inducted into the American Institute of Certified Planners' College of Fellows in 2000.

Jay C. Henry, 66

Jay C. Henry, an architecture professor at the University of Texas at Arlington and an expert on Texas architecture, died March 15, 2005. He joined the UTA faculty in 1972 and, during his career, had also taught at the university's School of Architecture in Rome and the Texas Consortium Program in London. The author of more than 50 conference papers and more than a dozen scholarly articles and reviews, Henry's work appeared in *Perspective, Cite, Texas Review of Books, Texas Architect*, and the *Journal of the Society of Architectural Historians*. His book *Architecture in Texas, 1895–1945* was published in 1993. He received his bachelor of architecture degree from the Catholic University in America in 1962, his master's degree from the University of Washington in Seattle, and his PhD from the University of California, Berkeley.

Walter Hopps, 72

Walter Hopps, founding director of the Menil Collection in Houston, TX, died March 20, 2005. He was a leading curator of 20th-century modern art who helped bring to prominence to some of the period's most important artists. Born in Los Angeles in 1933, Hopps' love of modern art was ignited through his friendship with Walter and Louise Arensberg, owners of a world-class modern art collection. While studying at the University of California, Los Angeles, he and some fellow students opened an exhibition space and held shows for Craig Kauffman and Edward Kienholz (with whom Hopps later opened the Ferus Gallery in 1957) exposing the talents of Ed Ruscha, Ken Price, Robert Irwin, and Billy Al Bengston. Soon Hopps was organizing exhibitions at the Pasadena Art Museum, eventually joining the staff in 1962 where he later became a director of the institution. While there, Hopps organized the first American retrospectives of Kurt Schwitters, Marcel Duchamp, and Joseph Cornell as well as an American Pop Art exhibition, a first of its kind in the country. In 1976 at the then National Collection of Fine Arts in Washington (now the Smithsonian Institution's American Art Museum), Hopps presented the first midcareer survey of the work of Robert Rauschenberg. He began working with Houston art collector Dominique de Menil in 1980. As she made plans to build a museum to house the works she had amassed with her husband John, Hopps helped her select the architect Renzo Piano. The highly acclaimed museum opened in 1987 with Hopps as director, and in 1989 he became its curator of 20th-century art. His exhibitions there included works of Andy Warhol, Max Ernst, and sculptor John Chamberlain. In 1996 he curated an Edward Kienholz retrospective at the Whitney Museum of American Art in New York, and in 1997, a James Rosenquist retrospective (with Sarah Bancroft) at the Guggenheim Museum in New York. In 2001 the Menil established the $15,000 Walter Hopps Award for Curatorial Achievement.

Joseph J. Jacobs, 88

Joseph J. Jacobs, founder of the international engineering and construction firm Jacobs Engineering Group, died Oct. 23, 2004. He grew this Pasadena, CA company from its founding in 1947 to a worldwide entity earning $2.27 billion in revenue and employing more than 35,000. The youngest of seven children from a Lebanese immigrant family, Jacobs took various jobs to finance his degrees in chemical engineering from the Polytechnic Institute of Brooklyn, eventually earning a BS, MS, and PhD. After moving to Pasadena in 1947, Jacobs established Jacobs Engineering, which became a world leader in the design, construction, and operation of plants in the pharmaceutical, petroleum, chemical, and biotechnology industries. Jacobs served as CEO until 1992, when he stepped down to act as chair in order to devote more time to his philanthropic causes, which included the Jacobs Family Foundation in supporting local youth at risk and economic development. In 1983, Jacobs was awarded the prestigious Hoover Medal from President Reagan in recognition of his engineering, education, and humanitarian efforts. Jacobs served on the board of his alma mater and Harvey Mudd College in Claremont, CA. Jacobs' books include his autobiography, *The Anatomy of an Entrepreneur: Family, Culture and Ethics* and *Compassionate Conservation: Assuming Responsibility and Respecting Human Dignity*.

Philip Johnson, 98

Iconic 20th-century architect, scholar, art collector, and provocateur Philip Johnson died Jan. 25, 2005. Born to wealth, Johnson traveled frequently as a young man developing an eye for design and modern art, eventually becoming the first curator of the architecture department at the Museum of Modern Art in New York in the early 1930s. He did not formally pursue architectural practice until he enrolled in the Harvard Graduate School of Design in 1941 at the age of 35, studying under Walter Gropius and Marcel Breuer. Architecture was art first and foremost to Johnson and like the great painters, his career was marked by shifts in style.

His lengthy and controversial career included revelations of a youthful flirtation with fascism and later in life that he was gay, but more importantly, it was hallmarked by a constant evolution of style in his work, from modernism to postmodernism to classicism to deconstructivism, that left critics unsure of his motives and his direction. As Paul Goldberger noted in Johnson's obituary in the *New York Times*, "...what fascinated him most was the idea of the new, and once he had helped establish Modernist architecture in the United States, he moved on..." He was an avid patron of young architects and cultural institutions his entire life. Johnson kept current on trends, openings, and styles and was relentlessly social. Highly quotable, he became himself a media figure and perhaps the most recognized architect of the century.

Following a course of study in the humanities at Harvard, Johnson graduated in 1927 and traveled in Europe where he saw for himself the great works of the early modernists. Through an exhibition he staged at the MOMA in 1932—"Modern Architecture"—and a book he wrote with Henry-Russell Hitchcock that year entitled *The International Style*, Johnson was instrumental in introducing the work of Ludwig Mies van der Rohe, Gropius, Le Corbusier, and other modernists to audiences in the United States. He even negotiated Mies' first American commission. Between 1936 and 1940, Johnson dabbled in right-wing politics, following closely the careers of Huey Long and Adolf Hitler. He was unable to contribute professionally to the causes of those he admired, and eventually his interest faded.

After graduating from architecture school and serving in the US Army during World War II (following an FBI investigation of his political activities), Johnson rejoined the Museum of Modern Art in 1946 as he established his own architecture practice. His relationship with MOMA would last the rest of his life, though he left to concentrate solely on his architectural practice in 1955. The 1951 west wing addition to the museum and the highly acclaimed 1953 sculpture garden were designed by Johnson, and over the years he gave the museum many pieces from his modern art collection. The selection of Cesar Pelli to design a 1978 update to MOMA chilled Johnson's relationship with the institution for several years, though he would later reside in Museum Tower above the museum, also a Pelli project. Eventually the museum named its architecture gallery the Philip Johnson Gallery.

Many of Johnson's early works reflected a strong Mies influence, perhaps none more strongly than 1949's Glass House in New Canaan, CT. Johnson designed the house and eventually a surrounding compound for himself, spent weekends more often than not at this retreat, and it was there that he died. Over the years the compound expanded to include an art gallery, a sculpture garden, a library, and a gatehouse. He willed the property to the National Trust for Historic Preservation in order to open it to the public as a museum following his death. Though many of his designs garnered mixed reviews over the years, the Glass House has been a source of praise since it was built and is generally considered to be one of the finest mid-century residential designs in the United States.

Johnson's first large-scale commercial project is also considered a classic of its genre—the Seagram Building in Manhattan—designed with Mies and completed in 1958. The archetype of postwar modernism, it however marked the beginning of a departure from the International Style for Johnson. He incorporated classical elements into the 1961 Amon Carter Museum in Ft. Worth, TX; the New York State Theater at Lincoln Center in 1964; and the Bobst Library at New York University, designed in 1965 and completed in 1973. He formed a partnership with John Burgee in 1967, and together the pair would design many prominent projects for developers and corporations. These included the glass-fronted IDS complex in Minneapolis in 1972 and Houston's Pennzoil Place, famous for its profile, as two trapezoidal towers standing only 10 feet apart form an optical illusion from every angle. In the late 1970s and early 80s the firm was extremely prolific, designing signature skyscrapers and office buildings in Atlanta, Boston, Chicago, San Francisco, Houston, Denver, Detroit, Pittsburgh, Louisville, and Dallas. All featured heavy finishes and nods to architectural styles of times past. But the distinctly postmodern AT&T Headquarters in New York (now the Sony Building) was perhaps the most controversial with its pink granite façade, 90-foot Italianate archway, and a top shaped like a Chippendale chest. Johnson and Burgee also designed California's Crystal Cathedral, a 4000-seat mega-church for televangelist Robert Schuller, in 1980. Described as an "ecclesiastical greenhouse," the structure is wider and higher than Paris' Notre Dame cathedral.

In 1991 his partnership dissolved as Burgee sought to control the firm. Johnson continued to receive commissions on his own and then with partner Alan Ritchie as they formed Philip Johnson/Alan Ritchie Architects. The two continued working together until Johnson's death. Among their collaborations were several projects for Donald Trump, including the glass tower at 1 Central Park West in New York.

Philip Johnson was awarded the Gold Medal of the American Institute of Architects, and in 1979 he received the first Pritzker Prize for Architecture. Though even Johnson once referred to himself as a "whore" for the number of large projects he was awarded by developers, Paul Goldberger noted in the *New York Times,* "…He created several designs, including the Glass House, the sculpture garden of the Museum of Modern Art, and the pre-Columbian gallery at Dumbarton Oaks in Washington that are widely considered among the architectural masterworks of the 20th century."

Greg Jordan, 48

Interior designer Greg Jordan, named one of 2005's Deans of Design by *Architectural Digest* magazine, died April 20, 2005. An accidental designer, he moved to New York to be a novelist in 1980. But at the urging of a friend who admired his flair for the craft, he pursued his vision of high-end, traditional design and soon built a client list of stars and socialites. A native of Monroe, LA, Jordan brought classicism, gentility, and manners to his work, and clients became friends. His rising career was catapulted when a room he designed for the Kips Bay Decorator Show house in 1992 led to a project for Blaine and Robert Trump, brother of (The) Donald. Eventually Jordan's client list would include Johnson & Johnson heiress Elizabeth Johnson, actress Ashley Judd, and Seinfeld creator Larry David. In 2004, encouraged by David, he expanded to Los Angeles, opening a studio and shop on Melrose Place. He was a graduate of Wabash College in Crawfordsville, IN.

John Anthony Kassay, 85

John Anthony Kassay, educator and author of the definitive book on shaker furniture, died Feb. 17, 2005. *The Book of Shaker Furniture* was published in 1980 and has since become a classic work on the subject, featuring Kassay's own drawings following years of research. He taught woodworking technology and construction in the Design and Industry Department of San Francisco State University from 1957 to 1987 before being named an emeritus professor. A contributor to woodworking and industrial arts periodicals, Kassay was also the author of *The Book of American Windsor Furniture: Styles and Technologies*, published in 1998. During World War II he served with General George Patton's Third Army, earning both a Purple Heart and a Bronze Star. On the GI Bill he earned a bachelor's degree at East Central University in Ada, OK, in 1949, and then his master's degree at Pittsburgh State University in Kansas. Epsilon Pi Tau, the professional fraternity for education in technology, awarded Kassay its 1999 Distinguished Service Award.

Edna Kimbro, 57

Edna Kimbro, an expert on the history and preservation of adobe structures, died June 26, 2005. She was responsible for saving many of California's mission-era adobe buildings, as well as improving conservation techniques for the structures and pioneering new forms of seismic retrofitting for earthen architecture. In the mid-1970s, she and her husband bought and renovated an 18th-century adobe house in Santa Cruz that had once been part of an early California pueblo. It was this project that sparked Kimbro's interest in adobe conservation, and she wasted no time tackling other sites and learning as much as possible about preserving this important part of California's history. After her own house, Kimbro turned her sights to a residence for Native Americans at Mission Santa Cruz from the 1820s, working to raise money for the project and to get the site designated a California state historic park. A native of Monterey, she studied art history at the University of California, Santa Cruz, and later she was credentialed as an architecture conservator. Kimbro was widely consulted on preservation projects, researching, writing reports, and preparing conservation recommendations. She was named the Monterey district historian for the California Department of Parks and Recreation in the early 1980s, a position she held many years. In 1989 Kimbro participated in a program sponsored by the International Center for the Study and Preservation and Restoration of Cultural Property that brought together architects and engineers from countries where mud-brick building techniques are still in use. Held in Rome, one of the many subjects the meeting offered was seismic retrofitting for earthen structures. Shortly after she returned, Kimbro's own home, the 1840 Castro Adobe, was damaged by the Loma Prieta earthquake. She immersed herself in the study of seismic stabilization and initiated a study by the Getty Conservation Institute in the mid-1990s. The institute funded a survey of Southern California adobe structures including seismic testing, and Kimbro led a group of conservationists as they experimented with a variety of new techniques. The Getty Institute published several technical books she authored and co-authored on the subject. Eventually Kimbro would lobby the state of California to protect and renovate the Castro Adobe, built by Mexican rancher Jose Joaquin Castro. It is now a National Historic Site and a State Historic Landmark. In 2003 Kimbro received a lifetime achievement award from the California Mission Studies Association, an organization she helped found. Her many projects around California included Monterey's Royal Presidio Chapel and Rancho Camulos in Ventura County.

Alexander Kouzmanoff, 89

Alexander Kouzmanoff, former chair of architecture at Columbia University's Graduate School of Architecture, Planning, and Preservation and an award-winning architect died Oct. 9, 2005. His 1977 design for the underground annex of the Avery Architectural and Fine Arts Library at Columbia was renown for its thoughtful layout and excellent space planning and was awarded the Albert S. Bard Award from the City Club of New York and an award of excellence from the New York State Association of Architects. His firm, Alexander Kouzmanoff Associates, was founded in 1967, and its many projects included several buildings for the State University of New York system. He completed both his bachelor's and master's degrees at the University of Illinois and worked from 1947 to 1952 for Harrison & Abromowitz. While there he worked on the design of the United Nations Headquarters, the Los Angeles Opera, and US embassies in Havana and Rio de Janiero. Following five years of work as a consultant, he joined the Columbia faculty in 1952 and was appointed chair of the graduate school architecture program in 1971. He was named a fellow of the American Institute of Architects in 1977. Kouzmanoff's son Jan now leads his firm, reorganized in 1992 as Kouzmanoff Bainton Architects.

Norman D. Kurtz, 69

Norman D. Kurtz, a mechanical engineer, evangelist for green building techniques, and whose firm, Flack + Kurtz, worked on some of the highest-profile projects of recent decades, died May 13, 2003. These included Petronas Towers in Kuala Lumpur, Malaysia; the William J. Clinton Presidential Center in Little Rock, AR; and the World Financial Center and new Bloomberg L.P. headquarters, both in Manhattan. In the 1970s, Kurtz began educating other members of the building team and designing more sustainable, energy-conserving functionality into buildings on their drawing boards following the US energy crisis. An adjunct professor of engineering at the Princeton University School of Architecture where he earned his BS, Kurtz earned his MS from Stanford University. He was a lecturer at universities including the Massachusetts Institute of Technology and Harvard Graduate School of Design. Kurtz had been president and CEO of the 350-person Flack + Kurtz before stepping into the role of chair in 2003. The firm was acquired by London-based WSP in 2000, and his founding partner Peter Flack retired in 1996.

Naomi Leff, 66

Interior designer Naomi Leff died Jan. 30, 2005. Perhaps most famous for her 1986 design and refurbishment of New York City's Rhinelander Mansion into the Polo Ralph Lauren's flagship store on Madison Avenue, her design office handled strictly A-list clients and projects. Her residential design clients included Steven Spielberg, David Geffen, Barry Diller, and Tom Cruise and Nicole Kidman. A native of New York, Leff received a BS from SUNY Cortland and a master's degree in sociology from the University of Wisconsin–Madison before enrolling herself in Pratt Institute where she received a master's in environment design with a minor in architecture. From 1975 until 1980 when she founded Naomi Leff & Associates, Leff was a senior designer for Bloomingdale's. She also designed interiors for luxury retailers Neiman-Marcus and Bergdorf Goodman as well as the Park Hyatt Beaver Creek Resort in Telluride, CO, the Shearson Lehman Hutton Saddle Ridge Conference Center in Beaver Creek, CO, and many interiors for yachts and private planes.

Phyllis Williams Lehmann, 91

The art historian and archeologist known for reuniting the hand of the Winged Victory of Samothrace with two of its long-lost fingers, Phyllis Williams Lehmann, died Sept. 29, 2004. Lehmann was an authority on the architecture and monuments of Samothrace, Greece, a remote, mountainous island in the north Aegean, which was the center of one of the most famous mystery cults of Greek antiquity, and considered crucial in the development of arts in the Hellenistic period. After receiving a bachelor's degree from Wellesley College in 1934, she worked for two years at the Brooklyn Museum as an assistant in charge of the classical collection. In 1938, while working on her graduate degree at New York University's Institute of Fine Arts, she first visited Samothrace to work on the excavation. In 1943, she received her PhD, then married archeologist Karl Lehmann, the excavation's director, the following year. She became the assistant field director in 1948 and upon her husband's death in 1960 assumed the role as acting director, a position she held until 1965. A member of the Smith College faculty from 1946 to 1978, she served as dean of the college from 1965 until 1970. Lehmann's many books include *The Pedimental Sculptures of the Hieron in Samothrace* and *Samothrace III: The Hieron*, which received the Alice Davis Hitchcock Book Award from the Society of Architectural Historians in 1969, the year after she was made an honorary citizen of Samothrace.

Karl Linn, 81

Karl Linn, the landscape architect for Ludwig Mies van der Rohe's Seagram Building in New York who later devoted himself to building community gardens, died Feb. 3, 2005. Linn also designed the interior landscaping for the Seagram Building's Four Seasons Restaurant, but in the late 1950s, he devoted himself to starting community garden programs in low-income neighborhoods. The move was a reaction to the trend toward suburban trophy yards, referring to these as "landscapes of affluence." Trained as a psychoanalyst, Linn believed in the restorative power of gardening and of people working together. He founded the Neighborhood Renewal Corps, based in Philadelphia, in 1961, to renew blighted urban areas, and a year later he started a similar program in Washington, DC. Natives of eastern Germany and the only Jews in their town, Linn's family fled to Palestine in 1934 and established a farm near Haifa. Linn worked the land and eventually graduated from the Kadoorie Agricultural School in Palestine. In 1946 he went to Switzerland to study psychoanalysis, and he then immigrated to New York where he practiced and helped found a school for emotionally disturbed children. When he returned to landscape architecture in the early 1950s, he sought to work the connection between his psychotherapeutic practice and the healing power of gardening. In 1989 he cofounded the Urban Habitat Program, a part of the Earth Island Institute, and had previously been a founder of Architects/Designers/Planners for Social Responsibility. Linn was a teacher at the University of Pennsylvania's School of Fine Arts and the Massachusetts Institute of Technology. He was also a fellow of the American Society of Landscape Architects.

Lelio Marino, 69

Lelio (Les) Marino, founder of the Cambridge, MA-based Modern Continental Construction Co., died Nov. 12, 2004. His firm's big break came in 1996 with the start of Boston's $14.6-billion Central Artery/Tunnel project; the firm ultimately won more than $3 billion in contracts. Armed with only a wheelbarrow and a shovel, Marino started the company in 1967 with his partner and friend, Kenneth Anderson, after emigrating from Italy in 1958. Based on his guiding principles of love, discipline, justice, and respect, Marino stressed the importance of extensive organizational communication, management approachability, employee participation on all levels, and a clear mission statement for the firm. His management style is best summarized by his belief that "the manager must serve the company and the company must serve the employees. Nothing else works." Marino's sense of commitment extended into the arena of health, motivating him to rise every day at 3:30 a.m. to exercise for 90 minutes before beginning work at 7 a.m. Marino's focus on health also inspired him to establish a restaurant, farm, and a health clinic. Marino's firm became a New England leader in safety management, receiving several Gold and Silver Safety awards from the Central Artery's safety incentive program. Blossoming from its roots as a small road and drainage contractor to the largest heavy-civil firm in New England, Marino's principles were always evident in the company's successes.

Richard Cedric Marshall, 84

Richard Cedric Marshall, a San Francisco Bay-area architect and educator who devoted his career to designing innovative schools, died Oct. 23. 2004. He was an early advocate of open-plan schools, one of the first architects in the 1960s to design flexible floor plans that worked with new ways of teaching. His 50-year career was devoted to making schools more configurable, yet more intimate in scale. He began his career with prominent California school designers John Lyon Reid Architects, working for the firm from 1950 to 1959. While there he spent a year as acting head of the Department of Architecture at the University of Calcutta in Howrah, India. In 1959 he formed Marshall, Leefe & Ehrenkrantz with James Leefe and Ezra Ehrenkrantz. From 1964 to 1975 he partnered with Chester Bowles Jr. forming Marshall & Bowles. He worked to prepare a master plan for San Rafael schools in 1968 that called for their two large schools to be rescaled, forming "schools within a school," and helping deinstitutionalize their learning facilities. From 1971 to 1972 Marshall served as advisor and consultant for the African Region, Khartoum, Sudan for UNESCO. He spent the year advising West African governments on school planning and construction. He designed the Fremont High School in Oakland in 1973 with the firm of Esherick, Homsey, Dodge & Davis, setting up an office trailer next to the site in order to make himself available to the staff, students, and community. Two students who met Marshall there went on to careers as architects. In 1982 Marshall and Kam Lee formed the practice Marshall/Lee. Marshall was also an educator himself, teaching architecture and school planning at the University of California at Berkeley; Healds College in San Francisco; and in India and Africa. He was elected the American Institute of Architects College of Fellows in 1976. He served many years on the school's committee of the AIA at all levels—local, state, and national—and was a past chair of the Fellowship Nominating Committee. During his career, Marshall designed schools across California, in Moraga, Piedmont, San Lorenzo, San Rafael, Tomales, Livermore, Oakland, and San Francisco. He also designed the Bank of California branches at Stevens Creek, Palo Alto, and San Carlos;

the Plumbing and Pipe Fitting Industry Local Union 38 headquarters building on Market Street in San Francisco; and many buildings at the Konocti Harbor Inn Resort at Clear Lake. He studied forestry as an undergraduate at UC Berkeley and returned to the school to study architecture following service in the Air Force. He completed his last year of study at the Ecole des Beaux Arts in Paris, France.

J. Edward Martin, 88

Los Angeles architect and structural engineer, J. Edward Martin, whose firm oversaw the construction of nearly half of the downtown's office towers, including the city's first high-rise, the Union Bank building, died Nov. 22, 2004. Martin was the second generation to run the firm, AC Martin Partners, which was started by his father, Albert C. Martin, in 1906. A Los Angeles native, Edward graduated in 1939 from the University of Illinois with a bachelor's degree in architectural engineering. During the war, Martin, working as a public service officer, is credited (along with a handful of other civil engineers) with salvaging and recommissioning 19 sunken vessels extracted from the bottom of Pearl Harbor. After the war, Martin and his brother, Albert Jr., ran the firm, with Edward overseeing management and Albert focusing on design. Pioneering computer design and seismic technology during an era of unprecedented construction growth, the diversification of AC Martin Associates extended to hospitals, shopping malls, government buildings, aerospace complexes (especially for TRW and Lockheed), and entire communities. Martin's son, Chris, is now at the firm's helm. One of his fondest memories was walking with his father through the renovation of City Hall, which was originally designed by his grandfather.

Ehrman B. Mitchell Jr., 80

Philadelphia architect Ehrman B. Mitchell Jr., a founding partner of Mitchell/Giurgola and 1979 president of the American Institute of Architects, died Jan. 18, 2005. With Romaldo Giurgola, he founded the firm in 1958, and by 1960 the pair was awarded a marquee project—the design of the visitor's center for the Wright Brothers National Memorial in North Carolina. Renown for rich, contextual but modern designs, the firm designed many prominent Philadelphia buildings, including the Penn Mutual Tower, the United Way headquarters, and the 1976 Liberty Bell Pavilion. Mitchell/Giurgola, now MGA Partners, won the 1965 commission to design the Washington, DC, headquarters of the American Institute of Architects but withdrew to protest design revisions. Mitchell led a challenge in 1972 to a practice in Philadelphia of architects donating 5 percent of their fees on government projects to the Democratic Party, leading to a grand-jury investigation. In 1980 the firm was selected to design Australia's parliament complex in Canberra. Mitchell retired in 1985.

Marian Scott Moffett, 55

Marian Scott Moffett, professor of architectural history and theory at the University of Tennessee, Knoxville, died Sept. 26, 2004. After earning her PhD in architecture from the Massachusetts Institute of Technology in 1975, she joined the faculty of the University of Tennessee. Moffett served as president of the faculty senate (1985–86), associate to the vice chancellor for academic affairs (1993–1999), associate provost (2000–2001), and associate dean in the College of Architecture and Design (2003–2004). She received numerous awards, including the Chancellor's Citation for Extraordinary Service to the University. Moffett's knowledge of music and architecture, coupled with her keen intelligence and people skills, contributed to her exceptional teaching abilities. Moffett's professional work encompassed both global and local subjects. She coauthored *A World History of Architecture, The History of Western Architecture,* and *Buildings Across Time: An Introduction to World Architecture,* in addition to her personal study of vernacular buildings presented in *East Tennessee Cantilever Barns.*

Jean Muller, 80

French engineer Jean Muller, a pioneering bridge designer and one of *Engineering News Record* magazine's engineering leaders, died March 17, 2005. He began his career as a protégé of Eugene Freyssinet, the inventor of prestressed concrete, and is credited with the development of the post-tensioning method of bridge construction. Working for Freyssinet at STUP in the late 1940s, now Freyssinet International, Muller led the design and construction of a three-bowstring bridge in Caracas, Venezuela, setting a record for clear span length at that time—150 meters. In the early 1950s Muller led the New York office of Freyssinet International, bringing their post-tensioning technique to the United States with the design of the bridge over Louisiana's Lake Pontchartrain. Toward the end of the decade he returned to France and joined Campenon Bernard, working on concrete dams, oil rigs, containment vessels for nuclear materials, and the 1962 Choisy-le-Roi bridge in France. On that project, Muller is credited with the first use of the match-cast precast segmental construction method for concrete bridges. According to *Engineering News Record,* Muller also designed Normandy's Brotonne Bridge, "the first concrete box-girder with a single plane of cable stays." He formed Figg & Muller Engineers in 1978 with Gene Figg, producing such US landmarks as the cable-stayed concrete Sunshine Skyway bridge in Tampa, FL, and Seven Mile Bridge in the Florida Keys. In 1988 Muller formed J. Muller International, working in Europe, North America, and Southeast Asia. Among the firm's many high-profile projects: the Monterrey railway viaduct in Mexico, the H-3 Windward Viaduct in Hawaii, and the multi-span post-tensioned concrete box girder Confederation Bridge in Canada.

Connecting Prince Edward Island with New Brunswick, the Confederation Bridge is the longest bridge in the world constructed over waters that freeze as well as the longest bridge in Canada. Muller was the recipient of many industry awards worldwide, including being named a fellow of the American Consulting Engineers Council in 1981 and a Chevalier of the Legion of Honour in 1992. He was one of *Engineering News Record's* top 125 engineering leaders in a 1999 survey.

Robert K. Murase, 66

Robert K. Murase, a landscape architect responsible for some of the Northwest's most acclaimed gardens and parks, died July 19, 2005. A Japanese-American, Murase practiced worldwide and across the United States and was greatly influenced by his friend, the sculptor Isamu Noguchi. His style has been described both as spiritual and muscular, with stone as a signature element, cut in unorthodox geometry. He is perhaps best known for projects such as the Japanese American Historical Plaza in Portland, OR, where he lived, the Garden of Remembrance in downtown Seattle, and the courtyard of the Japanese American Museum in Los Angeles. Interned during World War II, Murase's family later settled in San Francisco, and he graduated with a degree in landscape and sculpture from the University of California, Berkeley. He apprenticed with Robert Royston and Lawrence Halprin before moving his wife and children to Kyoto, Japan. It was there that he researched, taught, designed, and befriended Noguchi, departing after nine years in the country. While there he designed a garden for the Myodo Kyo Kai Buddhist Temple in 1975, earning an Honor Award from the American Society of Landscape Architects. In 1979 he helped establish the Portland office of EDAW, a national landscape design firm, founding his own firm, Murase and Associates, three years later with wife Judy acting as business manager. Today the firm employs 24 and maintains a second office in Seattle. Among Murase's many projects: the gardens of the Oregon Convention Center in Portland; the Esther Short Park in Vancouver, Canada; landscapes for the Grand Canyon transit center; the St. Croix National Scenic Riverway in Wisconsin; the Sumitomo Museum in Kyoto, Japan; and work on the campuses of Nike in Beaverton, OR, and Microsoft in Redmond, WA. In Murase's obituary, Randy Gragg, architecture critic for *The Oregonian* newspaper, described his Japanese-American Historical Plaza in Waterfront Park as "...one of the great places in Portland." In a separate remembrance of the designer, Gragg described the park as "turning the dark historic rupture of Japanese internment into a frank, heartfelt recollection of a century of Japanese experience and the timeless importance of the Bill of Rights." Murase was a fellow of the American Society of Landscape Architects.

Dwayne C. Nuzum, 68

Dwayne C. Nuzum, an architect and former chancellor of the University of Colorado at Colorado Springs, died Jan. 18, 2005. He served in that position from 1986 to 1992 and had also been the dean of the College of Architecture and Planning at the Denver campus of the University of Colorado, most recently chairing its Department of Planning and Design. Nuzum had also served as executive director of the Colorado Commission on Higher Education. A native of Boulder, Colorado, he received his bachelor's degree in architecture from the University of Colorado in 1962 and a master's degree in architecture from the Massachusetts Institute of Technology. In 1965 Nuzum received a PhD in town planning from the Delft Technical Institute in the Netherlands on a Fulbright grant. He served on the boards of numerous civic organizations including the Colorado Historical Foundation, the City and County of Denver Convention Center Urban Design Review Committee, and the Colorado Center for Community Development.

Brian Pohanka, 50

Civil war historian and battlefield preservationist Brian Pohanka died June 15, 2005. An advisor on Civil-War-era films such as *Glory* and *Cold Mountain*, Pohanka's interest in the period began as a young boy, and he became an expert in the field. He helped found the Association for the Preservation of Civil War Sites, now the 70,000-member Civil War Preservation Trust. Much of his preservation work concerned telling the stories of the battles, the soldiers, and their place in the war, bringing the rich history of the endangered battlefields alive. He helped stop development projects on battlefields in northern Virginia and was named Battlefield Preservationist of the Year in 2004 by the Civil War Preservation Trust and the Central Virginia Battlefields Trust. He was the senior researcher and writer on the 27-volume Civil War series from Time-Life Books and a consultant for the History Channel's *Civil War Journal.* Pohanka kept his beard trimmed in a historically accurate style and was a captain of Company A of the Fifth New York Volunteer Infantry, a group of reenactors. He even met his wife at one; both were in period dress. A native of Washington, DC, he was doing research on the Civil War at the National Archives by the age of 12. Pohanka received a degree in history from Dickinson College in Carlisle, PA, and authored many works including *Mapping the Civil War* (1992), *Distant Thunder: A Photographic Essay on the Civil War* (1988), and *Myles Keough: An Irish Dragoon in the 7th Calvary* (1991).

Neville Quarry, 71

Australian architect and educator Neville Quarry died in October, 2004. He was awarded the Royal Australian Institute of Architects Gold Medal in 1994 and the International Union of Architects's Jean Tschumi Prize in 1981 for "important work in the training of young architects and fostering professional international collaboration." He was a practicing architect, but it was as a professor of architecture that he is best remembered. While studying for his master's degree at Rice University, Quarry worked as a teaching assistant, then, in 1961, returned to Australia where he became a senior lecturer at the University of Melbourne until 1970. For the next six years, Quarry joined the faculty at Papua New Guinea's PNG University of Technology where he was the founding head of the school's new architecture program. In 1976 he returned to the NSW Institute of Technology (now University of Technology Sydney) where he was head of the School of Architecture until he retired in 1989. A tireless critic, writer, and lecturer, Quarry was the author of the book *Award Winning Australian Architecture*. In the 1960s he had edited *Cross Section*, a critical review of Australian architecture. In the 1980s he organized the International Series of lectures that brought talents such as Frank Gehry and Michael Graves to Australian audiences. After he retired, Quarry currated Australia's exhibitions to the Venice Biennale of Architecture. His other honors included an architecture prize from the NSW RAIA for the Quarry Residence in Paddington (1986) and the Papua New Guinea Independence Medal in 1975. He was named a Member of the Order of Australia in 1995. He continued to design residences following his retirement.

Jane Silverstein Ries, 96

The first female landscape architect in Colorado, Jane Silverstein Ries, died July 6, 2005. In 1929 Ries was one of the first females to enroll at the Lowthorpe School of Landscape Architecture. Although she began her career in 1933 by working for the Denver landscape architect Irvin J. McCrary, she left after six months to start her own firm. During her 56-year career, Ries designed many important civic improvement projects, including the Denver Botanical Gardens, the Denver Art Museum, and the Colorado Governor's Mansion. In addition to her mentoring role to women, Ries was an early advocate of sustainable design, beautiful green spaces, and raising the standards of urban life in an era when such concerns were not yet in vogue. Ries was a fellow in the American Society of Landscape Architects and was the 2005 recipient of the ASLA Medal, the organization's highest honor.

Arthur Rosenblatt, 73

Instrumental in reshaping the Metropolitan Museum of Art, the architect Arthur Rosenblatt, died Jan. 11, 2004. After completing his bachelor's degree in architecture in 1956 from the Carnegie Institute of Technology (now Carnegie Mellon University), Rosenblatt was hired by Thomas Hoving, director of the Met, as a design consultant in 1966. Until 1986, Rosenblatt was responsible for the Met's architecture and planning as administrator, vice director, and vice president, when $1 billion was spent on construction and renovation projects for the Sackler, Lehman, and Rockefeller wings and the Temple of Dendur. Hoving's memoir, *Making the Mummies Dance: Inside the Metropolitan Museum of* Art, states that Hoving relied on Rosenblatt's streetwise ability to pacify community opposition during this expansion. As director of the United States Holocaust Memorial Museum in Washington, DC, during the five-year construction period before it opened (1986–88), Rosenblatt selected James Ingo Freed of I.M. Pei & Partners to design the building, in association with Notter, Finegold & Alexander. Also involved with the restoration of the New York Public Library and Bryant Park, Rosenblatt is credited with founding RKK&G Museum and Cultural Facilities Consultants in 1995 and coauthoring *Building Type Basics for Museums.*

Paul Rothstein, 47

Paul Rothstein, an innovative associate professor at Arizona State University, died unexpectedly on March 8, 2005. His students clearly appreciated his teaching skills, voting him Outstanding Professor for five of the six years he taught at ASU. Rothstein also was on a mission to transform product development into a social responsible, entrepreneurial, and collaborative practice. His initiative to develop InnovationSpace, an interdisplinary product development program at ASU that commercializes sustainable product design concepts, was one practical aspect of this goal. In addition to teaching, Rothstein focused on exploring, developing, and articulating new methods and processes for sparking user-centered business and design innovation. He also lectured widely, conducting research funded by corporations such as 3M, Honeywell, and Telex, and offered professional workshops relating to experience design and the application of field research in design. Prior to ASU, Rothstein taught at the Illinois Institute of Technology's Institute of Design.

Gene Schrickel Jr., 78

Lifelong Arlington, TX, resident and landscape architect Gene Schrickel Jr., died July 3, 2005. After earning his BS degree in landscape architecture from Texas A&M University in 1950, Schrickel was involved in the design of many Arlington parks, golf courses, and major landscape projects at the University of Texas at Arlington.

Schrickel was instrumental in the passage of legislation for registration of landscape architects in Texas, serving as president of the Texas chapter of the American Society of Landscape Architects. He was also director of the Council of Park and Recreation Consultants, trustee of the American Society of Landscape Architects, and was appointed by the governor to the Texas Board of Architectural Examiners.

John Ormsbee Simonds, 92

John Ormsbee Simonds, a pioneering modernist landscape architect and former president of the American Society of Landscape Architects, died May 26, 2005. Influenced by gardens he saw in Asia and studying under Walter Gropius and Marcel Breuer at the Harvard Graduate School of Design in the late 1930s, Simonds formed a firm in Pittsburgh, PA, with his brother Phil—Simonds and Simonds—in 1940. He designed the Chicago Botanic Garden, Mellon Square, and Equitable Plaza in Pittsburgh, as well as many parks in that city. The firm is credited with reviving Pittsburgh's Lake Elizabeth by renovating Allegheny Commons Park on its north side. An urban planner, Simonds designed more than 80 communities, including Miami Lakes and Pelican Bay in Florida. A member of the Carnegie Mellon University faculty for 13 years, Simonds was also the author of *Landscape Architecture* in 1963, a college textbook that is on its fourth edition and has sold more than 100,000 copies. He was commissioned by the state of Virginia to prepare an environmental action plan; his report, *Virginia's Common Wealth*, is still being referred to today. A fellow of the ASLA, Simonds received the ASLA Medal in 1973 and in 1999 was honored with the ASLA President's Centennial Medal, awarded for the first time for "unparalleled contributions to landscape architecture and service to the ASLA in the 20th century." He was also a fellow of the Royal Academy of Design in Great Britain. The firm, Simonds and Simonds, was renamed Environmental Planning and Design. Simonds retired in 1983.

Robert Slutzky, 75

Painter and educator Robert Slutzky died May 3, 2005. His writings and teachings on the relationship between art and architecture, both primarily in the modern idiom, influenced many of today's progressive practicing architects. He is perhaps best known for a pair of essays entitled "Transparency: Literal and Phenomenal," written in the mid 1950s with colleague and architectural theorist Colin Rowe. Both were on the faculty of the University of Texas at Austin, and their work was circulated for years in various forms through architecture schools until it was published for the first time in 1963. "Transparency" was both a call for an elevation of the ideals of modern architecture and also a rumination on the relationship between architectural space and the painted canvas. In the early 1950s, following his study at New York City's Cooper Union for the Advancement of Science and Art, where he would later spend many years as a professor of art and architecture, Slutzky studied with Josef Albers at Yale University, earning his MFA. During his career he would collaborate with innovative modern architects including Peter Eisenman, Richard Meier, and John Hejduk, with whom he served on the Texas faculty. At the time of his death, he was a professor of fine arts at the University of Pennsylvania.

Richard Solomon, 62

Architect Richard Solomon, director of the Graham Foundation for Advanced Studies in the Fine Arts, died July 14, 2005. The Chicago-based Graham Foundation, established in 1956, seeks to foster public debate and develop new approaches to architecture, for example recently sponsoring research into prefabricated shelters, Quonset huts, and, in 2004, a contest to reimagine Chicago's lakefront. Before assuming directorship of the Graham Foundation in 1993, Soloman edited *Inland Architect* magazine and taught architectural design as an adjunct professor at the University of Illinois at Chicago. His firm, Richard Jay Solomon & Associates, designed a commuter train station for Metra in Northbrook, IL, among other projects. Solomon received his bachelor's degree from the Massachusetts Institute of Technology and a master's degree in environmental design from Yale University. A former member of the board of directors of the Society of Architectural Historians, he also served as a member of the board of overseers of the Department of Architecture at the Illinois Institute of Technology and the advisory council of the School of Architecture at Princeton University.

Ezra Stoller, 89

Celebrated architectural photographer, Ezra Stoller, who helped the public appreciate the unprecedented style of modernist buildings, died on Oct. 29, 2004. Trained as an architect, Stoller used his architectural expertise in taking and making his photographs to assist people in comprehending the beauty of most of the important buildings of the 1950s and 1960s, including Eero Saarinen's TWA Terminal at Dulles Airport, Frank Lloyd Wright's Guggenheim Museum in New York, Ludwig Mies van der Rohe's and Philip Johnson's Seagram building in New York, and Louis I. Kahn's Salk Institute for Biological Studies in La Jolla, CA. Using just the right angle and the right light, leading architects of the world sought him to have their building "Stollerized." "While I cannot make a bad building good, I can draw out the strengths in a work that has strength," Stoller said. William S. Saunders, the author of *Modern Architecture: Photographs by Ezra Stoller*, expanded on this concept by his observation that "he had a pretty deep appreciation of the kinds of strengths of modern architecture: simplicity, proportion, balance. He was dedicated to showing buildings in the best possible way." To this end, Stoller often waited days watching the light move across the surface of the building to snap the best shot in black and white with his large-format camera. Stoller received a bachelor's degree in 1938 from the School of Architecture and Allied Arts at New York University and founded Esto Photographics in 1966. In 1961 Stoller was honored by the American Institute of Architects with the Architectural Photography Medal.

Israel Stollman, 81

Israel Stollman, whose name for decades has been synonymous with urban planning, died Feb. 2, 2005. In addition to being known for his comprehensive understanding of the field, in 1978 Stollman was instrumental in the consolidation of two planning groups, the American Society of Planning Officials and the American Institute of Planners, into one national organization—the American Planning Association. Born to Russian Jewish immigrants on New York's Lower East Side in 1923, Stollman received his BS in social science, with a self-devised major in housing and planning from the City College of New York in 1947 and went on to earn his master's degree in city planning the following year from the Massachusetts Institute of Technology. After Stollman established and chaired the graduate program in city and regional planning at Ohio State University from the mid-1950s until 1968, he spent the next decade forming America's premier planning organization, the American Planning Association. Stollman is remembered as a highly ethical man, who "did everything with dignity, respect, and grace." A collector of stereopticon views of cities dating as far back as the 1850s, Stollman recently donated 20,000 slides to the Getty Museum.

Steven Strom, 56

Steven Strom, chair of the Department of Landscape Architecture at New Jersey's Rutgers University since 1987, died July 28, 2005. He also directed the Center for Land Planning at the New Jersey Agricultural Experiment Station and was elected a fellow of the American Society of Landscape Architects in 2002. Before joining the faculty at Rutgers, Strom taught landscape architecture at the University of Wisconsin–Madison. He initiated foreign study programs at both schools. A past president of the council of Educators in Landscape Architecture, he was a recipient of that organization's Outstanding Educator award. With fellow professor Kurt Nathan, Strom wrote the textbook *Site Engineering for Landscape Architects*, now in its fourth edition. He was a graduate of Rutgers and received his master's in landscape architecture from the University of Massachusetts, Amherst.

Kenzo Tange, 91

The most influential figure in postwar Japanese architecture, Kenzo Tange, died March 22, 2005. After having transformed barren Hiroshima into a tranquil peace park in the 1940s and 50s, Tange went on to design many important buildings throughout the world, earning him one of architecture's highest honors—the Pritzker Prize in 1987. In awarding this prize, an international jury acknowledged the duality of his style. "Tange arrives at shapes that lift our hearts,' the citation said, "because they seem to emerge from some ancient and dimly remembered past and yet are breathtakingly of today." The synthesis of these two elements combining the structural daring of modernism with traditional forms parallels his coexistent admiration of Le Corbusier's style (which he gained from working in the office of Kunio Maekawa, an important disciple of Corbu after graduating from the University of Tokyo's architecture department in 1938) and traditional Japanese architecture. His two sports arenas for the Tokyo Olympics in 1964, whose swooping suspended roofs are often described as among the most beautiful structures of the 20th century, evoke the simplicity of archaic temple forms while manifesting Le Corbusier's expressive tendencies of the time. Tange's Yamanashi Press and Broadcasting Center at Kofu, completed in 1967, advanced his Metabolist urban principles, which proposed buildings with endlessly replaceable components as a solution for Japan's urban congestion. The flexibility of this design has allowed the intended gaps in the building to become filled in with terraces and roof gardens, fulfilling his abiding desire: "I like to think there is something deep in our own world or reality that will create a dynamic balance between technology and human existence, the relationship between which has a decisive effect on contemporary cultural forms and social structure."

W. Dorwin Teague, 94

W. Dorwin Teague, son of famed industrial designer Walter Dorwin Teague and an accomplished product designer in his own right, died Sept. 16, 2005. An engineer, the younger Teague devoted his career to designing decidedly unflashy products but ones that were smaller, lighter, or better-performing than their predecessors. He designed a better cash register for the National Cash Register Company, the mimeograph machine for A.B. Dick, and held the first patent on the reclining dentists' chair. The chair significantly improved dental visits both for patients and for doctors who could now sit comfortably during an examination. The design won a 1960 certificate of merit from the Industrial Designers Institute. Teague left the Massachusetts Institute of Technology to work for his father's firm. One of his first designs there was for the Marmon 16 automobile, shortly before the automaker shut down during the Depression. During the 1940s and 50s, he was an engineer for Bendix Aviation

Corporation where he designed the Lark surface-to-surface and the Loki surface-to-air liquid propellant rockets. He formed his own firm, Dorwin Teague, Inc., in 1966. His work during his lengthy career included designs for ice buckets, can openers, vacuum cleaners, a waterbed, bicycle brakes, and many other objects. He authored a 1998 memoir entitled *Industrial Designer: The Artist as Engineer.*

Walter Thabit, 83

Longtime East Coast city planner and advocate for diversity in redevelopment Walter Thabit died March 15, 2005. He spent his career working to encourage the incorporation of low-income housing into plans intended to revitalize blighted areas. Thabit studied design at Brooklyn College and received master's degrees in sociology from the New School University and city planning from the Massachusetts Institute of Technology. He began his career as a planning analyst in New York and served from 1954 to 1958 as director of the master plan section in Baltimore's Department of City Planning. Before becoming a planner for East New York, Brooklyn, he spent several years as a planning consultant. Thabit wrote about his experiences in East New York in his 2003 book *How East New York Became a Ghetto.* From 1976 to 1980 he was senior planner for New York's Landmarks Preservation Commission and then served as an associate city planner in New York's Department of Transportation from 1980 to 1988. In response to redevelopment proposals that called for displacing many citizens, Thabit worked with more than a dozen communities in New York, New Jersey, and Pennsylvania to develop alternate plans. He founded Planners for Equal Opportunity in 1964, a 600-member progressive group, which later became the Planners Network.

A. Hays Town, 101

Beloved Baton Rouge architect A. Hays Town died Jan. 6, 2004. "Archetype of the gracious, Southern gentleman," stated San Francisco architect Michael Stanton, Town expressed the local architectural archetypes in his attention to detail, proportion, siting, materials, and other contextualistic elements. He was a soulful artist whose lovingly, hand-sketched drawings uncannily captured their design essence, observes architect Skipper Post. Davis Rhorer, director of the Downtown Development District of Baton Rouge who has spent the last two decades preserving Town's buildings, remarked that "it's almost hard to describe, except you could walk into a room or see a home and it felt right." This sense of appropriateness is a common thread that connects his earlier, modernist phase of commercial buildings with his residential "Creole" style from the 1960s, (characterized by Acadian porches, Spanish rooflines, and Creole doorways), and has greatly influenced designers. Among Town's well-known buildings are Baton

Rouge's Blue Cross building on Florida Street, the First Baptist Church, Dunham Chapel, and the Baptist Student Center at Louisiana State University, which express his reuse of old building materials and his unique blend of modern vernacularism. In 1922 Town graduated from Southwestern Louisiana Institute with a degree in engineering and from the Tulane School of Architecture in 1926.

John Turley, 79

Chicago architect John Turley died Feb. 19, 2005. After becoming enamored with Mies van der Rohe's buildings while working as a photographer, Turley moved to Chicago and became one of Mies' top students while earning his bachelor's degree from the Illinois Institute of Technology in 1955. While employed by Mies and eventually as a partner of Skidmore, Owings & Merrill, he worked on dozens of structures far and near, including the Wills Tobacco Factory in Bristol, UK; the First Wisconsin building in Madison; and Chicago's John Hancock Center and Sears Tower. In his spare time Turley was a woodworker who crafted bowls and furniture in his basement workshop. He was also active in a service group to help impoverished Chicago residents get job training and find work. Always an advocate of Chicago architecture and the arts, Turley enjoyed mentoring younger architects who were trying to become established.

Kitty Baldwin Weese, 87

Kitty Baldwin Weese, influential Chicago modern furniture retailer and widow of famed Chicago architect Harry Weese, died March 18, 2005. With partner Jody Kingrey, Kity Weese co-owned and operated the Baldwin Kingrey design store on Michigan Avenue in Chicago from 1947 to 1957, when it was sold. It was among the first stores in the United States to sell and stock entirely modern inventory. Their first shipment of inventory sold out before it made it to the floor. Most of the furniture they stocked was designed by architects, including Alva Aalto, Charles and Ray Eames, and Eero Saarinen. Weese gave her husband credit for suggesting she open the store, though she graduated with a degree in psychology from Huntingdon College in Alabama. During World War II, she had been a psychologist for the US State Department. After she and Kingrey sold the store, Weese concentrated on raising three children and traveling worldwide with her husband, the founder of the eponymous Harry Weese & Associates. He designed Washington DC's Metro subway system as well as the Time and Life Building in Chicago and several projects in Columbus, IN, an architectural mecca thanks to the patronage of the local Cummins Engine Foundation. Kitty Weese opened an interior design practice in 1970, mostly designing commercial interiors. Author John Brunetti wrote a book about the store entitled *Baldwin Kingrey: Midcentury Modern in Chicago.*

Robert F. Wellner, 85

Engineer and bridge designer Robert F. Wellner died Feb. 9, 2005. senior vice president at Figg Engineering Group in Tallahassee, FL, he helped design many large bridge projects across the United States, including the Natchez Trace Parkway Arches in Nashville, TN; the Clark Bridge over the Mississippi River at Alton, IL; the Chesapeake & Delaware Canal Bridge near St. Georges, DE; the I-93 Central Artery in Boston; the JFK Air Train in New York; and bridges for the Pennsylvania Turnpike Commission over the Susquehanna River and the Allegheny River. Wellner was a registered professional engineer in 14 states, though he undertook the work as a second career. From 1954 to 1983, he worked for Bethlehem Steel, retiring as the manager of construction marketing. He had received his BS in civil engineering from the University of South Carolina before serving in the Navy from 1951 to 1954. He was a member of the American Society of Civil Engineers and had served on the board of directors in the Planning and Design Division of the American Road & Transportation Builders Association until 2004. In 2002 he was awarded Honorary Lifetime Membership in the American Segmental Bridge Institute.

Name Index

Name Index

Name Index

Name Index

Name Index

Name Index

Name Index

Name Index

Name Index

Name Index

Name Index

Name Index

Name Index

Name Index

Name Index

Name Index

Name Index

Name Index

Name Index

Name Index

Name Index

Name Index

Name Index

Name Index

Name Index

Name Index

Name Index

Site Index

Site Index

Site Index

Site Index

Site Index

Site Index

Site Index

Site Index

Site Index

Site Index

Available from Östberg...

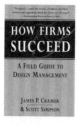

How Firms Succeed: A Field Guide to Design Management
James P. Cramer and Scott Simpson

A hands-on guide to running any design-related business—from a two-person graphics team to middle-management to CEOs of multinational firms—offering advice on specific problems and situations and providing insight into the art of inspirational management and strategic thinking.

"*How Firms Succeed* is a fountainhead of great ideas for firms looking to not just survive, but thrive in today's challenging marketplace."
—*Thompson E. Penney, FAIA*
President/CEO, LS3P Architecture, Interior Architecture, Land Planning and President, American Institute of Architects, 2003

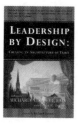

Leadership by Design: Creating and Architecture of Trust
Richard N. Swett

Ambassador Richard Swett's groundbreaking new book investigates the unique civic leadership strengths of the architecture profession. Leadership by Design is an eloquent plea to architects, leaders and citizens alike to expand the tool chest as we seek new leadership to design new solutions for the complex challenges facing our nation and the world.

"This book reveals that the 'citizen-architect' has always been in our midst and begins an important dialogue about how that role should be designed for the future."
—*Robert A.M. Stern, FAIA*
Robert A.M. Stern Architects and Dean, Yale School of Architecture

Almanac of Architecture & Design
James P. Cramer and Jennifer Evans Yankopolus, editors

The only complete annual reference for rankings, records, and facts about architecture, interior design, industrial design, landscape architecture, planning and historic preservation.

"The reader who uses this book well will come away with a richer sense of the texture of the profession and of the architecture it produces."
—Paul Goldberger, *The New Yorker*

America's Best Architecture & Design Schools

This special 40-page issue of *DesignIntelligence* offers the only ranking of architecture and design schools in the United States. conducted annually since 2000, this study is the only one that polls professional practice leaders—the constituency most qualified to comment on which schools consistency produce the best graduates. National and regional rankings and a commentary and analysis of the current state of design education are just a few of the offerings.

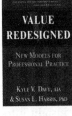

Value Redesigned: New Models for Professional Practice
Kyle V. Davy and Susan L. Harris

In *Value Redesigned*, Davy and Harris reveal a vivid landscape where innovative new models for professional practice are already beginning to flourish, showing firms avenues of escape from the vicious cycle of commoditization and low prestige that is epidemic within the architecture and engineering community. Aligned with the dynamics of the emerging knowledge-based economy, these new models of practice offer bold value propositions, combining new ways of creating value with innovative pricing strategies.

"Value Redesigned is a timely and important book for all professionals and professional firms involved in the built environment projects. This is a must read for any one who cares about the future of their own firm and the future of the industry."
—*Al Barkouli, PE*
Executive Vice President, David Evans and Associates, Inc.

Design plus Enterprise: Seeking a New Reality in Architecture & Design
James P. Cramer

Using specific examples, *Design plus Enterprise* illustrates how using business principles architects can create better design services—and thereby, a better society. It also demonstrates how smart design can drive economic success.

"This is must reading for every architect...It clearly points out how design and the designer are enriched by recognizing that the profession of architecture is both a business and a way of enhancing the environment"
—M. Arthur Gensler Jr., FAIA
Chairman, Gensler Architecture, Design & Planning Worldwide

Available from Östberg...

Communication by Design: Marketing Professional Services
Joan Capelin

How to communicate—and, especially why—to clients, prospects, staff, and the public is the basis of this powerful book. It is targeted to business principals as well as anyone who aspires to a leadership position in a firm, association, or business joint venture.

"Capelin offers thought-provoking practical lessons in marketing leadership—illustrated by interesting insights and implementable ideas. Read this book, put her advice into action, and your firm will flourish."

—*Howard J. Wolff*
Senior Vice President/Wimberly Allison Tong & Goo

DesignIntelligence

The Design Future Council's monthly "Report on the Future" provides access to key trends and issues on the cutting edge of the design professions. Each month it offers indispensable insight into management practices that will make any firm a better managed and more finically successful business.

"We read every issue with new enthusiasm because the information always proves so timely. No other publication in our industry provides as much useful strategic information."

—*David Brody Bond LLP*

Compensation Survey of Architecture and Design Firms

DesignIntelligence's annual *Compensation Survey* provides a refreshing glimpse into the process of salary and compensation administration. Condensed into composite figures for medium, large, and very large professional practices, this 20-page report covers actual compensation rates for the top twenty-percent of firms in the United States today. It has been hailed as "necessary reading" for leaders in professional practices and as "a commonsense blueprint and guide on salary trends."

"...not just a collection of charts and graphs but a thoughtful integration of hard data and very intelligent writing."

—James Brogan, Director of IT, Kohn Pedersen Fox Architects

Order Form

Publication	Price	Qty.	Total
How Firms Succeed: A Field Guide to Design Management	$39.00		
Communication by Design: Marketing Professional Services	$34.95		
Leadership by Design: Creating an Architecture of Trust	$39.50		
Design Plus Enterprise: Seeking a New Reality in Architecture & Design	$29.00		
Almanac of Architecture & Design	$49.50		
Value Redesigned: New Models for Professional Practice	$39.50		
America's Best Architecture & Design Schools[†]	$34.95[†]		
DesignIntelligence (1 year subscription)	$365.00		
Compensation Survey of Architecture and Design Firms	$19.95		

	Subtotal	
Shipping: $4.95 for 1st item; $1.00 each additional item	**Shipping**	
*GA residents add 6%	**Tax***	
	Total	

[†] A PDF version of *America's Best Architecture & Design Schools* may be downloaded immediately from our Web site at www.greenway.us.

Method of Payment

☐ Check ☐ Credit Card

_____

Card Number   Exp. Date   Signature

Contact/Shipping Information

_____

Name   Title

_____

Company

_____

Address

_____

City   State   Zip

_____

Telephone   Fax

_____

Email

Your completed order form may be faxed to us at 770.209.3778 or mailed to:
Greenway Communications, 30 Technology Parkway South, Suite 200, Norcross, GA 30092
All our publications can also be purchased online at www.di.net. 800.726.8603

The Greenway Group, Inc.

The Greenway Group, Inc. is a multi-faceted firm that supports design excellence through the promotion of innovative business practices, a focus on the future, and knowledge sharing. Its consulting division, Greenway Consulting (www.greenway.us), specializes in future-based strategic advisory services, executive coaching, mergers and acquisitions, executive recruitment, strategic planning, brand analysis, futures forecasting, and business modeling for the A/E/C industry. Counsel House Research, Greenway's research arm, supports many of Greenway Consulting's initiatives with its extensive databases and pursues customized research projects such as the annual architecture and interior design school rankings. Its communications division, Greenway Communications, publishes the annual *Almanac of Architecture & Design*, as well as many design management titles under its Östberg Library of Design Management imprint, and the Archidek series of educational, collectable architecture trading cards. Greenway also manages the non-profit think-tank, the Design Futures Council; its mission is to explore trends, changes, and new opportunities in design, architecture, engineering, and building technology to foster innovation and improve the performance of member organizations. The Council also publishes the monthly *DesignIntelligence* (www.di.net), the international design marketplace's strategic management newsletter. Greenway Group is firmly committed to helping organizations grow faster, smarter and healthier through shared knowledge and strategic insights for the future.

About the Editors

James P. Cramer

James P. Cramer is the founder and chairman of The Greenway Group, Inc.; co-chair of the Washington DC-based think-tank, the Design Futures Council; editor-in-chief of *DesignIntelligence*, a monthly letter on trends, strategies, and changes published by the Design Futures Council; and adjunct professor of architecture at the University of Hawaii. He researches, consults, and gives seminars for leading professional firms around the world and is the author of over 135 articles and several  books, including the critically acclaimed *Design + Enterprise, Seeking a New Reality in Architecture,* and co-author of *How Firms Succeed, A Field Guide to Management Solutions.* Cramer is the former chief executive of The American Institute of Architects in Washington, DC, past president of the American Architectural Foundation, and a former publisher of *Architecture* magazine. He is also a fellow of the Western Behavioral Sciences Institute in La Jolla, CA, and a Richard Upjohn Fellow of The American Institute of Architects.

Jennifer Evans Yankopolus

Jennifer Evans Yankopolus is the co-editor of the *Almanac of Architecture & Design* and an architectural historian. She is also the editor of the Archidek series of collectable, educational architecture trading cards and an editor for the Östberg press where she helps projects to achieve the imprint's goal of promoting design excellence. She has a master's degree in architecture history from the Georgia Institute of Technology. She also studied at Drake University, where she received her B.S. in business administration and earned a master's degree in heritage preservation from Georgia State University. As a researcher, architectural historian, and project director, she brings a historical perspective to Greenway's initiatives.

Comment Form

Invitation For Comments and Suggestions

Please include any ideas, comments, or suggestions for the *Almanac of Architecture & Design.*

Suggestions and Comments

_____

_____

_____

_____

_____

_____

_____

_____

_____

_____

Contact Information

_____
Name

_____
Address

_____
City   State   Zip

_____
Telephone

_____
Fax

_____
Email

Please return this form to:
Greenway Communications
ATTN: Almanac
30 Technology Parkway South, Suite 200
Norcross, GA 30092
Tel 770.209.3770
Fax 770.209.3778

Östberg™

Library of Design Management

Every relationship of value requires constant care and commitment. At Östberg, we are relentless in our desire to create and bring forward only the best ideas in design, architecture, interiors, and design management. Using diverse mediums of communications, including books and the Internet, we are constantly searching for thoughtful ideas that are erudite, witty, and of lasting importance to the quality of life. Inspired by the architecture of Ragnar Östberg and the best of Scandinavian design and civility, the Östberg Library of Design Management seeks to restore the passion for creativity that makes better products, spaces, and communities. The essence of Östberg can be summed up in our quality charter to you: "Communicating concepts of leadership and design excellence."